A Moment's Liberty

The Shorter Diary

Virginia Woolf

A
Moment's
Liberty

The Shorter Diary
Virginia Woolf

ABRIDGED AND EDITED BY

ANNE OLIVIER BELL

INTRODUCTION BY

QUENTIN BELL

Harcourt Brace Jovanovich, Publishers

SAN DIEGO   NEW YORK   LONDON

HBJ

Copyright © 1984, 1982, 1980, 1978, 1977 by Quentin Bell and
Angelica Garnett
Editorial notes copyright © 1990 by Anne Olivier Bell
Introduction copyright © 1990 by Quentin Bell

Library of Congress Cataloging-in-Publication Data
Woolf, Virginia, 1882–1941.
A moment's liberty: the shorter diary/Virginia Woolf; edited by Anne
Olivier Bell; introduction by Quentin Bell.
p.   cm.
ISBN 0-15-161894-1
1. Woolf, Virginia, 1882–1941— Diaries. 2. Novelists, English — 20th
century — Diaries. I. Bell, Anne Olivier. II. Title.
PR6045.072Z466   1990
828'.91203 — dc20   90-33428
[B]

Printed in the United States of America

First American edition
A B C D E

Contents

Introduction

THIS is an abridged version of the diaries which Virginia Woolf wrote in the years between 1915 and 1941. Those diaries were published in full between 1977 and 1984 in five profusely annotated and carefully indexed volumes, and were furnished with an introduction by me. The purpose of that introduction was to preface a hitherto unpublished text, one which could hardly fail to interest scholars or enthusiasts for whom, indeed, the learned apparatus of those volumes was supplied. This present work is aimed at a more general public, which may well include many who are unfamiliar with the other writings of the diarist. In fine, my earlier task was to introduce the diaries; my present one, to introduce Virginia Woolf the writer.

Such an essay is appropriate inasmuch as the diary is on the whole a very simple and straightforward, though hastily written, record, and for this reason a good starting-point for anyone who has had the very sensible idea of adventuring into this fertile province of literature. The novice will very likely have heard ill of the writer I am trying to present. She was, we are frequently told, snobbish, elitist, and malicious. The reader will be able to form his or her own opinion of this. Here I would only point out that some other diarists, as for instance Pepys and Boswell, also had their faults of character but that, to put it mildly, their occasional lapses from perfection do not make them less readable. But there are other charges, more serious in the eyes of a prospective reader, which should be examined. It must be allowed that in Virginia Woolf's novels there are passages which baffle the common reader. In her critical writings she is always lucid; but in the fictions her disregard of what I should call narrative, her interest in the obscure emotions and the workings of the human mind, and her indifference to the more humdrum facts of everyday life, result in obscurities which can confound us. *The Waves* is not an easy read, and most of the earlier fictions present difficulties which are sometimes formidable. The diary, on the other hand, is almost always plain sailing. Virginia Woolf sets herself, at the end of her working morning or between tea and dinner, to record the pains and delights of her days. No prose could be less 'studied', and if anything is at all unclear it is because the diarist is in a hurry to dash down her experiences. Writing about herself and her life she does not disdain the commonplace. Whereas the characters – if they can be called characters – in *The Waves* scarcely seem to have such a thing as an income, Virginia Woolf, as a diarist, does not refrain from making notes on the price of eggs.

In that earlier introduction to which I have alluded, I committed myself to the kind of value judgment which I usually avoid, and declared that the diaries rank with the greatest of her novels, that they are a masterpiece. But the question may now arise: do they still look like a masterpiece now that they have been boiled down to a fifth of their original size? I think they do. Indeed I would suggest that in some respects the deletions of the editor have enhanced the merits of the original text.

The story which unfolds in these pages may be divided into three parts. Firstly, the years of recovery (1915–22) – recovery, that is, from the terrifying mental breakdowns of Virginia Woolf's early married life and, with the restoration of her health, the beginnings of her reputation as a writer, the publication of her first and second novels, and of a few strikingly original short stories which indicated the direction that she was to take. Secondly, the years of ascent (1922–31), in which, writing what are now her most celebrated novels, she formed and developed her own style, each book, beginning with *Jacob's Room* and culminating in *The Waves*, bringing new problems, new triumphs, and new fame. Thirdly, the final phase (1931–41), the phase of wealth, celebrity and distress. This coincides with a deterioration in her world and in the world at large, which was drifting with fearful speed towards barbarism and war, a catastrophe for which her grand remedy was feminism. Those years saw her long and painful struggle to write *The Years*, and the final triumph, as we can now see it, of *Between the Acts*, a novel which was published posthumously and which might have been altered if she could have been saved from the fear of insanity and from suicide.

In each period we see the writer sustaining old friendships and starting new ones. From the first Virginia was a central figure, with her sister Vanessa Bell, in what is called Bloomsbury, and her Bloomsbury friendships were formed long before these diaries were begun. The Great War had done something to disperse and to change the group, but familiar figures like Maynard Keynes, Desmond MacCarthy, Lytton Strachey, E. M. Forster and Roger Fry provide material for some valuable portraits; and to these may be added more recently introduced younger fellow-writers, Katherine Mansfield and T. S. Eliot. We do get an occasional glimpse of the corridors or waiting rooms of power: the afternoon when Virginia's cousin Herbert Fisher, then a cabinet minister, invited himself to tea and told her that the war had been won; or the memorable visit to the Woolfs' Sussex house of Sidney and Beatrice Webb, planning a socialist future for Britain. Such encounters did bring her momentarily close to the world of military and political action, although in neither case was she left with much admiration for the chief actors.

In the second period, as she enters her forties, we find the author rising and adventuring into the world of rank and fashion, if we may thus describe Lady Colefax and Lady Cunard, and that much more important connection (for it was sentimental) with Knole and the Sackvilles. At the other end of the social spectrum we may notice – indeed we cannot possibly escape – the long tragi-comic saga of Nelly Boxall, the Woolfs' living-in servant who, it seemed, could neither live with Virginia nor without her, so was continually giving notice and continually withdrawing it, exasperating her mistress who however was sufficiently attached to her to be culpably weak in dealing with her moods.

It was a token of her success that Virginia was now invited to meet the leaders of her profession. T. S. Eliot had for long been a friend, but now she encountered celebrated older writers such as Arnold Bennett, H. G. Wells, Shaw, Yeats, Max Beerbohm and George Moore; and to this phase of her career we owe a memorable portrait of Thomas Hardy. Also, for her curiosity was catholic, a description of the total eclipse of the sun in 1926.

In the last phase there were still new friends to be made, notably Dame Ethel Smyth, one of the most remarkable as well as one of the most tiresome of her admirers. She also enjoyed the company of younger poets and writers – William Plomer, Christopher Isherwood, Stephen Spender and others. But the 1930s was a time of mourning: Lytton Strachey was the first to die, and after him Dora Carrington, Roger Fry, Ottoline Morrell, Ka Arnold-Forster and other, younger, people: Francis Birrell, Stephen Tomlin, and her nephew, Julian Bell.

To these lists of persons, which I hope will give the reader a notion of the kind of society to be met with in these pages, one should add a multitude of other things: birds and weather, landscape and London streets, the pleasures of walking, of conversation, of listening to music; the peculiarities of university life, the insufficiencies of ceremonies; the list is endless and would soon become pointless; but it is perhaps worth observing that Virginia is one of the few women to give us a first-hand description of a military operation: she witnessed and described one of the most crucial engagements of the Battle of Britain – even if she was unaware of its significance.

It has been said that Bloomsbury was an exclusive society which repulsed all would-be visitors with icy scorn and had no use for outsiders. To some extent this was true of Virginia's sister, but it is not true of the other members of that group, especially Virginia. There were, to be sure, some relationships which she found irksome, as for instance that with her mother-in-law Mrs Woolf, but her no doubt tedious conversations with unwelcome guests, however exasperating when experienced, became, when confided to her diary, a theme of great comic value. From the point of view of Leonard or of her doctor, such encounters could be dangerous: they might give rise to headaches and make of her a solitary invalid, with nothing to record but her own state of mind (not that such observations were without interest), or worse still might bring the diary to a halt. But whenever she has the strength to write and give expression to her curiosity, sympathy, malice or sense of humour, she becomes immensely readable. Inevitably, in a manuscript which was written in haste by a writer who normally arrived at her meaning by a series of successive drafts, there must be some superfluities which she would have struck out. Here in the abridged version an attempt is made to give added momentum and clarity by means of tactful deletion. One hopes that the intelligent reader will see the material advantages of this operation. But of course in avoiding one difficulty one may fall into another: the pleasure of reading these pages may lead him to complain that the book is too short.

QUENTIN BELL, *1989*

Editorial Note

WHEN Virginia Woolf died in 1941, she left a series of diaries, thirty volumes in all, written between 1915 and her death. From these her husband Leonard extracted those passages primarily concerned with her own preoccupations as a writer, and published them in 1954 under the title *A Writer's Diary*. After his death in 1969 his wife's copyrights were inherited by her sister Vanessa Bell's surviving children, and it fell to them to decide on any further publication of her remaining manuscripts, including her letters and diaries. The decision was taken that both these should be published in full. Accordingly the *Letters*, edited by Nigel Nicolson and Joanne Trautmann, appeared in six volumes between 1975 and 1980, and the *Diaries*, edited by me, in five volumes from 1977 to 1984, both series being extensively and scrupulously annotated and indexed. In the nature of things, this formidable array of volumes is somewhat intimidating to the general reader, who may have neither time, money, nor inclination to expend on such a scale. So now the Hogarth Press – the publishing business started on a hand-press in the Woolfs' Richmond dining room almost three-quarters of a century ago – is publishing a single-volume selection of Virginia Woolf's letters under the title *Congenial Spirits*, and this volume, *A Moment's Liberty*, an abridged version of her diary.

In reducing the original five volumes to one I have had to jettison some four-fifths of their contents. My purpose has been to preserve the overall character of the original, to follow the autobiographical thread, and to present a comprehensible and readable distillation of the 2,000 or so pages of Virginia's manuscript diaries. To do so I have omitted a host of figures altogether and rationed the appearances of others; I have (reluctantly) omitted the diaries Virginia kept on her travels – which may well deserve separate publication; I have deliberately reduced the space allowed to Virginia's reflections on the conception, progress and reception of her work, for these are given full scope in *A Writer's Diary*; and for the rest, I have cut and condensed wherever I could do so without impairing the quality, language, and sense of the original text. I have also, with heroic self-abnegation, omitted all my informative footnotes. (For the deprived, they are always to be found in the five-volume complete edition.) Instead, I have provided introductory summaries to each year to give a background to the subjects engaging Virginia's interest; and I have included in the Index brief details of the people she mentions.

As this shortened diary is designed to be easily read and enjoyed, I have amended Virginia Woolf's wayward punctuation, have spelled out the many abbreviations she employed in her rapid rush to set down her thoughts and impressions, and have occasionally inserted (in square brackets) a name or a word or two to help the reader.

Virginia Woolf's diaries have since 1979 been housed in the admirable Henry W. and Albert A. Berg Collection of English and American Literature in the New York Public Library (Astor, Lenox, and Tilden Foundations), together with a great number of her other manuscripts.

It remains for me to thank my step-sister Chloe Green and my daughter-in-law Imogen Bell for particularly valuable and expert help in time of need.

ANNE OLIVIER BELL

1915

Adeline Virginia (b. 1882) was the third of the four children of the second marriage of Leslie Stephen – Victorian man of letters and editor of the Dictionary of National Biography *– and his wife Julia, widow of Herbert Duckworth. The family, with the children of both parents' earlier marriages, lived in a large house at Hyde Park Gate, Kensington, with a staff of servants headed by the cook Sophie, removing each summer for several months to St Ives in Cornwall. Julia Stephen died in 1895, and (Sir) Leslie in 1904; that autumn, led by Vanessa, the eldest, the younger Stephens set up house at 46 Gordon Square, Bloomsbury, an unfashionable district where they felt able to loosen the shackles of Kensington convention. When Thoby Stephen left Trinity College, Cambridge – where his brother Adrian was to follow him – he brought his friends to Gordon Square, and his sisters were able first to be present at and soon to participate in the sort of free-ranging discussions on all manner of subjects which these intelligent and high-spirited young men had enjoyed at the University, and which were denied to most nicely-brought-up young ladies of that period. Among these visitors several were to become lifelong friends – Lytton Strachey, Saxon Sydney-Turner, Desmond MacCarthy. Two – Clive Bell and Leonard Woolf – were to become the husbands of Vanessa and Virginia Stephen.*

In 1906 Thoby Stephen died of typhoid fever contracted on a family expedition to Greece, and shortly afterwards Vanessa married his friend Clive Bell; Virginia and Adrian, leaving 46 Gordon Square to the Bells, moved a short distance to Fitzroy Square and subsequently, in 1911, to Brunswick Square, where they shared their household with the economist Maynard Keynes, Duncan Grant the painter and, home on leave after seven years as a colonial administrator in Ceylon, Leonard Woolf. The following year, in August, Virginia and Leonard were married. Virginia's nervous instability had long been an anxiety to her family; now Leonard was to bear it in aggravated form: she fell into depressions, refused to eat, and, in 1913, attempted suicide. Under his devoted care she gradually recovered, living for the most part in the country house she had leased before her marriage, Asheham in Sussex; and, after the outbreak of war in 1914, she was fit enough to return to London – or rather, its outskirts. In October she and Leonard took lodgings at 17 The Green, Richmond-on-Thames, with a Belgian landlady, Mrs Le Grys, and set about looking for a home of their own.

The Stephen sisters had resolved in their nursery that Vanessa would be a painter and Virginia a writer, and neither of them ever wavered from their chosen destinies.

From *1904 Virginia had published reviews and articles, mainly in* The Times Literary Supplement; *her first novel,* The Voyage Out, *had been accepted by her half-brother the publisher Gerald Duckworth in 1913, although its appearance was delayed until March 1915 owing to her breakdown, and she was at work on her second,* Night and Day. *Leonard Woolf, who resigned from the Colonial Service in order to marry Virginia, had published two novels,* The Village in the Jungle *in 1913 and* The Wise Virgins *in 1914. But although Virginia had inherited a modest private income, this was insufficient to support two – particularly in view of the heavy medical and nursing expenses she had incurred, and Leonard turned to journalism as a source of income, becoming more and more concerned with political matters.*

Virginia Woolf wrote her diary at 17 The Green, Richmond, each day between 1 January and 2 February 1915; ten days later there are three further pages, and then no more.

1915

Friday 1 January
We were kept awake last night by New Year Bells. At first I thought they were ringing for a victory.

Saturday 2 January
This is the kind of day which if it were possible to choose an altogether average sample of our life, I should select. We breakfast; I interview Mrs Le Grys. She complains of the huge Belgian appetites, & their preference for food fried in butter. If they eat thus in their exile, how must they eat at home, she wonders? After this, L. and I both settle down to our scribbling. We lunch; and read the papers, agree that there is no news. I read *Guy Mannering* upstairs for twenty minutes; and then we take Max for a walk. Halfway up to the Bridge, we found ourselves cut off by the river, which rose visibly, with a little ebb and flow, like the pulse of a heart. One of the queer things about the suburbs is that the vilest little red villas are always let, and that not one of them has an open window, or an uncurtained window. One house had curtains of yellow silk, striped with lace insertion. The rooms inside must be in semi-darkness; and I suppose rank with the smell of meat and human beings. I believe that being curtained is a mark of respectability – Sophie used to insist upon it. And then I did my marketing. Saturday night is the great buying night; and some counters are besieged by three rows of women. I always choose the empty shops, where I suppose one pays a halfpenny a pound more. And then we had tea, and honey and cream; and now L. is typewriting his article; and we shall read all the evening and go to bed.

Sunday 3 January
It is strange how old traditions, so long buried as one thinks, suddenly crop up again. At Hyde Park Gate we used to set apart Sunday morning for cleaning the table silver. Here I find myself keeping Sunday morning for odd jobs – typewriting it was today – and tidying the room – and doing

accounts which are very complicated this week. I have three little bags of coppers, which each owe the other something. We went to a concert at the Queen's Hall, in the afternoon. Considering that my ears have been pure of music for some weeks, I think patriotism is a base emotion. By this I mean that they played a National Anthem and a hymn, and all I could feel was the entire absence of emotion in myself and everyone else. If the British spoke openly about W Cs, and copulation, then they might be stirred by universal emotions. As it is, an appeal to feel together is hopelessly muddled by intervening greatcoats and fur coats. I begin to loathe my kind, principally from looking at their faces in the tube. Really, raw red beef and silver herrings give me more pleasure to look upon. But then I was kept standing forty minutes at Charing Cross Station, and so got home late, and missed Duncan [Grant] who came here. Moreover, London on a Sunday night now, with all its electric globes half muffled in blue paint, is the most dismal of places. There are long mud coloured streets, and just enough daylight and insufficient electric light to see the naked sky, which is inexpressibly cold and flat.

Monday 4 January
Philip [Woolf] came after luncheon, having four days leave. He is sick to death of soldiering – told us tales of military stupidity which pass belief. The Colonel says "I like well dressed young men – gentlemen" and gets rid of recruits who sink below this level. In addition to this, the demand for cavalry at the front is exhausted, so that probably they will stay at Colchester for ever. Another dark, rainy day. An aeroplane passed overhead.

Tuesday 5 January
We worked as usual: as usual it rained. After lunch we took the air in the Old Deer Park, and marked by a line of straw how high the river had been; and how a great tree had fallen across the towing path, crushing the railing beneath it. Three bodies were seen yesterday swiftly coursing downstream at Teddington. Does the weather prompt suicide? *The Times* has a queer article upon a railway smash, in which it says that the war has taught us a proper sense of proportion with respect to human life. I have always thought we priced it absurdly high; but I never thought *The Times* would say so. L. went off to Hampstead to give the first of his lectures to the Women's Guild. He did not seem nervous: he is speaking at this moment. The Belgians downstairs are playing cards with some friends, and talk – talk – talk – while their country is destroyed. After all, they have nothing else to do.

Wednesday 6 January

L. went off at 10 a.m. to give his second lecture at Hampstead. The first was a great success, as I knew it would be. He finds the women much more intelligent than the men; in some ways too intelligent, and apt on that account, not to see the real point. No one except a very modest person would treat these working women as he does. Clive [Bell], or indeed any other clever young man, would give himself airs; and however much he admired them pretend that he didn't.

I wrote all the morning, with infinite pleasure, which is queer, because I know all the time that there is no reason to be pleased with what I write, and that in six weeks or even days, I shall hate it. Then I went to London, and asked at Gray's Inn about Chambers. They had a set vacant; and I at once envisaged all sorts of charms, and let myself into them with a thrill of excitement. But they would be perfect for one, and impossible for two. Next I saw a flat in Bedford Row, which promised divinely, but on asking at the agents, was told they had just been instructed to let it furnished only – And now, of course, I am convinced that there is no flat in London to equal it! I could wander about the dusky streets in Holborn and Bloomsbury for hours. The things one sees – and guesses at – the tumult and riot and busyness of it all –

Now I have to decide whether I shall go up again, to a party at Gordon Square. On the one hand, I shirk the dressing and the journey; on the other I know that with the first chink of light in the hall and chatter of voices I should become intoxicated, and determine that life held nothing comparable to a party. I should see beautiful people, and get a sensation of being on the highest crest of the biggest wave – right in the centre and swim of things. On the third and final hand, the evening's reading by the fire here – and smoking and talking to L. in what stands for slippers and dressing gown – are heavenly too. And as he won't urge me to go, I know very well that I shan't. Besides, there is vanity: I have no clothes to go in.

Thursday 7 January

No – we didn't go to the Gordon Square party. Leonard got back too late, and it rained; and really, we didn't want to go. I started off after lunch today, first to go to the Foundling Hospital and ask whether they would let us have Brunswick Square – or half the house; then to the Omega [Workshops] to buy Janet [Case] a shawl, and then to tea with Janet. Brunswick Square is already practically let to a retired Ceylon Civil Servant, called Spence, who may however be willing to let the two upper floors, which would suit us very well. I became, of course, possessed with a passion to have Brunswick Square. When I got out, it was raining. I walked to the Omega however and bought my stuff from a foolish young woman in a

Post Impressionist tunic. I went to Hampstead, and was allowed up to Janet. She is in bed, and will have to stay in bed for weeks. Still, she is trained to be brave, and so unselfish by nature that other people really interest her. We talked about Leonard, and life in London and Hardy's poems which she can't re-read – too melancholy and sordid – and the subjects not interesting enough. I don't agree. It grew late; and she suggested that I should dine there and go with L. to the Peace Debate at the Women's Guild. I couldn't face dinner, so I retreated to the Public Library. On the way I walked through one of the worst downpours I have ever been in. My shoes squeaked so with wet as I walked up the Library that I was ashamed. Then I dined at a cabman's eating house – the only dining place, and very good. Coarse, but clean and sober. At eight I met L. at 28 Church Row. The rooms are old white panelled rooms; one was full of working women. It was a comfort to see how they roar with laughter, like schoolgirls. It was very good. The women impressive as usual – because they seem to feel, and to have such a sense of responsibility.

Friday 8 January
I went to Chancellors [Richmond Estate Agents], to ask whether there was any news of Hogarth [House]. At first the man said no. When I told him that we might take a house in London, he at once confessed that he had twice seen the present tenant, and that she does not like the house. Is this invented, and, if not, is there some good reason why she does not like it? It seems likely that we shall have to choose between Brunswick and Hogarth – unless both fail us.

Sunday 10 January
I was sitting typewriting this morning when there came a tap at the door; and someone whom I thought at first was Adrian, appeared; it was Walter Lamb however, fresh from the King. Whenever he has seen the King he comes to tell us. He insisted that we should go for a walk with him in Richmond Park. What did we talk about? We forgot about the King, and Walter told us a long inexpressibly dreary story about the inefficiency of the French soldiers. Whatever Walter says, has the same flat, smooth, grey surface; and his voice alone would dull the fieriest poesy in the world. His life now lies among respectable, semi-smart, rich people, whom he half-despises, so that his accounts are always a little condescending. The one passion of his life is for eighteenth century building. He is perfectly suited by Kew, and the Royal Academy, and the Royal family. He refused to lunch with us, saying that he had lived on pheasants all the week, and rhubarb was forbidden him, on account of his acidity.

I heard last night that old Spence won't let any part of Brunswick Square.

6

Monday 11 January

Leonard was in his bath this morning, and I was lying in bed, when I heard a commotion next door, and then someone rushed downstairs crying in a strange, unnatural voice "Fire! Fire!" As it was obvious that the house was not on fire, to any large extent, I put on my waterproof and slippers before I looked out of the window. I then smelt paper burning. I then went into the passage, and found smoke pouring from the open door of the next room. There was clearly time to escape, so I withdrew; and heard Lizzy return with the lodger; and heard her begin "I only put a bit of paper to draw the fire –" Later, I heard that the paper had caught; the draperies on the mantelpiece had caught; the screen had caught; the woodwork had caught. As every room in the house is lined with dry old wood, loosely papered over, ten minutes, I think, would have put the fire beyond water jugs – The wonder is how we have escaped so far, considering Lizzy. Yesterday she smashed two very nice bits of china for us.

We went up to London this afternoon: L. to see the editor of the *New Statesman* about an article on Diplomacy, I to go over a flat in Mecklenburgh Square. I went on to Day's Library and L. to the London Library. He has to write an article of 1200 words by Wednesday noon.

Tuesday 12 January

Cecil [Woolf] came to luncheon, in mufti, I observed. In fact they are both entirely sick of the army, and see no chance of going to the front. Nevertheless, Cecil thinks of being a permanent soldier, because the life is better than a Barrister's life. On the other hand, he and Philip may go to the colonies. The odd thing about the Woolf family, to me, is the extreme laxness of it. In my family, the discussions and agitations that went on about the slightest change in one's way of life were endless; but with the Woolfs it doesn't much seem to matter whether they turn farmer, run away with another man's wife, or marry a Polish Jew tailor's daughter. Perhaps the Woolfs haven't a family tradition. It gives a sense of freedom anyhow. From all this, obviously I have nothing to say.

Wednesday 13 January

L. went off to the *New Statesman* office this morning with his article. I lunched here, and then went to Day's, to get more books. The West End of London fills me with aversion; I look into motor cars and see the fat grandees inside, like portly jewels in satin cases. The afternoons now have an elongated pallid look, as if it were neither winter nor spring. I came back to tea. L. arrived – having seen Gordon Square and Maynard [Keynes] (who says German finance is crumbling) and Saxon [Sydney-Turner], who is recovering from influenza.

Thursday 14 January

We were woken this morning (I see this is going to become a stock phrase like 'Once upon a Time' in a faery story) by a thumping throbbing sound as if a motor omnibus were on the roof, endeavouring to start. Experience told now, however, that Lizzy had merely made a huge kitchen fire, when there was no water in the pipes. When L. turned on the tap, steam issued, as if it were Siegfried's dragon at Covent Garden, and then came floating bits of pipe, and the water was rust red. We wrote all the morning. After lunch we set off to Kingston in order to buy some charming cups, which are to be had there for a penny each. If Lizzy doesn't go, and continues to behave as though each day were her last, we must give her something cheap to break her rage against. We came home on top of a bus. Leonard is going up to hear the Fabians discourse; I think I shall indulge in a picture palace.

Friday 15 January

I went to my picture palace; and L. to his Fabians; and he thought, on the whole, that his mind and spirit and body would have profited more by the pictures than by the Webbs, and the doctors, who were talking about their etiquette. There were two or three superb pictures; but as usual, the drama is very boring. I wish one liked what everyone likes. The Hall was crowded, roars of laughter, applause &c.

We walked to Hogarth this afternoon, to see if the noise of schoolchildren is really a drawback. Well – I wonder what we shall do. I'd give a lot to turn over thirty pages or so, and find written down what happens to us. We are dining early, and going to a Hall – an unheard of dissipation – though there was a time when I went out to operas, evenings, concerts &c, at least three times a week. And I know we shall both feel, when its over, 'really a good read would have been better.'

Saturday 16 January

I think the Hall (Coliseum) last night *was* worth while – in spite of drawbacks. What I like in Halls are 'turns' – comic singers, or men imitating Prima Donnas, or Jugglers. I don't like one act plays. It takes me a whole act to get into a play, and so one act plays are mostly sheer boredom. Therefore I was disappointed to have three one act plays. However, there was a man who sang like a Prima Donna; and a patriotic Revue. We left, just as an Eastern jar, coloured grey and violet, shot up in the middle of the stage.

We wrote this morning. I took Max along the River, but we were a good deal impeded, by a bone he stole, by my suspenders coming down, by a dogfight in which his ear was torn and bled horribly. I thought how happy

I was, without any of the excitements which, once, seemed to me to constitute happiness. L. and I argued for some time about this. Also about the worthlessness of all human works except as a means of keeping the workers happy. My writing now delights me solely because I love writing and don't, honestly, care a hang what anyone says.

Monday 18 January

This afternoon we went over the houses in Mecklenburgh Square; which has led to a long discussion about our future, and a fresh computation of income. The future is dark, which is on the whole, the best thing a future can be, I think.

Tuesday 19 January

We walked in Richmond Park this afternoon; the trees all black, and the sky heavy over London; but there is enough colour to make it even lovelier today than on bright days, I think. The deer exactly matched the bracken. But L. was melancholy. When I analyse his mood, I attribute much of it to sheer lack of self confidence in his power of writing; as if he mightn't be a writer, after all; and being a practical man, his melancholy sinks far deeper than the half assumed melancholy of self conscious people like Lytton, and Sir Leslie and myself. There's no arguing with him.

Wednesday 20 January

Having finished a chapter, I went off buying small fragments of things part of the morning – For one thing, I saw a mass of pinkish stuff in the fishmongers, and bought it – Cods' Roe. Maynard Keynes came to dinner. We gave him oysters. He is like quicksilver on a sloping board – a little inhuman, but very kindly, as inhuman people are. We gossiped at full speed. Then we talked about the war. We aren't fighting now, he says, but only waiting for the spring. Meantime we lavish money, on a scale which makes the French, who are fearfully out at elbow, gape with admiration. We are bound to win – and in great style too, having at the last moment applied all our brains and all our wealth to the problem.

Friday 22 January

When L. pulled the curtains this morning, practically no light came in; there was a kind of greyish confusion outside – soft swirling incessant snow. This has gone on all day almost, sometimes changing to rain. The Green itself is very lovely; and lights up the room with its pure white glare. But the streets become brown directly. Of course, in this House of Trouble, the pipes burst; or got choked; or the roof split asunder. Anyhow in the middle of the morning I heard a steady rush of water in the wainscot; and

Mrs Le Grys, Lizzy and various people have been clambering about the roof ever since. The water still drips through the ceiling into a row of slop pails. We are going to hear the Fabians at Essex Hall.

Saturday 23 January

The Fabians were well worth hearing; still more worth seeing. The interest was watching Mrs [Beatrice] Webb, seated like an industrious spider at the table; spinning her webs (a pun!) incessantly. The hall was full of earnest drab women, and of broad nosed, sallow, shock headed young men, in brown tweed suits. They all looked unhealthy and singular and impotent. It was all very dull and sensible, and the idea that these frail webspinners can affect the destiny of nations seems to me fantastic. But it was well worth going, – and I have now declared myself a Fabian. Oliver and Ray [Strachey] dined with us. Oliver as usual, very prompt, impatient and rather testy. Ray solid and capable and soothing. We discussed the war.

Monday 25 January

My birthday – and let me count up all the things I had. L. had sworn he would give me nothing, and like a good wife, I believed him. But he crept into my bed, with a little parcel, which was a beautiful green purse. And he brought up breakfast, with a paper which announced a naval victory (we have sunk a German battleship) and a square brown parcel, with *The Abbot* in it – a lovely first edition. So I had a very merry and pleasing morning – which indeed was only surpassed by the afternoon. I was then taken up to town, free of charge, and given a treat, first at a Picture Palace, and then at Buzzards [Tea Rooms]. I don't think I've had a birthday treat for ten years; and it felt like one too – being a fine frosty day, everything brisk and cheerful, as it should be, but never is. We exactly caught a non-stop train, and I have been very happy reading father on Pope, which is very witty and bright, without a single dead sentence in it. In fact I don't know when I have enjoyed a birthday so much – not since I was a child anyhow. Sitting at tea we decided three things; in the first place to take Hogarth, if we can get it; in the second, to buy a printing press; in the third to buy a bull dog, probably called John. I am very much excited at the idea of all three – particularly the press. I was also given a packet of sweets to bring home.

Wednesday 27 January

Mrs Woolf and Clara came to dinner. Mrs Woolf has the mind of a child. She is amused by everything, and yet understands nothing – says whatever comes into her head – prattles incessantly, now good humoured, now ill humoured. She told us how she used to go to bed with a basket of socks by her side, so as to start darning first thing in the morning.

Thursday 28 January
Leonard off again to lunch with the Webbs. I decided to go to London, for the sake of hearing the Strand roar, which I think one does want, after a day or two of Richmond. Somehow, one can't take Richmond seriously. One had always come here for an outing, I suppose; and that is part of its charm, but one wants serious life sometimes. A new servant has come today. Lizzy left, carrying a brown paper parcel and whistling loudly – I wonder where she has gone?

Saturday 30 January
L. went to Chancellors this morning about Hogarth. They will let us know on Monday for certain.

Sunday 31 January
O dear! We quarrelled almost all the morning! and it was a lovely morning, and now gone to Hades for ever, branded with the marks of our ill humour. Which began it? Which carried it on? God knows. This I will say: I explode; and L. smoulders. However, quite suddenly we made it up (but the morning was wasted), and we walked after lunch in the Park, and came home by way of Hogarth, and tried to say that we shan't be much disappointed if we don't get it. After tea I started reading *The Wise Virgins*, and I read it straight on till bedtime, when I finished it. My opinion is that its a remarkable book; very bad in parts; first rate in others. A writer's book, I think, because only a writer perhaps can see why the good parts are so very good, and why the very bad parts aren't very bad. I was made very happy by reading this; I like the poetic side of L. and it gets a little smothered in Blue-books, and organisations.

Monday 1 February
We went up to London – L. to the London Library, I to Day's. I walked with him across the Green Park. In St James Street there was a terrific explosion; people came running out of Clubs; stopped still and gazed about them. But there was no Zeppelin or aeroplane – only, I suppose, a very large tyre burst. But it is really an instinct with me, and most people, I suppose, to turn any sudden noise, or dark object in the sky, into an explosion, or a German aeroplane. And it always seems utterly impossible that one should be hurt.

We have just been rung up by Chancellors, who wish us to see the owner of Hogarth tomorrow. In fact it seems quite likely at this moment that we shall get Hogarth. I wish it were tomorrow. I am certain it is the best house to take.

Tuesday 2 February

Well, it is tomorrow; and we are certainly nearer to Hogarth than we were.
We have done little else and thought of little else all day.

There are no entries in VW's diary for the next ten days

Saturday 13 February

There was a great downpour this morning. I am sure however many years
I keep this diary, I shall never find a winter to beat this. It seems to have
lost all self control. We wrote; and after luncheon L. went to the Library,
and I went to a concert at the Queen's Hall. I got by luck a very good
place, for the Hall was nearly full – and it was a divine concert. But one of
the things I decided as I listened (its difficult not to think of other things)
was that all descriptions of music are quite worthless, and rather unpleasant;
they are apt to be hysterical, and to say things that people will be ashamed
of having said afterwards. They played Haydn, Mozart no. 8, Brandenburg
Concerto, and the Unfinished. I daresay the playing wasn't very good, but
the stream of melody was divine. It struck me what an odd thing it was –
this little box of pure beauty set down in the middle of London streets, and
people – all looking so ordinary, crowding to hear, as if they weren't
ordinary after all, or had an ambition for something better. I was annoyed
by a young man and woman next to me who took advantage of the music
to press each other's hands. And other people eat chocolates, and crumbled
the silver paper into balls.

Sunday 14 February

Rain again today. I cleaned silver, which is an easy and profitable thing to
do. It so soon shines again. Philip came, and he and L. went for a walk. He
lunched with us and stayed talking till 3.30, wanting to talk about himself
perhaps and had to go back to Colchester, where the only tolerable thing
is the oysters.

Monday 15 February

We both went up to London this afternoon; L. to the Library, and I to
ramble about the West End, picking up clothes. I am really in rags. It is
very amusing. With age too one's less afraid of the superb shop women.
These great shops are like fairies' palaces now. I swept about in Debenham's
and Marshall's and so on, buying, as I thought, with great discretion. The
shop women are often very charming, in spite of their serpentine coils of
black hair. Then I had tea, and rambled down to Charing Cross in the dark,

making up phrases and incidents to write about. Which is, I expect, the way one gets killed. I bought a ten and elevenpenny blue dress, in which I sit at this moment.

1917

Virginia Woolf's record of daily life at The Green, Richmond, early in 1915 was brought to an end by the onset of a very severe mental breakdown. Soon after she became ill – mad, she called it – Leonard took possession of Hogarth House in Paradise Road, Richmond, and it was here and at her rented country house, Asheham in Sussex, that Virginia slowly recovered under the care of professional nurses, the last of whom left towards the end of the year, when she was able to resume a comparatively normal, if cautious, life. In February 1916 her household was augmented by two living-in servants, Nelly Boxall the cook and her impetuous friend Lottie Hope, who were to serve and to exasperate Virginia for many years to come. As Leonard became more and more involved in political activities, Virginia resumed her connection with The Times Literary Supplement, *and from 1916 onwards she contributed a regular stream of book reviews to this and other periodicals. Early in 1917 the Woolfs realised their intention (recorded by Virginia on her birthday in 1915) to buy a printing press, and that summer they issued their first hand-printed publication,* Two Stories. Written and Printed by Virginia and L. S. Woolf, *and then began to set* Prelude, *the long short story by Katherine Mansfield, whom they had met some time earlier. Thenceforth the preoccupations and satisfactions of the 'Hogarth Press' were an ever-present factor in their lives.*

Richmond is some distance from central London, but nevertheless the Woolfs maintained an active social life. Friends readily came out to meals, to walk with them in the neighbouring parks or to stay overnight; they themselves frequently went up by train to meetings, concerts, libraries, parties and so forth in London. Their circle included those drawn in through Leonard's political interests – in particular the doughty Margaret Llewelyn Davies, the General Secretary of the Women's Co-operative Guild; ramifications of family on both sides; and old friends such as Desmond MacCarthy and Roger Fry who were joined by a younger generation – Cambridge graduates like 'Ka' Cox, Karin Costelloe (who had married Adrian Stephen in 1914), Alix Sargant-Florence and, from the Slade School of Fine Art, Saxon Sydney-Turner's Egeria, Barbara Hiles, and Lytton Strachey's devotee, Dora Carrington.

Inevitably the war was a continuing background to their lives; four of Leonard's brothers joined the army; one was killed; and he himself was called up in May 1916 but, concerned rather for Virginia's than his own welfare, he obtained from their doctors certificates of unfitness for military service (he suffered from an uncontrollable

14

nervous tremor of the hands). Many of their circle had conscientious objections to the war, including Virginia's brother Adrian and her brother-in-law Clive Bell – who was nominally doing farm work on the estate of the Liberal MP Philip Morrell and his aristocratic wife Lady Ottoline at Garsington, near Oxford, which they had made a refuge for artists, intellectuals, and Conscientious Objectors. Clive and Vanessa, whose sons Julian and Quentin were born in 1908 and 1910, had some time since effected an amicable detachment, though both retained rooms in their former home in Gordon Square, the lease of which had been taken over by Maynard Keynes. Clive was engaged in a long affair with Mary Hutchinson; and Vanessa had fallen in life-long love with the painter Duncan Grant (both incidentally cousins of Lytton Strachey); and it was to enable him and his friend David (Bunny) Garnett to obtain agricultural work (upon which their exemption from military service depended) that Vanessa had moved her household to Charleston, an isolated farmhouse which Leonard had found about four miles from Asheham, which was to remain her, Duncan and Clive's country home until their deaths some half a century later.

1917

Hogarth House, Paradise Road, Richmond

Monday 8 October

This attempt at a diary is begun on the impulse given by the discovery in a wooden box in my cupboard of an old volume, kept in 1915, and still able to make us laugh at Walter Lamb. This therefore will follow that plan – written after tea, written indiscreetly, and by the way L. has promised to add his page when he has something to say. We planned today to get him an autumn outfit in clothes, and to stock me with paper and pens. This is the happiest day that exists for me. It rained steadily of course. London seems unchanged. We walked through Gough Square; Dr Johnson's house a fine, very well kept place, not so shabby as I expected. A little square, folded in behind Chancery Lane, and given over to printing presses. This is the best part of London to look at – not I now think to live in.

Tuesday 9 October

We had a horrid shock. L. came in so unreasonably cheerful that I guessed a disaster. He has been called up. It was piteous to see him shivering, physically shivering, so that we lit his gas fire, and only by degrees became more or less where we were in spirits; and still, if one could wake to find it untrue, it would be a mercy.

We took a proof of the first page of K[atherine] M[ansfield]'s story, *The Prelude*. It looks very nice, set solid in the new type. We had a short walk by the river. As it is a fine, fairly still evening, perhaps I shall have a raid to describe tomorrow. I forget how many people rang us up this morning, Alix [Sargant-Florence] for one, who wants to start her work apparently; and we have a liver and bacon Clumber [spaniel] in view, the property of a man taken for the army.

Wednesday 10 October

No air raid; no further disturbance by our country's needs. We walked down the river, through the park, and back to an early tea. At this moment, L. is bringing the 17 Club into existence. I am sitting over the fire, and we

have the prospect of K. Mansfield to dinner, when many delicate things fall
to be discussed. We notice how backward the leaves are in falling and
yellowing here compared with Asheham. It might still be August, save for
the acorns scattered on the path – suggesting to us the mysterious dispensation which causes them to perish, or we should be a forest of oaks.

Thursday 11 October
The dinner last night went off; the delicate things were discussed. We could
both wish that one's first impression of K.M. was not that she stinks like a
– well civet cat that had taken to street walking. In truth, I'm a little shocked
by her commonness at first sight; lines so hard and cheap. However,
when this diminishes, she is so intelligent and inscrutable that she repays
friendship. We discussed Henry James, and K.M. was illuminating I thought.
Today poor L. had to go the round of doctors and committees. His
certifications are repeated. He weighs only 9 stone 6 pounds.

Sunday 14 October
We were rung up and asked to dine with the Bells in Soho, and this, I regret to say, led to much argument: the night was wet, and L. didn't want –
old arguments in short were brought out, with an edge to them. So we
went dolefully enough, and found the place, behind the Palace [Theatre],
dined with Roger [Fry], Nina Hamnett, Saxon and Barbara [Hiles] and a
party such as might figure in a Wells novel; I enjoyed it though, and L.
was a model of self-control. Clive's remarks tended to prove that he is at
the centre of everything, but not so aggressive as usual.

Then on Saturday – what happened? Saturday was entirely given over
to the military. We are safe again, and, so they say, for ever. Our appearance
smoothed every obstacle. I waited in a great square, surrounded by barrack
buildings, and was reminded of a Cambridge college – soldiers crossing,
coming out of staircases, and going into others; but no gravel and no grass.
A disagreeable impression of control and senseless determination. A great
boarhound, emblem of military dignity I suppose, strolled across by himself.
L. was a good deal insulted: the doctors referred to him as 'the chap with
senile tremor', through a curtain. Mercifully the impression slowly vanished
as we went about Richmond. Herbert [Woolf] came to tea, bringing the
dog, Tinker, a stout, active, bold brute, brown and white, with large
luminous eyes. We have taken him for a walk, but directly he is loosed, he
leaps walls, dashes into open doors, and behaves like a spirit in quest of
something not to be found. We doubt rather if we can cope with him.

We are to have Alix and Lilian [Harris] to dinner.

Monday 15 October
Alix and Lilian were much as usual last night. Alix has the same air of level headed desperation, solid, capacious, but as low in tone as a coal cellar. However we found her very anxious to take on our work; and comes to learn tomorrow.

Tuesday 16 October
We started printing in earnest after lunch, and Alix came punctually; was instructed, and left on her high stool while we took the air with Tinker, who jumped from a parapet into a boat covered with tarpaulin, crashed through, and out again, unhurt though surprised. We came back, and Alix solemnly and slowly explained that she was bored, and also worried by her two hours composing, and wished to give it up. A sort of morbid scrutiny of values and of motives, joined with crass laziness, leads her to this decision; and I expect it will lead her to many more. She has a good brain, but not enough vitality to keep it working.

Wednesday 17 October
I went up to the show of pictures at Heal's this afternoon. Ottoline [Morrell] was not at her ease; closely buttoned up in black velvet, hat like a parasol, satin collar, pearly, tinted eyelids, and red gold hair. Needless to say one saw nothing of the pictures. Aldous Huxley was there – infinitely long and lean, with one opaque white eye. We had tea with Roger. I was very much conscious of strain – Ott languid, and taking refuge in her great ladyhood, which is always depressing. I walked with her in the downpour to Oxford Street, she buying me crimson carnations, without cordiality.

Friday 19 October
The sweetness of Ka [Cox]'s nature, so we thought, is triumphing over the bureaucracy which threatened to straitwaistcoat all her charm. Not but what office life isn't a pool past which one has to lead her. She spent the night, was down with her leather case in hand to catch an early train. I had a letter from Nessa about servants, and so went up to Mrs Hunt's [Domestic Agency] this afternoon. Not a parlourmaid to be had. With some skilful manipulation of trains, I reached the Æolian Hall, paid my shilling and heard a very long and very lovely Schubert octet. Coming out, I saw a grey, shockheaded woman without a hat – Alix; and we had tea at Spikings. She has a kind of independence and lack of concern for appearances which I admire. But as we walked up and down Dover Street she seemed on the verge of rolling up the usual veil of laughter and gossip and revealing her sepulchral despair – poor woman. "Where are you going now Alix?" "I really don't know." "Well, that sounds dismal! Don't you look forward to

say eleven tomorrow morning?" "I merely wish it didn't exist that's all!"
So I left her, hatless, aimless, unattached, wandering in Piccadilly.

Saturday 20 October

Happily, or she might say unhappily, for Alix she didn't presumably wander
in Piccadilly all night, or the great bomb which ploughed up the pavement
opposite Swan & Edgar's might have dug her grave. It turns out that a
Zeppelin came over, hovered unseen for an hour or two and left.

Sunday 21 October

Lytton [Strachey] came to luncheon, and Goldie [Goldsworthy Lowes Dick-
inson] to dinner – so we must have talked for six or seven hours. We walked
down the river and through the Park, Lytton in good spirits, having finished
a book of 100,000 words [*Eminent Victorians*], though now pretending that it
can't be published. He means to leave London and live 'for ever' in the country.
It seems a good thing that one's friends should try experiments. Poor old
Goldie is evidently beyond that stage. This war seems to possess him, to leave
little over. In fact he looked very shrunk and worn; infinitely good, charming,
devoted, every ounce of vitality rightly applied – no time for experiments, not
enough curiosity perhaps, though extreme kindliness and sympathy, which
in the case of young men, becomes amorous.

Monday 22 October

The moon grows full, and the evening trains are packed with people leaving
London. We saw the hole in Piccadilly this afternoon. Traffic has been
stopped, and the public slowly tramps past the place. Swan & Edgar has every
window covered with sacking or planks; you see shop women looking out
from behind: 'business goes on as usual' so they say. Our London Library
stands whole, however, and we found our books, and came home in the tube,
standing the whole way to Hammersmith, and have just come in.

Tuesday 23 October

Another lapse in this book, I must confess; but if I do it against my humour
I shall begin to loathe it; so the one chance of life it has is to submit to
lapses uncomplainingly. I remember though that we walked, printed, and
Margaret [Llewelyn Davies] came to tea. How pale these elderly women
get! The rough pale skin of toads, unfortunately: Margaret in particular
easily loses the flash of her beauty. This time we were whelmed in the
Co-op revolution; I get an occasional swinge of the tail which reminds me
of the extremely insignificant position I have in this important world. I get
a little depressed, a little anxious to find fault – a question of not being in
the right atmosphere. L. I suppose feels the same about Gordon Square.

Thursday 25 October

Saxon and Barbara dined with us; Saxon as usual when with her – gentle and giving off a sound as of a boiling, but not over boiling, kettle; speechless of course. As she has only simple direct things to say, L. and I were a little sleepy; but we have arranged that she is to take up printing. I am going to Asheham on Monday with Saxon.

Sunday 28 October

Still no raids, presumably the haze at evening keeps them off, though it is still and the moon perfectly clear. The numbers who have gone out of London this week must feel a little foolish.

Friday 2 November

L. is giving a lecture at Birkenhead at this precise moment, and will then I suppose travel all night across England before reaching me. I feel as if I'd moved about a great deal; kept moving to keep myself warm. I mean Asheham and Charleston were rather in the nature of distractions, so as not to think how strange and solitary I was. Not solitary in the literal sense of course. Yesterday at Charleston it rained all day, so I sat in; writing in the morning; sitting in the Studio after luncheon. Duncan painted a table, and Nessa copied a Giotto. I unpacked all my bits of gossip. They are very large in effect, these painters; very little self-conscious; they have smooth broad spaces in their minds where I am all prickles and promontories. Nevertheless to my thinking few people have a more vigorous grasp or a more direct pounce than Nessa. Two little boys with very active minds keep her in exercise. I like the feeling that she gives of a whole nature in use. In working order I mean; living practically, not an amateur, as Duncan and Bunny [Garnett] both to some extent are of course. I suppose this is the effect of children and of responsibility, but I always remember it in her. A love of the actual fact, is strong in her.

But I was glad to come home, and feel my real life coming back again – I mean life here with L. One's personality seems to echo out across space, when he's not there to enclose all one's vibrations. This is not very intelligibly written; but the feeling itself is a strange one – as if marriage were a completing of the instrument, and the sound of one alone penetrates as if it were a violin robbed of its orchestra or piano. A dull wet night, so I shall sleep.

Saturday 3 November

I woke 5 minutes before 7, and lay listening, but heard nothing, and was about, at 8 o'clock, to flatten out all my expectations when I heard L. at the door and there he was! With the softness of a mouse he had let himself in and breakfasted. We talked for as long as we could; divine contentment at being once more harmonious.

Tuesday 6 November
The melancholy fact is that Tinker, at the present moment, 5.30, is lost. He was let out in the garden and presumably escaped. We took the bus to Kingston; visited for the last time let us hope in our lives, the Recruiting Office, and after waiting in the familiar room with the two wooden benches, the towel hanging up and the khaki coat, L. was summoned, and given his paper which states that he is 'permanently and totally disabled.' We suppose this might fetch £500 if sold. However we were rather dashed by the loss of the spaniel whom we had come to like.

Saturday 10 November
Another melancholy fact is that I've let all these days pass – two of them because I was out late, the third, Friday, because I was too gloomy, and we were both too argumentative, to make writing possible. However to deal with the dissipations first. Nessa was up, and I had a Bloomsbury afternoon. I went to the Omega where Roger was convoying three chattering Frenchwomen round the show, and giving the impression as usual that French manners and language have a peculiar relish for him. The pictures glimmered through the dusk; and I was chiefly impressed by the Gertlers; Vanessa, too, very good; Duncan, I thought, a little pretty or tending to be. Nessa came and we left, I buying an apricot coloured coat on my way. I had tea in Gordon Square, which always puzzles me under the new arrangement, there being no sitting room. This was the prelude to a party on Thursday, to which I went, through the wet and the dirt, a very long expedition for two hours of life, though I enjoyed it. The usual sensation of being in a familiar but stimulating atmosphere, in which all the people one's in the habit of thinking of, were there in the body. A great many mop headed young women in amber and emerald sitting on the floor. I spent most of my time with Oliver [Strachey], and as the clock struck 10 I got up and went – an example of virtue if ever there was one. And now we see how the gloom came about. L. was testy, dispiriting, and tepid. We slept. I woke to a sense of failure and hard treatment. This persisted, one wave breaking after another, all day long. We walked on the river bank in a cold wind, under a grey sky. Both agreed that life seen without illusion is a ghastly affair. Illusions wouldn't come back. However they returned about 8.30, in front of the fire, and were going merrily till bedtime, when some antics ended the day.

Monday 12 November
Today we've been to London, as usually happens on Monday. We went to the Omega, and in came Roger, which embarrassed me a little, partly because of his own pictures, and also because I don't like talking of art in

front of him. He was in process of painting a table though, and disappeared. Then we went to Gordon Square, and who should open the door but Clive? He asked us in, and there was Mary Hutchinson in one of the big armchairs, a piteous half moon of a woman, to my thinking. She seems so crushed and submissive always.

Tuesday 13 November
We began our printing off this afternoon, and we printed 300 copies of the first page [of *Prelude*], but we should be glad of another press, though the results are very good for the most part. L. is making up a lecture he's giving at Hammersmith; I'm to preside over the Women's [Co-operative] Guild.

Wednesday 14 November
L. gave his lecture; I presided over my guild. It always puzzles me to know why the women come, unless they like sitting in a room not their own, gas and light free, other women on other chairs. They don't pay much attention apparently.

Thursday 15 November
We printed off another page, very successfully, which took till tea time, and then we went round in the semi-darkness to the little printer [owner of The Prompt Press] who will come round any moment now to see the room for the press.

Monday 19 November
The little printer came round at the end of the last page, and stayed perhaps one hour. We have advanced £10, and for that bought the cutting press, and stipulated that the printing press shall be here by January 14. On Friday we went to a concert, walking out when the English piece came on. Tea at Spikings, with some of the upper classes; who looked like pet dogs threatened with a cold bath. They were talking of the scarcity of motor cars. I bought a pair of stockings and then home. The stockings were in preparation for Garsington. We came back from that adventure two hours ago. It's difficult to give the whole impression, save that it wasn't much unlike my imagination. People strewn about in a sealingwax coloured room: Aldous Huxley toying with great round disks of ivory and marble – the draughts of Garsington; [Dorothy] Brett in trousers; Philip [Morrell] tremendously encased in the best leather; Ottoline, as usual, velvet and pearls; two pug dogs. Lytton semi-recumbent in a vast chair. Too many nick nacks for real beauty, too many scents, and silks, and a warm air which was a little heavy. Droves of people moved about from room to room all Sunday. After tea I had perhaps an hour over a log fire with Ottoline. On

the whole I liked [her] better than her friends have prepared one for liking her. Her vitality seemed to me a credit to her, and in private talk her vapours give way to some quite clear bursts of shrewdness. The horror of the Garsington situation is great of course; but to the outsider the obvious view is that Ottoline and Philip and Garsington House provide a good deal, which isn't accepted very graciously. In such conditions I think Ott deserves some credit for keeping her ship in full sail, as she certainly does. We were made immensely comfortable; a good deal of food; the talk had frequent bare patches, but then this particular carpet had been used fairly often. By talking severely to Philip, L. made him come up to Parliament today. He is a weak amiable long suffering man, who seems generally to be making the best of things, and seeing the best of people whom by nature he dislikes.

Thursday 22 November
On Wednesday Barbara came to make a start, and the machine thereupon completely struck work, and as our stock of K's ran out, she could only set four lines. This she did however, quickly and without fault, so that she promises well. She bicycled from Wimbledon, her small crop head, bright cheeks, brilliant waistcoat give her a likeness to some vivacious bird; but I don't know that I think this very emphatic appearance particularly interesting.

I dined with Roger and met Clive. We sat at the low square table covered with a bandanna, and eat out of dishes each holding a different bean or lettuce; delicious food for a change. We drank wine, and finished with soft white cheese, eaten with sugar. Then, taking a splendid flight above personalities, we discussed literature and aesthetics. Roger asked me if I founded my writing upon texture or upon structure; I connected structure with plot, and therefore said 'texture'. Then we discussed the meaning of structure and texture in painting and in writing. Then we discussed Shakespeare, and Roger said Giotto excited him just as much. This went on till I made myself go precisely at 10. And we discussed also Chinese poetry; Clive said the whole thing was too distant to be comprehensible. Roger compared the poetry with the painting. I liked it all very much (the talk I mean); the atmosphere puts ideas into one's head, and one can speak them straight out and be understood – indeed disagreed with. Old Roger takes a gloomy view, not of our life, but of the world's future.

Monday 26 November
Today I went into London with my manuscript; and Leonard – which entry was broken off somehow – but my recollection is that L. found Desmond [MacCarthy] at the London Library; together they look up the word f—— in the slang dictionary, and were saddened and surprised to

see how the thumb marks of members were thick on the page. My afternoon was by comparison chaste; though I'm hardly proud of the fact that I completely lost my way in seeking Printing House Square. A kind man in uniform took me to *The Times* at last.

Monday 3 December
On Saturday L. gave a lecture at Hampstead. But we had to race off in the Tube to Leicester Square to dine with Barbara, Saxon and a young woman; then on to *Figaro* at the Old Vic. It's perfectly lovely; breaking from one beauty into another, and so romantic as well as witty – the perfection of music, and vindication of opera.

On Sunday we heard of Cecil [Woolf]'s death, and Philip's wounds.

Wednesday 5 December
Our apprentice weighs rather heavily upon us. For one thing her presence is rather in the way of our complete comfort. It may be her youth; something highly polished so as to reflect without depth about her – On the other hand, she's nice, considerate; one can be open with her. The real drawback is her work. Today has been spent by L. in the futile misery of trying to print from one of her pages which won't lock up. As the other page had to be entirely taken down and re-set, her work amounts to *nil*; less than nil, considering L.'s time wasted. A bitter cold day too.

Thursday 6 December
Nothing was further from our minds than air raids; a bitter night, no moon up till eleven. At 5 however I was wakened by L. to a most instant sense of guns: as if one's faculties jumped up fully dressed. We took clothes, quilts, a watch and a torch, the guns sounding nearer as we went down stairs to sit with the servants wrapped in quilts in the kitchen passage. Slowly the sounds got more distant, and finally ceased; we unwrapped ourselves and went back to bed. In ten minutes there could be no question of staying there; guns apparently at Kew. Up we jumped, more hastily this time. Servants apparently calm and even jocose. Guns at one point so loud that the whistle of the shell going up followed the explosion. Then silence. Cocoa was brewed for us, and off we went again. Having trained one's ears to listen one can't get them not to for a time; and as it was after 6, carts were rolling out of stables, motor cars throbbing, and the prolonged ghostly whistlings which meant, I suppose, Belgian work people recalled to the munitions factory. At last in the distance I heard bugles; L. was by this time asleep, but the dutiful boy scouts came down our road and wakened him carefully.

Today we have printed, and discussed the raid, which, according to the

Star I bought was the work of twenty-five Gothas, attacking in five squadrons and two were brought down. A perfectly still and fine winter's day, so about 5.30 tomorrow morning perhaps –

Friday 7 December

But there was no raid; and as the moon wanes, no doubt we are free for a month. Happily no apprentice today, which gives a sense of holiday. Nessa was up about a governess, so I ended my afternoon in one of the great soft chairs at Gordon Square. I sat alone for twenty minutes, reading a book on Children and Sex. When Nessa came we had tea and it was discovered that Clive and Mary were in the house; the same party as usual. As usual to my liking; so much alive, so full of information of the latest kind; real interest in every sort of art; and in people too. I rather expect L. to disagree with all this. I judge by the amount of animation of brain produced in myself. Not that Mary Hutchinson opens her lips, but she has an air of mute sympathy. Nessa had to go round to Roger's, and I walked with her, buying sausages and cheese for a supper party on the way. Roger is becoming one of the successes of the day as a painter of perfectly literal and very unpleasant portraits.

Sunday 9 December

Lytton came to tea. I was alone, for L. went to Margaret. I enjoyed it very much. He is one of the most supple of our friends; I don't mean passionate or masterful or original, but the person whose mind seems softest to impressions, least starched by any formality or impediment. There is his great gift of expression of course, never (to me) at its best in writing; but making him in some respects the most sympathetic and understanding friend to talk to. Moreover, he has become, or now shows it more fully, curiously gentle, sweet tempered, considerate; and if one adds his peculiar flavour of mind, his wit and infinite intelligence, he is a figure not to be replaced by any other combination. Intimacy seems to me possible with him as with scarcely any one; for, besides tastes in common, I like and think I understand his feelings – even in their more capricious developments; for example in the matter of Carrington. He spoke of her, by the way, with a candour not flattering, though not at all malicious. "That woman will dog me" – he remarked. "She won't let me write, I daresay." "Ottoline was saying you would end by marrying her." "God! the mere notion is enough – One thing I know – I'll never marry anyone –" "But if she's in love with you?" "Well, then she must take her chance." "I believe I'm sometimes jealous –" "Of her? that's inconceivable –" "You like me better, don't you?" He said he did; we laughed. He brought us his Gordon. Next day he was to take the book to Chatto & Windus.

Tuesday 11 December

The infliction of our apprentice. I own that I sounded the very depths of boredom with Barbara. She gives out facts precisely as she received them – minute facts about governesses and houses. And no doubt of her own adequacy crosses her mind; all so nice, honest, sensible, how can there be a flaw; And the time passed; she missed her train; waited on for another – waited until 6.10 – and my evening fretted away without sensation, save of one standing under the drip of a water spout.

Wednesday 12 December

This morning ruined by the tears and plaints of Lottie [Hope], who thinks her work too hard, and finally demanded higher wages, which she could easily get, and so could Nell [Boxall]. I lost my temper, and told her to get them then. Up came Nelly in a conciliatory mood regretting Lottie's outburst, though pointing out the hardships of our printing-room, so untidy – work endless; had meant to ask a rise in February – everyone's wages raised. We were very amicable; but Lottie's taunts seemed to me unpleasant – At last she went.

Thursday 13 December

By careful arrangement I limited the reconciliation scene with Lottie to fifteen minutes at eleven sharp. She sobbed; repented; took back everything she'd said; all a fabrication about overwork, and the more people we had and the more mess we made the better she liked it. She kissed me and went off, like a chastened child, leaving me with a mixture of pity and (I suppose) self complacency. The poor have no chance; no manners or self control to protect themselves with; poverty degrades, as Gissing said.

Monday 17 December

Monday, as I think I've noted before, is our marketing day – but I'm forgetting Molly MacCarthy and Walter Lamb last night –

I forget who it was that came in at this moment; and I have excuse for forgetting, since it is now *Thursday 3 January 1918*, and we're just back from Asheham. I remember though that the last days were full of people. Walter and Molly as I began to relate. And then, I can remember that we had Ka; who contemplates resignation; and then, the night after, Bob [R. C. Trevelyan]; with his pockets bulging with Georgian poetry, his talk all of books and prices asked for printing, and number of copies sold, in the midst of which Nelly burst in to say that the Take Cover had sounded. So we had our dinner party in the cellar; Bob talking at such a rate that it was necessary to listen at the window for the guns, loud enough though they were. After that – the very next night – we went to the 17 Club dinner; a great deal of eating by some two hundred people at long tables. Next day we went to Asheham, and the journey was the worst in our record – five hours; spent mostly outside Clapham Junction; fog, bitter cold; every move stopping short in a minute or two. Motored out, I remember, and found the roads under snow; but very pleasant coming into the drawing room, save that we were without milk. One of the coldest and finest of Christmases. Rather to our relief, we spent it alone. There was the usual visit from Maynard and Clive. But what I like most about Asheham is that I read books there; so divine it is, coming in from a walk to have tea by the fire and then read and read – say *Othello* – say anything. It doesn't seem to matter what. And then the trees, spare and leafless; the brown of the plough, and yesterday, downs mountainous through a mist. Solitary sportsmen beat up duck and snipe on the marshes. Windows were almost always frozen in the morning, and each blade rough with frost. Partridges would come and sit in the field, lifeless little lumps they looked, half stiff with cold perhaps.

Clive, by the way, enlivened Christmas by a small book of verse – the prose fantastically foppish, the verse very pretty and light, to my mind (by which I mean not altogether to L.'s mind).

So we come to an end of the year, and any attempt to sum it up is beyond me, or even to cast a final glance at the evening paper, with news from Russia, which has just come in and drawn L. to remark: "A very interesting state of things –" "And what's going to happen?" "No human being can foretell that."

The End

1918

Although little reference to it is made in her diary, concurrently with all her other activities, social, domestic and journalistic, Virginia was writing her second novel, Night and Day, *which she reported 'finished' in November this year, although it was six months before she submitted it to her half-brother the publisher Gerald Duckworth. The most notable extension of her customary round was her now frequent resort to the 1917 Club in Soho, a meeting place for socialists and intellectuals which Leonard had helped to bring into existence. On her expeditions to London she found it convenient to drop in there in the afternoon, after perhaps delivering her copy for Bruce Richmond, the editor of* The Times Literary Supplement *(1918 and 1919 were her most prolific years as a journalist), or getting books from the London Library, in the expectation of finding tea, congenial company and gossip.*

Leonard meanwhile was becoming increasingly involved in the Labour movement, writing, researching and lecturing; in September he was appointed editor of the International Review. *Virginia's own contribution to the betterment of society was to preside over the local branch of Margaret Llewelyn Davies's Women's Co-operative Guild, which met at Hogarth House and for which she found speakers, often from among her own friends.*

The possibilities inherent in their embryo Hogarth Press continued to attract both Leonard and Virginia, in spite of their amateurishness as printers; moreover it attracted writers too. While still working on Katherine Mansfield's Prelude, *they were approached with a request that they might print James Joyce's* Ulysses, *refused by commercial printers fearful of prosecution under obscenity laws. Virginia was both repelled and impressed by the manuscript, and Leonard would have liked to undertake it, but of course the task was far beyond their capacities. In November T. S. Eliot came to dine at Hogarth House, the beginning of a long and respected friendship; his seven* Poems *became the fourth publication of the Hogarth Press, and was followed four years later by* The Waste Land, *both set up and printed by the Woolfs themselves.*

The war growled on in the background, but finally came to its end, after surges and relapses of hope; Virginia notes the privations and alarms it caused; but though travel was precarious and difficult, she and Leonard managed to make several country visits to friends including the Morrells at Garsington, to Lytton Strachey, now installed at Tidmarsh in Berkshire attended by his devoted Carrington, to Roger Fry near Guildford, and to their own Asheham; and it was while they were here that on

28

Christmas Day Vanessa gave birth at Charleston to Angelica, her daughter by Duncan Grant, and Julian and Quentin, her two little Bell sons, were brought over to stay with their Aunt Virginia.

1918

HOGARTH HOUSE, RICHMOND

Friday 4 January
There's no reason after all why one should expect special events for the first page of a new book; still one does: and so I may count three facts of different importance: our first use of the 17 Club; talk of peace; and the breaking of my tortoiseshell spectacles. This talk of peace (after all the most important of the three) comes to the surface with a kind of tremor of hope once in three months; then subsides; then swells again. What it now amounts to, one doesn't even like to guess; at any rate, one can't help feeling something moving. The 1917 Club is a success, on the basis of one tea. We met Alix, already an habitué by the fire; together with a knot of very youthful revolutionaries, one officer, and two sallow democratic officials. The rooms are light, bear traces of Omega, and are less formal than usual. Before this, I did my usual round; L. passing his afternoon in committees.

Saturday 5 January
We went to Hampton Court. We walked across Bushy Park, and along a raised bank beneath trees to the river. It was cold, but still. Then we took a tram to Kingston and had tea at Atkinsons, where one may have no more than a single bun. Everything is skimped now. Most of the butcher's shops are shut; the only open shop was besieged. You can't buy chocolates, or toffee; flowers cost so much that I have to pick leaves instead. We have cards for most foods. The only abundant shop windows are the drapers. Other shops parade tins, or cardboard boxes, doubtless empty. (This is an attempt at the concise, historic style.) I suppose there must be some undisturbed pockets of luxury somewhere still; but the general table is pretty bare. Papers, however, flourish, and by spending sixpence we are supplied with enough to light a week's fires.

Sunday 6 January

Alix and Fredegond [Shove] for supper. The talk, after flaunting round Clive, Barbara, Garsington &c, settled upon conscience, social duties, and Tolstoy. Gerald [Shove] read Tolstoy the other day, and determined to give up tobacco, but now argues that Tolstoy's commands were for men of looser life than he, so that he may smoke cigarettes. He thinks seriously of starting a nursery garden after the war, and threatens to give up their capital. "What's the use of that?" L. demanded. "That's the worst of all things to do. We don't want people to live on thirty shillings a week." "Psychologically it may be necessary if one is to abolish capitalism" I remarked. "I don't agree" said Alix. "Besides who would he give his capital to?" "In the ideal state everyone would have £300 a year" L. went on. "Please tell me some reason that I can remember to take back to Gerald" Fredegond pleaded. I forget now what the reason was. "He's got an awful conscience" she continued. "He ate a large Christmas dinner, and then he and his brother sent out for preserved fruit and when they had finished them they were miserable. 'We've behaved like pigs!' they cried. They were both miserable." L. gave us a great many reasons why we should keep what we have, and do good work for nothing. I still feel, however, that my fire is too large for one person. I'm one of those who are hampered by the psychological hindrance of owning capital.

Tuesday 8 January

To the printer's today, and find him calmly asserting that he can't really send the Press on the 14th. Can't find anyone to move it. This is cool as he took our ten pounds on the understanding we should have the press without fail.

Wednesday 9 January

The 17 Club is something of a lure; certainly promises better conditions for tea than a shop. So, having gone for my spectacles, I went to Gerrard Street. Found Fredegond and Faith [Henderson] there, also a large semi-circle of Cambridge youths, and one or two others. I was amused at the repetition of certain old scenes from my own past – the obvious excitement, and sense of being the latest and best (though not outwardly the most lovely) of God's works, of having things to say for the first time in history; there was all this; and the young men so wonderful in the eyes of the young women, and young women so desirable in the eyes of the young men, though this was not perceptible to me sitting elderly upon my sofa. However, then I was summoned to have my tea at the far end of the room; and Lytton came in. We tried still to overhear young Cambridge, and Lytton finally decamped, on my daring him, to that party.

I then had some private talk with Faith. According to her Nick [Bagenal, her brother] is getting a great deal of pain from the Saxon Barbara Nick combination. His claims are disregarded; Barbara prefers Saxon; and seems to be ashamed of the unintellectuality of Nick. She won't take him to see her Bloomsbury friends. Bloomsbury, I think, will have one more corpse to its credit; for poor Barbara's attainments aren't such as to give her a very secure footing there; and to my thinking a marriage with Nick offers more solid value than a cold blooded and only semi-real attachment with Saxon.

Friday 11 January
Another sedentary day, which must however be entered for the sake of recording that the Lords have passed the Suffrage Bill. I don't feel much more important – perhaps slightly so. Its like a knighthood; might be useful to impress people one despises.

Saturday 12 January
The hope of peace all broken up again; policies once more running in every direction, as far as one can tell.

Monday 14 January
We had Saxon to dinner on Saturday. He was at his lowest ebb. Even his gestures are weariful. He has been nowhere, seen no one. Played chess with Leonard, was beaten which didn't add to his spirits, and left burdened with the mysteries of this unintelligible world.

On Sunday, Clive came to tea; he hadn't long settled in when the Shoves arrived; and we spent an hour or two in gossip. After Clive went, Fredegond and Gerald stayed to dinner, and were more at their ease. Fredegond has a great turn for mimicry. She mimicked Karin [Stephen] bursting into tears one night from a sense that Maynard &c didn't want to see her. In fact the dominion that 'Bloomsbury' exercises over the sane and the insane alike seems to be sufficient to turn the brains of the most robust. Happily, I'm 'Bloomsbury' myself, and thus immune; but I'm not altogether ignorant of what they mean. And its a hypnotism very difficult to shake off, because there's some foundation for it. Oddly, though, Maynard seems to be the chief fount of the magic spirit. Talk about capital with Gerald; he says he means to part with his, but I guess that he always has some scruple to play with as an intellectual exercise.

Friday 18 January
Another skip, partly due to my writing a long letter to Nessa, which drained up some of the things I should have said here. But I like this better than

letter writing. On Thursday and Friday we worked away at printing. Unvarying cold and gloom, which turns now to rain, now to snow. This is the Hell of the year. We seem to mark time in the mud.

Monday 21 January

[On Sunday] Lytton came to tea; stayed to dinner, and about 10 o'clock we both had that feeling of parched lips and used up vivacity which comes from hours of talk. But Lytton was most easy and agreeable. Among other things he gave us an amazing account of the British Sex Society which meets at Hampstead. They were surprisingly frank; and fifty people of both sexes and various ages discussed without shame such questions as the deformity of Dean Swift's penis; whether cats use the w.c.; self abuse; incest – incest between parent and child when they are both unconscious of it, was their main theme, derived from Freud. I think of becoming a member. Lytton at different points exclaimed *Penis*: his contribution to the openness of the debate. We also discussed the future of the world; how we should like professions to exist no longer; Keats, old age, politics, Bloomsbury hypnotism – a great many subjects.

Wednesday 23 January

I see I've forgotten yesterday; but it was uneventful. L. went up to a meeting, Barbara was left in control of the Press, and I took a walk by myself. I went along the river to Marble Hill. I must retract what I said about the Hell of the year. We have glimpses of Heaven. I sat by the river watching a boat launched, and half expected to see buds on the willows. River very high, swift and yellow, testifying to the floods higher up. They say its been raining heavily; I daresay it has, but such is the civilisation of life in London that what with fires, electric light, underground railways and umbrellas, how can one take notice of the weather. We dined early and had the Guild. As usual, L. and I were the only people to speak; as usual it was only when talk drifted near food that one of the women broke silence. She wanted a bread shop. Oddly phlegmatic these women for the most part; with a passive sort of pleasure in sitting there and watching like so many pale grey sea anemones stuck to their rocks. Still, the children, the housework – excuses enough if one troubled to look.

Today we printed; and I made two little excursions into Richmond. The bakers' windows now provide almost nothing but little plates of dull biscuits; sections of plain cake; and little buns without any plums. If you see a plum, it is invariably a decoy plum; there are no others. This transformation scene has been stealing on imperceptibly; last year were we still allowed iced cakes? Its unthinkable!

Friday 25 January

My Birthday. L. slid a fine cow's horn knife into my hand this morning. Nelly has knitted me a pair of red socks which tie round the ankle, and thus just suit my state in the morning. Barbara came, and together we 'dissed' four pages, and L. printed off the second four at the printers – altogether a fine day's work. At this rate Katherine's story will be done in five weeks.

Saturday 26 January

Today we went to Kew. Snowdrops, dwarf cyclamen, some miniature rhododendrons out; also the points of some squills or crocuses coming through the grass and dead leaves.

Monday 28 January

I went to have my tooth finished, winding up for tea at the Club, which becomes as Goldie said "quite a family party". You come in to find half a dozen pairs of legs radiating from chairs towards the fire. You hear, or I heard, 'its a case of revolution or evolution' and then, if you've heard enough, you seek the *Manchester Guardian*, and hide yourself for precisely ten seconds. Fredegond, with apologies, breaks through the barrier. "But they're so fearfully dull, and I must talk something that isn't politics". That something, so far as I remember, was Ottoline, Alix, poetry, love. Home I went, and there was a raid of course. From 8 to 1.15 we roamed about, between coal hole, kitchen, bedroom and drawing room. I don't know how much is fear, how much boredom; but the result is uncomfortable, most of all, I believe, because one must talk bold and jocular small talk for four hours with the servants to ward off hysteria. Next morning ——

Tuesday 29 January

– the after effects of the raid were swept aside by Barbara. "Virginia, I shan't come on Friday because I'm going to be married." "You're going to marry – ?" "Yes, Nick [Bagenal]." "And Saxon?" "Saxon doesn't mind. Nothing's to be changed. We're all agreed."

These are the terms. I don't myself think that she wishes to be married; but has convinced herself that she should. She showed no wish to be congratulated or in any way fussed over. She stayed and printed as usual.

Wednesday 30 January

Up to a concert and tea with Ottoline. She is perched in the smallest bedroom of a Bloomsbury hotel, moulting, depressed, untidy, overdressed. Not much talk of interest to me, though friendly and not so overpowering in certain directions as usual.

Friday 1 February
A day of fog in patches. Last night the worst fog they say for thirty years, and old gents who escaped the raid walked in numbers over the edge of platforms and were crushed. A cook stepped into the Thames; people walked by rapping our railings to keep the road.

Tuesday 5 February
Karin came to give her lecture. She arrived at tea time. I can't help being reminded by her of one of our lost dogs – Tinker most of all. She fairly races round a room, snuffs the corners of the chairs and tables, wags her tail as hard as she can, and snatches at any scrap of talk as if she were sharp set; and she eats a great deal of food too, like a dog. This extreme energy may be connected with deafness. She has become a Bolshevik. Socialism is nibbling at our friends in a curious way. She and Adrian have scruples about the size of their income, and wish to earn money. She gave her paper on League of Nations well, though speaking too quick. She stayed the night. But I see that Adrian must find her energy, her not fastidious or critical but generous and warm blooded mind, her honesty and stability, a great standby –

Saturday 2 March
What is the use of finishing a sentence left unfinished a month ago? Here we are; evening; I came back from Asheham, or rather Charleston, an hour ago. After Karin went that Wednesday, rather a monotonous time began for me. Influenza began on the Friday; I was kept in bed eight days; on the next Tuesday we went to Asheham. For nine of our ten days we saw no one; but the days melted into each other like snowballs roasting in the sun. On Thursday Nessa came for the night, and I went back with her to Charleston for Friday night, L. taking the servants up to town. On Saturday morning Nessa, Duncan and I sat in the studio and gossiped. Part of the time we discussed art. They say there's no one worth considering as a painter in England today – no one like Katherine Mansfield or Forster even with whom its worth discussing one's business. In France this is reversed. Nessa showed me Saxon's letters. He has been very unhappy, and made out his moments of exaltation and depression with his usual minuteness. I left at 1.15, walking in a high wind with two parcels slung across my shoulders, to Glynde; through the park. Back here for tea.

Tuesday 5 March
The Guild meets tonight for Nick [Bagenal] to address it.

Wednesday 6 March
Again one has to wonder why the women come – what inducement there is in such a passive employment as sitting silent, half asleep, in a chair for an hour. Nick was in the right style for them too; simple, detailed, casual, much at his ease. He spoke for an hour. His matter of fact way of speaking and common sense also struck me. He seemed in good spirits; proud of Barbara, and telling me how after the war they'd like to live in the country and make good furniture after designs by Carrington.

We now have a mania for gambling over Demon patience. I lost four shillings over this in a week.

Friday 8 March
Going up in the lift at Holborn the other day I stood next a boy of fourteen or so, whose head only was visible among the crowd. I noticed that it was an extremely interesting, sensitive, clever, observant head; rather sharp, but independent looking. One couldn't tell from his cap whether he was well off or not. I came to the conclusion that he was the son of an officer with whom he stood. When we got into the street I looked at once at his legs. His trousers had holes in them. From that one could judge what a wretched affair his life will be.

Saturday 9 March
We went to a meeting called a 'Suffrage Rally' in Kingsway this afternoon. The hall was fairly well filled; the audience almost wholly women, as the speakers were too. The pure essence of either sex is a little disheartening. Moreover, whether its a meeting of men or of women, one can't help wondering why they do it. I get one satisfactory thrill from the sense of multitude; then become disillusioned, finally bored and unable to listen to a word. In truth this meeting seemed to beat the waves in vain. The vote being won, only great eloquence could celebrate the triumph. None were eloquent.

We had tea at the 17 Club. One room was crowded, and silent; at the end of the other Aldous Huxley and a young woman in grey velvet held what should have been a private conversation.

Monday 11 March
I spent seven shillings on books this afternoon; a fact to be recorded, since its the only mention of buying books this year, or last, perhaps. As a matter of fact I've accumulated twelve shillings as *Times* money; add five shillings for a birthday present, and I have seventeen shillings – an unparalleled sum. First, however, I beat the town for chocolate or sweets. In the whole of the stores, not one ounce of choc to be had; but some simple square

drops, such as one used to buy in a bag for a penny. Half a crown will now buy a pound of them. Half a crown in the old days would have bought a coal-scuttle full. Then I went on the top of a bus, for the day was of the quality of June, only fresher, and sadder too, to Nutt's shop to get a Leopardi; then to Mudie's where I bought Mill on Liberty; then to the Charing Cross Road where I bought *The Happy Hypocrite* by Max Beerbohm; and *Exiles of the Snow*, by Lancelot Hogben. In this way I laid out seven shillings.

Poor Hogben's book is precisely the dreary imitative stuff one might have expected; or even worse than one might have expected – what Lytton would call 'illiterate'; under the influence of Swinburne, incredibly ungifted, and weakly rebellious.

Tuesday 12 March

I may say that I'm 'rejected by *The Times*'. Its the second week of my rejection; and it has the result of making me write my novel [*Night and Day*] at an astonishing rate. If I continue dismissed, I shall finish within a month or two. It becomes very absorbing.

Thursday 14 March

My dismissal is revoked. A large book on Pepys arrived, which I spent the evening reading, and now another on Swinburne awaits me at the Railway station. I'm divided whether one likes to have books, or to write fiction without interruption.

Monday 18 March

On Saturday the chatter began. Lytton and Carrington came to tea – she apple red and firm in the cheeks, bright green and yellow in the body, and immensely firm and large all over. The talk has run off my mind, so that I don't suppose there was anything said of great importance. Carrington going out of the room for a second, Lytton explained that he would like to stay with us without her, could it be managed. He asked me to review his book. I agreed without thinking. On second thoughts I don't much want to write under surveillance, or to ask for the book of a friend. On Sunday the burden of visitors was oppressive. Gerald [Duckworth] and Saxon lunch; Saxon tea; Barbara, Nick, Middleton Murry dinner. Gerald's likeness to a pampered overfed pug dog has much increased. The feebleness of his hold on life save through the stomach must be fearful. His commercial view of every possible subject depressed me, especially when I thought of my novel destined to be pawed and snored over by him. Saxon at his least urbane and most insignificant. He was beaten at chess, and went, as if not wishing to meet Nick and Barbara. Nick was the only cheerful one of us.

Poor Murry snarled and scowled with the misery of his lot. He works all day, and writes when he comes home. Worst of all, Katherine has been very ill with haemorrhage from the lungs, out in France, and has to be brought home, which is difficult, in order to see how bad she is. But I thought him very much more of a person and a brain than I had thought him before. I had a good deal of talk about books with him, such as one couldn't have with Nick – though he's read Jane Austen, and can keep his end up by natural good sense and taste. Barbara was almost blotted out; scarcely spoke, I think. They went first; Murry stayed on, for a time, discussing French writers and Thomas Hardy. He will never write another novel, he says. Poetry is a short cut and "life seems to me now very precarious."

Friday 5 April
Off we went to Asheham on Thursday [21 March], in such a burst of summer heat that people in the Tube pulled blinds down. The daffodils were out and the guns could be heard from the downs. Even to me, who have no immediate stake, and repudiate the importance of what is being done, there was an odd pallor in those particular days of sunshine. Our visitors broke in upon the moods which weave so thick a texture into life alone at Asheham. First Lytton. Then we waited, with eyes upon the avenue, for the appearance of Barbara. She never came though, and upon Sunday I had a letter telling the almost incredible story of her repeated attempts to get into a train; how for three days she went to Victoria; never got in, and finally spent Easter alone in her studio, expecting, so we are told, to find herself in some nine months short of a fortnight, the mother of a child. Lytton was with us one day less than a week. We had short, and to me, very intimate talks; intimate in the sense that he will understand from the sight of the tail what the whole body of the thought is in one's mind. These thoughts were for the most part about books; but books include a good deal of life. I suspect that he is now inclined to question whether Eminent Victorians, four in number, and requiring four years for their production, are quite enough to show for his age and pretensions. I suppose the contrast (and to me there is a contrast) between his achievements and L.'s achievements made itself felt to him. Then he was sick one morning. His ebb of health is very low; and certainly health does make one careful, perhaps a little peevish, spiritually. Then James [Strachey] and Noel [Olivier] came. Our patience wore rather thin. Visitors do tend to chafe one, though impeccable as friends. L. and I discussed this. He says that with people in the house his hours of positive pleasure are reduced to one; he has I forget how many hours of negative pleasure; and a respectable margin of the acutely unpleasant. Are we growing old? But this time food

difficulties certainly increased one's discomfort. One day we came back from a long walk to find the third of a loaf of bread on the table. No more to be had in the house. This was due to bad management on Nelly's part, but then at Asheham it's very easy to manage badly and needs considerable thought, cycling and carrying, to manage even tolerably. The relief of being back in comparative plenty and anyhow next door to shops is quite recognisable. We came up on Friday.

Saturday 6 April
This morning I had a letter from Barbara telling me that Nick was danger-ously wounded on the 30th; they have operated. The last news said he was well through the operation. If he recovers, perhaps he won't be sent out again – but who knows? At least she has had the blow soon. But the state of waiting for telegrams and letters, and this baby in prospect, must be as fair a combination of torture as human beings can invent for each other. Rain all day till this moment when it has turned brilliant. Plum blossom in the garden, and flowers very healthy looking.

Sunday 7 April
We are just back from tea with Barbara and Saxon in the Studio. Nick is already moved to another hospital and has written himself, so at least he must be in no immediate danger. The couple in the interior were almost too perfect an illustration of the post impressionist spirit for my taste. Even the black and white cat seemed decorated by the Omega. Whitewash in which the hairs of the brush remain, a striped pole, Burnet for the covers, china dogs for the mantelpiece, check cottons wherever you looked, and to the censorious eye one or two uncertainties of taste or reversions to an earlier stage, as for example a bead necklace hanging on a nail. I don't think Saxon had anything to say; he reminded me of a hen who has laid an egg – but only one. We did not like Hampstead. The vulgarity of Richmond is always a relief afterwards.

Monday 8 April
There is an awkward moment between coming back from London and dinner which is the salvation of this book. For some reason one can't settle to read, and yet writing seems the proper channel for the unsettled irritable condition one is generally in. Perhaps this condition is intensified by tea at the 17 Club, particularly if one happens to meet Roger in the Charing Cross Road, in his wideawake hat with four or five yellow French books under his arm. He is the centre of a whirlwind to me. Under this influence I was blown straight into a book shop, persuaded to lay out three shillings and seven pence on a French novel, made to fix a day for coming to Durbins,

invited to a play and fairly overwhelmed – made to bristle all over with ideas, questions, possibilities which couldn't develop in the Charing Cross Road. Of course he was in a hurry to keep an appointment, and to produce one or two plays somewhere – ill too, so he said, but somewhat relieved in his mind by reading Fabre, who makes him see that after all our war, hideous though it is – but here we parted.

Wednesday 10 April
A very wet dark day. Printed. I set one page in one hour and fifteen minutes – my record. At this rate, the book might be done in a month. I had a letter from Miss Harriet Weaver yesterday asking whether we would consider printing Joyce's new novel [*Ulysses*], which no other printer will do, owing presumably to its sentiments. They must be very warm, considering the success he had with his last. She is to come here, though we can hardly tackle a book. I like this dipping into the great bran pie.

Saturday 13 April
A cold dismal day, and very bad news in the newspapers. Stout red-faced elderly men are visibly perturbed. And Ireland has Conscription. If one didn't feel that politics are an elaborate game got up to keep a pack of men trained for that sport in condition, one might be dismal; one sometimes is dismal; sometimes I try to worry out what some of the phrases we're ruled by mean. I doubt whether most people even do that. Liberty, for instance.

Last night Desmond rang us up. I'm afraid our friends' motives won't stand scrutiny. His book comes out on Monday; he, though forgetting everything, yet remembers a vague joking promise of mine, uttered at least a year ago, to review it in *The Times*. He is sending me a copy. I'm now debating how to deal with these damned authors –

Thursday 18 April
Harriet Weaver appeared. Here our predictions were entirely at fault. I did my best to make her reveal herself, in spite of her appearance, all that the Editress of *The Egoist* ought to be, but she remained inalterably modest, judicious, and decorous. Her neat mauve suit fitted both soul and body; her grey gloves laid straight by her plate symbolised domestic rectitude; her table manners were those of a well bred hen. We could get no talk to go. Possibly the poor woman was impeded by her sense that what she had in the brown paper parcel was quite out of keeping with her own contents. But then how did she ever come in contact with Joyce and the rest? Why does their filth seek exit from her mouth? Heaven knows. She is incompetent from the business point of view and was uncertain what arrangements to make. We both looked at the MS which seems to be an attempt to push

the bounds of expression further on, but still all in the same direction. And so she went.

Then I went to [Roger Fry's house near] Guildford. I don't see how to put three or four hours of Roger's conversation into the rest of this page; it was about all manner of things: on growing old; on loneliness; on religion; on morality; on Nessa; on Duncan; on French literature; on education; on Jews; on marriage; and on the *Lysistrata*. We woke next morning to find the hills covered in snow, and came up in a bitter wind and rain to the Omega; so to Gordon Square; where first the new Delacroix and then the Cézanne were produced. There are six apples in the Cézanne picture. What can six apples not be? I began to wonder. There's their relationship to each other, and their colour, and their solidity. To Roger and Nessa, moreover, it was a far more intricate question than this. It was a question of pure paint or mixed; if pure which colour; emerald or viridian; and then the laying on of the paint; and the time he'd spent, and how he'd altered it, and why, and when he'd painted it – We carried it into the next room, and Lord! how it showed up the pictures there, as if you put a real stone among sham ones.

All day it rained, and L. was out to tea. I went to the Guild, which pleased me by its good sense, and the evidence that it does somehow stand for something real to these women. In spite of their solemn passivity they have a deeply hidden and inarticulate desire for something beyond the daily life; I believe they relish all the pomp of officers and elections because in some way it symbolises this other thing. They wish me to get them a speaker on Sex Education, Mrs Hiscoke telling us that she had had to get a friend to explain the period to her own daughter, and she still feels shy if the daughter is in the room when sexual subjects are discussed. She's twenty-three years old.

Today I got Desmond's book, sent, I'm sorry to say, by request of the author.

Sunday 21 April
The weather goes on with its wind and rain and occasional snow. I went to a concert at the Palladium this afternoon; but on the whole I regretted it. A man called Julian Clifford played Mozart as if it were a Dream Waltz, slowly and sentimentally with a kind of lugubrious stickiness. I must now write to Desmond, who has been telephoning, I fear, with thoughts of that review.

Friday 26 April
There are five or six days missed out – I don't remember why, but partly at least because there wasn't much to say. On Wednesday Lottie spilt half

a case of type on the floor, so that I had to spend four hours in sorting every compartment – about the most trying work there is.

Wednesday 1 May

On Saturday we went to Hampton Court, the first visit for a long time. We had a tremendous talk about the Equator. In the middle of a demonstration with two pebbles, Jack Radcliffe passed (or so I thought). This diverted my attention. A serious reprimand had to be administered. It was discovered that I took the Equator to be a circular mark, coloured dull red, upon the end of a football. The ignorance and inattention combined displayed in this remark seemed so crass that for about twenty minutes we couldn't speak. However, I was forgiven, and told about the tropics of Cancer and Capricorn. The question originally was about the time of moon and sun rise and setting in different months.

On Sunday Desmond came after dinner. He has the hard sea-worthy look of an old salt, cased in stiff black, with a few gold scrolls about him. But within this shell he is as tender and vague as ever, and very tired after his day's work [at the Admiralty] which results, he is alarmed to find and so are we, in practical action upon his evidence. He yawned, and couldn't stir himself up, though L.'s yawns were partly the cause of this. Late at night he took to reading Joyce's MS aloud, and in particular to imitating his modern imitation of a cat's miau, but L. went to bed, and though capable of spending a night in this manner, I had compunction, and decoyed Desmond upstairs, collecting books as we went. Next morning, having observed that breakfast at 8.30 would possibly be early enough, he stayed talking about books till 10, and rambled off quite out of tune for his office.

Friday 3 May

By Bus and tube to Hampstead, and to tea with Margaret [Llewelyn Davies]. Janet [Case] was there in those decorous draperies with which people compromise between art and fashion in Hampstead. Lilian [Harris] semi-recumbent upon a green pillow, Margaret immensely fat and broad; all black. I felt this to be the heart of the woman's republic. L. came in, and we had a long semi-political argument arising out of Milk combines, about government.

Monday 6 May

I went to London on my usual round; the one I like best. In my beatific state I forgot the principal thing I'd gone for: a typewriter ribbon; but never mind; that will be another day's treat. Mudie's [Library] I don't altogether like because I'm kept waiting, but I love Holborn, and the Charing Cross Road, and I rather like turning into the 17 Club, and finding or expecting to find someone I want to talk to. I don't like buying hats though. Presently Leonard came, with Adrian. Adrian looks immensely long, and his little bow tie somehow gives him a frivolous rather than distinguished air, as if a butterfly had settled on him by mistake. He has some job in an office. We gossiped. Blood is a very strong tie; so much can be taken for granted, after the first shyness. We went on to the London Library, and so home.

Tuesday 28 May

To take up the pen directly upon coming back from Asheham shows I hope that this book is now a natural growth of mine – a rather dishevelled, rambling plant, running a yard of green stalk for every flower. But first let me recall Janet, Desmond, Katherine Mansfield and Lilian; there were others – yes, there was Harry Stephen and Clive. Each left me with a page full of comments, but useless now partly I think from my habit of telling these incidents over to people, and the telling leaves a groove in my mind which gives a hardness to the memory, stereotypes it, makes it a little dull. Katherine was marmoreal, as usual, just married to Murry, and liking to pretend it a matter of convenience. She looks ghastly ill. As usual we came to an oddly complete understanding. My theory is that I get down to what is true rock in her, through the numerous vapours and pores which sicken or bewilder most of our friends. It's her love of writing I think. But she is off to Cornwall.

At Asheham we had Roger, a picnic, and I spent a night at Charleston. That is by way of company. But the important thing was the weather. We had the best display of flowers yet seen – wall flowers in profusion, columbines, phlox, and as we went huge scarlet poppies with purple stains in them. The peonies even about to burst. Last night at Charleston I lay with my window open listening to a nightingale, which beginning in the distance came very near the garden. Fishes splashed in the pond. May in England is all they say – so teeming, amorous, and creative. I talked a good deal with Nessa – much about servants and other possibilities. Roger and I croaked a kind of frogs' chorus together – how we loved and admired and were only snubbed for our pains – Nessa sitting almost silent, stitching a dress by lamplight.

Thursday 6 June

These gaps are accounted for by the weather. Its not weather for drawing up to the fire and settling in. Carrington came to tea with me [and] stayed over two hours; and I think that by itself is a sign of youth. She is odd from her mixture of impulse and self consciousness; so eager to please, conciliatory, restless, and active. I suppose the tug of Lytton's influence deranges her spiritual balance a good deal. She has still an immense admiration for him and us. She looks at a picture as an artist looks at it; she has taken over the Strachey valuation of people and art; but she is such a bustling eager creature, so red and solid, and at the same time inquisitive, that one can't help liking her. She posted me up in all the gossip. Lytton complains that the critics haven't attacked his judgments. They have copied each other and complimented him without much fineness. Still his book goes into another edition. I haven't yet read it through.

Friday 7 June
L. was told the other day that the raids are carried out by women. Women's bodies were found in the wrecked aeroplanes. They are smaller and lighter, and thus leave more room for bombs. Perhaps it is sentimental, but the thought seems to me to add a particular touch of horror.

Monday 17 June
Another gap of ten days. Ray [Strachey] for the night. Ray lectured the Women's Co-operative Guild. How strange it is to see one's friends taking their fixed shape! She has the look of conscious morality which is born of perpetual testifying to the right. She has grown heavier, more dogmatic. She speaks in all the counties of England. She has lost such feminine charm as she had; she seems mature. But she is made of solid stuff; and this comes through and pleased me, and L. likes her better than the cropheads. Ray tends to think us a set of gifted but good for nothing wastrels.

Murry and the Sangers came here to supper last Sunday. Murry was pale as death, with gleaming eyes, and a crouching way at table that seemed to proclaim extreme hunger or despair. Charlie has his wintry brightness still; but after dinner such a duet of despair was croaked by Murry and Dora as warmed the cockles of Dora's heart. 'At Christmas' said Murry, 'I was near suicide; but I worried out a formula which serves to keep me going. Its the conception of indifferentism. I have hope no longer. I live in two layers of conscience' (but I forget what these were). Dora egged him on, and sounded his praises. But to us he seemed less nice, perhaps more anxious for effect, this time than before.

Monday 24 June
[Mark] Gertler and Kot [S. S. Koteliansky] dined with us. Gertler is a plump white young man, got up for the occasion very sprucely in sponge-bag trousers. The word he would wish one to use of him is evidently 'powerful'. There is something condensed in all Jews. His mind certainly has a powerful spring to it. He is also evidently an immense egoist. He means by sheer will power to conquer art. I felt about him, as about some women, that unnatural repressions have forced him into unnatural assertions. He

examined our furniture and pictures. He likes shiny lodging house things best, he said. He has never felt akin to anyone. He thinks himself very much cleverer than most painters. Kot sat indulgently silent.

We had a visit from Margaret; which opened with a tremendous broadside of co-operative shop: lamentations, aspirations and too sanguine expectations; all exaggerated, so I felt, in comparison with their real value. Margaret stayed till the last train. She is a fine specimen of the public woman; a type, after all, no less marked than the literary type, though not yet so fully observed and recorded. Their eccentricities keep me amused, when to tell the truth, I've ceased to follow their plots and denunciations. They have the habit of considering themselves driven to death, overwhelmed with work, without a possibility of rest; and never once since I've known her has Margaret owned to any state of health save that of being very tired. But these peculiarities are not more than jokes to me; and the directness and superb vigour of her character always overcome me with admiration.

Before tea this afternoon I finished setting up the last words of Katherine's story – 68 pages.

Thursday 27 June
Mrs Woolf and Herbert dined with us on Tuesday. She has, I think, the qualities of a person who has never altogether grown up, in spite of nine children and all her cares. She gossips and enjoys herself, and somehow deals with life very freely and easily and with the liveliest childlike interest in it all, mixed with the most absurd conventions. She chattered away. "But Rasselas says the truth – a very fine truth" she observed. "Happiness is never perfect – I've never found perfect happiness – always something missing, Virginia." Herbert cordial, distant, and detached as usual.

Monday 1 July
We've talked a great deal since I wrote last. First there was the party at the Club on Friday. All sorts of people one half knew from the papers – men with shaggy hair and great eyebrows – women cadaverous or flamboyant – [Ramsay] Macdonald, Huysmans, Mrs Despard, [J. H.] Thomas and so on. We dined with Adrian and Karin, a good dinner; at 9 we went on to Ray's party – a dull affair, neither respectable nor bohemian. On Saturday I went to tea with Janet – but my hand shakes so with carrying parcels that I can't write.

Friday 5 July
Today L. printed off the last of *Prelude*, only the title page and dedication still to do.

Tuesday 9 July

I can't fill up the lost days, though it is safe to attribute much space in them to printing. The title page was finally done on Sunday. Now I'm in the fury of folding and stapling, so as to have all ready for glueing and sending out tomorrow and Thursday. By rights these processes should be dull; but its always possible to devise some little skill or economy, and the pleasure of profiting by them keeps one content.

Wednesday 10 July

We have sent off our first copies this evening, after spending the afternoon in glueing and covering. They surprised us when done by their professional look. I must read the book through after dinner, partly to find possible faults, but also to make up my mind how much I like it as literature.

Adrian and Karin dined here last night, and he spoke to the Guild on Peace – very composed, clear, well spoken. He has traces of the judicial mind and manner. The women would all have peace tomorrow, on any terms, and abuse our government for leading us on after a plan of their own. When asked to join a Peace Meeting in Hyde Park on Sunday, Mrs Langton, as spokeswoman, intimated that on no account could they violate the Sabbath. What a terrible grip Christianity still has – she became rigid and bigoted at once, as if God himself had her in his grasp. That I believe is still the chief enemy – the fear of God. But I was tactful enough to keep this view dark.

Friday 12 July

Great storms have been beating over England the last three days, God being, as usual, spiteful in his concessions, and now threatening to ruin the harvest. I owe God a grudge for his effect upon the Guild.

I suppose a great many tongues are now busy with Katherine Mansfield. I myself find a kind of beauty about the story; a little vapourish I admit, and freely watered with some of her cheap realities; but it has the living power, the detached existence of a work of art. I shall be curious to get other opinions.

Tuesday 16 July

Monday was as usual a day for London and tea at the Club. I was so foolish as to fritter three shillings – one and sixpence on the blue penholder with which I write, and when I don't write, suck; one and sixpence on paper, at a grossly extravagant shop in Pall Mall. I justified these extravagances by the fact that you can get into the National Gallery for nothing. I spent an hour wandering there. But I see why I like pictures; its as things that stir me to describe them. I don't want to read stories or emotions or anything into them. But the atmosphere of picture galleries, always gloomy, is worse than ever now, when the glory of war has to be taught by a life-size portrait of Lord Kitchener, and almost life-size battle scenes.

Wednesday 17 July

We glued fifty copies of *Prelude*. So far our present supply is ample. It seems doubtful whether we shall sell more than a hundred. Clive writes a tolerant but not enthusiastic letter about it.

Thursday 18 July

All the copies that we glued yesterday have gone white in the back. We don't know the cause. [Bruce] Richmond rang up to offer me Rupert [Brooke]'s Life [by Edward Marsh] for next week. I told him that I should like to explain Rupert to the public. He agreed that there was much misunderstanding. "He was a very jolly sort of fellow" he said. I'm trying to get letters out of James [Strachey].

Tuesday 23 July

On Saturday we went to Tidmarsh [Berkshire]. From the point of view of country there is nothing that we at least can say for it; though the house and garden are nice enough. Lytton and Carrington were alone. No servant was visible and most of the waiting seemed to be done by Carrington. She is silent, a little subdued, makes one conscious of her admiring and solicitous youth. If one were concerned for her, one might be anxious about her position – so dependent on Lytton and having so openly burnt the conventional boats. She is to run her risk and take her chances evidently. Lytton was fresh from the Duchess of Marlborough and [Lord] d'Abernon, who is taking his play in hand. Whatever there is in the way of London society is, I suppose, now open to him. He is making his investigations not with a view to a permanent settlement; rather to round off his view of human nature. He declared he knows more different sorts of people than any of us; but we disputed this. A great deal of talk about Rupert. The book is a disgraceful sloppy sentimental rhapsody, leaving Rupert rather tarnished. Lytton very amusing, charming, benignant, and like a father to Carrington. She kisses him and waits on him and gets good advice and some sort of protection. He came up with us on Monday.

Saturday 27 July

On Wednesday I had one of my field days. To London, first to meet James at the Club. He was to tell me about Rupert for my article. His first words however were "Have you heard of Ka's engagement to Arnold-Forster?" This annoyed me considerably. I am glad that she should marry, though she bade fair to be a marked spinster, but marriage with Will Arnold-Forster will be merely a decorous and sympathetic alliance, making her more of a servant of the state than ever. Then, as James had a medical examination, we couldn't say much about Rupert, save that he was jealous, moody, ill-balanced, all of which I knew, but can hardly say in writing. Fredegond appeared next; having spread my rumour about Ka, which may not be true, and I hope it isn't, I went up to Gordon Square; Nessa in and out of the room all the time; and of course Clive and Mary appeared; and then everything goes over the same little rapids. We all dined at the Mont Blanc. Clive has never forgiven me – for what? His personal remarks always seem to be founded on some reserve of grievance, which he has decided not to state openly. But he paid for my dinner, and we wound up good temperedly. The rain pelted down and I rushed for my train.

By rights of importance I should remark that today L. was asked to stand for Parliament. I haven't yet turned my mind that way. A natural disposition to think Parliament ridiculous routs serious thought. But perhaps it isn't so ridiculous as speeches make one suppose.

Monday 29 July
I'm paralysed by the task of describing a week end at Garsington. I suppose we spoke some million words between us; listened to a great many more, chiefly from the mouth of Mrs [Mary Agnes] Hamilton, who strains at her collar like a spaniel dog, and has indeed the large hazel staring eyes of one of them. There was Gertler, Brett, Ottoline, three children and Philip. Happily the weather was fine, the food good, and we flowed about happily enough, and without serious boredom. In fact, for some reason I was rather well content. My bed was like layer upon layer of the most springy turf; and then the garden is almost melodramatically perfect, with its grey oblong pool, and pink farm buildings, its soft whitish grey stone and enormous smooth dense green yew hedges. Down these paths we wandered; once or twice with Ott; once with Mrs Hamilton. She hasn't a penny of her own; and has the anxious hard working brain of a professional, earning her living all the time. I'm not sure though that she didn't compare very well with Ott. Some time after tea we three meandered off 'to the woods'. But we never got there of course. Halfway up a hill in the sun, she stopped, leant on her parasol, looked vaguely across the landscape, and began a discourse upon love. "Isn't it sad that no one *really* falls in love nowadays? Its the rarest, rarest thing – I mean they don't see each other ideally. They don't feel that every word is something too wonderful just because the other has spoken it." Here, chiefly in order to get us home, I said that love meant a great many different things; and that to confine it to romantic love was absurd. I also maintained that one could love groups of people, and

landscapes. Unluckily this remark led Ott to lean on her parasol once more, and look longingly at a wheatfield. "Yes. I love that – just for itself – the curve of that wheatfield seems to me as divine as any human being. I love literature too –" "I love quite absurd things – the Independent Labour Party for instance," said Mrs Hamilton. At last we got moving again, and we asked the poor old ninny why, with this passion for literature, she didn't write. "Ah, but I've no time – never any time. Besides, I have such wretched health – But the pleasure of creation, Virginia, must transcend all others." I said it certainly did. We trailed back through the village, where all the peasants were lounging in the road, with their pipes and their dogs and their babies. The most affable and, I'm afraid, obsequious greetings were exchanged; the dazzling appearance of Ott and her pearls seeming to strike the agricultural labourer neither as wrong nor ridiculous, but as part of the aristocratic show that he's paid for. No one laughed. They seemed all very anxious to please. "Very nice people, aren't they?" she said when we came in; and I daresay nothing for the next three hundred years will make them otherwise.

I was taken to Gertler's studio and shown his solid 'unrelenting' teapot (to use Brett's word). He is a resolute young man; and if good pictures can be made by willing them to be good, he may do wonders. No base motive could have its way with him; and for this reason I haven't great faith in him. Its too moral and intellectual an affair; or perhaps the natural gift is not abundant enough to cover his conscience and will power. He says straight out what he thinks; his art an agony often, as he told me. But at last he understands that he wishes to paint form in the brightest colours. Form obsesses him. I advised him, for art's sake, to keep sane; to grasp, and not exaggerate. But he can think pianola music equal to hand-made, since it shows the form, and the touch and the expression are nothing.

ASHEHAM HOUSE

Wednesday 31 July
Arrived at Asheham. I sit as if in the open air – the drawing room providing only a shell of shade in the intense heat. The air dances over the field. The garden is overgrown, and the flowers crushed out.

We spent yesterday doing jobs in London. I saw a dead horse on the pavement – a literal case of what politicians call dying in harness, and rather pathetic to me – to die in Oxford Street one hot afternoon, and to have been only a van horse; and by the time I passed back again he was removed.

Saturday 3 August
There's nothing but rustic news to record, since as we expected the Murrys have put us off. Katherine writes that she's ill. I can't help guessing that she may be rather hopelessly ill. The weather hasn't held good. Yesterday was as wet a day as England often produces. We went mushrooming in the evening, and got a handkerchief full. So one of our great excitements has begun again. Perhaps we're rather pleased to be alone after all.

Monday 12 August
(I believe this is near about the anniversary of our wedding day, six years ago).

Friday 16 August
My visit to Charleston and L.'s to York are both partly responsible for this skip. My visit to Charleston was spent mostly in sitting in the drawing room and talking to Nessa while she made herself a small brown coat. Duncan wandered in and out; sometimes digging a vegetable bed, sometimes painting a watercolour of bedroom china, pinned to a door. In the evening there was the lumpish Bunny, inclined to be surly; and Nessa inclined to take him up sharply. What did we discuss? There was Ka's engagement, concerning which Duncan had a good deal to say; one of his statements being that Arnold-Forster is forty-five, and always has been. When Nessa and I were alone, I suppose we discussed the two parrokeets and money, which is not any longer such a distant, speculative sort of commodity as it used to be – at least to her. We discussed the children too; the sort of talk that runs on when one knows all the facts, but wishes to ascertain how they've changed position; Gertler's notions of painting; Duncan's fame; Bunny's socialism. Bunny thus defines his position: all capitalists are wrong; therefore for him to live upon Vanessa is good, inasmuch as she enjoys money that she has no right to, and could not possibly spend her interest better than by maintaining him. This evolved from a sentimental declaration by him that he ought to spend his life in giving honey to his friends for nothing. His brain must be a tangle of sentiments and half-realised socialism. I bicycled back on Wednesday and found L. and we were very happy, until it came to the fat bacon – when, alas –!

Monday 19 August
It is possible that we may have solved the problem of having visitors – not to see them. At this moment Adrian and Karin are in the house, as an occasional sound from the drawing room proves. But we only meet at meals; so that it is possible to think of things to say in the intervals.

Carrington came for the weekend. She is the easiest of visitors as she never stops doing things – pumping, scything, or walking. After trudging out here, she trudged to Charleston, and only came in at eleven last night, just as we were shutting the windows. Poor lugubrious Bunny escorted her, protesting that a ten mile walk was nothing compared to the joy of having some one to talk to. She trudged off again this morning to pack Lytton's box or buy him a hair brush in London – a sturdy figure, dressed in a print dress, made after the pattern of one in a John picture; a thick mop of golden red hair, and a fat decided clever face, with staring bright blue eyes.

Saturday 24 August

I confess that I shirk the task which has accumulated for seven days of describing our visitors. They are with us for another week; so I need not try to hit them this very moment. I hesitate a little to write evil of my guests, nor do I think evil – exactly. I refer, in rather crablike fashion, to something coarse, material, insensitive about Karin. She has no concealed vices. Would she be more interesting if she had? She is not stupid; or dull; or trivial; on the contrary she is bright, capable and stirring: stirring Adrian to read books upon economics, and even stirring him to learn shorthand which according to her is useful in a literary career. She intends him to have a career. Outwardly we are all good friends, talkative and in agreement, and not relying on gossip merely to despatch dinner with. We talk about the Labour Party, and politics, and anarchy, and government. And in her way she's a nice honest creature, not so sure of herself when it comes to taste; and knowing it too – though taste has led her, alas, to embroider a pair of shoes which Adrian obediently wears.

Friday 30 August

Here we are almost at the end of August, and finishing off Adrian and Karin's visit. They go to Charleston tomorrow. There is an element of criticism in our relationship, based partly on Karin's manners, appetite and appearance. Her appetite is frankly a schoolboy's. "What beef!" she exclaimed today. "Don't you feel elated at the sight of good meat?" Meals add a sort of romance to her life such as I in my way get, shall we say, from the post or the newspapers. L. on the other hand is irritated, and being irritated by superficial disagreeables finds deeper causes for them than I altogether agree with. Our usual method is to begin "Why did Adrian marry her?" Then I say "I can quite understand it – she has energy" and so on. Then L. says "I'd a thousand times rather have married Ka – in fact I'd rather have married any one in the whole world. I couldn't sit in the same room with her." Still, I do see why Adrian married her. First and foremost she makes him like other people. He has always, I believe, a kind of suspicion that whereas other people are professionals, he remains an amateur. She provides him with household, children, bills, daily life, so that to all appearances he is just like other people. I believe he needs constant reassurance on this point; and takes delight in her substantiality. He is very proud of her vitality. I suppose it provides him with a good deal of the stuff of life, which he does not provide for himself.

Yesterday I bicycled to Charleston, lunched, and came home in the evening. It was the first autumn day, warm, softly blue, and blurred with haze. Duncan spent the night before with us. He stumbled along until, by means which he only knows the secret of, he had us all laughing until the tears came. His chief effort was a description of Lady Strachey reading aloud. Then we discussed the bursting of people's bladders, the National Gallery, incest, perhaps, and other gossip. All sitting in the drawing room, until it grew too dark to see. We have lamps almost at dinner; but not quite.

Sunday 8 September

At anyrate today I am the wife of an Editor. Leonard got a letter to tell him that he is to get his first number [of the *International Review*] out in January. The idea is very amusing and stimulating too. I like playing with imaginary offices, and sheets of notepaper, and little boys with buttons, and myself walking up the steps to take a cup of tea, and surveying the Strand from the window. Then long galley proofs; distinguished foreign visitors; telegrams from distant capitals; general importance and glory; yes, a very nice prospect even on its picturesque side, which I admit is the one most perceptible to me.

Ka, another letter says, is to be married at 11 tomorrow. I can't help reading into her letter a sort of protest as to the merits of Will, and her love for him. Yet even so, I think of her as a rounder warmer more complete person than she was single. I suppose I had got into the habit of seeing her faithful solitary lonely till the end of time; I like happiness too well to be very fastidious about the husband.

Yesterday poor Bunny came for the night, bringing eight combs of honey, for which he charges half-a-crown each. How we were robbed at Brighton! Three shillings for a mixture of milk and saccharine. Poor old Bunny! He is as if caked with earth, stiff as a clod; you can almost see the docks and nettles sprouting from his mind; his sentences creak with rust. He can only lay hands on the simplest words. However by dint of kindly treatment we softened him. We wanted to know about mushrooms; and upon all funguses he is an authority. Then he could tell us about the agricultural labourers' Union, which is being half secretly organised even among our Freds and Wills. He has a humanity which is not at all theoretical.

He talks to the German prisoners, who are social democrats, only fought because they would be shot for refusing, and consider the whole war a device of the aristocracy. Bunny looks forward to a democratic future. I sacrificed half my morning and sat with him hemming handkerchiefs.

Tuesday 10 September
I spent the first five minutes with this book before me trying to fish two drowned flies out of my ink pot on the tip of my pen; but I begin to see that this is one of those undertakings which are quite impossible – absolutely impossible. Not Darwin or Plato could do it with the tip of my pen. At Asheham I naturally bethink me of Darwin and Plato; but in this I am not singular. My intellectual snobbishness was chastened this morning by hearing from Janet that she reads *Don Quixote* and *Paradise Lost* and her sister Lucretius in the evenings. Janet holds the characteristic view that *Don Quixote* is more humorous than Shakespeare. The coarseness of Shakespeare I can see would distress her; she would deal with it intellectually. All her generation use their brains too scrupulously upon books, seeking meaning rather than letting themselves run on for pleasure, which is more or less my way, and thus naturally richest and best.

Wednesday 18 September
I have let the first freshness of the Webbs fade from my mirror. I wonder how I can recapture the curious discomfort of soul which Mrs Webb produces each time I see her again? In the intervals one forgets; in a second it comes over one again. There's something absolutely unadorned and impersonal about her. She makes one feel insignificant, and a little out of key. She represses warmth or personality. She has no welcome for one's individuality. She divines a little what one's natural proclivities are, and she irradiates them with her bright electric torch.

It was a pouring wet day, on Saturday; not a day for geniality. Webb however has some coat to shake; she is bare as a bone. We sat down to tea, without George Young. They eat quickly and efficiently and leave me with hunks of cake on my hands. After tea we were soon disposing of our topics, and I began to feel nervous, lest our cupboards should be bare. Then George Young appeared, having like all Youngs, rejoiced in his battle with distance and wet. Liked the walk, he said. While he changed, Mrs Webb rapidly gave me her reasons for saying that she had never met a great man, or woman either. At most, she said, they possessed remarkable single qualities, but looked at as a whole there was no greatness in them. Shakespeare she did not appreciate, because a sister, who was a foolish woman, always quoted him wrong to her as a child. Goethe might conceivably have been a great man. Then, this having been dealt with, down came

L. and George Young, and they all pounced together upon some spot of interest floating far out beyond my ken. I think it was to do with the General Election and the views of the private soldiers.

After dinner Mrs Webb plunged from brisk argument to unconcealed snoring. Then Sidney had his turn. I thought he spoke a little quick to conceal the snores, but you have only to ask him a question and he can go on informing you till you can hold no more. He sketched his idea of a Supernational Authority. The work of Government will be enormously increased in the future. I asked whether I should ever have a finger in the pie? "O yes; you will have some small office no doubt. My wife and I always say that a Railway Guard is the most enviable of men. He has authority, and he is responsible to a government. That should be the state of each one of us." And then we discussed L.'s plans of a state so contrived that each person has to do some work. Here there was a long argument upon the growing distance between men of different social grades and professions. I asked (in reporting conversations one's own sayings stand out like lighthouses) one of my most fruitful questions; viz: how easy is it for a man to change his social grade? This brought down a whole shower-bath of information, but let us say that the Webbs' shower-baths are made of soda water. They never sink one, or satiate. Webb told us how many scholarships were won in London in a given year, and also reported upon the educational system of East Sussex, which bad though it is, is slightly better than that of West Sussex. "I myself" he said "came too early to profit by secondary education. My parents were lower middle class shopkeepers, possessed, like so many of their kind, with a blind determination to educate their sons somehow, but without the ghost of a notion how to set about it. They hit on the plan of sending me and my brother abroad to France and Germany; and so we learnt French and German at least. I can still read them, though I seldom do." Our talk must have dealt fully with education, for I remember that Mrs Webb woke with a start and delivered herself of a statement upon the German 'wrong turning', and put Young right on some point about the division of character and intellect. He was simple enough to separate them and to prefer what he was quite unable to define. She thrust him through and through with her rapier, but he persisted.

Next day, which was said to begin for the Webbs at 5.30, when they begin tea-drinking in their bedroom, I had to withdraw in order to do battle with a very obstinate review. My ideas were struck stiff by the tap of Mrs Webb's foot, up and down the terrace, and the sound of her rather high, rather mocking voice, discoursing to L. while she waited either for Webb to come or the rain to stop. They walked on the downs, till lunch. I must now skip a great deal of conversation and let us suppose that Sidney and Beatrice and I are sitting on the roadside overlooking Telscombe, smoking cigarettes, in bright sunshine. The downs were at their best; and set Mrs Webb off upon landscape beauty, and recollections of India, which she turns to when lying awake at night, relishing the recollection more than the reality. Sidney, one perceives, has no organ of sight whatever, and pretends to none. Mrs Webb has a compartment devoted to nature. So briskly narrating their travels and impressions, which were without respect for British rule, we set off home. I saw them from behind, a shabby, homely, dowdy couple, marching with the uncertain step of strength just beginning to fail, she clutching his arm, and looking much older than he, in her angularity. Their clothes looked ill dusted, and their eyes peering in front of them. My few private words came, as I knew they would come, when Mrs Webb detached us two together, passing Southease Church. She asked me about my novel, and I supplied her with a carefully arranged plot. I wished, so at least I said, to discover what aims drive people on, and whether these are illusory or not. She promptly shot forth: "Two aims have governed my life; one is the passion for investigation by scientific means; the other the passion for producing a certain good state of society by those investigations." Somehow she proceeded to warn me against the dissipation of energy in emotional friendship. One should have only one great personal relationship in one's life, she said; or at most two – marriage and parenthood. Marriage was necessary as a waste pipe for emotion, as security in old age when personal attractiveness fails, and as a help to work. We were entangled at the gates of the level crossing when she remarked, "Yes, I daresay an old family servant would do as well." In old age people become of little account, she said; one speculates chiefly upon the possibility, or the impossibility of a future life. This grey view depressed me more and more; partly I suppose from the egotistical sense of my own nothingness in her field of vision. And then we wound up with a light political gossip and chapter of reminiscences, in which Mr and Mrs Webb did their parts equally. And so to bed; and to my horror, in came Mrs Webb early next morning to say Goodbye, and perched in all her long impersonality on the edge of my bed, looking past my stockings drawers and po. This has taken so long to write that we are now arrived at

Monday 23 September

and so many things have accumulated, that I can hardly proceed to that masterly summing up of the Webbs which I intended. I had meant to point out the good qualities which come from such well kept brisk intellectual habits; how open minded they showed themselves; how completely and consistently <u>sensible</u>. That, I think, deserves a line under it. Good sense seems to me their invariable characteristic. Sidney is the warmer and more human of the two, and one could even commit the impropriety of liking him personally, which one can hardly do in the case of Mrs Webb. How stoically with his perpetual little smile, he remarked that they are now sixty, and therefore may expect a stroke within the next five years; but if he could arrange things with the divine messenger, he would compound somehow to die precisely at the same moment with 'my wife'.

I went over to Charleston last Tuesday and was shown his shells by Quentin; sat with Nessa and laid bare my sorrows, which she can more than match; and then Clive and Mary arrived in a motor car for tea – so many were their parcels and bags; and indeed Mary produced chocolates, cakes and sweets in abundance. I'm ashamed to say that that is my chief impression. She was, as usual, mute as a trout – I say trout because of her spotted dress, and also because, though silent, she has the swift composure of a fish. I walked home shoving my bicycle, too badly punctured to ride.

Then on Saturday we went to Lewes by train and bought a two-handled saw, and fish, and envelopes, and then met Gertler at the station and came out here. Whether our exclamations on parting from our guests are good evidence, I don't know, but on this occasion we both cried "Good God, what an egoist!" We have been talking about Gertler to Gertler for some thirty hours; it is like putting a microscope to your eye. One molehill is wonderfully clear; the surrounding world ceases to exist. But he is a forcible young man, as hard as a cricket ball; and as tightly rounded and stuffed in at the edges. We discussed – well, it always came back to be Gertler. He hoards an insatiable vanity. However, as I say, he has power and intelligence, and will, one sees, paint good interesting pictures, though some rupture of the brain would have to take place before he could be a painter.

HOGARTH HOUSE, RICHMOND

Saturday 12 October
The first week in London is always one of the richest; and the rich weeks always tend to pass unrecorded. I have my anniversary to celebrate also; this diary is one year old, and looking back I see how exactly one repeats one's doings. For example this week we went to buy an overcoat for L.; last year we bought boots. Again there was the question of a party; again what I may euphemistically call an 'argument'. Nessa was in London too; and I dined with her and Clive, only there was Duncan too, and we dined at Gordon Square. But Lord Grey's meeting has no counterpart last year; nor could I possibly have written then, as I can now write that tomorrow morning's paper may bring news of an armistice. Possibly the fighting will be over this time next week. Whatever we have done this week has had this extraordinary background of hope; a tremendously enlarged version of

the feeling I remember as a child as Christmas approached. The Northcliffe papers do all they can to insist upon the indispensability and delight of war. Grey's meeting was impressive as meetings go, which is not saying very much of course. He said nothing but what one has read and agreed with about a League of Nations, but he said it simply, and for a 'great statesman' to have sense and human feeling and no bombast does produce an odd sense of wonder and humility in me, as if human nature were worth something after all. There was an enormous audience, and as we left people were passing about the rumour that the Kaiser had abdicated.

I went on to my dinner at Gordon Square; thence to the Coliseum with Nessa, where we had to sit out an infinite length of Miss Clarice Mayne, after which we saw our [Diaghilev] ballet – Sche – (I can't achieve either the spelling or the speaking of it) which isn't one of the best, and when I saw it I remembered it better done at Covent Garden. Maynard who has the generosity and something of the manner now of an oriental prince, had hired a brougham for Nessa – an infinitely small, slow, antiquated carriage drawn by a very liverystables looking quadruped. Roger, Duncan, Maynard, Nessa and I all crammed in and padded along slowly across London to Chelsea. Somehow we passed Ottoline, brilliantly painted, as garish as a strumpet, displayed in the midst of omnibuses under an arc lamp; and she reappeared in the Sitwell's drawing room. I had made acquaintance with the two Sitwell brothers the day before and had been invited to the party. That very morning a review by me of Edith Sitwell's poems had appeared in *The Times*. Edith Sitwell is a very tall young woman, wearing a permanently startled expression, and curiously finished off with a high green silk head-dress, concealing her hair, so that it is not known whether she has any. Otherwise, I was familiar with everyone, I think. My complete mastery of evening parties is shown by the indifference with which I am deserted, and the composure with which I decide upon my next choice. I was a good deal impressed by this; and how calmly too, I looked at my watch, and saw it was time to leave, and went out alone, and drove to Sloane Square, not excited, not depressed, but contemplative and introspective.

Tuesday 15 October

I did not think I should so soon have to describe a meeting with a cabinet minister – though I admit that we seem to be drifting into a circle where the great officials are sometimes to be found. This is the doing of the *International Review*, mainly; but Herbert Fisher's visit was very obviously due to old family affection. I was sitting down alone to tea on Sunday, L. being gone to Sutton to speak about our colonies and the servants out, when the bell rang. On opening the door, there were Olive and M. Heseltine and Herbert Fisher. The Heseltines went off, and Herbert came in, as they had arranged beforehand. Was I nervous or proud? I don't think I felt a moment's agitation. For one thing he has lost his lean intellectual look; his hollow cheeks are filled; his eyes with that pale frosty look which blue eyes get in age; his whole bearing very quiet, simple, and when not speaking, rather saddened and subdued. Anyhow we talked without stopping and without difficulty.

"We've won the war today" he said at once. "The Germans have made up their minds they can't fight a retreat. The General Staff has faced the fact, and they've had what I think the considerable courage to admit it. There is now a good prospect of a complete defeat of the German army." Foch says "I have not yet had my battle". Despite the extreme vindictiveness of our press and the French press, Herbert believed that we are going to baulk Foch of his battle, partly because the Germans will accept any terms to avoid it. "Lloyd George has told me again and again that he means to be generous to the Germans. We want a strong Germany, he says." The Kaiser will probably go. "O I was a great admirer of the Germans in the beginning. I was educated there, and I've many friends there, but I've lost my belief in them. The proportion of brutes is greater with them than with us. They've been taught to be brutal. But it hasn't paid. No one can face another war. Why in ten years they could blot out London by their aeroplanes. But the proportion of men who have never been hurt, or even seen anything horrible is very large; thousands and thousands of soldiers all wanted the war conditions of life to go on 'without these bloody shells.' There'll be trouble when they come back. They'll find their old lives too dull. I'm going to educate them, its true; but that won't begin yet – not in my time. Very likely I shall go back to Oxford to teach."

So we talked on. I tried to think it extraordinary but I found it difficult – extraordinary, I mean, to be in touch with one who was in the very centre of the very centre, sitting in a little room at Downing Street where, as he said, the wireless messages are racing through from all over the world, a million miles a minute; where you have constantly to settle off-hand questions of enormous difficulty and importance – where the fate of armies does more or less hang upon what two or three elderly gentlemen decide. Importance seems to give people an appearance of simplicity; they are very courteous; but somehow no longer spontaneous people; the taint of the family butler is on them. But this was more visible when L. came in. Alone with me Herbert was very friendly and quiet; and gave himself no airs of dignity.

Friday 18 October
It is quite obvious of course that for some reason perhaps not creditable to me I think Herbert Fisher worth many more words than Ka say, or Saxon,

both of whom have dined here since. My theory is that for some reason the human mind is always seeking what it conceives to be the centre of things – I don't know what I call it; but I distinctly visualise it as a possession rather more in Herbert Fisher's hands than in other people's. I write hurriedly, giving no account of our suspension over what one of the papers calls 'the precipice of peace'. The truth is that nothing much more definite is yet known about peace.

Thursday 24 October

We are just in from Kingston – today being a holiday, and there heard the paper boys shouting out about the President [Wilson]'s message, which we bought and devoured. The main points are that he is keeping negotiations going; he discriminates too, between the German people and the Kaiser; he will consider an armistice with the one but only complete surrender with the other. Anyhow, the question is now laid before England and France.

Saturday 26 October

We had a day in London yesterday – somehow the charm of those days is not quite what it was. Am I getting blasé – is the 17 Club less enthralling? We went to the Omega show, met Roger there, were invited to tea at his studio, discussed the change in Duncan's style, representation, reality, and so on again. We dined at a very hot place in Soho. On again to the Club, where Leonard made his speech about Austria Hungary. As usual I find him not only very clear but with the right degree of passion to be interesting.

Monday 28 October

As I write this, the post brings a letter from [T. S.] Eliot asking to come and see us. To my great surprise a voice upon the telephone developed into the voice of Lady Mary Murray; asking us to lunch yesterday. We changed lunch to tea and went off to More's Gardens, a block of flats on the Embankment. A tea party is the least natural of situations, and produces the utmost amount of discomfort I think. Still it was the respectability that weighed me down. There are certain dun coloured misty days in autumn which remind me of the Murrays' atmosphere. The cleanliness of Gilbert was remarkable; a great nurse must rub him smooth with pumice stone every morning; he is so discreet, so sensitive, so low in tone and immaculate in taste that you hardly understand how he has the boldness to beget children. Maliciously enough, I felt that his simplicity was maintained in the face of years of worship and adulation, and that the proper thing to say is 'How wonderfully simple dear Gilbert Murray is!' But his niceness was unmeasured. The Toynbees came in. I had a long rigmarole with Arnold about his office and his learning and so forth; I think I frighten him; or perhaps I'm not used to the Oxford manner. Its suavity and politeness are strange to me.

Wednesday 30 October

Just in from a walk in the Park on this incredibly lovely autumn day. We talked of peace: how the sausage balloons will be hauled down, and gold coins dribble in; and how people will soon forget all about the war, and the fruits of our victory will grow as dusty as ornaments under glass cases in lodging-house drawing-rooms. How often will the good people of Richmond rejoice to think that liberty has been won for the good people of Potsdam? I can believe though that we shall be more arrogant about our own virtues. *The Times* still talks of the possibility of another season, in order to carry the war into Germany, and there imprint a respect for liberty in the German peasants. I think the distance of the average person from feelings of this sort is the only safeguard and assurance that we shall settle down again neither better nor worse.

Sunday 3 November

On Saturday, we had one of our Hampstead afternoons, L. going to Margaret, I to Janet. I've done the same thing so often. I've found her in that green distempered room, with the ugly pictures. Tea is prepared. I am pressed to eat more of everything. Questioned about butter and coal. And then Janet talked to me about literature, and I fell into a passing gloom. She says that a great many novels are written, and it seems fairly evident that none are 'immortal'. I suppose I referred this to my own novels. But I fancy that what depressed me was not only the personal question, but the smell of musty morality; the effect of talking to some one who seems to want all literature to go into the pulpit; who makes it all infinitely worthy and safe and respectable. I was also depressed at the implied criticism of *The Voyage Out*, and the hint that I had better turn to something other than fiction. Its the curse of a writer's life to want praise so much, and be so cast down by blame, or indifference. The only sensible course is to remember that writing is after all what one does best; that any other work would seem to me a waste of life; that on the whole I get infinite pleasure from it; that I make one hundred pounds a year; and that some people like what I write.

Saturday 9 November

We began to set up *Kew Gardens* this week – Thursday was the first day of it I think. On Wednesday I went up to Hampstead; found the tall ugly villa looking over the valley where the Murrys live. Katherine was up, but husky and feeble, crawling about the room like an old woman. How far she is ill, one can't say. She impresses one a little unfavourably at first – then more favourably. I think she has a kind of childlikeness somewhere which has been much disfigured, but still exists. Illness, she said, breaks down one's privacy so that one can't write –

Monday 11 November

Twenty-five minutes ago the guns went off, announcing peace. A siren hooted on the river. They are hooting still. A few people ran to look out of windows. The rooks wheeled round, and wore for a moment the symbolic look of creatures performing some ceremony, partly of thanksgiving, partly of valediction over the grave. A very cloudy still day, the smoke toppling over heavily towards the east; and that too wearing for a moment a look of something floating, waving, drooping. So far neither bells nor flags, but the wailing of sirens and intermittent guns.

Friday 15 November

Peace is rapidly dissolving into the light of common day. You can go to London without meeting more than two drunk soldiers; only an occasional crowd blocks the street. But mentally the change is marked too. Instead of feeling that the whole people, willing or not, were concentrated on a single point, one feels now that the whole bunch has burst asunder and flown off with the utmost vigour in different directions. We are once more a nation of individuals. Some people care for football; others for racing; others for dancing; others for – oh well, they're all running about very gaily getting out of their uniforms and taking up their private affairs again. The streets are crowded with people quite at their ease; and the shops blazoning unshaded lights. Yet its depressing too. We have stretched our minds to consider something universal at any rate; we contract them at once to the squabbles of Lloyd George, and a General Election. The papers are unreadable.

The first effect of peace on our circle is to set Desmond loose, and to bring Gerald Shove up to London saying that he must find a way of making £500 a year. Before long the crowd of out of work intellectuals looking for places will be considerable. Desmond is doing what he knows how to do supremely well – going later and later to the office every day and taking longer for lunch, and sometimes not going back again. This he proposes to continue for a fortnight; then to fold up his blue and gold coat for ever – unless by cutting off the brass buttons he can make it do for an ordinary coat. His spirits are very high.

I was interrupted somewhere on this page by the arrival of Mr Eliot. Mr Eliot is well expressed by his name – a polished, cultivated, elaborate young American, talking so slow, that each word seems to have special finish allotted it. But beneath the surface, it is fairly evident that he is very intellectual, intolerant, with strong views of his own, and a poetic creed. I'm sorry to say that this sets up Ezra Pound and Wyndham Lewis as great poets, or in the current phrase 'very interesting' writers. He admires Mr Joyce immensely. He produced three or four poems for us to look at – the fruit of two years, since he works all day in a Bank, and in his reasonable way thinks regular work good for people of nervous constitutions. I became more or less conscious of a very intricate and highly organised framework of poetic belief; owing to his caution, and his excessive care in the use of language we did not discover much about it.

Saturday 30 November
I see I've been rather slack, and I can't remember now exactly what's made me slack. Certainly not the General Election. Saxon dined here, talking of death without enthusiasm. He knew for certain that he would die on a certain day last summer and then – didn't. One night we went to the Russian dancers [at the Coliseum]; and it was incongruous enough to see what they offered the tolerant good tempered public who had been bellowing like bulls over the efforts of a man to nail a carpet down. They were tolerant, but, as I fancied, a little bit contemptuous of all this posing and springing against a flat blue wall. What a queer fate it is – always to be the spectator of the public, never part of it. This is part of the reason why I go weekly to see Katherine Mansfield up at Hampstead, for there at any rate we make a public of two.

Saturday 7 December
On Thursday I lunched with Roger in order to hear the following story. Mrs McColl to Mr Cox of the London Library: "Have you *The Voyage Out* by Virginia Woolf?" "Virginia Woolf? Let me see; she was a Miss Stephen, daughter of Sir Leslie. Her sister is Mrs Clive Bell I think. Ah, strange to see what's become of those two girls. Brought up in such a nice home, too. But then, they were never *baptised*."

Roger and I get on very well now; more genuine and free than we were, under the shadow of Gordon Square. At last, inevitably late, I go on to the 17 Club. Alix I found intoning pompously downstairs, with a perverted likeness to a colonel of the upper classes holding forth upon the iniquity of Bolshevism. Her theme is the iniquity of colonels; the method seems much the same; even the voice.

Monday 16 December
Back from a week-end with Roger. Lips, therefore, rather sore with talk, though his range is so wide, and we both have such a number of things to say that I, certainly, was neither bored nor satiated. It was polling day in

Guildford, as in other parts of the world, and Roger very gloomy about the future of the world. All Sunday, in spite of rain and fog he painted till the sky was black, having been grey through the time of daylight. I feel little hope about his pictures, but had to counterfeit an opinion as to the effect produced on the solidity of a bowl by a morning's work on it. He said that he grudged every hour of daylight spent not painting. We visited the National Gallery together this morning; I thought a Rembrandt 'very fine' which to him was mere melodrama. A little El Greco conveyed little till he illumined it; showed how it held more real colour than any other picture there. Then Ingres was repulsive to me; and to him one of the most marvellous of designs. I always feel, too, that to like the wrong thing, or fail in sufficiently liking the right, jars on him, like false notes, or sentimentality in writing.

Tuesday 17 December

I go to Asheham on Friday. Nessa has asked us to have the children for a fortnight when the new baby is born. This is now imminent, and she fixes the 28th for the exact day. We shall have one week entirely alone, at Asheham, the greatest and most unmixed pleasure this world affords; enhanced very much in my mind by the absence of servants. I am going to read through my novel and determine what to do with it.

We have printed off the text of *Kew Gardens*.

1919

As the war receded there were renewed contacts with circles which to a large extent Virginia had outgrown. Since the death of Sir Leslie Stephen in 1904 and his children's removal to Bloomsbury and to a very different outlook on society, Virginia, far more than Vanessa, harboured a certain loyalty to, as well as a writer's curiosity about, old friends and family connections from the 'respectable' Kensington world in which she had been brought up. Members of the aristocracy – Thynnes, Cecils – whom she had got to know through her intimate friendship with Violet Dickinson, a county neighbour of the Duckworth family, break surface from time to time in her diary. The death of 'Aunt Anny' – Thackeray's daughter, whose sister was Leslie Stephen's first wife, and whom Virginia had portrayed in Night and Day – is recorded; she died, aged eighty-one, at Freshwater in the Isle of Wight, the home ground of an earlier generation of eminent Victorians – Tennyson, G. F. Watts and his momentary bride Ellen Terry, and Virginia's own great-aunt Julia Margaret Cameron, the pioneer photographer – about whom she later wrote Freshwater, her only play. But in general she was more concerned with the future than the past, and with her developing relationships with new friends like Katherine Mansfield and T. S. Eliot. In May the Hogarth Press published Eliot's Poems, her own Kew Gardens, and a long poem by J. Middleton Murry (Katherine's husband), who had recently been appointed editor of the Athenaeum, to which journal Virginia was to make frequent contributions during this year and next, as well as producing almost weekly reviews for the TLS. In October her second novel, Night and Day, was published by her half-brother Gerald Duckworth.

But the most serious upheaval in the Woolfs' affairs this year was caused by their receiving in March six months' notice to vacate Asheham, which Virginia had rented since 1911. Reluctant to leave the neighbourhood she had grown to love, and where her sister now also had her foothold, Virginia impulsively bought a small house for £300 in the county town of Lewes; but dispirited by Leonard's tepid reaction to her enterprise, they subsequently secured Monks House at Rodmell, across the Ouse valley from Asheham, into which they moved their belongings in September and which was to remain their country home for the rest of both their lives.

1919

Hogarth House, Richmond

Monday 20 January
The fortnight in bed was the result of having a tooth out, and being tired enough to get a headache – a long dreary affair, that receded and advanced much like a mist on a January day. One hour's writing daily is my allowance for the next few weeks; and having hoarded it this morning, I may spend part of it now, since I am much behindhand with the month of January. I note however that this diary writing does not count as writing, since I have just reread my year's diary and am much struck by the rapid haphazard gallop at which it swings along, sometimes indeed jerking almost intolerably over the cobbles. Still if it were not written rather faster than the fastest typewriting, if I stopped and took thought, it would never be written at all; and the advantage of the method is that it sweeps up accidentally several stray matters which I should exclude if I hesitated, but which are the diamonds of the dustheap. If Virginia Woolf at the age of fifty, when she sits down to build her memoirs out of these books is unable to make a phrase as it should be made, I can only condole with her and remind her of the existence of the fireplace, where she has my leave to burn these pages to so many black films with red eyes in them. But how I envy her the task I am preparing for her! There is none I should like better. Already my thirty-seventh birthday next Saturday is robbed of some of its terrors by the thought. Partly for the benefit of this elderly lady, I intend to spend the evenings of this week of captivity making out an account of my friendships and their present condition, with some account of my friends' characters; and to add an estimate of their work, and a forecast of their future works.

Wednesday 22 January
Two days more were spent in bed, and today counts as my first of complete health.

How many friends have I got? There's Lytton, Desmond, Saxon; they belong to the Cambridge stage of life; very intellectual, cut free from Hyde

Park Gate; connected with Thoby; but I can't put them in order, for there are too many. Ka and Rupert and Duncan, for example, all come rather later; they belong to Fitzroy days; the Oliviers and all that set are stamped as the time of Brunswick Square; Clive I put a little aside; later still there are the cropheads, Alix, Carrington, Barbara, Nick, Bunny. I must insert too the set that runs parallel but does not mix, distinguished by their social and political character, headed perhaps by Margaret and including people like Goldie, Mrs Hamilton, and intermittent figures such as the Webbs. I have not placed Ottoline or Roger, and again there are Katherine and Murry and outlying figures such as Ray and Oliver. Gertler I must omit (and Mary Hutch too) for reasons which if my account gets written I might give; and Eliot I liked on the strength of one visit and shall probably see more of, owing to his poems which we began today to set up.

This is a very partial account, but I shall never place half of them accurately unless I start straight away. Lytton and Desmond and Saxon then. Well, I cherish a considerable friendship for each of them; the worst of it is how seldom we meet. With Lytton and Desmond till last month tethered to a stool in the Admiralty, months pass without a sight of them. The season of letter writing is over for all of us, I think; or perhaps we need different correspondents. Brilliant letters we wrote each other once, partly for the sake of being brilliant, and we were getting to know each other then, and there was a thrill about it (I speak of my own feelings.) But when we do meet, there is nothing to complain of. Lytton again is famous these last six months, but as that was a matter of course since his first six months there is not much surprise or change in it. Nothing is easier or more intimate than a talk with Lytton. If he is less witty, he is more humane. I like Carrington though. She has increased his benignity. O yes, if he were to walk in at this moment we should talk about books and feelings and life and the rest of it as freely as we ever did, and with the sense, on both sides I think, of having hoarded for this precise moment a great deal peculiarly fit for the other.

Friday 24 January
To resume. There are three words knocking about in my brain to use of Stracheys, – a prosaic race, lacking magnanimity, shorn of atmosphere. Roger's version is that all, except Lady Strachey, lack generosity. But then one must combine with this a great variety of mental gifts, and gifts of character – honesty, loyalty, intelligence of a spiritual order. One might almost attribute what I mean in Lytton's case at least to lack of physical warmth, lack of creative power, a failure of vitality warning him not to be spendthrift but to eke out his gifts parsimoniously, and tacitly assume his right to a superior share of comfort and opulence. In matters of emotion

this has a slightly stingy appearance. Mentally of course it produces that metallic and conventionally brilliant style which prevents his writing from reaching, to my judgment, the first rate. It lacks originality, and substance; it is brilliant, superbly brilliant journalism, a supremely skilful rendering of the old tune. But when I think of a Strachey, I think of someone infinitely cautious, elusive and unadventurous. To the common stock of our set they have added phrases, standards, and witticisms, but never any new departure; never an Omega, a Post-Impressionist movement, nor even a country cottage, a Brunswick Square or a printing press. We Stephens, yes, and even Clive, with all his faults, had the initiative, and the vitality to conceive and carry our wishes into effect because we wished too strongly to be chilled by ridicule or checked by difficulty. Even in the matter of taking Tidmarsh Lytton had to be propelled from behind, and his way of life insofar as it is unconventional, is so by the desire and determination of Carrington.

Thursday 30 January

Such is the cold today that I doubt I can go on with my disquisition. I must note for future use, the superb possibilities of Freshwater, for a comedy. Old Cameron dressed in a blue dressing gown and not going beyond his garden for twelve years, suddenly borrows his son's coat, and walks down to the sea. Then they decide to proceed to Ceylon, taking their coffins with them, and the last sight of Aunt Julia is on board ship, presenting porters with large photographs of Sir Henry Taylor and the Madonna in default of small change.

Tuesday 4 February

Let me try to account for the fact that Lytton has 'dominated' (why, even the word is his) a generation at Cambridge, and make it square with my disparaging remarks. How did he do it, how is he so distinct and unmistakable if he lacks originality and the rest? Is there any reputable escape from this impasse in saying that he is a great deal better than his books? or am I too chary of praise for those books? Am I jealous? Do I compare the six editions of *Eminent Victorians* with the one of *The Voyage Out*? Perhaps there's a hint of jealousy; but, if I underrate, I think the main cause is that while I admire, enjoy up to a point and up to a point agree, I'm not interested in what he writes.

Desmond has *not* rung up. That is quite a good preface to the description of his character. The difficulty which faces one in writing of Desmond is that one is almost forced to describe an Irishman: how he misses trains, seems born without a rudder to drift wherever the current is strongest; how he keeps hoping and planning, and shuffles along, paying his way by talking so enchantingly that editors forgive, and shopmen give him credit and at least one distinguished peer leaves him a thousand in his will.

Saturday 15 February

What a disgraceful lapse! Eleven days unrecorded. Still I think if I were a painter I should only need a brush dipped in dun colour to give the tone of those eleven days. I should draw it evenly across the entire canvas. Yesterday, Friday, I had one of my occasional galas. Dressed in my best I went to Sickert's pictures, which I here pronounce the pleasantest, solidest most painter-like show in England. And there I met Clive and Mary; Clive in his fur coat, Mary in the more subdued style of the New English [Art Club]. Later, Clive, Mary and I strolled chattering like a perch of parrokeets, to Verreys. Mary had a dutiful visit to pay her husband in hospital. So we sat and talked in an inner room – a pleasant, dissipated place, parquet floor, curved bar, little tables, green and gold flourishes, dilapidated George the IVth style, and empty at this hour, save for some dubious ladies. Our intercourse was very gay, vibrant, like that of stringed instruments. Duncan passed through – a strange shaggy interlude, but always and inevitably harmonious. He blinked as if newly exposed to the light, crumbled his brioche, and gulped down his coffee, stammering out his half articulated but immensely expressive words. Somehow, too soon, he hoisted himself into an astonishing long straight black coat, like a non-conformist minister's, hitched down his red waistcoat, and started off in a vague determined way to Victoria Station. And then we sat on, Clive and I, talking of writing, of my writing chiefly, which he praises sufficiently to give his strictures a good deal of force. Mary came in and interrupted, or rather influenced the current of our discourse, for she hardly spoke, and then we turned out into Regent Street where the lamps were lit, and the shop opposite had all its windows full of bright clothes against a green stage scene, and so strolling in the spring twilight and laughing still we made our way through Soho, and I left them, in a street with many jewellers' windows.

Tuesday 18 February

Here I sit waiting for Alix, who can't be coming to disburden herself of confidences as I supposed; and thus my mind returns by way of her fickleness to my friends. Where was I? Desmond, and how I find him sympathetic compared with Stracheys. It is true; I'm not sure he hasn't the nicest nature of any of us. I don't think that he possesses any faults as a friend, save that his friendship is so often sunk under a cloud of vagueness and effectively prevents us from meeting. Perhaps such indolence implies a slackness of fibre in his affections too – but I scarcely feel that. It arises rather from the consciousness which I find imaginative and attractive that things don't altogether *matter*. Somehow he is fundamentally sceptical. Yet who is more tolerant, more appreciative, more understanding of human nature? It goes without saying that he is not an heroic character. He finds pleasure too pleasant, cushions too soft, dallying too seductive, and then, as I sometimes feel now, he has ceased to be ambitious. His 'great work' (it may be philosophy or biography now, and is certainly to be begun, after a series of long walks, this very spring) only appears, I believe, in that hour between tea and dinner, when so many things appear not merely possible but achieved. Yet it is true that he has the floating elements of something brilliant, beautiful – some book of stories, reflections, studies, scattered about in him, for they show themselves indisputably in his talk. I can see myself going through his desk one of these days, shaking out unfinished pages from between sheets of blotting paper and deposits of old bills, and making up a small book of table talk, which shall appear as a proof to the younger generation that Desmond was the most gifted of us all. But why did he never do anything? they will ask.

At any rate in his own intermittent way Desmond is faithful. So much one may affirm of Saxon too, who comes next on my list. But Saxon's fidelity is almost that of the senile old collie, or broken down ass – the pensioner who can draw upon a memory of the past for a seat at one's table in perpetuity. He has little to give at the moment, life has not been generous to him. His possessions are old friendships, old memories – things we've talked of ages ago. Unlike the rest of us he has had no renewal of life in marriage; his hopes in that direction have been crushed. Therefore he comes disconsolately, asking rather than giving; asking at this moment that I shall accept Barbara at his hand – return her to him enriched with the glow of my approval. However, poor Saxon's life is now in the uncomfortable and unbecoming season which is so painfully well repro-duced out of doors. Sleet, and mud and chill, and nothing growing. He has summed up his own position accurately as that of one who finds himself lonely if alone, and bored if in company. But faithful – there is something worth having in Saxon's fidelity; something that makes his most meagre visitation not altogether fruitless. One is aware, even after two hours of tepid and almost entire silence, that he is strictly true, genuine, unalloyed.

At any rate I rest on the thought of Saxon with some relief after hovering for the past two months in a state of uncertainty over the thought of Katherine [Mansfield] Murry. It is at this moment extremely doubtful whether I have the right to class her among my friends. Quite possibly I shall never see her again. Upstairs I have letters in which she speaks of finding the thought of me a joy, dwelling upon my writing with excitement; I have letters making appointments, pressing for visits, adding postscripts of thanks and affection to visits already paid. But the last is dated December, and it is now February. The question interests, amuses, and also slightly, no very decidedly pains me. The truth is, I suppose, that one of the conditions unexpressed but understood of our friendship has been precisely that it was almost entirely founded on quicksands. We have been intimate, intense perhaps rather than open; but to me at anyrate our intercourse has been always interesting and mingled with quite enough of the agreeable personal element to make one fond – if that is the word – as well as curious. I was at pains to go up to Hampstead every week since mid October or November, I suppose. And then what happened? I go away for Christmas, and we send small bright presents. I add to mine one if not two long and affectionate letters; I propose to come as soon as I get back. My time in bed prevented this. But meanwhile, for no reason given or to be guessed at with any certainty, she falls silent; I get no thanks, no answers, no enquiries.

Friday 21 February
But all this is made to appear rather fine drawn and exaggerated by the simple fact that I have a letter this morning from Katherine herself asking me to tea on Monday and explaining how some new treatment gives her fever for two days and makes it impossible for her to see people.

Tuesday 25 February
The truth is I shirk the gigantic task of giving an account of Sunday's teaparty, at which I met Sir Henry Newbolt and Lady, Lady Cromer, the Bruce Richmonds, and a scattering of gallant bald cavalry officers, and mounds of South Kensington dowager respectability who must be nameless. But the amiability of South Kensington is disarming. A kind of modesty veils what is so prominent and disagreeable in the intellectuals. They have an air of saying "I am no one – no one at all. My only function is to be agreeable. Another cup of tea? Do for goodness sake take this arm chair – and let me fetch you a slice of bread and butter –" That's my impression of the moment; though for some reason it doesn't encourage one to say anything more interesting than Thank you and please don't trouble, and other phrases of the kind. Of no. 23 Cromwell Houses, fronting the stuffed beasts [the Natural History Museum], and quite capable of staring them out of countenance, I will only say that it is furnished on the great South Kensington principle of being on the safe side and doing the thing handsomely. Good Mrs Samuel Bruce went to the Autotype Company and ordered the entire Dutch school to be sent round framed in fumed oak. And so they were; and just covered the staircase walls, leaving an inch or two's margin in between. The drawing room – no, I can't write it all out; memory preserves only the shoulders of a horse on a gilt easel, and three large

seascapes, like slabs of thick bread and butter. The company was decorous and fur bearing as usual; and the music like the voice of spirits in another world enticing the hopelessly damned. But how nice they are too!

Very well: but now we come to another of the ornate and decorated tribe; try as she will she can never lay aside her coronet; I mean poor dear old Ottoline. We dined at Gatti's together last night. She has the slim swaying figure of a Lombardy poplar – the ridges and hollows of the cheeks are the only sign of her years (forty-seven I make them); and a feeble mincing step on the street, like that of a cockatoo with bad claws. She has an indomitable spirit – plucking life out with those same gouty claws as if she were young and had illusions by the score. As we sat at dinner Ott picked up scraps of talk from the other diners, and admired their profiles. And so round to Gordon Square where we found Clive at the top of the house, where I used to stand and write, in the largest arm chair ever seen, by the finest fire, with a screen across the door to keep the draught out, as affable as a cockatoo and as brightly coloured as a macaw. I left them together and lost my train.

Wednesday 5 March
Just back from four days at Asheham, and one at Charleston; I sit waiting for Leonard to come in, with a brain still running along the railway lines, which unfits it for reading. But oh, dear, what a lot I've got to read! The entire works of Mr James Joyce, Wyndham Lewis, Ezra Pound, so as to compare them with the entire works of Dickens and Mrs Gaskell; besides that George Eliot; and finally Hardy. And I've just done Aunt Anny [Lady Ritchie], on a really liberal scale. Yes, since I wrote last she has died, a week ago today to be precise, at Freshwater, and was buried up at Hampstead yesterday. I suppose my feeling for her is half moonshine; or rather half reflected from other feelings. Father cared for her; she goes down the last, almost, of that old 19th Century Hyde Park Gate world. Unlike most old ladies she showed very little anxiety to see one; felt, I sometimes think, a little painfully at the sight of us, as if we'd gone far off, and recalled unhappiness, which she never liked to dwell on. Also, unlike most old Aunts she had the wits to feel how sharply we differed on current questions; and this, perhaps, gave her a sense, hardly existing with her usual circle, of age, obsoleteness, extinction. For myself, though, she need have had no anxieties on this head, since I admired her sincerely; but still the generations certainly look very different ways.

Asheham was, I suppose, a qualified success only. Starting out to fetch milk on one of these days we met Gunn [the bailiff] and heard our fate. We're to go in September. He wants Asheham to live in with his old mother. Oh dear Oh dear! Each time I walked up the drive I thought how nothing was ever so perfect. If it weren't for the devil of starting something new in me, I should be in despair. On the whole we incline to aim at Itford farm house – a house that could be made very attractive, with its view and its sun. We have grown out of gentlemen's houses.

Charleston is by no means a gentleman's house. I bicycled round there in a flood of rain, and found the baby asleep in its cot, and Nessa and Duncan sitting over the fire, with bottles and bibs and basins all round them. Duncan went to make my bed. Their staff at this moment consists simply of Jenny, the sharp Jewish looking cook; and she having collapsed, spent the afternoon in bed. By extreme method and unselfishness and routine on Nessa's and Duncan's parts chiefly, the dinner is cooked, and innumerable refills of hotwater bottles and baths supplied. One has the feeling of living on the brink of a move. In one of the little islands of comparative order Duncan set up his canvas, and Bunny wrote a novel in a set of copy books. Nessa scarcely leaves the baby's room, or if she appears for a moment outside, she has instantly to go off and talk to Dan, Jenny's young man and the future support of Charleston, or to wash napkins, or bottles, or prepare meals. Then Quentin had just been suspected of measles – The atmosphere seems full of catastrophes which upset no one; the atmosphere is good humoured, lively, as it tends to be after three months of domestic disaster. In these circumstances, I daresay I had no more than thirty minutes consecutive talk with Nessa. But I broke off in full tide, and had to trudge through the mud to Glynde – such mud that when I went into the land agent, the sleek little clerk looked from my head to my boots in expostulation – as if such a figure couldn't possibly require a house with seven bedrooms and a bathroom. Unhappily there seems little chance of finding one. I've said nothing of my niece, who must be called so formally, since they've cancelled Susanna Paula, and can think of nothing else. She is a wistful, patient, contemplative little creature, examining the fire very meditatively, with a resigned expression, and very large blue eyes.

Wednesday 12 March

Clive gave me dinner at the Café Royal, which did not much interest me as a show, rather to his disappointment. However towards the end of dinner a woman of doubtful character dining alone with a man threw her glass on the floor, made a great rattle of knives and plates, upset the mustard pot and marched out like an indignant turkey cock. Was this moment, with the eyes of the diners upon her, what repaid her? Was it for this that she protested? Anyhow she left her man very crestfallen, trying to appear nonchalant; and I daresay that was what she wanted. I couldn't help thinking of the dreary scene in the flat next morning – the tears, the recriminations, the reconciliation – and next Sunday they'll dine, I suppose, at another restaurant.

This morning we had notice to quit [Asheham] from Hoper [the owner], and the further blow that he will not let us have the Itford Farm.

Wednesday 19 March

Life piles up so fast that I have no time to write out the equally fast rising mound of reflections, which I always mark down as they rise to be inserted here. I meant to write about the Barnetts, and the peculiar repulsiveness of those who dabble their fingers self approvingly in the stuff of others' souls. The Barnetts were at any rate plunged to the elbow; red-handed if ever philanthropists were. Is it chiefly intellectual snobbery that makes me dislike them? – is it snobbery to feel outraged when she says 'Then I came close to the Great Gates' – or reflects that God = good, devil = evil. Has this coarseness of grain any necessary connection with labour for one's kind? And then the smug vigour of their self-satisfaction! Never a question as to the right of what they do – always a kind of insensate forging ahead until, naturally, their undertakings are all of colossal size and portentous prosperity. Perhaps the root of it all lies in the adulation of the uneducated, and the easy mastery of the will over the poor. And more and more I come to loathe any dominion of one over another; any leadership, any imposition of the will. But I can only scratch the surface of what I feel about these two stout volumes [*Rev. Canon S. A. Barnett: His Life, Work and Friends* by his wife, Henrietta Barnett, 1918].

On Monday after many failures I met Murry at the Club and we had our talk about the *Athenaeum*. Success has already begun to do for Murry what I always said it would do. He is more freshly coloured, even in the cheeks, than when we last met. Why, he chuckled like a schoolboy; his eyes shone; his silences were occupied with pleasant thoughts, I think; not that he would admit that to edit the *Athenaeum* was much more preferable to a place in a government office. He talked so much about his plans, and with such zest that we sat there from 4.45 to 6.30, or past, and I had to rush. We went over all his names, and tried to think of others, but agreed that once our intimate friends were gone through the field was mown of its poppies. Katherine will do four novels every week – pray to God she don't do mine! I feel the acid in her once more – since she doesn't take the trouble to write a card to fix an engagement; but I shall try to go up there tomorrow and judge the situation with my own eyes.

Today we finished printing Eliot's poems – our best work so far by a long way, owing to the quality of the ink.

Saturday 22 March

The inscrutable woman remains inscrutable I'm glad to say; no apologies, or sense of apologies due. At once she flung down her pen and plunged, as if we'd been parted for ten minutes, into the question of Dorothy Richardson; and so on with the greatest freedom and animation on both sides until I had to catch my train. But something – something dark and catastrophic possibly to do with Murry – has taken place since we met. So much she hinted; but said she wished now to forget it – But this was a momentary revelation as I left. Otherwise, as I say, we chattered about the *Athenaeum* mostly, and I was much complimented to hear how much they wish for my writing. And again, as usual, I find with Katherine what I don't find with the other clever women a sense of ease and interest, which is, I suppose, due to her caring so genuinely if so differently from the way I care, about our precious art. Though Katherine is now in the very heart of the professional world – four books on her table to review – she is, and will always be I fancy, not the least of a hack.

Thursday 27 March

Our dinner last night at the Isola Bella was rather a brilliant affair in the Bohemian style, with a great deal of wine, and talk of books and pictures, and a general air of freedom and content. At the end of dinner the Padrone (Clive chattered Italian with the greatest gusto) brought a large sketch book, in which Nessa and Duncan and Roger all drew pictures, and we were rewarded by a bottle of Marsala. We talked by the way a great amount of *Athenaeum* gossip, all secretly delighted with our own importance; Clive and Roger to do art criticism, the most brilliant list of contributors on record.

Wednesday 2 April

Yesterday I took *Night and Day* up to Gerald [Duckworth], and had a little half domestic half professional interview with him in his office. I don't like the Club man's view of literature. For one thing it breeds in me a violent desire to boast: I boasted of Nessa and Clive and Leonard; and how much money they made. Then we undid the parcel, and he liked the title, but found that Miss Maud Annesley has a book called *Nights and Days* – which may make difficulties. But he was certain he would wish to publish it; and we were altogether cordial. I had tea at Gordon Square; then dinner at the Isola Bella; talk with Clive and Duncan; Clive insisting that Eliot dislikes me, and further trying to convince us that Nessa, Roger, himself, Lytton and I are the most hated people in London; superficial, haughty, and giving ourselves airs – that, I think, is the verdict against the ladies. I admit I hate not to be liked.

Thursday 10 April

A great skip, how accounted for I scarcely know. I have to read one book a day – such is the life of a hack. The Eliots, Walter and Marjorie [Strachey] dined here on Sunday; I amused myself by seeing how sharp, narrow, and much of a stick Eliot has come to be, since he took to disliking me. His wife a washed out, elderly and worn looking little woman, who was relieved to find Walter Lamb with his stories about the King provided for her; and indeed Walter seemed to both the ideal of manhood. Gumbo held forth in her most vivacious and commanding style.

Saturday 12 April

These ten minutes are stolen from *Moll Flanders*, which I failed to finish yesterday in accordance with my time sheet, yielding to a desire to stop reading and go up to London. But I saw London, in particular the view of white city churches and palaces from Hungerford Bridge through the eyes of Defoe. I saw the old women selling matches through his eyes; and the draggled girl skirting round the pavement of St James's Square seemed to me out of *Roxana* or *Moll Flanders*. Yes, a great writer surely to be thus imposing himself upon me after two hundred years. A great writer – and Forster has never read his books! I was beckoned by Forster from the [London] Library as I approached. We shook hands very cordially; and yet I always feel him shrinking sensitively from me, as a woman, a clever woman, an up-to-date woman. Feeling this I commanded him to read Defoe, and left him, and went and got some more Defoe, having bought one volume on the way.

Herbert Fisher astounded us by asking himself to lunch tomorrow, and we have been to Kew, and seen the Magnolia trees in blossom.

Thursday 17 April

We saw the magnolia tree in blossom next day with the Minister for Education himself. He is a strange mixture of ascetic and worldling. The lean secluded man now finds himself dazzled by office, and with all his learning and culture swept away by men of vitality and affairs. Such a tribute as he paid to Winston [Churchill] might have been paid by some dazzled moth to a lamp. He seems to see nothing clearly, or else some notion of responsibility forbids him to say what he thinks. He hums and haws when asked a plain question. His whole aspect is that of a worn and half obliterated scholar made spruce by tailors and doing his best to adopt the quiet distinguished manner of those who govern. In private he is a kindly, even affectionate gentleman, simple by nature, though tarnished with a supercilious superficial manner which leads him to dally urbanely and in a way which belittles them with art and letters and everything but politics. We took him to Kew, and chatted of Oxford and Walter Pater, and how Chesterton is a genius, and George Moore another, by way of relief from politics. And he approved of nature too, and likened the Thames beneath a shower to a picture in the Louvre. He stood still on the bank for some minutes, taking in the impression, not as a person who is accustomed to looking at things looks, but rather as a man who collects objects for the good of his soul. So it was too with the buds of the magnolia at Kew.

I could fill this page with gossip about people's articles in the *Athenaeum*, since I had tea with Katherine yesterday and Murry sat there mud-coloured and mute, livening only when we talked his shop. He has the jealous partiality of a parent for his offspring already. Heinemann has rejected Katherine's stories; and she was oddly hurt that Roger had not invited her to his party. Her hard composure is much on the surface.

Thursday 24 April

On Easter Monday we went up to visit the Murrys and see Hampstead Heath. Our verdict was that the crowd at close quarters is detestable; it smells; it sticks; it has neither vitality nor colour. How slow they walk! How passively and brutishly they lie on the grass! How little of pleasure or pain is in them! But they looked well dressed and well fed; and at a distance among the canary coloured swings and roundabouts they had the look of a picture. Very little noise they made; the large aeroplane that came flying so steadily overhead made more noise than the whole crowd of us. Why do I say 'us'? I never for a moment felt myself one of 'them'. Yet the sight had its charm: I liked the bladders, and the little penny sticks, and the sight of two slow elaborate dancers performing to a barrel organ in a space the size of a hearthrug. Katherine and Murry and Murry's brother met us at their door. We thought she would have enjoyed herself, from the likeness of her prose to the scene; on the contrary, she was disgusted. We had rather a stiff tea.

Last night the Coles [G.D.H. and Margaret] dined here, and gave me my first view of them. Sharp, positive, hard minds; in tense taut bodies; in Cole's case the mouth seems fixed in a kind of snarl at the world. A positive domineering young man he seemed; and she, with less force, equally sure of herself. A good laugh would do them both good; yet how laugh with those tight stretched drums for cheeks, and those curled sneering lips? I don't accuse either of them of a desire to be savage or destructive; I write from the outsider's unsympathetic point of view. But Leonard, though he works at their works, is still humane and deliberate. Its the perpetual strife that strings them up in this way, I think; no speculative or contemplative imaginative power seems to be left them. This I write from the recollection of them which came to me on waking. 'I don't like the Coles' I said to myself, before I had time to set my faculties to work upon this judgment.

Tomorrow we go down to Asheham for ten days; alone; leaving the servants to clean here, and intending to find a house for £35 if we can, for that is our solution at present.

Monday 5 May

The day mother died twenty something years ago. The smell of wreaths in the hall is always in the first flowers still; without remembering the day I was thinking of her, as I often do – as good a memorial as one could wish. Ah but how happy we've been at Asheham! It was a most melodious time. Everything went so freely; – but I can't analyse all the sources of my joy.

Wednesday 7 May

To recapitulate the events of Asheham is no longer in my power, or perhaps, since they were mainly of a spiritual nature requiring some subtlety to relate, I'm too lazy to try. Happiness – what I wonder constitutes happiness? I daresay the most important element is work, and that rarely fails either of us now.

A letter from Gerald to say he has read *Night and Day* with 'the greatest interest' and will be delighted to publish it. I suppose, as I go to the trouble of copying his words verbatim, that I was a good deal pleased by them. The first impression of an outsider, especially one who proposes to back his opinion with money, means something; though I can't think of stout smooth Gerald smoking a cigar over my pages without a smile.

I got over to Charleston and had a night and morning alone with Vanessa – so far as she can ever be alone. Living is fairly bare at the moment. They have all the necessaries; but not an ornament. My life, by comparison, seems padded at every turn. But they all looked as vigorous as possible. As usual, a good deal of domestic talk; sleep in the ground floor room at night, where this time last year about I heard the nightingales, and the fishes splashing in the pond, white roses tapped at the window; that night when I was told that [baby] Angelica was in evidence. Nothing but wind and rain this time, and no coal in the house.

Monday 12 May

We are in the thick of our publishing season: Murry, Eliot, and myself are in the hands of the public this morning. I read a bound copy of *Kew Gardens* through, having put off the evil task until it was complete. The result is vague. It seems to me slight and short.

On Friday I had tea with Katherine and Murry, with whom I now adopt a manner of motherly badinage; which is less fatiguing than the intellectual pose.

Friday 16 May

This week we've had Ottoline, and Lytton, and I've been to see Violet Dickinson. Let me attempt Ottoline, since her hat and veil on the sofa beside me recall her. She struck her unmistakable note on entering the room; rayed with green and blue, like the Cornish sea, and magnificently upright and held together; her blue blood giving her the carriage of assurance and self-respect which is rare among the intellectuals. Certain layers of powder showed upon the steeps of her face – but when you reflect that she's close on fifty – and has cropped her hair like a boy! Of course we talked personalities; and she was kindly, and well wishing, though considerably bewildered, and bewailing as usual her disasters in friendship, and inclined to blame everyone but herself. L.'s verdict was that she was 'very nice'; the first time he has ever said that. Perhaps she was on her good behaviour – but if so, she was capable of wrapping herself in her great Spanish cloak, and sallying out into the street without her hat; she's altogether such a fancy dress character that a hat more or less seems immaterial. We put her into her train with young officers who looked up startled; and despatched her to Waterloo.

Next day there was Lytton. I need not repeat the stock observations upon his mellow good humour. It is more to the point to chronicle a renewed sense of affection, which has never been seriously in abeyance. We scrutinised the condition of his soul, with his help, very closely. Ottoline had professed some alarm. We came to the conclusion that it would be absurd not to have this butterfly's season among the great.

I broke from Lytton with regret, and paid my visit to Violet; but she would have been hurt had I shirked it, to judge at least by her pleasure at seeing me. Its odd how people of fifty remain exactly fifty. She hasn't changed a hair for twenty years, which must be the length of our friendship. We take things up precisely as we left them; a year's gap makes no difference. When I come onto the verge of the respectable classes I'm always much struck by their unexpectedness: Violet is as much of a democrat as I am; as little of an Imperialist; she blames England; she has no hate of Germany; she sends clothes to Russia; and yet she lives in Manchester Street, and consorts chiefly with people like the Horners and the Thynnes. Beatrice Thynne has inherited a quarter of a million; two large properties, and one of the finest libraries in England; she has no idea what to make of them; visits them in a distracted way to see which she'd like to live in; can't make up her mind to settle in either, and finally spends most of her time in Gray's Inn, looked after by a charwoman.

Sunday 18 May

Our seductive sweetness appears still to be drawing bees from all quarters. As we left lunch there was a great rapping on the door, and the hall immediately filled with strangers, who eventually became Roger, Pamela [his daughter], and a strange silent foreign woman whom from her grey hair I took to be Margery Fry. We pitched on the grass, under a shower of apple blossom; and there sat until tea; and then Logan [Pearsall Smith] came; and we only fell silent at half past six or even later; nor was there a moment of repose, neither for tongue nor brain. [Logan] is a very well brushed, bright eyed, rosy cheeked man, seemingly entirely satisfied with life, which he appears to have mastered: visiting each of its flowers, like a bee. These flowers he keeps stored in his waistcoat pocket: lines from Jeremy Taylor, Carlyle, Lamb, &c. An epicurean, I suppose; a little frosty, I conjecture; though kindly and humane of course, rather than human.

Sunday 25 May

The day recalls the fact that we lunched with the Webbs this time last week. The Webbs were very quotable. Mrs Webb's brilliant idea of municipal bricks for children, inscribed with the names of organisations so that in putting them together they would learn their civic duties was almost too much in character to be suitable. Even Sidney had his mild joke at her.

Lytton came to tea on Friday and half maliciously assured me that my industry amazed him. My industry and my competence, for he thinks me the best reviewer alive, and the inventor of a new prose style, and the creator of a new version of the sentence. He asserted that he was disgusted by his own stereotyped ways: his two semi-colons; his method of understatement; and his extreme definiteness. Without agreeing, I conveyed my sense of his dangers, and urged him to write plays – stories – anything to break the mould of the early Victorians. After a volume on Victoria in the same manner, he is going to attempt it. But the money – he must make money – he can't write reviews.

Monday 9 June

A week at Asheham has intervened. An odd thing happened to me at Asheham, where I count upon becoming clearer and more concentrated. The very opposite of this took place. I dozed and drowsed and seemed to feel the sun in my brain sending all my thoughts to seek repose in the shadow. I write there at an open window looking onto the field; and the field was gilt with buttercups; the sheep were tempting in their indolence; in short, I used to find the morning gone and only a few lines written. The loveliness of Asheham once again brimmed the cup and overflowed. Wild ideas seized us of building a house. To give up every foothold in that region seemed unthinkable. With the notion of building a house running strongly in my mind I went to Charleston for a night and was there disabused of such fantasies very completely. Nessa and I quarrelled as nearly as we ever do quarrel now over the get up of *Kew Gardens*, both type and woodcuts; and she firmly refused to illustrate any more stories of mine under those conditions, and went so far as to doubt the value of the Hogarth Press altogether. An ordinary printer would do better in her opinion. This both stung and chilled me. Anyhow I left in a rather crumpled condition, and paused in Lewes in no cheerful mood, with three hours, moreover, to spend there. To pass the time, more than anything, I asked Mrs Wycherley [Estate Agent] about houses; and she bethought her of one newly on the market, small, old, actually in Lewes, and perhaps a little humble for one used to lodge at Asheham. Off I went up Pipes Passage, under the clock, and saw rising at the top of the sloping path a singular shaped roof, rising into a point, and spreading out in a circular petticoat all round it. An elderly and humble cottage woman, the owner, showed me over. How far my satisfaction with the general oddity and character of the whole place were the result of finding something that would do, that one could conceive living in, that was cheap (freehold £300) I don't know; but as I inspected the rooms I became conscious of a rising desire to settle here; to have done with looking about; to take this place, and make it one's permanent lodging. In short I took it there and then, being egged on by Wycherley's hesitation, and hints of a purchaser who had already asked for the refusal. The end of the story, which I must curtail, is that we have bought the Round House, and are now secure of a lodging on earth so long as we need sleep or sit anywhere.

Tuesday 10 June

I must use up the fifteen minutes before dinner in going on again, in order to make up the great gap. We are just in from the Club and from tea with James. His news is that Maynard in disgust at the peace terms has resigned; kicked the dust of office off him, and is now an academic figure at Cambridge. But I must really sing my own praises, since I left off at the point when we came back from Asheham to find the hall table stacked, littered, with orders for *Kew Gardens*. They strewed the sofa, and we opened them intermittently through dinner, and quarrelled, I'm sorry to say, because we were both excited, and opposite tides of excitement coursed in us, and they were blown to waves by the critical blast of Charleston. All these orders – 150 about, from shops and private people – come from a review in *The Times Literary Supplement* in which as much praise was allowed me as I like to claim. And ten days ago I was stoically facing complete failure! The pleasure of success was considerably damaged, first by our quarrel, and second, by the necessity of getting some 90 copies ready, cutting covers, printing tables, glueing backs, and finally despatching, which used up all spare time and some not spare till this moment.

Saturday *14 June*

Yesterday I had a Hampstead field day; first the Murrys, then Adrian and Karin, and finally dinner – it was 8.30 by the time I got it – with Ray and Dorothy Bussy. A very severe review of Murry, a severe review of Eliot, appeared in the *TLS* on Thursday. I don't see why they choose to come down so hard upon Murry; and I wish they hadn't. I attribute the extreme depression of him and Katherine at least partly to this. And I felt gorged and florid with my comparative success. Poor Murry pretended not to mind, but much like a small boy sticking it out that caning doesn't hurt. A poem is a very sensitive part to be beaten. But Katherine looks so ill and haggard that I suppose health may make a great part of her depression. She is going to San Remo for a year in September. Murry means to live alone in the country. I don't see how, all this being so, they can look forward to their future. Anyhow I went off rather sombre, leaving them to their spare lonely meal, nothing seeming to grow or flourish round them; leafless trees.

Wednesday *18 June*

I went off, as I now remember, to call on Adrian, as I was early for Ray; and found that strange couple just decided to become medical students. After five years' training they will, being aged thirty-five and forty-one or so, set up together in practice as psycho-analysts. Here is another chance; visions of success and a busy crowded, interesting life beguile him. Halfway through, I suppose, something will make it all impossible; and then, having forgotten his law, he will take up what – farming or editing a newspaper, or keeping bees perhaps. I don't see that it matters at all, so long as they always have some carrot dangling in front of them.

Yesterday, Tuesday, I was treated to ices at Gunter's by Clive. It was all the same as before. Little tables; long rather dark shop; numbers of gilt chairs; discreet buffet; elderly waitresses in black; and couples scattered all about silently, or almost silently, absorbing ices and sugared cakes. We strolled out of the solemn cave and sauntered through the purest 18th Century London to the Green Park where we sat on hard green chairs, and watched people passing down the little slope towards the Palace. This being, I suppose, the sixth week without rain the grass is already haycoloured and slippery. We gossiped, speculated, and reminisced. Very easy, agreeable talk to my mind, and then what an age I've known him! How much we've been through side by side – these infrequent meetings are little islands upon which one stands surveying the flood racing away in the past; looking out over the future, safely and with very little anxiety just at present. He talks of going to Paris in the autumn, to see what's on; and he's given up his book, and finds that articles of 2,000 words exactly suit him. He thinks of subjects in his bath. He makes money. He spends it on ices and dinners at the Café Royal. He dines out every night, enjoys every moment, and feels his senses quicker and stronger as time goes on. We agreed in finding life very delightful, though very different for each of us.

Monday 23 June
If I hadn't had since midday to settle myself, I should still be twanging and twittering with Garsington. But parties don't fluster me as they used. I don't much care now about the great question of hair; I am resigned to my station among the badly dressed, though the speeding up of my blue dress, and doubts as to its beauty scarcely seem to confirm that statement. However this may be, I enjoyed Garsington saying to myself 'The worst moment will be when I come into the drawing room in my blue dress before dinner.' I planned thus to get dressed quick and come in before Ott which is not difficult as Ott never gets dressed quick. Mercifully I need not face Garsington squarely and draw its picture. I observed that the sealing wax red drawing room is a good deal smaller this visit than last, and last visit than first. That's what happens to people too. The population was floating and changing. Goldie and I were permanent; Aldous Huxley came for one night. I shall leave out several names if I try to count them. I think Goldie was the principal element in the week end, that is to say that he took upon him the brunt of Sunday morning, and meal times; three hours sitting on a hard seat with Ott and me, Philip sometimes, Gertler occasionally, and Aldous off and on was a trial; but for us all it was well surmounted. I did not guess the time once. When Philip suggested a visit to the pigs I was ready but not over-ready. Ott needled away at her embroidery, losing her needle once, and crouching on all fours behind the seat, while Goldie and I went on talking. This seemed to me to typify her modest position; so long as people talk she doesn't much want to interfere, and she listens, especially if people's characters are discussed. Yet it struck me as strange –

Thursday 3 July
What struck me as strange? Perhaps I meant to finish by trying to define the sense of purposelessness which now and then besets me – Suppose we do settle exactly what Roger's character is, and what degree of spite to allow Clive – well this is too far gone for recapturing, though there was a queer enough sequel a day or two later at Asheham. We went there on the Thursday following, and came back yesterday. I can't give much space to Philip's letter though; [it] was all about my lack of heart and his terror of

me; to which I have rejoined 'if I'm Bloomsbury, you're Mayfair'; to his bewilderment, as I hope. But this is moonshine. The solid fact is that we own, besides the Round House, Monks House at Rodmell, with three quarters of an acre of land.

We own Monks House (this is almost the first time I've written a name which I hope to write many thousands of times before I've done with it) for ever. It happened thus. As we walked up the steep road from [Lewes] station last Thursday on our way to inspect the Round House, we both read out a placard stuck on the auctioneers' wall. 'Lot 1. Monks House, Rodmell. An old fashioned house standing in three quarters of an acre of land to be sold with possession.' "That would have suited us exactly" L. said as we passed, and I, loyal to the Round House, murmured something about the drawbacks of Rodmell, but suggested anyhow a visit to the place; and so we went on. I think a slight shade of anti-climax had succeeded my rather excessive optimism; at any rate, the Round House no longer seemed so radiant and unattainable when we examined it as owners. I thought L. a little disappointed. The bedrooms were very small. The garden not a country garden. Anyhow it seemed well to plan a visit to Rodmell on the following day. I bicycled over against a strong cold wind. This time I flatter myself that I kept my optimism in check. 'These rooms are small', I said to myself; 'The kitchen is distinctly bad. There's an oil stove, and no grate. Nor is there hot water, nor a bath, and as for the earth closet I was never shown it.' These prudent objections kept excitement at bay; yet even they were forced to yield place to a profound pleasure at the size and shape and fertility and wildness of the garden. There seemed an infinity of fruitbearing trees; unexpected flowers sprouted among cabbages. There were well kept rows of peas, artichokes, potatoes; and I could fancy a very pleasant walk in the orchard under the apple trees, with the grey extinguisher of the church steeple pointing my boundary. On the other hand there is little view – There is little ceremony or precision at Monks House. It is an unpretending house, long and low, a house of many doors, on one side fronting the street of Rodmell, and wood-boarded on that side, though the street of Rodmell is at our end little more than a cart track running out on to the flat of the water meadows. There are, if memory serves me, no less than three large outhouses of different kinds, and a stable; and a hen house – Our fruit and vegetables are said to flourish under the care of a single old man who for forty years has spent his spare time in tending these trees for the late Mr Jacob Verrall. All this made a happy kind of jumble in my brain, together with the store of old fashioned chairs and tables, glass and furniture with which every inch of room space is crowded. I came back and told my story as quietly as I could, and next day L. and I went together and made a thorough inspection. He was pleased beyond his expectation. The truth is he has the making of a fanatical lover of that garden. In short, we decided walking home to buy if we could, and sell Round House, as we conjecture we can. Eight hundred we made our limit, which, according to Wycherley, gave us a good chance of possession.

The sale was on Tuesday. I don't suppose many spaces of five minutes in the course of my life have been so close packed with sensation. The room at the White Hart was crowded. I looked at every face for signs of opulence, and was cheered to discover none. But then, I thought, getting L. into line, does *he* look as if he had £800 in his pocket? Bidding began. Someone offered £300. "Not an offer," said the auctioneer, who was immediately opposed to us as a smiling courteous antagonist, "a beginning." The next bid was £400. Then they rose by fifties. Wycherley standing by us, silent and unmoved, added his advance. Six hundred was reached too quick for me. The auctioneer egged us on. I daresay there were six voices speaking, though after £600, four of them dropped out, and left only a Mr Tattersall competing with Mr Wycherley. We were allowed to bid in twenties; then tens; then fives; and still short of £700. Seven hundred reached, there was a pause; the auctioneer raised his hammer, very slowly; held it up a considerable time; urged and exhorted all the while it slowly sank towards the table. "Now Mr Tattersall, another bid from you – ten pounds? five pounds? no more? for the last time then –" *dump*! and down it came on the table, to our thanksgiving – I purple in the cheeks, and L. trembling like a reed – "sold to Mr Wycherley." We stayed no longer. Out we went into the High Street, and very nearly quarrelled over the address of Roger's house.

Thursday 8 July
We went on however, L. to Asheham, and I to Charleston, where there was Maynard, and a good deal of brisk talk. He is disillusioned he says. No more does he believe, that is, in the stability of the things he likes. Eton is doomed; the governing classes, perhaps Cambridge too. These conclusions were forced on him by the dismal and degrading spectacle of the Peace Congress, where men played shamelessly, not for Europe, or even England, but for their own return to Parliament at the next election. He resigned, and is now a don at Cambridge, daily rejecting profitable offers made him by houses of business, willing, according to Duncan, to pay £4,000 a year for his attendance for a short time daily. We all came up to London early next day. We had an afternoon's gaiety at the Ballet, and then went back to Gordon Square, everything a little glittering and unreal, as usual after the country and in Nessa's presence.

Friday, the 4th, I went to tea with Katherine, since I begin to feel my visits numbered, how seriously I don't know, but once she gets abroad, what's to bring her back? Murry, poor man, pale and sad as usual, for she is again only just out of bed.

Thursday 10 July
Last night I dined at the Savoy Grill Room with Clive. It is long since I had taken part in the great ceremony of dinner with others believing in it, assisting at it, and dressing for it. Fish and meat and melon and ices have come to their own again. Clive parted with a good deal of paper money. He pointed out to me Picasso and Mme Picasso making off for the ballet. We drove back to Gordon Square and talked about the problems of literature. I wonder if I talk nonsense about writing to Clive? On the whole I believe that he has an odd gift for making one talk sense. He's so eager that one should talk sense; his enthusiasm is the engaging thing about him – deducting the tribute of his enthusiasm for me. Moreover, whatever one may think of his taste in life, however one may feel him a little battered and dusty in the pursuit of pleasure, still there's his honesty; his vivacity; his determination not to be bored, and not to bore. In his own way he is somehow a figure.

Saturday 12 July
In public affairs, I see I've forgotten to say that peace was signed; perhaps that ceremony was accomplished while we were at Asheham. I've forgotten the account I was going to write out of the gradual disappearance of things from shop windows; and the gradual, but still only partial reappearance of things. Sugar cakes, currant buns, and mounds of sweets. The effect of the war would be worth describing, and one of these days at Monks House – but why do I let myself imagine spaces of leisure at Monks House? I know I shall have books that must be read there too. But this dressing up of the future is one of the chief sources of our happiness, I believe. There's still a good deal of the immediate past asserting its claim on me. I met Morgan Forster on the platform at Waterloo yesterday; a man physically resembling a blue butterfly – I mean by that to describe his transparency and lightness. I like Forster very much, though I find him whimsical and vagulous to an extent that frightens me with my own clumsiness and definiteness. Then I bought my bag of coffee, and so up to Katherine, with whom I spent my hour very happily. Indeed, I like her more and more; and think we have reached some kind of durable foundation.

Saturday 19 July
One ought to say something about Peace Day, I suppose, though whether its worth taking a new nib for that purpose I don't know. In ten minutes or so the Richmond procession begins. I fear there will be few people to

applaud the town councillors dressed up to look dignified and march through the streets. Rain held off till some half hour ago. The servants had a triumphant morning. They stood on Vauxhall Bridge and saw everything. Generals and soldiers and tanks and nurses and bands took two hours in passing. It was they said the most splendid sight of their lives. But I don't know – it seems to me a servants' festival; something got up to pacify and placate 'the people' – and now the rain's spoiling it. There's something calculated and politic and insincere about these peace rejoicings. Moreover they are carried out with no beauty, and not much spontaneity. Yesterday in London the usual sticky stodgy conglomerations of people, sleepy and torpid as a cluster of drenched bees, were crawling over Trafalgar Square, and rocking about the pavements in the neighbourhood. The one pleasant sight I saw was due rather to the little breath of wind than to decorative skill; some long tongue-shaped streamers attached to the top of the Nelson column licked the air, furled and unfurled, like the gigantic tongues of dragons, with a slow, rather serpentine beauty. (And now, in the rain, under a grey brown sky, the bells of Richmond are ringing – but church bells only recall weddings and Christian services.) I can't deny that I feel a little mean at writing so lugubriously; since we're all supposed to keep up the belief that we're glad and enjoying ourselves. So on a birthday, when for some reason things have gone wrong, it was a point of honour in the nursery to pretend. Years later one could confess what a horrid fraud it seemed; and if, years later, these docile herds will own up that they too saw through it, and will have no more of it – well – should I be more cheerful?

Sunday 20 July
Perhaps I will finish the account of the peace celebrations. What herd animals we are after all! – even the most disillusioned. At any rate, after sitting through the procession and the peace bells unmoved, I began after dinner to feel that if something was going on, perhaps one had better be in it. I routed up poor L. and, seeing that the rain was stopped, we went out just before ten. Explosions had for some time promised fireworks. The doors of the public house at the corner were open, and the room crowded; couples waltzing; songs being shouted, waveringly, as if one must be drunk to sing. A troop of little boys with lanterns were parading the Green, beating sticks. Not many shops went to the expense of electric light. A woman of the upper classes was supported dead drunk between two men partially drunk. We followed a moderate stream flowing up the Hill. Illuminations were almost extinct half way up, but we kept on till we reached the terrace. And then we did see something – not much indeed, for the damp had deadened the chemicals. Red and green and yellow and blue

balls rose slowly into the air, burst, flowered into an oval of light, which dropped in minute grains and expired. Rising over the Thames, among trees, these rockets were beautiful; the light on the faces of the crowd was strange; yet of course there was grey mist muffling everything, and taking the blaze off the fire. It was a melancholy thing to see the incurable soldiers lying in bed at the Star and Garter with their backs to us, smoking cigarettes, and waiting for the noise to be over. We were children to be amused. So at eleven we went home. Today the rain has left us in no doubt that any remaining festivities are to be completely quenched.

Thursday 24 July
Last night we had Forster and the Bussys. Morgan is easily drowned even by the vivacity of the Bussys. He is an unworldly, transparent character, whimsical and detached, caring very little I should think what people say, and with a clear idea of what he wishes. I don't think he wishes to shine in intellectual society; certainly not in fashionable. He is fantastic and very sensitive; an attractive character to me. He resembles a vaguely rambling butterfly; since there is no intensity or rapidity about him. To dominate the talk would be odious to him. He subsided in a chair; or strolled about the room, turning over the pages of a book. Even when the Bussys had gone, we made little direct headway. He will come to Asheham if we pay his fare. He has only £26 in the bank. I liked this simple way of explaining things.

Monks House, Rodmell

Sunday 7 September
I suppose this is the first day upon which I could easily sit down and write in my long suffering and by this time I hope tolerant diary. The move was accomplished in one day, thanks chiefly to the organisation of L. who tied all the books in lots. Two waggon loads, one leaving about ten, another at six did the job, and we managed to roost about the house somehow or other that night. Much remains to be done inside the house, though the main arrangements are now made. But for some days one's mind is distracted by perpetually dwelling upon the changes round one; it works with an effort. This is wearing off slightly, though I write this as if I were raising seven stone on my pen instead of the usual number of ounces. However from all the difficulties, advantages and disadvantages of the place, I think the upshot is wholly favourable. One gains much in the way of variety here; there are more walks, and endless interests in the garden, though nothing of the flawless beauty of Asheham.

Thursday 12 September

Duncan and Nessa have just been over unexpectedly to tea. Other people's incursions always leave me tremulous. They break in upon a mood of depression, deep according to L.; to me of the consistency of September mist. Why is it, I wonder? Partly that for ten days I don't think I've had a letter; then I expect something unpleasant from Macmillans [USA]. Here I make my forecast. 'We have read *Night and Day* with the deepest interest, but hardly think it would appeal to our public over here.' Though I foretell this, and see that written down it is negligible as criticism, yet I want to have that unpleasant moment over. And the publication of *Night and Day* may perhaps send an occasional tremor through me for all my boasting. If that is pronounced a failure, I don't see why I should continue writing novels. These are the usual writer's melancholies.

Saturday 13 September

Well, Macmillan's letter came this morning, and is neither so good nor so bad as it might have been. They read with great interest, think *Night and Day* a fine work, but not likely to appeal to a wide public in America, and too long to be, at this season, worth reprinting. But they propose to take 500 or 1000 sheets from Gerald; the same number of *The Voyage Out*, and understand that I will offer them my next book. On the whole, I'm rather pleased than otherwise. I shall accept, I suppose, since there's scarcely time to try elsewhere. But I don't think Macmillan had much to do with my depression. Do I envy Nessa her overflowing household? Perhaps at moments; everything flourishing and humane there; perhaps I can't help a contrast which never occurs when I'm in full flood of work. I made these comparisons yesterday, when I lunched there and spent the afternoon and rode home. I had meant to say something about these queer spiritual states. They interest me, even when I'm the subject. And I always remember the saying that at one's lowest ebb one is nearest a true vision. I think perhaps nine out of ten people never get a day in the year of such happiness as I have almost constantly; now I'm having a turn of their lot.

Sunday 14 September

Well, I don't think my turn of their lot is a very serious matter. We went for our first Sunday walk today. In order to counteract the tremendous draw of the garden we have arranged two walks a week, on Sundays and Wednesdays. Today we went on the downs towards Kingston. We saw the sea at Brighton and the sea at Eastbourne to right and left of us. I must try a little Plato now – to prove that concentration is as easy here as elsewhere.

Sunday 21 September

By paying five shillings I have become a member of the Lewes public library. It is an amusing place – full of old ghosts; books half way to decomposition. A general brownness covers them. They are as much alike outwardly as charity schoolchildren. Most have shed their boards years ago, and been recovered in brown paper.

Sunday 28 September

Cut off as we are from all human intercourse I cannot be sure even of the date. It is said that the entire railways of England are on strike; the miners, and perhaps the transport workers, are with them. This happened yesterday morning, or rather late the night before; and though we got our papers through late in the evening, we are without posts. The signalman gave us some information yesterday, and believes himself to be striking against a reduction of fourteen shillings a week in his wages. His strike pay comes to sixteen shillings a week. How with prices what they are the strike can be kept up more than a day or two is difficult to see. He expects a settlement tomorrow; but like all the rest, he knows far less about the reasons and machinations than we do – L. at any rate. At present, what with Sunday and the quiet one imagines on the lines, a queer deep silence seems to lie upon us. We post letters knowing they won't get further than Lewes. There is talk of a motor car service. The Government make a show of courageous determination. We are on war rations, and told to be brave and good. Not since coaching days has the village of Rodmell been so isolated as it is at the present moment. Yet a state of siege has a certain smugness and self-sufficiency about it. No one can interrupt. If it lasts another day or two the food difficulty will begin. Then there's the question of getting back on Thursday.

Yesterday we went over to Asheham, plundered the hollow of its mushrooms, and then got in at the drawing room window. I don't know whether its one's accommodating temper that painted the place a little shut in and dismal, with the vast hollow behind and the straight view between trees in front. I thought it lacking in variety, this time, and colour – but I expect this is one of the devices of the imagination. Anyhow Monks improves, after the fashion of a mongrel who wins your heart. We have been planting tiny grains of seed in the front bed, in the pious or religious belief that they will resurrect next spring as Clarkia, Calceolaria, Campanula, Larkspur and Scabious. I shan't recognise them if they do; we are planting at a venture, inspired by seedsman's language: how they stand high and bear bright blue petals.

Tuesday 30 September

This is opened to record the Strike bulletin. Nothing has happened. All railways are silent. I went into Lewes yesterday and found a kind of modified Sunday prevailing. There were numbers of motors with luggage and the pampered rich. Rumour – shop keepers, that is to say – predicts a long strike. Who's in the right, they don't say: 'anyhow its bad for us'. In our private world the discomfort is mostly what we imagine for the future. We can make no plans anyhow. The papers are just in, shrunk to single sheets, and untrustworthy in their extreme – *Daily Mail* and *Herald*; trustful in the middle perhaps, *Daily News*. So far nothing but persistent hostility on both sides; no overtures.

Wednesday 1 October

The strike remains, so far as we can judge, the same. On the other hand, rumours of the strike change from hour to hour. A post came this morning. The postman is reported to say that all trains are running as usual. The signalman appears. Situation unchanged; much depressed. Then Dedman [gardener] comes to pick apples. A notice is in the post office, he says, that trains are as usual. Nelly goes to Lewes. Comes back 'frightened' so she says. A few trains only, into which you get at your own risk. We went down to the signalman with books and offers of help. His wife met us; he being at Newhaven. A fiery, impulsive, vigorous woman about to bear her fifth child. She was urging him to give in. Public opinion was against them, she said. Then she explained that they had only saved six shillings. With their strike pay this can't long keep off hunger. Then she couldn't see the rights of it. "They're like children who've had their sweet and don't want to give up their penny" she said, often enough to show that she'd used the argument often to him. They must give it up sooner or later, so why not now.

HOGARTH HOUSE, RICHMOND

Tuesday 7 October

Home yesterday. The 'docile herds' whom I describe on Peace Day are not so deluded after all. They have held the country up for eleven days, I think. We did a little to support them too, and kept one man on strike who would have gone back without our pound. Still, what's to be read in the papers is hardly fit for my private page.

I began reading the first volume of my diary; and see that its second anniversary is now reached. I don't think the first volume makes such good reading as the last; a proof that all writing, even this unpremeditated scribbling, has its form, which one learns. Is it worth going on with? The trouble is, that if one goes on a year or so more, one will feel bound on that account to continue. I wonder why I do it. Partly, I think, from my old sense of the race of time: 'Time's winged chariot hurrying near' – Does it stay it?

Saturday 11 October
For the first time I went up to London yesterday in the first place to buy gloves; in the second to have tea at Nessa's flat. Lytton we ran into at the Club on coming back – composed, agreeable, permanently shone upon, and completely sure of himself – ah, but infinitely charming into the bargain. Success, I believe, produces a kind of modesty. It frees you from bothering about yourself. He was flattering to me, as usual; but then I'm *not* a success. Did I not hear from Macmillan today that Messrs Duckworth's charges are prohibitive? So my chance of appearing in America is gone. But I'm showered under with review books.

Tuesday 21 October
This is Trafalgar day, and yesterday is memorable for the appearance of *Night and Day*. My six copies reached me in the morning, and five were despatched, so that I figure the beaks of five friends already embedded. Am I nervous? Oddly little; more excited and pleased than nervous. In the first place, there it is, out and done with; then I read a bit and liked it; then I have a kind of confidence, that the people whose judgment I value will probably think well of it, which is much reinforced by the knowledge that even if they don't, I shall pick up and start another story of my own.

Thursday 23 October
The first fruits of *Night and Day* must be entered: 'No doubt the work of the highest genius' Clive Bell. Well, he might not have liked it; he was critical of *The Voyage Out*. I own I'm pleased; yet not convinced that it is as he says. The people whose judgment I respect won't be so enthusiastic as he is, but they'll come out decidedly on that side, I think. Moreover, in a way which I can't defend to L., I do respect Clive's judgment. It's erratic, but always springs from a direct feeling. I think I feel most doubtful about Morgan; after getting his report I shall be quite at ease. Three or four people count, and the rest, save as a senseless clapping of hands or hissing, are nowhere.

Thursday 30 October
If I could treat myself professionally as a subject for analysis I could make an interesting story of the past few days, of my vicissitudes about *Night and*

Day. After Clive's letter came Nessa's – unstinted praise; on top of that Lytton's: enthusiastic praise; a grand triumph; a classic; and so on; Violet's sentence of eulogy followed; and then, yesterday morning, this line from Morgan: 'I like it less than *The Voyage Out*.' Though he spoke also of great admiration, and had read in haste and proposed re-reading, this rubbed out all the pleasure of the rest. Yes; but to continue. About 3 in the afternoon I felt happier and easier on account of his blame than on account of the others' praise – as if one were in the human atmosphere again, after a blissful roll among elastic clouds and cushiony downs. Yet I suppose I value Morgan's opinion as much as anybody's. Then there's a column in *The Times* this morning; high praise; and intelligent too. I hope this week will see me through the reviews, I should like intelligent letters to follow; but I want to be writing little stories; I feel a load off my mind all the same.

Saturday 1 November

Never have I been so pressed with reviewing. I think I might slack off if *Night and Day* succeeds. Happily the book begins to recede from the front of my mind.

Thursday 6 November

Sydney [Waterlow] and Morgan dined with us last night. The doubt about Morgan and *Night and Day* is removed; I understand why he likes it less than *The Voyage Out* and, in understanding, see that it is not a criticism to discourage. Perhaps intelligent criticism never is. All the same, I shirk writing it out, because I write so much criticism. We talked very easily, the proof being that we (I anyhow) did not mind silences. Morgan has the artist's mind; he says the simple things that clever people don't say; I find him the best of critics for that reason. Suddenly out comes the obvious thing that one has overlooked.

Saturday 15 November

I have never been so neglectful of this work of mine; but there have been substantial difficulties. We were with Lytton last Sunday; on Monday I was at the dentist, and back just in time for Molly Hamilton; Tuesday I wrote letters; Wednesday, at a concert, with Violet Dickinson immediately after; Thursday Molly MacCarthy, for tea and after tea; Friday to Margaret and Lilian, and so here I am, sitting after Saturday tea, a large warm meal, full of currants and sugar and hot tea cake, after a long cold walk.

If I shut my eyes and thought of Tidmarsh, what should I see? Carrington a little absorbed with household duties; secreting canvas in the attic; Saxon mute and sealed till Sunday night, when he flowered for a time and talked of Greek; Lytton – a more complex situation. Good and simple and tender

– a little low in tone; a little invalidish. If I'd married him, I caught myself thinking, I should have found him querulous. He would have laid too many ties on one, and repined a little if one had broken free. He was in his usual health (as they say); but the sense of living so much for health, and assembling so many comforts round him with that object is a little depressing. But what I feel for Lytton is as true as ever it was. We sit alone over the fire and rattle on, so quick, so agile in our jumps and circumventions. On his table were the latest editions of Voltaire. His books were as primly ranged and carefully tended as an old maid's china. I was in the vein to feel highly 'creative', as indeed he said he thought me. But he declared himself entirely without that power. He can invent nothing he says; take away his authorities, and he comes to a full stop. Perhaps this is true of all Stracheys.

Molly Hamilton still strains at her leash like the spaniel of my legend. It is a rough eager mind, bold and straightforward, but O dear – when it comes to writing! Her courage impresses me – the sense she gives of a machine working at high pressure all day long – the machine of the professional working woman. A tailor made coat costing £16 is essential she said to exact respect in an office.

I think Violet Dickinson must be skipped. So we skip to Molly who took her tea in the kitchen, and lastly we approach the heights of Hampstead – the immaculate and moral heights of Hampstead. Had I the energy left I would write out that scene of revelation and explanation with Margaret, since in thirty minutes we traversed more ground than in the past three years. Tentatively she began it – how Janet and she felt that perhaps – they might be wrong, but still in their view – in short my article on Charlotte Brontë was so much more to their liking than my novels. Something in my feeling for human beings – some narrowness – some lack of emotion – here I blazed up and let fly. So you go on preaching humanity, was the gist of what I said, when you've withdrawn, and preserve only the conventional idea of it. But its you that are narrow, she retaliated. On the contrary, I'm the most sympathetic, the most human, the most universal of people. But the idea of herself as a forcible intense woman, excluding the greater half of the human heart staggered her. She took the blow well. It was as if one had suddenly drawn some curtain. She must think it over, and write to me she said.

Friday 28 November

This gap can easily be accounted for by recalling the old saying (if it is one) that when things happen, people don't write. Too many things have happened. Within this last fortnight the *International Review* has come to an end; both servants are going; two publishers have offered to publish *Night and Day* and *The Voyage Out* in America; Angelica has stayed with us –

together with a greater number than usual of dinners, letters, telephone calls, books to review, reviews of my book, invitations to parties and so forth. It was the dinner parties that led Nelly to give notice last Monday. She did it in a way which makes me think she would be glad now to change her mind. She would this moment if I asked her. But on the whole I'm not going to ask her. Let alone the recurring worry of these scenes we both incline to try a new system of dailies, which never ceases to attract us. We mean to make the attempt now. No one could be nicer than Nelly, for long stretches. But the fault is more in the system of keeping two young women chained in a kitchen to laze and work and suck their life from two in the drawing room than in her character or mine.

Katherine Mansfield wrote a review which irritated me – I thought I saw spite in it. A decorous elderly dullard she describes me; Jane Austen up to date. Leonard supposes that she let her wish for my failure have its way with her pen. But what I perceive in all this is that praise hardly warms; blame stings far more keenly; and both are somehow at arms length. Yet it's on the cards, I suppose, that *Night and Day* is a marked success.

I'm reading Ethel Smyth [*Impressions that Remained*, 1919]. I wish it were better – (odd that I wrote that genuinely meaning it). What a subject! But of course, not knowing how to write she's muffed it. The interest remains, because she has ridden straight at her recollections, never swerving and getting through honestly, capably. Honesty is her quality; and the fact that she made a great rush at life; friendships with women interest me.

Friday 5 December
This last week L. has been having a little temperature in the evening, due to malaria, and that due to a visit to Oxford; a place of death and decay. I'm almost alarmed to see how entirely my weight rests on his prop. And almost alarmed to see how intensely I'm specialised. My mind turned by anxiety, or other cause, from its scrutiny of blank paper, is like a lost child – wandering the house, sitting on the bottom step to cry.

Saturday 6 December
On Tuesday I lunched with the [Lord Robert] Cecils. Perhaps this is my first appearance as a small Lioness. The Bibescos wished to meet me; Lord Cranborne has a great admiration for me. Lord Robert was congenial as usual, long, loose, friendly and humorous, in spite of the crucifix on his watch chain. Lord Cranborne much of a Cecil in appearance, modest and gentle, with a long sallow face, no chin, and shiny blue coat and trousers. I stayed talking with Nelly [Cecil] when the rest were gone – about adders, about servants, George Eliot, and *Night and Day*.

Sunday 28 December
Probably the last entry this year, and not likely to be the most articulate. Twenty-two days gap to be accounted for chiefly by illness: first L.'s which dribbled on; then much in the same way I was attacked – eight days in bed, down today on the sofa, and away to Monks House tomorrow. It was influenza – what they call a low type, but prolonged, and sponging on the head as it always does. Not much to say therefore, even if I could say it. But I've read two vast volumes of the Life of [Samuel] Butler and am racing through Greville Memoirs – both superbly fit for illness. Oh yes, I've enjoyed reading the past year's diary, and shall keep it up. I'm amused to find how its grown a person, with almost a face of its own.

L.'s book not yet out; but we have six copies in advance. Servants determined to stay for ever and ever. No news of the sale of *Night and Day*, but private opinion highly pleasing to me. *International Review* amalgamated with *Contemporary* [*Review*], and L. to keep his office and his virgins. We think we now deserve some good luck. Yet I daresay we're the happiest couple in England.

1920

As she entered her thirty-ninth year the tentative form for a new novel began to take shape in Virginia's imagination; it developed into Jacob's Room, *which was to occupy her for the next two years or so. This novel was an important development, her discovery of a style suited to her mind and imagination. Meanwhile in the Hogarth Press, the Woolfs continued with their modest endeavours – a story by E. M. Forster, biblical stories by Logan Pearsall Smith, and Gorky's* Reminiscences of Tolstoi, *the first of a series of short Russian works brought to them by the Ukrainian exile Koteliansky, which led Leonard, and later Virginia, to study Russian in order to collaborate with him over the translations. Towards the end of the year the business of the Press occupied so much of the Woolfs' time they once again determined to enlist a helper; and in October Ralph Partridge, ex-officer, Oxford graduate, protégé of Lytton Strachey and the ardent wooer of Carrington, started part-time work at Hogarth House.*

Towards the end of 1919 Vanessa and her children had returned to London so that the boys might go to school; and Gordon Square, where they now occupied two floors at the top of Adrian and Karin Stephen's house, no. 50, again became a magnet for Virginia. She, beginning to 'feel a little famous', half enjoyed and half deplored the social demands increasingly made upon her, both as hostess and guest, from which she and Leonard escaped from time to time to Rodmell, removing there, as became their fixed custom, for eight to ten weeks in summer, and inviting their friends for weekend visits. This year saw the inauguration by Desmond's wife Molly MacCarthy of the 'Memoir Club' in which the members – all intimate friends – would meet for dinner and then read aloud their frank reminiscences – a seed-bed for biographical revelations which survived until the 1950s.

At the end of April Katherine Mansfield, who for her health's sake had spent the winter by the Mediterranean, returned to her Hampstead home, and once again Virginia – in spite of the hurt of Katherine's caustic review of Night and Day *in the* Athenaeum *– was drawn by a shared passion for their 'precious art' into renewing her affectionate relationship with this enigmatic, and now seriously ill, fellow writer. In August she went up to London from Rodmell to say goodbye to her for the last time; Katherine returned to the Riviera in September, and Virginia never saw her again.*

1920

MONKS HOUSE, RODMELL

Wednesday 7 January

This is our last evening. We sit over the fire waiting for post – the cream of the day, I think. Yet every part of the day here has its merits. The house is empty by half-past eleven; empty now at five o'clock; we tend our fire, cook coffee, read, I find, luxuriously, peacefully, at length. Every day or nearly I've walked towards a different point and come back with a string of matchings and marvels. Five minutes from the house one is out in the open, a great pull over Asheham; and, as I say, every direction bears fruit. Once we went over the cornfield and up onto the down. The long down grass pale, and as we pushed through it, up got a hawk at our feet, seeming to trail near the ground, as if weighted down – attached to something. It let the burden fall, and rose high as we came up. We found the wings of a partridge attached to a bleeding stump, for the hawk had almost done his meal. We saw him go back to find it. Further down the hill-side a great white owl 'wavy in the dusk', flew behind the hedge as we came past. Village girls were returning, and calling out to friends in doors. So we cross the field and churchyard, find our coke burnt through to red, toast the bread – and the evening comes.

L. has spent most of his time pruning the apple trees, and tying plums to the wall. To do this he wears two jackets, two pairs of gloves; even so the cold bites through. These last days have been like frozen water, ruffled by the wind into atoms of ice against the cheek; then, in the shelter, forming round you in a still pool.

HOGARTH HOUSE, RICHMOND

Saturday 10 January

So the New Year is broached: ten days of it already spent. The 1917 Club has the merit of gathering my particular set to a bunch about 4.30 on a week day. There, returning on Thursday, I found Clive (I heard him from the stairs), Morgan, Fredegond and dim background figures just worth a nod turning out to be Oliviers – varieties of Oliviers. Now Clive showed as gaslight beside Morgan's normal day – his day not sunny or tempestuous but a day of pure light, capable of showing up the rouge and powder, the dust and wrinkles, the cracks and contortions of my poor parrokeet. He makes me feel the footlights myself. The blend of the two was not agreeable; or rather not comfortable.

Wednesday 14 January

Leonard's book [*Empire and Commerce in Africa*] is out today. To judge by his calm, you would not think it. Great gales in the way of weather; a French ship sunk in the Bay of Biscay; a Cornish steamer too wrecked off Swanage; and on our windows such a battering at night that we woke twice. Violent gusts leaping out of the heart of complete calm – a suggestion of animal savagery; or human frenzy. But what with glass and brick we humans do pretty well.

Saturday 17 January

Now Desmond for the night; I'm writing dully, wishing, though I love Desmond, for a solitary night. He has been made successor to Eagle [J. C. Squire] on the *Statesman*.

Tuesday 20 January

Years ago as a child I made up a wise saw to the effect that if one didn't expect a party to be nice it was and t'other way round. So Desmond's visit was easy, refreshing, and passed without hitch. We had a fine store of talk to keep us going. The story of his voyage – the squall at sea; arrival at Cape Town; Mrs Paley's surprise – his wire 'Desmond sailed' arriving 'Desmond failed' – (as indeed he might probably have done) – all this in the lovely soft voice. Then much talk of the *New Statesman* – projects without number. Secretly, I think, he was much excited and pleased. Five hundred assured, two hundred and fifty of it dependent on a weekly article, signed Affable Hawk (this is a dead secret). Off we went after tea to Roger's, all across Europe to the Brecknock Arms [Camden Town]. As we both depend upon holding to a button naturally we did not arrive easily. The house very high and narrow, with many large rooms, and a bright lining of pictures. Roger to my eyes slightly shrunken, aged? Can one use that word of him? And I don't know how much I colour him from my own depression – for I guessed he didn't much care for *Night and Day*. He showed freakish by side of Desmond's benevolence.

Wednesday 21 January
It would be easy to take up the line that Roger's praise is not worth having, since it is balanced by what appears an irrational prejudice. If the prejudice is on your side, well and good. I sometimes fancy that the only healthy condition is that of doing successful work. Roger's work never meeting with the right sort of appreciation, he suffers perpetually from an obscure irritation. The main form it takes is irritation against England; I fancy I can trace it elsewhere also. He is testy without much occasion, and too easily reverts to grievance, how art critics hate him, how its only in France that they care for his pictures – If I'm sincere, however, I see that I'm led to infer all this from what I note in my own disposition under a cloud. For one thing, I find it difficult to write. I held my pen this morning for two hours and scarcely made a mark. The marks I did make were mere marks, not rushing into life and heat as they do on good days. Perhaps Roger was the first cloud; Desmond may have contributed a little; and then how many silly things I did yesterday.

Saturday 24 January
Oh dear, this talk of novels is all turned sour and brackish by a visit to Mrs Clifford. She must have supplied herself with false teeth since I saw her – twenty years ago; and her hair frizzed out is surely browned by art; but she remains otherwise the same – large codfish eyes and the whole figure of the nineties – black velvet, morbid, intense, jolly, vulgar – a hack to her tips, with a dash of the stage – 'dear', 'my dear boy'; "Did you know Leonard, that I was only married for three years, and then my husband died and left me with two babies and not a penny – so I had to work – oh yes, I worked, and sold the furniture often, but I never borrowed." However the pathetic is not her line. But if I could reproduce her talk of money, royalties, editions, and reviews, I should think myself a novelist; and the picture might serve me for a warning. Having years ago made a success, she's been pulling the wires to engineer another ever since, and has grown callous in the process. Her poor old lips pout for a pat of butter; but margarine will do. She keeps her private and very rancid supply on some of the little tables that those distressing rooms are lumbered with: she has a review of herself in the *Bookman* and a portrait, and a paper of quotations about *Miss Fingal*. Moreover, I had a feeling that in these circles people do each other good turns; and when she proposed to make my fortune in America, I'm afraid a review in *The Times* was supposed to be the equivalent. Brave, I suppose, with vitality and pluck – but oh, what an atmosphere of rancid cabbage and old clothes stewing in their old water! We went away laden with two of the cheap flaring books – "Are you going to take my mangy works! To tell the truth I'm in debt –" Yes, but was that why we

were asked to tea? Not altogether, I suppose, but partly; subconsciously. And now, you see, all colour is taken from my boasting, a second edition of *The Voyage Out* needed; and another of *Night and Day* shortly. Oh dear there must be an end of this! Never write for publishers again anyhow.

Monday 26 January

The day after my birthday; in fact I'm thirty-eight. Well, I've no doubt I'm a great deal happier than I was at twenty-eight; and happier today than I was yesterday having this afternoon arrived at some idea of a new form for a new novel. Suppose one thing should open out of another – and yet keep form and speed, and enclose everything, everything? For I figure that the approach will be entirely different this time: no scaffolding; scarcely a brick to be seen; all crepuscular, but the heart, the passion, humour, everything as bright as fire in the mist. The theme is a blank to me. Anyhow, there's no doubt the way lies somewhere in that direction; I must still grope and experiment but this afternoon I had a gleam of light.

Yesterday being my birthday and a clear bright day into the bargain showing many green and yellow flushes on the trees, I went to South Kensington and heard Mozart and Beethoven.

Saturday 31 January

At present the battle in our circles is between James and Desmond. James wishes to 'stab humbug dead'. Desmond and I wish, on the contrary, to revive it like a phoenix from its ashes.

Wednesday 4 February

The mornings from 12 to 1 I spend reading *The Voyage Out*. I've not read it since July 1913. And if you ask me what I think I must reply that I don't know – such a harlequinade as it is – such an assortment of patches – here simple and severe – here frivolous and shallow – here like God's truth – here strong and free flowing as I could wish. The failures are ghastly enough to make my cheeks burn – and then a turn of the sentence, a direct look ahead of me, makes them burn in a different way. On the whole I like the young woman's mind considerably – and my word, what a gift for pen and ink! I can do little to amend.

Friday 13 February

Again many lapses and the same excuses. For some time now life has been considerably ruffled by people. Age or fame or the return of peace – I don't know which – but anyhow I grow wearied of 'going out to tea'; and yet can't resist it. To leave a door shut that might be open is in my eyes some form of blasphemy. That may be; meanwhile I neither write my diary nor read my Greek. There was a lunch party at the Café Royal on the day of Duncan's private view to record: twelve guests; everything handsomely done; I stimulated and fuddled with wine; a queer assortment of the usual and the unusual. I fancy Duncan would rather have done without fuss, and he slunk off after lunch, leaving us to visit the show. Meanwhile I say nothing and have nothing to say of Duncan's pictures. They spun in my head like the white wine I'd drunk; so lovely, so delicious, so easy to adore. However I only caught glimpses here and there as well dressed people moved across them. Next day I bought one of Duncan's pictures.

I must skip over forgotten days and alight at Ottoline's last night. Yet I don't know that I can describe an evening party – Philip and I sitting together watched the door open and people come in. There were more of the shady smart sort than of old; or so they looked to me since I did not know them. There were Eliots and Huxleys and Forster and – all the rest. My single diversion was a dialogue with W. J. Turner, an inarticulate, infinitely modest man, with nice vague eyes, seeming to wish to tell the truth; yet too shy to be ready with it. At a party now I feel a little famous – the chances are people like Turner whose names I know, also know my name. I must have one coloured figure though in my black and white; I must spare a phrase for the sealing-wax green of Ottoline's dress. This bright silk stood out over a genuine crinoline. She did control the room on account of it. Yet I dreamt all night of her disillusioned with a weak pouting face, revealing her inner discontent. Indeed I can't help thinking her unhappy!

Sunday 15 February
But the Webbs! I find the hour of 1.30 on a cold blowy day, precisely fitting to them. As we walk down Grosvenor Road the old papers blow and the middle classes parade in their Sunday clothes. The houses have a red raw look. Factory chimneys face the windows across the river. There is no sun or warmth. Then there's the mutton and the cabbage and apple tart – all adequate but joyless. Bad cigarettes. A little whisky. The drawing room now a glacial white with water colours hung accurately apart. Mrs Webb displaying shark like teeth. Webb daubed red, and clumsily thick in person. No longer am I frightened; only dreary and dismal, and rasped all over by the sense of so hideous a prospect. Mrs Webb told me it was wrong to prevent L. from going into Parliament; we want men of subtle intellect and – But what is 'right' and who are 'we'? Frostily friendly she said goodbye. One deals with the situation more easily, but the horror of it increases with familiarity. Shall we become like that too? I stamp up and down the platform to warm myself; steep my hands in hot water, crouch over the fire, but still I'm irritated and exacerbated.

Wednesday 3 March

So then at the end of that week we went to Rodmell, and are back again two days ago. But I've numbers of old clothes in my dirty clothes basket – scenes, I mean, tumbled pell mell into my receptacle of a mind, and not extracted till form and colour are almost lost. I suppose 'going out to tea' continued; oh, there was a dinner at Gordon Square, when Mary, becoming almost peevish in her bedroom refused to part with hairpins: I made a note of that scene. Desmond was there: Desmond warm, affectionate, the oldest friend, so I sometimes feel; perhaps the best.

Then there was Roger's speech at the Club and my first effort – five minutes consecutive speaking – all very brilliant, and opening the vista of that form of excitement not before glimpsed at. Dined with Nessa and Duncan in Soho. Saw the woman drop her glove. A happy evening. Then off to Monks – and here I should write large and bright about the SPRING. It has come. It has been with us over a fortnight. Daffodils all out; garden set with thick golden crocuses; snowdrops almost over; pear trees budding; birds in song; days like June with a touch of the sun – not merely a painted sky but a warm one. Now we've been to Kew. Almond trees out.

Saturday 6 March

Tuesday and Wednesday here in Richmond printing. Then on Thursday, dine with the MacCarthys, and the first Memoir Club evening. A highly interesting occasion. Seven people read – and Lord knows what I didn't read into their reading. Sydney [Waterlow], to whom the occasion was one of some importance, signified as much by reading us a dream – in reality a parable – altogether a queer, self-conscious, self analytic performance, interesting to me. Clive purely objective; Nessa starting matter of fact; then overcome by the emotional depths to be traversed; and unable to read aloud what she had written. Duncan fantastic and tongue – not tied – tongue enchanted. Molly literary about tendencies and William Morris, carefully composed at first, and even formal; suddenly saying "Oh this is absurd – I can't go on" shuffling all her sheets. "These meagre Welsh, these hard-headed Scots – I detest them – I wanted to be the daughter of a French marquise by a misalliance with –" That was the tone of it. Roger well composed; story of a coachman who stole geraniums and went to prison. Good: but too objective. I doubt that anyone will *say* the interesting things but they can't prevent their coming out. Before this by the way, I saw Nessa's new home, no. 50 [Gordon Square] and looked in upon Adrian and Karin doing biology in their dining room.

Tuesday 9 March

In spite of some tremors, I think I shall go on with this diary for the present. I sometimes think that I have worked through the layer of style which suited it – suited the comfortable bright hour after tea. Never mind: I fancy old Virginia, putting on her spectacles to read of March 1920 will decidedly wish me to continue. Greetings! my dear ghost. Several good books can be written still; and here's the bricks for a fine one.

To return to the present owner of the name: on Sunday I went up to Campden Hill to hear the Schubert Quintet – to see George Booth's house – to take notes for my story – to rub shoulders with respectability – all these reasons took me there, and were cheaply gratiffed at seven-and-sixpence. Whether people see their own rooms with the devastating clearness that I see them, thus admitted once for one hour, I doubt. Chill superficial seemliness; but thin as a March glaze of ice on a pool. A sort of mercantile smugness. Horsehair and mahogany is the truth of it; and the white panels, Vermeer reproductions, Omega table and variegated curtains rather a snobbish disguise. The least interesting of rooms: the compromise; though of course, that's interesting too. I took against the family system. Old Mrs Booth enthroned on a sort of commode in widow's dress; flanked by devoted daughters; with grandchildren somehow symbolical cherubs. Such neat dull little boys and girls. There we all sat in our furs and white gloves.

Monday at the Club, which I see I've ceased to describe.

Thursday 18 March

If this diary were the diary of the soul I could write at length of the second meeting of the Memoir Club. Leonard was objective and triumphant; I subjective and most unpleasantly discomfited. I don't know when I've felt so chastened and out of humour with myself – a partner I generally respect and admire. 'Oh but why did I read this egotistic sentimental trash!' That was my cry, and the result of my sharp sense of the silence succeeding my chapter. It started with loud laughter; this was soon quenched; and then I couldn't help figuring a kind of uncomfortable boredom on the part of the males; to whose genial cheerful sense my revelations were at once mawkish and distasteful. What possessed me to lay bare my soul! I saw Nessa yesterday, and she guessed at none of this – which indeed Leonard firmly assured me was a miasma on my part due to late nights &c.

Saturday 10 April

We sped to Rodmell, which accounts for another formidable break. By the way, Morgan keeps a diary, and in his diary Morgan writes conversation – word for word, when the humour takes him. I don't know that the humour takes me to describe our Easter at Monks House. To describe Monks House would be to trench upon literature, which I can't do here; since we only slept by snatches last night, and at 4 am turned a mouse out of L.'s bed. Mice crept and rattled all night through. Then the wind got up. Hasp of the window broken. Poor L. out of bed for the fifth time to wedge it with a toothbrush. So I say nothing about our projects at Monks, though the view across the meadows to Caburn is before me now; and the hyacinths blooming, and the orchard walk. Then being alone there – breakfast in the sun – posts – no servants – how nice it all is!

I'm planning to begin *Jacob's Room* next week with luck. (That's the first time I've written that.)

Thursday 15 April
Rain has come – what I mind much more is the black sky: so ugly. Yesterday I think I was unhappy all day long. What book can I settle to read? I want something that won't colour my morning's mood – something a little severe. My notion is to write this [book] in chapters straight off; not beginning one unless I can count on so many days clear for finishing it.

Saturday 17 April
To the Bach Festival [at Central Hall, Westminster] last night; as I settled into my seat, a voice said Virginia! It was Walter Lamb. The egg shaped man – the billiard ball man – sat by me, and told me a great deal about Bach. Bach was very beautiful, though the human element in the choir always distracts me. *They* aren't beautiful; all in greens, greys, pinks, blacks, fresh from the suburbs and high tea. The hall seemed to suit them better than the music.

Tuesday 20 April
Saw the birth of Ka's son in *The Times* this morning, and feel slightly envious all day in consequence. To the Bach choir last night; but one of our failures. I'd made out on waking such a perfect day; and one by one my events missed fire. Such a good morning's writing I'd planned, and wasted the cream of my brain on the telephone. Then the weather; great bouncing gusts all set about with rain soaking one; buses crowded; left typewriting paper in the bus; a long time waiting at the Club – Then Bach unaccompanied isn't easy – though at last I was swept up to the heights by a song. Anna Magdalena's song. I walked a few steps beyond Herbert Fisher coming out; followed him across the empty lamplit purlieus of Westminster, saw him step so distinguished, yet to my eye so empty, into Palace Yard, and so to take part in ruling the Empire. His head bent – legs a little wavering – small feet – I tried to put myself inside him, but could only suppose he thought in an exalted way which to me would be all

bunkum. Indeed, I feel this more and more. I've had my dive into their heads and come out again, I think.

Saturday 24 April

Morgan came for a night. Very easy going. I wish I could write his talk down. "I must now write a postcard. Yes, I must really catch the first post if possible. I'll take it myself – is there time still? I'll tell you what it is. The seat is being painted. The boy is so stupid he'll paint it after its been rained upon. Then it will be ruined." "Nonsense" said L. "It won't hurt it." "But are you sure?" "Positive." "Oh then I'll let it alone – if you're quite sure. My mother is having the seat painted green. She wouldn't let me do it, and the boy is dreadfully stupid. I found him putting on the paint without having scraped the old paint off first." &c . . .

This is very like Morgan; so too his reliance on Leonard. "Where d'you get your boots? Are Waterman pens the best?"

Wednesday 5 May

We have had a Thursday to Tuesday at Rodmell; which accounts, as I say, making my apology to this book, in which so few pages seem to have been written. As we sat down to dinner on Saturday, Desmond rapped at the door. Desmond (this is L.'s saying not mine, and I quote it to avoid speaking grudgingly myself) produces a sense of frowst in the room. It rained; he lay back, smoking cigarettes, eating sweets and opening novels which he never read. Being an editor has drugged the remnants of ambition in him, and he is now content. Content is disillusioning to behold: what is there to be content about? It seems, with Desmond now, always afternoon.

Saturday 8 May

Yesterday I had tea with Saxon at the Club; and, remembering old lonely evenings of my own, when the married couple seemed so secure and lamplit, asked him back to dinner. I wonder though whether his loneliness ever frightens him as mine used to frighten me. I daresay office work is a great preservative.

Tuesday 11 May

It is worth mentioning, for future reference, that the creative power which bubbles so pleasantly on beginning a new book quiets down after a time, and one goes on more steadily. Doubts creep in. Then one becomes resigned. Determination not to give in, and the sense of an impending shape keep one at it more than anything. I'm a little anxious. How am I to bring off this conception?

L. is up in London seeing his constituents. Eight gentlemen are waiting on him to learn his views. Though it was summer till 3.30, it is now brushed with blackness, and I must shut the window and put on my jersey. Nessa comes back on Friday. Clive and Mary are in Paris.

Tuesday 18 May

Gordon Square begins again and like a snake renews its skin outworn – that's the nearest I can come to a quotation. [No. 50] Gordon Square different – like a looking glass version of 46. You are let in, by a strange servant, go up bare steps, hear children crying at various stages, go up and up – till you reach what is, in the real Gordon Square, servants' bedrooms. Nessa is right at the top. Well we talked till I left at 8; interrupted though by Lytton, Angelica, and Julian. Lytton said that James and Alix are to be married in three weeks. But though satisfactory, I find no excitement in this. They know each other too well to stir one's imagination thinking of their future, as one does with most engagements. Then, talk talk; and as we were despatching the superficial and reaching the easy-intimate, I had to tear off, in the rain, to Wigmore Hall. Sat between Oliver and Saxon; and these musical people don't listen as I do, but critically, superciliously, without programmes.

Thursday 20 May

Up yesterday with peonies to Nessa. Then I went on with L. to dine with the Coles in Chelsea. The Coles are Webbs in embryo – with differences of course. I'm used to being at ease with clever young men, and to find myself stumped, caught out, leg before the wicket at every turn is not pleasant. Never was there such a quick, hard, determined young man as Cole; covering his Labour sympathies, which are I suppose intellectual, with the sarcasm and sneers of Oxford. Then there's a bust of [William] Morris on the side board, too much to eat, Morris curtains, all the works of all the classics, and Cole and Mrs hopping on the surface like a couple of Cockney sparrows. The whole effect as of electric light full in the eyes – unbecoming at my age. One can see Mrs Cole rapidly becoming the cleverish elderly fox terrier type of intellectual woman – as it is not a shade or valley in her mind. Cole, grinning like a gutterpipe demon took us to the door – so spry, alert, virile, and ominous.

I have written to Katherine. No answer.

Monday 24 May

A real bank holiday – blazing weather, sound of buses unceasing – crowds like queues in the streets – and we spent it properly going to Hurlingham to see polo, of which I must make this rapid note. You get the impression that the turf is india-rubber – so lightly do the horses spring – touching it and up again – Captain Lockit galloping down with his stick like a Persian rider with a lance. A large white ball is then thrown in the midst. The horses twirl and dart; almost like long lean cats their scamper after the ball; only as they come past you hear a roar in the nostrils. But the bounce and agility of them all knotted together pawing the ball with their feet indescribable; passing in a second from full gallop to delicate trot as the ball is dribbled almost between their feet. This is the game of the officers of England. Each had eight ponies, and one lasted in this frenzy of freshness only seven minutes. Anyhow it was well worth seeing.

Summer has set in two days ago. Yesterday for the first time we lunched out of doors.

Wednesday 26 May

L. has been adopted as the Labour candidate of the seven Universities; may even be writing his letter of acceptance upstairs now. We are having the kitchen re-built at a cost of £80 at Monks House. And the night Morgan and Nessa dined here we saw a fire. Three minutes of excitement – great flames shooting up behind the playground; then a glow as of red yellow gauze, with sparks rising and falling; then a lovely sight when the hose shot into the air, wrapping itself in light and soaring like a rocket. A pouring crackling noise all the time, and now and then wood crashing.

This morning Katherine writes a stiff and formal note thanking me for my kind postcard, and saying she will be delighted to see me, though 'grown *very* dull'. What does this mean – *she* hurt with *me*? Anyhow I go on Friday to find out, unless stopped as is always possible.

Monday 31 May

Back from Monks an hour ago, after the first week-end – the most perfect, I was going to say, but how can I tell what week-ends we mayn't spend there? The first pure joy of the garden I mean.

I had my interview with Katherine Mansfield on Friday. A steady discomposing formality and coldness at first. Enquiries about house and so on. No pleasure or excitement at seeing me. It struck me that she is of the cat kind: alien, composed, always solitary and observant. And then we talked about solitude, and I found her expressing my feelings, as I never heard them expressed. Whereupon we fell into step, and as usual, talked as easily as though eight months were minutes – till Murry came in. We chatted as usual. Aldous was our butt. But Murry going at length, Katherine and I once more got upon literature. A queer effect she produces of someone apart, entirely self-centred; altogether concentrated upon her 'art'; almost fierce to me about it, I pretending I couldn't write. "What else is there to do? We have got to do it." Then asked me to write stories for the *Athenaeum*.

"But I don't know that I can write stories" I said, honestly enough, thinking that in her view, after her review of me, anyhow, those were her secret sentiments. Whereupon she turned on me, and said no one else could write stories except me – *Kew Gardens* the right 'gesture', a turning point. "Well but *Night and Day?*" I said, though I hadn't meant to speak of it. "An amazing achievement" she said. "Why, we've not had such a thing since I don't know when –" "But I thought you didn't like it?" Then she said she could pass an examination in it. Would I come and talk about it – lunch – so I'm going to lunch; but what does her reviewing mean then? Anyhow, once more as keenly as ever I feel a common certain understanding between us.

Saturday 5 June

I've gone back into winter clothes; its bitter windy; and the sun sparks and glints instead of burning. It burnt on Derby Day though – the day I lunched with Katherine and had two hours of priceless talk – priceless in the sense that to no one else can I talk in the same disembodied way about writing; without altering my thought more than I alter it in writing here. (I except L. from this.) We talked about books, writing of course: my own. Then I said "You've changed. Got through something"; indeed there's a sort of self command about her as if having mastered something subterfuges were no longer so necessary. She told me of her terrific experiences last winter – experience of loneliness chiefly; alone in a stone house [at Ospedaletti] with caverns beneath it into which the sea rushed; how she lay on bed alone all day with a pistol by her; and men banged at the door. Murry sent a balance sheet of his accounts; came at Christmas with plum pudding and curd cheese; "Now I'm here, its all right". Then she went to him for assurance; didn't get it; and will never look for that particular quality again. I see what she means, vaguely. She is nervous about her book coming out; fearing lest she hasn't done enough. Anyhow, I enjoyed myself; and this fragmentary intermittent intercourse of mine seems more fundamental than many better established ones.

Tuesday 8 June

One of my field days yesterday – National Gallery – there met Clive – ices at Gunters – dine with Nessa. My drive to Waterloo on top of a bus [was] very vivid. A bright night; with a fresh breeze. An old beggar woman, blind, sat against a stone wall in Kingsway holding a brown mongrel in her arms and sang aloud. There was a recklessness about her; much in the spirit of London. Defiant – almost gay, clasping her dog as if for warmth. How many Junes has she sat there, in the heart of London? How she came to be there, what scenes she can go through, I can't imagine. O damn it all, I say, why can't I know all that too? Perhaps it was the song at night that seemed strange; she was singing shrilly, but for her own amusement, not begging. Then the fire engines came by – shrill too; with their helmets pale yellow in the moonlight. Sometimes everything gets into the same mood; how to define this one I don't know – It was gay, and yet terrible and fearfully vivid. Nowadays I'm often overcome by London; even think of the dead who have walked in the city. Perhaps one might visit the churches. The view of the grey white spires from Hungerford Bridge brings it to me; and yet I can't say what 'it' is.

Thursday 17 June
Today is Cup Day at Ascot; which I think marks the highest tide of the finest society's greatest season – all superlatives that mean little to me – save as I catch the hum of wheels in Piccadilly on a fine afternoon, and passing carriages look in and see powdered faces like jewels in glass cases. One must be young to feel the stir of it. Yet the fine weather gives us too our sudden acceleration: dinner parties; Memoir Club; invitations; coming one on top of another.

I lunched at Gordon Square for Roger's show: got stuffed in the head with wine and talk and sat there not very comfortably. A toast to Roger missed fire somewhat – so, I fear do the pictures, which fill three rooms garishly, as with coloured sheets of tin, not one being yet bought. Lytton and I stood in a window, and he told me how he lived for ambition; he wants influence not fame; not Maynard's influence, but the influence of some old gentleman on whose 80th birthday people present addresses – he wants to deal little words that poison vast monsters of falsehood. This I declared to be unattainable. But I believe it to be what he wishes. Tea at Gunters; dinner at Nessa's; and so home, a little bruised about the lips, thirsty for a great draught of solitude, which was not given me; since we dined next with the Murrys, next with Roger, and last night had the Memoir Club here, of which I'm too sleepy to give any notice.

Wednesday 23 June
Poor Roger has only sold three or four sketches. There the innumerable pictures hang, like ugly girls at a dance, and no one bids a penny piece. According to Nessa, he can talk of nothing else, and they're at their wits ends to say the right things – since what is to be said, save that bad pictures don't sell?

Tuesday 29 June
Back from Rodmell, which was disappointing, as if held to our lips the cup of pleasure was dashed from them. One day was consumed by Saxon and Barbara. Poor Barbara has the fixed lines of premature maturity. Such a

grind and a drudge her life is as fills me with pity – For she seemed to have no choice. First Nick, then the child – and all her lines laid down for her for life, by the hand of fate, for she can't leap them. Our generation is daily scourged by the bloody war. Even I scribble reviews instead of novels because of the thick skulls at Westminster and Berlin. Saxon was airy and sprightly. The kitchen a success I think, but then I'm not a cook.

Tuesday 6 July
Too much to write as usual, but we work like navvies at binding Morgan [*The Story of the Siren*], and have no time for frivolity. Festivities get wedged in where convenient. It looks as though Morgan might boom, though I don't, as a critic, see altogether what the reason is.

Tuesday 13 July
Oh the servants! Oh reviewing! Nelly has vacillated between tears and laughter, life and death for the past ten days; can't feel an ache anywhere without sending for me or L. to assure her that aches are not certainly fatal. Then she cries. Never, never, never will she get over it, she says. The doctor comes. Innumerable pills and draughts consumed. Sweats, sleepless nights, recur. And nothing the matter save what one of us would call an upset inside and take a pill for. This drives us to accept invitations, since if anyone comes here, the atmosphere lowers. But where have we been? Indeed I see myself cutting covers incessantly.

Now for Oh reviewing! – Three weeks I think have passed without a word added to *Jacob*. How is one to bring it through at this rate. Yet its all my fault – why should I do *The Cherry Orchard* and Tolstoy for Desmond, why take up the Plumage Bill for Ray? But after this week I do no more.

MONKS HOUSE, RODMELL

Monday 2 August
Bank Holiday. I'm in the middle of baking a cake, and fly to this page for refuge, to fill in moments of baking and putting in my bread. Our season ended unexpectedly; the blind falling with the light still in the sky. If I were not ashamed of my egotism, I could give a literal meaning to my metaphor – seeing that I had to leave Nessa's great party at 11 in order to be home, not to disturb L., and be ready for packing and going next morning. Poor L., utterly driven for a month at last confessed to feeling tired, and was indeed on the verge of destruction. As a hobby, the Hogarth Press is clearly too lively and lusty to be carried on in this private way any longer. Moreover, the business part of it can't be shared, owing to my incompetence.

The future, therefore, needs consideration. This being so, we fled a week earlier than intended. On Monday I went up, to say good bye to Katherine Mansfield, was inveigled into a night at 46 [Gordon Square] and could write many pages on my reflections on sleeping in London again. The ease and rapidity of life in London a good deal impressed me – everything near at hand, to be compassed between lunch and tea, without setting out and making a job of it. Katherine asked me to review her book; I cried off on the ground that to review spoils the reading. They are coming to Eastbourne, so my farewell is deferred.

Thursday 5 August

I write *Jacob* every morning now, feeling each day's work like a fence I have to ride at, my heart in my mouth till its over, and I've cleared, or knocked the bar out. (Another image, unthinking it was one.)

Tuesday 10 August

I have spent the whole afternoon yellow washing the earth closet. I can now reckon up my labours: dining room distempered and cleaned; bannisters painted blue; stairs white; and now the earth closet. Coming home on Sunday, a hot still day, Leonard initiated a scheme for the future of the Press. We are going to offer [Ralph] Partridge a share in it, baiting this perhaps minute titbit with the plumper morsel of secretaryship to L. About the middle of dinner L. developed this further: why not buy a complete printing outfit? Why not? Run a shop too, perhaps. Ramifications spring unceasingly from this centre. Its a pleasant thing, come autumn, to make plans. Nelly still mysteriously diseased, and that being so we implore her to stay away –

Friday 20 August

Mrs Dedman cajoled us there by calling it a Sussex funeral, and promised that the bearers would wear smock frocks. But only six were to be found in the village; so the plan was given up; Mr Stacey was lowered to his grave by black farm labourers, two of whom managed to tumble into the grave as they lowered him. Smock frocks exist however, as she proved by showing us grandfather's, and a fine piece of stitchery it is, with a pattern appropriate to Rodmell, distinct from all other villages. The entire male population of Kingston village came out of church after the coffin; brown faces, white hairs, showing on top of coal black coats. The clergy acted with such portentous gloom that even now I daresay they scarcely feel comfortable. The day was cold; a thunder shower purple in the sky. As usual the service seemed chill, awkward, unmanageable; everyone subduing their natural feelings, and seeming to play a part because the others did.

The coffin was a pale grey, wreaths attached by strings. Whether the Catholic form is warmer, I know not. I saw one man shredding a few grains of dust at the right moment. But the ceremonial spirit is entirely absent. We never catch fire. Then the awkwardness of old Sunday coats and hats. I feel Sunday clinging to my clothes like the smell of camphor.

Wednesday 25 August

For the third time this summer, I went to London on Monday, paid five shillings for a plate of ham, and said goodbye to Katherine. I had my euphemism at parting; about coming again before she goes; but it is useless to extend these farewell visits, and after all, visits can't do away with the fact that she goes for two years, is ill, and heaven knows when we shall meet again. These partings make one pinch oneself as if to make sure of feeling. Do I feel this as much as I ought? Am I heartless? And then, after noting my own callousness, of a sudden comes the blankness of not having her to talk to. So on my side the feeling is genuine. She wants to live in an Italian town and have tea with the doctor. But we propose to write to each other – She will send me her diary. Shall we? Will she? If I were left to myself I should; being the simpler, the more direct of the two. Strange how little we know our friends.

So I missed my train; and what I wanted most in the world was to catch it and travel back with L.

Tuesday 31 August

The last day of August – and what a day! November in the city without the lights. Then the schoolchildren singing, and as I write Lottie chatter-chattering – so I'm out of mood. Detestable grey sky – life has too few days to waste them thus. I must walk my temper off upon the downs. But first I've Partridge and Carrington to deal with. Another step has been taken in life: we have a partner and a secretary at a cost of £100. Rash, I suppose; but then what's the point of life if one's not rash? Anyhow we step out boldly, and if the Press is to live, it had better run a risk or two. The young man, aged twenty-six, just left Oxford, is a superb body – shoulders like tough oak; health tingling beneath his skin. Merry shrewd eyes. He has been religious; is now socialistic; literature I don't suppose counts for much: he's written an essay on Milton, which Carrington was not struck by. Carrington is ardent, robust, scatterbrained, appreciative, a very humble disciple, but with enough character to prevent insipidity. A little ashamed of Partridge, I thought her. But what shoulders! what thickness of bone! Well, how will it turn out? What shall we print?

Wednesday 8 September

Lytton, Mary, Clive, came here yesterday, discussed immortality; and I find my bid for it is as letter writer. What about poor *Jacob* then? and hadn't I better drive my pen through sheets that pay of a morning, in the intervals of writing letters? Oh vanity, vanity! how it grows on me – how I swear to crush it out – Learn French is the only thing I can think of. Then I didn't like Mary; she saying sharp things and then hard, and I unable to say out loud 'Well then, why come and sit on my lawn?' Why does she? L. at tea put me right: Mary Hutchinson is one of the few people I dislike, I said. No: he replied: one of the many you dislike and like alternately.

Wednesday 15 September

Nelly by the way has now had, I suppose, every organ in her body examined, and is pronounced healthy with the exception of her teeth. So that shot of mine seems the true one.

Lytton has been with us from Friday to Tuesday. We walked all the way to Kingston, talking, back over the flats, talking. Save for shadows that cross and leave him ruffled, he is now uniformly amiable. At night we had the first two or three chapters of [*Queen*] *Victoria* – Disgraceful to say I was twice overcome with sleep, owing to our wood fire; but the liveliness of it is such as to make one forget whether its good or not. I don't know what qualities it has. I suspect it depends too much upon amusing quotations, and is too much afraid of dulness to say anything out of the way. Not at all a meditative or profound book; on the other hand, a remarkably composed and homogeneous book. A miracle in the matter of condensation and composition I suspect. But we are to read it when done. Blessed with fine weather, I could look from my window, through the vine leaves, and see Lytton sitting in the deck chair reading. He wore a white felt hat, and the usual grey clothes; was long and tapering as usual; looking so mild and ironical, his beard just cut short. As usual, I got my various impressions: of suavity, a gentle but inflexible honesty; lightning speed; something peevish and exacting; something incessantly living, suffering, reflecting moods. Still he can withdraw in that supercilious way that used to gall me; still show himself superior to me, contemptuous of me – of my morality that is, not of my mind. Well, I can walk and talk with him by the hour.

Sunday 19 September

Eliot is separated only by the floor from me. The odd thing about Eliot is that his eyes are lively and youthful when the cast of his face and the shape of his sentences is formal and even heavy. Rather like a sculptured face – no upper lip; formidable, powerful, pale. Then those hazel eyes seeming to escape from the rest of him. We talked – America, Ottoline, aristocracy, printing, Squire, Murry, critics. "And I behaved like a priggish pompous little ass" was one of his comments upon his own manner at Garsington. He is decidedly of the generation beneath us – I daresay superior – younger, though.

Monday 20 September
To go on with Eliot, as if one were making out a scientific observation – he left last night directly after dinner. He improved as the day went on; laughed more openly; became nicer. I kept myself from being submerged, though feeling the waters rise once or twice. I mean by this that he completely neglected my claims to be a writer, and had I been meek, I suppose I should have gone under – felt him and his views dominant and subversive. He is a consistent specimen of his type, which is opposed to ours. Unfortunately the living writers he admires are Wyndham Lewis and Pound – Joyce too, but there's more to be said on this head. He told me he was more interested in people than in anything. He can't read Wordsworth when Wordsworth deals with nature. His turn is for caricature. He wants to write a verse play in which the four characters of Sweeney act the parts. Now he wants to describe externals. Joyce gives internals. His novel *Ulysses* presents the life of man in sixteen incidents, all taking place (I think) in one day. This, so far as he has seen it, is extremely brilliant, he says. Perhaps we shall try to publish it. Joyce himself is an insignificant man, wearing very thick eyeglasses, a little like Shaw to look at, dull, self-centred, and perfectly self assured. There is much to be said about Eliot from different aspects; his mind is not yet blunted or blurred. He wishes to write precise English; but catches himself out in slips; and if anyone asked him whether he meant what he said, he would have to say no, very often. Now in all this L. showed up much better than I did; but I didn't much mind.

Sunday 26 September
But I think I minded more than I let on; for somehow *Jacob* has come to a stop, in the middle of that party too, which I enjoyed so much. Eliot coming on the heel of a long stretch of writing fiction (two months without a break) made me listless; cast shade upon me; and the mind when engaged upon fiction wants all its boldness and self-confidence. He said nothing – but I reflected how what I'm doing is probably better done by Mr Joyce. Then I began to wonder what it is that I am doing: to suspect, as is usual in such cases, that I have not thought my plan out plainly enough – so to dwindle, niggle, hesitate – which means that one's lost.

Went to Charleston for the night; and had a vivid sight of Maynard by lamplight – like a gorged seal, double chin, ledge of red lip, little eyes, sensual, brutal, unimaginative: one of those visions that come from a chance attitude, lost so soon as he turned his head. I suppose though it illustrates something I feel about him.

Eliot has sent me his poems, and hopes to maintain contact during the winter.

Friday 1 October

Here we are at the last day; the boxes with apples standing open – Yes, undoubtedly the best summer so far, in spite of execrable weather, no bath, one servant, and an earth closet down a winding glade. To that verdict we both set our hands. Even the schoolchildren's voices, if one thinks of them as swifts and martins skirling round the eaves, exhilarate instead of annoying. We now give them apples, rejecting their pence, and requiring in return that they shall respect the orchard. They had already stripped several trees. Nelly, by the way, returns. I must try to say nothing sharp, though inclined to. After all, without education, – there are excuses.

One of the charms of Rodmell is the human life: everyone does the same thing at the same hour. Everyone is in his, or their garden; lamps are lit, but people like the last daylight. What I mean is that we are a community.

HOGARTH HOUSE, RICHMOND

Monday 18 October

This is a long break, and perhaps I should not fill it now if it were not that I am in from the Club, and can't settle to anything. Yet we have been back seventeen days, have seen a number of people, and harboured more thoughts than there are words in my mind. Who have we seen? The usual people, Nessa and Duncan, Clive, Mary, Stracheys, Stephens, Ka, Arnold-Forsters, – Kot, too, who came to bring us Tchekhov, and was so excited over it and other projects as to twang like a fiddle, instead of solemnly resounding as usual like a full barrel of beer. We are well launched upon the work of the Press. Partridge – Ralph I should call him – is putting his ox's shoulder to the wheel, and intends to do 'hurricane' business. We are bringing out *Three Stories* by L.; my book [*Monday or Tuesday*]; (printed for an experiment by McDermott): and have in view Tchekhov, Eliot, Roger, possibly Lytton's essays.

Monday 25 October

(first day of winter time). Why is life so tragic; so like a little strip of pavement over an abyss? I look down; I feel giddy; I wonder how I am ever to walk to the end. But why do I feel this? Now that I say it I don't feel it. The fire burns; we are going to hear *The Beggar's Opera*. Only it lies about me; I can't keep my eyes shut. It's a feeling of impotence: of cutting no ice. Here I sit at Richmond, and like a lantern stood in the middle of a field my light goes up in darkness. Melancholy diminishes as I write. Why then don't I write it down oftener? Well, one's vanity forbids. I want to appear a success even to myself. Yet I don't get to the bottom of it. Its having no children, living away from friends, failing to write well, spending too much on food, growing old – I think too much of the whys and wherefores; too much of myself. I don't like time to flap round me. Well then, work. Yes, but I so soon tire of work – can't read more than a little, an hour's writing is enough for me. Out here no one comes in to waste time pleasantly. If they do, I'm cross. The labour of going to London is too great. Nessa's children grow up, and I can't have them in to tea, or go to the Zoo. Pocket money doesn't allow of much. Yet I'm persuaded that these are trivial things: its life itself, I think sometimes, for us in our generation so tragic – no newspaper placard without its shriek of agony from some one. Unhappiness is everywhere: just beyond the door; or stupidity which is worse. Still I don't pluck the nettle out of me. To write *Jacob's Room* again will revive my fibres, I feel. And with it all how happy I am – if it weren't for my feeling that it is a strip of pavement over an abyss.

Wednesday 10 November

Nessa's room at Gordon Square is becoming what the drawing room at 46 was five or six years ago. I go there and find that astonishing brightness in the heart of darkness. Julian coming in with his French lesson; Angelica hung with beads, riding on Roger's foot; Clive claret coloured and yellow like a canary; Duncan vague in the background, sitting astride a chair, looking with blurred eyes rather dimly. Altogether I sometimes feel that not to have a refuge here would be a bad thing – I don't know. Ralph hints at a plan of sharing a London house with us – which tempts me, on some days.

Sunday 13 November

L. now translating Tchekhov, and I must set to on my share, I suppose. Ralph comes twice a week or so, an indomitable, perhaps rather domineering, young man; loves dancing; in the pink of health; a healthy brain.

Tuesday 23 November

We see too many people for me to describe them, had I the time. I have lived the past two weeks methodically, printing till dark, allowing myself a day off, arranging things rather successfully; so my strip of pavement (I bag that phrase for *Jacob*) widens.

Sunday 5 December

The Memoir Club was fearfully brilliant – I mean I was; and Leonard so much more impressive with so much less pains; and Morgan very professional; and Mary never laughed once at my jokes. Well, I shall laugh loud at hers next Wednesday to make up. Eliot and Goldie dined here t'other night – a successful party. A cold in the head made me desperate like wine – nothing seemed to matter. I laughed in the grim marble face and got a twinkle back. What a big white face he has beside Goldie's mobile brown monkey one! A mouth twisted and shut; not a single line free and easy; all caught, pressed, inhibited; but great driving power somewhere – and my word what concentration of the eye when he argues! We discussed criticism, and I find he thinks himself a poet. A little human laughter comes very welcome to him, as I guess, and I think he would willingly break up his formal ways. My guess is that he wishes to detach himself from sets, and welcomes us as an escape. Then – what? Gerald Duckworth engaged – does that count as news? dinner at the Toynbees, but I can't go into that. What do I want to go into? How hard we work – that's what impresses me this winter: every compartment stuffed tight, chiefly owing to the press. Whether we can keep it up, I don't know. Then both so popular, so well known, so much respected – and Leonard forty, and I nearing it, so there's not much to boast of. In my heart, too, I prefer the nondescript anonymous days of youth. I like youthful minds; and the sense that no one's yet anybody.

Sunday 12 December

Nearing the end of the year. Everything muffled in snow and crisp with frost, streets knobbed and slippery; hands grimy as cold for some reason always makes them. Here we sit over the fire, expecting Roger – whose book is out; as everyone's book is out – Katherine's, Murry's, Eliot's. None have I read so far.

Scenes now come to mind. Gordon Square at tea time – All those branches twisting themselves so fluently, like the Laocoon; so I saw them from Ralph's upper room. Then there's Lytton coming round to tea. At once we plunge, even on the cold pavement, into literature. So we pace to Nessa's door. And Ralph? Well, I wouldn't marry Ralph – A despot. True. But what's to happen to Carrington? She can't live indefinitely with me – Perhaps with him? Door opens, in I go; up I go; children there; sit over the stove; Nessa draws pictures for Angelica. And home again.

Molly Hamilton next. I'm enlarging my sphere, not very widely, but I take pains to accept what's offered. When accepted, I feel that I must make the most. It's not for nothing that I go out to tea. So there we sit, scratching on the match box. "I'm assistant editor to the *Review of Reviews* – at a salary of £570!" she cried. And so her mother can live in London; and she's launched; poor Molly can do all this by chaining herself to the desk. There the desk was and books laid out as you see them in shops. Did the match burst into flame? Yes, I think so, about happiness, and human beings. I forget my first view of Molly, going down the Strand the night of the Cenotaph; such a lurid scene, like one in Hell. A soundless street; no traffic; but people marching. Clear, cold, and windless. A bright light in the Strand; women crying Remember the Glorious Dead, and holding out chrysanthemums. Always the sound of feet on the pavement. Faces bright and lurid – poor Molly's worn enough by that illumination. I touched her arm; whereupon she jumped, like some one woken. A ghastly procession of people in their sleep.

Sunday 19 December
I ought to say how happy I am, since one of these pages said how unhappy I was. I can't see any reason in it. My only guess is that it has something to do with working steadily; writing things out of my head; and never having a compartment empty. I can't help suspecting that both Mr and Mrs Woolf slowly increase in fame; that helps to fill compartments. My book seems to me rather good. L.'s book seems to him (so I interpret) rather good. I am entreated to write for the *TLS*.

So we reach the end of the year; which is for us cheerful, I think. For one thing we want to get to Rodmell; to see what has happened to the garden. I shall like a soft grey walk. Then the post. Then reading. Then sitting in the chimney corner. We take the servants and ensure comfort, for by contriving it, we're now on the best of terms with them. Left to myself I should invite people down – then probably regret it. But this is dawdling and rambling – never mind – this poor book must take what it can get and be thankful. (I use my new blotter, just given me by L., for the first time.)

1921

During the first half of 1921, besides working on Jacob's Room, *Virginia was as usual making frequent contributions to journals, although one of her favoured outlets, the* Athenaeum, *was now ceasing its independent existence owing to the decision of its editor, Middleton Murry, to join his ailing wife Katherine Mansfield abroad. In February Virginia attended his farewell dinner in Gordon Square.*

In 1920 Leonard had been selected as the Labour Party candidate for the Combined Universities' parliamentary seat, and though in general he pursued the attendant fatigues of this calling without Virginia's physical support, in March this year she accompanied him to Manchester when he addressed his potential constituents in the University there. And soon afterwards they took the train to spend Easter in her beloved Cornwall.

By early June Virginia's energetic social, literary and printing activities had brought her to a state of collapse, which necessitated a period of rest and quiet. After a further two months' summer break at Monks House, she returned to Richmond early in October, and finished Jacob's Room *a month later, though a further eight months were to elapse before she considered it fit to show to Leonard.*

This autumn, after summer holidays spent at Charleston, Vanessa with her children and Duncan had decamped to St Tropez where Roger Fry also was staying, thus removing one segment of Virginia's intimate circle; but there were other friends to see, walks to take in Richmond Park, more reviewing for the TLS, *and the ever-present demands of the Hogarth Press which, with the advent of their new assistant Ralph Partridge and of a new printing machine, increased rather than diminished. The Woolfs found themselves ineluctably becoming professional publishers, although most of the necessary operations – type-setting, stitching, binding, and still some of the actual printing – were carried out by themselves in the living rooms of their home. Virginia's own* Monday or Tuesday, *published early in April, was a characteristic product of this period. And their second collaboration with Koteliansky,* The Note Books and Reminiscences of Anton Tchekhov *by Maxim Gorky, also published in April, attracted a wider renown and brought further manuscripts to the Hogarth Press. However the problems attendant on such success – in particular the need for a working assistant – became a perennial source of strain. The regular presence of Ralph Partridge (who this year succeeded in persuading Carrington to marry him) in their house and at mealtimes grew more and more trying to the Woolfs; and though Virginia admired his vitality and enjoyed his confidences, they became less and less convinced of its benefits.*

1921

HOGARTH HOUSE, RICHMOND

Tuesday 25 January

Here have I waited twenty-five days before beginning the new year; and the twenty-five is, not unfortunately my twenty-fifth, but my thirty-ninth birthday; and we've had tea, and calculated the costs of printing Tchekhov; now L. is folding the sheets of his book, and Ralph has gone. I'm at a crisis in *Jacob*: want to finish in 20,000 words, written straight off in a frenzy. And I must pull myself together to bring it off. Lytton has asked to dedicate *Victoria* to me, which pleases me, and I stipulate, from vanity, for my name in full.

Monday 31 January

Just back from Tidmarsh, from the Club, from Harrison's [dentist], from losing two books on a bus. Lytton keeps his books amazingly tidy, like books on the stage. L. much depressed on Sunday morning and working out how many hours remained, before breakfast. Indeed, Saturday night was hard going. Lytton lapsed into gentle indifference, tired, depressed perhaps. Carrington I think grows older, and her doings are of the sort that age. Next day was better. Carrington and Ralph tactfully made out lists of summer flowers in the dining room. "You ought to have dedicated *Victoria* to Carrington" I said. "Oh dear no – we're not on those terms at all." "Ottoline will be enraged" I said. Yes, he thought she might be. The manuscript was there, and once I began reading it, I couldn't stop myself. Talk of going to Italy at Easter with the party but – One of the 'buts' is the Press. I sometimes think that L. and I are settling in too soundly. And now, am I to learn Russian with him and Kot? If he can read it and solace his age with it I shall be furious. But I'm broiling as I write and can't settle to anything, and detest going away, and vow never to do it, but to work, work, work –

Saturday 5 February

Jealousy or ambition has won the day, and I've just had my first Russian lesson and mortgaged my time to the extent of doing three lessons weekly. L. is mumbling Russian as I write. Have I done a great deal of work in pursuance of my vow? Books begin to drop in, and so long as I can do them every other week I rather like the relief from *Jacob*; I am beginning the last lap; and it is a sprint towards the end, difficult to keep up.

Wednesday 16 February

Russian is snatching all the time spared for this book. I can only keep up with L. by running as hard as I can. Everyone prophesies an early end. But I feel myself attached to an express train. With Kot and Leonard dragging me, I must be pulled through somehow.

We have dined twice at the Cock [Tavern]. Pale, marmoreal Eliot was there last week, like a chapped office boy on a high stool with a cold in his head, until he warms a little, which he did. We walked back along the Strand. "The critics say I am learned and cold" he said. "The truth is I am neither." As he said this, I think coldness at least must be a sore point with him. Then there was Murry's farewell dinner at 46 [Gordon Square]. I sat next Murry. He posed, I thought; looked anguished and martyred. Then, at the end, I asked after Katherine. Poor man! he poured himself out. We sat on after the others had gone. Apparently she is worse – dying? God knows. She is desperately depressed, thinks her book bad, can't write. Murry asked me to write to her. She feels herself out of things, left alone, forgotten. As he spoke with great feeling, and seemed to be very miserable, I liked him, felt with him, and think there can be no doubt that his love for Katherine anyhow is sincere.

Friday 18 February

I have been long meaning to write a historical disquisition on the return of peace; for old Virginia will be ashamed to think what a chatterbox she was, always talking about people, never about politics. Moreover, she will say, the times you lived through were so extraordinary. They must have appeared so, even to quiet women living in the suburbs. But indeed nothing happens at one moment rather than another. The history books will make it much more definite than it is. The most significant sign of peace this year is the sales; just over; the shops have been flooded with cheap clothes. Pre-war prices, so they say. Food has fallen a penny here, a penny there, but our books scarcely show a change. Servant girls aged twenty get £45 wages. And *The Times* pays me three guineas instead of two for a column. But I think you'll find all this written more accurately in other books, my dear Virginia: for instance in Mrs Gosse's diary and Mrs Webb's. I think it true to say that during the past two months we have perceptibly moved towards cheapness – *just* perceptibly. It is just perceptible too that there are very few wounded soldiers abroad in blue, though stiff legs, single legs, sticks shod with rubber, and empty sleeves are common enough. Also at Waterloo I sometimes see dreadful looking spiders propelling themselves along the platform – men all body, legs trimmed off close to the body. There are few soldiers about.

To change the subject, Rose Macaulay dined here last week – something like a lean sheep dog in appearance – harum scarum – humble – too much of a professional, yet just on the intellectual side of the border. Might be religious though: mystical perhaps. Not at all dominating or impressive; I daresay she observes more than one thinks for. Clear pale mystical eyes. A kind of faded moon of beauty: oh and badly dressed.

Monday 21 February

We dined with Roger the other night; and found Sydney [Waterlow]. After dinner we turned over sketches in the studio – not the pleasantest occupation for a cold night. Still old Roger has a quality of imagination which attracts me – loose and warm and genuine, in contrast to the costive judicial Sydney, who was catching us out all the time. Sydney looks melancholy; is touched with grey. This gives him an air of distinction. Then we had Quentin and Julian for Sunday, packed Julian home with a temperature, and I put him to bed. Quentin ran in to see Angelica. I liked to think of all this set going in the younger generation.

Tuesday 1 March

We came back from Rodmell yesterday; and Rodmell was all gold and sunshine. The one dismal element was provided by the human race. We went to tea at the Rectory. My book [*Monday or Tuesday*] is back from the printer, who has added the final eyesore – a brown back. There it is in masses, and I can't read it, for fear of howlers, printer's as well as writer's.

Morgan goes to India, and I think for ever. He will become a mystic, sit by the roadside, and forget Europe, which I think he half despises. In thirty years time he may turn up again, give us an amused look, and return to the East, having written a little unintelligible poetry. He has no roots here. And the news made me melancholy. I like him, and like having him about. But we shan't see him again. He sails on Friday.

Sunday 6 March

But perhaps I colour my view of Morgan from my painter's box. At any rate, Bob [Trevelyan] at the Cock the other night made it all seem very reasonable and desirable – "a trip to India just the thing for him – a relief after his ... well, his mother is trying sometimes – very fond of him of course; devoted to him and he ..." This in the usual Bob style, hinting little defects and mysteries with one corner of his mouth, praising with the other.

Nessa approves of *Monday or Tuesday* – mercifully; and thus somewhat redeems it in my eyes. But now I wonder a little what the reviewers will make of it – this time next month. The general line will be that I am becoming too much in love with the sound of my own voice; not much in what I write; indecently affected; a disagreeable woman. The truth is, I expect, that I shan't get very much attention anywhere.

Sunday 13 March

Eliot dines here tonight, alone, since his wife is in a nursing home, not much to our regret. But what about Eliot? Will he become 'Tom'? What happens with friendships undertaken at the age of forty? Do they flourish and live long? I suppose a good mind endures, and one is drawn to it, owing to having a good mind myself. Not that Tom admires my writing, damn him.

Nessa has influenza; slightly; and I'm glad to see how solicitous dear old Duncan is, waiting on her, and taking thought for her, better I think than Clive ever did.

Friday 18 March

Just back from two days at Manchester. I fancied myself writing this account, and how good it would be; what lots of things I had to say; and now the pen brings blankness. Well I was kept awake by business men talking in slow steady almost continuous voices in the room above till 1.30; and we were up early, breakfasted and caught a train, and so home, travelling all through the great rocky moors of Derbyshire – places so solitary they might be eighteenth century England; great sweeps of country all sunny and gloomy with bare rocks against the sky; and then behold a row of east end slum houses, with a strip of pavement and two factory chimneys set down in the midst. The houses are all stone, bleak, soot stained, different from our cottages; not cottages at all, but streets. Suddenly, in the palm of a wide valley you come on a complete town – gasworks, factories, and little streams made to run over stone steps and turn engines I suppose. "Yes" I said to Mrs Unwin, "Derbyshire is a very fine country." We were standing in a pit at the University, below us a row of chairs, on which sat Professors Unwin, Findlay, Goldman (a financier) and Weiss. Leonard then got up and made his speech, a very vigorous one. We sat round on hard benches, with ink pots, or the holes for them, in front of us.

All Manchester streets are the same, and all strung with tramlines. You hear bells striking all the time. Then there are no tea shops, but great cafés; and no little shops, but all big drapers. Then there's Queen Victoria, like a large tea cosy, and Wellington, sleek as a mastiff with paw extended; none of this was quite English, or at least London. The people were lower middle class, no sprinkling of upper class. But my observation of the university type was more profound. Mr and Mrs Weiss gave a dinner in the refectory before L.'s second speech; and there they all were – professors and wives, elderly people, depressed looking, with the manner of dons, but not the extreme confident eccentricity of first rate brains. But how supercilious I thought myself, and ultimately how much pure merit seemed in them. The women were dowdy; oh yes, but they too had fought for the right. Professor Unwin told me he had been arrested three times for attending seditious meetings during the war. Mrs Weiss said her husband had resigned because the University refused to accept a Conscientious Objector, upon which they thought the better of it. And yet there is no surface brilliancy; not a scrap of romance. It is a little familiar professional society, trying to keep up the standards, which (perhaps wrongly) I suppose must be hard work in Manchester, or am I merely snobbish in thinking it harder to say clever things and write clever books in Manchester than in Cambridge? Old Mrs Herford and Professor Findlay sat patiently looking at the tablecloth with nothing to say, like two old horses who have been working in the fields all day together. L., in the large room after dinner, was emphatically first rate. "Are you a politician?" they asked me. "Do you do much organising work?" I said I listened. Why was I there then? Oh for the fun of spending ten pounds in Manchester and seeing the Zoo. So we went to the Zoo; and I daresay I could write something interesting about that – a pale stone desert given over to charwomen and decorators; a few bears; a mandrill, and a fox or two – all in the desolation of depression.

Tuesday 22 March

Here we are on the verge of going to Cornwall. This time tomorrow we shall be stepping onto the platform at Penzance, sniffing the air, looking for our trap, and then – Good God! – driving off across the moors to Zennor – Why am I so incredibly and incurably romantic about Cornwall? One's past, I suppose; I see children running in the garden. A spring day. Life so new. People so enchanting. The sound of the sea at night. And now I go back 'bringing my sheaves' – well, Leonard, and almost forty years of life, all built on that, permeated by that: how much so I could never explain.

ZENNOR, CORNWALL

Wednesday 30 March
This is the last evening, and L. is packing, and I'm not in the mood for writing, but feel superstitiously that I should like to read something actually written in Cornwall. By looking over my left shoulder I see gorse yellow against the Atlantic blue. And we've been lying on the Gurnard's Head, on beds of samphire among grey rocks with buttons of yellow lichen on them. You look down onto the semi-transparent water – the waves all scrambled into white round the rocks – gulls swaying on bits of seaweed – rocks now dry now drenched with white waterfalls pouring down crevices. We took a rabbit path round the cliff, and I find myself a little shakier than I used to be. Still however maintaining without force to my conscience that this is the loveliest place in the world.

HOGARTH HOUSE, RICHMOND

Friday 8 April
Ten minutes to eleven a.m. And I ought to be writing *Jacob's Room*; I can't, and instead I shall write down the reason why I can't – this diary being a kindly blank faced old confidante. Well, you see, I'm a failure as a writer; my book [*Monday or Tuesday*] out (prematurely) and nipped, a damp firework. A short notice [in the *TLS*] scrambled through, put in an obscure place, rather scrappy, complimentary enough, but quite unintelligent. I mean by that that they don't see that I'm after something interesting. So that makes me suspect that I'm not. Oh and Lytton's book is out and takes up three columns: praise, I suppose. My temper sank and sank till for half an hour I was as depressed as I ever am. To rub this in we had a festival party at 41 [Gordon Square]: to congratulate Lytton; which was all as it should be; but then he never mentioned my book; and for the first time I have not his praise to count on. What depresses me is the thought that I have ceased to interest people – at the very moment when, by the help of the Press, I thought I was becoming more myself.

Roger is staying with us. I think he has the nicest nature among us – so open, sincere, and entirely without meanness; always generous, I think, and somehow hearty? He throws out a tremendous laugh. We went to the Bedford Music Hall last night, and saw Miss Marie Lloyd, a mass of corruption – long front teeth – a crapulous way of saying 'desire', and yet a born artist – scarcely able to walk, waddling, aged, unblushing. A roar of laughter went up when she talked of her marriage. She is beaten nightly by her husband. I felt that the audience was much closer to drink and beating and prison than any of us. The coal strike is on.

Sunday 10 April

I must note the symptoms of the disease, so as to know it next time. The first day one's miserable: the second happy. There was an Affable Hawk on me in the *New Statesman* which at any rate made me feel important (and its that that one wants).

Tuesday 12 April

I must hurriedly note more symptoms of the disease, so that I can turn back here and medicine myself next time. Well; I'd worn through the acute stage, and come to the philosophic semi-depressed, indifferent, when L. dropped into my ear the astonishing news that Lytton thinks 'The String Quartet' 'marvellous'. This did for a moment flood every nerve with pleasure, so much so that I forgot to buy my coffee and walked over Hungerford Bridge twanging and vibrating. I'm not nearly as pleased as I was depressed; and yet in a state of security. What I had feared was that I was dismissed as negligible.

Friday 15 April

Lytton rang up this morning, and I asked him about his book. "Are you smothered in laurels?" "Well, rather depressed," he said, and so he sounded. "I'm in the middle; and then I shall write to you about it." "And I'm writing to you about yours" he answered. He's sold, so they say, 5,000 copies this week, and another edition is printing. I have sold just 300. Well, but that doesn't prove my immortality, as I insinuate. One ought to write more of this occasion, since I suppose in twenty years' time the publication of *Queen Victoria* will be thought an important matter; but these things aren't important to us.

A queer sort of stillness seems already settling down on us, as of Sunday. This is the foreboding of the General Strike. L. has just come in with a paper which says that nothing has been done to patch up the strike. Therefore at 10 tonight, unless something happens meanwhile, all trains, trams, buses, mines, and perhaps electric light works come to an end. The servants have been to the Co-ops and brought back a week's groceries. We have a bundle of candles. Our most serious lack is coal, as Nelly forgot to order any. Still, Heaven knows why, I don't believe the strike will happen.

Sunday 17 April

And I was perfectly right. The strike didn't happen. The Triple Alliance had split: the railwaymen and transport workers refusing to go on with it, and leaving the miners by themselves. Presumably the miners will have to give in, and I shall get my hot bath, and bake home made bread again; yet it seems a pity somehow, – if they're to be forced back and the mine owners triumphant. I think this is my genuine feeling, though not very profound. It is fairly obvious that working people are well enough satisfied to prefer going on working.

Monday 18 April
Just back from lunching with a Cabinet Minister. I mean, of course, Herbert Fisher. We think he asked us in order to apologise for – everything. He said he had neither the physical force nor the combativeness to carry things through. He said he hated Parliament. A political life is dull, and wastes all one's time he said; one is always listening to dull speeches, frittering time away. He leaves home at 10, gets back at 11 p.m. and then has a bundle of papers to go through. And then he was careful to explain that the public is ridiculously in the dark about everything. Only the Cabinet knows the true spring and source of things he said. That is the only solace of the work. A flood tide of business flows incessantly from all quarters of the world through Downing Street; and there are a few miserable men trying desperately to deal with it. They have to make tremendous decisions with insufficient evidence on the spur of the moment. Then he pulled himself up, and said, solemnly, that he is going to Geneva to initiate peace – disarmament. "You are the great authority upon that, I understand", he said to Leonard. Anyhow I confess it seemed to me, sitting opposite to Leonard in that brown ugly room with its autotypes of Dutch pictures, that Leonard was an authority and Herbert a thin-shredded thread paper of a man.

Friday 29 April
Every afternoon for a week I've been up to the Æolian Hall; taken my seat right at the back; put my bag on the floor and listened to Beethoven quartets. Do I dare say listened? Well, but if one gets a lot of pleasure, really divine pleasure, and knows the tunes, and only occasionally thinks of other things – surely I may say listened. We are just back from the 5th. We had tea with Lytton, Carrington and Ralph.

Tuesday 3 May
Hamilton Fyfe in the *Daily Mail* says that Leonard's story will rank with the great stories of the world. Am I jealous? Only momentarily. But the odd thing is that I immediately think myself a failure. I feel fine drawn, misty, attenuated, inhuman, bloodless and niggling out trifles that don't move people. A full stop in *Jacob*, owing partly to depression. But I must pull together and finish it off. I can't read it as it is.

Sunday 15 May

Whit Sunday – dull, wet, and cold; so that on the whole we don't blame the coal strike for keeping us here over the fire instead of Monks House. By this time I think Carrington will have made up her mind one way or t'other. She must have had an odious Sunday. But still she *must* make up her mind. So I told Ralph on Friday, broaching that topic after all these months of silence. He did it himself, rather, by telling me of his gloom of the night before: his loneliness. He was very shrewd and bitter about Carrington. "She thinks herself one of the little friends of all the world" he said. Then he said she was selfish, untruthful, and quite indifferent to his suffering. So people in love always turn and rend the loved, with considerable insight too. He was speaking the truth largely. But I expect he was biassed; and also I expect – and indeed told him – that he is a bit of an ogre and tyrant. He wants more control than I should care to give – control I mean of the body and mind and time and thoughts of his loved. There's his danger and her risk; so I don't much envy her making up her mind this wet Whit Sunday.

Monday 23 May

So Carrington did make up her mind to become Partridge – no, that is precisely what she is determined not to do; and signs herself aggressively Carrington for ever. If people ever took advice I should feel a little responsible for making up Ralph's mind. I mean I am not sure that this marriage is not more risky than most. Certainly she is not in love; and he has the obdurate Anglo-Indian in him. But still, if she couldn't face the prospect of a week-end breach, or of a journey alone to Italy, she had no alternative. So they were married on Saturday.

We have been to Rodmell, and as usual I come home depressed – for no reason. Merely moods. Have other people as many as I have? That I shall never know. And sometimes I suppose that even if I came to the end of my incessant search into what people are and feel I should know nothing still.

Thursday 26 May

I sat in Gordon Square yesterday for an hour and a half talking to Maynard. Sometimes I wish I put down what people say instead of describing them. The difficulty is that they say so little. Maynard said he liked praise; and always wanted to boast. He said that many men marry in order to have a wife to boast to. But, I said, its odd that one boasts considering that no one is ever taken in by it. Its odd too that you, of all people, should want praise. You and Lytton are passed beyond boasting – which is the supreme triumph. There you sit and say nothing. I love praise, he said. I want it for the things

I'm doubtful about. He was going to some official dinner. He gets £120 for an article –

Thursday 2 June
The day after Derby Day, the very height of the season, I suppose; anyhow of leaf and flower. People turn up regularly though with little planning on our part. Madge Vaughan on Friday; Kot on Saturday; Roger; Fredegond. Will these names recover anything in ten years' time of the last week of May 1921? Madge asked to come; so we had her. She is curiously changed. She has become ordinary. Yet she has her gaiety and her vitality which protect one from the worst boredom. But not Leonard or Roger. They were out of hand with misery. And this was the woman I adored! I see myself now standing in the night nursery at Hyde Park Gate, washing my hands, and saying to myself 'At this moment she is actually under this roof.'

Sunday 5 June
Murry has written against our Tchekhov in the *Nation*. As for Kot, yesterday he couldn't keep his seat for fury. He verged on the voice and language of the public house. Is Murry 'a damned swindler'? Suppose we admired Murry's writing, would he change his tune? In my theory he's all parched for praise – run mad for lack of it. Yet it goes against my psychology to think people scoundrels. I don't know – at this moment I incline to think him a damned swindler – only a swindler so plausible that he'll become Professor of English Literature in the University of Oxford.

Tuesday 7 June
Eliot, by the way, saw no truth in Murry's article. "He is extremely clever" he said. "But you don't mean that in a good sense", I said. "Oh no; not at all." And Eliot astounded me by praising *Monday or Tuesday*. This really delighted me. It pleases me to think I could discuss my writing openly with him. *Ulysses* he says is prodigious.

MONKS HOUSE, RODMELL

Monday 8 August
What a gap! How it would have astounded me to be told when I wrote the last word here, on June 7th, that within a week I should be in bed, and not entirely out of it till the 6th of August – two whole months rubbed out. These, this morning, the first words I have written – to call writing – for sixty days; and those days spent in wearisome headache, jumping pulse, aching back, frets, fidgets, lying awake, sleeping draughts, sedatives, digi-

talis, going for a little walk, and plunging back into bed again – all the horrors of the dark cupboard of illness once more displayed for my diversion. Let me make a vow that this shall never, never, happen again; and *then* confess that there are some compensations. To be tired and authorised to lie in bed is pleasant; then, scribbling 365 days of the year as I do, merely to receive without agitation of my right hand in giving out is salutary. I feel that I can take stock of things in a leisurely way. Then the dark underworld has its fascinations as well as its terrors. Later, I had my visitors, one every day; so that I saw more people than normally even. Roger, Lytton, Nessa, Duncan, Dorothy Bussy, Pippa [Strachey], Carrington, James and Alix – all these came; and were as detached portraits – cut out, emphatic, seen thus separately compared with the usual way of seeing them in crowds. Lytton, I note, is more than ever affectionate. One must be, I think, if one is famous. One must say to one's old friends 'All my celebrity is nothing – nothing – compared with this.' And that was what he did say too.

Tuesday 9 August
Nessa &c have had a splendid summer of dissipation. I don't envy it; I don't want it; I want nothing but quiet and an active brain. Yet I have a worm of uncertainty moving at the foundations of this pleasant life: cultivated voices and a cultivated dog barking wake us on Sunday mornings. The truth is, Rodmell is a colony for Georgian poets, and though I am all for letting live, and not reading their works, it is hard and indeed intolerable that I should have to let them live next door to me.

Wednesday 10 August
But how is one to arrive at the truth? I have changed the *Daily News* for the *Morning Post*. The proportions of the world at once become utterly different. The *Morning Post* has the largest letters and the double column devoted to the murder of Mrs Lindsay; Anglo-Indians, Anglo-Scots, and retired old men and patriotic ladies write letter after letter to deplore the state of the country; applaud the *Morning Post*, the only faithful standard bearer left. They lament the downfall of England, which is flourishing as usual in the *Daily News*. But the *Daily News* has become a vivacious scrapbag. News is cut up into agreeable scraps, and written in words of one syllable. I may well ask, what is truth?

Thursday 11 August
A fortnight already gone. It goes too quick – too quick. If only one could sip slowly and relish every grain of every hour! For, to speak the truth, I've thought of making my will for the first time during these past weeks.

Sometimes it seems to me that I shall never write out all the books I have in my head, because of the strain. The devilish thing about writing is that it calls upon every nerve to hold itself taut. That is exactly what I cannot do – Now if it were painting or scribbling or making patchwork quilts or mud pies, it wouldn't matter.

Thursday 18 August
Nothing to record; only an intolerable fit of the fidgets to write away. Here I am chained to my rock: forced to do nothing; doomed to let every worry, spite, irritation and obsession scratch and claw and come again. This is to say that I may not walk, and must not work. Whatever book I read bubbles up in my mind as part of an article I want to write. No one in the whole of Sussex is so miserable as I am; or so conscious of an infinite capacity of enjoyment hoarded in me, could I use it. I hear poor L. driving the lawn mower up and down, for a wife like I am should have a label to her cage. She bites! Still if one is Prometheus, if the rock is hard and the gadflies pungent, gratitude, affection, none of the nobler feelings have sway. And so this August is wasted. Only the thought of people suffering more than I do at all consoles; and that is an aberration of egotism, I suppose. Seldom penetrated by love for mankind as I am, I sometimes feel sorry for the poor who don't read Shakespeare, and indeed have felt some generous democratic humbug at the Old Vic, when they played *Othello* and all the poor men and women and children had him then for themselves. Such splendour, and such poverty. I am writing down the fidgets, so no matter if I write nonsense.

Saturday 10 September
I recovered, and we took to seeing houses – without the least success, except that the rides to and from were successful. Much more important (to me) than anything else, was my recovery of the pen; and thus the hidden stream was given exit, and I felt reborn. I started an article upon the obscure, and should have finished it today had not Lytton come. However I gained by the exchange. We talked and talked; and always dislodged some new nugget, the deeper we went. He is going to write a play, "I am going to meet my Waterloo" – that is to say he is going to have a shot at the creative. If that fails, he dooms himself to history for ever – perhaps a history of English literature. Writing is an agony, we both agreed.

Monday 12 September
It is true that we are alone again, but I cannot take up my pen, partly, I think, from superstition. I said goodbye to James and Alix [Strachey] at 9 this morning; therefore the whole day is contaminated. James remains precisely where he was – the only human being, Alix says, fit for the

contemplative life, which is the highest. To look on comprehendingly is, she says, better than to create. But James claims no such eminence. He is the least ambitious of men – low, muted, gentle, modest – selfish of course, but not blind-selfish, not at all possessive, masculine, or dominating. I caught Alix in profile and saw her old, masterly, advanced; always in the same coat and skirt, which indeed renews itself as if it were her natural covering.

Lytton, by the way, talked about s——y; and agreed that the b.'s are all namby pambies and sentimentalists. He is himself, he said. To be a b. one must be unvirile, unpossessive, very nice indeed, but tending to be sentimental. And then their tastes become so degraded.

Wednesday 14 September
There was a very great storm three nights ago. I had to light my candle for support. Next morning our plum tree was down, and a great tree snapped some feet from the ground in the churchyard. The cottagers have been busy snatching up the twigs; the larger branches belonging, perhaps, to the Rector. More rain fell that night than in the three previous months, yet L. is not satisfied. Our garden is a perfect variegated chintz: asters, plumasters, zinnias, geums, nasturtiums and so on: all bright, cut from coloured paper, stiff, upstanding as flowers should be. I have been planting wallflowers for next June.

Thursday 15 September
It is the loveliest of evenings – still; the smoke going up straight in the quarry; the white horse and strawberry coloured horse feeding close together; the women coming out of their cottages for no reason, and standing looking; the cock pecking in the midst of his hens in the meadow; starlings in the two trees; Asheham fields shorn to the colour of white corduroy; Leonard storing apples above my head. Will this recall anything? I am so anxious to keep every scrap, you see.

A letter from Morgan this morning. He seems as critical of the East as of Bloomsbury, and sits dressed in a turban watching his Prince dance, quite unimpressed. He is not impressed by *Queen Victoria* either. Flimsy, he says, compared with Macaulay, which was perhaps what I meant.

I heard from Roger the other day, all in a hubblebubble about Murry's sneering pinpricking article. He is so angry that he can talk of nothing else. We must go on doing what we like in the desert Roger says, and let Murry climb the heights, as he certainly will.

The birds are moving about like nets full of fish; they turn sideways and vanish; sideways again, and become full of black spots.

Monday 19 September
Miss Green [Leonard's secretary] has been for the week-end, and a more comfortable guest does not exist. One need not bother about her; yet, at meal times, she proves brisk and fresh. Her father was a professor, or teacher, of geology at Oxford. Her mother, a Unitarian, and a liberal, with a great admiration for Gladstone. When Minna was nine her father died. She has lived all over England; and is fearfully independent – marches about, protected by her extreme plainness, unmolested, and unnoticed; yet has a strong will of her own; and observes, and won't be put upon. She is one of the regiment of the wage earning women's republic. Now she is off to spend a fortnight in Germany – a country which she thinks very beautiful. I said there were too many signposts and plaster statues. She would have none of it.

Wednesday 28 September
Eliot's visit passed off successfully, and yet I am disappointed to find that I am no longer afraid of him –

HOGARTH HOUSE, RICHMOND

Wednesday 2 November
This was the very last thing I wrote at Rodmell – so I suppose. I ought to run over the five weeks or so left out; and really cannot; for I have seen so many people; and so much has happened; though we are where we are. A printing machine is waiting at Richmond Station, and will be delivered at 8 a.m. tomorrow. Ralph is putting his back to the wheel, a very solid obdurate back. Some of our luncheons have been stormy, or rather silent, with sudden raps of opposition from the third party. But we have got along so far. In two days' time – during the week-end at any rate – I hope to finish *Jacob*. And one of these days I must read it. We go to Rodmell on Friday. I see I can think of nothing worth saying.

Tuesday 15 November
Really, really – this is disgraceful – fifteen days of November spent and my diary none the wiser. But when nothing is written one may safely suppose that I have been stitching books; or we have had tea at 4 and I have taken my walk afterwards; or I have had to read something for next day's writing, or I have been out late. We went to Rodmell, and the gale blew at us all day; off arctic fields; so we spent our time attending to the fire. The day before this I wrote the last words of *Jacob* – on Friday November 4th to be precise, having begun it on April 16th, 1920; allowing for six months

interval due to *Monday or Tuesday* and illness, this makes about a year. I have not yet looked at it.

We dined with Clive on Friday. Aldous and Mary and Maynard there. All the time I felt Mary solicitous, even affectionate; and sure enough, as I left she took my hand, said "I don't like this plan of quarrelling" and asked me to come and see her.

Poor Lilian – poor Margaret. They sit beside the corpse of the Women's Guild; the blinds are drawn; they are sad and white, brave, tearless, but infinitely mournful. When one leaves a life work at sixty, one dies. One ought to work – never to take one's eyes from one's work; and then if death should interrupt, well, it is merely that one must get up and leave one's stitching – one won't have wasted a thought on death. Margaret says in her work one gets superannuated. One must give it up. A very cruel work then; and she is left without husband or child.

Wednesday 16 November
It is pouring; but we say Thank God it is warmer. It has been freezing for a week. We go to bed under red blankets, quilts, fur coats. But now, as I say, it is raining. I take in the *Westminster Gazette*. For some politics are beginning to interest me, as I suppose they interest City men – like a football match. One might become a virulent Socialist – or a Conservative? It is a game. I mean by that that I don't think of ends (nor does any one else) but of means. I get no letters nowadays, so I read my paper. Did I describe the advent of the Press? Nelly panic struck, thinking it would come through the kitchen floor. How do you invent these fears? I asked her. But never have we been so peaceful domestically for so long.

Friday 25 November
L.'s forty-first birthday. My apology for not writing is quite truthfully, the Hogarth Press. Roger's woodcuts, 150 copies, have been gulped down in two days. I have just finished stitching the last copies – all but six. Last week-end we spent at Tidmarsh. I remember so little; for with old, worn, creased, shabby, intimate friends, it runs so easily; no rapids, or waterfalls; room for everything; and no damned brilliance. And it was all very warm and the details – such as cups and plates – were exquisite. Carrington and Ralph have a gigantic four poster bed.

Saturday 3 December
I dined with the Sangers last night, and enjoyed society. I wore my new black dress, and looked, I daresay, rather nice. That's a feeling I very seldom have; and I rather intend to enjoy it oftener. I like clothes, if I can design them. So Bertie Russell was attentive, and we struck out like swimmers

who knew their waters. Bertie is a fervid egoist – which helps matters. And then, what a pleasure – this mind on springs. "If you had my brain you would find the world a very thin, colourless place" he said. "But my colours are so foolish" I replied. "You want them for your writing" he said. "God does mathematics. That's my feeling. It is the most exalted form of art." "Art?" I said. "Well there's style in mathematics as there is in writing" he said. "I get the keenest aesthetic pleasure from reading well written mathematics. My brain is not what it was. I'm past my best – and therefore, of course, I am now celebrated. In Japan they treated me like Charlie Chaplin – disgusting. I shall write no more mathematics. Perhaps I shall write philosophy. The brain becomes rigid at fifty – and I shall be fifty in a month or two. I have to make money." "Surely money is settled upon Russells by the country?" I said. "I gave mine away years ago, to help promising young men who wanted to write poetry. From twenty-eight to thirty-eight I lived in a cellar and worked. Then my passions got hold of me. Now I have come to terms with myself. I am no longer surprised at what happens. I don't expect any more emotional experiences. I don't think any longer that something is going to happen when I meet a new person." I said I disagreed with much of this. Yet perhaps I did not expect very much to happen from talking to Bertie. I felt that he had talked to so many people. Thus I did not ask him to come here – I enjoyed it though a good deal; and got home and drank cocoa in the kitchen.

Sunday 11 December
Both the servants have German measles, and for three days we have been servants instead of masters.

Sunday 18 December
Here it is practically the end of the year, and more pages left blank than seems to me altogether wholesome. But my diary dwindles, perversely enough, when the stuff for it is most abundant. There was Roger here for tea and dinner yesterday; the day before I had to go plundering the shops for presents after tea; Thursday, I had to put in semicolons to my Henry James article and then rush to catch a train to Hampstead to dine with Brett and Gertler. Tomorrow we dine with Adrian. Roger's visit went off specially well. I mean we are grown rather intimate, and sit talking at our ease – practically of everything. I see in this one of the good effects of middle age. Roger grudges every minute now that he doesn't paint. So we reflected upon these strange, on the whole merciful, dispensations, by which Roger always sees masterpieces ahead of him and I see great novels – We have our atmosphere of illusion, without which life would be so much duller than it is.

Our luck seems, at last, to be in again. With luck we may have £400 instead of £250; and we might buy a motor car; and we might buy the meadow; and we might run up another lodge, and we might take in a new strip of garden. And so on and so on.

Monday 19 December

I will add a postscript on the nature of reviewing. "Mrs Woolf? I want to ask you one or two questions about your Henry James article –" First (only about the right name of one of the stories). "And now you use the word 'lewd'. Of course, I don't wish you to change it, but surely that is rather a strong expression to apply to anything by Henry James? I haven't read the story lately of course – but still my impression is –" "Well, I thought that when I read it; one has to go by one's impressions at the time." "But you know the usual meaning of the word? It is – ah – *dirty* – Now poor dear old Henry James – At anyrate, think it over, and ring me up in 20 minutes." So I thought it over and came to the required conclusion in twelve minutes and a half.

But what is one to do about it? He [Bruce Richmond] made it sufficiently clear not only that he wouldn't stand 'lewd', but that he didn't much like anything else. I feel that this becomes more often the case, and I wonder whether to break off, or to pander, or to go on writing against the current. Anyhow, for the present I shall let it be.

To add to Leonard's trophies, the Webbs have asked him to edit a book; the League of Nations Union offer to reprint *International Government*; and *The Village in the Jungle* is sold among other rare first editions at six shillings. All very good.

1922

Virginia started the year with influenza, the sequelae of which lasted into the summer and involved consultations with doctors and specialists. But despite her uncertain health, she enjoyed a lively social life. Friends came to see her at Richmond; she and Leonard were able to spend Easter and Whitsun at Monks House, and to visit Lytton Strachey and his co-habitees at Tidmarsh; and in July she went once again to Garsington at the invitation of Lady Ottoline Morrell. At the beginning of August the Woolfs removed to Sussex; and here too they were beset with visitors, including Lytton Strachey, T. S. Eliot, and E. M. Forster, back from India. Vanessa and her household were again in residence at Charleston, a few miles off.

Vexed by the editorial timidity of the TLS, *Virginia determined at the start of the year to give up reviewing – she wrote but five all told this year – and concentrated on revising* Jacob's Room, *which Leonard read in July and pronounced her best work. It was published (though not printed) by the Hogarth Press – its largest undertaking so far – in October (thereafter all Virginia's books were published by the Press), and had a mixed reception. But already in the summer she had begun a story she referred to as* Mrs Dalloway, *and this gradually expanded into a full-length novel, given poignancy by the accidental death in October of an important figure from her youth, Kitty Maxse, who was to some extent the model for Mrs Dalloway.*

In July Leonard accepted a post writing on political matters for the weekly Nation & Athenaeum; *and in November his electioneering activities were concluded by the General Election, in which he came bottom of his poll, although the Labour Party as a whole made considerable gains. But concurrently with his political interests, the Woolfs were increasingly concerned with the question of their Hogarth Press. This year it issued nine titles; and the problem of coping with the work involved became acute: Leonard in particular found Ralph Partridge more and more irritating and less and less dependable; Ralph, for his part, encouraged by Lytton Strachey, foresaw an influential and expanding future for himself in the management of the Press. There were endless discussions; alternative solutions proposed; well-to-do aspiring partners investigated; established publishers' enticing offers considered . . . In the end a solution presented itself as if in answer to Virginia's prayer: an intelligent young woman longing to dedicate herself to printing. Ralph was to go; Marjorie Thomson would replace him; and Leonard and Virginia would keep control of their own creation.*

On 14 December, dining with Clive Bell, Virginia made a new acquaintance: Mrs Harold Nicolson, who preferred to be known by her maiden name, Vita Sackville-West.

1922

HOGARTH HOUSE, RICHMOND

Tuesday 3 January
Home last night, after ten or eleven days at Monks House – days when the wind blew from every quarter at the top of its voice, and great spurts of rain came with it, and hail spat in our fire, and the lawn was strewn with little branches, and there were fiery sunsets over the downs. In the morning I wrote with steady stoicism my posthumous article upon Hardy. No more reviewing for me, now that [Bruce] Richmond re-writes my sentences to suit the mealy mouths of Belgravia; it is odd how stiffly one sets pen to paper when one is uncertain of editorial approval. That is the true reason why I give up; joined with the economic reason that I make as much by other means. Leonard planted, pruned, sprayed, though the cold and the wet and the wildness made his behaviour a heroism to be admired, not comprehended. Tonight my reading begins.

Sunday 22 January
'Tonight my reading begins' did I say? And two nights later I was shivering over the fire and had to tumble into bed with the influenza. Happily, it has been a mitigated lapse – not complete like the summer's. Nessa just back from France, alighting for a fortnight, and then off again to Paris. But what am I to say about her? All very gay in French boots, hat, and check shirt; with that queer antique simplicity of surface which I compare to the marble cheeks of a Greek statue.

Saturday 4 February
Another fortnight spent in bed. Indeed, almost as I put down my pen I was seized with a second attack, lay in bed like a piece of timber, and am still in bed, sitting up, looking at the fire, and my temperature a shade above normal. I think this second attack was more wearisome than the first, and I have seen very few people. Nessa came again. How painful these meetings are! Let me try to analyse. Perhaps it is that we both feel that we can exist independently of the other. The door shuts between us, and life flows on

again and completely removes the trace. That is an absurd exaggeration. The truth is she was a little depressed, ostensibly because no one had mentioned painting to her in the course of three weeks. "I have seen all the cleverest people," she said "and not one mentioned painting. I hung two of our latest paintings in Maynard's room, and he never noticed them." "Surely Clive?" I said. "Oh Clive knows nothing whatever about it" she replied. All this tends to make her turn to Paris as her dwelling place. But then there are the children, Julian at school, Quentin coming home nightly. And then there is Duncan. "And after all there is nothing binding in our relationship", she said. "Its quite different from yours." And so this ruffled me. I set out to prove that being childless I was less normal than she. She took offence (the words are too strong). Told me I shouldn't enjoy café life in Paris. Told me I liked my own fireside and books and my friends' visits; implied that I was settled and unadventurous. Implied that I spent a great deal upon comfort. As we had only two hours together, and she left for Paris next morning, and perhaps I shan't see her till May, I felt a sort of discontent, as the door closed behind her. Indeed, we are at the moment a little tremulous again. What to do about Ralph? – about the Press? Ralph works in the basement, and leaves the machine dirty. Yesterday he slipped off leaving L. to go down and clean up. Upon this crystallised all our grumblings of the past – They are to the effect that he is lazy, undependable, now industrious, now slack, all corroded by Lytton – the old story, which one has heard so often from the victims of the old serpent. Should we part company? I suspect the work is not possible for an educated and vigorous young man.

Tuesday 14 February
[On] Monday [Dr] Fergusson came in and pronounced that my eccentric pulse had passed the limits of reason and was in fact insane. So I was laid in bed again, and set up my state in the drawing room, where I now write sitting up in bed, alongside the fire, so that perhaps I shall be up and creeping this time next week. Katherine Mansfield bursts upon the world in glory next week [*The Garden Party*]; I have to hold over *Jacob's Room* until October, and I somehow fear that by that time it will appear to me sterile acrobatics. Nevertheless, such is life, that I am very tolerably amused; see a good many people. And Adrian is so happy and genial that I am really pleased. An unambitious man, with good brains, money, wife and children is, I daresay, the most fortunate of us all. "Oh well" he said talking of his medical career, "it's something to do. It's easier now to go on than to stop" he said. Like the whole family, he has this distinguished, cool, point of view, which always makes him good company, and admits him to any society – if he wished for any society, which needless to say, he doesn't.

Wednesday 15 February

I thought to myself, as Lytton was talking, Now I will remember this and write it down in my diary tomorrow. And as I thought that, everything melted to mist. People don't say things, except in biographies. True, Lytton was smooth and mild and melancholy beyond his wont; but with intimates, when talk is interesting, one sentence melts into another; heads and tails merge; there is never a complete beast. But he was back again in his old pre-*Eminent Victorians* despondency, partly, I guessed, because the publishers are chilly about his essays; partly because he can't think of a plot for a play.

Friday 17 February

I meant to write about death, only life came breaking in as usual. I like, I see, to question people about death. I have taken it into my head that I shan't live till seventy. Suppose, I said to myself the other day, this pain over my heart suddenly wrung me out like a dish cloth and left me dead? – I was feeling sleepy, indifferent, and calm; and so thought it didn't much matter, except for L. Then, some bird or light I daresay, or waking wider, set me off wishing to live – wishing chiefly to walk along the river and look at things.

Saturday 18 February

Three dozen eggs at present prices work out at 10/6. Three dozen = 36. Four eggs for breakfast work out at twenty-eight a week. This leaves eight over for cooking. I have an egg now every night for dinner. I make these calculations not with a view to an essay upon national economy, though that comes in. My weekly books – these are in my mind. For according to the papers, the cost of living is now I don't know how much lower than last year; whereas my books remain about the same. You can't question Nelly much without rubbing a sore. She threatens at once to send up a cheap meal "And Mr Woolf won't like that." There! Not a very grievous itch; and quelled by the sight of the new Byron letters just come from Mudies. But after six weeks influenza my mind throws up no matutinal fountains. A little air, seeing the buses go by, lounging by the river, will, please God, send the sparks flying again.

Monday 6 March

The cat lets this mouse run a few steps once more. I have walked for ten minutes only, according to the directions of Dr Sainsbury, who after examining me for an hour said – many things; among them that we can't go abroad. But I am back again, after two months this very day, sitting in my chair after tea, writing; and I wrote *Jacob* this morning, and though my temperature is not normal, my habits are: and that is all I care for.

Sunday 12 March
This book dwindles. Yet many portraits are owed to it – I have seen people – and people. Eliot, Clive, Violet, – if no one else. Of these Eliot amuses me most – grown supple as an eel; yes, grown positively familiar and jocular and friendly, though retaining I hope some shreds of authority. I mustn't lick all the paint off my Gods. He is starting a magazine; to which twenty people are to contribute; and Leonard and I are among them! So what does it matter if Katherine Mansfield soars in the newspapers, and runs up sales skyhigh? Ah, I have found a fine way of putting her in her place. The more she is praised, the more I am convinced she is bad. What, then, did we discuss? He has written a poem of forty pages, which we are to print in the autumn. This is his best work, he says. He is pleased with it; takes heart, I think, from the thought of that safe in his desk. Clive, via Mary, says he uses violet powder to make him look cadaverous. I am seeing Clive rather frequently. He comes on Wednesdays; jolly, and rosy, and squab: a man of the world; and enough of my old friend, and enough of my old lover, to make the afternoons hum. But, oh dear me, after nine weeks claustration, I want to vault the wall, and pick a few flowers. The ethical code of Bloomsbury allows poaching; and I'm amused to see how a change of relationship, a middle-aged relationship, offers new experiences.

Then I hit Morgan on the wing. He had come to London that very day, and so came here, and was, we thought, depressed to the verge of inanition. To come back to Weybridge, to come back to an ugly house a mile from the station, an old, fussy, exacting mother, to come back having lost your Rajah, without a novel, and with no power to write one – this is dismal, I expect, at the age of forty-three. The middle age of b——s is not to be contemplated without horror. But he was charming, transparent; and told us as much as we could get out. A year's absence fills one too full for many drops to issue upon turning the bottle upside down. He told us about the sparrows that fly about the Palace – No one troubles about them. "I used to shout at them sometimes. The squirrels sat on the piano. I used to row on the lake which was nice. The Indians were too heavy to row. There were black hills. A very nice climate, but dull. There were sparrows only. In other parts the birds were so lovely – I thought of you Virginia (which pleased me). It is a very nice life; but one wants other people to talk to. It is much nicer than this. I felt no enthusiasm at seeing my native cliffs again." That was obvious. Off he went, carrying a very heavy metal plate, to dine with Aunt Rosalie at Putney.

Friday 24 March
Still invalided, I sit and receive visitors almost daily; and say nothing about them here. People are neglected, and accumulate, up and up and up. Clive

is the most persistent; we talked from 4.30 to 10.15 the other day. It is clear that I am to rub up his wits; and in return I get my manners polished. I hear of supper parties; elicit facts about drink and talk and goings on. He enjoys *every*thing – There is no truth about life, he says, except what we feel. It is good if you enjoy it, and so forth. Obviously we reach no heights of reason. Nor do we become completely intimate. A little colour is added to taste. We have our embrace; our frill of sentiment. Impossible, as Nessa says, to talk without it. But I perceive, chiefly through his letters, that once a fortnight is the pitch of our relationship.

Thursday 30 March
It is snowing now, large loose watery flakes; they fall straight; there is no wind. Muddy water is in the evening sky, and we began summer time last Sunday, so the evening sky is prolonged.

Thursday 27 April
Just back – not from the Club, but from Rodmell, and fingers are so cold I can't close them on my pen. It is blackening for another downpour. This is the worst spring on record. Twenty-seven days of bitter wind, blinding rain, gusts, snowstorms, storms every day. So Rodmell was mitigated joy.

Sunday 11 June
Disgraceful! disgraceful! disgraceful! From the 27th day of April to this, not a word has been recorded. And I only write now to excuse myself from copying out a page or two of *Jacob*. The depression of a return from Rodmell is always acute. Perhaps this continued temperature may be some sort of cause for my ups and downs. Yet the ten days at Rodmell passed smoothly. One lives in the brain there – I slip easily from writing to reading with spaces between of walking – walking through the long grass in the meadows, or up the downs. And so of course, coming back from Rodmell – blank – reason for blank forgotten as well as blank's contents.

Friday 23 June
I think I've been working too hard; talking too much; to open this book. Working at copying *Jacob* after tea. As for the talk, it has been all about love and lies with Ralph. We have had a mad bull in the house – a normal Englishman in love; and deceived. His stupidity, blindness, callousness, struck me more powerfully than the magic virtues of passion. I began by believing his story – that Carrington had lied in matters of such importance that their relations were now forever damaged. But he concealed some essentials; how he had treated her, so as to foster lies. His passions are like those in books. And he thinks this fine. "But I am like that." "You're a

maniac" I said. Indeed I shouted it in the train coming back from Roger's lecture. "I should have left you if you had treated me like that." He does not answer. It was the stupidity of virility that impressed me.

We have seen a great many people. Roger's lectures provide a rendezvous. Eliot dined last Sunday and read his poem. He sang it and chanted it and rhythmed it. It has great beauty and force of phrase; symmetry; and tensity. What connects it together, I'm not so sure. But he read till he had to rush, and discussion thus was curtailed. One was left, however, with some strong emotion. *The Waste Land*, it is called; and Mary Hutch, who has heard it more quietly, interprets it to be Tom's autobiography – a melancholy one. Yes, Mary kissed me on the stairs. That was after the Memoir Club. Lytton and Morgan read; and our standard is such that little is left for me to hint and guess at. They say what they mean, very brilliantly; and leave the dark as it was before. Morgan, who is now out and about again, very calm, serene, like a kettle boiling by some private fire, spent the night here, and we sat round the table and discussed his book. *Jacob* is being typed by Miss Green, and crosses the Atlantic on July 14th. Then will begin my season of doubts and ups and downs.

Monday 17 July

Back from Garsington, and too unsettled to write – but then this does not count as writing. It is to me like scratching; or, if it goes well, like having a bath – which of course, I did not get at Garsington. I don't know that any incident burnt through the long windy cold day. I liked old [Augustine] Birrell's stories. He is a very well matured vintage: the barrel round and tight and mellow; and the wine within bright and sweet, and not lacking tang either. Ottoline has her little green book room with the gilt pillars stuffed with pretty yellow books. There I sat, crouching over the fire, and we talked, rather on our guard – a little toothless perhaps. Much disillusioned she said she was, but now indifferent to disillusionment. So we had the case of Aldous Huxley – a pretty poor one. There is Murry pleading and whining to be taken in, with a view to Oxford honours, so Birrell shrewdly said. Still we were low in tone – had she not had an operation on her bladder two days before? But energy ran like whips through her.

Leonard has been offered [H. N.] Brailsford's post [leader-writer and foreign affairs specialist] on the *Nation*; and has taken it.

I am finishing *Jacob's Room*. Grizzel [a dog] now belongs to us. We dine in the drawing room – the dining room being given over to print and Ralph (he annoys us both considerably). My temperature goes on, as usual, and Dr Hamill thinks that my right lung is suspicious. Fergusson says no. And perhaps I shall have to see Sainsbury to settle it.

Wednesday 19 July

Today Ralph has a story that Maynard and Lytton are to buy the *English Review* from Austin Harrison, set him up as drudge, pay their contributors £10.10 a thousand words, and beat all rivals. If Ralph wants it, then I think Lytton may agree; not otherwise. At Garsington they were getting up a subscription to give Tom £300, and so free him from journalism. These two bits of gossip seem to belong together.

Saturday 22 July

My conscience drives me again to write. Clive came to tea yesterday, and offered me only the faded and fly-blown remnants of his mind. He had been up late. So had I – at the pictures. For my own part, all my strings are jangled by a night out. Dissipation would rot my writing (such as it is, I put in, modestly). The question yesterday was about Lytton and the *English Review*. Would it be good or bad for his writing? Ralph says that he is very depressed; blocked by the play he can't write – and never will be able to write, say I; and if he lubricated himself with journalism, he might reel off some history or biography, and so pass by the play unmoved; and this is his line, and a good one too, I say. If Lytton takes it, Ralph is to be business manager, and leave us. Well? We are polite, but we don't sigh. Ralph is in mischief again. Poor young man! For really he was never meant for intellectual whirlpools. No; he was meant for punts in backwaters, gramophones, ices, flirtations, a pretty wife, large family, and interests in the City. We have bad luck with our prentices. Next time we must stipulate for eunuchs.

Hamill sticks to it that my right lung is wrong. Fergusson finds nothing. Pneumonia germs have been discovered. And my case is to be laid before Sainsbury on the 9th – all rather a bore.

Wednesday 26 July

On Sunday L. read through *Jacob's Room*. He thinks it my best work. He calls it a work of genius; he thinks it unlike any other novel; he says that the people are ghosts; he says it is very strange; he found it very interesting, and beautiful, and without lapse (save perhaps the party) and quite intelligible. I cannot write this as formally as it deserves, for I was anxious and excited. But I am on the whole pleased. Neither of us knows what the public will think. There's no doubt in my mind that I have found out how to begin (at forty) to say something in my own voice; and that interests me so that I feel I can go ahead without praise.

Friday 28 July

The affairs of the Partridges have engrossed us for two hours again. Partridge's conduct is that of the village Don Juan. Again, he behaves like a bull in a garden. He is a male bully, as L. says. I am reminded of the tantrums of Adrian and Clive. There is something maniacal in masculine vanity.

MONKS HOUSE, RODMELL

Thursday 3 August

Twice a year I make good resolutions – in August and October. My good resolution for August is to work methodically, yet with the grain not against it. Often, my wisdom teaches me, good resolutions wither because forced. And modern science teaches us to respect pleasure, or that is my reading.

We ended our season last Monday at the Commercio [Restaurant], with Clive and Roger. Roger came in with his hair flying and his coat flying carrying canvases – his mouth open, his eyes searching round – and we had our usual talk. Clive had his bits of gossip. To Gordon Square afterwards; Nessa had the mumps downstairs. Duncan drifted in, soft haired, vague, gentle as usual. Roger undid his canvases, and leant two portraits of Logan [Pearsall Smith] against the sofa. "Yes, I think that is the best portrait I have done so far" he said. He is fifty-five I suppose; and still thinks he is about to begin to paint as he should – a merciful dispensation – a carrot to lure him across the desert. But it is no desert to Roger. Every faculty is used and burnished, and some fairly on the way to be worn out. He suffers, consults doctors, aches and shivers, but eternally goes on. The perfect man, as I told him, and as indeed I believe him to be. He is off to spend the summer painting with Derain. It is his obsession now – to paint, paint, paint. Nothing else is worth doing.

Yesterday I walked to the top of Asheham hill, and found colonies of mushrooms on the way. The house now looks a little rigid and fixed, the country shut in, and severe compared with this. But the garden here is a lovely patch – open and airy with views of the hills.

Wednesday 16 August

I should be reading *Ulysses*, and fabricating my case for and against. I have read 200 pages so far – not a third; and have been amused, stimulated, charmed, interested by the first two or three chapters – and then puzzled, bored, irritated, and disillusioned as by a queasy undergraduate scratching his pimples. And Tom, great Tom, thinks this on a par with *War and Peace*! An illiterate, underbred book it seems to me: the book of a self taught working man, and we all know how distressing they are, how egotistic, insistent, raw, striking, and ultimately nauseating. When one can have the cooked flesh, why have the raw? But I think if you are anaemic, as Tom is, there is a glory in blood. Being fairly normal myself I am soon ready for the classics again. I may revise this later. I do not compromise my critical sagacity. I plant a stick in the ground to mark page 200. For my own part I am laboriously dredging my mind for *Mrs Dalloway* and bringing up light buckets.

I see I have said nothing about our day in London – Dr Sainsbury, Dr Fergusson, and the semi-legal discussion over my body, which ended in a bottle of quinine pills, and a box of lozenges, and a brush to varnish my throat with. Influenza and pneumonia germs, perhaps, says Sainsbury, very softly, wisely, and with extreme deliberation. "Equanimity – practise equanimity Mrs Woolf" he said, as I left; an unnecessary interview from my point of view; but we were forced into it by one step after another on the part of the bacteriologists. I take my temperature no more till October 1st.

Meanwhile there is the question of Ralph. This – it is the old question of his lumpiness, grumpiness, slovenliness, and stupidity versus his niceness, strength, fundamental amiability and connections.

Tuesday 22 August

I should like very much to account for my depression. Sydney Waterlow spent the week-end here; and reproduced in his heavy lifeless voice exactly the phrases in which Murry dismisses my writing. I cannot write *Mrs Dalloway*. Indeed it is fatal to have visitors, even like Clive for one day, in the middle of a story. I had just got up steam. All that agony now has to begin again. And Sydney is always a feather bed on a hot night – ponderous, meritorious, stuffy. No one ever suffered so acutely from atmosphere as I do; and my leaves drooped one by one; though heaven knows my root is firm enough. Ah, but how divinely happy we were until 12.30 on Thursday when Clive boarded the enchanted island with news from the world. Never have I been so happy in my life. The day was like a perfect piece of cabinet making – beautifully fitted with beautiful compartments. The odd thing is that neither of us wishes for visitors. Of course they threaten us from all sides – no: leave me, leave me, is all I say: to work my brain.

Saturday 26 August

Today is fine, and yesterday we went to Charleston by the Bus, for the first time. After all, one must respect civilisation. Charleston is as usual. One hears Clive shouting in the garden before one arrives. Nessa emerges from a great variegated quilt of asters and artichokes; not very cordial; a little absent minded. Clive bursts out of his shirt; sits square in his chair and bubbles. Then Duncan drifts in, also vague, absent minded, and incredibly wrapped round with yellow waistcoats, spotted ties, and old blue stained painting jackets. His trousers have to be hitched up constantly. He rumples his hair. However, I can't help thinking that we grow in cordiality, instead of drifting out of sight. And why not stand on one's own legs, and defy them, even in the matter of hats and chaircovers? Surely at the age of forty . . .

I dislike *Ulysses* more and more – that is think it more and more unimportant; and don't even trouble conscientiously to make out its meanings. Thank God, I need not write about it.

Sunday 3 September

Perhaps the greatest revolution in my life is the change of nibs – no longer can I write with my old blunt tree stump – people complained. But then the usual difficulties begin – what is to take its place? I should be reading the last immortal chapter of *Ulysses*; but I'm hot with Badminton in the orchard, and we dine in thirty-five minutes. I'm fretful with people. Every day will now be occupied till Tuesday week.

Wednesday 6 September

Visitors leave one in tatters; yet with a relish for words. Phrases roll on my tongue – which, really one can't produce for the delectation of my mother-in-law and Flora: who are now on their way back to Lewes; Carrington and Partridge being on their way to Chiddingly; the Sangers being on their way up Asheham Hill; and Lytton beginning to consider being on his way here.

We had our premeditated interview last night, with Ralph lying on the bed up here. Did his face show any change as Leonard went on – very forcible, measured, and impersonal. "Things have been unsatisfactory in my opinion" and so on. Ralph put up no more defence than a flock of sheep, which is disarming. Carrington is going to sit out his infidelities; which she does with her lips shut. She is going to paint. But she will never be a young woman again.

We had a great chatter party on Monday – Maynard, Nessa, Duncan, the Sangers. But how could I repeat the talk? Maynard is going to build a house: Nessa and Duncan are going to draw an income for ten years from it. It is to be a hotel, perfectly appointed, in a field off Beanstalk Lane – eight suites of rooms, with eight bathrooms, kitchens, waterclosets, surrounding a courtyard; in short a Peacock novel in stone; soon filled with characters. No doubt we have re-arranged life almost completely. Our parents were mere triflers at the game – Maynard, besides being our greatest living economist, has a dancer for a mistress, and is now preparing to stage a Mozart ballet; interviews the Coliseum Manager; is an expert on contracts. Then Duncan is going to dance with Lydia [Lopokova]. And Roger – but I need not go through the list; for my point is the same – we have all mastered the art of life, and very fascinating it is.

I finished *Ulysses*, and think it a misfire. Genius it has I think; but of the inferior water. It is underbred, not only in the obvious sense, but in the literary sense. A first rate writer, I mean, respects writing too much to be tricky; startling; doing stunts. I'm reminded all the time of some callow board school boy, full of wits and powers, but so self-conscious and egotistical that he loses his head, becomes extravagant, mannered, uproarious, ill at ease, makes kindly people feel sorry for him, and stern ones merely annoyed; and one hopes he'll grow out of it; but as Joyce is forty this scarcely seems likely. I have not read it carefully; and only once; and it is very obscure; so no doubt I have scamped the virtue of it more than is fair. I feel that myriads of tiny bullets pepper one and spatter one; but one does not get one deadly wound straight in the face – as from Tolstoy, for instance; but it is entirely absurd to compare him with Tolstoy.

Thursday 7 September
Having written this, L. put into my hands a very intelligent review of *Ulysses*, in the American *Nation*; which, for the first time, analyses the meaning; and certainly makes it very much more impressive than I judged. Still I think there is virtue and some lasting truth in first impressions; so I don't cancel mine.

Tuesday 12 September
Lytton drove off an hour ago; and I have been sitting here, unable to read or collect myself – such is the wreckage dealt by four days of conversation. I told Lytton I should try to write down his talk – which sprang from a conversation about Boswell. But said Lytton, I never do talk. One night he gave us a complete account of the prison system, based on reports which he has been reading – thoroughly, with mastery, and a kind of political ability which impresses me. He would have been an admirable ruler of an Indian province. However, as usual, there was one main theme to which we returned – Ralph and Carrington. Both weigh upon poor old Lytton who feels himself in the position of a father, is slightly in love, yet sees, with his usual candour, all the faults and drawbacks.

Tuesday 26 September
A great many things have happened, unrecorded. This has been the most sociable summer we've ever had. Sometimes I feel as if, instead of sleeping

through the months in a dark room, I'd been up in the light all night. Clive and Mary came: Mary in grey silk stockings; was very affable; sat on the floor. Morgan came on Friday; Tom on Saturday. My talk with Tom deserves writing down, but won't get it for the light is fading; and one cannot write talk down either, as was agreed at Charleston the other day. There was a good deal of talk about *Ulysses*. Tom said the book would be a landmark, because it destroyed the whole of the 19th Century. It left Joyce himself with nothing to write another book on. He thought that Joyce did completely what he meant to do. But he did not think that he gave a new insight into human nature – said nothing new like Tolstoy. (Light now fails – 7.10 after a bad rainy day.)

Wednesday 27 September
While Tom and I talked in the drawing room, Morgan wrote an article up here; or flitted through; humble, deprecating, chubby like a child; but very observant. Tom's head is all breadth and bone compared with Morgan's. He still remains something of the schoolmaster, but I am not sure that he does not paint his lips. After Joyce, however, we came to ticklish matters – the Eliot fund; the upshot of it was that Tom won't leave the Bank under £500, and must have securities – not pledges. So next morning, when Ott's letter and circular arrived, aiming at £300, I had to wire to her to stop.

   For the rest the week-end was chilly and stormy. We had one blow on the hills. Tom left before dinner. Then we snuggled in, and Morgan became very familiar; anecdotic; simple; gossiping about friends and humming his little tunes. I was impressed by his complete modesty (founded perhaps on considerable self assurance). Compliments scarcely touch him. There is something too simple about him – for a writer perhaps – mystic, silly, but with a child's insight; oh yes, and something manly and definite too.

Wednesday 4 October
Our last whole day. From the weather point of view, the summer has been altogether disappointing. It has promised and then withheld. We have not had seven consecutive good days. Spiritually speaking, we have made some progress in Rodmell society. I was struck by the bloodlessness of philistines the other day at the Rectory. They seem far less alive than we intellectuals, so pale, so watery, so mild. I am a little uppish, though, and self assertive, because [Donald] Brace wrote to me yesterday 'We think *Jacob's Room* an extraordinarily distinguished and beautiful work, and we delight in publishing it' – or words to that effect. As this is my first testimony from an impartial person I am pleased.

Hogarth House, Richmond

Saturday 8 October
Back again, over the fire at Hogarth House. But the day has been spoilt for me – so strangely – by Kitty Maxse's death; and now I think of her lying in her grave at Gunby. I read it in the paper. I hadn't seen her since, I guess 1908. I could not have kept up with her; she never tried to see me. Yet, yet – these old friends dying without any notice on our part always – it begins to happen so often – saddens me: makes me feel guilty. I wish I'd met her in the street. My mind has gone back all day to her; in the queer way it does.

Saturday 14 October
Kitty fell, very mysteriously, over some bannisters. How did it happen? Some one presumably knows, and in time I shall hear. "It seems rather melancholy that it should come to an end like this" Nessa said; but she was putting Angelica to bed, and we could not dig in our past. I have seen Nessa, Maynard, Lydia [Lopokova], Desmond, Saxon, Lytton, Frankie Birrell and Margery Fry, all within this week; and had two letters, from Lytton and Carrington, about *Jacob's Room*; and here we are on the verge of publication. My sensations? – they remain calm. I want to be through the splash and swimming in calm water again. I want to be writing unobserved. *Mrs Dalloway* has branched into a book; and I adumbrate here a study of insanity and suicide: the world seen by the sane and the insane side by side – something like that; and to be more close to the fact than *Jacob*; but I think *Jacob* was a necessary step, for me, in working free.

Sunday 29 October
There was the *Times* review on Thursday – long, a little tepid, I think; saying that one can't make characters in this way; flattering enough. Of course, I had a letter from Morgan in the opposite sense – the letter I've liked best of all. We have sold 650, I think; and have ordered a second edition. My sensations? – as usual, mixed. I shall never write a book that is an entire success. This time the reviews are against me, and the private people enthusiastic. Either I am a great writer or a nincompoop. But I want to be quit of all this. I don't want to be totting up compliments, and comparing reviews. I want to think out *Mrs Dalloway*.

Our position becomes more and more complicated. Clearly we cannot go on publishing seriously with Ralph attached to us like a drone. At anyrate the labour and worry of getting out a long book makes me decided not to do it again on the present system. We have to go to Tidmarsh next week to explain the position. Carrington says that Lytton is most anxious for some arrangement, and the uncertainty is trying Ralph's nerves. Yet this nervous man makes no attempt to do the most ordinary things for us. L. has to tie parcels every morning. Ralph catches no earlier or later trains. Thursday morning he spent at the tailor's.

The election is beginning to roar in the newspapers. L. has a chance of getting in. We have bitten off a large piece of life – but why not?

Tuesday 7 November
We had a stormy week-end at Tidmarsh, and I'm afraid I have concluded that Ralph must go. His jealousy, and irrationality, combined with his fixed determination to make a permanent hobby out of what's a profession to us, make the position less and less possible. Yet, I am sorry, and like him, and the association. On the other hand what fun to spring off and make a good job of it! Suppose one could get a young man or woman of wits who would work violently and rashly.

Monday 13 November
Reviews are now favourable and utterly contradictory, as usual. I am quite able to write away without bother from self-consciousness, now; which shows that my splash is over. And now I have a multitude of pleasant jobs on hand, and am really very busy, and very happy, and only want to say Time, stand still here; which is not a thing that many women in Richmond would say I think. I walked in the Park, bought two wild duck and six snipe, all fresh and bleeding, just shot at Beaconsfield by two poachers I suspect. I paid eight and sixpence, thus introducing a good deal of stir in Hogarth House kitchen.

Monday 27 November
I need not say that my wild duck stank like old sea weed and had to be buried. But I cannot dally over this incident, which in tamer days might have provided some fun, because I have such a congeries of affairs to relate. There is the Press to be chronicled. At the Club we overheard one of those usual shabby, loose, cropheaded, small faced bright eyed young women [say] that she was tired of teaching and meant to become a printer. When she went into the writing room, I followed her, plucked her out, and revealed us to her as proprietors of the Hogarth Press. Yesterday she and 'a friend' came to tea. This friend we called mistakenly Jones; he being [C. E. M.] Joad, of the 1917 Club; a philosopher; a sturdy short man, with very bright round eyes, hair touched with grey, cocksure, reposing much weight upon the sterling quality of his intellect, and thus dispensing with the graces and amenities, as usual with sterling young men. He tipped one of my chairs on two legs, and ate a large tea, keeping close watch over Marjorie's interests at every point. For it

was evident that she was ready to bind herself hand and foot to us, and make fantastic promises. Still, she has been thoroughly educated, must earn her living, and has written, Joad says, a first rate novel. Well its not quite written, she said; being of course far more modest and less self confident than Cyril. "We are going to be married in February" she said. "And I mean to go on working after I'm married." I should say she is twenty-five or six; quick, impulsive, but with a steel thread in her from earning and learning, which is an invaluable property, and one that gives an edge to the rest. In short she might take us on and make a life work of it. Joad, who detests my books, may be an obstacle; since he may try to impose his literary views upon us; but I don't know. Moreover, we both liked him, and her too (but she was less self assertive, passed the cake, praised the dog, and sensitively appraised the situation with antennae quivering, woman like). We all kept our heads very creditably, insisted upon strict business dealings, and are to meet again on Sunday week. But where then does Ralph come in? He looks a little glum, and says very little.

Sunday 3 December
But these are historic days. The Hogarth Press is in travail. Heinemanns made us a most flattering offer – to the effect that we should give our brains and blood, and they would see to sales and ledgers. But we sniff patronage. If they gain, we lose. We have decided for freedom and a fight with great private glee. This brought on an argument with Ralph last Friday; he brought forth a plan obviously concocted at Tidmarsh, by which we are to become a company, Lytton, L. and I for partners, with Ralph remaining as he is. Lytton is said to hint a possibility that we should have all his work. At first tempting, this plan becomes to us less and less feasible. At this moment we incline to Miss [Marjorie] Thomson and freedom. Why, after all, should we conciliate Ralph? And is it not better to end this perpetual strain of friendship's burden – hurting Lytton's feelings that is, by failing to consider how fast poor Ralph's heart beats after a conversation with us? But there is a serious reason, and not mere restlessness, in our need for re-organisation. We are both giving all our spare time, and still there is far more work than we can do. At this rate, we have work for not three people but four or five or six.

This autumn has been perhaps the busiest of my dilatory life. People and books – I sing that to the tune of Women and Wine, which comes in *The Beggar's Opera*. I dined with Mary on Friday, met Clive and Aldous; Aldous very long, rather puffy, fat faced, white, with very thick hair, and canary coloured socks, is the raconteur; the young man of letters who sees life. We all said we despised reviewers and told little stories to our own advantage.

Friday 15 December

I have fifteen minutes before my solitary dinner, L. dining with Sangers, after a terrific Hogarth Press discussion ending in the final parting with Ralph. I am too muzzy headed to make out anything. This is partly the result of dining to meet the lovely gifted aristocratic Sackville-West last night at Clive's. Not much to my severer taste – florid, moustached, parakeet coloured, with all the supple ease of the aristocracy, but not the wit of the artist. She writes fifteen pages a day – has finished another book – publishes with Heinemanns – knows everyone. But could I ever know her? I am to dine there on Tuesday. The aristocratic manner is something like an actress's – no false shyness or modesty – makes me feel virgin, shy, and schoolgirlish. Yet after dinner I rapped out opinions. She is a grenadier; hard; handsome; manly; inclined to double chin. Dear old Desmond moped like a tipsy owl in his corner, affectionate and glad to talk to me, I think. He said something about the French admiring *Jacob*, and wishing to translate it.

As for Ralph – that question certainly can't be settled before L. comes in. Why did he make me, and L., so furious by saying, in his sulky schoolboy voice, that if this crisis hadn't happened, he would have had a nice surprise to offer us at Easter? – something of Lytton's presumably. I think the kernel of our discontent lies in that sentence. So far as I can see, Ralph's disappearance would leave us more freedom, but give us more work. We should have to make further arrangements. But the basis would be sound, which is the great thing. If we keep Ralph, there will be constant disease. I think by our own merits now we attract all the young.

1923

Virginia began the year in a mood of depression – dispelled for a moment by a grand and enjoyable fancy-dress party in Gordon Square – which persisted until the spring; it was caused in part by her continuing ill-health, and aggravated by financial anxieties. Leonard had been receiving a regular income from the Nation & Athenaeum; *the control of the paper now changed hands, Maynard Keynes becoming Chairman of the new board, and Leonard's future was uncertain. The burden of maintaining two houses, two servants, the Hogarth Press and its adherents, all weighed on Virginia, and she forced herself to take on more paid journalism and postpone work on the two books now occupying her thoughts – a collection of essays which became* The Common Reader, *and the development of her* Mrs Dalloway *stories into a full-length novel (which for a time she called* The Hours). *The constant presence in her house of Ralph Partridge – who did not leave until March – and the new assistant Marjorie Thomson, added to her discomfort. And the news of Katherine Mansfield's death in January intensified her feelings of uneasy dejection.*

The previous year Virginia had been involved in an abortive scheme to enable T. S. Eliot to leave his employment in a bank so that he might devote his energies to writing; now she saw an opportunity to further this aim by getting him appointed literary editor of the Nation *under its new management; but instead Leonard was offered the post; and the Woolfs set off at the end of March for a four-week holiday in Spain – their first foreign journey since their honeymoon – in a much happier frame of mind. They travelled via Paris and Madrid to the extreme south, where they stayed with Gerald Brenan – a friend of the Partridges – for a week.*

Back in Richmond, Virginia again responded to the allurements of social life; Vanessa was in Gordon Square; the indefatigable hostess Lady Sibyl Colefax began to invite Virginia to her luncheon parties; she attended the first performance of the Sitwells' Façade; *she spent a weekend at Garsington; and the inconvenience and limitations of living in the suburbs became an increasing source of discontent. But it was some months before she could get Leonard to concede that her health no longer warranted this exile, and agree to her looking for a house for them in Bloomsbury.*

In September the Woolfs interrupted their summer stay at Monks House and made their way to Studland in Dorset where Maynard Keynes had rented a house with his future wife, the Russian ballerina Lydia Lopokova. Here their fellow guests were two young men, Raymond Mortimer, a rising literary critic, and George (Dadie) Rylands, who the following year was to join the Hogarth Press for a while, and who became a great favourite with *Virginia*.

At *Monks House* and again in *Richmond* in the autumn, *Virginia* worked steadily at both her books, and at articles – the first version of her 'Mr Bennett and Mrs Brown' appeared in *New York* in November and was reprinted in the Nation & Athenaeum *in December. The Woolfs were at Monks House for ten days at Christmas; they spent a night at Charleston, and bored Vanessa with talk of the* Nation.

1923

HOGARTH HOUSE, RICHMOND

Tuesday 2 January

If I were a dissembler I should date this the last day of 1922. So it is to all
intents. We came back from Rodmell yesterday, and I am in one of my
moods, as the nurses used to call it, today. And what is it and why? A desire
for children, I suppose; for Nessa's life; for the sense of flowers breaking
all round me involuntarily. Here's Angelica – here's Quentin and Julian.
They make my life seem a little bare sometimes; and then my inveterate
romanticism suggests an image of forging ahead, alone, through the night;
of suffering inwardly, stoically; of blazing my way through to the end –
and so forth. The truth is that the sails flap about me for a day or two on
coming back. And it is all temporary: yes let me be quite clear about that.
Years and years ago, after the Lytton affair, I said to myself, walking up
the hill at Bayreuth, never pretend that the things you haven't got are not
worth having; good advice I think. And then I went on to say to myself
that one must like things for themselves; or rather, rid them of their bearing
upon one's personal life. One must venture on to the things that exist
independently of oneself. Now this is very hard for young women to do.
Yet I got satisfaction from it. And now, married to L., I never *have* to make
the effort. Perhaps I have been too happy for my soul's good? And does
some of my discontent come from feeling that? I could not stay at 46 [Gordon
Square] last night, because L. on the telephone expressed displeasure. Late
again. Very foolish. Your heart bad – and so my self reliance being sapped,
I had no courage to venture against his will. Then I react. Of course its a
difficult question. For undoubtedly I get headache or the jump in my heart;
and then this spoils his pleasure, and if one lives with a person, has one
the right – So it goes on.

Middle Age then. Let that be the text of my discourse. I'm afraid we're
becoming elderly. We are busy and attach importance to hours. I have my
correspondence to finish, says L. today. I don't laugh. But we must not let
our hobbies and pleasures become objects of fetish worship. L., I think,
suffers from his extreme clarity. He sees things so clear that he can't swim,

float and speculate. And now we have such a train attached to us that we have to go on. Nessa, though, who might so easily plead ties and circumstances, rides much more freely than we do. She will spend Easter travelling with the children, for instance. We have to make money – that is true. We have to have a house; two houses; two servants; a press; a Thomson; a Ralph. Yet most of this is for my sake; and am I honest in wishing it otherwise? I will leave it here, unfinished, a note of interrogation – signifying some mood that recurs, but is not often expressed.

Sunday 7 January

Let the scene open on the doorstep of number 50 Gordon Square. We went up last night, carrying our bags, and a Ceylonese sword. There was Mary Hutchinson in lemon coloured trousers with green ribbons. And so we sat down to dinner; off cold chicken. In came Roger and Adrian and Karin; and very slowly we coloured our faces and made ready for number 46. The drawing room was full, miscellaneous, and oriental for the most part. Suppose one's normal pulse to be 70: in five minutes it was 120; and the blood, not the sticky whitish fluid of daytime, but brilliant and prickling like champagne. This was my state, and most people's. We collided, when we met; went pop, used Christian names, flattered, praised, and thought (or I did) of Shakespeare. At any rate, I thought of him when the singing was doing – Shakespeare I thought would have liked us all tonight. Gumbo distorted nursery rhymes; Lydia [Lopokova] danced; there were charades; Sickert acted Hamlet. We were all easy and gifted and friendly and like good children rewarded by having the capacity for enjoying ourselves thus. I daresay no one said anything very brilliant. I sat by Sickert, and liked him, talking in his very workmanlike, but not at all society manner, of painting, and Whistler; of an operation he saw at Dieppe. There is something indescribably congenial to me in this easy artists' talk; the values the same as my own and therefore right; no impediments; life charming, good and interesting; no effort; art brooding calmly over it all; and none of this attachment to mundane things, which I find in Chelsea.

As parties do, this one began to dwindle, until a few persistent talkers were left by themselves. Lytton and I sat side by side on the sofa. "And what do you think of the Tidmarsh Press?" [he said]. And this was his crafty way of telling me that Ralph means to set up on his own, after the Hogarth model, after Easter. Lytton was anxious to sound me. Should we think it poaching? I said I should say sharp things, but there was quite enough work for two. But Lytton was not altogether urbane. He is possessive. His baby shall have his toy, and he shan't share it with anyone else this time. Well – so be it. Love is the devil. No character can stand against it. But this passed in our trivial champagne-pricking way. And so, at 3 I suppose, back to no. 50. And so we breakfasted together this morning, with the church bells ringing, and all the houses full of Stracheys, Grants, Stephens and Bells and Partridges – a wet grey morning, in the heart of London, where I am so seldom at that hour.

Tuesday 16 January
Katherine has been dead a week, and how far am I obeying her 'do not quite forget Katherine' which I read in one of her old letters? It is strange to trace the progress of one's feelings. Nelly said in her sensational way at breakfast on Friday "Mrs Murry's dead! It says so in the paper!" At that one feels – what? A shock of relief? – a rival the less? Then confusion at feeling so little – then, gradually, blankness and disappointment; then a depression which I could not rouse myself from all that day. When I began to write, it seemed to me there was no point in writing. Katherine won't read it. Katherine's my rival no longer. Then, as usual with me, visual impressions kept coming and coming before me – always of Katherine putting on a white wreath, and leaving us, called away; made dignified; chosen. And she was only thirty-three. And I could see her before me so exactly, and the room at Portland Villas. I go up. She gets up, very slowly, from her writing table. A glass of milk and a medicine bottle stood there. Everything was very tidy, bright, and somehow like a doll's house. She (it was summer) half lay on the sofa by the window. She had her look of a Japanese doll, with the fringe combed quite straight across her forehead. Sometimes we looked very steadfastly at each other, as though we had reached some durable relationship through the eyes. Hers were beautiful eyes – rather doglike, brown, very wide apart, with a steady slow rather faithful and sad expression. Her nose was sharp, and a little vulgar. Her lips thin and hard. She looked very ill – very drawn, and moved languidly, drawing herself across the room, like some suffering animal. I suppose I have written down some of the things we said. And then she was inscrutable. Did she care for me? Sometimes she would say so – would kiss me – would look at me as if (is this sentiment?) her eyes would like always to be faithful. She would promise never never to forget. That was what we said at the end of our last talk. She said she would send me her diary to read, and would write always. For our friendship was a real thing, we said. It would always go on whatever happened. What happened was, I suppose, faultfindings and perhaps gossip. The surroundings – Murry and so on – and the small lies and treacheries, the perpetual playing and teasing, cut away much of the substance of friendship. Yet I certainly expected that we should meet again next summer, and start fresh. And I was jealous of her writing – the only writing I have ever been jealous of. For two days I felt that I had grown middle aged, and lost some spur to write. That feeling is going. I no longer

keep seeing her with her wreath. I don't pity her so much. Yet I have the feeling that I shall think of her at intervals all through life. Probably we had something in common which I shall never find in anyone else. I think I never gave her credit for all her physical suffering and the effect it must have had in embittering her.

I have been in bed, 101, again.

Sunday 28 January
A certain melancholy has been brooding over me this fortnight. I date it from Katherine's death. The feeling so often comes to me now – Yes, go on writing of course but into emptiness. I'm cock – a lonely cock whose crowing nothing breaks – of my walk. However then I had my fever, and violent cold, was in and out of bed for a week. In casting accounts, never forget to begin with the state of the body.

We have now had Thomson twice – Marjorie I should and do call her, and she comes tomorrow full time. She has a little too much powder and scent for my taste, and drawls. In short she is not upper class. But she has honest intent eyes, and takes it seriously, which, as she is quite without training, is as well. My only fear is lest she should prove a flibbertigibbet. Her quickness of movement, keenness, and dependability are so far a great gain on Ralph. There he sits thick as an oak and as angular. We have heard no more of the Tidmarsh Press.

Much talk of the *Nation*, which, as I should have recorded, is sold to Maynard and a group, and our future once more quite uncertain.

Wednesday 7 February
Nessa's wedding day. Reflections suppressed. I must describe Cambridge. We walked from the station, cold, starry, dismal; then familiar; King's College Chapel; hasty wash and dress, and dine with [J. T.] Sheppard. He was in evening dress. A good deal of raw time had to be manufactured. I had romanced so much about Cambridge that to find myself sitting there was an anti-climax. Then off in the motor to the ADC [Theatre]. I think I was genuinely excited, rather than moved, by *Oedipus Rex*. The plot is so well tied; the story's race so fast. Then the young men's faces, pink and plump under their wigs, moved me. And so to bed; with King's bell saying very pompously all through the night the hour. We were happy and busy all Sunday, first Sheppard, then Pernel [Strachey]; sitting on the Backs, strolling up to Newnham, then lunching with the Shoves. So to the [G. E.] Moores. Then to Maynard's: I must say the pleasantest sitting room I have ever been in, owing to the colours and paintings, curtains and decorations of Bell and Grant. Here we dined well. The party began after a few brilliancies on my part about religion: emotional capital which I did not

know how to invest, I said. And Maynard kept the old ball smartly rolling. Indeed we were rather talk-dazed. And as people arrived, I suppose one's eyes tire; one's brain stales.

The depression which I mentioned comes partly from the uncertainty about the *Nation*. Leonard thinks himself a failure. And what use is there in denying a depression which is irrational? Can't I always think myself one too? And our depression comes too from the time of year, wet and wan, and from Thomson's drawling voice, and Ralph's stubbornness. I think Thomson and Ralph daily for lunch and tea, and the need for bright talk, depress also; and I shall be glad when the 15th March arrives.

Saturday 10 February
The omens are, I think, more favourable. Then we have £40 from income tax return – I seem to see a feather floating favourably from that region where the Gods abide. So I said as we walked in the cemetery this afternoon. It is now our plan (a day old) to walk from 2 to 3; print from 3 to 5; delay our tea; and so make headway. Ralph sticks on, defiant, argumentative, and gives one the lowest opinion of the manly virtues.

Monday 19 February
How it would interest me if this diary were ever to become a real diary: but then I should have to speak of the soul, and did I not banish the soul when I began? What happens is, as usual, that I'm going to write about the soul, and life breaks in. Talking of diaries sets me thinking of old Kate [Stephen], in the dining room of 4 Rosary Gardens; and how she opened the cabinet and there in a row on a shelf were her diaries from January 1, 1877; all the same to a t. And I made her read an entry; one of many thousand days, like pebbles on a beach: morning, evening, afternoon, without accent. Oh how strangely unaccented she is, sitting there all of a piece, with the mute sagacity of elephant or grey mare! Orderly solidity marked every atom there. The vases stood on mats: each was supplied with a tuft of mimosa and maidenhair. The Christmas cards – six – were ranged on the mantelpiece. Red tiles newly dusted. Green walls. Objects that came from India. And said Kate I intend to live to 1944 when I shall be eighty-four. And on her last day she will say to the charwoman who attends her, Bring me the diaries which you will find in the cabinet; and now, put them on the fire. I scarcely tried to disturb what had the sculptured classic appearance of alabaster fruit beneath glass.

In scribbling this, I am led away from my soul, which interests me nevertheless. For it is the soul I fancy that comments on visitors and reports their comments, and sometimes sets up such a to-do in the central departments of my machinery that the whole globe of me dwindles to a button head. I think this dwindling is often the result of talking to second rate people. They make the world pinchbeck.

We had a surprise visit from the Nicolsons. She [Vita] is a pronounced Sapphist, and may, thinks Ethel Sands, have an eye on me, old though I am. Snob as I am, I trace her passions five hundred years back, and they become romantic to me, like old yellow wine. Harold is simple downright bluff; wears short black coat and check trousers; wishes to be a writer, but is not I'm told and can believe, adapted by nature. Soul, you see, is framing all these judgments, and saying, this is not to my liking, this is second rate, this vulgar; this nice, sincere, and so on. My soul diminished, alas, as the evening wore on.

And we are still in suspense. Maynard is on the war path. And also I am trying to pull wires, to seat Tom at the *Nation* as literary editor. Yes, I am grown up. I give advice. I am a little bored indeed, and could wish that poor dear Tom had more spunk in him, less need to let drop by drop of his agonised perplexities fall ever so finely through pure cambric. One waits; sympathises; but it is dreary work.

Tuesday 6 March
Undoubtedly this has been a very unpleasant quarter. I date our misery from January 3rd. The main grievance has been this *Nation* affair, which hangs over us, lifting, then lowering, as it is at the present moment – low and black over our heads. On April 7th our income ceases; Maynard has made us no definite offer – but that I think is assured so far as L. goes. But that is only £120 p.a. and we shall have to scrape up the rest rather dismally, doing journalism, I suppose. But it is not the money trouble that worries us: but something psychological. The gloom is more on L.'s side than on mine. Mine is a gloom like a mist that comes and goes. I dip into different circles – and come home either exalted or depressed. Then the social question rises between L. and me. Are we becoming 'respectable'? Shall we dine with the [Bruce] Richmonds? L. says no. I regret it. Yes, somehow I regret it seriously, this shutting of the door upon suburban studies. I love the chatter and excitement of other people's houses. I want to make life fuller and fuller. Never mind, I say; once I get my claws into my writing and I'm safe. Eliot slightly disillusions me too; he is peevish, plaintive, egotistical; what it amounts to is that poverty is unbecoming.

Saturday 17 March
We now read plays at 46 [Gordon Square]. 46 is become a centre. For how long we don't know, as Maynard's marriage approaches. 46 has been very pleasant to me this winter. Two nights ago the Nicolsons dined there. Exposed to electric light eggs show dark patches. I mean we judged them

both incurably stupid. He is bluff, but oh so obvious; she, Duncan thought, took the cue from him, and had nothing free to say. There was Lytton, supple and subtle as an old leather glove, to emphasise their stiffness. It was a rocky steep evening.

And then? Ralph is gone, casually, without good bye. I have seen Osbert Sitwell, Sebastian Sprott and Mr [Raymond] Mortimer. As Nessa says, we are becoming fashionable.

Friday 23 March
L. has just come in with an offer from Maynard of the literary editorship of the *Nation*. Well, that's unexpected. Here have I been toiling these three weeks to make Eliot take it; finally he shied; and this is the result. No doubt there are drawbacks, but it means safety for the moment, indeed luxury. And to me it opens interesting vistas – but here I am with the typhoid germs and can't write.

*   *   *

Friday 11 May
The long break deserves a line, since I shall scarcely commemorate it otherwise. Have I not, with infinite labour, written for the first number of the *Nation* 'To Spain'? Am I not sitting waiting for L. to 'come back from the office' like other wives? It annoys me to be like other wives. Ah there he is! No: damn it; only Nelly gone out. As I say, I cannot go into the journey, Spain, Paris, et cetera. I stayed in Paris by way of facing life. I meant to use this diary to pull myself up from a fortnight's debauch of journalism, *Nation*'s affairs, and so on. So far we don't feel the *Nation* blood of our blood. It may turn that way. We work very hard at it. It has temptations and attractions. I like having the pick of new books. People crowd and press for work. It is mildly amusing to say, now don't worry, I'm not going to give you any. I have been so often in their position. But these delights are not very profound.

Sunday 13 May
Karin was here yesterday. Adrian is altogether broken up by psychoanalysis. His soul rent in pieces with a view to reconstruction. The doctor says he is a tragedy: and this tragedy consists in the fact that he can't enjoy life with zest. I am probably responsible. I should have paired with him instead of hanging on to the elders. Karin says we shall see a great change in three months. For my part, I doubt if family life has all the power of evil attributed to it, or psycho-analysis of good.

Morgan told me that when he and Mortimer discussed novelists the other day they agreed that Lawrence and I were the only two whose future interested them. They think of my next book, which I think of calling *The Hours*, with excitement. This does encourage me.

Monday 4 June

But I cannot describe Garsington. Thirty-seven people to tea; a bunch of young men no bigger than asparagus; walking to and fro, round and round; compliments, attentions, and then this slippery mud – which is what interests me at the moment. A loathing overcomes me of human beings – their insincerity; their vanity – A wearisome and rather defiling talk with Ott last night is the foundation of this complaint – and then the blend in one's own mind of suavity and sweetness with contempt and bitterness. Her egotism is so great. Yet on Saturday night I liked her. Lord David [Cecil] is a pretty boy. Puffin [Anthony] Asquith an ugly one – wizened, unimpressive, sharp, like a street boy. [Edward] Sackville-West reminded me of a peevish shop girl. They have all the same clipped quick speech and politeness, and total insignificance. What puts me on edge is that I'm writing like this here, and spoke so differently to Ott. I'm over peevish in private, partly in order to assert myself. I am a great deal interested suddenly in my book. I want to bring in the despicableness of people like Ott; I want to give the slipperiness of the soul. I have been too tolerant often.

And then there was Mrs Asquith. I was impressed. She is stone white; with the brown veiled eyes of an aged falcon; and in them more depth and scrutiny than I expected; a character, with her friendliness, and ease, and decision. Oh if we could have had Shelley's poems, and not Shelley the man! she said. Shelley was quite intolerable, she pronounced; she is a rigid frigid puritan; and in spite of spending thousands on dress. She rides life, if you like; and has picked up a thing or two, which I should like to plunder and never shall.

Wednesday 13 June

Nessa is back and the London season of course in full swing. So I judged yesterday in the Æolian Hall, listening, in a dazed way, to Edith Sitwell vociferating through the megaphone. There was Lady Colefax in her hat with the green ribbons. Did I say that I lunched with her last week? That was Derby Day and it rained, and all the light was brown and cold, and she went on talking talking, in consecutive sentences like the shavings that come from planes, artificial, but unbroken. It was not a successful party, Clive and Lytton and me.

I should be describing Edith Sitwell's poems [*Façade*], but I kept saying to myself 'I don't really understand ... I don't really admire.' The only view, presentable view that I framed, was to the effect that she was monotonous. She has one tune only on her merry go round. And she makes her verse keep step accurately to the Hornpipe. This seems to be wrong.

Tuesday 19 June

I took up this book with a kind of idea that I might say something about my writing – which was prompted by glancing at what Katherine Mansfield said about *her* writing in *The Dove's Nest*. But I only glanced. She said a good deal about feeling things deeply; also about being pure, which I won't criticise, though of course I very well could. But now what do I feel about *my* writing? – this book, that is, *The Hours*, if that's its name? One must write from deep feeling, said Dostoevsky. And do I? Or do I fabricate with words, loving them as I do? No I think not. In this book I have almost too many ideas. I want to give life and death, sanity and insanity; I want to criticise the social system, and to show it at work, at its most intense – But here I may be posing. Am I writing *The Hours* from deep emotion? Of course the mad part tries me so much, making my mind squint so badly that I can hardly face spending the next weeks at it.

One thing I do feel pretty certain about and here confide it to my diary – we must leave Richmond and set up in London. The arguments are so well known to me that I can't bother to write them down. Leonard remains to be converted, and my God, the move – the horror – the servants. Still this is life – never to be sitting down for longer than one feels inclined.

Thursday 28 June

This may be life; but I doubt that I shall ever convert L. and now sit down baffled and depressed to face a life spent, mute and mitigated, in the suburbs, just as I had it in mind that I could at last go full speed ahead. For the capacities in me will never, after forty, accumulate again. And I mind missing life far more than he does, for it isn't life to him in the sense that it is life to me. But half the horror is that L. instead of being, as I gathered, sympathetic, has the old rigid obstacle – my health. And I can't sacrifice his peace of mind, yet the obstacle is surely now a dead hand, which one should no longer let dominate our short years of life – oh to dwindle them out here, with all these gaps, and abbreviations! Always to catch trains, always to waste time, to sit here and wait for Leonard to come in, to spend hours standing at the box of type with Marjorie, to wonder what its all for – when, alternatively, I might go and hear a tune, or have a look at a picture, or find out something at the British Museum, or go adventuring among human beings. Sometimes I should merely walk down Cheapside. But now I'm tied, imprisoned, inhibited. All I can do is to pretend I'm writing something very important, or reading with a view to a book I shall never write. This is the pith of my complaint. For ever to be suburban. L. I don't think minds any of this as much as I do. But then, Lord! what I owe to him! What he gives me! Still, I say, surely we could get more from life than we do – isn't he too much of a Puritan, of a disciplinarian, doesn't he through birth and training accept a drastic discipline with too Spartan a self control? There is, I suppose, a very different element in us; my social side, his intellectual side. This social side is very genuine in me. Nor do I think it reprehensible. It is a piece of jewellery I inherit from my mother – a joy in laughter, something that is stimulated by contact with my friends. Moreover, for my work now, I want freer intercourse, wider intercourse – and now, at forty-one, having done a little work, I get my wages partly in invitations. I might know people. In Richmond this is impossible. Either we have arduous parties at long intervals, or I make my frenzied dashes up to London, and leave, guiltily, as the clock strikes 11.

Saturday 8 July
It is now the hottest day of the year, and I don't want to grumble; having seen many people – Anyhow, if a move is to be made, it can't be till the autumn, or new year. Anyhow, I am content at present, or moderately so. I can't help thinking myself about as successful journalistically as any woman of my day. But that is not saying much. I wish I could write *The Hours* as freely and vigorously as I scribble *Freshwater, a Comedy*. Its a strange thing how arduous I find my novels; and yet *Freshwater* is only spirited fun; and *The Hours* has some serious merit. By the way, on re-reading this book I resolved to write rather more carefully, and to record conversations verbatim. It is difficult to write carefully, as I am always having at this book by way of killing time, filling time, or writing out the fidgets. As for recording conversations, nothing is harder.

Sunday 22 July
A great many conversations to record: dined with [Raymond] Mortimer and Scofield Thayer the other night and went on with them to Mary's. Mortimer is Oxford; he is all angle and polish. Wears a swallow tail white waistcoat; wants brilliancy not intimacy, is half a dandy. Scofield Thayer was a cautious hardheaded American, edited the *Dial*. Like Mortimer he buys modern pictures. But the talk was too formal and too conventional to bear writing out; or I can't do it. A good account of flying from Thayer: "The pilot said he wouldn't start. The company had sold three seats instead of two. But I had taken my passage ten days before. I wouldn't budge. Some luggage was left. One man took his dachs. But we felt overweighted. Then we got above a storm. One leant over and saw the lightning dashing up at one's face. It was terrible. I looked at my feet. One man kept going to the side and being sick. The other kept saying It is bad It is bad. And

we all knew we were overweighted. Suddenly the engines stopped. We pitched up and down. We expected the whole thing to crash. The dog sat quite calm. Then after ten minutes the engine began again. Towns looked like the handle of that salt cellar. Never again, no. And the pilot said he'd been guiding with one hand and fumbling with the other and suddenly touched the right spring by chance, and the engine started. But we might just as well have dashed to the ground."

Friday 28 July

These days before going, as we do on Wednesday, are too dissipated for serious reading writing living or thinking. This half year has kept me on the hop. I like that; agitating though it is. I've taken my fences, as I say, and got some good gallops for my trouble. Never settle, is my principle in life; and I try to put it in practice, but in talk more than in action I daresay. My theory is that at forty one either increases the pace or slows down. Needless to say which I desire. But, to be just, my activity is also mental. I'm working variously and with intention. And I'm going to work hard, hard, hard, in every sense at Rodmell. Also I shall explore – take a motor bus ride along the downs one day – see Steyning and Arundel and so on.

Monks House, Rodmell

Monday 6 August

I have ruined my morning's work by making bread and buns, which require constant voyages to the kitchen. We went over to Charleston yesterday. Although thinking quite well of ourselves, we were not well received by the painters. There they sat like assiduous children at a task in a bedroom – Roger, Nessa, and Duncan; Roger on chair in foreground; Nessa on sofa, Duncan on bed. In front of them was one jar of flowers, and one arrangement of still life. Roger was picking out his blue flower very brightly. For some reason, the talk was not entirely congenial. Clive was sitting in the drawing room window reading Dryden. Hollyhocks, decapitated, swam in a bowl; there was a loaf for tea, and a long slab of cake. Roger, I can't help think-ing, has become a little querulous with years. His grievances torment him; he talks of them too much. After tea, Angelica had her dolls' tea party in the window, and beat Clive, and when he cried, ran of her own accord and picked him a flower – which was a sensible womanly act. She is sensitive – minds being laughed at (as I do). "Don't laugh at me" she said, petulantly, to Roger.

Saturday 29 August

I've been battling for ever so long with *The Hours*, which is proving one of my most tantalising and refractory of books. Parts are so bad, parts so good. I'm much interested; can't stop making it up yet – yet. What is the matter with it?

Clive has an egg – a turkey's egg – for a head now – quite bald; never a hair will grow any more. Mary was shrinking, childlike, not attending when I read my play, but very anxious to say the right thing. Chocolates she brought; she wore tight grey Alpaca, with large buttons, and she powdered and re-powdered in the drawing room. Going to the dogs was discussed.

Thursday 30 August

My goodness, the wind! Last night we looked at the meadow trees, flinging about, and such a weight of leaves that every brandish seems the end. I read such a white dimity rice puddingy chapter of Mrs Gaskell at midnight in the gale, *Wives and Daughters* – I think it must be better than *Old Wives' Tale* all the same.

Wednesday 5 September

Our week end was Francis Birrell and Raymond Mortimer. Frankie spills out the whole contents of his head like a nice little boy; never stops talking. Mortimer is a curious half breed. An Oxford young man, inclined to smartness, dress and culture. His soul is uneasy in Cambridge company. He flatters. He is not very simple, candid or talkative, like chatterbox Frankie who is as open as daylight. "My father is a solicitor – lives at Exmouth, and has really been a bachelor since the death of my mother. She died when I was quite small. No I don't mind being an only child at all. I am quite happy. If I had two thousand a year, I should never write. I should buy pictures and travel." We discussed writing novels on Asheham Hill. But he can't write novels himself. Doesn't see why he should; has no originality. Likes pictures perhaps best, because there's Picasso in painting and no one to match him in writing. At the same time we were talking about Clive Bell who had been to luncheon, talking a great deal. "He seems to me a perfectly happy and developed man, and he enjoys life too." Then Vanessa: "She has such a lovely voice, and then she's very lovely to look at. Her personality too is very impressive," he said. In short "You can't imagine what it has been to me getting to know Bloomsbury. They're different human beings from any I thought possible."

I began for the fifth but last time, I swear, what is now to be called *The Common Reader*, and did the first page quite moderately well this morning.

Tuesday 11 September

Here we are back from 'The Knoll', Studland. It was reckoned that we could have got to France in less time. I wanted to observe Lydia as a type for Rezia; and did observe one or two facts. It was very hot at Lulworth, and we sat with the sun in our eyes on a verandah having tea. Suddenly she got cross, frowned, complained of the heat, seemed about to cry, precisely like a child of six. She was concerned to know what Leonard meant by coupling her with me among the 'sillies'. "It means that you can both be beaten," Maynard said. Maynard is grown very gross and stout, especially when he wraps his leopard-spotted dressing-gown tight round his knees and stands in front of the fire. He has a queer swollen eel-like look, not very pleasant. But his eyes are remarkable, and as I truly said when he gave me some pages of his new book to read, the process of mind there displayed is as far ahead of me as Shakespeare's. True, I don't respect it so much. The poet Rylands was there and Mortimer. Dadie's hair (he became Dadie at 10 a.m. Monday at Poole Station) is precisely the colour and consistency of the husk of straw. Add to this a blue cornflower coloured tweed suit, his apple red face, and blue eyes and you have – well, merely a cornflower to me, but to Raymond the most intoxicatingly beautiful young man that it is possible to imagine. We motored to Lulworth on Sunday, or rather to Warbarrow, which we climbed and walked five miles over the down. My shoes interfered with my pleasure rather. But I thought of the year 1830, and how most of England then looked as this coast looked, bays with their sweep untenanted, only coast guards and grey cottages, and rowing boats making off to little ships. And then I caught a view or two which I've no doubt will keep for some years and then be used. The clear water was very moving to me, with the pale stones showing under it like jelly fish. Lulworth of course was all skittles. Then we stopped, Maynard liking I think to be showman, at Bindon Abbey, having just before seen the old Manor house where Tess [of the D'Urbervilles] slept, or lived. At Bindon Lydia lay in her pink jacket with the white fur in a Bishop's tomb – a kind of shaped tank sunk in the earth on the way up to the Calvary. She lay quite still, acting death, her muscular dancer's legs in white silk stockings lying with the soles of the feet touching, and Maynard and I standing by. What did she think about? About Maynard, and her death, and what would happen before? Heaven knows. We sat on the mound of the Calvary, and Maynard talked about palaeolithic man. To return: – Dadie has an ingratiating manner of pawing ladies old enough to be his mother. He threw out an idea that he might join the Press. The printing mania has come upon him. He asked lightly, for he is not emphatic and very happy I should think, with all his interests and successes, and no inhibitions and good health, and money in prospect, and an editor to print his poems, and a year more at Cambridge, and a possible fellowship and so forth – he asked lightly whether he might lodge with us in the holidays, and pay his way by working the press. So you see how the future branches and extends: I mean there are ways down the forest; roads leading to right and left hitherto unseen.

Tuesday 18 September
Leonard's day in London, and before I walk off to meet him I may as well write here. We have had visitors – Lytton and the Partridges, unexpectedly; then Nessa and Duncan; then Morgan for the week-end. There are times when I want no one, times when I relish the commonest animated slug. I am worn smooth with talk at the moment. Yet how good, kind, tender, and clever we all are! Not much talk of interest with Lytton. He pounced on our books. Oh books, books! he cried. Fame has made him confident, taken from him I suppose some charm, turned it to strength of some kind. Very well. We all grow old; grow stocky; lose our pliancy and impressionability. Even Morgan seems to me to be based on some hidden rock. Talking of Proust and Lawrence he said he'd prefer to be Lawrence; but much rather would be himself. He is aloof, serene, a snob, he says, reading masterpieces only. We had a long gossip about servants. But it grows cold and dark; I shall walk off to meet L.

HOGARTH HOUSE, RICHMOND

Monday 15 October
This last entry seems long ago. And I meant to record for psychological purposes that strange night when I went to meet Leonard and did not meet him. What an intensity of feeling was pressed into those hours! It was a wet windy night; and as I walked back across the field I said Now I am meeting it; now the old devil has once more got his spine through the waves. And such was the strength of my feeling that I became physically rigid. And there was something noble in feeling like this; tragic, not at all petty. Then cold white lights went over the fields; and went out; and I stood under the great trees waiting for the lights of the bus. And that went by; and I felt lonelier. But I could control all this, until, suddenly, after the last likely train had come in I felt it was intolerable to sit about, and must do the final thing, which was to go to London. Off I rode, without much time, against such a wind; and again I had a satisfaction in being matched with powerful things, like wind and dark. I battled, had to walk; got on; drove ahead; dropped the torch; picked it up, and so on again without any lights. Saw men and women walking together; thought, you're safe and

happy and I'm an outcast; took my ticket; had three minutes to spare, and then, turning the corner of the station stairs, saw Leonard, coming along, walking very quick, in his mackintosh. He was rather cold and angry (as perhaps was natural). And then, not to show my feelings, I went outside and did something to my bicycle. Also I went back to the ticket office, and said to the humane man there, "It's all right. My husband caught the last train. Give me back my fare", which he did. And I got the money more to set myself right with Leonard than because I wanted it. All the way back we talked about a row at the office; and all the time I was feeling My God, that's over. I'm out of that. Its over. Really, it was a physical feeling, of lightness and relief and safety. And yet there was too something terrible behind it – the fact of this pain, I suppose; which continued for several days. I think I should feel it again if I went over that road at night. But I have not got it all in, by any means.

My first activity has been to see houses. So far I have seen the outsides of two. And the problem is a difficult one. Its my wish to live in London, no one else's. How far can this wish bear the weight of the removal, the expense, the less pleasant surroundings, and so on? Here we are tight wedged in printing and editing. And we have Dadie in prospect. This young man with hair like the husk of corn, says he wishes to devote his life to the Hogarth Press, and is writing to that effect to Leonard. This will begin in June. He shall be a partner, and take over the work; and we shall supervise, and by degrees it will become more and more important, and we shall be the benefactors of our age; and have a shop, and enjoy the society of the young, and rummage and splash in the great bran pie, and so never, never stop working with brains or fingers or toes till our limbs fly asunder and the heart sprays off into dust. Such is my fancy picture.

Saturday 3 November

And now I've found a house: 35 Woburn Square. Yes, shall I write that address often? Certainly I hope to. For me it would be worth £500 a year in pleasure. Think of the music I could hear, the people I could see, easily, unthinkingly? And then comes before me the prospect of walking through the city streets; starting off early and walking say to Wapping. Why this so obsesses my mind I don't know. But I have wasted my time drawing a plan of 35 on the opposite page. Nothing runs away with time like these house dreams. I must read Sophocles. After twenty years I now know how to read Greek quick (with a crib in one hand) and with pleasure. This is for the eternal book. And my mind whips off to rents – how much can we ask for this house? I'm heartless about poor old Hogarth, where for nine years we have been so secure.

Friday 16 November

No we didn't take 35 Woburn Square, and the colour has gone out of it, and I don't want to write about it at the moment. I'm back from lunch [with] Lady Colefax and in rather a fritter, too much so to read Euripides. Indeed, I've been talking to Hugh Walpole – not an impressive man – a man who protests too much; an uneasy, prosperous, vain man, who harbours some grudge against clever intellectuals and yet respects them, would like to be one. He has the look of a kindly solicitor or banker; red cheeks; very small bright eyes; a genial, but not profound or cordial manner. An uninteresting mind, and really not able to cast a shadow even upon me. I did not feel knocked over, dashed to pieces, or anything very vividly, except that he was slightly in awe of me. As for Lady Colefax, there she sits painted and emphatic at the head of her table, broad cheeked, a little coarse, kindly, glass-eyed, affectionate to me almost, capable, apparently disinterested – I mean if she likes to listen to clever talk and buy it with a lunch of four courses and good wine, I see no harm in it. Its a taste, not a vice. Off we streamed at 3.

So to the Tate with Lytton. Lytton and I don't need much preliminary. "Here's my book – *Queen Victoria* – in French. I daresay it reads better in French." He has almost bought a house near Hungerford, in the downs. There are no drains and no water. Still I advised the leap, as I always advise leaps. And then there was [Boris] Anrep, and his tinted [Blake mosaic] floor, all raying out in greens and browns, like the waves of a sea; not a good metaphor, for it is really very compact, strong, and contained. Droves of schoolchildren kept sweeping over it. He explained it to me, smelling rather too much of whisky.

Monday 3 December

Back from Rodmell; unable to settle in; therefore I write diary. An odd psychological fact – that I can write when I'm too jangled to read. Moreover, I want to leave as few pages blank as possible; and the end of the year is only some three weeks off. Oh there's Adrian's catastrophe to record – now two weeks old. Nessa rang me up in the middle of dinner with Tom here. "Adrian and Karin are going to separate." You could have knocked me down with a feather. The devoted and inseparable couple! They'd been unhappy for years. They hadn't quarrelled. Nessa says, and Clive says, that Karin did it. She felt all I used to feel: the snub; the check; the rebuke; the fastidiousness; the lethargy. Poor old Adrian; undoubtedly the *DNB* crushed his life out before he was born. It gave me a twist of the head too. I shouldn't have been so clever, but I should have been more stable, without that contribution to the history of England.

Wednesday 19 December

I don't know if this is my last chance of writing. I am so stifled with work of all sorts, society of all sorts, and plans of all sorts, that I can't pour a pure stream from my tap. I must briefly touch on Dadie; house problem not settled; Maynard threatening to cut down reviews; Leonard at this moment threatening to resign; publishing, writing, doing Hardy and Montaigne and the Greeks and the Elizabethans and *The Hours*; accepted in America, neglected by all prize givers, very happy, very much on the go – that's my state, at the moment of writing, 6.14 p.m. on Wednesday aforesaid.

1924

On returning to Richmond from Monks House at the New Year, Virginia lost no time in pressing on with her plan to move into London, and by 9 January she had found her house – 52 Tavistock Square, Bloomsbury, on which, after the usual agitations, the Woolfs secured a ten-year lease from the Bedford Estate. In spite of Leonard's reservations, the problem of the servants, and all the practical dispositions to be made, Virginia's determination carried them forward, and the move took place on 13 March. In the meantime she still found time for some social distractions, including meeting Arnold Bennett and enjoying another encounter with the philosopher Bertrand Russell, who had been her sister-in-law Karin Stephen's tutor at Cambridge. At a farewell dinner given by the Nation to the poet Edmund Blunden, Virginia talked to Katherine Mansfield's widower Middleton Murry, and confirmed her low opinion of his character.

Installed in their new home on the top two floors of 52 Tavistock Square, Virginia felt herself at the hub of her world: Vanessa round the corner in Gordon Square; friends at hand to come or to go to; concerts, theatres, films within easy reach; and in the basement the busy life of the Hogarth Press, with Marjorie Thomson at work, Dadie Rylands coming as potential manager, and manuscripts pouring in. They published fourteen books this year, including small paper-bound works by Eliot, Roger Fry, E. M. Forster, Robert Graves and Virginia herself; and the first volumes of the Collected Papers of Sigmund Freud, Leonard having secured the English rights to the publications of the International Psycho-Analytical Library. Notwithstanding the increased bustle of her life, Virginia managed to write a great deal of journalism, largely unsigned contributions to the Nation; and in October, she records that she had finished Mrs Dalloway, which she had worked at steadily since moving house.

The Woolfs were at Monks House for Easter; in May they stayed with Lytton Strachey and attendant Partridges at Tidmarsh, and later in the year at Lytton's new home, Ham Spray House in Wiltshire; they went to Cambridge, where Virginia read a paper, 'Character in Fiction', to the Society of Heretics; in July they were at Garsington.

Although after first meeting Harold Nicolson and his wife Vita Sackville-West at Clive Bell's and on one or two further occasions Virginia had decided that they were both incurably stupid, the acquaintance was fostered by Vita, who in July this year invited Virginia to lunch with her father Lord Sackville at Knole, his vast baronial *mansion in Kent, and then to her own home, Long Barn, nearby. Virginia's imagination was stirred by the visit and her hostess, who was to become her most beloved woman friend. Vita came for a night to Monks House in September, overaweing Nelly by her rank, and making Virginia very conscious of the shabby imperfections of her own and Vanessa's cherished homes. But the initial benefit of this relationship was to the Hogarth Press, who published Vita's* Seducers in Ecuador *(dedicated to Virginia), and were to become her main publishers for many years to come.*

By the end of the year Dadie Rylands had decided that the life of a printer and publisher was not for him, and proposed a Cambridge friend, Angus Davidson, to succeed him, which he did on 10 December; he spent Christmas with the Woolfs at Monks House.

1924

HOGARTH HOUSE, RICHMOND

Thursday 3 January

This year is almost certainly bound to be the most eventful in the whole of our (recorded) career. Tomorrow I go up to London to look for houses; on Saturday I deliver sentence of death upon Nelly and Lottie; at Easter we leave Hogarth; in June Dadie comes to live with us; and our domestic establishment is entirely controlled by one woman, a vacuum cleaner, and electric stoves. Now how much of this is dream, and how much reality? I should like, very much, to turn to the last page of this virgin volume and there find my dreams true. It rests with me to substantiate them between now and then.

Wednesday 9 January

At this very moment, or fifteen minutes ago to be precise, I bought the ten years' lease of 52 Tavistock Square, London WC1. Subject of course to the lease, and to Providence, the house is ours; and the basement, and the billiard room, with the rock garden on top, and the view of the Square in front and the desolated buildings behind, and Southampton Row, and the whole of London – London thou art a jewel of jewels, and jasper of jocunditie – music, talk, friendship, city views, books, publishing, all this is now within my reach, as it hasn't been since August 1913, when we left Clifford's Inn for a series of catastrophes which very nearly ended my life, and would, I'm vain enough to think, have ruined Leonard's. So I ought to be grateful to Richmond and Hogarth, and indeed, I am grateful. Nowhere else could we have started the Hogarth Press, whose very awkward beginning had rise in this very room. Here that strange offspring grew and throve; it ousted us from the dining room, which is now a dusty coffin; and crept all over the house. And people have been here, thousands of them it seems to me. I've sat over this fire many an evening talking, and save for one fit of the glooms last summer, have never complained of Richmond, till I shed it, like a loose skin. I've had some very curious visions in this room too, lying in bed, mad, and seeing the sunlight quivering like gold

175

water on the wall. I've heard the voices of the dead here. And felt, through it all, exquisitely happy.

Saturday 12 January
Nelly has agreed to stay on alone as a general; and I am to find Lottie a place in Gordon Square. I see difficulty upon difficulty ahead. None of this would much matter if L. were happy; but with him despondent or grim, the wind is taken out of my sails, and I say, what's it all for? Its odd how entirely this house question absorbs one. It is a radical change, though. It means a revision of four lives. Yet for people of our age, which is in full summer, to dread risk and responsibility seems pusillanimous. We have no children to consider. My health is as good as it will be in this world, and a great deal better than it ever has been. The next ten years must see the press into fame or bankruptcy; to loiter on here is a handicap. But I've gone through all these matters time and time again, and wish I could think of something else. I've so much work on hand. Its odd how unimportant my work seems, suddenly, when a practical matter like this blocks the way.

Sunday 20 January
No final news of Tavistock Square yet. Here we are, going through a time of waiting. I shall be happy so soon as my claws are into the move. At present, I feel Oh God another journey? Must I go up by train? Where am I to change before dinner tomorrow, and so on.

Wednesday 23 January
And on Monday if I'd written here I should have had to say 'we have lost Tavistock Square'. It was a very unpleasant shock, and for my part I don't think we could easily have got over it. But my house finding genius was outraged; what's the good of me, it asked, if you let these sharpers trick you? And I warn you, 52 is your house. So, practically not only spiritually speaking it now is. I visited the office with cheque and signature before one today; and then spent a shilling on a plate of beef. Ah well! Now I can sigh contented over my fire, in spite of the rain, and the [rail] strike, and Lady Colefax and Ethel Sands, and all cares and sorrows and perplexities.

I have seen Roger; seen his pictures, which with the irrepressible vanity of the artist, he makes even the blind like me report on, by electric light, in a hurry. But enough of that; in every other way he abounds; cut him wherever you like, and the juice wells up. Lytton has bought his house. But now I am going to write till we move – six weeks straight ahead. A letter from Morgan today saying 'To whom first but you and Virginia should I tell the fact that I've put the last words to my novel [*A Passage to India*]?' He is moved, as I am always on these occasions.

Sunday 3 February

I didn't write however, because L. started the 'flu, the very next day, and gave me an unpleasant day; but there's an odd pleasure too, purely feminine I suppose, in 'looking after', being wanted; giving up my pen, and sitting with an invalid. But he was up in four days or less; and here we are, on the rails again, a very lovely spring day, which, by Heaven's grace, we have spent alone. No servants at the moment; no callers. The sun laid gold leaf over the trees and chimneys today. The willows on the bank were soft, yellow, plumy, like a cloud; like an infinitely fine spray. I reflect that I shan't be walking here again next spring. I am not sentimental about it: Tavistock Square with the pale tower is more beautiful I think, let alone the adorable omnibuses.

Owing to the influenza, I don't think I have seen more than a handful; went to Ethel Sands's; talked to Arnold Bennett, a loveable sea lion, with chocolate eyes, drooping lids, and a protruding tusk. He has an odd accent; a queer manner; is provincial; very much a character. I suspect he minds things, even my pinpricks. He is slow, kind, affectionate, hauls himself along a sofa.

Nelly went to the flat with me, and next day wrote out a time table, to show that by 3 p.m. she would still have to wash up luncheon and do Leonard's boots. Very well, I said, find a place with Lottie. But the end of a week's consideration is, apparently, that Nelly clings to us. The money is paid over, and the house presumably ours tomorrow. So I shall have a room of my own to sit down in, after almost ten years, in London.

Saturday 9 February

We have been measuring the flat. Now the question arises Is it noisy? No need to go into my broodings over that point. Fitzroy Square rubbed a nerve bare which will never sleep again while an omnibus is in the neighbourhood. My feeling about this move is that we're doing the courageous thing.

Morgan was here last night; *A Passage to India* done; and he is much excited, on the boil with it, consulting L. about terms; has been offered £750. So *he's* all right. Marjorie has put earrings in her ears and left Joad. Poor chit! At twenty-four. I was at Fitzroy then, and devilish unhappy too. I'm working at *The Hours*, and think it a very interesting attempt. (And its just as noisy here, if one listens, as it can possibly be in Tavistock Square. One gets into a habit of not listening. Remember this sage advice.) Karin has been confiding. Adrian wants to come back.

Saturday 23 February

Really I've a thousand things to do. I've just said to L. I'm so busy I can't begin, which unfortunately is too true of me. Then I bethink me that with life in its present rush, I may never again write a word of this book at Hogarth House, and so should take a few minutes to lay the sod, or whatever the expression is. Its very cold, barbarous weather. Twice we have meant to go to Rodmell and failed. Warmth is the one need I have. May's will move us on March 13th for fifteen pounds. I am going to force L. into the outrageous extravagance of spending twenty-five pounds on painted panels, by Bell and Grant. We are trying to hook together all the resources of civilisation – telephone, gas, electric light, and, at this distance, naturally find it arduous. The electric light man doesn't turn up. Lottie is going to Karin – I fancy I have forgotten that item. All could not have fallen out better, so far, I say, being by no means ready to bait the deity, who can always show his claws. That reminds me of the celebrated Mr [Bertrand] Russell the other night at Karin's. (She gives her weekly party in the great gay drawing room [at 50 Gordon Square] which is nevertheless a little echoing and lofty and very very chill.) He said "Just as I saw a chance of happiness, the doctors said I had got cancer. My first thought was that was one up to God. When I was getting better – I had very nearly died – the thing I liked was the sun: I thought how nice to feel the sun and the rain still. People came a long way after that. The old poets were right. They made people think of death as going where they could not see the sun. I have become an optimist. I realise now that I like life – I want to live. Before that illness, I thought life was bad." So to Charlie Sanger, who is good all through; and then on to [G. E.] Moore: "When he first came up to Cambridge, he was the most wonderful creature in the whole world. His smile was the most beautiful thing I have ever seen. I said to him once, Moore, have you ever told a lie? 'Yes' he said – which was the only lie he ever told." I asked him, as I ask everyone, to write his life for the press. "But my mind is absolutely relevant. I can't ramble. I stick to facts." "Facts are what we want. Now the colour of your mother's hair?" "She died when I was two – there you are, relevant facts. I remember my grandfather's death, and crying, and then thinking it was over. I saw my brother drive up in the afternoon. Hooray! I cried. They told me I must not say hooray at all that day." He had no one to play with. One does not like him. Yet he is brilliant of course; perfectly outspoken; familiar; talks of his bowels; likes people; and yet and yet – He disapproves of me perhaps? This luminous vigorous mind seems attached to a flimsy little car, like that on a large glinting balloon. And he has no chin, and he is dapper. Nevertheless, I should like the run of his headpiece. We parted at the corner of the Square; no attempt to meet again.

Wednesday 12 March

And I'm now going to write the very last pages ever to be written at Hogarth House. My head is stuffy and heavy. Last night we dined at [Edmund] Blunden's farewell party, thirty-five covers laid, six or seven speeches made. My little drama was provided by Murry, who, as people were going, came and sat beside me. "We're enemies." "Not enemies. We're in different camps. But I've never said a word against you, Virginia." We came into a swift confused wrangle about 'writing well', but here L. came up; said we must go. But I shan't meet Murry for ten years, and I want to finish the argument – "Shall I come to the *Adelphi*?" "Do" he said, yet so oleaginously, with a rolling, lustful, or somehow leering, eye, so that I kept thinking how he'd come down in the world, spiritually, what tenth-rate shillyshallying humbugs he must live among. And we said goodbye for ten years. How honest and trusty and sterling Francis Birrell was in comparison! So home that long cold exhausting journey for the last time. Some odds and ends of ideas came to me at the dinner. For one thing, how pungent people's writing is compared with people's flesh. We were all toothless insignificant amiable nonentities – we distinguished writers; Blunden despairing, drooping, crow-like, rather than Keats-like. And did we really all believe in Blunden's 'genius'? Had we read his poems? How much sincerity was there in the whole thing? The truth is these collective gatherings must be floated by some conventional song, in which all can join, like He's a jolly good fellow, which Squire started. Subtler impressions did occur to me, but I can't place them at the moment. Nor at the moment can I think of any farewell for this beautiful and lovable house, which has done us such a good turn for almost precisely nine years, so that, as I lay in bed last night, I nearly humanised it, and offered it my thanks.

*   *   *

The Woolfs' move from Hogarth House to 52 Tavistock Square, Bloomsbury, took place on 13 and 14 March. They were to inhabit the two top floors of the large four-storey house on the southern side of the square; the sitting tenants, Messrs Dollman & Pritchard, Solicitors, continued their tenure of the ground and first floors; the extensive basement was given over to the Hogarth Press; and a large billiard room built in place of a back garden became both VW's study and the storeroom for Hogarth Press books.

52 Tavistock Square, WC1

Saturday 5 April

Well, I will make a brief beginning – after three weeks' silence. But it has not been silence at all. The noise of bus and taxi has worried me, and the noise of the human tongue has disturbed me, pleasantly and otherwise, and now I'm half asleep. Leonard working as usual. But can I collect any first impressions? My first night in the basement I saw the moon, with drifting clouds, and it was a terrifying and new London moon; dreadful and exciting, as if the Richmond moon had been veiled. Oh the convenience of this place! and the loveliness too. We walk home from theatres, through the entrails of London. Why do I love it so much? ... for it is stony hearted, and callous. The tradespeople don't know one – but these disparaging remarks were interrupted and it is now

Tuesday 15 April

– and L. and I have been having one of those melancholy middle aged summings up of a situation which occur from time to time, but are seldom recorded. Indeed most of life escapes, now I come to think of it; the texture of the ordinary day. L. was desperately gloomy. Not a stroke of work done he says, since we came to London. This is largely imagination, I think, though its true fish keep drifting into the net. Gerald Brenan back; Roger rampant to paint us; Morgan, elflike, mocking, aloof; Nessa and Duncan. Then there was Angelica's accident which, for the psychology of it I should have described. Here was Nessa painting, and I answering the telephone. Louie [nurse] and Angelica have been knocked down by a motor and are in the Middlesex Hospital. I had to repeat it to Nessa: to destroy all that simmering everyday comfort, with the smell of paint in the room, and Tom just coming upstairs to tea. She ran out and away from the telephone instinctively, ran round in an aimless way for a second. Then off they dashed and I after them, and so to the hospital, holding hands in the cab; and then sheer agony, for there was Louie, with her foot bandaged, and no Angelica; only an evasive nurse, parrying enquiries and taking us behind a screen where Angelica lay in bed, still, her face turned away. At last she moved. "She's not dead" Duncan said. They both thought her dead. Then the young doctor came, and seemed silently and considerately but firmly to wish the mother to know that the case was hopeless: very grave; run over across the stomach. Yes there may have to be an operation. The surgeon had been sent for. So Nessa went back to sit there, and I saw again that extraordinary look of anguish, dumb, not complaining, which I saw in Greece, I think, when she was ill. The feelings of the people who don't talk express themselves thus. My feeling was 'a pane of glass shelters me. I'm only allowed to look on at this.' Its a queer thing to come so close to agony as this, and just to be saved oneself. What I felt was that death and tragedy had once more put down his paw, after letting us run a few paces. People never get over their early impressions of death I think. I always feel pursued. But there's an end of this. Nothing was wrong with Angelica – it was only a joke this time.

It takes a long time to form a habit – the habit of living at 52 Tavistock Square is not quite formed, but doing well. Already I have spent a week without being bothered by noise. One ceases to hear or to see. Dadie has been – a sensitive vain youth, with considerable grit in him, I judge. Sometimes the future appears perilous; problematical rather, the press that is, but always fruitful and interesting.

Monday 5 May
This is the twenty-ninth anniversary of mother's death. I think it happened on a Sunday morning, and I looked out of the nursery window and saw old Dr Seton walking away with his hands behind his back, as if to say It is finished, and then the doves descending, to peck in the road, I suppose, with a fall and descent of infinite peace. I was thirteen, and could fill a whole page and more with my impressions of that day, many of them ill received by me, and hidden from the grown ups, but very memorable on that account: how I laughed, for instance, behind the hand which was meant to hide my tears; and through the fingers saw the nurses sobbing.

But enough of death – its life that matters. London is enchanting. I step out upon a tawny coloured magic carpet, it seems, and get carried into beauty without raising a finger. And people pop in and out, lightly, divertingly, like rabbits; and I look down Southampton Row, wet as a seal's back or red and yellow with sunshine, and watch the omnibuses going and coming, and hear the old crazy organ. One of these days I will write about London. I have left the whole of society unrecorded. Tidmarsh, Cambridge, and now Rodmell. We had a queer little party here the other day – when the sinister and pedagogic Tom cut a queer figure. I cannot wholly free myself from suspicions about him – at the worst they only amount to calling him an American schoolmaster; a very vain man.

Saturday 21 June
I am oh so sleepy; in fact just woken from a hot drowse. If I weren't so sleepy, I would write about the soul. I think its time to cancel that vow against soul description. What was I going to say? Something about the violent moods of my soul. I think I grow more and more poetic. Perhaps I restrained it, and now, like a plant in a pot it begins to crack the earthenware. Often I feel the different aspects of life bursting my mind asunder. Morgan

is too restrained in his new book perhaps. I mean, what's the use of facts at our time of life? Why build these careful cocoons?

I look forward with a little alarm to Dadie coming, chiefly I think that it commits us more seriously. But that will wear off soon. It seems to me the beginning of ten years of very hard work. I don't see how Marjorie will fit in, altogether, and rather anticipate some rearrangement. So far, no gossip and no soul. Yet I've seen – Bob, Desmond, Lytton, Sebastian [Sprott], Dorothy Bussy, Mrs Eliot – this last making me almost vomit, so scented, so powdered, so egotistic, so morbid, so weakly.

I am writing, writing, and see my way clear to the end now, and so shall gallop to it, somehow or other.

Thursday 3 July
This is Dadie's second day. Marjorie is ill, which is all to the good; business is brisk; I sat in the basement two days ago and took five pounds. But I have let Garsington languish like a decaying wreath on my pen. That was last Sunday. And, treading close on Garsington was the enamelled Lady Colefax, actually in this room, like a cheap bunch of artificial cherries, yet loyal, hard, living on a burnished plate of facts; inquisitive; not at all able to sink to the depths; but a superb skimmer of the surface; which is bright, I suppose, and foam tipped. I can't bring myself to despise this gull as I ought. But aristocrats, worldlings, for all their surface polish, are empty, slippery, coat the mind with sugar and butter, and make it slippery too.

Saturday 5 July
Just back, not from the 1917 Club, but from Knole, where indeed I was invited to lunch alone with his Lordship. His Lordship lives in the kernel of a vast nut. You perambulate miles of galleries; skip endless treasures – chairs that Shakespeare might have sat on – tapestries, pictures, floors made of the halves of oaks; and penetrate at length to a round shiny table with a cover laid for one. A dozen glasses form a circle each with a red rose in it. One solitary peer sits lunching by himself, with his napkin folded into the shape of a lotus flower. Knole is a conglomeration of buildings half as big as Cambridge I daresay; if you stuck Trinity, Clare and King's together you might approximate. But the extremities and indeed the inward parts are gone dead. Ropes fence off half the rooms; the chairs and the pictures look preserved; life has left them. Not for a hundred years have the retainers sat down to dinner in the great hall. Then there is Mary Stuart's altar, where she prayed before execution. "An ancestor of ours took her the death warrant" said Vita. All these ancestors and centuries, and silver and gold, have bred a perfect body. She is stag like, or race horse like, save for the face, which pouts, and has no very sharp brain. But as a body hers is

perfection. So many rare and curious objects hit one's brain like pellets which perhaps may unfold later. But its the breeding of Vita's that I took away with me as an impression, carrying her and Knole in my eye as I travelled up with the lower middle classes, through slums. There is Knole, capable of housing all the desperate poor of Judd Street, and with only that one solitary earl in the kernel.

MONKS HOUSE, RODMELL

Saturday 2 August
Here we are at Rodmell, and I with twenty minutes to fill in before dinner. A feeling of depression is on me, as if we were old and near the end of all things. It must be the change from London and incessant occupation. Then, being at a low ebb with my book, I begin to count myself a failure. Now the point of the Press is that it entirely prevents brooding, and gives me something solid to fall back on. The country is like a convent. The soul swims to the top.

Julian has just been and gone, a tall young man who, inveterately believing myself to be young as I do, seems to me like a younger brother; anyhow we sit and chatter, as easily as can be. Its all so much the same – his school continues Thoby's school. He tells me about boys and masters as Thoby used to. It interests me just in the same way. He's a sensitive, very quick witted, rather combative boy; full of Wells, and discoveries, and the future of the world. And, being of my own blood, easily understood – going to be very tall, and go to the Bar, I daresay.

Sunday 3 August
L. has been telling me about Germany, and reparations, how money is paid. Lord what a weak brain I have – like an unused muscle. He talks; and the facts come in, and I can't deal with them. But by dint of very painful brain exercises, perhaps I understand a little more than Nelly does of the International situation. And L. understands it all – picks up all these points of the daily paper absolutely instantly, has them connected, ready to produce. Sometimes I think my brain and his are of different orders. Were it not for my flash of imagination, and this turn for books, I should be a very ordinary woman.

Friday 15 August
By the way, why is poetry wholly an elderly taste? When I was twenty I could not for the life of me read Shakespeare for pleasure; now it lights me as I walk to think I have two acts of *King John* tonight, and shall next read

Richard the Second. It is poetry that I want now – long poems. I want the concentration and the romance, and the words all glued together, fused, glowing: have no time to waste any more on prose. When I was twenty I liked Eighteenth Century prose; now its poetry I want, so I repeat like a tipsy sailor in front of a public house.

I don't often trouble now to describe cornfields and groups of harvesting women in loose blues and reds and little staring yellow frocked girls. But that's not my eyes' fault; coming back the other evening from Charleston, again all my nerves stood upright, flushed, electrified (what's the word?) with the sheer beauty – beauty abounding and superabounding, so that one almost resents it, not being capable of catching it all, and holding it all at the moment.

Sunday 7 September
In my last lap of *Mrs Dalloway*. There I am now – at last at the party, which is to begin in the kitchen, and climb slowly upstairs. It is to be a most complicated spirited solid piece, knitting together everything and ending on three notes, at different stages of the staircase, each saying something to sum up Clarissa.

We had Dadie twice to stay; Clive and Mary yesterday; I slept a night at Charleston; L. went to Yorkshire; rather an odd disjointed wet summer, with people dropping in, Nelly rather moping, but loyal. The garden here flourishes.

Monday 15 September
Vita was here for Sunday, gliding down the village in her large new blue Austin car, which she manages consummately. She was dressed in ringed yellow jersey, and large hat, and had a dressing case all full of silver and night gowns wrapped in tissue. Nelly said "If only she weren't an honourable!" and couldn't take her hot water. But I like her being honourable, and she is it; a perfect lady, with all the dash and courage of the aristocracy, and less of its childishness than I expected. She is like an over ripe grape in features, moustached, pouting, will be a little heavy; meanwhile, she strides on fine legs, in a well cut skirt, and though embarrassing at breakfast, has a manly good sense and simplicity about her which both L. and I find satisfactory. Oh yes, I like her; could tack her on to my equipage for all time; and suppose if life allowed, this might be a friendship of a sort. [She] took us to Charleston – and how one's world spins round – it looked all very grey and shabby and loosely cut in the light of her presence. As for Monks House, it became a ruined barn, and we picnicking in the rubbish heap.

Monday 29 September

A fortnight later: writing partly to test my new penkala (professing fountain-pen qualities), partly to exorcise my demon. Only Karin and Ann [aged eight]: only a hole blown in my last chapter. There I was swimming in the highest ether known to me, and thinking I'd finish by Thursday; Lottie suggests to Karin we'd like to have Ann: Karin interprets my polite refusal to her own advantage and comes down herself on Saturday, blowing everything to smithereens. More and more am I solitary; the pain of these upheavals is incalculable; and I can't explain it either. *She* saw nothing. "Disturbing the flow of inspiration?" she said this morning, having shouted outside the door till I had to fetch cotton wool. And its down in ruins my house; my wings broken; and I left on the bare ground. But what cares Karin! She slightly chortles to plant us with some of her burdens and makes off well pleased at having got her way. Here am I with my wrecked week – for how serene and lovely like a Lapland night was our last week together – feeling that I ought to go in and be a good aunt – which I'm not by nature. These wails must now have ending, partly because I cannot see.

And of course children are wonderful and charming creatures. I've had Ann in talking about the white seal, and wanting me to read to her. There's a quality in their minds to me very adorable: to be alone with them, and see them day to day would be an extraordinary experience. They have what no grown up has – that directness – chatter, chatter, chatter, on Ann goes, in a world of her own, with its seals and dogs; happy because she's going to have cocoa tonight, and go blackberrying tomorrow; the walls of her mind all hung round with such bright vivid things, and she doesn't see what we see.

52 TAVISTOCK SQUARE, WC1

Friday 17 October

It is disgraceful. I did run upstairs thinking I'd make time to enter that astounding fact – the last words of the last page of *Mrs Dalloway*; but was interrupted. Anyhow I did them a week ago yesterday. 'For there she was.' But in some ways this book is a feat; finished without break from illness, which is an exception; and written really in one year. The only difficulty is to hold myself back from writing others. I see already The Old Man. But enough, enough – yet of what should I write here except my writing? Odd how conventional morality always encroaches. One must not talk of oneself, &c; one must not be vain &c. Even in complete privacy these ghosts slip between me and the page.

The thought of Katherine Mansfield comes to me – as usual rather reprehensibly – thinking yes, if she'd lived, she'd have written on, and people would have seen that I was the more gifted. I think of her in this way off and on – that strange ghost, with the eyes far apart, and the drawn mouth, dragging herself across the room. Katherine and I had our relationship; and never again shall I have one like it.

Lytton dined here the other night – a successful evening. Oh I was right to be in love with him twelve or fifteen years ago. It is an exquisite symphony his nature when all the violins get playing as they did the other night; so deep, so fantastic. We rambled easily. We talked of his writing, and I think now he will write another book; of mine: of the School of Proust, he said; then of Maynard: one side of him detestable.

Saturday 1 November

We went to Hamspray on a wet misty day, and saw what the view might be in the sun; a flat meadow with trees in groups like people talking leading to the downs. We walked to the top with Carrington. Carrington was as if recently beaten by Ralph. Is she really rather dull, I asked myself? or merely a sun flower out of the sun? We came home in the rain.

Tuesday 18 November

We were, I was rather, at Mary's party last night, and suffer today. The upper classes pretended to be clever. Duff Cooper, Lady Diana and all that set, as they say; and my chief amusement came from seeing them as a set. That is the only merit of these parties, that individuals compose differently from what they do in private.

Dadie came back yesterday and we had a jolly afternoon – oh infinitely better than a party at River House! lie though I did to Mary on the telephone – I in two jackets, for it is freezing, and hair down; he in shirtsleeves. Thus one gets to know people; not poised on the edge of a chair on the slippery floor, trying to laugh, and being spurred by wine and sugar cakes. Clive of course changes into an upper class man, very loud, familiar, and dashing, at once. Lytton sits in his own green shade, only emerging when the gentle youths come in. I was impressed by Nessa, who went to this party for which we were all titivating and dressing up, in her old red brown dress which I think she made herself.

Saturday 13 December

This diary may die, not of London, but of the Press. For fourteen days we have been in the thick of a long press revolution – Dadie going, Marjorie going, Marjorie staying, Angus Davidson coming. That is the final result, but achieved only at the cost of forty million words. For my own part, I could never see Dadie as a permanent partner, Dadie in his silver grey suits, pink shirts, with his powdered pink and white face, his nerves, his manners, his love of praise. Angus, however, after three days, already seems to me permanent and dependable.

I am now galloping over *Mrs Dalloway*, re-typing it entirely from the start, a good method, I believe, as thus one works with a wet brush over the whole, and joins parts separately composed and gone dry.

Monday 21 December
Really it is a disgrace – the number of blank pages in this book! The effect of London on diaries is decidedly bad. This I fancy is the leanest of them all. Indeed it has been an eventful year, as I prophesied; and the dreamer of January 3rd has dreamt much of her dream true; here we are in London, with Nelly alone, Dadie gone it is true, but Angus to replace him. What emerges is that changing houses is not so cataclysmic as I thought; after all one doesn't change body or brain.

How sharply society brings one out – or rather others out! Roger the other night with Vita for instance. He became the nonconformist undergraduate at once, the obstinate young man (I could see him quite young with his honest uncompromising eyes), who will *not* say what he does not believe to be true. The effect on Vita was disastrous; and pure honesty is a doubtful quality; it means often lack of imagination. It means self assertiveness, being rather better than other people; a queer trait in Roger to unearth after so many years of smooth intercourse. For the most part he is so sympathetic. His Quaker blood protests against Vita's rich winy fluid; and she has the habit of praising and talking indiscriminately about art, which goes down in her set, but not in ours. It was all very thorny until that good fellow Clive came in, and addressed himself to conciliate dear old obtuse, aristocratic, passionate, Grenadier-like Vita.

All our Bloomsbury relationships flourish, grow in lustiness. Suppose our set to survive another twenty years, I tremble to think how thickly knit and grown together it will be. At Christmas I must write and ask Lytton if I may dedicate *The Common Reader* to him. And that's the last of my books to be dedicated, I think. What do we talk about? I wish I could write conversation. We go over the same things, undoubtedly. The press however is always casting up wreckage. People come most days. I enjoy my printing afternoons, and think it the sanest way of life – for if I were always writing, or merely recouping from writing, I should be like an inbreeding rabbit – my progeny becoming weakly albinos. One meets a good many men now. There's a little thrush like creature called Tomlin who wants to sculpt me.

1925

This year Virginia's diary opens on a note – that of petulant exasperation with her resident servant Nelly Boxall – which was to sound again and again until it was finally silenced by Nelly's departure in 1934. In the early months of the year Virginia suffered the usual winter ills, influenza and headaches, while revising and preparing her two books, Mrs Dalloway *and* The Common Reader, *for their publication by the Hogarth Press. Exceptionally, she sent advance proofs of the former to an old pre-war friend with whom she had been corresponding, the painter Jacques Raverat, who was dying in the south of France.*

In April, leaving the Hogarth Press in the nervous care of Angus Davidson, the Woolfs again made what was to become a regular spring excursion, this year to spend ten days by the Mediterranean at Cassis. On their return, while awaiting the publication of her books, Virginia resumed her close-packed intellectual and social life and her involvement in Hogarth Press affairs. One of their authors, the thirty-year-old Robert Graves, burst in on the Woolfs unknown and unannounced at tea-time one day; another evening an emotional T. S. Eliot confided in them the new turn his life was taking and his anxieties about his wife's psychological health. The hostess Lady Colefax sought Virginia's company; the Sitwells asked her to dine; she entertained new and old friends to tea, to dinner, and to after-dinner coffee and conversation at Tavistock Square. Her books were published, and had a mixed reception, the details of which she rather obsessively notes. In fact, a very busy and social summer, and one which exacted its toll soon after their summer migration to Rodmell, when Virginia collapsed at Charleston in the middle of Quentin Bell's birthday dinner, and thereafter had to submit to a period of enforced inactivity. But she was able to make a start on To the Lighthouse, *which had long been germinating in her mind.*

Late in September the newly married Maynard Keynes and Lydia Lopokova came to Monks House and regaled the Woolfs with their observations on conditions in Soviet Russia, where they had spent their honeymoon (Keynes's A Short View of Russia *was published by the Hogarth Press in December). But their visit renewed Virginia's headache, and on returning to Tavistock Square at the beginning of October, she continued her semi-invalid existence under doctor's orders, occasionally allowed out for a walk, able to receive a few visitors. In November, one of the (subsequently tarnished) idols of her youth, Madge Vaughan, died.*

Towards the end of the year the news that Vita Sackville-West was to join her diplomat husband in Persia forced Virginia to examine the nature of her feelings, aroused by a three-day visit to Vita's Kentish home, Long Barn. Builders were at work at Monks House, and the Woolfs spent Christmas with the Bell family at Charleston.

1925

Tuesday 6 January
What a flourish I began 1924 with! And today, for the 165th time, Nelly has given notice – Won't be dictated to; must do as other girls do. On the whole, I'm inclined to take her at her word. The nuisance of arranging life to suit her fads, and the pressure of 'other girls' is too much, good cook though she is, and honesty, crusty old maid too, dependable, in the main, affectionate, kindly, but incurably fussy, nervy, unsubstantial.

I spent the morning writing a note on an Elizabethan play; then I went into the printing room to see the time – found Angus [Davidson] and Leonard; Stayed and laughed. L. went off to the [*Nation*] office, when we had dog-walked round the Square; it being a black grained winter day; lengths of the pavement ink black where not lighted. Never shall I describe all the days I have noticed. Rodmell was all gale and flood; these words are exact. The river overflowed. We had seven days rain out of ten. Often I could not face a walk. L. pruned, which needed heroic courage. My heroism was purely literary. I revised *Mrs Dalloway*: the dullest part of the whole business of writing; the most depressing and exacting. L. read it; thinks it my best – but then has he not got to think so? Still I agree. Anyhow it is sent off to Clarks [printers], and proofs will come next week.

I did not see very much at Rodmell, having to keep my eyes on the typewriter. Angus was with us for Christmas, a very quiet, very considerate, unselfish deliberate young man, with a charming sense of humour – colourless, Lytton says: passive. But I think well of him, all the same.

Wednesday 18 March
This disgrace has been already explained – I think: two books to see through the press, mainly between tea and dinner; influenza; and a distaste for the pen.

*   *   *

Wednesday 8 April

Just back from Cassis. Often while I was there I thought how I would write here frequently and so get down some of the myriad impressions which I net every day. But directly we get back, what is it that happens? We strip and dive into the stream, and I am obsessed with a foolish idea that I have no time to stop and write, or that I ought to be doing something serious. Even now, I pelt along feverishly, thinking half the time, But I must stop and take Grizzle out; I must get my American books in order; the truth is, I must try to set aside half an hour in some part of my day, and consecrate it to diary writing. Give it a name and a place, and then perhaps, such is the human mind, I shall come to think it a duty, and disregard other duties for it.

I am under the impression of the moment, which is the complex one of coming back home from the South of France, shot with the accident I saw this morning and a woman crying Oh oh oh faintly, pinned against the railings with a motor car on top of her. All day I have heard that voice. I did not go to her help; but then every baker and flower seller did that. A great sense of the brutality and wildness of the world remains with me – there was this woman in brown walking along the pavement – suddenly a red film car turns a somersault, lands on top of her, and one hears this oh, oh, oh.

Since I wrote, which is these last months, Jacques Raverat has died; after longing to die; and he sent me a letter about *Mrs Dalloway* which gave me one of the happiest days of my life. Jacques died, as I say; and at once the siege of emotions began. I do not any longer feel inclined to doff the cap to death. I like to go out of the room talking, with an unfinished casual sentence on my lips. That is the effect it had on me – no leavetaking, no submission – but someone stepping out into the darkness.

I am waiting to see what form of itself Cassis will finally cast up in my mind. There are the rocks. We used to go out after breakfast and sit on the rocks with the sun on us. Then we would go for a walk in the afternoon, right up over the hill, into the woods. It was stony, steep and very hot. We heard a great chattering birdlike noise once, and I bethought me of the frogs. The ragged red tulips were out in the fields; all the fields were little angular shelves cut out of the hill, and ruled and ribbed with vines. Here and there was an angular white, or yellow or blue washed house, with all its shutters tightly closed; an incomparable cleanness and definiteness everywhere. At La Ciotat great orange ships rose up out of the blue water of the little bay. On the hill, which is stony as a desert, the nets were drying; and then in the streets children and girls gossiped and meandered all in pale bright shawls and cotton frocks, while the men picked up the earth of the main square to make a paved court of it. The Hotel Cendrillon is a white house, with red tiled floors, capable of housing perhaps eight people. The whole hotel atmosphere provided me with many ideas: oh so cold, indifferent, superficially polite, and exhibiting such odd relationships: as if human nature were now reduced to a kind of code, which it has devised to meet these emergencies, where people who do not know each other meet, and claim their rights as members of the same tribe. But L. and I were too too happy, as they say; if it were now to die &c.

Sunday 19 April
I'm out to make £300 this summer by writing, and build a bath and hot water range at Rodmell. But, hush, hush – my books tremble on the verge of coming out, and my future is uncertain.

Lytton came in the other night. He seemed to me autumnal: with that charming rectitude of spirit which no one else attains so perfectly I think. His justice of mind is considerable. But Christ is dismissed, to his disappoint-ment, for he grows more and more fussy about subjects: Christ, he says did not exist: was a figment; and so much is known that really he couldn't pull it all together in one book. We talked of old buggers and their lack of attraction for young men. My anti-bugger revolution has run round the world, as I hoped it would. The pale star of the bugger has been in the ascendant too long. Julian agrees emphatically.

Marjorie and her Tom [Marshall] looked in at the basement this evening, very happy, L. says. She is a nice trusty creature, and if I wished to see anyone, I daresay it would be her.

Monday 20 April
Happiness is to have a little string onto which things will attach themselves. For example, going to my dressmaker, or rather thinking of a dress I could get her to make, and imagining it made – that is the string, which as if it dipped loosely into a wave of treasure brings up pearls sticking to it. And my days are likely to be strung with them. I like this London life in early summer – the street sauntering and square haunting, and then if my books were to be a success; if we could begin building at Monks, and put up wireless for Nelly, and if – if – if. But really what I should like would be to have three pounds to buy a pair of rubber soled boots, and go for country walks on Sundays.

One thing, in considering my state of mind now, seems to me beyond dispute: that I have, at last, bored down into my oil well, and can't scribble fast enough to bring it all to the surface. I have now at least six stories welling up in me, and feel at last that I can coin all my thoughts into words. Now suppose I might become one of the interesting – I will not say great

– but interesting novelists? Oddly, for all my vanity, I have not until now had much faith in my novels.

Monday 27 April
The Common Reader was out on Thursday: this is Monday, and so far I have not heard a word about it, private or public; it is as if one tossed a stone into a pond, and the waters closed without a ripple. And I am perfectly content, and care less than I have ever cared.

I meant to dash off [Robert] Graves before I forget him. Figure a bolt eyed blue shirted shockheaded hatless man in a blue overcoat standing goggling at the door at 4.30 on Friday. "Mrs Woolf?" I dreading and suspecting some *Nation* genius, some young man determined to unbosom himself, rushed him to the basement, where he said "I'm Graves". Everybody stared. He appeared to have been rushing through the air at sixty miles an hour and to have alighted temporarily. So he came up, and, wily as I am, I knew that to advance holding the kettle in a dishclout was precisely the right method, attitude, pose. The poor boy is all emphasis, protestation and pose. He has a crude likeness to Shelley, save that his nose is a switchback and his lines blurred. But the consciousness of genius is bad for people. He stayed till 7.15 (we were going to *Caesar and Cleopatra* – a strange rhetorical romantic early Shaw play) and had at last to say so, for he was so thick in the delight of explaining his way of life to us that no bee stuck faster to honey. He cooks, his wife cleans; four children are brought up in the elementary school; the villagers give them vegetables; they were married in Church; his wife calls herself Nancy Nicholson. Calling herself Nicholson has sorted her friends into sheep and goats. All this to us sounded like the usual self consciousness of young men, especially as he threw in, gratuitously, the information that he descends from Dean, Rector, Bishop, von Ranke, &c &c &c, only in order to say that he despises them. Still, still, he is a nice ingenuous rattle headed young man; but surely once one could live simply without protestations. I tried, perhaps, to curry favour, as my weakness is. L. was adamant. Then we were offered a ticket for the Cup Tie, to see which Graves has come to London after six years; can't travel in a train without being sick; is rather proud of his sensibility. No I don't think he'll write great poetry: but what will you? The sensitive are needed too, the half-baked, stammering, stuttering, who perhaps improve their own quarter of Oxfordshire.

And on Sunday we had our first walk, to Epping.

Wednesday 29 April
Hastily I must record the fact of Tom's long gaslit emotional rather tremulous and excited visit last night, which informed us of his release from

the Bank; some heavensent appointment to take effect next October. He has been thinking over his state these past weeks, being alone, with time on his hands. He has seen his whole life afresh, seen his relations to the world, and to Vivien in particular, become humbler, suppler, more humane – accusing himself of being the American husband, and wishing to tell me privately what store Vivien sets by me, has done nothing but write since last June, because I told her to! He then went into her psychology. Then he said to L. Do you know anything about psycho-analysis? L. said yes, in his responsible way; and Tom then told us the queer story – how Martin the doctor set Vivien off thinking of her childhood terror of loneliness, and now she can't let him, Tom, out of her sight. There he has sat mewed in her room these three months, poor pale creature, or if he has to go out, comes in to find her in a half fainting state. We advised another doctor. But whether its doctors or sense or holiday or travel or some drastic method unknown that's to cure that little nervous self conscious bundle – heaven knows. The upshot was a queer sense of his emotion in coming to tell us all this – something not merely touching to my vanity but to my sense of human worth, I think; his liking for us, affection, trust in Leonard, and being so much at his ease in some subconscious way he said, with me, all making me lay my arm on his shoulder; not a very passionate caress, but the best I can do.

And now I'm a little fidgety about *The Common Reader*; not a single word of it from a soul.

Friday 1 May
The Common Reader came out eight days ago, and so far not a single review has appeared, and nobody has written to me or spoken to me about it or in any way acknowledged the fact of its existence, save Maynard, Lydia and Duncan.

Monday 4 May
Now there's one sneering review in *Country Life*, almost inarticulate with feebleness, trying to say what a Common Reader is, and another, says Angus, in the *Star*, laughing at Nessa's cover.

Saturday 9 May
As for *The Common Reader*, the *TLS* had close on two columns sober and sensible praise – neither one thing nor the other. And Goldie [Goldsworthy Lowes Dickinson] writes that he thinks 'this is the best criticism in English – humorous, witty and profound'. My fate is to be treated to all extremes and all mediocrities. But I never get an enthusiastic review in the *TLS*. And it will be the same for *Dalloway*, which now approaches.

Thursday 14 May

The first day of summer, leaves visibly drawing out of the bud, and the Square almost green. Oh what a country day – and some of my friends are now reading *Mrs Dalloway* in the country. But the odd thing is this: honestly I am scarcely a shade nervous about *Mrs D*. Why is this? The truth is that writing is the profound pleasure and being read the superficial. I'm now all on the strain with desire to stop journalism and get on to *To the Lighthouse*. This is going to be fairly short: to have father's character done complete in it; and mother's; and St Ives; and childhood; and all the usual things I try to put in – life, death, &c. But the centre is father's character, sitting in a boat, reciting We perished each alone, while he crushes a dying mackerel – However, I must refrain.

Yesterday was a terrific chatter day – Desmond on top of Dr Leys, Lord Olivier on top of Desmond, James and Dadie to finish off with, while L. had I forget how many press interviews and committees into the bargain. But I meant to describe my dear old Desmond, whom it rejoiced me to see again, and he held out both his hands, and I set him in his chair and we talked till 7 o'clock. He is rather worn and aged; a little, I think, feeling that here's forty-five on him and nothing achieved, except indeed the children, whom he dotes on. I saw him thinking of his welter of old articles lying dusty in boxes. So I said I would take the thing in hand and see it through, which touched him, for children are not enough, after all; one wants something to be made out of oneself alone – and five boxes of dusty articles are rather raggy and rotten for forty-five years. And he praised *The Common Reader* with enthusiasm; and will write on it; and so we chattered along, when L. came; and then the dinner party, I just having time for a race round the Square; both Dadie and James very easy and affable, indeed for Dadie I feel considerable affection – so sensitive and tender is he, and one of these days will get a pull on himself, and be less of a quicksilver. But what these scholars want is to get at books through writing books, not through reading them.

But I must remember to write about my *clothes* next time I have an impulse to write. My love of clothes interests me profoundly; only it is not love; and what it is I must discover.

Friday 15 May

Two unfavourable reviews of *Mrs Dalloway*: unintelligible, not art &c; and a letter from a young man in Earl's Court: 'This time you have done it – you have caught life and put it in a book . . .'

Sunday 17 May

The only judgment on *Mrs Dalloway* I await with trepidation (but that's too strong) is Morgan's. He will say something enlightening.

Just back (all my days here begin with this) from Sutton. Oh it is full summer weather – so hot one can't walk on the sunny side, and all London transmogrified. We came home on top of a bus all the way for a shilling, with the usual glimpses down lanes, into farmyards, at running streams, persisting in between villas, and behind sunbaked yellow or black motor roads. A little girl on the bus asked her mother how many inches are there in a mile. Her mother repeated this to me. I said you must go to school and they'll tell you. But she is at school said her mother. She's seven; and *he* (the baby on her knee) goes to school. He's three. So I gave them two biscuits left over, and the little girl (see my egotism) with her bright excitable eyes, and eagerness to grasp the whole universe reminded me of myself, asking questions of my mother. We saw Lambeth, and I imagined the frolics of clergymen in the boscage, which is very thick; crossed Westminster Bridge; admired the Houses of Parliament and their fretted lacy look; passed the Cenotaph, which L. compromised by sitting with his hat off all the way up Whitehall, and so home.

Wednesday 20 May

Well, Morgan admires. This is a weight off my mind. Better than *Jacob* he says; was sparing of words; kissed my hand, and on going said he was awfully pleased, very happy (or words to that effect) about it. He thinks – but I won't go into detailed criticism; I shall hear more; and this is only about the style being simpler, more like other people's this time.

I dined with the Sitwells last night. Edith is an old maid. I had never conceived this. I thought she was severe, implacable and tremendous; rigid in her own conception. Not a bit of it. She is, I guess, a little fussy, very kind, beautifully mannered, elderly too, almost my age, and timid, and admiring and easy and poor, and I liked her more than admired or was frightened by her. Nevertheless, I do admire her work, and that's what I say of hardly anyone: she has an ear, and not a carpet broom; a satiric vein; and some beauty in her. Nothing could be more conciliatory and less of an eagle than she; odd looking too, with her humorous old maid's smile, her half shut eyes, her lank hair, her delicate hands, wearing a large ring, and fine feet, and her brocade dress, blue and silver. Nothing of the protester or pamphleteer or pioneer seemed in her – rather the well born Victorian spinster. So I must read her afresh. The three Sitwells have considerable breeding about them; I like their long noses, and grotesque faces. As for the house, Osbert is at heart an English Squire, a collector, but of Bristol glass, old fashion plates, Victorian cases of humming birds, and not of foxes' brushes and deers' horns. His rooms are all stuck about with these objects. And I liked him too. But why are they thought daring and clever? Why are they the laughing stocks of the music halls and the penny-a-liners? Not much talk; all easy goodnatured generalities after dinner, Francis [Birrell] bawling, [Arthur] Waley sombre and demure, and I very indulgent with my compliments.

Monday 1 June

Bank holiday, and we are in London. To record my books' fates slightly bores me; but now both are floated, and *Mrs Dalloway* doing surprisingly well.

Tom came in yesterday, rather rockier than last time, not quite so flushed with emotion, and inclined to particularise the state of Vivien's bowels too closely for my taste. What is more to the point is that Tom is to be the editor of a new quarterly, which some old firm is issuing in the autumn, and all his works must go to them – a blow for us. He said nothing of my books. With great dignity, I did not ask for his opinion. People often don't read books for weeks and weeks. And anyhow, for my part, I hate giving an opinion.

Friday 5 June

To work off the intense depression left by Desmond. What does this come from? But I have just made this beautiful image – how he is like a wave that never breaks, but lollops one this way and that way and the sail hangs on one's mast and the sun beats down – And then I was ruffled by Nelly, but got over it, by spending £50 of charm. And we have had Vita, Edith Sitwell, Morgan, Dadie – old Vita presenting me with a whole tree of blue Lupins, and being very uncouth and clumsy, while Edith was like a Roman Empress, so definite, clear cut, magisterial, and yet with something of the humour of a fishwife – a little too commanding about her own poetry and ready to dictate – tremulously pleased by Morgan's compliments (and he never praised Vita, who sat hurt, modest, silent, like a snubbed schoolboy).

Sunday 14 June

A disgraceful confession – this is Sunday morning, and just after ten, and here I am sitting down to write diary and not fiction or reviews, without any excuse, except the state of my mind. After finishing those two books, though, one can't concentrate directly on a new one; and then the letters, the talk, the reviews . . . I can't settle in, contract, and shut myself off. I've written six little stories, scrambled them down untidily, and have thought out, perhaps too clearly, *To the Lighthouse*. And both books so far are successful. More of *Dalloway* has been sold this month than of *Jacob* in a year. I think it possible we may sell 2,000.

Waking this morning, rather depressed that *Mrs D.* did not sell yesterday, that we had [a dinner party] last night and not a single compliment vouchsafed me, that I had bought a glass necklace for one pound, that I had a sore throat and a streaming nose, rather under the weather, I say, I snuggled into the core of my life, which is this complete comfort with L., and there found everything so satisfactory and calm that I revived myself, and got a fresh start; feeling entirely immune. The immense success of our life is, I think, that our treasure is hid away; or rather in such common things that nothing can touch it. That is, if one enjoys a bus ride to Richmond, sitting on the Green smoking, taking the letters out of the box, combing Grizzle, making an ice, opening a letter, sitting down after dinner, side by side, and saying 'Are you in your stall, brother?' – well, what can trouble this happiness? And every day is necessarily full of it.

Tuesday 18 June
Old Lytton has fairly passed from our lives. No word about my books; no visits since Easter. I imagine that when he takes a new love, and he has Angus, he gets surly, like a stag; he feels a little ridiculous, uneasy, and does not relish the company of old cynical friends like ourselves.

Thursday 16 June
No, Lytton does not like *Mrs Dalloway*, and, what is odd, I like him all the better for saying so, and don't much mind. What he says is that there is a discrepancy between the ornament (extremely beautiful) and what happens (rather ordinary – or unimportant). So that as a whole, the book does not ring solid; yet, he says, it is a whole; and he says sometimes the writing is of extreme beauty. What can one call it but genius? he said! Fuller of genius, he said, than anything I had done. Perhaps, he said, you should take something wilder and more fantastic, a framework that admits of anything, like *Tristram Shandy*. But he thought me at the beginning, not at the end. And he said *The Common Reader* was divine, a classic; *Mrs D.* being, I fear, a flawed stone. Its odd that when Clive and others (several of them) say it is a masterpiece, I am not much exalted; when Lytton picks holes, I get back into my working fighting mood, which is natural to me.

Saturday 27 June
The first fruit of *The Common Reader* (a book too highly praised now) is a request to write for the *Atlantic Monthly*. So I am getting pushed into criticism. It is a great stand by – this power to make large sums by formulating views on Stendhal and Swift.

Sunday 19 July

By bringing this book down here to the Studio, I have rather stinted it I think, as my mornings have all been spent writing. So a whole tribe of people and parties has gone down the sink to oblivion. A happy summer, very busy; rather overpowered by the need of seeing so many people. I never ask a soul here; but they accumulate. Tonight Ottoline; Tuesday Jack Hutch; Wednesday Edith Sitwell, Friday dine with Raymond. These are my fixed invitations; and all sorts of unforeseen ones will occur. I run out after tea as if pursued. I mean to regulate this better in future. But I don't think of the future, or the past, I feast on the moment. This is the secret of happiness, but only reached now in middle age.

Monday 20 July

I should consider my work list now. I think a little story, perhaps a review, this fortnight; having a superstitious wish to begin *To the Lighthouse* the first day at Monks House. I now think I shall finish it in two months there. But this theme may be sentimental: father and mother and child in the garden; the death; the sail to the lighthouse. (I conceive the book in three parts: 1, at the drawing room window; 2, seven years passed; 3, the voyage.)

Last night Clive dined with us; and Nelly is rather waspish about it this morning. Ottoline came, in tea kettle taffeta, all looped and scolloped and fringed with silver lace, and talked about Rupert [Brooke] and Jacques [Raverat], and re-told, with emendations, the story of Ka and Henry Lamb and herself. She has been working over these old stories so often, that they hold no likeness to the truth – they are stale, managed, pulled this way and that, as we used to knead and pull the crumb of bread, till it was a damp slab. Then the old motor was heard hooting and there was Philip and Julian [Morrell], at which, at Julian that is, Clive cheered up, and was very brisk and obliging as he knows how. We argued the case of the aristocracy v. the middle class. I rather liked it. I like the sense of other people liking it, as I suppose the Morrells do, for they settle on us like a crowd of crows, once a week now. My vanity as a hostess is flattered. Sometimes a buttery crumb of praise is thrown to me – But enough, enough.

Thursday 30 July

I should here try to sum up the summer, since August ends a season, spiritual as well as temporal. Well; business has been brisk. I don't think I get many idle hours now, the idlest being, oddly enough, in the morning. When the dull sleep of afternoon is on me, I'm always in the shop, printing, dissing, addressing; then it is tea, and Heaven knows we have had enough visitors. Sometimes I sit still and wonder how many people will tumble on me without my lifting a finger.

On Tuesday at 12.30 Maynard retires to St Pancras Registry Office with Lydia, and Duncan to witness (against his will). So that episode is over. But, dear me, I'm too dull to write. Yet I have a thousand things to say.

Monks House, Rodmell

Saturday 5 September
And why couldn't I see or feel that all this time I was getting a little used up and riding on a flat tyre? So I was, as it happened; and fell down in a faint at Charleston, in the middle of Quentin's birthday party; and then have lain about here, in that odd amphibious life of headache, for a fortnight. This has rammed a big hole in my eight weeks which were to be stuffed so full. Never mind. I have made a very quick and flourishing attack on *To the Lighthouse* all the same. I am still crawling and easily enfeebled, but if I could once get up steam again, I believe I could spin it off with infinite relish.

Monday 14 September
A disgraceful fact – I am writing this at ten in the morning in bed in the little room looking into the garden, the sun beaming steady, the vine leaves transparent green, and the leaves of the apple trees so brilliant that, as I had my breakfast, I invented a little story about a man who wrote a poem, I think, comparing them with diamonds, and the spiders' webs (which glance and disappear astonishingly) with something or other else. I am writing this partly to test my poor bunch of nerves at the back of my neck – will they hold or give again, as they have done so often; partly to glut my itch ('glut' and 'itch'!) for writing. It is the great solace, and scourge.

Tom has treated us scurvily. On Monday I get a letter that fawns and flatters, implores me to write for his new quarterly; and proposes to discuss Press matters as soon as we get back; on Thursday we read in the *TLS* that his new firm is publishing *The Waste Land* and his other poems – a fact which he dared not confess, but sought to palliate by flattering me.

Tuesday 22 September
How my handwriting goes down hill! Another sacrifice to the Hogarth Press. Yet what I owe the Hogarth Press is barely paid by the whole of my handwriting. Haven't I just written to Herbert Fisher refusing to do a book for the Home University Series – knowing that I can write a book, a better book, a book off my own bat, for the Press if I wish! To think of being battened down in the hold of those University dons fairly makes my

blood run cold. Yet I'm the only woman in England free to write what I like. The others must be thinking of series and editors.

Thursday 24 September

Sad to think a week only left whole of this partially wrecked summer; however, I don't complain, seeing as how I have dipped my head in health again and feel stabilised once more about the spinal cord, which is always the centre of my being. Maynard and Lydia came here yesterday – Maynard in Tolstoy's blouse and Russian cap of black astrakhan – a fair sight, both of them, to meet on the high road! An immense good will and vigour pervades him. She hums in his wake, the great man's wife. But though one could carp, one can also find them very good company, and my heart, in this the autumn of my age, slightly warms to him, whom I've known all these years, so truculently, pugnaciously, and unintimately. We had a very brisk talk of Russia: such a hotch-potch, such a mad jumble, Maynard says, of good and bad. Briefly, spies everywhere, no liberty of speech, greed for money eradicated, people living in common, yet some, Lydia's mother for instance, with servants, peasants contented because they own land, no sign of revolution, aristocrats acting showmen to their possessions, ballet respected, best show of Cézanne and Matisse in existence. Endless processions of communists in top hats, prices exorbitant, yet champagne produced, and the finest cooking in Europe. Then the immense luxury of the old Imperial trains; feeding off the Tsar's plate. One prediction of theirs, to the effect that in ten years' time the standard of living will be higher in Russia than it was before the war, but in all other countries lower, Maynard thought might very well come true. Anyhow they are crammed and packed with sights and talks.

But the Keyneses, I need hardly say, renewed my headache, and when Lytton came, I was drooping over the fire, and could not do much battle with that old serpent. But to tell the truth, I am exacerbated this morning. It is 10.25, on a fine grey still day; the starlings are in the apple trees; Leonard is in London. But why am I exacerbated? By Roger. I told him I had been ill all the summer. His reply is – silence as to that; but plentiful descriptions of his own front teeth. Egotism, egotism – it is the essential ingredient in a clever man's life I believe. It protects; it enhances; it preserves his own vital juices entire by keeping them banked in. Also I cannot help thinking that he suspects me of valetudinarianism and this enrages me; and L. is away and I can't have my thorn picked out by him, so must write it out. There! it is better now; and I think I hear the papers come; and will get them, my woolwork, and a glass of milk.

Wednesday 30 September
This was I suppose successfully accomplished; and it is now Wednesday morning, damp and close and over all the sense already of transmigration, of shedding one habit for another. My autumn coat is grown.

52 TAVISTOCK SQUARE, WC1

Friday 27 November
Oh what a blank! I tumbled into bed on coming back – or rather [Dr] Ellie [Rendel] tumbled me; and keeps me still prostrate half the day. Next week I shall go to the ballet, my first night out. One visitor a day. Till two days ago, bed at 5. On the whole, I have not been unhappy, but not very happy; too much discomfort; sickness (cured by eating instantly); a good deal of rat-gnawing at the back of my head; one or two terrors; then the tiredness of the body – it lay like a workman's coat. Sometimes I felt old, and spent. Madge [Vaughan] died. Rustling among my emotions, I found nothing better than dead leaves. Her letters had eaten away the reality – the brilliancy, the warmth. Oh detestable time, that thus eats out the heart and lets the body go on. They buried a faggot of twigs at Highgate, as far as I am concerned. I drove to the gate, and saw Nessa and Leonard, like a pair of stuffed figures, go in.

Vita has been twice. She is doomed to go to Persia; and I minded the thought so much (thinking to lose sight of her for five years) that I conclude I am genuinely fond of her. Reading and writing go on. Not my novel though. And I can only think of all my faults as a novelist and wonder why I do it – a wonder which Lytton increases, and Morgan decreases. Lytton is off: The Loves of the Famous. Queen Elizabeth &c. I thought him at his most intimate last night; all plumy, incandescent, soft, luminous. Something slightly repels (too strong) Leonard. His character is not so good as Morgan's, he said, walking round the Square in the snow today. "There is something about all Stracheys –" Then, when we talk, L. and I, we rather crab Lytton's writing I observe. But all this vanishes with me when he comes, as yesterday, to talk, and talk, and talk. Nothing, in my sentimental heart, can stand against these old loyalties. If six people died, it is true that my life would cease: by which I mean, it would run so thin that though it might go on, would it have any relish? Imagine Leonard, Nessa Duncan Lytton Clive Morgan, all dead.

Monday 7 December
We shall spend Christmas at Charleston, which I'm afraid Leonard will not like much. We walked at Hampstead on Saturday. It was very cold. It had a foggy winter beauty. We went in to Ken Wood, and it was here that we discussed Lytton, gravely, like married people. But my God – how satisfactory

after, I think, twelve years, to have any human being to whom one can speak so directly as I to L.! He has the faults of a small nature said L. He is ungenerous. He asks, but never gives. But I have always known that – often I have seen the dull eyelid fall over him, if one asked a little too much: some sheath of selfishness that protects him from caring too much, or committing himself uncomfortably. He is cautious. He is a valetudinarian. But – I have known about Lytton's leathern eyelid since I was twenty. But L. said when they were at Cambridge Lytton was not like that to him. Morgan, said Leonard, as we trod back over the slippery hillocks seeing so little as we talked (and yet all this part of Hampstead recalls Katherine to me – that faint ghost, with the steady eyes, the mocking lips, and, at the end, the wreath set on her hair), Morgan has improved. Morgan is I think naturally more congenial to L. than Lytton is. He likes 'Sillies'; he likes the dependent simplicity of Morgan and myself. He likes settling our minds, and our immense relief at this. Well, well.

I am reading *A Passage to India*; but will not expatiate here, as I must elsewhere. (By the way, Robert Bridges likes *Mrs Dalloway*: says no one will read it; but it is beautifully written, and some more, which L. who was told by Morgan cannot remember.) Now, to write a list of Christmas presents. Ethel Sands comes to tea. But no Vita.

Monday 21 December
But no Vita! But Vita for three days at Long Barn, from which L. and I returned yesterday. These Sapphists *love* women; friendship is never untinged with amorosity. I like her and being with her, and the splendour – she shines in the grocer's shop in Sevenoaks with a candle-lit radiance, stalking on legs like beech trees, pink glowing, grape clustered, pearl hung. Anyhow she found me incredibly dowdy, no woman cared less for personal appearance – no one put on things in the way I did. Yet so beautiful, &c. What is the effect of all this on me? Very mixed. There is her maturity and full breastedness: her being so much in full sail on the high tides, where I am coasting down backwaters; her capacity I mean to take the floor in any company, to represent her country, to visit Chatsworth, to control silver, servants, chow dogs; her motherhood (but she is a little cold and offhand with her boys), her being in short (what I have never been) a real woman. In brain and insight she is not as highly organised as I am. But then she is aware of this, and so lavishes on me the maternal protection which, for some reason, is what I have always most wished from everyone. What L. gives me, and Nessa gives me, and Vita, in her more clumsy external way, tries to give me. Anyhow, I am very glad that she is coming to tea today, and I shall ask her, whether she minds my dressing so badly? I think she does.

We go down to Charleston tomorrow, not without some trepidation on my part.

1926

The year again began for Virginia with a period of ill-health and low spirits, the latter intensified by the absence in Persia of Vita Sackville-West, who now engrossed her feelings, and to whom she wrote long letters every few days. Nonetheless she was working on To the Lighthouse *with energy and confidence, though frequently distracted by the claims of the Hogarth Press – manuscripts to be read, parcels to pack, authors to see, etc. In March Leonard decided to resign his literary editorship of the* Nation & Athenaeum, *a decision applauded by Virginia, though in the event he was dissuaded by Maynard Keynes from carrying it out until early in 1930. In April the Woolfs went to Dorset for a few days' holiday, and soon afterwards Virginia finished the first part of* To the Lighthouse; *but then ordinary life was totally disrupted by the General Strike, the effects of which in Tavistock Square she records with a detail she suspects will prove tedious in later years. Vita returned to England in May and, after a first wary reunion, their intimacy quickened and flourished.*

Virginia's growing reputation brought increased social contact with the literary world; she greatly enjoyed meeting George Moore at one dinner party; yet a promising friendship with her contemporary Rose Macaulay received a setback when she and Leonard were her guests at another, unexpectedly formal, 'literary' dinner. She records the lunch-time talk of H. G. Wells and a visit to the Poet Laureate Robert Bridges near Oxford, shepherded by Lady Ottoline Morrell; she again observed the literary establishment with a cynical eye when Vita Sackville-West lectured to the Royal Society of Literature; and in July she and Leonard paid a visit to Thomas Hardy at his home near Dorchester, partly from motives of pure admiration, partly because Virginia had been commissioned by The Times Literary Supplement *to prepare an obituary tribute.*

On retreating to Monks House – where improvements, including the installation of a bath and two WCs had been made – at the end of July, Virginia was for a time prostrated with exhaustion; reviving in the cloudless August weather, she reached the end of To the Lighthouse, *but thereafter fell into a depression, which she analysed as arising from her being idle without being ill. In the autumn she was working on the revision of the first draft of her novel, seeing a great deal of Vita both in London and at Long Barn, being pursued by Lady Colefax, meeting her Bloomsbury familiars, and writing very little in her diary. On 22 December the Woolfs went to Cornwall to spend Christmas with Ka and Will Arnold-Forster at Zennor.*

1926

Tuesday 19 January
Vita having this moment (twenty minutes ago) left me, what are my feelings? Of a dim November fog; the lights dulled and damped. But this will disperse; then I shall want her, clearly and distinctly. Then not – and so on. One wants that atmosphere – to me so rosy and calm. She is not clever; but abundant and fruitful; truthful too. She taps so many sources of life; repose and variety, was her own expression, sitting on the floor this evening in the gaslight. I feel a lack of stimulus, of marked days, now Vita is gone; and some pathos, common to all these partings; and she has four days' journey through the snow.

Monday 8 February
Just back from Rodmell – to use again the stock opening. And I should explain why I've let a month slip perhaps. First, I think, the German measles or influenza; next Vita; then, disinclination for any exertion, so that I never made a book till last week. But undoubtedly this diary is established, and I sometimes look at it and wonder what on earth will be the fate of it. It is to serve the purpose of my memoirs. At sixty I am to sit down and write my life. I am rather tired, a little tired, from having thought too much about *To the Lighthouse.* Never never have I written so easily, imagined so profusely. Murry says my works won't be read in ten years' time.

Tuesday 23 February
Vita is a dumb letter writer, and I miss her. I miss the glow and the flattery and the festival. I miss her, I suppose, not very intimately. Nevertheless I do miss her, and wish it were May 10th.

I am blown like an old flag by my novel. This one is *To the Lighthouse.* I am now writing as fast and freely as I have ever written in the whole of my life; more so – twenty times more so – than any novel yet. Anyhow this goes on all the morning; and I have the devil's own work not to be flogging my brain all the afternoon. I live entirely in it, and come to the surface rather obscurely and am often unable to think what to say when we walk round the Square.

The publishing season is about to begin. Nessa says Why don't you give it up? I say, because I enjoy it. Then I wonder, but do I? What about Rome and Sicily? Am I a fanatical enthusiast for work, like my father? I think I have a strain of that, but I don't relish it. Tonight Francis Birrell and Rose Macaulay dine with us. To celebrate the occasion, I have bought a toast rack and a bedspread, which covers that atrocious chest of drawers which has worried me these two years. I am now so pleased with the colour that I go out and look at it.

Wednesday 24 February

They came last night, Francis and Rose Macaulay – I daresay I shall be calling her Rose one of these days. Rose – too chattery chittery at first go off; lean as a rake, wispy, and frittered. Some flimsy smartness and taint of the flimsy glittery literary about her: but this was partly nerves I think; and she felt us alien and observant doubtless. She has no humbug about her; only [is] frosted and rather cheaply gilt superficially with all that being asked to speak at dinners, to give opinions to newspapers. She is writing an article for an American paper on London after the War. It is this sort of thing that one distrusts in her. Why should she take the field so unnecessarily? But I fancy our 'leading lady novelists' all do as they are asked about this, and I am not quite one of them. I saw my own position a good deal lowered and diminished; and this is part of the value of seeing new people – still more of going to people's houses. One is, if anything, minimised: here in the eternal Bloomsbury, one is apt, without realising it, to expand. I like Francis. I like his laughter; and his random energy. We talked a lot of father, who, said Francis, dominates the Twentieth Century. "A remarkable man; for though he would not believe in God, he was stricter than those who did." Rose Macaulay said her parents called him always 'poor Leslie Stephen' because he had lost his faith. Also they said he was very gentle and charming.

Saturday 27 February

As for the soul: why did I say I would leave it out? I forget. And the truth is, one can't write directly about the soul. Looked at, it vanishes; but look at the ceiling, at Grizzle, at the cheaper beasts at the Zoo which are exposed to walkers in Regent's Park, and the soul slips in. Mrs Webb's book [*My Apprenticeship*] has made me think a little what I could say of my own life. But then there were causes in her life: prayer; principle. None in mine. Great excitability and search after something. Great content – almost always enjoying what I'm at, but with constant change of mood. I don't think I'm ever bored. Yet I have some restless searcher in me. Why is there not a discovery in life? Something one can lay hands on and say 'This is it'? What is it? And shall I die before I can find it? Then (as I was walking through Russell Square last night) I see mountains in the sky: the great clouds, and the moon which is risen over Persia; I have a great and astonishing sense of something there, which is 'it' – A sense of my own strangeness, walking on the earth is there too. Who am I, what am I, and so on; these questions are always floating about in me. Is that what I meant to say? Not in the least. I was thinking about my own character; not about the universe. Oh and about society again; dining with Lord Berners at Clive's made me think that. How, at a certain moment, I see through what I'm saying; detest myself; and wish for the other side of the moon; reading alone, that is. What did we talk about? Tom and the Sitwells; Eddie Marsh and Lady Colefax, and I felt one could go on saying these things for ever, and they mean nothing.

Tuesday 9 March

Then I was at two parties: Ethel [Sands]'s tea; Mary's dinner. Ethel's was a ghastly frizzly frying pan affair. I chattering in front of the footlights. As for Mary's party, there, save for the usual shyness about powder and paint, shoes and stockings, I was happy, owing to the supremacy of literature. This keeps us sweet and sane, George Moore and me I mean. He has a pink foolish face; blue eyes like hard marbles; a crest of snow white hair; little unmuscular hands; sloping shoulders; a high stomach; neat, purplish well brushed clothes; and perfect manners, as I consider them. That is to say he speaks without fear or dominance; accepting me on my merits; every one on their merits. Still in spite of age uncowed, unbeaten, lively, shrewd. "As for Hardy and Henry James though, what shall one say? I am a fairly modest man; but I admit I think *Esther Waters* a better book than *Tess*. But what is there to be said for that man? He cannot write. He cannot tell a story. The whole art of fiction consists in telling a story. But my good friend (to me – half hesitating to call me this), what have you to say for Hardy? You cannot find anything to say. English fiction is the worst part of English literature. Compare it with the French – with the Russians. Henry James wrote some pretty little stories before he invented his jargon. But they were about rich people. You cannot write stories about rich people," because, I think he said, they have no instincts. But Henry James was enamoured of marble balustrades. There was no passion in any of his people. And Anne Brontë was the greatest of the Brontës and Conrad could not write, and so on.

Saturday 20 March
But what is to become of all these diaries, I asked myself yesterday. If I
died, what would Leo make of them? He would be disinclined to burn them;
he could not publish them. Well, he should make up a book from them, I
think; and then burn the body. I daresay there is a little book in them; if
the scraps and scratches were straightened out a little. God knows. This is
dictated by a slight melancholia, which comes upon me sometimes now,
and makes me think I am old; I am ugly; I am repeating things. Yet, as far
as I know, as a writer I am only now writing out my mind.

Wednesday 24 March
"I'm going to hand in my resignation this morning" said L. making the
coffee. "To what?" I asked. "The *Nation*." And it is done; and we have six
months only before us. I feel ten years younger. It was a temporary
makeshift job, amusing at first, then galling, and last night, after an argument
of the usual kind about literary articles and space and so on with Maynard
and [the editor] Hubert [Henderson], L. came to the decision to resign now.
The mercy of having no ties, no proofs, no articles to procure, and all that,
is worth a little more exertion elsewhere. I'm amused at my own sense of
liberation. To upset everything every three or four years is my notion of a
happy life. But I suppose freedom becomes a fetish like any other. These
disjointed reflections I scribble on a divine, if gusty, day; being about to
dine at a pot-house with Rose Macaulay – not a cheerful entertainment;
but an experience perhaps.

Saturday 27 March
We went off on a blowing night to dine at Rose Macaulay's 'pot-house',
as I so mistakenly called it. There were ten second rate writers in second
rate dress clothes – L. by the way was in his red brown tweed. Then the
pitter patter began: the old yard was scratched over by these baldnecked
chickens. The truth was that we had no interests private: literature was our
common ground; and though I will talk literature with Desmond or Lytton
by the hour, when it comes to pecking up grains with these active stringy
fowls my gorge rises. What d'you think of the Hawthornden Prize? Why
isn't Masefield as good as Chaucer, or Gerhardi as good as Tchekhov?
Sylvias and Geralds and Roberts and Roses chimed and tinkled round the
table. I said "Holy Ghost?" when Mr O'Donovan said "The whole of the
coast." Lodged on a low sofa in Rose's underground cheerful, sane, breezy
room I talked to a young cultivated man, mild aesthete, but thank God, not
a second rate journalist. All the same I kept saying to myself, Thank God
to be out of that; out of the *Nation*; no longer brother in arms with Rose

and Robert and Sylvia. It is a thinblooded set; so 'nice', 'kind', respectable, cleverish and in the swim.

Then our set at Nessa's last night was hardly at its best. L. and Adrian silent and satirical; Old Sickert rather toothless and set; I driven to chatter, not well; but Nessa and Duncan don't consolidate and order these parties. L. was off early this morning to Rodmell where Philcox is in the thick of building and drains: so I had no time to uncrease my rose leaf; had to try and work; could not settle; suddenly shook my coat, like a retriever; and pondered where shall I spend the day? decided on Greenwich, arrived there at 1; lunched; everything fell out pat; smoked a cigarette on the pier promenade, saw the ships swinging up, one, two, three, out of the haze; adored it all; yes, even the lavatory keeper's little dog; saw the grey Wren buildings fronting the river; and then another great ship, grey and orange; with a woman walking on deck; and then to the Hospital: first to the Museum where I saw Sir John Franklin's pen and spoons (a spoon asks a good deal of imagination to consecrate it). I played with my mind watching what it would do – and behold if I didn't almost burst into tears over the coat Nelson wore at Trafalgar with the medals which he hid with his hand when they carried him down, dying, lest the sailors might see it was him. There was too his little fuzzy pigtail, of golden greyish hair tied in black; and his long white stockings, one much stained, and his white breeches with the gold buckles, and his stock – all of which I suppose they must have undone and taken off as he lay dying. Kiss me Hardy &c – Anchor, anchor. I read it all when I came in, and could swear I was there on the *Victory*. Then it was raining a little, but I went into the Park, which is all prominences and radiating paths; then back on top of a bus, and so to tea. I think my rose leaf is now uncrumpled. Certainly I shall remember the ships coming up and Nelson's coat long after I have forgotten how silly and uncomfortable I was at Nessa's on Friday.

Sunday 11 April
Mrs Webb's life makes me compare it with mine. The difference is that she is trying to relate all her experiences to history. She is very rational and coherent. She has always thought about her life and the meaning of the world: indeed, she begins this at the age of four. She has studied herself as a phenomenon. Thus her autobiography is part of the history of the Nineteenth Century. She makes herself fit in very persuasively and to my mind very interestingly. She taps a great stream of thought.

Friday 30 April
I have not said anything about Iwerne Minster. Now it would amuse me to see what I remember it by. Cranbourne Chase: the stunted aboriginal

forest trees, scattered, not grouped in cultivations; anemones, bluebells, violets, all pale, sprinkled about, without colour, livid, for the sun hardly shone. Then Blackmore Vale: a vast air dome and the fields dropped to the bottom; the sun striking, there, there; a drench of rain falling, like a veil streaming from the sky, there and there; and the downs rising, very strongly scarped (if that is the word) so that they were ridged and ledged; then an inscription in a church 'sought peace & ensured it', and the question, who wrote these sonorous stylistic epitaphs? And then tea and cream – these I remember; the hot baths; my new leather coat; Shaftesbury, so much lower and less commanding than my imagination, and the drive to Bournemouth, and the dog and the lady behind the rock, and the view of Swanage, and coming home.

And then it was horror: Nelly; faced her going; was firm yet desolated; on Tuesday she said "Please ma'am may I apologise"; and I had enough look into the 'servant question' to be glad to be safe again with Nelly. Now I vow come what may, never never to believe her again. "I am too fond of you ever to be happy with anyone else" she said. Talking of compliments, this is perhaps the greatest I could have.

Yesterday I finished the first part of *To the Lighthouse*, and today began the second. I cannot make it out – here is the most difficult abstract piece of writing – I have to give an empty house, no people's characters, the passage of time, all eyeless and featureless with nothing to cling to: well, I rush at it, and at once scatter out two pages. Is it nonsense, is it brilliance?

Wednesday 5 May
An exact diary of the Strike would be interesting. For instance, it is now a quarter to two; there is a brown fog; nobody is building; it is drizzling. The first thing in the morning we stand at the window and watch the traffic in Southampton Row. This is incessant. Everyone is bicycling; motor cars are huddled up with extra people. There are no buses. No placards. No newspapers. Water, gas and electricity are allowed; but at 11 the light was turned off. I sat in the Press in the brown fog, while L. wrote an article for the *Herald*. Then Clive dropped in, the door being left open. He is offering himself to the Government. Maynard excited, wants the Hogarth Press to bring out a skeleton number of the *Nation*. It is all tedious and depressing, rather like waiting in a train outside a station. One does not know what to do. And nature has laid it on thick today – fog, rain, cold. A voice, rather commonplace and official, wishes us good morning at 10. This is the Voice of Britain, to which we can make no reply. The voice is very trivial, and only tells us that the Prince of Wales is coming back, that the London streets present an unprecedented spectacle.

Thursday 6 May
Everything is the same, but unreasonably, or because of the weather, or habit, we are more cheerful, take less notice, and occasionally think of other things. Clive dines in Mayfair, and everyone is pro-men; I go to Harrison [dentist], and he shouts me down with "Its red rag versus Union Jack, Mrs Woolf". Frankie [Birrell] dines out, and finds everyone pro-government. Bob [Trevelyan] drops in and says Churchill is for peace, but [Prime Minister] Baldwin won't budge. Clive says Churchill is for tear gas bombs, fight to the death, and is at the bottom of it all. So we go on, turning in our cage. It feels like a deadlock, on both sides; as if we could keep fixed like this for weeks. What one prays for is God: the King or God; some impartial person to say kiss and be friends – as apparently we all desire. Just back from a walk to the Strand. One notices lorries full of elderly men and girls standing like passengers in the old third class carriages. Children swarm. The shops are open but empty. Over it all is some odd pale unnatural atmosphere – great activity but no normal life. Business improved today. We sold a few books. Clive calls in to discuss bulletins – indeed, more than anything it is like a house where someone is dangerously ill; and friends drop in to enquire, and one has to wait for doctors' news.

Friday 7 May
No change. 'London calling the British Isles. Good morning everyone.' That is how it begins at 10. The only news is that the archbishops are conferring, and ask our prayers that they may be guided right. Very little work done by either of us today. Leonard went to the [*Nation*] office, I to the British Museum; where all was chill serenity, dignity and severity. Written up are the names of great men; and we all cower like mice nibbling crumbs beneath. I like this dusty bookish atmosphere. Most of the readers seemed to have rubbed their noses off and written their eyes out. Yet they have a life they like – believe in the necessity of making books, I suppose; verify, collate, make up other books for ever. It must be fifteen years since I read here. I came home and found L. and Hubert [Henderson] 'taking a cup of tea', which means an hour and a half's talk about the Strike. L. says if the State wins and smashes the Trades Unions he will devote his life to Labour; if the archbishop succeeds, he will be baptised. Now to dine at the Commercio to meet Clive.

Sunday 9 May
There is no news of the strike. The broadcaster has just said that we are praying today. And L. and I quarrelled last night. I dislike the tub thumper in him; he the irrational Christian in me. Baldwin broadcast last night: he rolls his rs; tries to put more than mortal strength into his words. 'Have

faith in me. You elected me eighteen months ago. What have I done to forfeit your confidence? Can you not trust me to see justice done between man and man?' Impressive as it is to hear the very voice of the Prime Minister, descendant of Pitt and Chatham, still I can't heat up my reverence to the right pitch. No I don't trust him: I don't trust any human being, however loud they bellow and roll their rs.

Monday 10 May
Quarrel with L. settled in studio. Oh, but how incessant the arguments and interruptions are! As I write, L. is telephoning to Hubert. We are getting up a petition. There was a distinct thaw (we thought) last night. So we went to bed happy. Today ostensibly the same deadlock; beneath the surface all sorts of currents, of which we get the most contradictory reports. I to the House of Commons this morning with L.'s article to serve as stuffing for Hugh Dalton in the Commons this afternoon. All this humbug of police and marble statues vaguely displeasing. But the Government provided me with buses both ways, and no stones thrown. After lunch to bookshop; to London Library; walk home; Clive; then Maynard ringing up to command us to print the *Nation* as the *New Statesman* is printed; to which I agreed, and L. disagreed; then dinner; more telephones ringing at the moment, 9.5.

Tuesday 11 May
I may as well continue to write while I wait – here interruptions began which lasted from 12.30 to 3. I believe it is false psychology to think that in after years these details will be interesting. The war is now barren sand after all. But one never knows: and waiting about, writing serves to liberate the mind from the fret and itch of these innumerable details. Events are that the Roneo workers refuse to set up L.'s article in the *Nation*, in which he says that the strike is not illegal or unconstitutional. Presumably this is a little clutch of the Government throttle. Mr Baldwin has been visiting the Zoo. Tonight the names [the petition] are to be handed in; and then perhaps silence will descend upon us. But then everyone rings up – the most unlikely people. Yesterday Ralph [Partridge] and Frances Marshall were in a railway accident. One man was killed – the result of driving a train without signals, by the efforts of ardent optimistic undergraduates. Day's Library boy was set upon by roughs, had his cycle overturned, but kept his books and was unhurt after calling here.

Wednesday 12 May
Strike settled (ring at bell). The Strike was settled about 1.15 – or it was then broadcast. They told us to stand by and await important news. Then a piano played a tune. Then the solemn broadcaster assuming incredible

pomp and gloom and speaking one word to the minute read out: Message from 10 Downing Street. The TUC leaders have agreed that Strike shall be withdrawn. Instantly L. dashed off to telephone to the office; we finished lunch; then I rang up Clive – who proposes that we should have a drink tonight. I saw this morning five or six armoured cars slowly going along Oxford Street; on each two soldiers sat in tin helmets, and one stood with his hand at the gun which was pointed straight ahead ready to fire. But I also noticed on one a policeman smoking a cigarette. Such sights I dare say I shall never see again; and don't in the least wish to.

Thursday 13 May

I suppose all pages devoted to the Strike will be skipped, when I read over this book. Oh that dull old chapter, I shall say. Excitements about what are called real things are always unutterably transitory. Yet it is gloomy – and L. is gloomy, and so am I unintelligibly – today because the Strike continues – no railwaymen back: vindictiveness has now seized our masters. Government shillyshallies. Anyhow it will take a week to get the machinery of England to run again. In short, the strain removed, we all fall out and bicker and backbite. Such is human nature – and really I don't like human nature unless all candied over with art. We dined with a strike party last night and went back to Clive's. A good deal was said about art there.

Thursday 20 May

I think nothing need be said of the Strike. As tends to happen, one's mind slips after the crisis, and what the settlement is, or will be, I know not.

Vita comes to lunch tomorrow, which will be a great amusement and pleasure. I am amused at my relations with her: left so ardent in January – and now what? Also I like her presence and her beauty. Am I in love with her? But what is love? Her being 'in love' with me, excites and flatters; and interests. What is this 'love'? Oh and then she gratifies my eternal curiosity: who's she seen, what's she done – for I have no enormous opinion of her poetry. I should have been reading her poem tonight.

Tuesday 25 May

Tomorrow we go to Rodmell – to find the bath and the WC and drawing room with the wall pulled down. I have finished – sketchily I admit – the second part of *To the Lighthouse* – and may, then, have it all written over by the end of July. A record – seven months, if it so turns out.

So Vita came: and I register the shock of meeting after absence; how shy one is; how disillusioned by the actual body; and she was shabbier, come straight off in her travelling clothes; and not so beautiful, as sometimes perhaps; and so we sat talking on the sofa by the window, she rather silent,

I chattering, partly to divert her attention from me; and to prevent her thinking 'Well, is this all?' as she was bound to think, having declared herself so openly in writing. So that we each registered some disillusionment; and perhaps also acquired some grains of additional solidity – This may well be more lasting than the first rhapsody. But I cannot write. Suddenly the word instinct leaves me.

Wednesday 9 June

Then I got the 'flu, last Saturday; so have seen no one. Yes, Rodmell is a perfect triumph, I consider. In particular, our large combined drawing eating room with its five windows, its beams down the middle, and flowers and leaves nodding in all round us. The bath boils quickly; the water closets gush and surge (not quite sufficiently though). The weather again failed us. We then went to a party at Edith Sitwell's (I in my new dress) 'to meet Miss [Gertrude] Stein', a lady much like Joan Fry, but more massive; in blue sprinkled brocade, rather formidable. Edith distraught; and cherries in handfuls, and barley water.

Wednesday 30 June

This is the last day of June and finds me in black despair because Clive laughed at my new hat, Vita pities me, and I sank to the depths of gloom. This happened at Clive's last night after going to the Sitwells with Vita. Oh dear I was wearing the hat without thinking whether it was good or bad; and it was all very flashing and easy; and [I] sat by Vita and laughed and clubbed. When we got out it was only 10.30 – a soft starry night: it was still too early for her to go. So she said "Shall we go to Clive's and pick him up?" and I was then again so lighthearted, driving through the Park, and finally came to Gordon Square and there was Nessa tripping along in the dark, in her quiet black hat. Then Duncan came, carrying an egg. Come on all of us to Clive's, I said; and they agreed. Well, it was after they had come and we were all sitting round talking that Clive suddenly said, or bawled rather, what an astonishing hat you're wearing! Then he asked where I got it. I pretended a mystery, tried to change the talk, was not allowed, and they pulled me down between them, like a hare; it was very forced and queer and humiliating. So I talked and laughed too much. Duncan prim and acid as ever told me it was utterly impossible to do anything with a hat like that. And Leonard got silent, and I came away deeply chagrined, as unhappy as I have been these ten years; and revolved it in sleep and dreams all night; and today has been ruined.

Thursday 1 July

But all this has obscured Garsington; [Robert] Bridges; and [H. G.] Wells. These great men are so much like the rest of us. Wells remarkable only for a combination of stockishness with acuity: he has a sharp nose, and the cheeks and jowl of a butcher. He likes, I judge, rambling and romancing about the lives of other people; he romanced about the Webbs: said their books were splendid eggs, well and truly laid, but addled. Described Beatrice, as by a gipsy and a Jew: a flashing creature, become Quaker as we all do as we get on. That has nothing to do with Christianity. Are you a Quaker, I asked. Of course I am. One believes that there is a reason for things (I think he said). But he did not rise steadily off the ground for long. Lunch is a hot stodgy hour too. I could see from the plaintive watery look on Mrs Wells' face that he is arrogant lustful and bullying in private life. The virtues he likes are courage and vitality.

As for Bridges: he sprang from a rhododendron bush, a very lean tall old man, with a curly grey hat, and a reddish ravaged face, smoky fierce eyes, with a hazy look in them; very active; rather hoarse, talking incessantly. We sat in his open room and looked past blue spikes of flowers to hills, which were invisible, but when they show, all this goes out he said – his one poetical saying. He is direct and spry, very quick in all his movements, racing me down the garden to look at pinks, then into his library, where I asked to see the Hopkins manuscripts; and sat looking at them with that gigantic grasshopper Aldous [Huxley] folded up in a chair close by. Ottoline undulated and vagulated. I said how much I like his poems – true of the short ones: but was mainly pleased and gratified to find him so obliging and easy and interested.

Sunday 4 July

Then Wells came again; and stayed till 4. He is getting to the drowsy stage: the sixties. He talked about his new book, the thoughts one has at sixty. What other ideas has he? Desmond asked. Well, to do away with Sunday. There should be a holiday once in ten days. That was his own stint. Ten days work, then four or five days off. The present system was wasteful. The shadow of the week-end begins on Friday, is not over till Monday afternoon. He struck me again as an odd mixture of bubble and solidity – likes to blow a phrase now and then. We got him on Hardy – a very simple, subtle old peasant man much impressed by clever people who write; very humble; wrote his early books in chapters as the printers wanted them. Then he got up to go: we asked him to stay and tell us about Henry James. So he sat down. Oh I should be delighted to stay and talk the whole afternoon, he said. Henry James was a formalist. He always thought of clothes. He was never intimate with anyone – not with his brother even:

had never been in love. Wells has learnt nothing from Proust – his book like the British Museum. One knows there are delightful interesting things in it, but one does not go there. One day it may be wet – I shall say God, what am I to do this afternoon? And I shall read Proust as I might go to the British Museum. Would not read Richardson – a man who knows all about feminine psychology – nobody ought to know that. I said on the contrary he knew very little: was conventional. Honour, chastity and so on. Wells said we had changed our ideas completely. That idea of chastity had vanished. Women were even more suggestible than men. He said we are happier perhaps – children are certainly more at ease with their parents. But he thought they were beginning to miss restraints. They were wondering what things were for. Henry James could not describe love – there comes the ahh – laying on of hands. This Wells could do himself. I am a journalist. I pride myself upon being a journalist he said. In all this he showed himself, as Desmond said afterwards, perfectly content to be himself, aware of his powers – aware that he need not take any trouble, since his powers were big enough.

Thursday 22 July
The summer hourglass is running out rapidly and rather sandily. Many nights I wake in a shudder thinking of some atrocity of mine. I bring home minute pinpricks which magnify in the middle of the night into gaping wounds. However I drive my pen through de Quincey of a morning, having put *To the Lighthouse* aside till Rodmell. There all virtue, all good is in retreat. Here nothing but odds and ends – going to the dentist, buying combs; must dine with Osbert Sitwell tonight though, and go to Hardy tomorrow.

Sunday 25 July
At first I thought it was Hardy, and it was the parlourmaid, a small thin girl, wearing a proper cap. She came in with silver cake stands and so on. Mrs Hardy talked to us about her dog. How long ought we to stay? Can Mr Hardy walk much &c I asked, making conversation. She has the large sad lack lustre eyes of a childless woman; great docility and readiness, as if she had learnt her part; not great alacrity, but resignation, in welcoming more visitors; wears a sprigged voile dress, black shoes, and a necklace. We can't go far now, she said, though we do walk every day, because our dog isn't able to walk far. He bites, she told us. She became more natural and animated about the dog, who is evidently the real centre of her thoughts. Then again the door opened, more sprucely, and in trotted a little puffy cheeked cheerful old man, with an atmosphere cheerful and businesslike in addressing us, rather like an old doctor's or solicitor's, saying "Well now –"

or words like that as he shook hands. He was dressed in rough grey with a striped tie. His nose has a joint in it, and the end curves down. A round whitish face, the eyes now faded and rather watery, but the whole aspect cheerful and vigorous. He sat on a three cornered chair at a round table, where there were the cake stands and so on; a chocolate roll; what is called a good tea; but he only drank one cup, sitting on his three cornered chair. He was extremely affable and aware of his duties. He did not let the talk stop or disdain making talk. He talked of father – said he had seen me, or it might have been my sister but he thought it was me, in my cradle. He had been to Hyde Park Place – oh Gate was it. A very quiet street. That was why my father liked it. Odd to think that in all these years he had never been down there again. He went there often. Your father took my novel – *Far from the Madding Crowd*. We stood shoulder to shoulder against the British public about certain matters dealt with in that novel – you may have heard. Some other novel had fallen through that was to appear; and he asked me to send my story. So I sent it in chapter by chapter, and was never late. Wonderful what youth is! I had it in my head doubtless, but I never thought twice about it – it came out every month.

He puts his head down like some old pouter pigeon. He has a very long head; and quizzical bright eyes, for in talk they grow bright. He said when he was in the Strand six years ago he scarcely knew where he was, and he used to know it all intimately. At this rate London would soon be unrecognisable. But I shall never go there again. And he smiled in his queer way, which is fresh and yet sarcastic a little: anyhow shrewd. Indeed, there was no trace to my thinking of the simple peasant. He seemed perfectly aware of everything; in no doubt or hesitation; having made up his mind; and being delivered of all his work; so that he was in no doubt about that either. He was not interested much in his novels, or in anybody's novels. "I never took long with them" he said. Can you write poetry regularly? I asked (being beset with the desire to hear him say something about his books); but the dog kept cropping up. How he bit; how the inspector came out; how he was ill; and they could do nothing for him. Would you mind if I let him in? asked Mrs Hardy, and in came Wessex, a very tousled, rough brown and white mongrel, got to guard the house, so naturally he bites people, said Mrs Hardy. Well, I don't know about that, said Hardy, perfectly natural, and not setting much stock by his poems either it seemed. Did you write poems at the same time as your novels? I asked. No, he said. I wrote a great many poems. I used to send them about, but they were always returned, he chuckled. I wanted him to say one word about his writing before we left and could only ask which of his books he would have chosen, if like me, he had had to choose one to read in the train. I had taken *The Mayor of Casterbridge*. "And did it hold your interest?" he asked. I stammered that I could not stop reading it, which was true, but sounded wrong. Anyhow he was not going to be drawn, and went off about giving a young lady a wedding present. None of my books are fitted to be wedding presents, he said. You must give Mrs Woolf one of your books, said Mrs Hardy, inevitably. Yes I will. But I'm afraid only in the little thin paper edition, he said.

He said to a friend who begged him not to give up poetry, "I'm afraid poetry is giving up me." The truth is he is a very kind man, and sees anyone who wants to see him. He has sixteen people for the day sometimes. Do you think one can't write poetry if one sees people? I asked. "One might be able to – I don't see why not. Its a question of physical strength" said Hardy. But clearly he preferred solitude himself. Always however he said something sensible and sincere; and thus made the obvious business of compliment giving rather unpleasant. He seemed to be free of it all; very active minded; liking to describe people; not to talk in an abstract way.

Now we began to look at the grandfather clock in the corner. We said we must go – tried to confess we were only down for the day. I forgot to say that he offered L. whisky and water, which struck me that he was competent as a host, and in every way. So we got up and signed Mrs Hardy's visitors' books; and Hardy took my *Life's Little Ironies* off, and trotted back with it signed, and Woolf spelt Wolff, which I daresay had given him some anxiety. Then Wessex came in again. I asked if Hardy could stroke him. So he bent down and stroked him, like the master of the house. Wessex went on wheezing away. What impressed me was his freedom, ease, and vitality. He seemed very 'Great Victorian', doing the whole thing with a sweep of his hand and setting no great stock by literature; but somehow, one could imagine, naturally swept off into imagining and creating without a thought of its being difficult or remarkable; becoming obsessed; and living in imagination. Mrs Hardy thrust his old grey hat into his hand and he trotted us out on to the road. And so we left, and he trotted in again.

The whole thing – literature, novels &c – all seemed to him an amusement, far away, too, scarcely to be taken seriously. Yet he had sympathy and pity for those still engaged in it. But what his secret interests and activities are – to what occupation he trotted off when we left him – I do not know.

MONKS HOUSE, RODMELL

Saturday 31 July
Here is a whole nervous breakdown in miniature. We came on Tuesday. Sank into a chair, could scarcely rise; everything insipid; tasteless, colourless.

Enormous desire for rest. Wednesday – only wish to be alone in the open air. Air delicious – avoided speech; could not read. Thought of my own power of writing with veneration, as of something incredible, belonging to someone else; never again to be enjoyed by me. Mind a blank. Slept in my chair. Thursday. No pleasure in life whatsoever; but felt perhaps more attuned to existence. Character and idiosyncracy as Virginia Woolf completely sunk out. Humble and modest. Difficulty in thinking what to say. Read automatically, like a cow chewing cud. Slept in chair. Friday. Sense of physical tiredness; but slight activity of the brain. Beginning to take notice. Making one or two plans. Saturday (today) much clearer and lighter. Thought I could write, but resisted, or found it impossible. A desire to read poetry set in on Friday. This brings back a sense of my own individuality. But today senses quickening. Curiosity about literature returning.

Friday 3 September
For the rest, Charleston, Tilton, *To the Lighthouse*, Vita, expeditions: the summer dominated by a feeling of washing in boundless warm fresh air – such an August not come my way for years; bicycling; no settled work done, but advantage taken of air for going to the river, or over the downs. The novel is now easily within sight of the end, but this, mysteriously, comes no nearer.

Sunday 5 September
I am frightfully contented these last few days, by the way. I don't quite understand it. Perhaps reason has something to do with it. Charleston and Tilton knocked me off my perch for a moment: Nessa and her children; Maynard and his carpets. My own gifts and shares seemed so moderate in comparison; my own fault too – a little more self control on my part, and we might have had a boy of twelve, a girl of ten. This always rakes me wretched in the early hours. So I said, I am spoiling what I have. And thereupon settled to exploit my own possessions to the full; I can make money and buy carpets; I can increase the pleasure of life enormously by living it carefully. No doubt, this is a rationalisation of a state which is not really of that nature. Probably I am very lucky. Then, I am extremely happy walking on the downs. I like to have space to spread my mind out in. Whatever I think, I can rap out, suddenly, to L. We are somehow very detached, free, harmonious. Hence I come to my moral, which is simply to enjoy what one does enjoy, without teasing oneself oh but Nessa has children, Maynard carpets.

I am almost entirely surrounded by sheep. God knows, I wish we could buy the terrace, and have a garden all round the lodge – but this is not a serious diminution of joy.

Monday 13 September

The blessed thing is coming to an end I say to myself with a groan. Oh the relief of waking and thinking its done – the relief, and the disappointment I suppose. I am talking of *To the Lighthouse*. Morgan said he felt 'This is a failure' as he finished *A Passage to India*. I feel – what? A little stale this last week or two from steady writing. But also a little triumphant.

Wednesday 15 September

A State of Mind. Woke up perhaps at 3. Oh its beginning its coming – the horror – physically like a painful wave swelling about the heart – tossing me up. I'm unhappy unhappy! Down – God, I wish I were dead. Pause. But why am I feeling like this? Let me watch the wave rise. I watch. Vanessa. Children. Failure. Yes, I detect that. Failure failure. (The wave rises). Oh they laughed at my taste in green paint! Wave crashes. I wish I were dead! I've only a few years to live I hope. I can't face this horror any more – (this is the wave spreading out over me). This goes on; several times, with varieties of horror. Then, at the crisis, instead of the pain remaining intense, it becomes rather vague. I doze. I wake with a start. The wave again! The irrational pain: the sense of failure; generally some specific incident, as for example my taste in green paint, or buying a new dress, or asking Dadie for the week-end, tacked on. At last I say, watching as dispassionately as I can, Now take a pull of yourself. No more of this. I reason. I take a census of happy people and unhappy. I brace myself to shove to throw to batter down. I begin to march blindly forward. I feel obstacles go down. I say it doesn't matter. Nothing matters. I become rigid and straight, and sleep again, and half wake and feel the wave beginning and watch the light whitening and wonder how, this time, breakfast and daylight will overcome it; and then hear L. in the passage and simulate, for myself as well as for him, great cheerfulness; and generally am cheerful, by the time breakfast is over. Does everyone go through this state? Why have I so little control? It is the cause of much waste and pain in my life.

Tuesday 28 September

Intense depression: I have to confess that this has overcome me several times since September 6th (or thereabouts). It does not come from something definite, but from nothing. I discovered that, for the first time for many years, I had been idle without being ill. This is a warning then; never to cease the use of the brain. Then, owing to mismanagement, no one came to stay, and I got very few letters; and the high pure hot days went on and on; and this blankness persisted, and I began to suspect my book of the same thing; and there was Nessa humming and booming and flourishing over the hill; and one night we had a long long argument. Vita started it by coming over, and L. (I say) spoilt the visit by glooming because I said he had been angry. He shut up, and was caustic; but admitted that my habits of describing him and others had this effect often. I saw myself, my brilliancy, genius, charm, beauty (&c &c – the attendants who float me through so many years) diminish and disappear. One is in truth an elderly dowdy fussy ugly incompetent woman, vain, chattering and futile. Then he said our relations had not been so good lately. I admitted that I had been irritated, first by the prevalency of dogs (Grizzle on heat too). Secondly by his assumption that we can afford to saddle ourselves with a whole time gardener, build or buy him a cottage, and take in the terrace to be garden. Then, I said, we shall be tying ourselves to come here; shall never travel; and it will be assumed that Monks House is the hub of the world. This it certainly is not, I said, to me; nor do I wish to spend such a measure of our money on gardens, when we cannot buy rugs, beds or good armchairs. L. was, I think, hurt at this, and I was annoyed at saying it, yet did it, not angrily, but in the interests of freedom. Too many women give way on this point, and secretly grudge their unselfishness in silence – a bad atmosphere. Our atmosphere decidedly cleared, after this, and I am once more full of work, and quite unable, I see, to make plain even to my own eyes, my season of profound despondency.

But it is always a question whether I wish to avoid these glooms. In part they are the result of getting away by oneself. These nine weeks give one a plunge into deep waters; which is a little alarming, but full of interest. One goes down into the well and nothing protects one from the assault of truth. Down there I can't write or read; I exist however. I am. Then I ask myself what I am? and get a closer though less flattering answer than I should on the surface – where, to tell the truth, I get more praise than is right. I am glad to find it on the whole so interesting, though so acutely unpleasant.

Thursday 30 September
I wished to add some remarks to this, on the mystical side of this solitude; how it is not oneself but something in the universe that one's left with. It is this that is frightening and exciting in the midst of my profound gloom, depression, boredom, whatever it is: one sees a fin passing far out. What image can I reach to convey what I mean? Really there is none I think. All I mean to make is a note of a curious state of mind. I hazard the guess that it may be the impulse behind another book.

I was depressed again today because Vita did not come (yet relieved at the same time); had to hold L.'s ladder in the garden, when I wanted to write or to try on Nessa's dress; and slightly afraid that this dress is not very successful. But I am shelving the dress problem on these principles. I am having cheap day clothes; and a good dress from Brooke; and am being less pernickety about keeping to limits, as I have only to write and stir myself to make, I wager, quite £50 extra in the year for my own extravagances. No longer shall I be afraid to lunch out because 'I've no clothes'. Soon, this time next week, I shall have no time for glooming or introspection. It will be "When may I come and see you?"

52 TAVISTOCK SQUARE, WC1

Saturday 30 October
It will be when may I come and see you! – too true a prophecy, though made in the damp and solitude of Rodmell. So the week slips or sticks through my fingers; rage misery joy, dullness elation mix. I am the usual battlefield of emotions; alternately think of buying chairs and clothes; plod with some method revising *To the Lighthouse*; quarrel with Nelly; and so we go on. Among external things, we were at Cambridge for the week-end; kept warm at the Bull – and there's a good subject – the Hotel. A whole life opened to me. Then [Sir Edmund] Gosse introducing Vita at Royal – something [Society of Literature]. I never saw the whole hierarchy of literature so plainly exposed. Gosse the ornament on the tea pot: beneath him file on file of old stout widows whose husbands had been professors, beetle specialists doubtless, meritorious dons; and these good people, reflecting all the depths of the suburbs tinctured with literature, dear Vita told them were 'The Hollow Men'. Her address was read in sad sulky tones like those of a schoolboy; her rich pendulous society face, glowing out under a black hat at the end of the smoky dismal room, looked very ancestral and like a picture under glass in a gallery. She was fawned upon by the little dapper grocer Gosse, who kept spinning round on his heel to address her compliments and to scarify Bolshevists; in an ironical voice which seemed to ward off what might be said of him; and to be drawing round the lot of them thicker and thicker, the red plush curtains of respectability. I don't regret my wildest, foolishest, utterance, if it gave the least crack to this respectability. But needless to say, no word of mine has had any effect whatever. Gosse will survive us all.

Tuesday 23 November
. . . a discussion at tea about Angus. He don't do, L. says: will never make a manager. These difficulties recur. Next year L. thinks we could sell to advantage. It [the Hogarth Press] gives one a full life: but then life is so full already. Colefax complicates the scene – Colefax is the death of

this book. Aren't I always reading her scrawls or answering them. This culminated last week in her dining alone with me, off cold chicken. I found us talking socially, not intimately, she in pearls (shams Vita says) popping up one light after another: like the switch board at the telephone exchange at the mention of names. She is, I maintain, a woman of the world: has all her senses tuned to that pitch. The machine doesn't work in private, though she was very anxious, poor aspiring, slightly suspicious and uneasy woman, that it should. Now, aged fifty, she asks, Is this life? – rushing round, dining and giving dinners; never able to concentrate in a corner, and secretly, in my opinion, not desiring it but pretending it, as she has the habit of pretence. This is all right in her, but wrong in me. So we don't altogether amalgamate; but I have my reservations, she hers. In came Dadie, to our relief, somewhat.

Fame grows. Chances of meeting this person, doing that thing, accumulate. Life is as I've said since I was ten, awfully interesting – if anything, quicker, keener at forty-four than twenty-four – more desperate I suppose, as the river shoots to Niagara – my new vision of death. "The one experience I shall never describe" I said to Vita yesterday. She was sitting on the floor in her velvet jacket and red striped silk shirt, I knotting her pearls into heaps of great lustrous eggs. She had come up to see me – so we go on – a spirited, creditable affair, I think, innocent (spiritually) and all gain, I think; rather a bore for Leonard, but not enough to worry him. The truth is one has room for a good many relationships. Then she goes back again to Persia.

I am re-doing six pages of *Lighthouse* daily. My present opinion is that it is easily the best of my books.

1927

Back in Tavistock Square after a chilly Christmas in Cornwall, Leonard read and approved To the Lighthouse, *which was put into proof, corrected by Virginia, and published in May. In the early months of the year Virginia felt bereft of her intimates; Vanessa and Duncan were at Cassis, where Clive was to join them; Vita, with whom Virginia had spent two nights in January at the Sackvilles' ancestral home, Knole, rejoined her husband in Persia, and again Virginia felt the want of her intensely; and it was the recollection of Vita and a perception of the historical continuity of her forebears at Knole that set off a profusion of ideas which was to result in her fantasy* Orlando.*

This year the Hogarth Press published over forty books and pamphlets, and Leonard's doubts about the amiable Angus Davidson's capacity to 'manage' led to the latter's reluctant resignation at the end of the year, after which Leonard himself managed the business until 1931 with what Virginia called 'competent underlings'.

The Woolfs' spring holiday took them via Cassis as far afield as Sicily, with a week in Rome on the return journey. On coming home Nelly the cook was found to be ill; To the Lighthouse *was published and sold well; Vita returned from Persia and again occupied the foreground of Virginia's life. A sharp spell of headache at the end of May gave her the excuse thereafter to fend off unwanted visitors and invitations, but did not prevent her from joining a party with Vita and Harold Nicolson which took an overnight train to Yorkshire to observe the total eclipse of the sun on 29 June. The success of* To the Lighthouse *enabled the Woolfs to buy a motor car in July; Virginia herself took driving lessons but gave up after a while, and it was Leonard who habitually drove.*

Before settling in at Monks House early in August, Virginia crossed the Channel to spend three days near Dieppe with her American painter friends Ethel Sands and Nan Hudson; she then spent a happy summer in Sussex, writing easily, motoring about the countryside, seeing a good deal of Vita, of her family and her friends, observing country life; and, just before leaving, plunging into the 'greatest rapture known to me' – the inspired writing of Orlando. *This kept her absorbed and vigorous during the later months of the year, with little time or inclination to air her discontents in her diary; enjoying her work, enjoying her pleasures, enjoying her success. On Christmas Eve the Woolfs went to Sussex for nine days.*

1927

Sunday 23 January

Well Leonard has read *To the Lighthouse*, and says it is much my best book, and it is a 'masterpiece'. He said this without my asking. I came back from Knole and sat without asking him. He calls it entirely new – 'a psychological poem' is his name for it. Having won this great relief, my mind dismisses the whole thing, as usual; and I forget it, and shall only wake up and be worried again over proofs and then when it appears.

We went to Cornwall. Will [Arnold-Forster] is a water-blooded waspish little man, all on edge, vain, peevish, nervous. Ka is matronly, but substantial. Some views I retain – one of the valley in the evening light – but others were only a dull impression of life suspended and frozen. We came home for these reasons a day early, and next morning I had a letter from the *New York Herald Tribune* asking me to go there, passage paid, £120 in my pocket and, perhaps, expenses, and write four articles. We accepted, on conditions; but have not heard yet. Meanwhile we hesitate, for if Leonard came, we should probably be £150 out of pocket. The adventure is tempting. But the grind of moneymaking is scarcely to be endured unnecessarily. We could go to Greece, or Italy, for less.

At Knole, Vita took me over the four acres of building, which she loves; too little conscious beauty for my taste: smallish rooms looking on to buildings; no views; yet one or two things remain: Vita stalking in her Turkish dress, attended by small boys, down the gallery, wafting them on like some tall sailing ship – a sort of covey of noble English life: dogs walloping, children crowding, all very free and stately; and a cart bringing wood in to be sawn by the great circular saw. They had brought wood in from the Park to replenish the great fires like this for centuries; and her ancestresses had walked so on the snow with their great dogs bounding by them. All the centuries seemed lit up, the past expressive, articulate; not dumb and forgotten; but a crowd of people stood behind, not dead at all; and so we reach the days of Elizabeth quite easily. After tea, looking for letters of Dryden's to show me, she tumbled out a love letter of Lord

Dorset's (Seventeenth Century) with a lock of his soft gold tinted hair which I held in my hand a moment. One had a sense of links fished up into the light which are usually submerged. Otherwise no particular awe or any great sense of difference or distinction. They are not a brilliant race. I came home to Marjorie Strachey, Tom Eliot, Nessa and Roger. A little constricted our society: but how lively and agile compared with the [aristocracy?]

Thursday 3 February

I ask, why another volume? What is the purpose of them? L. taking up a volume the other day said Lord save him if I died first and he had to read through these. And do I say anything interesting? I can always waste an idle hour reading them; and then, oh yes, I shall write my memoirs out of them one of these days.

That reminds me of the Webbs: those thirty-six strenuous hours at Liphook, in an emphatic lodging house, with blue books in the passages; and those entirely devoted – by which I mean those entirely integrated people. Their secret is that they have by nature no divisions of soul to fritter them away: their impact is solid and entire. Without eyes and ears (but Mrs Webb listens in and prefers Mozart to Handel, if I may guess) one can come down with more of a weight upon bread and butter or whatever the substance is before one. On a steely watery morning we swiftly tramped over a heathy common talking, talking. In their efficiency and glibness one traces perfectly adjusted machinery; but talk by machinery does not charm, or suggest: it cuts the grass of the mind close at the roots. I'm too hurried to write. Mrs Webb is far less ornamental than of old: wispy untidy drab, with a stain on her skirt and a key on her watch chain; as if she had cleared the decks and rolled her sleeves and was waiting for the end, but working.

Saturday 12 February

But I am forgetting, after three days, the most important event in my life since marriage – so Clive described it. Mr Cizec has bingled me. I am short haired for life. Having no longer, I think, any claims to beauty, the convenience of this alone makes it desirable. Every morning I go to take up brush and twist that old coil round my finger and fix it with hairpins and then with a start of joy, no I needn't. In front there is no change; behind I'm like the rump of a partridge. This robs dining out of half its terrors. For the rest – its been a gay tropical kind of autumn, with so much Vita and Knole and staying away: we have launched ourselves a little more freely perhaps from work and the Press. But now with Nessa away, Clive away, Duncan away, Vita away, the strenuous time sets in: I'm reading and writing at a great pace; mean to make all the money we want for Greece and a motor car.

Yesterday rather a flat talk with Angus. L. says he doesn't 'manage'. Angus refuses to budge an inch. He can't see the point of it. As he says, too, what's he to do if he leaves? He doesn't much want to leave. Though sometimes 'fed up' he likes it better than most work. But I'm persuaded we need, the Press needs, a fanatic at the moment; not this quiet easygoing gentlemanliness. I am annoyed at doing cards, and envelopes; and L. does twice the work I do.

Monday 28 February

My brain is rather stale. Do I like *The Lighthouse*? I think I was disappointed. But God knows. I have to read it again.

And now the wind is making the tin screen over the gas fire rattle. How we protect ourselves from the elements! Coming back last night [from Rodmell] I thought, owing to civilisation, I, who am now cold, wet, and hungry, can be warm and satisfied and listening to a Mozart quartet in fifteen minutes. And so I was. That ring may be Tom. No. Tom don't run upstairs – only the lower classes do that.

And I don't think I shall go out in the rain, though I am going to spend this week in long romantic London walks. I have successfully broken the neck of that screaming grey goose – society. There's nothing to be afraid of in dining with Ethel or Sibyl – and I'm shingled now. One spins round for a moment and then settles on one's feet. But about the Soul: the soul has sunk to the bottom. I am empty headed tonight.

Saturday 5 March

Both rather headachy and fatigued. A holiday, without dinner to order, or telephone to answer, or people to talk to, will be a divine miracle. We go to Cassis on the 30th; then to Sicily; so home by Rome. What could be more to my heart. Often I sit and think of looking at things. The greed of my eye is insatiable. To think of seeing a new place fills me with excitement. I now make up pictures of Sicily. Think of the Campagna grey in the evening.

Monday 14 March

Although annoyed that I have not heard from Vita by this post nor yet last week, annoyed sentimentally, and partly from vanity – still I must record the conception last night of a new book. Suddenly between twelve and one I conceived a whole fantasy to be called 'The Jessamy Brides' – why, I wonder? I have rayed round it several scenes. Two women, poor, solitary at the top of a house. One can see anything (for this is all fantasy), the

Tower Bridge, clouds, aeroplanes. Everything is to be tumbled in pell mell. Sapphism is to be suggested. Satire is to be the main note – satire and wildness. The Ladies are to have Constantinople in view. Dreams of golden domes. My own lyric vein is to be satirised. Everything mocked. And it is to end with three dots . . . so. For the truth is I feel the need of an escapade after these serious poetic experimental books whose form is always so closely considered. I want to kick up my heels and be off. I think this will be great fun to write; and it will rest my head before starting the very serious, mystical poetical work which I want to come next.

Monday 21 March
Almost in a week now we shall be starting. I dislike the days before going. I went to buy clothes today and was struck by my own ugliness. Like Edith Sitwell I can never look like other people – too broad, tall, flat, with hair hanging. And now my neck is so ugly.

Edith Sitwell came to tea: transparent like some white bone one picks up on a moor, with sea water stones on her long frail hands which slide into yours much narrower than one expects like a folded fan. She has pale gemlike eyes; and is dressed, on a windy March day, in three decker skirts of red spotted cotton. She half shuts her eyes; coos an odd little laugh. All is very tapering and pointed, the nose running on like a mole. She said I was a great writer, which pleased me. So sensitive to everything in people and books she said. She got talking about her mother blaspheming in the nursery, hysterical; terrible; setting Edith to kill bluebottles. She is a curious product, likeable to me: sensitive, etiolated, affectionate, lonely, having to thread her way (there is something ghostlike and angular about her) home to Bayswater to help cook dinner. In other ages she would have been a cloistered nun; or an eccentric secluded country old maid. It is the oddity of our time that has set her on the music hall stage. She trips out into the limelight with all the timidity and hauteur of the aristocratic spinster.

* * *

Sunday 1 May
We came back on Thursday night from Rome; from that other private life which I mean to have for ever now. One is nobody in Italy: one has no name, no calling, no background. Altogether I don't think I've ever enjoyed one month so much. What a faculty of enjoyment one has! I liked everything. I wish I were not so ignorant of Italian, art, literature and so on. However, I cannot now write this out, or go into the great mass of feeling which it composed in me. Nelly was found, at 11.30, when we got back, in bed, with some mysterious affection of the kidney. This was a jar; the coffee was a

jar; everything was a jar. And then I remember how my book is coming out. But I think, honestly, I care very little this time – even for the opinion of my friends.

Thursday 5 May

Book out. We have sold (I think) 1690 before publication – twice *Dalloway*. I write however in the shadow of the damp cloud of the *TLS* review, gentlemanly, kindly, timid and praising beauty, doubting character, and leaving me moderately depressed. I know why I am depressed: a bad habit of making up the review I should like before reading the review I get.

Wednesday 11 May

Vita back; unchanged, though I daresay one's relation changes from day to day. Clive and she together. I think Clive is pretty miserable: his stay at Cassis a failure, so far as writing goes. And then the question rises, has he not gone too far in eating, drinking, love making, to stop dead now? He seemed random and unsettled. He talked (always shifting away from himself yet returning ambiguously to that centre) about going mad: sometimes thought he was going mad.

My book. What is the use of saying one is indifferent to reviews when positive praise, though mingled with blame, gives one such a start on, that instead of feeling dried up, one feels, on the contrary, flooded with ideas? I gather from vague hints, through Marjorie Thomson, through Clive, that some people say it is my best book.

Monday 16 May

The book. Now on its feet so far as praise is concerned. Nessa enthusiastic – a sublime, almost upsetting spectacle. She says it is an amazing portrait of mother; a supreme portrait painter; has lived in it; found the rising of the dead almost painful. Then Ottoline, then Vita, then Charlie [Sanger], then Lord Olivier, then Tommy [Tomlin], then Clive – he came in, ostensibly to praise this 'amazing book – far the best you've ever written', and sat on, but how wandering and unhappy. I have scarcely seen him in this mood ever before. But what is it? Has he lost faith? Has the dancing mist of rhapsody failed him – he who was based so solidly on such beef and beer or champagne rather. Suppose one woke and found oneself a fraud? It was part of my madness – that horror. But then as Clive said, you go mad but you bound up again – the inference being that he was to stay mad.

Monday 6 June (Whit Monday)

I have been in bed a week with a sudden and very sharp headache, and this is written experimentally to test my brain. The *Lighthouse* has sold 2,200 and we are reprinting. And now, with Morgan's morganatic, evasive, elusive letter this morning, the *Lighthouse* is behind me: my headache over; and after a week at Rodmell, my freedom from inspection, my deep dive into my own mind will begin. How odd, it comes into my mind, is Nessa and my jealousy of each other's clothes! I feel her, when I put on my smart black fringed cape, anguished for a second. Then she says she is going to wear earrings: I say at once that I will; this she resents. Yet we are both fundamentally sensible, and so recover from our umbrage. I think, however, I am now almost an established figure – as a writer. They don't laugh at me any longer. Soon they will take me for granted. Possibly I shall be a celebrated writer.

Saturday 18 June

This is a terribly thin diary for some reason: half the year has been spent, and left only these few sheets. Perhaps I have been writing too hard in the morning to write here also. Three weeks wiped out by headache. We had a week at Rodmell, of which I remember various sights, and the immense comfort of lying there lapped in peace. Lay out all day in the new garden, with the terrace. There were blue tits nested in the hollow neck of my Venus. Slowly ideas began trickling in; and then suddenly I rhapsodised and told over the story of the Moths, which I think I will write very quickly: the play poem idea; the idea of some continuous stream, not solely of human thought, but of the ship, the night, &c, all flowing together: intersected by the arrival of the bright moths. A man and a woman are to be sitting at table talking. Or shall they remain silent? It is to be a love story: she is finally to let the last great moth in. Perhaps the man could be left absolutely dim. France: near the sea; at night; a garden under the window. But it needs ripening. I do a little work on it in the evening when the gramophone is playing late Beethoven sonatas. (The windows fidget at their fastenings as if we were at sea.)

We saw Vita given the Hawthornden [Prize]. A horrid show up, I thought: not of the gentry on the platform – Squire, Drinkwater, Binyon only: of us all: all of us chattering writers. My word! how insignificant we all looked! How can we pretend that we are interesting, that our works matter? The whole business of writing became infinitely distasteful. But there may be a stream of ink in them that matters more than the look of them – so tightly clothed, mild, and decorous – showed. I felt there was no one full grown mind among us. In truth, it was the thick dull middle class of letters that met; not the aristocracy.

Wednesday 22 June

Harold Nicolson and Duncan dined with us, and Nessa came in afterwards, very silent, inscrutable and, perhaps, critical. As a family we distrust anyone outside our set, I think. We too definitely decide that so and so has not the necessary virtues. I daresay Harold has not got them; at the same time, there is a good deal in him I like: he is quick and rash and impulsive; not in our sense very clever; uneasy; seeming young; on the turn from diplomat to intellectual; not Vita's match; but honest and cordial. L. says he's too commonplace. I liked my little duet with him. He wears a green, or blue, shirt and tie; is sunburnt; chubby; pert; vivacious. Talked of politics, but was flimsy compared with Leonard – I thought. Said it was with L. and me that he felt completely at his ease. Told stories which sound rather empty in the bare Bloomsbury rooms.

Thursday 23 June

Never have I spent so quiet a London summer. I have set my standard as an invalid, and no one bothers me. No one asks me to do anything. Quiet brings me cool clear quick mornings, in which I dispose of a good deal of work, and toss my brain into the air when I take a walk.

Vita's book [*The Land*] verberates and reverberates in the press. A prize poem – that's my fling at it – for with some relics of jealousy, or it may be of critical sense, I can't quite take the talk of poetry and even great poetry seriously. Oh and Sibyl [Colefax] has dropped me: and I don't feel the fall. And Adrian came to tea on Sunday, and fairly sparkled. At last I think he has emerged. Even his analysis will be over this year. At the age of forty-three he will be educated and ready to start life. So we Stephens mature late. And our late flowers are rare and splendid. Think of my books, Nessa's pictures – it takes us an age to bring our faculties into play.

Thursday 30 June

Now I must sketch out the Eclipse.

About 10 on Tuesday night several very long trains, accurately filled (ours with civil servants) left King's Cross. In our carriage was Vita and Harold, Quentin, L. and I. Before it got dark we kept looking at the sky: soft fleecy; but there was one star, over Alexandra Park. The Nicolsons got sleepy: Harold curled up with his head on Vita's knee. She looked like Sappho by Leighton, asleep; so we plunged through the midlands; made a very long stay at York. Then at 3 we got our sandwiches. Then we had another doze, or the Nicolsons did; then here was a level crossing, at which were drawn up a long line of motor omnibuses and motors, all burning pale yellow lights. It was getting grey – still a fleecy mottled sky. We got to Richmond about 3.30; it was cold, and the Nicolsons had a quarrel about

Vita's luggage. We went off in the omnibus, saw a vast castle (who does that belong to said Vita, who is interested in castles). All the fields were aburn with June grasses and red tasselled plants, none coloured as yet, all pale. Pale and grey too were the little uncompromising Yorkshire farms. As we passed one, the farmer, and his wife and sister came out, all tightly and tidily dressed in black, as if they were going to church. At another ugly square farm, two women were looking out of the upper windows. These had white blinds drawn down half across them. We were a train of three vast cars, one stopping to let the others go on; all very low and powerful; taking immensely steep hills. The driver once got out and put a small stone behind our wheel – inadequate. There were also many motor cars. These suddenly increased as we crept up to the top of Bardon Fell. Here were people camping beside their cars. We got out, and found ourselves very high, on a moor, boggy, heathery, with butts for grouse shooting. There were grass tracks here and there, and people had already taken up positions. So we joined them, walking out to what seemed the highest point looking over Richmond. One light burnt down there. Vales and moors stretched, slope after slope, round us. It was like the Haworth country. But over Richmond, where the sun was rising, was a soft grey cloud. We could see by a gold spot where the sun was. But it was early yet. We had to wait, stamping to keep warm, Leonard kept looking at his watch. Four great red setters came leaping over the moor. There were sheep feeding behind us. There were thin places in the cloud, and some complete holes. The question was whether the sun would show through a cloud or through one of these hollow places when the time came. We began to get anxious. We saw rays coming through the bottom of the clouds. Then, for a moment, we saw the sun, sweeping – it seemed to be sailing at a great pace and clear in a gap; we had out our smoked glasses; we saw it crescent, burning red; next moment it had sailed fast into the cloud again; only the red streamers came from it; then only a golden haze, such as one has often seen. The moments were passing. We thought we were cheated; we looked at the sheep; they showed no fear; the setters were racing round; everyone was standing in long lines, rather dignified, looking out. I thought how we were like very old people, in the birth of the world – druids on Stonehenge. At the back of us were great blue spaces in the cloud. But now the colour was going out. The clouds were turning pale; a reddish black colour. Down in the valley it was an extraordinary scrumble of red and black; there was the one light burning; all was cloud down there, and very beautiful, so delicately tinted. The 24 seconds were passing. Then one looked back again at the blue: and rapidly, very very quickly, all the colours faded; it became darker and darker as at the beginning of a violent storm; the light sank and sank; we kept saying this is the shadow; and we thought now it is over – this is the shadow; when suddenly the light went out. We had fallen. It was extinct. There was no colour. The earth was dead. That was the astonishing moment: and the next when as if a ball had rebounded, the cloud took colour on itself again; and so the light came back. I had very strongly the feeling as the light went out of some vast obeisance; something kneeling down and suddenly raised up when the colours came. They came back astonishingly lightly and quickly and beautifully in the valley and over the hills, at first with a miraculous glittering and aetheriality. The colour for some moments was of the most lovely kind – fresh, various – here blue, and there brown: all new colours, as if washed over and repainted. It was like recovery. We had been much worse than we had expected. We had seen the world dead. We were bitterly cold. I should say that the cold had increased as the light went down. One felt very livid. Then – it was all over till 1999. What remained was a sense of the comfort which we get used to, of plenty of light and colour. This for some time seemed a definitely welcome thing. Yet when it became established, one rather missed the sense of its being a relief and a respite, which one had had when it came back after the darkness. How can I express the darkness? It was a sudden plunge, when one did not expect it: being at the mercy of the sky; our own nobility; the druids; Stonehenge and the racing red dogs; all that was in one's mind. Also to be picked out of one's London drawing room and set down on the wildest moors in England was impressive. For the rest, I remember trying to keep awake in the gardens at York and falling asleep. Asleep again in the train. It was hot and we were messy. The carriage was full of things. Harold was very kind and attentive. We got home at 8.30 perhaps.

Monday 4 July
Back from Long Barn. Such opulence and freedom, flowers all out, butler, silver, dogs, biscuits, wine, hot water, log fires, Italian cabinets, Persian rugs, books – this was the impression it made: as of stepping into a rolling gay sea, with nicely crested waves. Yet I like this room better perhaps: more effort and life in it, to my mind. Vita very opulent, in her brown velvet coat, pearl necklace, and slightly furred cheeks (they are like Saviour's Flannel). I liked Harold too. He is a spontaneous childlike man; has a mind that bounces when he drops it; an air of immaturity. I should judge him very generous and kind hearted. Vita very free and easy, always giving me great pleasure to watch, and recalling some image of a ship breasting a sea, nobly, magnificently, with all sails spread, and the gold sunlight on them.

Monday 11 July
In a mood of random restlessness – Nelly having for the 125th time 'given notice' this morning. I am sick of the timid spiteful servant mind. But I

have never mentioned the absorbing subject – the subject which has filled our thoughts to the exclusion of Clive and Mary and literature and death and life – motor cars. Every evening we go round with Pinker [dog] for a game in Gordon Square; we sit there in between the sulphur coloured storms; under the shelter of trees with the rain pattering between the leaves. We talk of nothing but cars. Then sometimes, word is brought that Mrs Bell is at the door in her car. I rush out, and find her rather nervously in control of a roomy shabby Renault with Fred beside her. Three times I have been for a little tour with her. And yesterday we commissioned Fred to find us and bring instantly to our door a Singer. We have decided on a Singer. And the reason why I am distracted now is that Fred is going to ring me up and say if I am to have my first lesson this evening. This is a great opening up in our lives. One may go to Bodiam, to Arundel, explore the Chichester downs, expand that curious thing, the map of the world in one's mind. It will I think demolish loneliness, and may of course imperil one's privacy. The Keyneses have one too – a cheap one. Nessa thinks it will break down at once. Nessa takes a very sinister view of the Keyneses. She anticipates ruin of every sort for them, with some pleasure too. Here's Leonard – And now I must quickly dress for Clive's party; there's a plethora of parties this week.

With any luck *The Lighthouse* will reach 3000 this week.

Saturday 23 July
Since making the last entry I have learnt enough to drive a car in the country alone. On the backs of paper I write down instructions for starting cars. We have a nice little shut up car in which we can travel thousands of miles. The world gave me this for writing *The Lighthouse*, I reflect, a book which has now sold 3,160 (perhaps) copies; will sell 3,500 before it dies, and thus far exceeds any other of mine. All images are now tinged with driving a motor. Here I think of letting my engine work, with my clutch out.

It has been, on the whole, a fresh well ordered summer. I am not so parched with talk as usual. My illness in May was a good thing in some ways; for I got control of society at an early stage, and circumvented my headache, without a complete smash. I enjoyed the Eclipse; I enjoyed Long Barn (where I went twice); I enjoyed sitting with Vita at Kew for three or four hours under a cloudy sky, and dining with her: she refreshes me, and solaces me. I have worked very methodically and done my due of articles, so that with luck I shall have made £120 *over* my proper sum by September. That is, I shall have made £320 by journalism, and I suppose at least £300 by my novel this year. The Press is going on. Novels are the great bloodsuckers. I fancy that we don't do as well as we should with novels.

Monks House, Rodmell

Monday 8 August

I was to have written here such a brilliant account of my three days at Dieppe, and now shall not, I suppose. We have motored most days. We opened one little window when we bought the gramophone; now another opens with the motor.

Wednesday 10 August

Yes, the motor is turning out the joy of our lives, an additional life, free and mobile and airy, to live alongside our usual stationary industry. We spin off to Falmer, ride over the Downs, drop into Rottingdean, then sweep over to Seaford, call in pouring rain at Charleston, pass the time of day, return for tea, all as light and easy as a hawk in the air. Soon we shall look back at our pre-motor days as we do now at our days in the caves. After a week here, Leonard has become perfectly efficient; I am held back by insufficient lessons, but shall be expert before September is half through. Various little improvements in the house keep me on the thrill with hope and despair. Perhaps if I make an extra sum we might build a bed sitting room for me in the attic, enlarge L.'s study, and so have a desirable, roomy, light house. For if we had £300 every year to spend, it is difficult to think of anything, except this, travel, and pocket money, to spend it on. Here at the age of forty-five are Nessa and I growing little wings again after our lean years.

Sunday 4 September

Many scenes have come and gone unwritten, since it is today 4th September, a cold grey blowy day, made memorable by the sight of a kingfisher, and by my sense, waking early, of being again visited by 'the spirit of delight'. 'Rarely rarely comest thou, spirit of delight' [Shelley]. That was I singing this time last year; and sang so poignantly that I have never forgotten it, or my vision of a fin rising on a wide blank sea. No biographer could possibly guess this important fact about my life in the late summer of 1926: yet biographers pretend they know people.

Tuesday 20 September

A thousand things to be written had I time: had I power. A very little writing uses up my capacity for writing. But I can think of more books than I shall ever be able to write. How many little stories come into my head!

We motored to Long Barn and back yesterday, through suburbs for the most part. All Hampstead, red, sanitary, earnest, view gazing, breeze requiring, is lodged in the heights of Ashdown Forest. And Quentin came, and the Keyneses came, and Morgan came. Quentin won't let us play him Wagner: prefers Bach. Nessa's children are terrifyingly sophisticated: so Morgan said when Angelica, rigged up in a long black shawl, acted Lady Cornflax and Lady Ottoline at Charleston. They have grown up without any opposition: nothing to twist or stunt. Hence they have reached stages at sixteen or seventeen which I reached only at twenty-six or twenty-seven. But the summer has never burnt; and is now ashes. But we are very happy – seldom more so, I think. Perhaps things are doing rather well – and L. said the other day, "The strange thing is that we always come to the same opinion about things" – which pleased me.

Sunday 25 September

Now let me become the annalist of Rodmell. Thirty-five years ago, there were 160 families living here where there are now no more than eighty. It is a decaying village, which loses its boys to the towns. Not a boy of them, said the Rev. Mr Hawkesford, is being taught to plough. Rich people wanting week-end cottages buy up the old peasants' houses, for fabulous sums. Monks House was offered to Mr Hawkesford for £400: we gave £700. He refused it, saying he didn't wish to own country cottages. Now Mr Allison will pay £1200 for a couple, and we he said might get £2000 for this. He is an old decaying man, run to seed. He is sinking into old age, very shabby, loose limbed, wearing black wool mittens. His life is receding like a tide, slowly; or one figures him as a dying candle, whose wick will soon sink into the warm grease and be extinct. He tumbles into an armchair; and tells over his stock of old village stories, which always have this slightly mocking flavour, as though, completely unambitious, and by no means successful himself, he recouped himself by laughing slyly at the humours of the more energetic. He smokes endless cigarettes, and his fingers are not very clean. Talking of his well, he said "It would be a different thing if one wanted baths" – which for some seventy years, presumably, he has done without. Of his clerical character there is little visible. I asked him if he had work to do: a question which amused him a little. Not work, he said; but a young woman to see. And then he settled into the armchair again, and so sat out a visit of over an hour and a half.

Wednesday 5 October

I write in the sordid doss house atmosphere of approaching departure. Pinker is asleep in one chair; Leonard is signing cheques at the little deal table under the glare of the lamp. The fire is covered with ashes, since we have been burning it all day. Envelopes lie in the grate. I am writing with a pen which is feeble and wispy; and it is a sharp fine evening with a sunset,

I daresay. If my pen allowed, I should now try to make out a work table, having done my last article for the *Tribune*, and now being free again. And instantly the usual exciting devices enter my mind: a biography beginning the year 1500 and continuing to the present day, called *Orlando*: Vita; only with a change about from one sex to another. I think, for a treat, I shall let myself dash this in for a week.

52 TAVISTOCK SQUARE, WC1

Saturday 22 October

'I shall let myself dash this in for a week' – I have done nothing, nothing else for a fortnight; and am launched somewhat furtively but with all the more passion upon *Orlando: A Biography*. It is to be a small book, and written by Christmas. I walk making up phrases; sit, contriving scenes; am in short in the thick of the greatest rapture known to me. Talk of planning a book, or waiting for an idea! This one came in a rush. But the relief of turning my mind that way about was such that I felt happier than for months; as if put in the sun, or laid on cushions; and after two days entirely gave up my time chart and abandoned myself to the pure delight of this farce. I am writing *Orlando* half in a mock style very clear and plain, so that people will understand every word. But the balance between truth and fantasy must be careful. It is based on Vita, Violet Trefusis, Lord Lascelles, Knole, &c.

A great many incidents to record. They come always in a rush together, these bright October days, with everyone just back, fresh from solitude, cheerful, busy, sociable. Nessa has initiated, informally, Sunday evenings; and there Old Bloomsbury is to gather, after dinner – Helen [Anrep], Clive, Roger and so on. Then there's Clive. He has laid his stairs with the vividest green, five inches thick: has every comfort and convenience. I dine there to meet Harold [Nicolson] and Tom [Eliot]: Tom, of course, in white waistcoat, much the man of the world; which sets the key, and off they go telling stories about 'Jean' (Cocteau), about Ada Leverson, Gosse, Valéry, &c &c and L. and I feel a little Bloomsburyish perhaps; no, I think this sort of talk is hardly up to the scratch. Harold does it best.

We saw the pale dove grey coffin of Mrs Wells slide through the gates at Golders Green. It had tassels like bell pulls on it. Wells sat in bottle blue overcoat by [Bernard] Shaw, sobbing. One saw his white handkerchief going in and out of his pocket. Poor Jane! It was desperate to see what a dowdy shabby imperfect lot we looked; how feeble; how ugly for the most part. And yet we were doing our best to say something sincere about our great adventure (as Wells almost called it). And he has been adventurous and plunged about in his bath and splashed the waters, to give him his due. Afterwards we stood about congratulating.

Sunday 20 November
I will now snatch a moment from what Morgan calls 'life' to enter a hurried note. My notes have been few; life a cascade, a glissade, a torrent: all together. I think on the whole this *is* our happiest autumn. So much work; and success now; and life on easy terms. My morning rushes, pell mell, from 10 to 1. I write so quick I can't get it typed before lunch. This I suppose is the main backbone of my autumn – *Orlando*.

Vita comes; Dottie [Wellesley] comes; Clive incessant; Tom; Roger; we have our Bloomsbury evenings; for the first time I have been spending money, on a bed, on a coat (the coat, at the moment, I regret). But the money psychology is odd; and that it doesn't give me enormous pleasure to spend. I doubt that I want anything enough; yet worry about spending wrongly; and must buy an evening dress which worries me too. Domestic life, Nelly, that is, good as gold.

Wednesday 30 November
A very happy autumn this, I repeat. After Christmas discontent will set in no doubt, when I must write criticism. But I will steal a march on that depression. Moreover, aren't I proud at the moment. Ruth Draper admires me: I am to meet her on Friday. So tonight I go to the pit to see Ruth Draper. Lunch with Sibyl; dine with Ethel; and a new dress, made from one a hundred years old. These are the little waves that life makes; which keep us tossing and going up and down on top of them.

Tuesday 20 December
This is almost the shortest day and perhaps the coldest night of the year. We are in the black heart of a terrific frost. The pavement was white with great powdery flakes the other night, walking back with Roger and Helen; this was from Nessa's last Sunday – last, I fear, for many a month. But I have as usual 'no time'. Angus is finally to go: we had another semi-painful interview in the Studio; when he interrupted L.'s dismissal with his own resignation. Not enough money.

Nessa's children's party last night. The little creatures' acting moved my infinitely sentimental throat. And yet oddly enough I scarcely want children of my own now. This insatiable desire to write something before I die, this ravaging sense of the shortness and feverishness of life, make me cling, like a man on a rock, to my one anchor. I don't like the physicalness of having children of one's own. I can dramatise myself as parent, it is true, And perhaps I have killed the feeling instinctively; as perhaps nature does.

I am still writing the third chapter of *Orlando*. I have had of course to give up the fancy of finishing by February and printing this spring. It is drawing out longer than I meant. How extraordinarily unwilled by me but potent in its own right by the way *Orlando* was! as if it shoved everything aside to come into existence.

Yes, I repeat, a very happy, a singularly happy autumn.

Thursday 22 December

I just open this for a moment, being dull of the head, to enter a severe reprimand of myself. I am meretricious; mediocre; a humbug; am getting into the habit of flashy talk. Tinsel it seemed last night at the Keyneses. Dadie says I have no logical power and live and write in an opium dream. And the dream is too often about myself. Now, with middle age drawing on, and age ahead, it is important to be severe on such faults. So easily might I become a harebrained egotistic woman, exacting compliments, arrogant, narrow, withered. To correct this, and to forget one's own sharp absurd little personality, reputation and the rest of it, one should read; see outsiders; think more; write more logically; above all be full of work; and practise anonymity. Silence in company; or the quietest statement, not the showiest, is also 'indicated' as the doctors say. It was an empty party, rather, last night. Very nice here, though.

1928

Thomas Hardy died on 11 January; his ashes were interred in Westminster Abbey, and Leonard and Virginia attended the ceremony in Poets' Corner. Her valedictory article on Hardy's novels, commissioned in 1919, was published in the TLS *on 19 January. Virginia's usual seasonal low spirits were compounded by headaches, by the absence of Vanessa and Duncan who now had a secure winter refuge at Cassis; and by the effect on Vita of her father's death and her consequent sense of being disinherited – Knole and the Sackville estates being entailed on the male heir, her uncle. But Virginia finished writing* Orlando *towards the end of March, and she and Leonard then took three weeks off, driving in their Singer car across France to Cassis and back, before settling to the laborious task of revision. Leonard read the manuscript at the end of May and sent it to press.*

Another death and funeral – that of the respected classical scholar Jane Harrison – again shows Virginia's curiosity about and critical observation of conventional ceremonies; and her ambivalent attitude to public esteem is also evident in her reaction to the award of this year's Femina Vie Heureuse *prize for* To the Lighthouse: *disappointment when she thought she had been passed over; disparagement when she received it at the hands of the best-selling novelist Hugh Walpole (with whom nevertheless she was to strike up an odd friendship).*

At the beginning of the year Virginia had been invited to speak to the Arts Society of Newnham College, and though in the event it was October before she could fulfil this engagement and a similar one at the other Cambridge women's college, Girton, she was gathering ideas for her talk on 'Women and Fiction' throughout the preceding months – talks which were to be expanded and published a year later as A Room of One's Own.

The two summer months at Monks House were animated and sociable; the purchase of an adjoining field gave the Woolfs a greater sense of permanency in the village; the fine weather and the mobility conferred by their motor car enabled them to make day visits to Vita and to her close friend Lady Dorothy Wellesley in Kent. Their own visitors included E. M. Forster, concerned like Leonard about the implications of the forthcoming Bow Street trial of the lesbian novel The Well of Loneliness; *and old Mrs Woolf, Leonard's mother, whose demands on filial consideration both exhausted and discomposed Virginia. The summer ended with Virginia apprehensively setting off to spend a week travelling alone with Vita in Burgundy.*

Orlando *was published on* 11 *October and, notwithstanding its rather mixed reception, sold better than any of her books, and a third printing was ordered by the end of the year. But apart from her absorption in the preparation of her Cambridge lectures, she had no clear impulse towards another book. Descriptions in a letter from Vanessa of great moths invading her house at Cassis at night hovered in her imagination, and began to take hold; but it was to be many months before these stirrings were to be developed. In the meantime, she was enjoying the social fruits of her success – invitations from the prominent hostess Lady Cunard, dinner parties to meet Max Beerbohm or George Moore, as well as the more familiar pleasures of her own circle.*

1928

Tuesday 17 January

Yesterday we went to Hardy's funeral [in Westminster Abbey]. What did I think of? Of Max Beerbohm's letter, just read; or a lecture to the Newnhamites about women's writing. At intervals some emotion broke in. But I doubt the capacity of the human animal for being dignified in ceremony. One catches a Bishop's frown and twitch; sees his polished shiny nose; suspects the rapt spectacled young priest gazing at the cross he carries of being a humbug; next here is the coffin, an overgrown one; like a stage coffin, covered with a white satin cloth; bearers elderly gentlemen rather red and stiff, holding to the corners; pigeons flying outside; insufficient artificial light; procession to Poets' Corner; dramatic 'in sure and certain hope of immortality' perhaps melodramatic. After dinner at Clive's Lytton protested that the great man's novels are the poorest of poor stuff; and can't read them. Over all this broods for me some uneasy sense, of change, and mortality, and how partings are deaths; and then a sense of my own fame – why should this come over me? – and then of its remoteness; and then the pressure of writing two articles on Meredith and furbishing up the Hardy [for the *TLS*]. And a sense of the futility of it all.

Saturday 11 February

I am so cold I can hardly hold the pen. The futility of it all – so I broke off; and have indeed been feeling that rather persistently, or perhaps I should have written here. Hardy and Meredith together sent me torpid to bed with headache. I know the feeling now, when I can't spin a sentence, and sit mumbling and turning; and nothing flits by my brain which is as a blank window. So I go to bed, stuffing my ears with rubber; and there I lie a day or two. Such 'sensations' spread over my spine and head directly I give them the chance; such anguishes and despairs; and heavenly relief and rest; and then misery again. Never was anyone so tossed up and down by the body as I am, I think. But it is over: and put away.

For some reason, I am hacking rather listlessly at the last chapter of

Orlando, which was to have been the best. Always always the last chapter slips out of my hands. One gets bored. For the rest, Bloomsbury today revives. Clive is back: whereupon Mary asks us to lunch: and so we return to some flicker of the snowdrop pallor of very early spring.

Saturday 18 February

I am happy to say I have still a few pounds in the Bank, and my own cheque book too. This great advance in dignity was made in the autumn. My mind is woolgathering away about Women and Fiction, which I am to read at Newnham in May. The mind is the most capricious of insects – flitting fluttering. I had thought to write the quickest most brilliant pages in *Orlando* yesterday – not a drop came, all, forsooth, for the usual physical reasons, which declared themselves today. It is the oddest feeling: as if a finger stopped the flow of ideas in the brain.

Sunday 18 March

I have lost my writing board; an excuse for the anaemic state of this book. Indeed I only write now, in between letters, to say that *Orlando* was finished yesterday as the clock struck one. Anyhow the canvas is covered. There will be three months of close work needed, imperatively, before it can be printed; for I have scrambled and splashed, and the canvas shows through in a thousand places. But it is a serene, accomplished feeling to write, even provisionally, The End, and we go off on Saturday, with my mind appeased. I have written this book quicker than any: and it is all a joke; and yet gay and quick reading I think; a writer's holiday. So we go motoring across France on Saturday, and shall be back on April 17th for the summer.

Thursday 22 March

Yes it's done – *Orlando* – begun on 8th October, as a joke; and now rather too long for my liking. All this I dismiss from a mind avid only of green fields. The sun; wine; sitting doing nothing. I have been for the last six weeks rather a bucket than a fountain; sitting to be shot into by one person after another. A rabbit that passes across a shooting gallery, and one's friends go pop-pop. Morgan and Desmond were here to tea. Morgan more of the blue butterfly than ever. Unless I talk, he says nothing. And any shadow sends him flitting. Desmond comes in, round as a billiard ball; and this is true of his dear bubbling lazy mind; which has such a glitter and lustre now from mere being at ease in the world that it puts me into a good temper to be with him. Roger and Helen, Ka and Will [Arnold-Forster], the other night. Roger malicious a little, and vain. There is an innocence in this vanity which is likeable; but I am touchy for the reputation of Bloomsbury. I thought I could see Ka and Will comparing us, and being glad we were not impeccable. They compare us with the political world: we them with our own.

Watery blowy weather; and this time next week we shall be in the middle of France.

*　　*　　*

Tuesday 17 April
Home again, as foretold, last night, and to settle the dust in my mind, write here. We have been across France and back – every inch of that fertile field traversed by the admirable Singer. And now towns and spires and scenes begin to rise in my mind as the rest sinks. I see Chartres in particular, the snail, with its head straight, marching across the flat country, the most distinguished of churches. The rose window is like a jewel on black velvet. Grey weather dashed all over this; and I remember coming in at night in the wet often, and hearing the rain in hotels. Often I was bobbing up and down on my two glasses of vin du pays. Always some good food and hot bottles at night. And there was Nessa and Clive – Oh and my prize [the *Prix Femina*] – £40 from the French. And Julian. And one or two hot days and the Pont du Gard in the sun; and Les Baux; and mounting all the time steadily was my desire for words, till I envisaged a sheet of paper and pen and ink as something of miraculous desirability. And there was St Rémy and the ruins in the sun. I forget now how it all went – how thing fitted to thing; but the eminences now emerge.

Saturday 21 April
A bitter windy rainy day. There is no blue, no red, no green in this detestable spring. Furs are in the shops. Life is either too empty or too full. Happily, at forty-six I still feel as experimental and on the verge of getting at the truth as ever. Oh and Vita – to take up the burden of facts – has had a stupendous row with her mother – in the course of which she was made to take the pearl necklace from her neck, cut it in two with a pocket knife, deliver over the twelve central pearls, put the relics, all running loose, in an envelope the solicitor gave her. Thief, liar, I hope you'll be killed by an omnibus – so 'my honoured Lady Sackville' addressed her, trembling with rage in the presence of a secretary and a solicitor and a chauffeur. The woman is said to be mad. Vita very gallant and wild and tossing her head.

Dined with Lydia and Maynard: two couples, elderly, childless, distinguished. He and she both urbane and admirable. Grey comes at Maynard's temples. He is finer looking now: not with us pompous or great: simple, with his mind working always, on Russian, Bolshevists, glands, genealogies; always the proof of a remarkable mind when it overflows thus vigorously into bypaths. Lydia is composed and controlled. She says very sensible things.

We went, also, to Jane [Harrison]'s funeral, getting 'there' (somewhere out of the world where buses pass only one every fifteen minutes), just as the service ended. We walked to the grave; the clergyman, a friend, waited for the dismal company to collect; then read some of the lovelier, more rational parts of the Bible; and said, by heart, Abide with me. A bird sang most opportunely; with a gay indifference, and if one liked, hope, that Jane would have enjoyed. Then the incredibly drab female cousins advanced, each with a fat bunch of primroses and dropped them in; and we also advanced and looked down at the coffin at the bottom of a very steep brazen looking grave. But though L. almost cried, I felt very little – only the beauty of the Come unto me all ye that are weary; but as usual the obstacle of not believing dulled and bothered me. Who is 'God' and what the Grace of Christ? and what did they mean to Jane?

Friday 4 May
And now there's the *Femina* Prize to record – an affair of dull stupid horror: a function; not alarming; stupefying. Hugh Walpole saying how much he disliked my books; rather how much he feared for his own. Afterwards there was the horror of having looked ugly in cheap black clothes. I cannot control this complex. I wake at dawn with a start. Also the 'fame' is becoming vulgar and a nuisance. It means nothing; and yet takes one's time. Americans perpetually. We have seen an endless number of people.

Thursday 31 May
It is very quiet at the moment. Whitsun is over. We were at Rodmell and saw the races. The sun is out again; I have half forgotten *Orlando* already, since L. has read it and it has half passed out of my possession. [He] thinks it in some ways better than *The Lighthouse*; about more interesting things, and with more attachment to life, and larger. The truth is I expect I began it as a joke, and went on with it seriously. Hence it lacks some unity. He says it is very original.

June weather. Still, bright, fresh. Owing to the Lighthouse (car) I don't feel so shut in London as usual. Also London itself perpetually attracts, stimulates, gives me a play and a story and a poem, without any trouble save that of moving my legs through the streets. I walked Pinker to Gray's Inn Gardens this afternoon, and saw – Red Lion Square: Morris's house; thought of them on winters' evenings in the 'fifties; thought we are just as interesting; saw Great Ormond Street where a dead girl was found yesterday; saw and heard the Salvation Army making Christianity gay for the people: a great deal of nudging and joking on the part of very unattractive young men and women; making it lively, I suppose; and yet, to be truthful, when I watch them I never laugh or criticise, but only feel how strange and interesting this is: wonder what they mean by 'Come to the Lord'. I daresay exhibitionism accounts for some of it: the applause of the gallery; this lures boys to sing hymns; and kindles shop boys to announce in a loud voice that they are saved. It is what writing for the *Evening Standard* is for Rose Macaulay and I was going to say myself: but so far I have not done it.

Wednesday 20 June

So sick of *Orlando* I can write nothing. I have corrected the proofs in a week; and cannot spin another phrase. I detest my own volubility. Why be always spouting words? Also I have almost lost the power of reading. Correcting proofs five, six or seven hours a day, writing in this and that meticulously, I have bruised my reading faculty severely. Take up Proust after dinner and put him down. This is the worst time of all. It makes me suicidal. All seems insipid and worthless. Mercifully Nessa is back. My earth is watered again. She is a necessity to me – as I am not to her. I run to her as the wallaby runs to the old kangaroo.

Julian dines with us tonight to meet Miss Sylva Norman whom I fetched up from complete nonentity on the telephone last night. Another marvel of science. There she was in ten minutes after we thought of her saying she would LOVE to come. Julian is a vast fat powerful sweet-tempered engaging young man, into whose arms I let myself fall, half sister, half mother, and half (but arithmetic denies this) the mocking stirring contemporary friend. Mercifuily Julian has his instincts sane and normal: has a wide forehead, and considerable address and competence in the management of life.

Saturday 7 July

All last night I dreamt of Katherine Mansfield and wondered what dreams are; often evoke so much more than thinking does – almost as if she came back in person and was outside one, actively making one feel; instead of a figment called up and recollected, as she is, now, if I think of her. Yet some emotion lingers on the day after a dream; even though I've now almost forgotten what happened in the dream, except that she was lying on a sofa in a room high up, and a great many sad faced women were round her. Yet somehow I got the feel of her, and of her as if alive again, more than by day.

Monks House, Rodmell

Wednesday 8 August

I am, as I write, wherever I come to a stop, looking out of the lodge window at our field; and the little cottage boys with the cursed shrill voices playing cricket half way down it; and as usual I am sentimental and worried. Children playing: yes, and interrupting me; yes and I have no children of my own; and Nessa has; and yet I don't want them any more, since my ideas so possess me; and I detest more and more interruption; and the slow heaviness of physical life, and almost dislike people's bodies, I think, as I grow older. I write thus partly in order to slip the burden of writing narrative, as for instance: we came here a fortnight ago. And we lunched at Charleston and Vita came and we were offered the field and we went to see the farm at Lime Kiln. Yet no doubt I shall be more interested, come ten years, in facts; and shall want, as I do when I read, to be told details, details, so that I may look up from the page and arrange them into one of those makings-up which seem so much truer done thus, from heaps of non-assorted facts, than now I can make them, when it is almost immediately being done under my eyes.

Sunday 12 August

Yesterday at Charleston we had tea from bright blue cups under the pink light of the giant hollyhock. We were all a little drugged with the country: a little bucolic I thought. It was lovely enough – made me envious of its country peace: the trees all standing securely – why did my eye catch the trees? The look of things has a great power over me. Even now, I have to watch the rooks beating up against the wind, which is high. And still I say to myself instinctively 'What's the phrase for that?' But what a little I can get down with my pen of what is so vivid to my eye.

Tuesday 14 August

Just back from Long Barn and Dottie [Wellesley]'s new house, Penns in the Rocks. Can one really be in love with a house? Is there not something sterile in these passions? She is too anxious for other people to praise it. And I don't want possessions. I think this is true. I don't want to be Dottie collecting endless settees and armchairs round myself. But then I have now a pressing sense of the flight of time; and if one is so soon to arrive, why pack all these things? More truthfully, if one is so soon to start, why prepare all these impedimenta. I feel on the verge of the world, about to take flight. Dottie on the other hand feels 'I have at least, in spite of every other grudge on the part of fate, ten or fifteen thousand a year; and it is only fair that I should get from my money what I can.'

Friday 31 August
This is the last day of August, and like almost all of them of extraordinary beauty. Morgan was here for the week-end; timid, touchy, infinitely charming. One night we got drunk, and talked of sodomy, and sapphism, with emotion – so much so that next day he said he had been drunk. Morgan said that Dr Head can convert the sodomites. "Would you like to be converted?" Leonard asked. "No" said Morgan, quite definitely. He said he thought Sapphism disgusting: partly from convention, partly because he disliked that women should be independent of men.

Monday 3 September
The Battle of Dunbar, the Battle of Worcester, and the death of Cromwell – how often it seems I said that to my father at St Ives; standing bolt upright in the dining room at Talland House. And it is a perfect 3rd September day. Leonard gave me the blue glass jug today because I was nice to his mother. He went to Brighton to get it for me. Seldom have I felt as tired as I did last night. This shaky ramshackle old lady of seventy-six wore us out. Her talk never stops; never follows a line; is always about people; starts anywhere; at any moment. What makes it difficult is that she divines states of feeling to some extent, and would say pointedly "You must often think of your writing when you are not writing, Virginia," when through exhaustion I became silent. I felt the horror of family life, and the terrible threat to one's liberty that I used to feel with father, Aunt Mary or George [Duckworth, her half-brother]. It is an emotion one never gets from any other human relationship. She had the right to somehow put her claws in me. How strangely she made everything commonplace, ugly, suburban, notwithstanding a charm too. But to be attached to her as a daughter would be so cruel a fate that I can think of nothing worse; and thousands of women might be dying of it in England today: this tyranny of mother over daughter, or father; their right to the due being as powerful as anything in the world. And then, they ask, why women don't write poetry. Short of killing Mrs Woolf nothing could be done. Day after day one's life would be crumpled up like a bill for tenpence three farthings. Nothing has ever been said of this.

Monday 10 September
Desmond, who lunched here with Julian, has just gone. We spent the afternoon – hour after hour wasting away again, or why not say for once turning to gold and silver – coining gold and silver talk then – talk very intimate now, more so than ever: a continuation of our talk in Tavistock Square the other day: there he said he had now twelve years to live; nine to be exact; and here we talked of his work, money, women, children, and

writing; till I took him along the Roman Road; and back to tea. Do you suppose then that we are now coming like the homing rooks back to the tops of our trees? and that all this cawing is the beginning of settling in for the night? I seem to notice in several of my friends some endearing and affecting cordiality; and a pleasure in intimacy; as if the sun were sinking.

This has been a very animated summer: a summer lived almost too much in public. Often down here I have entered into a sanctuary; a nunnery; had a religious retreat; of great agony once; and always some terror: so afraid one is of loneliness: of seeing to the bottom of the vessel.

Monday 17 September
I have precisely five minutes before dinner. Quentin has swallowed those precious two hours in which I was to have read Dorothy Osborne: Quentin grown elegant and self conscious, liking to use French words; very sophisticated, showing in every movement now the shadow of our faults, as a set: uneasy, I doubt not; quick, sensitive; but wanting something of Julian's force and simplicity. So they change parts, growing, changing, turning from fat to thin. The drawing room smells with his paints.

Saturday 22 September
This is written on the verge of my alarming holiday in Burgundy. I am alarmed of seven days alone with Vita; interested; excited, but afraid – she may find me out, I her out. I'm afraid of the morning most; and three o'clock in the afternoon; and wanting something Vita does not want. And I shall spend the money that might have bought a table or a glass.

This has been the finest, and not only finest, but loveliest, summer in the world. Owning the field has given a different orient to my feelings about Rodmell. I begin to dig myself in and take part in it. And I shall build another storey to the house if I make money. But the news of *Orlando* is black. We may sell a third that we sold of *The Lighthouse* before publication. They say this is inevitable. No one wants biography. I doubt therefore that we shall do more than cover expenses – a high price to pay for the fun of calling it a biography. I must write some articles this winter, if we are to have nest eggs at the Bank.

52 TAVISTOCK SQUARE, WC1

Saturday 27 October
A scandal, a scandal, to let so much time slip, and I leaning on the bridge watching it go. Only leaning has not been my pose: running up and down,

irritably, excitedly, restlessly. And the stream viciously eddying. Why do I write these metaphors? Because I have written nothing for an age.

Orlando has been published. I went to Burgundy with Vita. We did not find each other out. It flashed by. Yet I was glad to see Leonard again. How disconnected this is! My ambition is from this very moment, eight minutes to six, on Saturday evening, to attain complete concentration again. I gave up reading and thinking on the 24th September when I went to France. I came back, and we plunged into London and publishing. I am a little sick of *Orlando*. I think I am a little indifferent now what anyone thinks. Joy's life's in the doing – I murder, as usual, a quotation. I mean its the writing, not the being read that excites me. The reception, as they say, surpassed expectations. Sales beyond our record for the first week.

Thank God, my long toil at the women's lecture is this moment ended. I am back from speaking at Girton, in floods of rain. Starved but valiant young women – that's my impression. Intelligent, eager, poor; and destined to become schoolmistresses in shoals. I blandly told them to drink wine and have a room of their own. Why should all the splendour, all the luxury of life be lavished on the Julians and the Francises, and none on the Phares and the Thomases? The corridors of Girton are like vaults in some horrid high church cathedral – on and on they go, cold and shiny – with a light burning. High gothic rooms; acres of bright brown wood; here and there a photograph. And we saw Trinity and King's this morning.

Wednesday 7 November
Since I wrote here I have become two inches and a half higher in the public view. I think I may say that I am now among the well known writers. I had tea with Lady Cunard – might have lunched or dined any day. It was not her atmosphere – this of solitary talk. She is too shrewd to expand, and needs society to make her rash and random which is her point. Ridiculous little parrokeet faced woman; but not quite sufficiently ridiculous. I kept wishing for superlatives; could not get the illusion to flap its wings. Flunkeys, yes; but a little drab and friendly. Marble floors, yes; but no glamour; no tune strumming, for me at least. And the two of us sitting there had almost to be conventional and flat. And then we went up and up to see pictures on stairs, in ballrooms, and finally to Lady Cunard's bedroom, hung entirely with flower pieces. The bed has its triangular canopy of rose red silk; the windows, looking on the [Grosvenor] Square, are hung with green brocade. Her poudreuse, painted and gilt, stood open with gold brushes and looking glasses, and there on her gold slippers were neatly laid gold stockings. All this paraphernalia for one stringy old hop o' my thumb. She set the two great musical boxes playing and I said did she lie in bed and listen to them? But no. She has nothing fantastic in that way

about her. Money is important. But no doubt she has her acuity, her sharp peck at life; only how adorable, I thought, as I tiptoed home in my tight shoes, in the fog, in the chill, could one open one of these doors that I still open so venturously, and find a live interesting real person, a Nessa, a Duncan, a Roger. Some one new, whose mind would begin vibrating. Coarse and usual and dull these Cunards and Colefaxes are – for all their astonishing competence in the commerce of life.

And I cannot think what to 'write next'. I mean the situation is, this *Orlando* is of course a very quick brilliant book. Yes, but I did not try to explore. And must I always explore? Yes I think so still. Because my reaction is not the usual. Yes, but *The Moths?* That was to be an abstract mystical eyeless book: a playpoem. And there may be affectation in being too mystical, too abstract. I rather think the upshot will be books that relieve other books: a variety of styles and subjects: for after all, that is my temperament, I think.

Desmond destroyed our Saturday walk; he is now mouldy and to me depressing. He is perfectly reasonable and charming. Nothing surprises, nothing shocks him. He has been through it all one feels. He has come out rolled, smoothed, rather sodden, rather creased and jumbled, like a man who has sat up all night in a third class railway carriage. His fingers are stained yellow with cigarettes. One tooth in the lower jaw is missing. His hair is dank. His eye more than ever dubious. He has a hole in his blue sock. Yet he is resolute and determined – that's what I find so depressing. He seems to be sure that it is his view that is the right one; ours vagaries, deviations. And if his view is the right one, God knows there is nothing to live for: not a greasy biscuit. And the egotism of men surprises and shocks me even now. Is there a woman of my acquaintance who could sit in my armchair from 3 to 6.30 without the semblance of a suspicion that I may be busy, or tired, or bored; and so sitting could talk, grumbling and grudging, of her difficulties, worries; then eat chocolates, then read a book, and go at last, apparently self-complacent and wrapped in a kind of blubber of misty self satisfaction? Not the girls at Newnham or Girton. They are far too spry; far too disciplined. None of that self-confidence is their lot.

Thursday 8 November
We went to Karin's party last night. The truth is the stimulus is too brisk; one rattles; and only a shout can be heard; and one must stand; and one gets caught, like a bramble on a river by some branch; and hooked up out of the eddy. An emerald green Russian talked to me of seals and then gave me a card; I am to lecture four times a week for eight weeks in America – oh yes – and she will arrange most advantageous terms. But won't mention money in a drawing room: so we lapse upon seals again.

Saturday 10 November

... the [*Well of Loneliness*] trial yesterday at Bow Street. We were all packed in by 10.30; the door at the top of the court opened; in stepped the debonair distinguished magistrate; we all rose; he bowed; took his seat under the lion and the unicorn, and then proceeded. Something like a Harley Street specialist investigating a case. All black and white, tie pin, clean shaven, wax coloured, and carved, in that light, like ivory. He was ironical at first: raised his eyebrows and shrugged. Later I was impressed by the reason of the law, its astuteness, its formality. Here have we evolved a very remarkable fence between us and barbarity; something commonly recognised; half humbug and ceremony therefore – when they pulled out calf bound books and read old phrases I thought this; and the bowing and scraping made me think it; but in these banks runs a live stream. What is obscenity? What is literature? What is the difference between the subject and the treatment? In what cases is evidence allowable? This last, to my relief, was decided against us: we could not be called as experts in obscenity, only in art. So Desmond was only asked his qualifications and then, not allowed to answer the obscene question, was dismissed. After lunch we heard an hour more, and then the magistrate, increasingly deliberate and courteous, said he would read the book again and give judgment next Friday at two, on the pale tepid vapid book which lay damp and slab all about the court. And I lost my little Roman brooch and that is the end of this great day, so far. A curious brown top lighted scene; very stuffy; policemen at the doors; matrons passing through. An atmosphere quite decent and formal, of adult people.

Sunday 25 November

Leonard's 48th birthday. We were at Rodmell, where all has fallen into our hands, rapidly, unexpectedly: on top of the field we get a cottage, and Percy [Bartholomew] is 'our man'.

Wednesday 28 November

Father's birthday. He would have been ninety-six, yes, today; and could have been ninety-six, like other people one has known; but mercifully was not. His life would have entirely ended mine. What would have happened? No writing, no books; – inconceivable. I used to think of him and mother daily; but writing *The Lighthouse* laid them in my mind. (I believe this to be true – that I was obsessed by them both, unhealthily; and writing of them was a necessary act.) He comes back now more as a contemporary. I must read him some day.

Last night was one of our evenings – apparently successful. People enjoyed it. Perhaps I didn't; perhaps I did. Halfway through Lytton vanished, brayed out of the room by Clive's vociferation, L. thinks. Clive makes it all very strident, gaslit, band played.

As for my next book, I am going to hold myself from writing till I have it impending in me: grown heavy in the mind like a ripe pear; pendant, gravid, asking to be cut or it will fall. *The Moths* still haunts me, coming, as they always do, unbidden, between tea and dinner, while L. plays the gramophone. I shape a page or two; and make myself stop.

Sunday 9 December

I have again seen too many people, without much intensity. Christmas impends. And we shall spend it alone here, I think, and go to Rodmell afterwards and plan a new room. And then to Berlin we say. Meanwhile Nessa and I give our Tuesday evenings, and too many people press to come. But why, I ask 'see' people? What's the point? These isolated occasions which come so often. May I come and see you? And what they get, or I get, save the sense of a slide passing on a screen, I can't say.

Tuesday 18 December

Here I should be pegging away at 'Fiction'; rather an interesting little book I think; but I was switched off to write a eulogy of Lady Strachey, burnt yesterday with a bunch of our red and white carnations on top of her. It is odd how little her death means to me – for this reason. About a year ago she was said to be dying; and at once I made up my usual visualisation; felt the whole emotion of Lady Strachey's passing – her memories and so on – that night; and then she did not die; and now when she does die, not a vision, not an emotion comes my way. These little tricks of psychology amuse me.

L. has just been in to consult about a third edition of *Orlando*. This has been ordered; we have sold over 6000 copies; and sales are still amazingly brisk. Anyhow my room is secure. For the first time since I married – 1912-1928 – sixteen years, I have been spending money. The spending muscle does not work naturally yet. I feel guilty; and yet have an agreeable luxurious sense of coins in my pocket beyond my weekly thirteen shillings which was always running out, or being encroached upon. Yesterday I spent fifteen shillings on a steel brooch. I spent three pounds on a mother-of-pearl necklace – and I haven't bought a jewel for twenty years perhaps! I have carpeted the dining room – and so on. I think one's soul is better for this lubrication. The important thing is to spend freely, without fuss or anxiety; and to trust to one's power of making more.

But to return to Max Beerbohm. I met him at Ethel [Sands]'s the other night. As I came in a thick set old man (such was my impression) rose, and I was introduced. No freakishness, no fancy about him. His face is solidified;

has a thick moustache; a red veined skin, heavy lines; but then his eyes are perfectly round, very large, and sky blue. His eyes become dreamy and merry when the rest of him is well groomed and decorous in the extreme. Halfway through dinner he turned to me and we began a 'nice', interesting, flattering, charming kind of talk. I said, as I think, that he is immortal. In a small way, he said; but with complacency. He asked me how I wrote. For he hacks every step with his pen, and therefore never alters. He thought I wrote like this. I told him I had to cut out great chunks. I wish you would send them to me, he said, simply. Indeed, he was nothing if not kind; but looked long and steadily – that queer painter's look, so matching, so considering, apart from human intent; yet with him not entirely. After dinner, he leant on the mantelpiece and Maurice Baring and I flittered round him like a pair of butterflies, praising, laughing, extravagant. But always he had to be led off to talk politely to this person and that; finally disappeared, very dignified, very discreet in his white waistcoat, pressing my hand in his plump firm one long; and saying what a pleasure &c. I own that I don't find much difference between the great and ourselves – indeed they are like us: I mean they don't have the frills and furbelows of the small; come to terms quickly and simply. But we got, of course, very little way.

And we dined last night with the Hutchinsons and met George Moore – like an old silver coin now, so white, so smooth; with his little flipper hands, like a walrus's; and his chubby cheeks, and little knees – yet always saying the thing that comes into his head; fresh, juvenile almost for that reason; and very shrewd. And what it comes to is that the great are very simple; quick to come to terms with; reserved; and don't pay attention to other people's books (Moore throws scorn on them all – Shaw – a shriek of vulgarity – poisoned with vulgarity – never wrote a good sentence in his life – Wells – I spare myself Wells – and Galsworthy –) and live in an atmosphere very serene, bright, and fenced off: for all that they are more to the point than ordinary people; go to the heart of things directly. Moore toddled off and got quickly into a cab, Jack said, for all his look of an old silver coin.

For the Christmas holidays Vita Sackville-West and her two sons had rejoined Harold Nicolson, now Counsellor at the British Embassy in Berlin, and urged the Woolfs to visit them there. Virginia and Leonard crossed from Harwich on 16 January and were joined in Berlin by Vanessa and Quentin Bell and Duncan Grant; they all spent a rather rackety and inharmonious week together, and the Woolfs returned the way they had come, Virginia reaching home in a state of collapse. During the ensuing period of invalidism, she was engrossed by the ideas adumbrated in her Cambridge lectures on 'Women and Fiction', which by the end of June she had written out in the form of a short book entitled A Room of One's Own and sent to the printer.

The Hogarth Press was prospering, largely due to the success of Orlando; it employed a staff of three in the office, under Leonard's authoritative and in the main benevolent direction. Their greater affluence enabled the Woolfs to embark on various improvements to Monks House and, at the end of the summer, to buy a cottage in Rodmell to accommodate a local servant – an alteration in her domestic organisation much to Virginia's liking, uncomfortable as she found her dependence upon and resentment of Nelly's constant presence in her home. When the Labour Party narrowly won the General Election at the end of May, Virginia was disconcerted by the realisation that Nelly, like herself, was now of the ruling party.

Early in June the Woolfs went by train to Cassis for ten days' holiday, lodging near Duncan and Vanessa. Home again, Virginia suffered from a sense of dejection and aimlessness, but gradually the impulse towards a new work took possession of her mind, and the rather nebulous ideas suggested by Vanessa's description of moths began to take form on paper, developing eventually into The Waves. The dejection however accompanied her to Monks House at the beginning of their summer stay, and was sustained by a disproportionate sense of grievance at the news that Vita had gone abroad with a new friend, Hilda Matheson, the talks director of the BBC; and by Nelly's provocations and withdrawals. Nonetheless a succession of weekend visitors, including William Plomer, the young writer from South Africa whose first book had been published by the Hogarth Press in 1926, was entertained; visits were made to Charleston, to Vita at Long Barn, to the Labour Party Conference at Brighton; and the proofs of A Room of One's Own were corrected and finally despatched. The book was published on 24 October after the Woolfs had returned to London; a few days later it was praised by Vita Sackville-West in what Virginia called a 'flamboyant broadcast', and sales soared: by the end of the year it had gone into a fourth *impression. Henceforward the Woolfs were what Leonard considered 'very well off'.*

Two changes in the circumstances of those close to her affected Virginia: Vanessa, whose children were now at Cambridge, in Paris, and at boarding school, gave up her home in Gordon Square and moved into a large studio adjacent to that occupied by Duncan Grant in Fitzroy Street; and Harold Nicolson, encouraged by his wife and both Leonard and Virginia, resigned from the diplomatic service and returned to England and a job on the Beaverbrook Press.

1929

Friday 4 January

Now is life very solid, or very shifting? I am haunted by the two contradic-
tions. This has gone on for ever: will last for ever; goes down to the bottom
of the world – this moment I stand on. Also it is transitory, flying,
diaphanous. I shall pass like a cloud on the waves. I am impressed by the
transitoriness of human life to such an extent that I am often saying a
farewell – after dining with Roger for instance; or reckoning how many
more times I shall see Nessa.

*　　*　　*

Thursday 28 March

It is a disgrace indeed; no diary has been left so late in the year. The truth
was that we went to Berlin on the 16th of January, and then I was in bed
for three weeks afterwards, and then could not write, perhaps for another
three, and have spent my energy since in one of my excited outbursts of
composition – writing what I made up in bed, a final version of *Women and
Fiction*. And as usual I am bored by narrative. I want only to say how I met
Nessa in Tottenham Court Road this afternoon, both of us sunk fathoms
deep in that wash of reflection in which we both swim about. She will be
gone on Wednesday for four months. It is queer how instead of drawing
apart, life draws us together. But I was thinking a thousand things as I
carried my teapot, gramophone records and stockings under my arm. It is
one of those days that I called 'potent' when we lived in Richmond.

I am going to enter a nunnery these next months; and let myself down
into my mind; Bloomsbury being done with. It is going to be a time of
adventure and attack, rather lonely and painful I think. But solitude will be
good for a new book. In old days books were so many sentences absolutely
struck with an axe out of crystal; and now my mind is so impatient, so
quick, in some ways so desperate. I feel on the verge of some strenuous

257

adventure. So when I wake early, I brace myself out of my terrors by saying that I shall need great courage: after all, I say, I made £1000 all from willing it early one morning. No more poverty I said; and poverty has ceased. I am summoning Philcox next week to plan a room – I have money to build it, money to furnish it. And we have the new car, and we can drive to Edinburgh in June if we like, and go to Cassis.

Nessa has taken a studio and will let 37, thus ending, for ever I suppose, her Gordon Square life. How much I admire this handling of life as if it were a thing one could throw about; this handling of circumstance. Angelica will go to school.

Saturday 13 April

I am sordidly debating within myself the question of Nelly; the perennial question. It is an absurdity, how much time L. and I have wasted in talking about servants. And it can never be done with because the fault lies in the system. How can an uneducated woman let herself in, alone, into our lives? What happens is that she becomes a mongrel; and has no roots anywhere. I could put my theory into practice by getting a daily of a civilised kind, who had her baby in Kentish Town; and treated me as an employer, not friend. Here is a fine rubbish heap left by our parents to be swept.

Hugh Walpole was here the other day, from 4.30 to 7.15, alone over the fire. The same uneasy talk as usual; brisk and breezy, hating war; and then this morbid egotism and desire to scratch the same place over and over again – his own defects as a writer and how to remedy them, what they spring from; all mixed up with his normal and usual sense of being prosperous and admired – from which, as he admits when I ask him, he gets great pleasure. He starts indeed to protest that he gives pleasure, does good, but can't bring that out in my presence; which is why he seeks my presence – a scratching stone to rid him of the worlds's mud. On the other hand, I like these bustling vigorous characters: I like talk of Russia, and war and great doings and famous people. If I don't see them I romanticise them.

Leonard is upstairs finishing the Hogarth Press accounts. Yesterday he gave the three stall hands a bonus. They sent up a bunch of roses later in the day. For the first time we have made over £400 profit. And seven people now depend on us; and I think with pride that seven people depend, largely, upon my hand writing on a sheet of paper. That is of course a great solace and pride to me. Its not scribbling; its keeping seven people fed and housed. They will be feeding off *Women and Fiction* next year for which I predict some sale. It made itself up and forced itself upon me as I lay in bed after Berlin. I used to make it up at such a rate that when I got pen and paper I was like a water bottle turned upside down.

Monday 29 April

Oh this cold spring! Dry as a bone, though, until today, but with never a blue sky. So that my red coat, which is like haws in winter suits it. I heard the nightingale at Vita's a week or two ago – the one warm night. And we were cold at Rodmell last week, when we went down to see Philcox, who will build two rooms for £320, and take only two months. It was cold; but how silent, how safe from voices and talk! How I resented our coming back; and quickly changed into the social sphere of my soul; and went to lunch with Sibyl; and there had, for my pains, precisely six minutes tolerable talk with Max Beerbohm. But dear me, how little talk with great men now disturbs me.

Poor Tom – a true poet, I think; what they will call in a hundred years a man of genius: and this is his life. I stand for half an hour listening while he says that Vivien can't walk. Her legs have gone. But what's the matter? No one knows. And so she lies in bed – can't put a shoe on. And they have difficulties, humiliations, with servants. And after endless quibbling about visiting – which he can't do these eight weeks, owing to moving house and fifteen first cousins come to England, suddenly he appears overcome, moved, tragic, unhappy, broken down, because I offer to come to tea on Thursday. Oh but we don't dare ask our friends, he said. Would you really come – all this way to see us? Yes I said. But what a vision of misery, imagined, but real too. Vivien with her foot on a stool, in bed all day; Tom hurrying back lest she abuse him; this is our man of genius. This is what I gathered yesterday morning on the telephone.

Sunday 12 May

A wet day, or we should be at Hampton Court with Roger and [Charles] Mauron. And I am glad of the rain, because I have talked too much. We have seen too many people – Sydney Waterlow perhaps the most notable, as a resurrection. A desperate looking pompous sad respectable elderly man; worldly; but quivering as usual in his shell. Any pin pricks him in the unarmoured skin. I liked him. Also we had a party: Roger a little old – to my mind he needs Nessa to fertilise and sweeten him. Some queer rancour often seems to exacerbate him. When his stomach heals his leg aches. And [William] Plomer came – a little rigid I fear; and too much of a gentleman; and little Blunden, the very image of a London house sparrow, that pecks and cheeps and is starved and dirty. And Julian, to me a very satisfactory young man at present; full of ardour, yet clear, precise, and genial too; much more apt to see the good than the bad.

Monday 13 May

... up came Saxon, on his holiday – going to *The Ring* of course, and having a day off. For how many years has he done this – strange methodical character that he is. We don't meet for months, and take up the subject again. He took out his cheque book and said he thought the pattern was changed, with the same interest in that minute detail as he had thirty years ago. He has the same umbrella hanging by a hook on his arm; the same gold watch chain; and his pirouetting attitudes; and sprightly bird-like ways. What then has life given you, I asked (myself). Well, he is free to go to the Opera, to read Plato, to play chess. And he will continue doing these things, as if they were the chosen things, till he dies. There is a certain dignity in this steady doing of things which seem chosen. Yet – thus one always ends a comparison of lives – I wouldn't for the whole world live yours.

The reason I dislike dining with Sibyl is that she exacts it; I am to give her a display of intimacy, which she cannot acquire, poor woman, for herself.

Wednesday 15 May

I went to Sibyl's dinner; but Heavens, how little real point there is to these meetings – save indeed that the food is good; and there is wine, and a certain atmosphere of luxury and hospitality. This, on the other hand, tends to drug one; one has been given something, for which one has to pay. And I don't like that feeling. The old white haired baby [George Moore] sat propped up in his high chair; his hair now white like flax, like silk; his cheeks tinted a child's pink; his eyes with their marble hardness; his boneless ineffective hands. For some reason, he paid me compliments, indeed referred to me as an authority on English; and even offered, which I daresay was kindly meant, though nothing has happened, to send me one of his books. What did we discuss? Mostly himself and his books, I think; and how he had known various old dim figures, far away in the past. He talked about Henry James, and a proof sheet which nobody could read; and he said that a sentence ought to form like a cloud at the end of the pen – don't you think so? he said to me.

Tuesday 28 May

It is an odd summer, this one, unexampled in our history. We are going off to Cassis on Tuesday for a week. This is a revolution. We have never been abroad so late in the year I think. The Election will be over. We shall be governed by a Tory or a Labour party – Tory I suppose. And I feel, rather oddly, that this is an important election. Walking down the King's Road with Sydney Waterlow the other night – having been to dine at his club – talking about the election, Sydney said that human nature has improved. We are all becoming gentler and wiser. Even the dogs are.

Friday 31 May

The oculist said to me this afternoon "Perhaps you're not as young as you were". This is the first time that has been said to me; and it seemed to me an astonishing statement. It means that one now seems to a stranger not a woman, but an elderly woman. Yet, although I felt wrinkled and aged for an hour, and put on a manner of great wisdom and toleration, buying a coat, even so, I forget it soon; and become 'a woman' again.

"We are winning" Nelly said at tea. I was shocked to think that we both desire the Labour Party to win – why? Partly that I don't want to be ruled by Nelly. I think that to be ruled by Nelly and Lottie would be a disaster. Last night at Charleston we heard election results spoken very distinctly in the drawing room. Driving home through Lewes there was not a single light downstairs. No one was even listening in. The streets were perfectly empty. One man was pump shipping against the station wall. I had imagined a crowd, flares, shouts, white sheets – only three black cats, out on business with the mice. So we shall be ruled by Labour.

We went down to Worthing to see Leonard's mother, laid like an old rose – rather lovely this time – in a narrow room; with the sea opposite. And she cried; and was very dismal. Nothing of life, as we see it, remains to her – [she] can't read or sleep, yet anxiously demands, does Leonard think she will get well? We had been saying driving down that one should take poison. She has every reason; and yet demands more life, more life, at seventy-eight. She quarrels; she can't walk; she is alone; she is looked after by nurses; lives in an hotel, but demands more life, more life. I was moved by her; could hardly speak. I suppose human nature, so emotional, so irrational, so instinctive, as it is in her, but not in me, has this beauty; this what they call 'elemental' quality. One may get it too, when one is seventy-eight. One may lie sobbing, and yet cry does doctor think I shall recover? One will not perhaps go to the writing table and write that simple and profound paper upon suicide which I see myself leaving for my friends.

We voted at Rodmell. I saw a white gloved lady helping an old farm couple out of her Daimler.

52 TAVISTOCK SQUARE, WC1

Saturday 15 June

Home last night from Cassis. The hottest holiday I have ever had. And in some ways different from others; partly that it was so hot; then that we were alone with Nessa and Duncan. I forget what the facts of our stay were. We were there for a week, coming the day before they expected us, oddly enough, as we did last year. I wrote a little article on Cowper, but lifting the words with difficulty in the heat, surrounded by black and white butterflies. And L. and I were very extravagant, for the first time in our lives, buying desks, tables, sideboards, crockery for Rodmell. This gave me pleasure; and set my dander up against Nessa's almost overpowering supremacy.

A sense of nothingness rolls about the house; due to the fact that we came back last night and are not going round in the mill yet. Time flaps on the mast – my own phrase I think. There are things I ought to do. I ought to correct *A Room of One's Own*. I ought to write several dull silly letters. Lytton once said that we can only live if we see through illusion. Now I must somehow brew another decoction of illusion. Well, if the human interest flags, I must not sit thinking about it here. I must make human illusion – ask someone in tomorrow after dinner; and begin that astonishing adventure with the souls of others again – about which I know so little.

Sunday 16 June
As I finished those words, in came Leonard to say that Desmond was coming round in two minutes – which he did, so that the sail filled out again and the ship went on. Desmond was shabby and baggy in grey. He was bubbling and simmering, off to dine at Kettners, and determined to be punctual. A vein of determination lies in him; and he is the most cooked and saturated of us all. Not an atom remains crude; basted richly over a slow fire – an adorable man, a divine man, for all his power of taking the spine out of me. Happily we did not get on to that – writing that is to say.

Sunday 23 June
It was very hot that day, driving to Worthing to see Leonard's mother, my throat hurt me. Next morning I had a headache. So we stayed on at Rodmell till today. At Rodmell I read through *The Common Reader*; I must learn to write more succinctly. I am horrified by my own looseness: the result is a wobble and diffusity and breathlessness which I detest. And so I pitched into my great lake of melancholy. Lord how deep it is! What a born melancholiac I am! The only way I keep afloat is by working. Directly I stop working I feel that I am sinking down, down. And as usual, I feel that if I sink further I shall reach the truth. That is the only mitigation; a kind of nobility. Solemnity. I shall make myself face the fact that there is nothing – nothing for any of us. Work, reading, writing, are all disguises; and relations with other people. Yes, even having children would be useless.

However, I now begin to see *The Moths* rather too clearly; or at least strenuously, for my comfort. I think it will begin like this: dawn; the shells on a beach; I don't know – voices of cock and nightingale; and then all the children at a long table – lessons; the beginning. Could one not get the waves to be heard all through? Or the farmyard noises? Some odd irrelevant noises. Well all this is of course the 'real' life; and nothingness only comes in the absence of this. Everything becomes green and vivified in me when I begin to think of *The Moths*.

Sunday 30 June
My melancholy has been broken, like a lake by oars, since I wrote. I have been so active. We have seen so many people. Last night we dined with Roger, tonight with Clive; Lytton came; Vita came; we had a party. I bought a dress in Shaftesbury Avenue. It was very hot, I think; and is now cold, indeed for the first time for weeks it is, or has been, raining.

This last half year I made over £1800; almost at the rate of £4000 a year; the salary almost of a Cabinet minister; and time was, two years ago, when I toiled to make £200. Now I am overpaid I think for my little articles. Well, after tomorrow I shall close down article writing, and give way to fiction for six or seven months till next March perhaps.

Desmond is being very brilliant about the Byron letters and the Boswell papers. Think! There are eighteen volumes of Boswell's diaries now to be published. With any luck I shall live to read them. I feel as if some dead person were said to be living after all – an odd effect, this disinterment of a mass more of Boswell when one had thought all was known, all settled. And father never knew. These papers were in a cabinet in Ireland.

MONKS HOUSE, RODMELL

Monday 5 August
Yes that is the date, and the last was June 30th – a tribute to the helter skelter random rackety summer I spent. Far the pleasantest memories, standing out like green weed on some civet grey pond, were the week ends here; with the hay cutting and the lights lambent; Leonard's new room, Hedgehog Hall, a-building, and my lodge being made into the palace of comfort which it now is. Yes it was a scattered summer; I felt as if the telephone were strung to my arm and anybody could jerk me who liked. A sense of interruption bothered me. And then I'm cross with Vita: she never told me she was going abroad for a fortnight – didn't dare; till the last moment, when she said it was a sudden plan. Lord Lord! I am half amused though; why do I mind? what do I mind? how much do I mind?

One of the facts is that these Hildas are a chronic case; and, like the damned intellectual snob that I am, I hate to be linked, even by an arm, with Hilda [Matheson]. Her earnest aspiring competent wooden face appears before me. A queer trait in Vita – her passion for the earnest middle-class intellectual, however drab and dreary. You can choose between us, I say, stopping writing; and I get some satisfaction from making up caustic phrases.

Thursday 8 August

This is written to while away one of those stupendous moments – one of those painful, ridiculous, agitating moments which make one half sick and yet I don't know – I'm excited too; and feel free and then sordid; and unsettled; and so on – I've told Nelly to go; after a series of scenes which I won't bore myself to describe. And so at lunch L. and I settled it; and I spoke two words, which she almost pulled out of my mouth in her eagerness to show herself delighted and eager and hard and untouched – a sordid painful scene after fifteen years; but then how many I have had, and how degrading they are. And if we don't break now we drift on endlessly – oh but all these old arguments I know by heart. In truth we never should have gone on, I daresay, if it hadn't been for the war; I don't know. I'm confirmed in my wish to have no resident servants ever again. That is the evil which rots the relationship.

Saturday 10 August

Well, Heaven be praised; it is all over and calm and settled. Nelly – how long ago that seems! – is staying. And I'm too deliciously relieved to have seen Vita this moment and find that her story to me was precisely true. Indeed I was more worried and angry and hurt and caustic about this affair than I let on, even to the blank page; yet afraid too of exaggeration. Of course, one is right about Nelly – right that she is, in bad moods, almost insufferably mean, selfish and spiteful; but – she is in a state of nature; untrained; uneducated, without the power of analysis or logic; but we shan't part now, I think. And I'm half pleased to find that it is harder to part after fifteen years than I thought. And I'm pleased – oh very pleased – about Vita.

Monday 19 August

I opened this book to record the blessed fact that for good or bad I have just set the last correction to *Women and Fiction*, or *A Room of One's Own*. I shall never read it again I suppose. Good or bad? Has an uneasy life in it I think: you feel the creature arching its back and galloping on, though as usual much is watery and flimsy and pitched in too high a voice.

William Plomer has been for the week end and gone. A compressed inarticulate young man, thickly coated with a universal manner fit for all weathers and people: tells a nice dry prim story; but has the wild eyes which I once noticed in Tom, and take to be the true index of what goes on within. Once or twice he almost cracked his crust – sitting on the stones this morning for instance. I think he shows up well against the Raymonds and the Frankies – is somehow solid; to their pinchbeck lustre.

And now, having written my little articles, I must think of that book again, and go down step by step into the well. These are the great events and revolutions in one's life – and then people talk of war and politics. I shall grind very hard; all my brakes will be stiff, my springs rusty. But I have now earned the right to some months of fiction.

Thursday 22 August

I thought on my walk that I would begin at the beginning: I get up at half past eight and walk across the garden. Today it was misty and I had been dreaming of Edith Sitwell. I wash and go into breakfast which is laid on the check tablecloth. With luck I may have an interesting letter; today there was none. And then bath and dress; and come out here and write or correct for three hours, broken at 11 by Leonard with milk, and perhaps newspapers. At one luncheon – rissoles today and chocolate custard. A brief reading and smoking after lunch; and at about two I change into thick shoes, take Pinker's lead and go out – up to Asheham hill this afternoon, where I sat a minute or two, and then home again, along the river. Tea at four, about; and then I come out here and write several letters, interrupted by the post, with another invitation to lecture; and then I read one book of *The Prelude*. And soon the bell will ring, and we shall dine and then we shall have some music, and I shall smoke a cigar; and then we shall read – La Fontaine I think tonight and the papers – and so to bed. But my skeleton day needs reviving with all sorts of different colours. Today it was grey and windy on the walk; yesterday generous and open; a yellow sun on the corn; and heat in the valley. Both days differ greatly; both are among the happiest of my life – I mean among the happy undistinguished days, ripe and sweet and sound; the daily bread; for nothing strange or exalted has happened; only the day has gone rightly and harmoniously.

Monday 16 September

Leonard is having a picnic at Charleston and I am here – 'tired'. But why am I tired? Well I am never alone. This is the beginning of my complaint. I am not physically tired so much as psychologically. I have strained and wrung at journalism and proof correction; and underneath has been forming my *Moths* book. Yes, but it forms very slowly; and what I want is not to write it, but to think it for two or three weeks say. (And they've gone to some lovely place – Hurstmonceux perhaps, in this strange misty evening; and yet when the time came to go, all I wanted was to walk off into the hills by myself. I am now feeling a little lonely and deserted and defrauded, inevitably.) And every time I get into my current of thought I am jerked out of it. We have had the Keyneses; then Vita came; then Angelica and Eve [Younger]; then we went to Worthing, then my head begins throbbing – so here I am not writing – that does not matter, but not thinking, feeling or seeing – Leonard appeared at the door at this moment; and they didn't go to Hurstmonceux or anywhere; so I missed nothing – one's first egotistical pleasure.

Another reflection – nothing is so tiring as a change of atmosphere. I am more shattered and dissipated by an hour with Leonard's mother than by six hours – no, six days, of Vita. (Nessa don't count.) The tremendous gear changing that has to take place grinds one's machinery to bits.

And then I am forty-seven: yes: and my infirmities will of course increase. To begin with my eyes. Last year, I think, I could read without spectacles; would pick up a paper and read it in a tube; gradually I found I needed spectacles in bed; and now I can't read a line without them. What other infirmities? I can hear, I think, perfectly: I think I could walk as well as ever. But then will there not be the change of life? And may that not be a difficult and even dangerous time? Obviously one can get over it by facing it with common sense – that it is a natural process; that one can lie out here and read; that one's faculties will be the same afterwards; that one has nothing to worry about in one sense – I've written some interesting books, can make money, can afford a holiday. Oh no; one has nothing to bother about; and these curious intervals in life – I've had many – are the most fruitful artistically – one becomes fertilised – think of my madness at Hogarth – and all the little illnesses – that before I wrote *To the Lighthouse* for instance. Six weeks in bed now would make a masterpiece of *Moths*. But that won't be the name. Moths, I suddenly remember, don't fly by day. And there can't be a lighted candle. Altogether, the shape of the book wants considering – and with time I could do it.

Saturday 21 September
Another of those curious plums, things falling unexpectedly in our way, has just happened. Annie the large eyed sad young woman has been to ask us to buy her a cottage, and let her do for us always, in fact be our servant here. She and her baby, aged two, have been turned out at a fortnight's notice to make room for two spinster dog breeders. She would make an ideal servant, I believe; she would be a great standby; one could come here as long as one liked – and poor dear Nelly could be left in London. It needs some thinking – meanwhile Annie is up against this terrific high black

prison wall of poverty – has to manage with a child on fifteen shillings a week.

Sunday 22 September

Though write letters I will and must, I will canter here a moment. It is a fine September morning; the rooks cawing, the shadows very long and shallow on the terrace. The body has gone out of the air. It is thinning itself for winter. An exacting and rather exhausting summer this has been. On the other hand, this is the best appointed summer we have ever had. Never has the garden been so lovely – all ablaze even now; dazzling one's eyes with reds and pinks and purples and mauves; the carnations in great bunches, the roses lit like lamps. Often we go out after dinner to see these sights. And at last I like looking about the drawing room. I like my rug; my carpet; my painted beams. And for some odd reason I have found lovelier walks this year than ever – up into the downs behind Telscombe. Partly it is the weather, perhaps; we have had day after day of cloudless warm sun.

Wednesday 25 September

But what interests me is of course my oil stove. We found it here last night on coming back from Worthing. At this moment it is cooking my dinner in the glass dishes perfectly I hope, without smell, waste, or confusion: one turns handles, there is a thermometer. And so I see myself freer, more independent – able to come down here with a chop in a bag and live on my own. I go over the dishes I shall cook – the rich stews, the sauces – the adventurous strange dishes with dashes of wine in them. Of course Leonard puts a drag on, and I must be very cautious, like a child, not to make too much noise playing.

Then, old Mrs Woolf – She has come to wear a charm and dignity to me, unknown before, now her old age is crumbling down all the cheerful sentimental small talk – she becomes curiously more human and wise. True she is peevish and bored as a child; but has attained some carelessness of show and pomp and respectability, as if she had washed her hands of most things and were playing on a beach. I must go into the kitchen to see my stove cooking ham now.

Wednesday 2 October

We have just been over Annie's cottage – so I suppose it is. And we therefore own another fair sized house; but the arrangement with Annie seems another of those plums which have dropped into our hands here. She will cook; my oil stove makes hot meals practicable at all hours; but I am dazed with the Brighton [Labour Party] conference (how my days of reflection have dwindled!). The audience makes an extraordinary baaing noise; and I thought how politics was no longer an affair of great nobles and mystery and diplomacy, but of commonsense, issuing from ordinary men and women of business – not very exalted, but straightforward, like any other business affair.

The light is dying; I hear the village boys kicking footballs; the atmosphere – winter, change, London's imminence – scatter finally my poor efforts at solid concentration. Yet I have, these last days, set my book alight I think – got it going. And all the Americans write and cable for articles. Leonard in the cold windy road is cleaning the car.

52 TAVISTOCK SQUARE, WC1

Friday 11 October
And I snatch at the idea of writing here in order not to write *Waves* or *Moths* or whatever it is to be called. These October days are to me a little strained and surrounded with silence. What I mean by this last word I don't quite know, since I have never stopped 'seeing' people. No; its not physical silence; its some inner loneliness. To give an example – I was walking up Bedford Place this afternoon, and I said to myself spontaneously, something like this. How I suffer, and no one knows how I suffer, walking up this street, engaged with my anguish, as I was after Thoby died – alone; fighting something alone. But then I had the devil to fight, and now nothing. And when I come indoors, it is all so silent. Yet I am writing – oh and we are very successful; and it is autumn; and the lights are going up; and Nessa is in Fitzroy Street – in a great misty room, with flaring gas and unsorted plates and glasses on the floor; and the Press is booming; and this celebrity business is quite chronic – and I am richer than I have ever been – and bought a pair of earrings today – and for all this, there is vacancy and silence somewhere in the machine. If I never felt these extraordinarily pervasive strains – of unrest, or rest, or happiness, or discomfort – I should float down into acquiescence. Here is something to fight: and when I wake early I say to myself, Fight, fight.

Its odd, now I come to think of it – I miss Clive.

Wednesday 23 October
I will here sum up my impressions before publishing *A Room of One's Own*. It is a little ominous that Morgan won't review it. It makes me suspect that there is a shrill feminine tone in it which my intimate friends will dislike. I forecast then that I shall get no criticism, except of the evasive jocular kind, from Lytton, Roger and Morgan; that the press will be kind and talk of its

charm and sprightliness; also I shall be attacked for a feminist and hinted at for a sapphist; Sibyl will ask me to luncheon; I shall get a good many letters from young women. I am afraid it will not be taken seriously. I doubt that I mind very much. It is a trifle, I shall say; so it is, but I wrote it with ardour and conviction.

We dined last night with the Webbs. We sit in two lodging house rooms (the dining room had a brass bedstead behind a screen), eat hunks of red beef, and are offered whisky. It is the same enlightened, impersonal, perfectly aware of itself atmosphere. And I compared them with L. and myself, and felt (I daresay for this reason) the pathos, the symbolical quality of the childless couple; standing for something, united.

Saturday 2 November

I dreamt last night that I had a disease of the heart that would kill me in six months. Leonard, after some persuasion, told me. My instincts were all such as I should have, in order, and some very strong: quite voluntary, as they are in dreams, and have thus an authenticity which makes an immense and pervading impression. First, relief – well I've done with life anyhow (I was lying in bed); then horror; then desire to live; then fear of insanity; then (no this came earlier) regret about my writing, and leaving this book unfinished; then a luxurious dwelling upon my friends' sorrow; then a sense of death and being done with at my age; then telling Leonard that he must marry again; seeing our life together; and facing the conviction of going, when other people went on living. Then I woke, coming to the top with all this hanging about me; and found I had sold a great many copies of my book – the odd feeling of these two states of life and death mingling as I ate my breakfast feeling drowsy and heavy.

Tuesday 5 November

Oh but I have done quite well so far with *A Room of One's Own*: and it sells, I think; and I get unexpected letters. But I am more concerned with my *Waves*. I've just typed out my morning's work; and can't feel altogether sure. There's *something* there but I can't get at it squarely.

On Sunday we were at Rodmell; and my room is now about three feet of brick, with the window frames in; rather an eyesore, for it cuts off the garage roof and the downs – both pleasanter sights than I had thought.

Sunday 17 November

A horrid date. Yes, I am feeling a little sick, a little shivery; I can't settle to anything; I am in a twitter; I find myself talking aloud: "After what happened the other morning, I am afraid I must now give you notice . . . After you told me to leave your room I went to Mr Woolf and said that I could not keep you as my maid any longer. I haven't made up my mind in a hurry. But the scenes at Rodmell were worse than ever. And now this is the last. This is the 17th of November. I shall expect you to go on the 17th December." Yes, this is what I have to say to Nelly at 9.30 tomorrow. And I am almost trembling with this nervous anticipation as I write. But it must be done.

Monday 18 November

Well it is over, and much better than I expected – at least for the present. To my question Do you want to give me notice? she replied "I have given you notice –" "Then you wish to go at the end of your month?" As we refused her an hour's extra help when she was ill, yes. But this was said without conviction – which means I'm afraid that she has no more intention of going than I have of taking ship to Siberia. So be it. I shall hope that the dust will be settled now for a week or two.

Sunday 8 December

Dear me; last Monday, as L. advised, I asked Nelly if she wished to go: and so (as I foreboded) she said reasonably no; and proposed solutions. We were landed; not emotionally; rather wearily and disillusionedly on my part, in a compromise for a month; if the trial is unsatisfactory then to part without further discussion for ever.

Just back from Rodmell. The roof is on; the floors are made; the windows in; giving, it seemed, vast sweeping views of flooded meadows; but there was only a blink of light even at midday; we were engulfed in whirling wet; working up to such a storm on Friday night as I have, I think, never been in. It went round and round; and there was thunder in the crash of the wind; and great zigzags of lightning; and hail drumming on the iron roof outside my room; and such a fury of noise one could not sleep. So at one I went up to L. and looked at the lighted windows in the village; and thought, really with some fear, of being out alone that moment. Dreams were all blown about, elongated, distorted, that night. A tree down in the churchyard. Trees down all the way up today. However, the mind was very still and happy. I read and read and finished I daresay three foot thick of MSS read carefully too; much of it on the border, and so needing thought.

Saturday 14 December

By the way, the sales of *A Room* are unprecedented – have beaten *Orlando*; feels like a line running through one's fingers; orders for 100 taken, as coolly as 12's used to be. We have sold, I think, 5500; and our next year's income is made.

Had I married Lytton I should never have written anything. So I thought at dinner the other night. He checks and inhibits in the most curious way.

L. may be severe; but he stimulates. Anything is possible with him. Lytton was mild and damp, like a wet autumnal leaf. Lonely, and growing elderly.

Sunday 15 December
Last night we went to *The Calendar* (by Edgar Wallace) with Ann [Stephen]; and there was a cheer, and behold a great golden Queen bowing in a very small bow windowed box. Also, when the lights went up, the King, red, grumpy, fidgeting with his hands; well groomed, bluff; heavy looking, with one white flower in his buttonhole, resenting the need, perhaps, of sitting to be looked at between one of the acts – his duty to be done. Once the Duchess of York sat with the Queen; a simple, chattering, sweethearted little roundfaced young woman in pink; but her wrists twinkling with diamonds, her dress held on the shoulder with diamonds. The Queen also like a lit up street with diamonds. An odd feeling came to me of the shop window decorated for the public: these our exhibits, our show pieces. Not very impressive – no romance or mystery – the very best goods.

MONKS HOUSE, RODMELL

Thursday 26 December
And I am sitting in my new room, with curtains, fire, table; and two great views; sometimes sun over the brooks and storm over the church. A violent Christmas; a brilliant serene Boxing day. I find it almost incredibly soothing – a fortnight alone – almost impossible to let oneself have it. Relentlessly we have crushed visitors: we will be alone this once, we say; and really, it seems possible. Then Annie is to me very sympathetic.

Before I went Clive came to tea. He asked me if I had been told that he had criticised *A Room*? I said no. He was a little rasped; said the jokes were lecture jokes. "Girls come round me" – too much of that – little ideas – nothing compared with *Orlando*. But his criticism is founded upon the theory that I can't feel sex: have the purple light cut off. But as always, his own axe wants grinding: that Love is enough – or if love fails, down one goes for ever. And I always feel, how jolly, how much hunting, and talking and carousing there is in you! How long we have known each other – and then Thoby's form looms behind – that queer ghost. I think of death sometimes as the end of an excursion which I went on when he died. As if I should come in and say well, here you are.

Saturday 28 December
Bernard Shaw said the other night at the Keyneses – and the Keyneses have just wrecked my perfect fortnight of silence, have been over in their

Rolls Royce – and L. made them stay, and is a little inclined to think me absurd for not wishing it – Bernard Shaw said to me, "*Heartbreak House* is the best of my plays. I wrote it after staying with you at the Webbs in Sussex – perhaps you inspired it. [George] Moore's an odd man – a very small talent cultivated with the utmost patience. We used to laugh at him in the old days. He was always telling us stories about himself and a lady – a grand lady – and she was always throwing something at his head and just missing it. Nobody was better tempered. But he was our laughing stock. And one day Zola said to me I've discovered your great English novelist! Who's that said I. His name is George Moore. And I burst out laughing – not our little George Moore, with his stories about himself? But it was. A lesson, you see, not to be too quick in judging one's friends."

1930

It was through, and with, Roger Fry that in January Virginia was asked to dine in Bedford Square by Fry's friend Henry ('Bogey') Harris, the wealthy connoisseur and art collector, where their fellow guests were political notables including the Labour Prime Minister, Ramsay MacDonald. Subsequently, while she was semi-immured during her usual winter indispositions, two very disparate visitors, one from the past, the other to loom large in the future, engaged her descriptive powers. Margery Snowden had been a fellow student of Vanessa's at the Royal Academy Schools at the beginning of the century, and remained her lifelong correspondent; Dame Ethel Smyth, the doughty old composer and feminist, fired by reading A Room of One's Own, *was determined to meet its author, and, having met her, threw herself with vigour into what became for her a passionate friendship, and for Virginia an engrossing if demanding new relationship.*

Leonard had finally succeeded in giving up his literary editorship of the Nation & Athenaeum *in mid-February; but the work of the Hogarth Press absorbed more and more of his time, so that by the end of the year he and Virginia decided once again to restrict its operations to the publication of their own books; but, as before, the decision was postponed. Virginia's books were being reissued in a Uniform Edition; Vita Sackville-West's* The Edwardians, *published this year, became a best-seller; manuscripts poured in, the literary ones read by Virginia herself; the Woolfs were glad to escape as often as possible to Rodmell. At the beginning of May they toured south-west England as far as St Ives, travelling their books. Soon after their return, Nelly their servant was admitted to hospital for an operation and, in spite of the inconvenience of organising substitute help, the relief of being free of her perpetual presence determined Virginia to dispense with her altogether and employ only non-resident domestics.*

Despite the distractions of visitors and visits – to Vita at Long Barn, to Ethel Smyth's Surrey home, to Leonard's brother Philip, the Estate Manager to James de Rothschild at Waddesdon Manor in Buckinghamshire – and her rather precarious state of health, Virginia completed her first draft of The Waves *by the end of April, and at once embarked on the second version, which she worked on for the following nine months. At Rodmell during the summer months she varied this work by reading and writing on Hazlitt. At the end of August she fainted in the garden, an alarming experience, but recovered after a week's immobility and resumed her active round of outings and meetings, entertaining Vanessa's family and, less willingly, Leonard's,*

273

seeing Vita and Ethel Smyth, inviting friends for weekends or meals. The Woolfs returned to Tavistock Square on 4 October, and Virginia, who had engaged a temporary cook-housekeeper, steeled herself to dismiss the still convalescent Nelly and, having done so, relented. Nelly returned to work at the beginning of 1931.

Three years earlier Lady Ottoline Morrell had returned to Bloomsbury from Garsington and re-established herself in Gower Street, and it was here, the day after T. S. Eliot and his now seriously deranged wife had been to tea with her, that Virginia encountered the poets W. B. Yeats and Walter de la Mare. She was now much in demand as a guest – so much so that she swore never to dine out again, a vow she signally failed to keep.

The Woolfs drove to Rodmell on Christmas Eve, and Virginia at once took to her bed with a cold and a temperature; but by the end of the year she was again thinking about, if not actually writing, The Waves.

1930

Thursday 9 January
I merely note that I am going to try to keep next week entirely free from 'seeing' people, bating my dinner at Bogey Harris's to meet the Prime Minister, and Angelica's party. I am going to see if I can keep seven days out of the clutch of the seers.

Sunday 12 January
Thanks to my pertinacity and industry, I can now hardly stop making up *The Waves*. Now I feel that I can rush on, after six months hacking, and finish; what is essential is to write fast and not break the mood – no holiday, no interval if possible, till it is done. Then rest. Then re-write. As for keeping a week free – I am now going to visit L.'s mother; then to the Frys after dinner. Marjorie Strachey to tea tomorrow; Duncan, I think, on Tuesday; Vita on Friday; Angelica on Saturday; Bogey Harris Wednesday; one day remains entire – Thursday – and that's the end of my week.

Thursday 16 January
A page of real life. Last night at Bogey Harris's. I came in, flung into the room in my red coat; an oval room, with painted ceiling, and books. "Lady Londonderry will be late; but we won't wait." I have forgotten the Prime Minister [Ramsay MacDonald] – an unimpressive man; eyes disappointing; rather heavy; middle class; no son of the people; sunk; grumpy; self-important; wore a black waistcoat; had some mediocrity of personality. In came Lady Londonderry very late; in ruby velvet, cut to the middle of the back. All went in to dinner, and I was too blind to read Sir Robert Vansittart on the man's card, so had to jumble for my neighbour's pursuit. Never mind. They all called each other Van, Bogey, Ramsay, Edie, across the table; engaged in governing England. And so upstairs, Lady Londonderry running ahead, opening doors, taking us into little rooms to look at majolica, at altarpieces. Then round the fire she started off, fluent, agreeable, hard hitting, telling stories – all indiscreet, open, apparently. We discussed Birth

275

Control. "Dear Edie, you won't let me convert you. But when you see your miners with those terrible illegitimate children – Eight in a room. One bed. What can you expect? Can't do anything else. What would you do? What should we do, if we lived like that?" "But we're not beasts. We can control ourselves. I detest Prohibition for that reason." Swept on, energetically, confidently. Lady Londonderry can do whatever she wishes. She looked like an early Victorian picture – a Lawrence, I thought; a small pinched well cut face; healthy; without paint; very pink, pearls knotted about her wrists. The rooms all set out with cases, chests, pictures, objects. "I never give more than ten pounds: I hunt about in rag and bone shops." Bogey is evidently one of those elderly comfortable men of taste and leisure who make a profession of society; a perfectly instinctive snob. Knows everyone; nothing to say, with all his talk of Lords and Ladies; something of a gorged look, which connoisseurs have; as if he had always just swallowed a bargain. Roger says he has 'flair'; Roger who looks like a ravaged scavenger and lives with sardine tins and linoleum; yes, but Roger's house seems alive, with a living hand in it, manipulated, stretched. I tried, sitting on a priceless settee, picked up in Whitechapel for ten pounds (I never give more) to analyse my sensations. The ladies showed a perfect commercial grasp of the situation. Ramsay was tossed between them like a fish among cormorants. I had the impression that they did not rate this acquisition high; but took it as a part of the day's work. Lady Londonderry had him to herself in a shaded room for an hour.

Sunday 26 January
I am forty-eight; we have been at Rodmell – a wet, windy day again; but on my birthday we walked among the downs, like the folded wings of grey birds; and saw first one fox, very long with his brush stretched; then a second; which had been barking, for the sun was hot over us; it leapt lightly over a fence and entered the furze – a very rare sight. How many foxes are there in England?

I forgot to say that when we made up our six months' accounts, we found I had made about £3,020 last year – the salary of a civil servant; a surprise to me, who was content with £200 for so many years.

Sunday 16 February
To lie on the sofa for a week. If I could stay in bed another fortnight (but there is no chance of that) I believe I should see the whole of *The Waves*. I believe these illnesses are in my case – how shall I express it? – partly mystical. Something happens in my mind. It refuses to go on registering impressions. It shuts itself up. It becomes chrysalis. I lie quite torpid, often with acute physical pain. Then suddenly something springs. Two nights

ago, Vita was here; and when she went, I began to feel the quality of the evening – how it was spring coming; a silver light; mixing with the early lamps; the cabs all rushing through the streets; I had a tremendous sense of life beginning; and all the doors opening; and this is I believe the moth shaking its wings in me; ideas rush in me. It is no use trying to write at this stage. I would like to lie down and sleep, but feel ashamed. Leonard brushed off his influenza in one day and went about his business feeling ill. But as I was saying, my mind works in idleness. To do nothing is often my most profitable way.

Thursday 20 February
She [Margery Snowden] came in wrapped in a dark fur coat; which being taken off, she appeared in nondescript gray stockinette and jay blue stripes. Her face is pale, and very small; indeed, has a curious preserved innocency which makes it hard to think that she is fifty. The preserved look seems to indicate lack of experience; as if life had put her in a refrigerator. She brought me a parcel, and this was a book from Ethel Smyth, with a letter. Then we talked – but it was her starved and anguished look that remains, and the attitude of mind. She seemed to be saying inwardly 'I have missed everything. There are Vanessa and Virginia; they have lives full of novels and husbands and exhibitions. I am fifty and it has all slipped by.' I gathered this from the jocose pertinacity with which she kept referring to herself. She said the climate of Cheltenham is so sleepy that she often can't paint; and after lunch they put on the gramophone. Nothing long distracted her from her central concern – I have had no life and life is over. Even clothes suggested the same old theme. In fact I have seldom got a more dismal impression of suffering: call it rather frustration, non-entity; being lifted on a shelf, and seeing things pass. Lord, how I praise God that I had a bent strong enough to coerce every minute of my life since I was born! This fiddling and drifting and not impressing oneself upon anything – this always refraining and fingering and cutting things up into little jokes and facetiousness – that's what's so annihilating. Yet given little money, little looks, no special gift – what can one do? How could one battle? How could one leap on the back of life and wring its scruff?

Friday 21 February
No two women could be more extravagantly contraposed than Margery Snowden and Ethel Smyth. I was lying here at four yesterday when I heard the bell ring, then a brisk tramp up the stairs; and then behold a bluff, military old woman (older than I expected), bounced into the room in a three cornered hat and tailor made suit. "Let me look at you." That over, "Now I have brought a book and pencil. First I want to make out the

genealogy of your mother's family. Old Pattle – have you a picture? No. Well now – the names of his daughters." This lasted out tea. Afterwards, we talked ceaselessly till 7 – when L. came in. We talked – she talked considerably more than I; and she got off: oh about music – "I am said to be an egoist. I am a fighter. I feel for the underdog. Believe me I have to go on coming to London, bullying, badgering – at last they promise me fourteen women in the orchestra. I go and find two. So I begin ringing up." She has a vein, like a large worm, in her temple which swells. Her cheeks redden. Her faded eyes flash. She has a broad rounded forehead. I like to hear her talk of music. She says writing music is like writing novels. One thinks of the sea – naturally one gets a phrase for it. Orchestration is colouring. Rhapsodies about *A Room*. There is something fine and tried and experienced about her besides the rant and the riot and the egotism – and I'm not sure that she is the egotist that people make out. She said she never had anybody to admire her, and therefore might write good music to the end. Has to live in the country because of her passion for games. Plays golf, rides a bicycle; was thrown hunting two years ago. Then fell on her arm and was in despair, because life would be over if she could not play games. "I am very strong" which she proved by talking till 7.30; then eating a biscuit and drinking a glass of vermouth and going off to eat a supper of macaroni when she got to Woking at 9.

Saturday 22 February
I'm not to go down to the studio till Monday; and so must canter my pen amateurishly here. Lytton came in after dinner. Very twinkly, lustrous, easy and even warm. Leonard made cigarettes. I lay on the sofa in the twilight of cushions. Lytton had been sent a book about Columbus and told us the story making it into a fantastic amusing Lytton book – Columbus a mad religious fanatic who sailed west and west because he had read in Isaiah a prophesy; his crew being convicts let out from prison; and they came to Cuba and he made them sign a statement that this was India, because it was too large to be an island; and they picked up gold and gems and went back to Spain and the King and Queen rose as he came in. Here are all the elements of a Lytton concoction, told with great gusto; irony; a sense of the incongruous and dramatic. Then we warbled melodiously about Dadie and Cambridge and so on. He has a new gramophone. He is editing Greville. He is very content too – and very well equipped, and buys books; and likes us; and is going to Cambridge this week-end. Its odd how little one remembers what is actually said.

Saturday 1 March
And then I went for a walk and brought on a headache, and so lay down again till today, when we propose to drive off – oh Thank God a thousand times – to Rodmell and there be at rest. This little affair has taken three weeks, and will land me in four, of non-writing inexpressiveness. Yet I'm not sure that this is not the very thing for *The Waves*.

Tuesday 11 March
My impressions of Margaret [Llewelyn Davies] and Lilian [Harris] at Monks House were of great lumps of grey coat; straggling wisps of hair; hats floppy and home made; thick woollen stockings; black shoes, many wraps, shabby handbags, and shapelessness and shabbiness and dreariness and drabness unspeakable. A tragedy in its way. Margaret at any rate deserved better of life than this dishevelled and undistinguished end. We showed them the garden, gave them tea (and I don't think an iced cake had come Lilian's way this six weeks) and then – oh the dismal sense of people stranded, wanting to be energised; drifting – all woollen and hairy. (It is odd how the visual impression dominates.) Must old age be so shapeless? The only escape is to work the mind. I shall write a history of English literature, I think, in those days. And I shall walk. And I shall buy clothes, and keep my hair tidy, and make myself dine out. Margaret has her tragic past. She is pathetic to me now – conciliatory and nervous, where she used to be trenchant and severe. What I miss is colour, energy, any clear reflection of the moment. I see those thick stockings and grey hairy wraps everywhere.

Friday 28 March
Yes, but this book is a very queer business. I had a day of intoxication when I said Children are nothing to this: when I sat surveying the whole book complete, and quarrelled with L. (about Ethel Smyth) and walked it off, felt the pressure of the form – the splendour and the greatness – as perhaps I have never felt them. How to end I don't know. Yet I think something is there; and I propose to go on pegging it down, arduously, and then re-write, reading much of it aloud like poetry.

Home from tea with Nessa and Angelica. A fine spring day. I walked along Oxford Street. The buses are strung on a chain. People fight and struggle. Knocking each other off the pavement. Old bareheaded men; a motor car accident; &c. To walk alone in London is the greatest rest.

Friday 11 April
Yesterday walked through the Waddesdon greenhouses with [the head gardener] Mr Johnson. There were single red lines taking root in sand.

Cyclamen by the hundred gross. Azaleas massed like military bands. Carnations at different stages. Vines being picked thin by sedulous men. Nothing older than forty years, but now ready made in perfection. A fig tree that had a thousand lean regular branches. The statues tied up, like dead horses, in sheets. The whole thing dead. Made, planted, put into position in the year 1880 or thereabouts. One flower would have given more pleasure than those dozens of grosses. And the heat, and the tidiness and the accuracy and the organisation. Mr Johnson like a nectarine, hard, red, ripe. He was taught all he knew by Miss Alice [de Rothschild], and accepted admiration as his due. Sir he called us.

Tuesday 29 April
And I have just finished, with this very nib-full of ink, the last sentence of *The Waves*. I think I should record this for my own information. But I have never written a book so full of holes and patches; that will need re-building, yes, not only remodelling. This is a reach after that vision I had, the unhappy summer – or three weeks – at Rodmell, after finishing *The Lighthouse*.

PM. And I think to myself, as I walk down Southampton Row, 'and I have given you a new book.'

Thursday 1 May
I have wasted the brilliant first of May which makes my skylight blue and gold; have only a rubbish heap in my head; can't read, and can't write, and can't think. The truth is, of course, I want to be back at *The Waves*. But then we are going touring Devon and Cornwall on Sunday which means a week off.

Sunday 18 May
The thing is now to live with energy and mastery, desperately. To despatch each day high handedly. So not to dawdle and dwindle, contemplating this and that. No more regrets and indecisions. That is the right way to deal with life now that I am forty-eight: and to make it more and more important and vivid as one grows old.

[Undated: late May]
This is all very well; but what if Nelly then gets taken ill with her kidneys, must have an operation. Soberly and seriously a whole fortnight has been blown from my life; because I have had to hang about to see [the doctor], to buy food, to arrange with Taupin [temporary cook], to arrange with the hospital; to go there in an ambulance. My mind in order to work needs to be stretched tight and flat. It has been broken into shivers.

Sunday 15 June

How many skips there are here! Nothing said of our tour through the West; nothing said of Nelly's operation; of Taupin, who lost my key, broke tumblers, and cooked with the faded inspiration of one who had been a good cook; and nothing said of the divine relief of my quiet evenings, without servants; and how we dine out at the Cock; and how we say, can't this last? Leonard is not apt at a crisis. I mean his caution sticks his back up. He foresees obstacles. He has a philanthropic side too, which I distrust. Must be good to dependants.

Monday 16 June

Oh to be rid of servants, for all the emotions they breed – trust, suspicion, benevolence, gratitude, philanthropy – are necessarily bad. And Nelly is now deposited on us for a day; turned out of hospital at a moment's notice. It is odd how those old scenes rankle in my mind – how unwilling I am to have her back. I think with real shrinking of having her in control again.

I don't know why, but I have stinted this book. The summer is in full swing. Its elements this year are Nessa and Duncan, Ethel Smyth, Vita and re-writing *The Waves*. Ethel Smyth drops in; dropped in yesterday for instance. I heard a ring, went up, and saw an old char in her white alpaca coat; sat her down; disburdened her of cardboard boxes: full of white pinks; and looked at her rather monumental old colonel's face (girt round with an inappropriate necklace, for she was going to lunch with [Sir Thomas] Beecham.) I get, generally, two letters daily. I daresay the old fires of Sapphism are blazing for the last time. In her heyday she must have been formidable – ruthless, tenacious, exacting, lightning quick, confident; with something of the directness and singleness of genius, though they say she writes music like an old dryasdust German music master. Her style in writing memoirs though is to her credit – indeed she has ridden post haste through life; and accumulated an astonishing number of observations, with which she qualifies her conversation so as to drive L. almost frantic. One speech of hers lasted twenty minutes unbroken, he says, the other night. She is a game old bird – an old age entirely superior in vitality to Margaret's.

Wednesday 23 July

Edith Sitwell has grown very fat, powders herself thickly, gilds her nails with silver paint, wears a turban and looks like an ivory elephant, like the Emperor Heliogabalus. I have never seen such a change. She is mature, majestic. Her fingers are crusted with white coral. She is altogether composed. A great many people were there – and she presided. But though thus composed, her eyes are sidelong and humorous. The old Empress remembers her scallywag days. We all sat at her feet – cased in slender black slippers, the only remnants of her slipperiness and slenderness. We hardly talked together, and I felt myself gone there rather mistakenly, had she not asked me very affectionately if she might come and see me alone. Her room was crowded with odds and ends of foreigners.

Saturday 26 July
Just back from a night at Long Barn, and am all of a quiver with home coming to L., to two newts in the bathroom, letters (from Ethel, and flowers), books, &c. A very nice homecoming; and makes me a little amazed at my own happiness. I daresay few women are happier – not that I am consistently anything; but feel that I have had a good draught of human life, and find much champagne in it. It has not been dull – my marriage; not at all.

MONKS HOUSE, RODMELL

Wednesday 6 August
This is written at Rodmell; oh yes, and it is the best, the freest, the comfortablest summer we have ever had. Figure to yourself feet swollen in boots. One takes them off – that is my state without poor dear Nelly; with nice bright Annie. The rain pelts – look at it (as the people in *The Waves* are always saying) now. My dinner is cooking. I have so many rooms to sit in, I scarcely know which to choose. And new chairs. And comfort everywhere, and some beginnings of beauty. But it is the freedom from servants that is the groundwork and bedrock of all this expansion. After lunch we are alone till breakfast. I say, as I walk the downs, never again, never again. Cost what it may, I will never put my head into that noose again.

I walk; I read; I write, without terrors and constrictions; I make bread. I cook mushrooms. I wander in and out of the kitchen. I have a resource besides reading. Why we ever suffered that discomfort so long, that presence grumbling, always anyhow (for that's unfair) at a different angle from ours –

Wednesday 20 August
Last night was Quentin's birthday. "Another Quentin birthday over" said Maynard, at the gate after the fireworks, counting perhaps the remaining years. The rockets went roaring up and scattered their gold grain. The willows were lit grey over the pond. The bonfire was forked, like branches in a wind. Nessa, in red, threw on a screen. Angelica, whirring and twirling like an old screaming witch, danced round it. "Childhood – true childhood"

said Lydia. For some minutes everything that was said had the quality of sayings in a Tchekhov play.

Ethel's letters are daily: for we have so much to make up. Should I curtail her and curb them? I think not. If one adventures, adventure wholly. And she is so courageous, remarkable, shrewd, that it would be mere poltroonery for me to hold off for fear of ridicule. So I let that old bonfire rage red and perhaps throw a screen on it.

Monday 25 August
Ethel came for a night on Friday, and let me pelt in a few notes of this curious unnatural friendship. I say unnatural because she is so old, and everything is incongruous. Her head is an enormous size over the temples. Music is there, she said, tapping her temples. That way lies insanity. She cannot refrain from repeating what I guess to be very worn compliments, often repeated to herself at dead of night. For she cannot get over unfortunately her own ill-treatment. A refrain occurs; and it is all the more marked for being in contrast with the generosity, sense, balance, and shrewdness of all else. Off her own music, and the conspiracy against her – for the Press are determined to burke her, though she fills every hall – that's the line of it – she is an admirable guest. Oh yes and more. I went through some odd vicissitudes, in the way of emotion. Lying in my chair in the firelight she looked eighteen; she looked a young vigorous handsome woman. Suddenly this vanishes; then there is the old crag that has been beaten on by the waves; the humane battered face that makes one respect human nature; or rather feel that it is indomitable and persistent. Then I am conscious, I suppose, of the compliment she pays me. But then she is over seventy. I had some interesting moments. About jealousy for instance. "D'you know, Virginia, I don't like other women being fond of you." "Then you must be in love with me Ethel." "I have never loved anyone so much. Ever since I saw you I have thought of nothing else &c. I had not meant to tell you." But what I like in her is not I think her love, for how difficult it is to make that intelligible – what I like is the indomitable old crag; and a certain smile, very wide and benignant. But dear me I am not in love with Ethel.

Tuesday 2 September
I was walking down the path with Lydia. If this don't stop, I said, referring to the bitter taste in my mouth and the pressure like a wire cage of sound over my head, then I am ill: yes, very likely I am destroyed, diseased, dead. Damn it! Here I fell down – saying "How strange – flowers". In scraps I felt and knew myself carried into the sitting room by Maynard; saw L. look very frightened; said I will go upstairs. The drumming of my heart, the

pain, the effort got violent at the doorstep; overcame me; like gas; I was unconscious; then the wall and the picture returned to my eyes; I saw life again. Strange, I said, and so lay, gradually recovering till 11 when I crept up to bed. Today, Tuesday, I am in the lodge and Ethel comes – valiant old woman! But this brush with death was instructive and odd. Had I woken in the divine presence it would have been with fists clenched and fury on my lips. "I don't want to come here at all!" So I should have exclaimed. I wonder if this is the general state of people who die violently. If so, figure the condition of Heaven after a battle.

I will use these last pages to sum up our circumstances. A map of the world. Leaving out the subject of Nelly, which bores me, we are now much freer and richer than we have ever been. For years I never had a pound extra, a comfortable bed, or a chair that did not want stuffing. This morning Hammond [Lewes furnishers] delivered four perfectly comfortable armchairs – and we think very little of it.

I seldom see Lytton; that is true. The reason is that we don't fit in, I imagine, to his parties nor he to ours; but that if we can meet in solitude, all goes as usual. Yet what do one's friends mean to one, if one only sees them eight times a year? Morgan I keep up with in our chronically spasmodic way. My Bell family relations are young, fertile and intimate. Julian and Quentin change so much. This year Quentin is shabby, easy, natural and gifted; last year he was foppish, finicky and affected. Julian is publishing with Chatto & Windus. As for Nessa and Duncan I am persuaded that nothing can be now destructive of that easy relationship, because it is based on Bohemianism. My bent that way increases – in spite of the prodigious fame. I am more and more attracted by looseness, freedom, and eating one's dinner off a table anywhere, having cooked it previously. Ease and shabbiness and content therefore are all ensured. Adrian I never see. I keep constant with Maynard. I never see Saxon. I am slightly repelled by his lack of generosity; yet would like to write to him. Perhaps I will. George Duckworth, feeling the grave gape, wishes to lunch with Nessa; wishes to feel again the old sentimental emotions. After all, Nessa and I are his only women relations. A queer cawing of homing rooks this is. I daresay the delights of snobbishness somewhat fail in later life – and we have 'made good' – that is his expression.

My map of the world lacks rotundity. There is Vita. Yes – she was here the other day, after her Italian tour, with two boys; a dusty car, sand-shoes and Florentine candlepieces, novels and so on tumbling about on the seats. I use my friends rather as giglamps: there's another field I see; by your light. Over there's a hill. I widen my landscape.

Monday 8 September

I will signalise my return to life – that is writing – by beginning a new book, and it happens to be Thoby's birthday, I remark. He would have been, I think, fifty today. After coming out here I had the usual – oh how usual – headache; and lay, like a fibre of tired muscle, on my bed in the sitting room, till yesterday. Now up again and on again; with one new picture in my mind: my defiance of death in the garden.

But the sentence with which this book was to open ran 'Nobody has ever worked so hard as I do' – exclaimed in driving a paper fastener through the fourteen pages of my Hazlitt just now. Time was when I dashed off these things all in the day's work. Now I spend I daresay a ridiculous amount of time, more of trouble, on them. I began reading Hazlitt in January I think. And I am not sure that I have speared that little eel in the middle – which is one's object in criticism. Never mind; it shall go today; and my appetite for criticism is, oddly, whettened. I have some gift that way, were it not for the grind and the screw and the torture –

Anyhow, this is the happiest summer since we had Monks House; the most satisfactory. The weather is September weather, bright, sunny, cool. We have a project of making my bedroom the sitting room – for the view. To let it waste, day after day, seems a crime: elderly eyes cannot waste.

Wednesday 24 September

I have taken up my staff again; I wish I could say that my book was my staff; but oh dear, how many people have I seen – dashing that support from my hand. Our friends work us very hard – and my two months respite [is] nibbled at by all who choose. I think I will spend August next year in Northumberland.

Monday 29 September

So all those days were completely ruined by the assiduity of our friends. When one has to tidy the table, pick fresh flowers, collect chairs and be ready at four, or at one, to welcome and all the rest of it, the circumjacent parts of the day are ruined. On the whole L.'s family do the trick most thoroughly. Everything is such an effort; so unreal; what I say is so remote from what I feel; their standards are so different from mine; I strain myself perpetually with trying to provide the right cakes, the right jokes, the right affection and inquiries. Naturally it often goes wrong, as on Friday. Mrs Woolf who is the vainest of women, began to pay herself the usual compliments upon her wonderful management of so many fatherless and penniless children. And then of course she will not be satisfied until I have also wondered and exclaimed at her amazing unselfishness and courage. Here of course I begin to see very plainly how ugly, how nosey, how irreparably middle class they all are. Indeed, my aesthetic sense is the one that protests most obstinately – how they cheapen the house and garden – how they bring in an atmosphere of Earls Court and hotels, how impossibly out of place and stuffy and towny and dressy and dowdy they look on the terrace, among apple trees and vegetables and flowers. But there I am pinned down, as firmly as Prometheus on his rock, to have my day, Friday 26th of September 1930, picked to pieces, and made cheap and ugly and commonplace; for the sting of it is that there is no possible escape – no escape that won't make old Mrs Woolf begin to dab her eyes and feel that she is not being welcomed – she who is so 'painfully sensitive' – so fond of cakes, so incapable of amusing herself, so entirely without any interest in my feelings or friends; so vampire-like and vast in her demand for my entire attention and sympathy. Lord Lord! how many daughters have been murdered by women like this! What a net of falsity they spread over life. How it rots beneath their sweetness – goes brown and soft like a bad pear! At the same time I cannot make out a case for myself as a maltreated person. No, because I have an interest beyond my own nose. But let me note that old age can only be made tolerable by having a firm anchor outside gossip, cakes, and sympathy. Think of imposing even one afternoon of such a burden upon Quentin, Julian and Angelica! I shall spend my day at the British Museum.

The great game of diplomacy is begun with Nelly. I have told [her doctor] that we will pay her wages, but not have her back till she is well.

52 TAVISTOCK SQUARE, WC1

Wednesday 15 October

I say to myself 'But I cannot write another word.' I say 'I will cut adrift – I will go to Roger in France – I will sit on pavements and drink coffee – I will see the Southern hills; I will dream; I will take my mind out of its iron cage and let it swim – this fine October.' I say all this; with energy; but shall I do it? Shan't I peter out here, till the fountain fills again? Oh dear oh dear – for the lassitude of spirit! Rarely rarely comest thou now, spirit of delight. You hide yourself up there behind the hotel windows and the grey clouds. It is dismal to broach October so languidly.

Alas, one day last week Nelly appeared – of course on her best behaviour – very much the old and trusted servant, with, I think, a dash of suspicion. Why did I not have her back and give her help, seeing that she had been with us fifteen years? – that I think was in her mind. But we kept it down; and she is off to Colchester for ten days and then – oh dear, I say again, oh dear.

Thursday 23 October
Ethel came in yesterday evening; rather battered in an old moleskin coat; in the triangular hat which the hotel proprietor at Bath has made into its shape with a few pins. Well, I begin to make note of her, because, among other things – how many others – she said would I like her to leave me some of her letters in her will? Would you like me to write something about you? I said. Oh yes; what fun! So I am to some extent Ethel's literary executor, a post I have always vaguely desired; and so I now make a few notes as she talks, for a portrait. She hopes not to live another seven years; gives me to understand that now that her last barren years have been fructified by knowing me, she can sing her nunc dimittis.

Monday 27 October
How comfortless and uneasy my room is – a table all choked with papers, &c. I'm now grinding out *Waves* again, and have perhaps an hour and a half to spend: a short time on Dante; a short time on MSS; a short time here – with another pen. Yesterday we went to Warlingham and sat in a gravel pit, like a Cézanne. I made this comparison to appease myself for not being in France. And we walked along a bridle path; and saw old quiet farms, and rabbits, and downs, all preserved as by a magic ring from Croydon. Never was the division between London and country so sharp. Home, and made dinner; and read MSS. But rather casually and unanimously we have decided within the last week to stop the Press. Yes; it is to come to an end. That is we are to go on only with my books and L.'s and what we print ourselves. In short, we shall revert next October to what we were in the Hogarth House days – an odd reversal, seeing that we are now financially successful. But what's money if you sell freedom? we say. And what's the point of publishing these innocuous novels and pamphlets that are neither good nor bad? So we make this decision, casually, walking round the Square after lunch and thus slip another shackle from our shoulders. This is what I call living with a pilot in the ship – not mere drifting ahead.

Sunday 2 November
And tonight the final letter to Nelly is to be sent; there it rests in my red bag, but I have great reluctance to read it over, as I had to write it. Yet I don't suppose she will mind acutely. For one thing, she has been prepared, I think, by our readiness to do without her; and then since the famous scene last November I think she has been aware of a change. These five months at any rate have proved that we are freer, easier and no less comfortable, indeed more comfortable, without her, for all her good humour, sense and niceness; which now that I have written the letter, I see once more in their

true proportions. Oh never again to have scenes with servants – that is my ambition.

Wednesday 5 November
The letter is sent; the shock over. And I come in and find the house empty and silent. A slight inaccuracy, if applied to the past few days. Ethel, Lyn [Irvine] and Hugh Walpole to tea on Monday; Vita, Clive and Hilda Matheson to dine; Hugh again later, and his piteous, writhing and wincing and ridiculous and flaying alive story of Willie Maugham's portrait [in *Cakes and Ale*]; Hugh, turning round on his bed of thorns again and yet again, and pressing them further and further in. Clive is home blind of one eye and much in need of society. I thought him, why heaven knows, rather admirable and touching, determined not to be a burden on his friends. And he can't read or write, and has hired a reader. Its the evenings that will be bad he said. Nessa characteristically writes from Cassis that she doesn't think much of it, and supposes that spectacles, 'which we all wear' will put it right.

Saturday 8 November
I pressed his hand when we said goodbye with some emotion: thinking This is to press a famous hand: it was Yeats's, at Ottoline's last night. He was born in 1865 so that he is now a man of sixty-five – and I am forty-eight; and thus he has a right to be so much more vital, supple, high charged and altogether seasoned and generous. He has grown very thick (last time I met him – and I may note that he had never heard of me and I was slightly embarrassed by Ottoline's painstaking efforts to bring me to his notice – was in 1907 or 8 I suppose, at dinner at 46 [Gordon Square]). He is very broad; very thick; like a solid wedge of oak. His face is too fat; but it has its hatchet forehead in profile, under a tangle of grey and brown hair; the eyes are luminous, direct, but obscured under glasses; they have however seen close, the vigilant and yet wondering look of his early portraits. I interrupted a long dream story of [Walter] de la Mare's when I came in: about seeing Napoleon with ruby eyes and so on. Yeats was off, with vehemence even, kindling and stumbling a little, on dreams; those which have colour are rare and mean – I forget what. de la Mare told another very cryptic dream about a book with circles in it; the outermost ring black, the inner blue and so on. Yeats identified this dream at once as the dream of the soul in some particular state – I forget what. And so on to dreaming states, and soul states; as others talk of Beaverbrook and free trade – as if matters of common knowledge. de la Mare had just been to the National Gallery, and had got no pleasure from the pictures. Yeats said he could get nothing from Rembrandt, nothing from El Greco. He then explained our pleasure in pictures, or other works of art, by an elaborate metaphor. Then,

discussing what poems we could come back to unsated, I said *Lycidas*; de la Mare said no. Not Milton for him: he could never recognise his own emotions there. Milton's woodbine was not his woodbine, nor Milton's Eve his Eve. Yeats said he could not get satisfaction from Milton; it was Latinised poetry (as somebody said, Milton had (in some way irreparably) damaged the English language). And so to modern poetry, and the question of the spade. Yeats said that 'we', de la Mare and himself, wrote 'thumbnail' poems only because we are at the end of an era. He said that the spade has been embalmed by thirty centuries of association; not so the steam roller. Poets can only write when they have symbols. And steam rollers are not covered in symbolism – perhaps they may be after thirty generations. He and de la Mare can only write small fireside poems. Most of emotion is outside their scope. All left to the novelists I said – but how crude and jaunty my own theories were beside his: indeed I got a tremendous sense of the intricacy of the art; also of its meanings, its seriousness, its importance, which wholly engrosses this large active minded immensely vitalised man. And I was impressed by his directness, his terseness. No fluff or dreaminess. He seemed to live in the centre of an immensely intricate briar bush, from which he could issue at any moment; and then withdraw again. And every twig was real to him. Indeed he seemed in command of all his systems, philosophies, poetics and humanities; not tentative any more. Hence no doubt his urbanity and generosity. Compare him with Tom for instance, who came to tea the day before, and may be, for anything I know, as good a poet. Poor Tom is all suspicion, hesitation and reserve. His face has grown heavier, fatter and whiter. There is a leaden sinister look about him. But oh – Vivien! Was there ever such a torture since life began! – to bear her on one's shoulders, biting, wriggling, raving, scratching, unwholesome, powdered, insane, yet sane to the point of insanity, reading his letters, thrusting herself on us, coming in wavering, trembling – "Does your dog do that to frighten me? Have you visitors? Is it accident? That's what I want to know" (all this suspiciously, cryptically, taking hidden meanings). Have some honey, made by our bees, I say; have you any bees? (and as I say it, I know I am awaking suspicion). "Not bees. Hornets." "But where?" "Under the bed." And so on, until worn out with half an hour of it, we gladly see them go. This bag of ferrets is what Tom wears round his neck.

On second thoughts, Yeats and de la Mare talk too much about dreams to be quite satisfactory. This is what makes de la Mare's stories (lent me by Ottoline) wobbly.

Wednesday 12 November
And I had my talk with Nelly last night. An odd, meandering, contradictory, mainly affectionate and even intimate talk. One of her preoccupations [is]

to establish her own hard lot and innocence of all offence among the [other Bloomsbury] servants. We had treated her badly, turning her off because of ill-health. But Nelly, you gave me notice ten times in the past six years – and more . . . But I always took it back. Yes but that sort of thing gets on the nerves. Oh ma'am I never meant to tire you. But then Nelly you forgot that when you were with us. But then for three years I've been ill. And I shall never like any mistress as much as I like you . . . And so on and so on – all the old tunes, some so moving; so pathetic; some (I'm glad to say) so irrational, hysterical and with that curious senseless reiteration of grievances which used to drive me frantic. The truth – but I could never tell her this – is that that kind of dependency and intimacy wears one down; is a psychological strain. And then the gossip. Oh I won't say how I've heard, but I've heard – And so at last, after every variety of feeling, I was left with the one feeling No I could not have you sleeping here again. [*Later*] And then I let her come back, for three months, from January 1st. How am I ever to apologise to myself sufficiently?

Tuesday 2 December
No I cannot write that very difficult passage in *The Waves* this morning, all because of Arnold Bennett and Ethel [Sands]'s party. I can hardly set one word after another. There I was for two hours, so it seemed, alone with Bennett in Ethel's little back room. And this meeting I am convinced was engineered by Bennett to 'get on good terms with Mrs Woolf' – when heaven knows I don't care a rap if I'm on terms with Bennett or not. Its true, I like the old creature: I do my best, as a writer, to detect signs of genius in his smoky brown eye; I see certain sensuality, power, I suppose; but O, as he cackled out, "What a blundering fool I am – what a baby – compared with Desmond MacCarthy – how clumsy." This innocence is engaging; but would be more so if I felt him, as he infers, a 'creative artist'. "Its the only life" he said (this incessant scribbling, one novel after another, one thousand words daily), "I don't want anything else. I think of nothing but writing." And at last I drew Lord David [Cecil] in. And we taunted the old creature with thinking us refined. He said the gates of Hatfield were shut – "shut away from life." "But open on Thursdays" said Lord David. "I don't want to go on Thursdays" said Bennett. "And you drop your aitches on purpose" I said, "thinking that you possess more 'life' than we do." "I sometimes tease" said Bennett "But I don't think I possess more life than you do. Now I must go home. I have to write one thousand words tomorrow morning." And this left only the scrag end of the evening; and this left me in a state where I can hardly drive my pen across the page.

Friday 12 December
This, I think, is the last day's breathing space I allow myself before I tackle the last lap of *The Waves*. I have had a week off – but I think I have got my breath again and must be off for three or perhaps four weeks more. Then, as I think, I shall make one consecutive writing of the interludes – and then – oh dear, some must be written again; and then corrections; and then send to Mabel [typist]; and then correct the type; and then give to Leonard, perhaps some time late in March. Then put away; then print, perhaps in June.

Tuesday 16 December
I will never dine out again. I will burn my evening dress. I have gone through this door. Nothing exists beyond. I have taken my fence; and now need never whip myself to dine with Colefax, Ethel, Mary again. These reflections were hammered in indelibly last night at Argyll House. The same party: same dresses; same food. To talk to Sir Arthur [Colefax] about Queen Victoria's letters, and the Dyestuff Bill, and – I forget – I sacrificed an evening alone with Vita, an evening alone by myself – an evening of pleasure. And so it goes on perpetually. Forced, dry, sterile infantile conversation. And I am not even excited at going. So the fence is not only leapt, but fallen. Why jump?

Thursday 18 December
Lord David, Lytton and Clive last night. Told them how I had burnt my evening dress in the gas fire – general agreement that parties are a folly. Clive specially emphatic.

Saturday 20 December
And Kingsley Martin lunched with us (sweeping up turkey as a char sweeps feathers) and said that the *Nation* and the *New Statesman* are to amalgamate; and he is to be editor (highly secret, like all nonsense) and would L. be literary editor? No; L. would not.

Monday 22 December
It occurred to me last night while listening to a Beethoven quartet that I would merge all the interjected passages into Bernard's final speech, and end with the words O solitude.

Monks House, Rodmell

Saturday 27 December

But what's the use of talking about Bernard's final speech? We came down on Tuesday, and next day my cold was the usual influenza, and I am in bed with the usual temperature, and can't use my wits or form my letters – and so my precious fortnight of exaltation and concentration is snatched; and I shall go back to the racket and Nelly without a thing done. Meanwhile it rains; Annie's child is ill; the dogs next door yap and yap; all the colours are rather dim and the pulse of life dulled. I moon torpidly through book after book.

The *Journal of a Somerset Rector*: the parson – Skinner – who shot himself emerges like a bloody sun in a fog. He shot himself in the beech woods above his house; spent a life digging up stones and reducing all places to Camelodunum; quarrelled, bickered; yet loved his sons; yet turned them out of doors – a clear hard picture of one type of human life – the exasperated, unhappy, struggling, intolerably afflicted. Oh and I've read Queen Victoria's letters; and wonder what would happen had Ellen Terry been born Queen. Complete disaster to the Empire? Queen Victoria was entirely unaesthetic; a kind of Prussian competence and belief in herself her only prominences; material; brutal to Gladstone; like a mistress with a dishonest footman. Knew her own mind. But the mind radically commonplace; only its inherited force and cumulative sense of power making it remarkable.

Monday 29 December

If I can get out, and move about, and yet not get a headache, I daresay in three days I shall be beginning to play gently with the waves. I don't have the temptation here of London. How difficult though to get back into the right mental state: what a queer balance is needed.

Tuesday 30 December

What it wants is presumably unity; but it is I think rather good (I am talking to myself over the fire about *The Waves*). Suppose I could run all the scenes together more? – by rhythm, chiefly – so as to make the blood run like a torrent from end to end. I want to avoid chapters. Now if it could be worked over with heat and currency that's all it wants. And I am getting my blood up (temperature 99).

But all the same I went to Lewes, and the Keyneses came to tea; and having got astride my saddle the whole world falls into shape; it is this writing that gives me my proportions.

1931

At the suggestion of Dadie Rylands, a solution to the heavy demands of the Hogarth Press presented itself in the person of John Lehmann, a Cambridge friend of Julian Bell. He began work at 52 Tavistock Square in January with the prospect of becoming manager after an eight months' apprenticeship. The same day, Virginia and Ethel Smyth, invited by Pippa Strachey, spoke to a meeting of the London Society for Women's Service of which she was Secretary; and this occasion stirred up a ferment of ideas in Virginia's mind on the subject of the relative position of the sexes which led her to envisage a book which in the course of the following years developed into two: The Years and Three Guineas. In the meantime however she was still working on The Waves, which she finished in an almost visionary burst of inspiration on 7 February.

Ethel Smyth's composition for voice and orchestra The Prison was first performed this year, and Virginia was enticed into attending a rehearsal and, three weeks later, its Queen's Hall performance and Lady Rosebery's party for Ethel afterwards. Vita at this time was engrossed by the creation of her new home and garden at Sissinghurst Castle in Kent, and by a new love affair, and Virginia saw her less often than formerly. The void left by this comparative withdrawal was to some extent filled by Ethel Smyth's persevering ardour, which Virginia was beginning to find rather overpowering, and to which she preferred to respond in long and frequent letters.

Virginia was much saddened by the death of Arnold Bennett in March; in spite of her criticism of his writing, she respected and liked him, and she and Leonard attended his memorial service at St Clement Dan.'s. A fortnight later, leaving John Lehmann in charge of the Hogarth Press, they took a rather wet holiday in western France, motoring as far south as the Dordogne, where they visited the birthplace of Montaigne. Virginia derived much imaginative sustenance from such glimpses of artists' chosen habitations.

The summer months in London were dedicated to retyping The Waves and to trying to limit the time spent 'seeing' people. Leonard read the finished copy at Monks House one weekend in July and declared it to be a masterpiece. In July too Virginia had to endure what was to her a form of torture: being stared at. With Vanessa's connivance, the sculptor Stephen ('Tommy') Tomlin persuaded her to give him six sittings to enable him to model her head, while Vanessa painted her.

At Rodmell in August Virginia corrected the proofs of The Waves, which she despatched to the printer only a month after Leonard's approval of the typescript, *and for relief occupied herself with writing* Flush, *a fanciful biography of Elizabeth Barrett Browning's spaniel. Besides the usual family and neighbourhood visits and visitors, this year brought Sibyl Colefax, the Kingsley Martins, John Lehmann, George and Lady Margaret Duckworth and Ethel Smyth to Monks House; Vita too came for a night. Politics and economics were meanwhile agitating the country and, inevitably, Maynard Keynes and Leonard. In August, Ramsay MacDonald resigned as Labour Prime Minister and, disowned by his own party, formed a National Government which was then re-elected by a large majority in the General Election on 30 October.*

The Waves *was published early in October, received warm praise from those Virginia most respected, was favourably reviewed, and sold surprisingly well – in contrast to Leonard's long considered book on the development of democratic psychology* After the Deluge, *a source of great mortification to him. However Virginia relaxed in her success, going to concerts and the theatre, to the motor show, asking people to dinner, spending weekends at Rodmell, and not straining at further writing. But by mid-November she was once again prostrated by debilitating headaches and forced to rest. Just before she and Leonard drove to Monks House for Christmas they learnt that Lytton Strachey was desperately ill, and the rest of the year was spent in a state of acute anxiety on his account, telephoning for news from the neighbouring cottage (whose lady-owners bred dogs, a source of constant aggravation to Virginia).*

1931

Monks House, Rodmell

Friday 2 January
Here are my resolutions for the next three months: the next lap of the year. First, to have none; not to be tied. Second, to be free and kindly with myself, not goading it to parties; to sit rather privately reading in the studio. To make a good job of *The Waves*. To care nothing for making money. As for Nelly, to stop irritation by the assurance that nothing is worth irritation: if it comes back, she must go. Then not to slip this time into the easiness of letting her stay.

52 Tavistock Square, WC1

Wednesday 7 January
Well, we have just got back, had our tea, and there are two hours to dinner. It is very quiet here, not a sound but the hiss of the gas. Oh but the cold was too great at Rodmell. I was frozen like a small sparrow. I looked out at dawn once or twice – a redness, like wood fire cinders, in a frosty sky; frost thick on the fields; the candles alight in some of the cottages, and so back to bed, wrapping my clothes round me. And every morning I took the bellows and chafed up my logs, and made a game of it, and almost always won my blazing fire by the time L. came up.

I shall go down and get the post. Already we are committed to 'see' six people before Monday – the only one of importance is John Lehmann.

Saturday 10 January
Lehmann may do: a tight aquiline boy, pink, with the adorable curls of youth; yes, but persistent, sharp. Shall I be paid if I come as apprentice? Can I have the Hogarth Press books? Not much atmosphere; save perhaps that his eyes are imaginative. Lord knows. And we ask four or five thousand as his share.

Tuesday 20 January

I have this moment, while having my bath, conceived an entire new book – a sequel to *A Room of One's Own* – about the sexual life of women: to be called *Professions for Women* perhaps – Lord how exciting! This sprang out of my paper to be read on Wednesday to Pippa [Strachey]'s society [The London Society for Women's Service]. Now for *The Waves*. Thank God – but I'm very much excited.

Friday 23 January

Too much excited, alas, to get on with *The Waves*. One goes on making up *The Open Door*, or whatever it is to be called. The didactive demonstrative style conflicts with the dramatic: I find it hard to get back inside Bernard again.

The speech took place: L. I think slightly exacerbated. Two hundred people; well dressed, keen, and often beautiful young women. Ethel in her blue kimono and wig. I by her side. Her speech rollicking and direct; mine too compressed and allusive. Never mind.

Monday 26 January

Heaven be praised, I can truthfully say on this first day of being forty-nine that I have shaken off the obsession of *Opening the Door*, and have returned to *The Waves*: and have this instant seen the entire book whole, and how I can finish it – say in under three weeks.

Wednesday 4 February

Today Ethel comes. On Monday I went to hear her rehearse [*The Prison*] at Lady Lewis's. A vast Portland Place house with the cold wedding cake Adam's plaster; shabby red carpets; flat surfaces washed with dull greens. The rehearsal was in a long room with a bow window looking onto other houses – iron staircases, chimneys, roofs – a barren brick outlook. There was a roaring fire in the Adam's grate. Ethel stood at the piano in the window, in her battered felt, in her jersey and short skirt, conducting with a pencil. There was a drop at the end of her nose. Miss [Elsie] Suddaby was singing The Soul, and I observed that she went through precisely the same attitudes of ecstasy and inspiration in the room as in a hall. Ethel's pince-nez rode nearer and nearer the top of her nose. She sang now and then; and once, taking the bass, made a cat squalling sound – but everything she does with such forthrightness, directness, that there is nothing ridiculous. She loses self-consciousness completely. She seems all vitalised; all energised; she knocks her hat from side to side. Strides rhythmically down the room to signify that this is the Greek melody; strides back; Now the furniture moving begins, she said, referring to some supernatural gambols connected with the prisoner's escape, or defiance, or death. I suspect the music is too literary – too stressed – too didactic for my taste. But I am always impressed by the fact that it is music – I mean that she has spun these coherent chords, harmonies, melodies out of her so practical vigorous strident mind. What if she should be a great composer? This fantastic idea is to her the merest commonplace: it is the fabric of her being. As she conducts, she hears music like Beethoven's. As she strides and turns and wheels about to us perched mute on chairs she thinks this is about the most important event now taking place in London. And perhaps it is.

Saturday 7 February
Here in the few minutes that remain, I must record, heaven be praised, the end of *The Waves*. I wrote the words O Death fifteen minutes ago, having reeled across the last ten pages with some moments of such intensity and intoxication that I seemed only to stumble after my own voice, or almost, after some sort of speaker (as when I was mad). I was almost afraid, remembering the voices that used to fly ahead. Anyhow it is done; and I have been sitting these fifteen minutes in a state of glory, and calm, and some tears, thinking of Thoby and if I could write Julian Thoby Stephen 1881–1906 on the first page. I suppose not. How physical the sense of triumph and relief is! Whether good or bad, its done; I mean that I have netted that fin in the waste of waters which appeared to me over the marshes out of my window at Rodmell when I was coming to an end of *To the Lighthouse*.

Tuesday 17 February
And I feel us, compared with Aldous and Maria [Huxley], unsuccessful. They're off today to do mines, factories . . . black country; did the docks when they were here; must see England. They are going to the Sex Congress at Moscow, have been in India, will go to America, speak French, visit celebrities, – while here I live like a weevil in a biscuit. Lord, how little I've seen, done, lived, felt, thought, compared with the Huxleys – compared with anyone. Here we toil, reading and writing, year in year out. No adventure, no travel. Here by some invisible rope, we are bound. My ship has sailed on. I toss among empty bottles and bits of toilet paper. All I like is my own capacity for feeling. If I weren't so miserable I could not be happy. Aldous takes life in hand. Whether that damages his writing I don't know . . . He is 'modern'. He is endlessly athletic and adventurous. He will be able to say he did not waste his youth. I fancy no one thing gives him the immense satisfaction things give me. That's all the comfort I find.

Monday 9 March
And then I went, more than a week ago, to Lady Rosebery's buffet. Sense of drum and blare; of Ethel's remorseless fangs; her irresistible vanity, and some pang too for her child's craving for a party – how tawdry, how paltry; her facing out the failure of *The Prison*: her desperate good cheer; her one bouquet; her old battered wigged head. How mixed my feelings were – and how exhausted and windswept and disillusioned I was – with my ears ringing, and no warmth, depth, comfort, slippers and ease anywhere; but all effort and strain.

Monday 16 March
These few and rather exacerbated entries show, I think, the backwash of *The Waves*. I am writing little articles of a morning, and should have been sketching the Houses of the Great this morning, but that I have not the material. This afternoon I shall try to see Carlyle's house and Keats's house.

Thursday 19 March
Ethel yesterday, very uneasy about her character; uneasy about her own greatness, requiring assurance, and snatching it rather hastily from such vague remarks as I could make. It seems possible to me that nature gave her everything except the power of expression in music; hence the race and violence and restlessness of her nature; the one outlet is stopped up. And she for ever batters at the door; it remains locked; she flows away over me, Lady Cunard – whoever it may be, with the vehemence of a tortured and baffled spirit. But she would die rather than allow this. Hence her terrific egotism; her insatiable desire for praise, since she is denied the only true satisfaction. An exhausting companion therefore.

Saturday 28 March
Arnold Bennett died last night; which leaves me sadder than I should have supposed. A lovable genuine man; well meaning; ponderous; kindly; coarse; rather dignified; deluded by splendour and success; but naive; much at the mercy of life for all his competence; a shop keeper's view of literature; yet with the rudiments, covered over with fat and prosperity and the desire for hideous Empire furniture, of sensibility. Some real understanding power, as well as a gigantic absorbing power. These are the sort of things that I think by fits and starts this morning; I remember his determination to write 1000 words daily; and how he trotted off to do it that night. Queer how one regrets the dispersal of anybody who seemed – as I say – genuine; who had direct contact with life. An element in life – even in mine that was so remote – taken away. This is what one minds.

Saturday 11 April

Oh I am so tired of correcting my own writing – these eight articles. I have however learnt I think to dash; and not to finick. Its the repulsiveness of correcting that nauseates me. And the cramming in and the cutting out. And articles and more articles are asked for. For ever I could write articles.

On Thursday we have our fortnight in France. I think I shall like La Rochelle best: I shall want to live there. I shall take a house there: I shall dream of walking there when I am old and full of sleep.

*   *   *

Sunday 3 May

Yes, that's all very well; but how to begin, and why begin? I mean what do these diaries amount to? O merely matter for a book, I think; and to read when I have a headache. After all, Percy could burn the lot in one bonfire. He could burn them at the edge of the field where, so we think, we shall lie buried. That was our conclusion after attending Arnold Bennett's funeral.

We are going to regulate 'seeing' people. There is to be a weekly black hole; a seething mass of people all eating tea together. We shall thus have more evenings free. Two days are to be set aside for reading MSS. These two decisions – the Black Hole, and Hogarth Press MSS, will I think make for an orderly and satisfactory summer.

Wednesday 13 May

Unless I write a few sentences here from time to time I shall, as they say, forget the use of my pen. I am now engaged in typing out from start to finish the 332 pages of that very condensed book *The Waves*. I do seven or eight daily; by which means I hope to have the whole complete by June 16th or thereabouts. This requires some resolution; but I can see no other way to make all the corrections, and keep the lilt, and join up, and expand and do all the other final processes. It is like sweeping over an entire canvas with a wet brush.

Tuesday 19 May

Lytton's book [*Portraits in Miniature*] very good. That's his line. The compressed yet glowing account which requires logic, reason, learning, taste, wit, order and infinite skill – this suits him far better, I think, than the larger scale, needing boldness, originality, sweep. Lytton and Raymond to dinner tonight. Desmond t'other night: much obliterated in the struggle for life.

Thursday 28 May

Soon after this, I started a headache – flashes of light raying round my eyes, and sharp pain; the pain cut into me by Ethel's voice, as she sat telling me – "You've got to listen" – about Adrian Boult, and how he ordered her to leave the room. And then to Rodmell, where the same thing happened – the light round my eyes, but as I could lie still in my bed in my big airy room, the pain was much less. If it were not for the divine goodness of L., how many times I should be thinking of death. At Monks House we had electric light, and the Frigidaire is working. When the electric light fused, we could hardly tolerate Aladdin lamps, so soon is the soul corrupted by comfort. Yesterday men were in the house all day boring holes for electric fires. What more comfort can we acquire? And, though the moralists say when one has a thing one at once finds it hollow, I don't at all agree. I enjoy my luxuries at every turn, and think them wholly good for what I am pleased to call the soul.

Thursday 2 June

Ethel again – All my ills, such as they are, spring from liver: I am a very strong woman, who needs calomel. I think that she wants me to be everlasting; that she dislikes other people's illnesses which interfere with her vitality; that she likes to rationalise everything; that she suspects, on principle, all shrinking, subtlety and sensibility. I don't know.

Monday 8 June

Dreams: I had three lately: one of Katherine Mansfield; how we met, beyond death, and shook hands; saying something by way of explanation and friendship; yet I knew she was dead. A curious summing up, it seemed, of what has passed since she died.

Tuesday 23 June

And yesterday, 22 June – when I think, the days begin to draw in, I finished my re-typing of *The Waves*. Not that it is finished – oh dear no. For then I must correct the re-re-typing. This work I began on May 5th, and no one can say that I have been hasty or careless this time; though I doubt not the lapses and slovenlinesses are innumerable.

A dark kind of summer. In spite of this, my little life has been adventurous and more stable than usual. There was Duncan's show; and considerable content, indeed a kind of bubbling rapture I think, in Fitzroy Street. I must ask Nessa why we are so happy. Clive is in Cassis. Julian has grown a bristling beard like a chimpanzee and is off with volumes of Pope to France. Tonight we go to the Gala Opera with Christabel [McLaren]. Stalls costing twenty-five shillings each.

Wednesday 24 June
Last night we went to the gala opera [Lyceum Theatre]; sat in the stalls, two rows from the stage, with Christabel and [Lady Abingdon], who came in late. Her fortune has been spent on her face. In the interval, old women like Roman matrons, ample, tightly girt; girls wand like; many large clear stoned necklaces and long dresses. I got the feeling of this traditional English life; its garden like quality; flowers all in beds and rows. Between the acts we all stood in the street; a dry brilliant night, with women all opening their cloaks; then came dribbling through us a draggled procession of poor women wheeling perambulators and carrying small, white-haired dazed children; going across Waterloo Bridge. Lady Abingdon stalked off without a good night or glance in our direction. Each of her nails was red, and cut out like a small rose petal. L. who had been reading *The Lady* said that this was considered in bad taste; and that men, according to *The Lady*, don't like it. So home, by cab. Oh and my hair stood the strain very well.

Tuesday 7 July
O to seek relief from this incessant correction and write a few words carelessly. A fine day I think and everything, so the tag runs in my head, handsome about us. L. is now floating on the tide of celebrity: asked to broadcast, asked to go to America, asked to write the Weekly Wayfarer in the *New Statesman*. And I am not jealous. Ethel has been penitent after her fashion. That is she came yesterday, after an intermission of almost a fortnight, and defended and explained herself in a speech which lasted twenty minutes by my watch. She raised her cup of tea six times to her lips but always thought of some new parenthesis or qualification and put it down untouched. Her zeal, sincerity and vitality of course convince; though I'm glad to drive my stake in firmly and so avoid complete overwhelming. I shout obloquies at her like gun shots. She takes them on her solid old body with a thud like that on an elephant's hide. I dominate by silence – a phenomenon to her very formidable. And off she goes at 6.45 subdued.

MONKS HOUSE, RODMELL

Friday 17 July
Yes. This morning I think I may say I have finished. L. will read it tomorrow; and I shall open this book to record his verdict. And I'm nervous, I confess. For one thing he will be honest, more than usually. And it may be a failure. And I can't do any more. As I say, I shall be nervous to hear what L. says when he comes out, say tomorrow night or Sunday morning,

to my garden room, carrying the MS and sits himself down and begins 'Well!'

Sunday 19 July

"It is a masterpiece" said L. coming out to my lodge this morning. "And the best of your books." This note I make; adding that he also thinks the first hundred pages extremely difficult, and is doubtful how far any common reader will follow. But Lord! what a relief! I stumped off in the rain in jubilation.

Friday 7 August

I sat to Tommy [Stephen Tomlin]. Oh dear, what a terrific hemp strong heather root obstinate fountain of furious individuality shoots in me – they tampered with it, Nessa and Tommy – pinning me there from 2 to 4 on six afternoons, to be looked at; and I felt like a piece of whalebone bent. This amused and interested me, at the same time I foamed with rage. And at last, at last, at last, on Thursday 30th we got into the car, slammed the door, and made off. And how satisfactory it has been, is being. I writing *Flush* of a morning, half seriously, to ease my brain, knotted by all that last screw of *The Waves*; L. doing his broadcast and correcting proofs; no one coming, except Bells; no one ringing up; no one to say dinner's ready, or to be stumping about in the kitchen. Annie, composed, neat, nimble, has everything disposed of by 3 – which reminds me I must go and put the pie in the oven, I think.

Monday 10 August

No I will not let this day be a bad one, though it has every sign of so being. First an argument with L. at breakfast about seeing his family; the usual rather embittered argument; and then a headache is incipient; which is caused partly by Charleston; where we were very gay. Now I sit in the lodge this grey pale morning and will not go on with *Flush*, because of my head; and we have a day in London tomorrow; and should begin to correct my first proofs; and perhaps shall when I've done this. No, I say, I will not let this day be a bad one: but by what means? Quiet and control. Eating apples – sleeping this afternoon. And now for *Waves*.

Saturday 15 August

Sibyl [Colefax] came by her own request yesterday; and I wondered after two hours jerking barren gossip, what satisfaction she got from it. Once she looked at the downs. The worst of being Sibyl is that one suspects every action of some motive. 'I am proving myself a woman who loves the country.' One never feels, This is what she likes, as I do when Vita stumbles over the marsh and hardly has a word to say. Sibyl looks at chairs and tables; sums one up; has a magpie's eye, a larder of facts which she will hand on at her next meeting. Then, as we stood at the door, she tried to make us invite her to stay. And I resisted. As you see, Sibyl's company does not lead to lofty reflections.

A wet wild August, the coldest for fourteen years; and the farmers here burning their hay. Meanwhile the country is in the throes of a crisis. Great events are brewing. Maynard visits Downing Street and spreads sensational rumours.

Sunday 16 August
I should really apologise to this book for using it as I am doing to write off my aimlessness; that is I am doing my proofs – and find that I must stop after an hour, and let my mind spread, after these moments of concentration.

The reason why Colefax is so dull is that she never feels or thinks for herself. That is why I should suffocate of dust if she spent a night here. Also she is forever collecting facts about one, not from interest, but from curiosity. It is a warning not to go to places like Argyll House again, because one is expected to make some return.

It is a good idea I think to write biographies; to make them use my powers of representation, reality, accuracy; and to use my novels simply to express the general, the poetic. *Flush* is serving this purpose.

Monday 17 August
Well now, it being just after 12.30 I have put the last corrections in *The Waves*: done my proofs; and they shall go tomorrow – never, never to be looked at again by me, I imagine.

Wednesday 19 August
My proofs did go: went yesterday; and I shall not see them again.

Tuesday 1 September
And so a few days of bed and headache and overpowering sleep, sleep descending inexorable, as I tried to read.

Thursday 3 September
Oh I was annoyed with Desmond's usual sneer at *Mrs Dalloway* – 'wool-gathering'. I was inspired to make up several phrases about Desmond's own processes – none of which, I suppose, will ever be fired off in print. But its true – a snub – even praise – from Desmond, depresses me more than the downright anger of Arnold Bennett – it saps my vitality.

I open this book again to record the fact that this is the 3rd of September. The Battle of Dunbar; the Battle of Worcester; and the death of Cromwell. A heavy flagging windy cloudy day with breadths of sun; not actually raining. Its odd how I always remember father saying that at St Ives on this day, and how I am always writing something in a diary on this day and generally it is crisp and clear.

Tuesday 15 September
I have come up here, trembling under the sense of complete failure – I mean *The Waves* – I mean L. accuses me of sensibility verging on insanity – I mean I am acutely depressed and already feeling rising the hard and horny back of my old friend Fight fight.

Wednesday 16 September
Oh but this morning I'm like a bee in the ivy bloom – can't write for pleasure. John [Lehmann] says "But I loved it, truly loved it, and was deeply impressed and amazed by its achievement in an entirely new method . . . There seems to me only the thinnest wall between such a novel and poetry." And its very difficult he adds; and so on.

Saturday 19 September
And the last few days have been heavenly – at last some heat; and then, with this book done, I'm calm; oh and walk; oh and have to record the horror of two bungalows on the top of the hill. Yes. This iniquity is being inflicted on the downs for ever by our 'prospective Labour candidate'. He shan't have my vote. I swept off into dreams of a house far away in Dorsetshire. But O – again – how happy I am: for the moment how sweet life is with L. here, in its regularity and order, and the garden and the room at night and music and my walks and writing easily and interestedly at Donne of a morning, and poems all about me. I've come to read poetry with intensity.

Monday 21 September
Here I am writing about Donne and we have 'gone off the Gold Standard' this morning. Maynard and [Richard] Kahn like people in the war. We sat talking economics and politics. Guards out: Tower defended (this a joke on Maynard's part). We're off, and I write about Donne. Yes; and what could I do better, if we are ruined; and if everybody had spent their time writing about Donne we should not have gone off the Gold Standard – that's my version of the greatest crisis &c &c &c – gabble gabble go the geese, who can't lay golden eggs.

Wednesday 30 September

I have come up here on this the last evening to clear up papers. All is softly grey: L.'s yellow dahlias are burning on the edge of the terrace. I have been over to Asheham, in the clear pale autumn afternoon, along Mandril walk, which we walked the night of our marriage. So its over, this summer too; and I regret it, and want to stay on, and soothe my mind with Elizabethan poets. Instead we go up tomorrow, and doesn't the lift of my heart tell me that strain, about *The Waves*, friends, reviewers, sales, &c will then begin to make a fiddle string in my side, stretched tight, on which lots of people will carelessly twang this winter. No help for it. So it always is with a book out. And it will be out in one week tomorrow.

52 TAVISTOCK SQUARE, WC1

Monday 5 October

A note, to say I am all trembling with pleasure, because Harold Nicolson has rung up to say *The Waves* is a masterpiece. Ah hah – so it wasn't all wasted then. I mean this vision I had here has some force on other minds. Now for a cigarette, and then a return to sober composition.

Friday 9 October

Really, this unintelligible book is being better 'received' than any of them. And it sells – how unexpected, how odd that people can read that difficult grinding stuff!

Wednesday 14 October

A note. *The Waves* has beaten all my books: sold close on 5,000; we are reprinting. The reviews I think the warmest yet. But Vita found it desperately dull – anyhow for 100 pages. What shall I say to Virginia? I can't get through it.

Saturday 17 October

More notes on *The Waves*. The sales, these past three days, have fallen; after the great flare up when we sold 500 in one day, the brushwood has died down, as I foretold. What has happened is that the library readers can't get through it and are sending their copies back. So, I prophesy, it will now dribble along till we have sold 6000 and then almost die, yet not quite. For it has been received, as I may say, quoting the stock phrases without vanity, with applause. I am in danger, indeed, of becoming our leading novelist, and not with the highbrows only. To show how slow a book it is, not only do Vita and Dotty find the first hundred pages boring in the extreme, but I have as yet (ten days after publication) had only three letters about it. Nessa's enthusiasm is the brightest spot.

Friday 23 October

Oh but I have been made miserable – damped and disheartened – because the *TLS* only gave half a column of belittlement to [Leonard's] *After the Deluge*. L. says – and honestly believes – that this puts an end to the book. He says his ten years' work are wasted, and that he sees no use in going on. Oh but the arguments which we have beaten out I daresay for six hours, walking in the Square, sitting over the fire – utterly cloud my mind. Its his curious pessimistic temper: something deeper than reason, that one can't deal with. Influenza has exactly the same effect, liberating the irrational despondency which I see in all Woolves, and connect with centuries of oppression. The world against us &c. How can one laugh off the half-column therefore? And when I say this morning incautiously "I'm reviewed in the *Manchester Guardian*", L. says 'Is it a long review?" And I say, feeling like a mother to a hurt and miserable little boy, Yes. Lord what human beings are!

Friday 30 October

Happily that morbidity of L.'s is over. Other things have intervened, and praise and some sale. And the General Election which has returned I think twenty-six Labour members to Parliament. Oh – yesterday we made an offer for 47 Gordon Square – a house where we may die; for its a 24-year lease. Strange to anchor there again.

Monday 16 November

But we are not to live and die in 47. The Bedford Estate won't house a publisher; would create a precedent; vans would stop at the door. Though [they] told us that we may stay on here past our term: the side of the Square is to be pulled down; but times are bad for building; and they will treat us with consideration.

Here I will give myself the pleasure of copying a sentence or two from Morgan's unsolicited letter on *The Waves*. 'I expect I shall write to you again when I have re-read *The Waves*. Its difficult to express oneself about a work which one feels to be so very important but I've the sort of excitement over it which comes from believing that one's encountered a classic.' I daresay that gives me more substantial pleasure than any letter I've had about any book. Yes, I think it does, coming from Morgan. To be noted, as curiosities of my literary history: I sedulously avoid meeting Roger and Lytton whom I suspect do not like *The Waves*. (*The Waves* has sold more than 7000. *The Deluge* is selling very well.)

Tuesday 17 November

Isn't it odd that I'm really, I believe, ostracised by some of my friends, because of *The Waves*, and lifted to the highest pinnacle by others because of it? But Morgan is the only one, either side, that matters.

MONKS HOUSE, RODMELL

Friday 25 December

(Christmas morning). Lytton is still alive this morning. We thought that he could not live through the night. It was a moonlit night. Nessa rang up at 10 to say that he has taken milk and tea after an injection. He had taken nothing for twenty-four hours and was only half conscious. This may be the turn, or may mean nothing. Now again all one's sense of him flies out and expands and I begin to think of things I shall say to him, so strange is the desire for life – the triumph of life.

After writing the last page, November 16th, I could not go on writing without perpetual headache; and so took a month lying down; have not written a line until the last fourteen days, when I heard about Lytton. He has been ill a month; I have lived through again all grades of feeling; then the telephone; then Angelica coming; then going to see James [Strachey]; then coming here last Tuesday, a dark drive, a tree reminding me of Lytton. Brighton yesterday. All very quiet, misty. Talk to L. last night about death; its stupidity; what he would feel if I died. And the feeling of age coming over us: and the hardship of losing friends.

Sunday 27 December

For forty-eight hours Lytton has been better, and now, Nessa says, realises that he is better, and eats; whatever he is allowed. I am therefore freely imagining a future with my old serpent to talk to, to laugh at, to abuse. I shall read his book on Shakespeare; I shall stay at Ham Spray; I shall tell him how L. and I sobbed on Christmas Eve.

But this page is one of my trials to test my brain. I am cross with Desmond, for talking about dreaming subjectivity and *The Waves*; I have been making phrases about his damnable tepidity – he who neither loves nor hates – in short I'm in a healthy condition. Lunching with the Keyneses, they took Lytton philosophically. "Is he alive?" Lydia asked. They did not go to Ham Spray because Lydia disapproves of the immorality of Carrington. "And what d'you feel about immortality, Maynard?" I asked. "I am an idealist," said Maynard, "and therefore on the whole I suppose I think that something may continue. Clearly the brain is the only exciting thing – matter does not exist. It follows therefore . . . but one is very vague." So, more or less, he said. And L. said death was stupid like a motor accident. And Maynard said he wished one could die at once: there should be death arranged for couples simultaneously, like himself and Lydia, me and Leonard. But he always supposed he would die before Lydia, and I, I said, before Leonard. Then Lydia and Leonard will marry. They will combine all these dogs – (dogs were wandering about). And so home. And I kissed Maynard. And they are coming to tea.

Tuesday 29 December

Lytton is, if anything, better. I need not ring up Nessa today, which is a matter of exquisite relief. It seems as if he were now to be seriously ill with ups and downs for some time. Well, we have lived through every grade of feeling – how strong, how deep – more than I guessed, though that cavern of horror is well known to me. In these acute states emotions are much simplified – there is none of the complexity that I feel this morning about Lytton, when I expect him to recover. I feel annoyance, humour, the desire to laugh with him.

It is a bitter windy morning, and Caburn when I came in was white with snow. Now it is black. Shall I ever 'write' again? Why take to it again? Books come gently surging round me, like icebergs. I could write a book of caricatures. Then there's *Flush*; there's *The Knock on the Door*; there's the appalling novel; there's *The Common Reader* . . . there's my little *Letter to a Poet*. But I'm deficient in excitement.

And L. has sold his 450; and I 9400 – what figures.

1932

The year opened under the shadow of Lytton Strachey's illness. A week before he died on 21 January, the Woolfs drove from London to his Wiltshire home, but were not able to see him. The news of his death reached them in Vanessa's studio during a party given for her thirteen-year-old daughter Angelica. Three weeks later they returned to Ham Spray to offer what support they could to the desolated and suicidal Carrington; she was found next day dying from a shot wound. During this melancholy period and the 'mausoleum talks' the circumstances generated among Lytton's many friends, Roger Fry was lecturing at the Queen's Hall in connection with the great exhibition of French Art at the Royal Academy. And Virginia was invited to give the Clark Lectures at Cambridge (which both T. S. Eliot and E. M. Forster had already done), an exceptionally flattering invitation which she at once refused, and then regretted her resolution. She was still ruminating a sequel to A Room of One's Own, which she now thought of calling A Tap or A Knock at the Door, and had set herself to prepare a sequel to The Common Reader, the volume of essays she had published in 1925, and this involved writing five new pieces and revising some twenty already published in various journals.

On 15 April the Woolfs, feeling they deserved an adventure, set off from Victoria Station with Roger Fry and his sister Margery for a tour in Greece; they were away four weeks. Virginia had been there in 1906 with her brothers and sister, but for her companions it was a new experience and one which, though strenuous, was stimulating and rewarding to all four.

The hot London summer was a very busy time for the Woolfs: innumerable social engagements – lunches, dinners, evening parties; visits to the cinema, the ballet, the Chelsea Flower Show; alternate weekends were spent when possible at Monks House. Virginia was trying to finish off the Common Reader volume, and again her exertions brought on fainting fits. An undercurrent to all this activity was John Lehmann's increasing discontent with his role in the Hogarth Press: he found Leonard a difficult taskmaster, the work too hard, the rewards too little, and Virginia, whom he revered, too aloof. Discussions, proposed rearrangements, interventions by Vanessa, failed to allay his grievances. But the Woolfs were shocked by his sudden decision to quit for good.

One of the Woolfs' first guests after moving to Rodmell for the summer was the prize-winning novelist Stella Benson, who had dined with them in July when visiting London from her home in Indo-China. Two days later the distressing news of the death of the Cambridge humanist G. L. Dickinson (Goldie) reached them; he was a dear and respected older friend, and a perceptive admirer of Virginia's writings. The country holiday followed its usual course, although Virginia suffered another alarming fainting fit early on, and took things gently, reading a good deal, contentedly writing Flush, and despatching her proofs of the second Common Reader. There was frequent contact with the Charlestonians and the Keyneses, the Woolf family visit, walks and car expeditions, one to stay a night with the Adrian Stephens in Essex. Unexpected visitors were the Eliots: she apparently more neurotic than ever, he considerate and indulgent of her behaviour, perhaps in the knowledge of his impending departure for a six-month lecture tour in America. It was during their visit that John Lehmann's letter announcing his departure from the Hogarth Press was delivered by the afternoon post.

Back in London after attending the Labour Party Conference at Leicester, Virginia went to the wedding in St Bartholomew the Great of Desmond MacCarthy's only daughter to Lord David Cecil; and it was on this day that the second Common Reader was published. Unusually, she seemed remarkably indifferent to its fate, being suddenly engrossed by a wholly new conception for a book, to be called The Pargiters, incorporating the ideas she had been turning over for her essay A Tap on the Door, but expanded to embody a family chronicle. This excited and absorbed her and she dashed it down at great speed through the autumn months. The effort strained her heart, and again she was advised to be careful, and gladly limited her social activities, mainly seeing people at home at tea-time – though she invited the novelist and journalist Rebecca West to dinner. The Woolfs went to Rodmell for Christmas, and Virginia grudgingly faced the task of polishing off Flush.

1932

Monks House, Rodmell

Friday 1 January

Yesterday we had Keyneses and Bells to tea. Lytton, as I must believe, very slow mending – O these dogs – that's my present curse. This irregular sharp bark is the devil. Nessa's description of the lounge at the Bear [Inn, Hungerford] filled with Stracheys reading detective novels in despair; Carrington moving about scarcely knowing people; Pippa violently self-controlled; Saxon helping by – I forget what; Tommy helping too; and the Stracheys, all grey, all woollen, all red nosed, swollen eyed, logical, quiet, exact, doing crossword puzzles; thinking of Lytton. And that afternoon (Christmas Eve) Lytton said "If its only keeping me alive a little longer, don't." And so they did nothing; but then he drank tea and milk with brandy and enjoyed them, and the Doctor happily had some serum, injected it, and so the turn – if turn they call it – began. This is a scene I can see; and see Lytton too, always reasonable, clear, giving his orders; and dying as he thought; and then, as reasonably, finding some strength returning, deciding to live. And L. and I sobbing here.

During the last days here, they have been putting up a great erection of girders on the bank opposite Asheham. Is this an overhead railway or an engine house? So another view of the downs is lost forever. And Annie repeats vague gossip that there is to be a series of factories between Newhaven and Lewes; are we doomed to go – or to stay on and be worried out of all walks, all views, and become crusted over with villas?

52 Tavistock Square, WC1

Wednesday 13 January

We came back from Rodmell last Sunday afternoon – a wet evening, and comfortable to be back, here high up in the air, beyond barking dogs. "I shall go bankrupt if those dogs bark any more" I said to Annie with some vehemence. John [Lehmann] labours, more nervously, and feels jaded, and wants a week off, and wants also to be our manager, not partner, but to stay in that capacity. So perhaps, and perchance, the dear old Press to which I owe so much labour – witness the pile of MSS before me – and fun – oh yes, a great deal of variety and oddity – may now settle down for life. For our lives. How long will they be? Can we count on another twenty years? I shall be fifty on 25th, Monday week that is; and sometimes feel that I have lived 250 years already, and sometimes that I am still the youngest person in the omnibus. (Nessa says that she still always thinks this, as she sits down.) And I want to write another four novels; and the *Tap on the Door*; and to go through English literature, like a string through cheese, or rather like some industrious insect, eating its way from book to book, from Chaucer to Lawrence. This is a programme, considering my slowness, to last out my twenty years, if I have them.

Lytton goes on, now better, now not so well.

Monday 18 January

And then we heard that Lytton was very ill again. So down we went to Ham Spray on Thursday. So hot, so fresh. The larks singing over the petrol pumps I remember on the Great West Road as we stopped to fill up. They were strained, silent. Then tears – Pippa sobbing on my shoulder at the Bear after lunch – hopeless almost – he is so ill – how can he get better? Then back to Ham Spray – how lovely, with its flat lawn, and the trees grouped and the down rising; this I noted with envy, thinking of my dogs barking, my downs ruined, as we sat at tea. I long sometimes for this sealed up, silent, remote country; long for its little villages; its muddy roads; its distance from Brighton and Peacehaven. And so home again, leaving them in the frail lovely house, with hospital nurses popping in and out; a light in Lytton's room, the shadow of a screen. Again today Carrington writes he is slightly better.

Thursday 21 January

And last night Lytton was dying – "much worse" Oliver telephoned; and this morning "much better again". So we go to Angelica's party in fancy dress. It is like having the globe of the future perpetually smashed – with Lytton – and then behold, it fills again.

Friday 22 January

Much better was much weaker. Lytton died yesterday morning.

I see him coming along the street, muffled up with his beard resting on his tie; how we should stop: his eyes glow. Now I am too numb with all the emotion yesterday to do more than think thoughts like this. Well, as I know, the pain will soon begin. How queer it was last night at the party –

Duncan, Nessa and I sobbing together in the studio – a sense of something spent, gone; the impoverishment; then the sudden vividness. Nessa said, What would one like if one died oneself? that the party should go on. He is the first of the people one has known since one was grown up to die, she said. It was very hopeless. Yes, twenty years of Lytton lost to us, stupidly; the thing we shall never have again.

Saturday 30 January
Oliver [Strachey] to dinner last night. "Lytton was a great man. Oh the excitement. I came back from India starved, and found – all that. They can't leave Carrington alone. She says she will kill herself – quite reasonable – but better to wait until the first shock is over and see. Suicide seems to me quite sensible." Oliver is a tough old buffer: with one flame inside of him. What the Americans call 'culture'. "*That's* the only thing: to realise the legacy that's been left us. To read. To do nothing from eighteen to twenty-two but read. That's what we did. That's why we shan't grow old – we shan't come to an end. But you can't do it if you don't do it then."

Thursday 4 February
One of the curious things I am now proving – now that I am going through the stages of Lytton's death – is that for us fame has no existence. We say we can't publish Lytton's letters for fifty years, if at all. We can't write about him. He has no funeral. I don't know where his ashes are to be buried. There is no commemoration any more, except when we meet and talk; or in the usual ways, alone at night, walking along the streets. The solid statue that father left – that exists no longer.

Monday 8 February
Why did I ever say I would produce another volume of *Common Reader?* It will take me week after week, month after month. However a year spent in reading through English literature will no doubt do good to my fictitious brain. Rest it anyhow. One day, all of a rush, fiction will burst in. I wake in the night with the sense of being in an empty hall: Lytton dead, and those factories building. What is the point of it; life, when I am not working, suddenly becomes thin, indifferent. Lytton is dead, and nothing definite to mark it. Also they write flimsy articles about him. And we go on – at Rodmell for the week-end; and went over to Caburn, and walked among those primeval downs: bowl shaped shadows; half circles; curves; a deep valley.

Thursday 11 February
My mind is set running upon *A Knock on the Door* (what's its name?) owing largely to reading 'Wells on Woman' – how she must be ancillary and

decorative in the world of the future, because she has been tried, in ten years, and has not proved anything. So in this mood I record Mary [Hutchinson]'s telling me last night how she loved cigars; but Jack refuses to let her smoke them – against his idea of what his wife should do – silly affectation – or to let her dress in a dress cut low at the back. Can't go out with you in that frock. Go and put on another. Its indecent. "He treats us – [their daughter] Barbara and me – as if we were tame leopards – pets belonging to him." As indeed they do, since neither has a penny except of Jack's earning and giving.

Saturday 13 February
I break off from my plain duty which is to read [Donne's] *Anatomy of the World* to record Roger's lecture last night. Roger rather cadaverous in white waistcoat. A vast sheet. Pictures passing. He takes his stick. Gets into trouble with the lanternist. Is completely at his ease. Elucidates, unravels with fascinating ease and subtlety this quality and that; investigates (with his stick) opposing diagonals; emphasises the immediate and instantaneous in French art. Here a Queen about to fling out her fingers; here a mother losing herself in pensive and tender reverie, while her child struggles and she restrains it, unconsciously, with perfect ease and control. So to Nessa's, where the stove was kindled, and there was hot soup and cold meat, and coffee and biscuits – all with the usual skill and organising capacity. There we laughed and exaggerated: about the lecture. And we talked about a new life of Jesus, which offers two proofs of his existence – witness Roger's intellectual vitality after speaking to the Queen's Hall for two hours – really excited about the reality of Jesus.

Tuesday 16 February
I have to dine with Ethel Sands tonight, and must have my hair curled. And I'm quivering and itching to write my – what's it to be called? – *Men are like that?* – no that's too patently feminist: the sequel then, for which I have collected enough powder to blow up St Paul's. It is to have four pictures.

Friday 26 February
And what a mint of people I've seen; dining with Ethel, having Desmond and Lord David and Ottoline and the Keyneses, and going to Monks House – so March-white and lovely, the fields, and the river, that bitter cold day; and then I saw – oh the Keyneses – yes – and talked of Lytton, and how Maynard thought we really carried unconvention too far – no service, no farewell. With Lytton there was no mark to say This is over.

And Ka shut me in the middle class bedroom effectively last night – so condescending, so self approving, with her docile stories of respectable lunches with the Cornish aristocracy. "And I do hope you will do more *Common Readers*. I prefer them to –" This little bit of patronage annoyed me more than it should. The day Ka came too we sold the ten thousandth copy of *The Waves*: which thus beats all my novels, unexpectedly.

Monday 29 February
And this morning I opened a letter, and it was from the Master of Trinity [College, Cambridge]: and it was to say that the Council have decided to ask me to deliver the Clark Lectures next year. Six of them. This, I suppose, is the first time a woman has been asked; and so it is a great honour – think of me, the uneducated child reading books in my room at 22 Hyde Park Gate – now advanced to this glory. But I shall refuse: because how could I write six lectures without giving up a year to criticism; without becoming a functionary; without sealing my lips when it comes to tilting at Universities; without putting off my *Knock at the Door*; without perhaps shelving another novel? But I am inclined to smile. Yes; all that reading, I say, has borne this odd fruit. And I am pleased; and still more pleased that I won't do it; and like to think that father would have blushed with pleasure could I have told him thirty years ago, that his daughter – my poor little Ginny – was to be asked to succeed him: the sort of compliment he would have liked.

Thursday 3 March
And now I am rather upset because the devil whispered, all of a sudden, that I have six lectures written in *Phases of Fiction*; and could furbish them up and deliver the Clark Lectures, and win the esteem of my sex, with a few weeks' work. Such is the perversity of my mind, I can now think of nothing else; my mind is swarming with ideas for lectures; things I can only say in lectures; and my refusal seems lazy and cowardly. Yet two days ago I was repugnant to the thought: longed only for freedom in which to write *A Tap at the Door*; and was convinced that I should be a time serving pot hunter if I accepted. Anyhow, I'm thankful that I wrote decidedly in the mood I was then in, before the devil whispered, and I went to my drawer and found that old MS; so well written, so full of thought – all the work done for me.

Saturday 12 March
So we went to Ham Spray – a lovely bright day, and got there at 1.30. "I thought you weren't coming" said Carrington. She came to the door, in her little jacket and socks with a twisted necklace. She was pale, small, suffering silently; very calm. She had hot soup for us. We sat in the cold dining room. "I didn't light the fire" she said. She had cooked us a nice hot lunch, succulent, with her own hands. We talked with effort; did she want us? Did

she resent our coming to spy on her? Then we sat on the verandah. We asked her to make us woodcuts for notepaper. And to do designs for Julia [Strachey]'s book. We tried to gossip; she laughed once or twice: and her eyes seemed to get bluer. Then it got cold and we went and sat in Lytton's study – all beautifully neat, his notepaper laid out – a great fire; all his books exactly fitting the shelves, with the letters over them. We sat on the floor round the fire. Then L. suggested a walk. She said she had some notes to write and would we go by ourselves. We only walked to the bottom of the long low down. Then L. went to do the car, and I wandered in the garden and then back into the sitting room. I was taking out a book when Carrington came in and asked if we would have tea before we went. She had made it. She and I went upstairs, arm in arm; and I said "Let me see the view from the window." We stood looking out – She said "Don't you think one ought to keep a room exactly as it was? I want to keep Lytton's rooms as he had them. But the Stracheys say this is morbid. Am I romantic about it d'you think" "Oh no, I'm romantic too," I said. She burst into tears, and I took her in my arms. She sobbed, and said she had always been a failure. "There is nothing left for me to do. I did everything for Lytton. But I've failed in everything else. People say he was very selfish to me. But he gave me everything. Lytton was like a father to me. He taught me everything I know. He read poetry and French to me." I did not want to lie to her. I said life seemed to me sometimes hopeless, useless, when I woke in the night and thought of Lytton's death. I held her hands. Her wrists seemed very small. She seemed helpless, deserted, like some small animal left. She was very gentle; sometimes laughing; kissing me; saying Lytton had loved his old friends best. She said he had been silly with young men. She had been angry that they had not understood how great he was. I said I had always known that. And this last year Lytton made up his mind to be middle aged. "And we were going to Malaga and then he was going to write about Shakespeare, And he was going to write his memoirs, which would take him ten years. It was ironical, his dying, wasn't it. He thought he was getting better. He said things like Lear when he was ill. I wanted to take you to see him the day you came, but I was afraid to – James and Pippa said one must not run any risk, and it might have upset him." And what else did we say? There was not much time. We had tea and broken biscuits. She stood by the fireplace. Then we said we must go. She was very quiet and showed no desire for us to stay. She kissed me several times. I said "Then you will come and see us next week – or not – just as you like?" "Yes, I will come, or not" she said. And kissed me again, and said Goodbye. Then she went in; and turned and I waved and she waved back and she went into the house.

Next morning at 8.30 the gardener heard a noise in her bedroom. He went in and found she had shot herself through the thigh. She died in three hours.

Thursday 17 March
So Carrington killed herself; and again what L. calls 'these mausoleum talks' begin again. We were the last to talk to her, and thus might have been summoned to the inquest; but they brought it in an accident. She maintained this, even to Ralph. Her foot slipped as she was shooting a rabbit. And we discuss suicide; and I feel, as always, ghosts changing. Lytton's affected by this act. I sometimes dislike him for it. He absorbed her, made her kill herself. Now we have to see Pippa, and James and Alix. Then to Rodmell; then – perhaps – to Greece with Roger and [his sister Margery]. A venture that would be: and I think we're both in the mood for ventures after this morbid time; so much talk of death; and there death is of course.

We went from Cambridge on Saturday to King's Lynn; through the lovely lonely coast that lies between that and Cromer; green meadows against the sea; and trees, and complete solitude, and now and then a line of little old houses; and some village spread out, as in a mediaeval picture, upon the rise of a dune; and lovely stubborn unknown place names; and wild roads; all this jumble somehow shadowed by Carrington's death; the name Partridge of course appearing on tombs and grocer's shops.

MONKS HOUSE, RODMELL

Thursday 24 March
Tomorrow is Good Friday and therefore we are at Rodmell on the loveliest spring day; soft; a blue veil in the air torn by birds' voices. I am glad to be alive and sorry for the dead: can't think why Carrington killed herself and put an end to all this. True, they are building the vast elephant grey sheds at Asheham, but I intend to see them as Greek temples; and Percy says they are building sixty cottages – but we wait to see if this is so. And the country is lovelier and lovelier, still with great empty spaces, where I want to walk, alone, and come to terms with my own head. Another book?

Tuesday 29 March
We went to Sissinghurst, and it was a fine goose grey morning. Harold came out in a torn jacket; Vita in breeches and pink shirt. We went over the grounds. Harold said "I'm getting nobler and nobler as we get poorer. I've refused an offer to write for the American papers. Oh but there are myriads of things to do here." Walls have been built and turf laid. "Yes we

want to turn those stables into guest bedrooms; and build a library across the courtyard," said Vita. All is planned. Harold has drawn it in his note book. So we ate cold salmon and raspberries and cream and little variegated chocolates and drank oh lots of drinks; and then climbed Vita's tower; lovely pink brick; but like Knole, not much view, save of stables that are to be guest rooms. So home. And then a very wet Sunday and a prodigious reading and drowsing.

52 TAVISTOCK SQUARE, WC1

Monday 11 April
The eddy of travel – wisps and straws – is already whirling round. I have a list of things to buy on my table. We start at 10 on Friday; shall be sailing down the Dalmatian coast this time next week. It is fiendishly cold, wet, blowing, like last year in France. I like this adventure of Greece all the same; and the fact that we are sociably going with Roger and Margery; and that – intimacy – will be part of our journey. The result of Lytton's death – this desire to be with friends.

As for external facts – it seems likely that our John [Lehmann] will not stay. That is he wishes to work half time in order to write.

Hail now; and camel coloured sky. I am waiting for lunch. Tomorrow we go to Monks House to take Pinker. This is a little girl's writing – like a child's letter.

*　　*　　*

MONKS HOUSE, RODMELL

Sunday 15 May
And now, Whit Sunday, here we are at Monks House, and Greece is perceptibly melting: just for a moment England and Greece stood side by side, each much enlivened by the other. When we landed, the English coast seemed long, low, sweeping, empty. I exclaimed at the extraordinary English green – with its silver mixture; and L. said the earth had an unbaked look – no red in it; and the lines of the hills so sloping. This was Greece still active in our eyes. But its force is waning. Already my mind is hard at work (in my absence) arranging, editing, bringing forward, eliminating, until it will present me, unasked, with visions, as I walk, of Aegina, of Athens – the Acropolis with the incandescent pillars; the view from the goatherd's

hill at Delphi. Last night's gossip at Charleston has further strewn sand over Greece. And my head has settled down; and my body is rapidly using itself to armchairs and soft beds and English meat and jam.

52 TAVISTOCK SQUARE, WC1

Tuesday 17 May
What is the right attitude towards criticism? What ought I to feel and say and do when Miss Bradbrook devotes an article in *Scrutiny* to attacking me? She is young, Cambridge, ardent. And she says I'm a very bad writer. It is perhaps true that my reputation will now decline. I shall be laughed at and pointed at. What should be my attitude? The right way is not to resent; not to . . . be long suffering and Christian and submissive either. Of course, with my odd mixture of extreme rashness and modesty (to analyse roughly) I very soon recover from praise and blame. But I want to find out an attitude. The most important thing is to investigate candidly the charge; but not fussily, not very anxiously.

Wednesday 25 May
Lord how I suffer! What a terrific capacity I possess for feeling with intensity – now, since we came back, I'm screwed up into a ball; can't get into step; can't make things dance; wonder how a year or twenty perhaps is to be endured; the inane pointlessness of all this existence; the old treadmill feeling, of going on and on and on; for no reason: Lytton's death; Carrington's; a longing to speak to him; all that cut away, gone; L.'s goodness, and firmness; and the immense responsibility that rests on him. What to do about the Press; about John; women; my book on professions; shall I write another novel; Nessa's children; society; buying clothes; Rodmell spoilt; all England spoilt; terror at night of things generally wrong in the universe; worst of all is this disjected barrenness. And my eyes hurt; and my hand trembles. A saying of Leonard's comes into my head in this season of complete inanity and boredom. 'Things have gone wrong somehow.' It was the night Carrington killed herself. We were walking along that silent blue street with the scaffolding. I saw all the violence and unreason crossing in the air; ourselves small; a tumult outside; something terrifying: unreason.

Thursday 26 May
And now today suddenly the weight on my head is lifted. I can think, reason, keep to one thing, and concentrate. Perhaps I owe it to my conversation with L. last night. I tried to analyse my depression: how my

brain is jaded with the conflict within of two types of thought, the critical, the creative; how I am harrassed by the strife and jar and uncertainty without.

Wednesday 1 June (Derby Day)
Oh dear, oh dear, I don't like dining with Clive – not altogether. It is true I conquered, at 8, my profound trepidation about my clothes. 'I won't wear my new dress' I said, 'in case I should be laughed at.' This philosophy shivered on the doorstep, when I saw two 20-horse-power cars drawn up, apparently at his door. Again I fluctuated and shivered, like a blown candle flame, when I came in and found only steamy, grubby, inarticulate Rex Whistler. Why have I dressed at all I asked. Then Lord David, then Bea Howe, then Mrs Quennell. That's all. So to dinner. And the boasting! Clive rattling out noble names; but I played my tricks: jumped over the candlestick; and co-operated with Clive in the great business of impressing. No, I don't think I like Clive's parties any more – I pick up too many thorns, one way and another. Anyhow, why not refuse the next party, and rummage on my own? My own pie is full enough.

Thursday 2 June
Lord David's party last night. Half across London. Derby night. Great motors full of men with buttonholes. A rose pink girl tripping across Shaftesbury Avenue hand in hand with a young man: all fluff and roses. Edwardes Square very large, leafy, silent, Georgian, refined; so to No. 41 with its white and green; a butler; an orange cat; Lord David and Elizabeth Bowen talking by the fire; then Puffin [Anthony Asquith], then John Sparrow. Not a good dinner: meagre, exiguous; and I took too many asparagus. All adroit kind nice talk – the note of the Asquiths and Cecils. "How very true" – "Yes, I agree entirely" – so different from Bloomsbury. There's more body to us. Still I don't complain. A little confabulation about Eddy [Sackville-West]; then about crying at crowds, at theatres, at films; what is tragic; about football. Talk about Auden and Naomi Mitchison: her review of Auden read aloud. Then they talked about the German youth movement; about bad people; about Murry; and I wore my new dress, too white and young perhaps; and so came home across London, and must now wash for Maynard's lunch and the Bernard Shaws – oh damn, oh damn – not an idea in my head or a wish to be brilliant.

Friday 3 June
I don't like old ladies who guzzle. My comment upon Ethel Smyth last night – no doubt a harsh one. But she champed and chopped; and squabbled over her duck; and then was over eaten and had to go home.

My comment upon the Shaws: he said "I am not sufficiently fond of myself to wish for immortality. I should like to be different. I should like to be a performer in music, and a mathematician. So I don't keep a diary. I destroy all my letters. Desmond MacCarthy says he's going to write my life – well, he may say so. He comes and talks – I can't tell the truth yet, about myself. The Webbs looked lonely somehow going off to Russia. I've always quarrelled with the Webbs. You see Webb has a gigantic faculty for absorbing information. And so, when I first knew him, I had to overcome an immense amount of useless knowledge. Webb would be much more effective if he'd one drop of the artist. But he has not one. Beatrice is in despair about it. Can't make a good speech therefore. People think my style as speaker is spontaneous, colloquial. It's the most artificial ever known. I've taken long railway journeys and spent them saying the letters of the alphabet aloud so as to make my vowels strike out. Then they forget I'm an Irishman – I think quicker than the English. No I don't mug things up – when I write history I don't read it. I imagine the sort of things people would have done and then I say they did them and then I find out facts – one always can – that prove it. The great pleasure of the Broadcasting to me is that I can sit at home and conduct the *Meistersinger* myself. I sit with the book of the score and conduct and I'm furious when they don't follow me." He is never still a moment – he clenches his fists – he flings himself this way and that; he sprang up to go, as if he were twenty-two, not seventy-four, as L. remarked. What life, what vitality! What immense nervous spring! That perhaps is his genius. Immense vivacity – and why I don't read him for pleasure. His face is bright red; his nose lumpy; his eyes sea green like a sailor's or a cockatoo's. He doesn't much notice who's there.

I heard Maynard say to Mrs Shaw "Well, we're about as bad as we can be. Never been so bad. We may go over the edge – but as its never been like this, nobody knows" – which was uttered in the low tone of a doctor saying a man was dying in the next room; but didn't want to disturb the company. This referred to the state of Europe, while we lunched – very well too.

Saturday 4 June
And last night we stopped the car in Hyde Park and I watched a people on the verge of ruin. How many Rolls Royces, and other low, pink, yellow, very powerful cars weren't booming through the park like giant dorbeetles, with luxurious owners, men and women, lying back, on their way to some party. A Rolls Royce means £5000 a year. Then the children in perambulators with nurses. Then the strollers and saunterers, that cloudy, rainy, thunder yellow evening. So back through the West End – more cars blocked; and we on the edge of a precipice.

Monday 13 June
Back from a good week-end at Rodmell – a week end of no talking, sinking at once into deep safe book reading; and then sleep: with the may tree like a breaking wave outside; and never a person to be seen, never an interruption: the place to ourselves: the long hours. Last week was such a scrimmage: oh so many people. Now Vita rings up: may she and Harold dine tonight; then Ethel; I look ahead to my fortnight's week end.

Saturday 18 June
John stays, on a revised basis, as adviser; and I am to consult and help him more, and not to sit here "with a red cross on your door, so that I daren't come in". My advice is that he shall be more malleable, and less pernickety. He craves influence and authority, to publish the books of his friends; wishes to start a magazine; is poor; must economise. Am I too aloof – partly so as not to chatter, partly to get to my own work? Ought one to be more sympathetic; but oh so many people to see and things to fit in already; nevertheless I'll try, if the new method is to be tried. He says Leonard is "so deep: and plans things; and never comes out at once with what he means; so that I don't know how to behave". I daresay we've spent ten hours talking about all this.

Nessa and Duncan's private view, Agnews.

Tuesday 28 June
I am trying to keep pace with the days and deliver the second *Common Reader* done on the last day of June – which I see with dismay is Thursday. It blazes, swoons, the heat. So hot yesterday – so hot.

Wednesday 6 July
Today is Wednesday and the *Common Reader* I confess is not yet quite done. But then – well, I had to re-write the last article, which I had thought so good, entirely. Many many people, too, and parties still to be transacted. These days have been very hot and busy.

Friday 8 July
And so I fainted, at the Ivy [Restaurant]: and had to be led out by Clive. A curious sensation. Feeling it come on; sitting still and fading out; then Clive by my side and a woman with salts. And the odd liberation of emotion in the cab with Clive; and the absolute delight of dark and bed: after that stony rattling and heat and Frankie [Birrell] shouting, and things being churned up, removed.

Monday 11 July
I will take a new pen and a new page to record the fact which is now a fact that I have slipped a green rubber band round the *Common Reader*, second series, and there it lies, at 10 minutes to one, ready to take upstairs. There is no sense of glory; only of drudgery done. Now I'm taking a holiday.

Saturday 16 July
Stella Benson last night: as quiet, as controlled, white, drawn as usual, also deaf; with steady honest eyes; said she had been to a great many parties. "I just say nothing. I feel none of these people matters. They say how much they liked my book [*Tobit Transplanted*] . . . I was given a medal. The old gentleman couldn't remember what for. He pinned it on. I go back in August. I hate Hong Kong. They play games. At Government House they give you a slip of paper with names of games on it: you have to put a cross next the one you play. Sitting out is one. James and I choose that. So we sit out together." That was her style in a very weak but persistent voice; she coughs; and then goes on with a mild persistent patience. The light faded in the drawing room, and she sat there lying back, telling us in a very low voice about the slave trade in Hong Kong.

Thursday 21 July
Oh but I'm so tired – I sometimes think people can't know what they do to me when they ask me to 'see' them: how they hold me in the scorching light: how I dry and shrivel: how I lie awake at night longing for rest – this is true. But know that I'm to be pitchforked up into the light and the glare again next day. Mary [Hutchinson] yesterday; Ethel today; Adrian tomorrow; and Julia Strachey. Since Monday, Nessa, Angelica, Tom and Elizabeth Bowen; Katherine [Furse] and [Mary Parker] Follett. And my head aches; and my back; and I'm sapped; wilted. Never mind. I shall lie in the cool at Monks House.

Friday 22 July
I do not like Ethel when she is doing the powerful stunt – or whatever stunt it is: proclaiming that all is over; denouncing me; protesting her love; whipping up a scene; being august; despairing; melodramatic and wobbly and weak all at the same time. No I do not like it: and also I am bored. This is the old fashioned version of an emotional scene – the tactics are to leave the other person in a hole – where indeed I would willingly have been left. Its the superficiality of these things that disenchants one: her lust for emotion. Or so I felt.

Monks House, Rodmell

Friday 5 August

Yesterday L. came in to my room at breakfast and said Goldie is dead. One of those muddles apparently: had an operation, secretly, a week ago; Roger saw him on Tuesday; talked; supposed him to be recovering; he died suddenly that night, of an internal haemorrhage. These are the dismal details of the end of that fine charming spirit. At night L. and I talked of death again the second time this year; we may be like worms crushed by a motor car. There may be a reason; if so not one we, as human beings, can grasp. Goldie had some mystic belief.

And now we have been to Lewes races and seen the fat lady in black with parts of her person spilling over the shooting seat on which her bulk is so insecurely poised: seen the riff raff of sporting society all lined up in their cars with the dickies bulging with picnic baskets; heard the bark of bookies; and seen for a second the pounding straining horses with red faced jockeys lashing them pound by; and beyond, the downs this windy sunny day looked wild and remote; and I could rethink them into uncultivated land again.

So people will go on dying until we die, Leonard said. Lytton, Carrington, Goldie – all last August to be spoken to – or let go, alas, because of the many times one would see them. That is one of my results: not to let friends lapse. But what can one do? One has to follow one's bent – mine often to be moody, irritable, longing for solitude.

Wednesday 17 August

Shall I then describe how I fainted again? – That is the galloping horses got wild in my head last Thursday night as I sat on the terrace with L. We were watching the downs draw back into fine darkness after they had burnt like solid emerald all day. Now that was being softly finely veiled. And the white owl was crossing to fetch mice from the marsh. Then my heart leapt; and stopped; and leapt again; and I tasted that queer bitterness at the back of my throat; and the pulse leapt into my head and beat and beat, more savagely, more quickly. I am going to faint I said and slipped off my chair and lay on the grass. Oh no I was not unconscious. I was alive; but possessed with this struggling team in my head: galloping, pounding. I thought something will burst in my brain if this goes on. Slowly it muffled itself. I pulled myself up, and staggered, with what infinite difficulty and alarm, back back back – how long it seemed – to the house; and gained my room and fell on my bed. Then pain, as of childbirth; and then that too slowly faded; and I lay presiding, like a flickering light, like a most solicitous mother, over the shattered splintered fragments of my body. A very acute and unpleasant experience.

Saturday 20 August
A curious day in London yesterday. I said to myself, standing at L.'s window, 'Look at the present moment because its not been so hot for twenty-one years.' Coming back we had the car shut and the windscreen open – thus sat in a hot rough gale: the coolest place is the front seat of a car going at forty or fifty miles with the windscreen open. For ten days this heat has lasted. After my faint my head soon throbs: or so I think. I think, a little, of dying suddenly. And reflect well then go about eating and drinking and laughing and feeding the fish. Odd – the silliness one attributes to death – the desire one has to belittle it, and be found as Montaigne said, laughing with girls and good fellows.

Friday 2 September
After this the wind blew – but that's long past; and it is a sea fret today, as we had meant to go to Canterbury. As we had meant – but – behold Tom and Vivien [Eliot] – she wild as Ophelia – alas no Hamlet would love her, with her powdered spots, in white satin, L. said; Tom, poor man, all battened down as usual, prim, grey, making his kind jokes with her. Then her chops and changes. Where is my bag? Where – where – then a sudden amorous embrace for me – and so on: trailing about the garden – never settling – seizing the wheel of their car – suddenly telling Tom to drive – all of which he bears with great patience: feeling perhaps that his seven months of freedom draw near. In the middle of their tea the post came with an astonishing letter from John to say that he does not intend to carry out our agreement. He has left the Press. L. says he will send no answer. What could one say indeed? What a blessing! That egotistical young man with all his jealousies and vanities and ambitions, his weakness and changeableness, is no loss. But we – or L. has lost an infinity of time.

A happy lively summer this – and I enjoy my freak of writing *Flush*.

52 TAVISTOCK SQUARE, WCI

Sunday 2 October
Yes. I will allow myself a new nib. Odd how coming back here upsets my writing mood. We are off to Leicester tomorrow, to the Labour Party Conference. Then back to the fever of publishing. My *Common Reader* doesn't cause me a single tremor. I am reading D. H. Lawrence with the usual sense of frustration. I don't escape when I read him; what I want is

to be made free of another world. This Proust does. To me Lawrence is airless, confined: I don't want this, I go on saying. And the repetition of one idea. I don't want that either. I don't want 'a philosophy' in the least. I don't believe in other people's reading of riddles. What I enjoy (in his *Letters*) is the sudden visualisation; but I get no satisfaction from his explanations of what he sees. And then its harrowing: this panting effort after something; and 'I have £6.10 left' and then Government hoofing him out, like a toad; and banning his book; the brutality of civilised society to this panting agonised man: and how futile it was. All this makes a sort of gasping in his letters. Then too I don't like strumming with two fingers – and the arrogance. After all English has one million words: why confine yourself to six? and praise yourself for so doing. But its the preaching that rasps me. I mean its so barren; so easy; giving advice on a system. He died though at forty-five. And why does Aldous say he was an 'artist'? Art is being rid of all preaching: things in themselves; whereas Lawrence would only say what proved something. I haven't read him of course. But in the *Letters* he can't listen beyond a point; must give advice; get you in to the system too. Hence his mind's schoolboy tweaking and smacking of anyone offered to him: Lytton, Bertie [Russell], Squire – His ruler coming down and measuring them. Why all this criticism of other people? Why not some system that includes the good?

Thursday 13 October
It was an odd sight – Desmond with Rachel on his arm. Everybody stood up. The white and red procession with the cross in front went ahead. Then very small, smooth, pale and sleek appeared Rachel and Desmond arm in arm. I have never seen him as a father. Now he was that – gentle, kind – leading his daughter. She was a wax work – with her diamond cross; very pale; very small; carrying a white book. Oh but the inadequacy of the service – the sense of its being the entirely obsolete and primitive voice of a defunct tribal magnate, laying down laws for the government of the tribe: and then these civilised sceptical people letting themselves pretend that they obey. That clogged and diluted all the real feeling. And David [Cecil]'s high collar and tails: and their sober decorous backs kneeling there: and the respectability and the wavering watery music: the perpetual compromise. The ceremony went decorously forward in that grey brown church [St Bartholomew the Great]. Now and then one heard a shout from the market. No I don't like the ceremony – oh I wanted some rapture – some precious stone to hold. None. None.

Today *The Common Reader* is out and I haven't given it a thought, being entirely absorbed in my Essay, which I began yesterday. But I still see the two doll figures kneeling – for all the world like a picture – what do I mean? I'm too sleepy to say. And now for Spender.

Wednesday 2 November
He [Stephen Spender] is a rattle headed bolt eyed young man, raw boned, loose jointed, who thinks himself the greatest poet of all time. I daresay he is – its not a subject that interests me enormously at the moment. What does? My own writing of course. I have entirely remodelled my 'Essay'. Its to be an Essay-Novel, called *The Pargiters* – and its to take in everything, sex, education, life &c; and come, with the most powerful and agile leaps, like a chamois across precipices, from 1880 to here and now. That's the notion anyhow, and I have been in such a haze and dream and intoxication, declaiming phrases, seeing scenes, as I walk up Southampton Row that I can hardly say I have been alive at all, since the 10th October. Everything is running of its own accord into the stream, as with *Orlando*. Then of course, being so excited, all this incandescence led to the galloping horses in my heart the night before last. I lay in bed reasoning that I could not come smash. Death I defy you, &c. But it was a terrific effort, holding on to the reins. So at 2.30 I woke L. and asked, very reasonably, for ice, which he got me. And my horses calmed down – he was so sensible. But Ellie [Dr Rendel] came yesterday and says I am putting a strain on my heart; so I take this as permission not to go to parties, not to do anything I dislike. And that's a great discovery. I think I shall have thus a very reasonable happy winter, writing *The Pargiters*, but for God's sake, I must be careful.

Thursday 10 November
A queer thing that Ott should come, after all these years, old, shabby, tender, to my sofa; and I liked her; its her integrity that's sloppy; that's what we all slipped on. Can't tell the truth about love – but then that's so interesting, and not discreditable, considering her upbringing – Welbeck, the young men servants. So she lent me her memoirs, full as they are of love letters, and copulation. I must now write to her.

Saturday 17 December
I have precisely four minutes before luncheon in which to record Rebecca West at dinner – oh yes a very clever woman, rather rubbed about the thorax; with a great supply of worldly talk; and much go and humour; a silky careening society voice; flowers from her afterwards to apologise for staying till 1.30. And then – oh ever so many people; and a wind up with L.'s family and then the Frys to dinner; and so to Rodmell on Tuesday.

Monday 19 December

Yes, today I have written myself to the verge of total extinction. By Heaven, I have written 60,320 words since October 11th. I think this must be far the quickest going of any of my books. But then those 60 thousand will have to be sweated and dried into 30 or 40 thousand – a great grind to come. Never mind. I have secured the outline and fixed a shape for the rest. I feel, for the first time, No I mustn't take risks crossing the road, till the book is done.

A very fruitful, varied and I think successful autumn – thanks partly to my tired heart: so I could impose terms; and I have never lived in such a race, such a dream, such a violent impulsion and compulsion – scarcely seeing anything but *The Pargiters*.

MONKS HOUSE, RODMELL

Friday 23 December

I must write off my dejected rambling misery – having just read over the 30,000 words of *Flush* and come to the conclusion that they won't do. Oh what a waste – what a bore! Four months of work, and heaven knows how much reading – not of an exalted kind either – and I can't see how to make anything of it. L. will be disappointed; and the money loss too – that's a bore. I took it up impetuously after *The Waves* by way of a change: no forethought in me; and so got landed; it would need a month's hard work – and even then I doubt it. And I'm thus led to end the year with a doleful plaint.

Saturday 31 December

I am so tired of polishing off *Flush* that I am taking a morning off, and shall use it here, in my lazy way, to sum up the whole of life. By that phrase I only mean I wish I could deliver myself of a picture of all my friends, thoughts, doings, projects at this moment. Vita is on the high seas, sailing to America. Our new car came, vicariously, yesterday – we are lent one. And I had a long letter from Ottoline, of sheer affection, and one still longer from Ethel Smyth, of dubious jealousy and suppressed temper and love strangled and out-bursting. And [Boris] Anrep wants to put me on the floor of the Bank of England as Clio, and – cards, thanks, catalogues of winter sales. And we shall be here till the 14th of January. And the dew pond is filling; the gold fish are dead; it is a clear pale blue eyed winter's day; and – and – and – my thoughts turn with excitement to *The Pargiters*, for I long to feel my sails blow out, and to be careering with Elvira, Maggie and the rest over the whole of human life.

And indeed I cannot sum this up, being tired in my head. I think of Lytton too. Yes, of course this autumn has been a tremendous revelation. It was a great season of liberation. Well – it is always doubtful how far one human being can be free. However, I secured a season of intoxicating exhilaration. Nor do I intend to let myself pay for it with the usual black despair. I intend.to circumvent that supervening ghost – that which always trails its damp wings behind my glories. I shall be very wary. To suppress oneself and run freely out in joy – such is the perfectly infallible and simple prescription. And to use one's hands and eyes; to talk to people; to be a straw on the river, now and then – passive, not striving to say this is this. If one does not lie back and sum up and say to the moment, this very moment, Stay you are so fair, what will be one's gain, dying? No: stay, this moment. No one ever says that enough. I am now going in, to see L. and say Stay this moment.

1933

From January until April Vita Sackville-West and her husband were away on a
lecture tour of America; Ethel Smyth's attempts to supplant her in Virginia's affections
became increasingly intrusive and, though her visits could not always be evaded,
Virginia for the most part fended her off by letter, pleading headache, absence, or
other engagements. But for once she was not ill during the early months of the year,
and was very fully occupied with her work and a lively social programme – so
occupied indeed that she wrote no diary for five weeks in February and March. 'That
silly book Flush' was finally polished off, sent to the printer in January, and the
proofs corrected after Easter; it was published in October, having already been selected
by the Book Society and the Book-of-the-Month-Club in New York, thus ensuring
considerable sales. But The Pargiters was Virginia's chief preoccupation throughout
the year, varied by reading and preparing an article on Goldsmith for the TLS. In
March another academic distinction – an Honorary Degree of Doctor of Letters –
was offered to Virginia by Manchester University, and again declined on the grounds
that she was opposed to writers accepting honours.

The celebrated German–Jewish conductor Bruno Walter, introduced by Ethel
Smyth, came to see the Woolfs in April; his passionate account, recorded by Virginia,
of the evils of the Nazi régime (Hitler had become Chancellor of Germany in January)
is her only reference to the growing menace of totalitarianism on the continent. But
Fascist Italy held no terrors for the Woolfs; on 5 May they set off in their new car
to drive through France to Siena and back, taking three weeks in all, an experience
the more enjoyable since Virginia had been learning Italian and was thus able to
talk to the people they encountered.

The summer in London was the usual mixture of work, duty (loyalty to Margaret
Llewelyn Davies took Virginia to the Jubilee Congress of the Women's Co-operative
Guild; family loyalty to visit her ailing half-brother Sir George Duckworth), lunch
and dinner parties, 'seeing' people, weekends at Rodmell, to where she and Leonard
removed for ten weeks at the end of July. Here it was much the same in a different
setting – more people: an American authoress, the family, Vita, Ethel Smyth, E. M.
Forster and T. S. Eliot, lately returned from America and separated from his wife;
and others. Virginia's response to this country life fluctuated between delight and
dejection, energy and exhaustion.

They returned to London and a busy publishing season, and this time Leonard
fell ill. Once again Virginia concluded that the Hogarth Press claimed too much of

their energies and should be given up; but it survived. Another illness took them to Croydon Airport, when they drove Vanessa and her younger son Quentin to catch an aeroplane, still an exceptional means of travel, for Switzerland where he was to spend months in a clinic for tubercular patients. Dining out with the Hutchinsons, Virginia observed the best-selling author Michael Arlen; and another dinner party, given by Clive Bell for her to meet Walter Sickert, was the outcome of a letter of admiration she wrote him after seeing an exhibition of his pictures; he responded by suggesting she should write about him, which she undertook to do. On 21 December the Woolfs went to Rodmell for Christmas.

1933

Monks House, Rodmell

Thursday 5 January
I am so delighted with my own ingenuity in having after only ten years or
so made myself, in five minutes, a perfect writing board, with pen tray
attached – and besides I'm so glad to be quit of page 100 of *Flush* – that I
can't help disporting myself on this free blue page, which thank God in
heaven, needs no re-writing. It is a wet misty day; and I daresay we shall
drive our new car twenty miles or so this afternoon, by way of a test. It is
like travelling first instead of third.

Sunday 15 January
I have come out here, our last morning, to write letters, so, naturally, I
write this book. But then I haven't written a line these three weeks – only
typed *Flush*, which, Heaven be praised, I 'finished', almost without inverted
commas, yesterday. Ah but my writing *Flush* has been gradually shoved
out, as by a cuckoo born in the nest, by *The Pargiters*. How odd the mind's
functions are! About a week ago, I began the making up of scenes –
unconsciously: saying phrases to myself; and so, for a week, I've sat here,
staring at the typewriter, and speaking aloud phrases of *The Pargiters*. This
becomes more and more maddening. It will however all be run off in a few
days, when I let myself write again.

52 Tavistock Square, wc1

Thursday 19 January
We began London briskly. [William] Plomer and Marjorie [Strachey] to
dine; and we went to Sadler's Wells and saw *Pomona* with Nessa's designs
– dresses, scenery – all very pale and bright – I mean Fra Angelico against
a background of Cassis – but dear (said to be from dieu) knows I can't keep
my wits at the ballet; can't throw a ring round so many wild horses – music,
dancing, decoration; and so hop on my perch, and merely make parrot

noises of appreciation – when, at Fitzroy Street [Vanessa's studio], we all had hot sausages. Roger was there – is he older, less volatile? He makes his signal to Helen sooner than of old and drives off in that blind bull of a car – but not before, as I maliciously observed, he had cross-questioned me about his lectures. This insistent egotism has its charm. I never asked him to read my essays.

Saturday 21 January
Well, *Flush* lingers on and I cannot despatch him. That's the sad truth. I always see something I could press tighter, or enwrap more completely. There's no trifling with words – can't be done: not when they're to stand 'for ever'. So I am battening down my *Pargiters* say till Wednesday – it shan't be later, I swear.

Thursday 26 January
Well, *Flush* is, I swear, despatched. Nobody can say I don't take trouble with my little stories. And now, having bent my mind for five weeks sternly this way, I must unbend them the other – the Pargiter way. No critic ever gives full weight to the desire of the mind for change. Now if I ever had the wits to go into the Shakespeare business I believe one would find the same law there – tragedy, comedy, and so on.

I think the Beau Monde has given me up; so I say I will rout further in the bran pie; and go to my Club and meet young working women. I am going to learn Italian.

Thursday 2 February
No we are not deserted by the world – oh dear no. And Galsworthy died two days ago, it suddenly struck me, walking just now by the Serpentine after calling on Mrs Woolf (who's been dying – is recovering). Galsworthy's dead; and Arnold Bennett told me he simply couldn't stick Galsworthy. That stark man lies dead.

Friday 17 February
I steal time from my Italian verbs. Yes I think I know them. I am having two lessons weekly from Bianca; she suggests three; but as I have to get in Ethel &c. Oh yesterday it was like being a snail shell and having a thrush tapping till the beak of her incessant voice broke my skull. And now she goes to Bath for five weeks – yes, to my relief I own. Because I can't bear being a snail shell. And she is so positive, so insistent. Being Ethel is so habitual to her.

I'm launched again in *The Pargiters*, in this blank season of the year – Nessa at Charleston, Clive in Jamaica, Roger in Tangier, Vita in America

– which of my friends is left? But Desmond dined the night before last; Morgan came in last night; [Winifred] Holtby today – so there's no lack of people.

Saturday 25 March

It is an utterly corrupt society I have just remarked, speaking in the person of Elvira Pargiter, and I will take nothing that it can give me &c &c; now, as Virginia Woolf, I have to write – oh dear me what a bore – to the Vice Chancellor of Manchester University and say that I refuse to be made a Doctor of Letters. Lord knows how I'm to put Elvira's language into polite journalese. What an odd coincidence! that real life should provide precisely the situation I was writing about! Nothing would induce me to connive at all that humbug. Nor would it give me, even illicitly, any pleasure. I really believe that Nessa and I are without the publicity sense. Now for the polite letters. Dear Vice Chancellor –

Tuesday 28 March

The polite letters have been sent. So far I have had, nor could have had any answer. No, thank Heaven, I need not emerge from my fiction in July to have a tuft of fur put on my head.

It is the finest spring ever known – soft, hot, blue, misty. Dinner with Lady Rhondda. I felt her a disappointed woman. Should have had ten children perhaps. She was sitting alone, shawled, dowdy, in an old Hampstead flat with a garden with great trees. She is what they call, I expect, 'inhibited' – something tentative, furtive. Discussed *Time & Tide*. She lives for *Time & Tide*. Then on to Clive; back from Jamaica. "The steward came in; and was surprised to find a young lady stark naked brushing her teeth." True Clive.

Thursday 6 April

Oh I'm so tired! I've written myself out over *The Pargiters* this last lap. This is a time of ending. I've ever so many people to see. Ott tomorrow. The people of Manchester have written, very politely, with additional respect for me, because I don't take honours. Nessa and the others at Charleston. Last night Lord Olivier, a jolly old bore, has been a dog in his day, dined here. And Pippa came in later – grown very thick, but looks unhappy.

Thursday 13 April

No I have worked myself too dry this time. There is not one idea left in the orange. But we go [to Rodmell] today, and I shall sun, with only a few books. No I will *not* write; I will *not* see people. But indeed I can't find words – use the wrong ones – that's my state: the familiar state after these three months writing – what fun that book is to me! And pressing in Italian, and seeing a mint of people – that state I say is quite familiar; and will vanish; yes, and then there's Italy to come. I have my new corduroys. And Ethel is 'cutting the painter' (between us – for the hundredth time).

Tuesday 25 April

No, we didn't see nobody at Rodmell. Lydia and Maynard arrived before we had been there half an hour; and we dined with them. That's all over – our ten days. Yes; I should now be correcting *Flush* proofs – I doubt that little book to some extent: but I'm in a doubting mood: the scrambled mood of transience, for on Friday 5th we go to Siena; so I can't settle.

But *The Pargiters*. I think this will be a terrific affair. I must be bold and adventurous. I want to give the whole of the present society – nothing less: facts, as well as the vision. And to combine them both. I mean, *The Waves* going on simultaneously with *Night and Day*. Is this possible? And there are to be millions of ideas but no preaching – history, politics, feminism, art, literature – in short a summing up of all I know, feel, laugh at, despise, like, admire, hate and so on.

Friday 28 April

We got out of the car last night and began walking down to the Serpentine. A summer evening. Chestnuts in their crinolines, bearing tapers; grey green water and so on. Suddenly L. bore off; and there was Shaw, dwindled shanks, white beard; striding along. We talked, by a railing, for fifteen minutes. He stood with his arms folded, very upright, leaning back; teeth gold tipped. Very friendly. That is his art, to make one think he likes one. A great spurt of ideas. "You forget that an aeroplane is like a car – it bumps – We went over the Great Wall. I caught the Chinese looking at us with horror – that we should be human beings! Of course the tour cost thousands; yet to see us, you'd think we hadn't the price of the fare to Hampton Court. Oh but my publicity! Its terrifying. An hour's bombardment at every port. I found myself on a platform with the whole university round me. They began shouting We want Bernard Shaw. So I told them that every man at twenty-one must be a revolutionary. After that of course the police imprisoned them by dozens. Oh I could only stand the voyage by writing. I've written three or four books. I like to give the public full weight. Books should be sold by the pound. What a nice little dog. But aren't I keeping you and making you cold" (touching my arm). Two men stopped along the path to look. Off he strode again on his dwindled legs. I said Shaw likes us. L. thinks he likes nobody. What will they think of Shaw in fifty years? He is seventy-six he said; too old for the tropics.

Saturday 29 April
Last night – to relieve myself for a moment from correcting that silly book *Flush* – oh what a waste of time – I will record Bruno Walter. He is a swarthy, fattish, man; not at all smart. Not at all the 'great conductor'. He is a little Slav, a little semitic. He is very nearly mad; that is, he can't get 'the poison' as he called it of Hitler out of him. "You must not think of the Jews" he kept on saying; "You must think of this awful reign of intolerance. You must think of the whole state of the world. It is terrible – terrible. That this meanness, that this pettiness, should be possible! Our Germany – which I loved – with our tradition – our culture – We are now a disgrace." Then he told us how you can't talk above a whisper. There are spies everywhere. He had to sit in the window of his hotel in Leipzig a whole day, telephoning. All the time soldiers were marching. They never stop marching. And on the wireless, between the turns, they play military music. Horrible horrible! He hopes for the monarchy as the only hope. He will never go back there. We must band together. We must refuse to meet any German. We must say that they are uncivilised. We will not trade with them or play with them – we must make them feel themselves outcasts – not by fighting them; by ignoring them. Then he swept off to music. He has the intensity – genius? – which makes him live everything he feels. Described conducting: must know every player.

* * *

52 TAVISTOCK SQUARE, WC1

Tuesday 30 May
Yes but of all things coming home from a holiday is undoubtedly the most damned. Never was there such aimlessness, such depression. Can't read, write or think. There's no climax here. Comfort yes: but the coffee's not so good as I expected. And my brain is extinct – literally hasn't the power to lift a pen. What one must do is to set it – my machine I mean – on the rails and give it a push. Lord – how I pushed yesterday to make it start running along Goldsmith again. There's that half finished article. Lord Salisbury said something about dished up speeches being like the cold remains of last night's supper. I see white grease on the pages of my article. Today it's a little warmer – tepid meat: a slab of cold mutton. It occurs to me that this stage, my depressed state, is the state in which most people usually are.

Wednesday 31 May
I think I have now got to the point where I can write for four months straight ahead at *The Pargiters*. Oh the relief – the physical relief! I feel as

if I could hardly any longer keep back – that my brain is being tortured by always butting against a blank wall – I mean *Flush*, Goldsmith, motoring through Italy; now, tomorrow, I mean to run it off. And suppose only nonsense comes? I'm disoriented completely after four weeks holiday – no three – but tomorrow we go to Rodmell again.

I thought, driving through Richmond last night, something very profound about the synthesis of my being: how only writing composes it; how nothing makes a whole unless I am writing; now I have forgotten what seemed so profound. Oh the agitation, oh the discomfort of this mood.

Tuesday 20 June
It is a very ugly thing, a ceremony. I detest them more and more. This refers to my waste of a morning at the W[omen's] C[o-operative] G[uild] Jubilee today. Margaret and Lilian, in grey blue and coffee colour – how characteristic! – presented a banner. The great hall full. The women all in pinks and blues. Fine old housekeepers; massive; determined. Now and then a great laugh; and very queer accents. But all was ceremony; and they say things that aren't true: they say we are on the brink of a new world; they talk of the triumph of co-operation. That's why I hate ceremonies – not a word that fits – all wind blown, gaseous, with elementary emotions. Years ago I got something out of the mere conglomeration, the stir, the multitude. But today, I was not annihilated, dispersed; I said to myself *The Pargiters* is more real, truer, harder, more veined with blood than all this, and longed to be back, working. How odd to spend a morning merely vacant, regardant! How many I spend concentrated! Then we shook, and smiled with others intervening, Margaret's, Lilian's hands; and found a back way out.

Monday 26 June
The present moment. 7 o'clock on June 26th: L. printing; hot; thunderous; I after reading *Henry IV Part I* saying what's the use of writing; reading, imperfectly, a poem by Leopardi; the present moment, in my studio. A bucket banged in the mews; dog barks; woman, 'I didn't know if you were out here.' Leaves door open; far away horns; a bee buzzing. King lays stone of London University. Doctors, scarlet, purple, in streets; poor little students in gowns; so to dine, and read; and music; thunder, I daresay; and so to open my windows, and go up: the moment done.

Thursday 6 July
Dinner at Roger's yesterday. Company: Sacheverell Sitwells, [Gerald] Brenans, Oliver [Strachey]. I sat next Georgia [Sitwell] and Roger. Talk of patent medicines. 'And then I found it was an aphrodisiac' Georgia says.

She buys every patent medicine, by way of sedative. Bounds, abounds, halloos dogs on the lawn: brown chocolate eyed; vital as they say, not intellectual. Made the salad with cheese. Mrs Brenan said to be sympathetic and soft and amusing by L. All chatter. Stayed late. Not much satisfaction – yet amusing enough, as such things are.

Also to sit with George [Duckworth] – a solid mound in pink pyjamas: Margaret tender and solicitous; given eau de Cologne; also Roger's show. Two days of misery writing Goldsmith, forced respite from *Pargiters*.

Friday 7 July
Being headachy after *Pargiters* and Goldsmith and ever so many people I have spent the whole morning reading old diaries, and am now (ten to one) much refreshed. This is by way of justifying these many written books. And we have a party tonight – Wests, Hutchinsons, Plomer – so I need rest my head. The diary amuses me.

Monday 10 July
And then I was in 'one of my states' – how violent, how acute, and walked in Regent's Park in black misery and had to summon my cohorts in the old way to see me through, which they have done more or less. A note made to testify to my old ups and downs; many of which go unrecorded though they are less violent I think than they used to be. But how familiar it was – stamping along the road, with gloom and pain constricting my heart; and the desire for death in the old way all for two, I daresay careless words.

It seems possible that Tom has finally deserted Vivien. Jack Hutch came to our frosty sticky party, with the meticulous fish blooded cultivated Andrews – Rebecca [West (Mrs Andrews)] merely a hard painted woman, that night, living in society – and Hutch told us how Vivien has heard by cable that Tom sailed [from America] on 26th and he has not arrived. She has by today worked herself into frenzy – in bed, with a nurse; and then Jack telephoned to Faber [Eliot's publisher] – L.'s idea – and they say mysteriously that they cannot discuss the matter on the telephone, but if Vivien will pull herself together she will realise that there is no reason for anxiety. This we interpret to mean that Tom is back; has told Faber that he is parting from her; but it is kept secret until he gives leave – which he may do today. I should expect that after his six months thought and absence he has decided to make the break here: has warned Vivien and provided for her. But she shuts the letters in the cupboard with the sealed string. L. is made her executor.

Thursday 20 July

This was quite a correct statement of the Eliot position. He has left her 'irrevocably'; and she sits meanwhile in a flat decorated with pictures of him, and altars, and flowers. We dine with the Hutchinsons tonight, and shall I expect found some sort of Vivien fund. It is said that there is a convent next door to Mary in which she might pass her days, praying for Tom.

I am again in full flood with *The Pargiters* after a week of very scanty pages.

MONKS HOUSE, RODMELL

Sunday 30 July

Settled in here again. A question how far places influence one's mood. Certain thoughts I always think: the downs spoilt, could we move, &c, leading to a well known round. Quentin ill with pleurisy; may have to have an operation. This is the first illness at Charleston. We dine there tonight. But I am organising life here, and so far rather well. Reading and walking and swimming into lucid depths, powerfully – that's how I put it. And people impend, but can be shelved for the moment.

Tuesday 8 August

Since we came here I have been twice to Charleston; seen the Keyneses; been to Worthing; had Elizabeth Read (a nice shrewd hard girl with a public mind) to tea; the Easedales and Norman Stewart (a clever, good fellow, scientist) to tea; expect Mrs Nef at three to discuss her scandalous memoirs; we go to London on Friday and Ethel comes on Sunday. Is this peace? I'm heavy brained today – its been so hot; I have read Mrs Nef from 10 to 12.20. Scandals about USA: but I am sworn to secrecy. I imagine a pretty youngish jumpy intellectual-fashionable American, completely disoriented; writes rather well; interesting; but all at sea.

Saturday 12 August

So naturally after Mrs Nef I was so tired – I shivered and shook. I went to bed for two days and slept I daresay seven hours, visiting the silent realms again. It strikes me – what are these sudden fits of complete exhaustion? I come in here to write: can't even finish a sentence; and am pulled under; now is this the sub-conscious pulling me down into her? the refusal of some part of the mechanism? Not quite. Because I'm not evading anything. I long to write *The Pargiters*. No. I think the effort to live in two spheres: the novel; and life; is a strain; Nefs almost break me, because they strain me so far from the other world; I only want walking and perfectly spontaneous childish life with L. and the accustomed when I'm writing at full tilt; to have to behave with circumspection and decision to strangers wrenches me into another region; hence the collapse.

Thursday 24 August

A week ago, having got my wind again, I dipped into *The Pargiters*, and determined to sweat it bare of flesh before going on, accumulating more scenes. I am rearranging too, all the first part, so as to bring it together. The death happens in the first chapter now. I have just killed Mrs Pargiter and can't shoot ahead to Oxford. For the truth is these little scenes embroil one, just as in life; and one can't switch off to a different mood all in a second. And now I have spent the morning reading the *Confessions* of Arsène Houssaye left here yesterday by Clive. What a vast fertility of pleasure books hold for me! I think I could happily live here and read forever. It is true, we have many interruptions. Yesterday, after knocking against a wild Alsatian that ran into the car – we gave him a great bang – he lay squirming – dead, I thought, then reeled up and went galloping over the field, unhurt, though he broke our lamps and bent the mudguard – after this unpleasant shock, Clive came and Julian and Frances Marshall, and played bowls. Still, we see too many people, to my view: the Kingsley Martins, who are to me mentally and physically unattractive people; she is ugly, stringy, earnest, plain. Kingsley eats so sloppily. And they force themselves upon us. Into the bargain, I have heard from Tom. Tom is all artifice and quips and quirks. A defence. One of these days perhaps he'll give up the trick, with marriage, or perhaps religion. All the same, our quiet days, in between times, are rightly balanced, full of peace, and possibilities. How happy, when people go, to get our dinner, and sit alone, and go to bed in my airy room, where the rising sun on the apples and asparagus wakes me, if I leave the curtain open. A happy day today without visitors.

Sunday 27 August

[Yesterday] morning we went in and found Lewes in festival – the corporation fidgetting about on a doorstep covered in dull red: the local tradesmen habited in blue robes with thin strips of fur, because the troops were coming, on their economy march to Arundel. We ran into them; dirty men in shirtsleeves, marching, with the flaps of their caps let down over their necks, it was so hot. The natives of Lewes stood at the bottom of Station Street waving handkerchiefs, bobbing their umbrellas up and down. Not an inspiring sight – the British army.

And I forgot to say that *Flush* has been chosen by the American Book Society. Lord!

Wednesday 30 August

And two days ago, sitting in the garden at Charleston, Clive in his queer jerky way said he had very bad news of Francis Birrell and brought out a letter from Raymond [Mortimer]. Francis has a tumour on his brain and is to be operated on, perhaps, today. So all night I dreamt of him, my dream giving me, as my dreams often do, the essence of a relationship which in real life will never find expression. I remember sitting beside him on a sofa, and how we kissed and kissed, as friends; though in my dream I do not think that I knew he was ill. I am rather haunted by it. Think of waiting all yesterday, for an operation which may well be fatal. What should I have felt had I been him? And why was I not him? The sense of friends dying is a very terrible one.

Saturday 2 September

With that usual dread of asking for news on the telephone, I rang up Raymond on Thursday and heard to my extreme relief, that Francis's case is not so bad nearly as it seemed. The growth is small, thought to be on the outside, and there seems no reason why he should not recover. Curious how all one's fibres seem to expand and fill with air when anxiety is taken off; curious also to me the intensity of my own feelings: I think imagination, the picture making power, decks up feelings with all kinds of scenes, so that one goes on thinking, instead of localising the event. All very mysterious. But anyhow I expanded, and felt very fond of that dear old rattling milk lorry, and hoped he would see me out. But let us think no more of death. Its life that matters, to quote my quotation from Montaigne.

Suddenly in the night I thought of 'Here and Now' as a title for *The Pargiters*.

L. is having the new pond made, the old one re-grouted, and is going to pave the front garden. *Flush*, I think with some pleasure, has made these extravagances possible.

I am reading with extreme greed a book by Vera Brittain, called *The Testament of Youth*. Not that I much like her. But her story, told in detail, without reserve, of the war, and how she lost lover and brother, and dabbled her hands in entrails, and was forever seeing the dead, and eating scraps, and sitting five on one WC, runs rapidly, vividly across my eyes. A very good book of its sort. The new sort, the hard anguished sort, that the young write; that I could never write. Nor has anyone written that kind of book before. Why now? What urgency is there on them to stand bare in public? She feels that these facts must be made known, in order to help – what? Herself partly I suppose. And she has the social conscience. But I give her credit for having lit up a long passage to me at least. I read and read and read.

Sunday 10 September
Why am I sitting here at 10.30 on a Sunday morning, writing diary, not
novel? Because of dear old Tom largely. Twenty-four hours (short interval
for sleep) solid conversation, preluded by two hours flimsy conversation
with the Hutchinsons. And at 1.30 Rosamond [Lehmann] and Wogan
[Philipps, her husband] to lunch; and at 4.30 Charleston to tea. Hence I am
sitting here. Tomorrow, in the divine peace of Monday, I shall walk on the
downs and think of Tom and my parched lips with some degree of pleasure.
He is ten years younger: hard, spry, a glorified boy scout in shorts and
yellow shirt. He is enjoying himself very much. He is tight and shiny as a
wood louse (I am not writing for publication). But there is well water in
him, cold and pure. Yes I like talking to Tom. But his wing sweeps curved
and scimitar-like round to the centre, himself. He's settling in with some
severity to being a great man. At forty-six he wants to live, to love; he has
seen nothing, nobody, for the last ten years. We had it out about Vivien at
breakfast. Some asperity on Tom's part. He won't admit the excuse of
insanity for her – thinks she puts it on. I thought him a little resentful of
all the past waste and exaction. I gather he will see a good deal of us. And
we agreed about the infamy of teaching English; the idiocy of lectures; the
whole hierarchy of professor, system and so on; at any rate I got him to
go some way with me in denouncing Oxford and Cambridge. He learnt (1)
self confidence at Oxford; (2) how to write plain English – that's all. I
daresay though he will become Professor of Poetry at Oxford one of these
days. His father was a brick merchant in St Louis; and they lived in the
slums among vacant lots; and his father always gave away money; and
died, alas, in 1919 before Tom had become – well, happily his mother lived
to see him what she called (and I daresay Tom too) a great man.

Saturday 23 September
This summer, I may say by way of criticism, and as a warning, has been
too broken up with people. Next year I intend to be more circumspect. For
the past fortnight I have lived, I say, as other people live – that is outwardly.
And it is a thorough wet day. The ponds are filling. L.'s new pond and
garden are almost done, and surprisingly good, I think. The summer is put
away folded up in the drawer with other summers. By God's grace we may
get ten or twelve days without visitors before going back, but I say this
not with conviction. The truth is, I like it when people actually come; but
I love it when they go. Old Ethel came, grown stout. And we go to Brighton
today to meet Morgan, and I shall read my memoir tonight, and so consider
myself quit of all duties to my friends. Monday begins my holiday.

Tuesday 26 September

I had so much of the most profound interest to write here – a dialogue of the soul with the soul – and I have let it all slip – why? Because of feeding the gold fish, of looking at the new pond, of playing bowls. Nothing remains now. I forget what It was about. Happiness. The perfect day, which was yesterday. And so on.

Monday 2 October

Yes. I had to write about the Memoir Club. Then they all came over, and we sat on the terrace; eleven people here. That's all over. Its October now; and we have to go to Hastings [Labour Party] Conference tomorrow and Wednesday, to Vita, and then back to London. I opened this book in order to make one of my self-admonishments previous to publishing a book. *Flush* will be out on Thursday and I shall be very much depressed, I think, by the kind of praise. They'll say its 'charming', delicate, ladylike. And it will be popular. Well now I must let this slip over me without paying it any attention. I must concentrate on *The Pargiters*.

Saturday 7 October

And now, letters, packing, going from the lodge to the house; a damp dull day so far, but it will clear. A very crowded gay summer in its way. Too crowded; but what happiness, coming back that night from London with L. for example: the country at midnight. And going up early; and bowls; and our solitary evenings; and cooking dinner.

52 TAVISTOCK SQUARE, WC1

Monday 9 October

Back again and our burden is on us. Mrs Woolf yesterday; today David Cecil; tomorrow Nessa Quentin Julian lunch; Hugh Walpole tea; Thursday Vita and [her sister-in-law] Mrs St Aubyn; and so it begins, with Sibyl and Rosamond in the background. I'm through the *Flush* wave though. A small one, compared with others. Desmond praises; *Morning Post* tears me between the rough, coarse yellow feeble teeth of poor Mr Grigson. So its over.

Friday 20 October

Did I say I was going to write *Here and Now*? Not a word done. L. had influenza. Up and about in two days of course. But last night I came to the decision to stop the career of the Hogarth Press; to revert to Richmond days. What is the use of drudging and sweating and curtailing Siena and entirely obliterating all Italy England Ireland and Greece for the sake of publishing Susan Lawrence and bad novels? No. Here we stop and take a fresh course. We go to Rodmell tomorrow and I shall there broach the new scheme. Look, I can't write, can't hold a pen, for all the bother and the worry. Its true we've had the devil's own week. But to me the Press has lost its spring and balance, and could regain it if it now made a constriction to the old ideals. We might start the magazine.

Sunday 29 October
Yesterday the *Granta* said I was now defunct. *Orlando, Waves, Flush* represent the death of a potentially great writer. This is only a rain drop; I mean the snub some little pimpled undergraduate likes to administer, just as he would put a frog in one's bed. But enough. Raymond came yesterday: Francis is still very much paralysed.

Sunday 12 November
I ought to have made a note on Nessa and the aeroplane – last Friday week – at Croydon. We took them there at 7. Had to be up by moonlight at 6.30. Drove across an empty delicately tinted London; Croydon a great space like a green race course. We stood on the top of the roof; saw the aeroplane whirl, till the propellors were lost to sight – simply evaporated; then the aeroplane takes a slow run, circles and rises. This is death I said, feeling how the human contact was completely severed. Up they went with a sublime air and disappeared like a person dying, the soul going. And we remained. I saw the plane become a little mark on the sky.

Thursday 23 November
Being too tired after dining with the Hutches last night to meet Michael Arlen to produce the finished article in *Here and Now*, perhaps I had better produce the raw. It was a real party – that is I wore my velvet dress. But I took it in my stride. And I had – oh voluminously – all Michael Arlen's confession, as I expected. He made £50,000 out of *The Green Hat*, which money he has perpetually to atone for – as by talking of D. H. Lawrence, and how he escaped his influence, how he made his own life, how he married his own wife, a dumb Greek called Atalanta – silent, he said, but a perfect lady – and has two children and can keep them all, with drains, games, servants – all this is protest and justification. Now he is writing an intelligent novel, from real experience, lacking to highbrows. Yet oh Mrs Woolf how I envy Aldous Huxley his background – his education. I was at a third rate public school, and lived in Earl's Court. His father died of a broken heart when Roumania came into the war. A little scraping dingy porous clammy monkey faced man.

Wednesday 29 November
I think I've got rid of vanity: of Virginia. Oh what a riddance. I've not read
an article on me by a man called Peel in the *Criterion*. I feel this is a great
liberation. I have cut the string that ties me to that quivering bag of nerves –
all its gratifications and acute despair. One sees people lunging and
striking at a thing like a straw horse and its not me at all. I sit back in
comfort and look round. I wonder if Nessa has always been like this? It is
calming. It is dignified. One does not seek uneasily for opinions on oneself.

Thursday 7 December
I was walking through Leicester Square just now when I read Death of
Noted Novelist on the poster. And I thought of Hugh Walpole. But it is
Stella Benson. Then why write anything immediately? I did not know her,
but have a sense of those fine patient eyes; the weak voice; the cough; and
sense of oppression. She sat on the terrace with me at Rodmell. And now,
so quickly, it is gone, what might have been a friendship. Its like the
quenching of something – her death out there in China; and I sitting here,
and writing about her. How mournful the afternoon seems, with the
newspaper carts dashing up Kingsway – 'Death of Noted Novelist' on the
placard. A very fine steady mind; much suffering; suppressed. There seems
to be some sort of reproach to me in her death, as in Katherine Mansfield's.
I go on, and they cease. Why? Why not my name on the posters? And I
have a feeling of the protest each might make: gone with their work
unfinished – each so suddenly. Stella was forty-one. A dreary island, she
lived on, talking to Colonels.

Sunday 17 December
I finished part 4 of *Here and Now* yesterday – therefore indulge in a
contemplative morning. To freshen my memory of the war, I read some
old diaries. How close the tears come, again and again; as I read of L. and
me at The Green: our quarrels; how he crept into my bed with a little
purse, and so on; how we reckoned our income and I was given tea free
for a treat. The sense of all that floating away for ever down the stream,
unknown for ever: queer sense of the past swallowing so much of oneself.
And today we make a loop with the past by going in our grand car to see
Margaret and Lilian. Well we are very happy. I think we live very fully,
freely, and adventurously. In short, what we made of that strange prelude
is good.
I dined with Clive to meet Sickert the other night. Sickert is sunk and
old till warmed with wine. He scarcely eats. At last he expanded, and sang
a French song and kissed Nessa's hand – spontaneously; mine more
formally. I think a difficult old man probably. But the ingrained artist.

Laughter – extravagance. How he was born in Germany, but not German. And lived at Munich till he was eight; and the German maid met the mad King – Sickert branches off. Then he went to Reading, a school kept by a drunken old woman, who beat a boy who had broken his arm. "And we thirty little wretches lay there cowed." How far he wants me to write about him, I don't know. I suspect he is changeable: that he forgets. He gets up at 5 and goes to his garage studio at 7 and has difficulty in lighting his stove. He reads three papers. He wore a pilot's cap with a green brim, but no overcoat, though it was freezing cold. He says one paints – let me see – the canvases galloped towards me. A fine Roman head, crisp hair, thick over the ears. Small dark eyes, broad forehead. "Oh Roger's a darling – but dear me . . ." great jokes about Roger. And so we went on, a little wine-flown, but friendly and communicative, and living on our capital – I mean that we were all artists – free masonry. I can't feel very sure though of any fact or relationship – I've not seen him these ten years, and then only to sing and joke. Yet he's chiselled, severe, has read: was reading Goldoni he said. And Flaubert's letters. And is *Madame Bovary* good? I'm a literary painter, romantic – You are the only person who understands me – kissing my hand. So home in the frost.

Thursday 21 December
This is the relic of a morning when I should tidy, pack, write letters and so on. We lunch at quarter to one, and then go, this yellow cold morning. No longer the great transition that it used to be.

1934

After returning to London from Rodmell in the middle of January, Virginia was at once caught up in a round of social engagements and by the end of the month was forced to rest – rest disturbed by the incursion of workmen carrying out improvements and redecorations to 52 Tavistock Square at the landlord's behest. This activity aggravated the underlying tensions with Nelly and led to rows, which corroded Virginia's peace of mind until she finally dismissed her. Nelly left at Easter after nearly eighteen years with the Woolfs, and was replaced by Mabel Haskins.

Virginia continued working on The Pargiters *(or as she now often called it,* Here and Now*), and finished her essay 'Sickert – A Conversation' after spending Easter at Rodmell (it was published by the Hogarth Press as a one-and-sixpenny pamphlet in October), and at the end of April set off for a fortnight's holiday in Ireland. Virginia had first met the novelist Elizabeth Bowen in 1932; and an invitation to visit her in her Irish home provided the impetus for the Woolfs' tour. They stayed a night at Bowen's Court, drove westwards to County Kerry – where they read in* The Times *of George Duckworth's death – on to Galway City and home by way of Dublin, Holyhead, and Stratford-on-Avon. This holiday was succeeded by a bout of ill-health which lingered off and on through the exceptionally hot summer days, frustrating Virginia's longing to press ahead with* The Pargiters. *At the end of June she was shaken by the horrifying news of the Nazi purge in Germany, when some 1200 people were killed on Hitler's orders.*

At Rodmell too there were domestic changes: Annie vacated the Woolfs' cottage on her marriage and her place was taken by another local girl, Louie Everest, who was to remain their servant until Leonard's death. But their ten weeks' country relaxation was clouded by anxiety over Frankie Birrell's operations, and then shattered by the unexpected death of Roger Fry on 9 September. Despite these distresses and the usual incursions of innumerable visitors, Virginia succeeded in reaching the end of the first draft of her book.

In London again, Virginia was agitated by an attack from Wyndham Lewis in his book Men Without Art, *which it took all her resolution and philosophy to overcome; and Roger Fry's death left a grievous void in her intimate circle. The idea was mooted that Virginia should write his life, a challenge which interested her, though she foresaw that Roger's sister Margery, his literary executor, might impose constraints. Meanwhile she faced up to the task of re-reading and re-writing* The Pargiters. *The sombre year ended with visits to the dying Frankie Birrell before the Woolfs departed before Christmas for three weeks at Monks House.*

1934

Tuesday 16 January

I have let all this time – three weeks at Monks – slip because I was there so divinely happy and pressed with ideas – another full flood of *Pargiters* or *Here and Now*. So I never wrote a word of farewell to the year; and now we are back again. (And have I a touch of the flue?)

Tuesday 30 January

Rather a rush of people; and a dinner to meet Noel Coward at Sibyl's on a cold foggy night. Nessa painting me again. Christmas mercifully over. Nessa very hard up. Question how to make money. Rather an old wives talk. Children, money, education, ways of life. Yesterday rather headachy; sleepy; strange trances in which I make up the last sentence read; to bed; sleep. Today, writing *Here and Now*, which draws out – hence my headache. Lunch with L.; went to the Danish Laundry about his collars. Women ironing. Back room with more women standing. Coppers I daresay downstairs. Looked at flats; L. home to print, I to wander to the Law Courts. Penetrated from end to end. Judge's Chambers: a kind of vault. King's Bench; &c. People scurrying; my sense of guilt at having no business there. So to bus; home.

Wednesday 14 February

But it was rather a bad headache: ten days recumbent, sleeping, dreaming, dipping into oh dear how many different books, how capriciously. And so to Rodmell for the week-end, and the bees buzzing in the hyacinths; the earth emerging very chastened and sharpened from winter under a veil; which became fog as we drove up, and is fog today. In addition, the house rings with the clamour of electricians: the new bath water engine being inserted; and then the Surveyor comes and says we are weighting the floors down with books: a heavy bill threatens; so out to buy ink for my new Waterman, with which I am to take notes for a new *Common Reader*. Now

348

I have just refused the National Portrait Gallery offer to draw me, thank God, and am very cautiously revising 'Sickert'.

Friday 16 February

Five minutes here before going to lunch with Nessa. A great Nelly row yesterday: which I hereby declare the last. It was about the workmen and her day out, and the end was that we had eggs for lunch and were forced to dine at the Cock, expensively and badly. No more of this, I say, and anticipate many days of ill ease, some violent scenes, and then pray God, after Easter, peace. Finished my Sickert article all the same. I put off *Here and Now* till next week.

Sunday 18 February

And I began *Here and Now* again this morning, Sunday, at the point where I left off all but three weeks ago for my headache. Here I note that from two to three weeks is the right space. It has not gone cold, as after six weeks; I still carry it in my mind.

The new electric boiler in and boiling our bath water this morning. The King of Belgium killed mountaineering. All last week they were fighting in Vienna: this somehow comes closer than usual to our safe London life: the people shot down.

Tuesday 20 February

To note the interesting stages of the duel with Nelly. Today I said, do you want this quarrel to go on? I would like to stop it now; but I shall discuss it later. Whereupon she said she wished it to end, but it was all my fault. So I am indifferent calm and Lord knows if I shan't give her notice tomorrow.

Sunday 4 March

A fine day, no fog; and I'm to sit to Nessa for the last time in ten minutes. Yesterday at Ethel Smyth's Mass [in the Albert Hall]. The Queen in the box: nodding from side to side; Ethel in her three cornered hat beside her; with her hand up. The Queen bowing, doing her duty graciously. So to Lyons [Tea Rooms] – I forget the Mass – where in that sordid crumby room assembled the garish Lady Diana [Cooper], Lady Cunard, and the pensive Lady Lovat and ourselves; amid clerks and shop girls eating cream buns. Lydia's *Doll's House* [Ibsen] tonight; on Wednesday Nessa's Private View. Sickert here to tea: very old – no illusions about his own greatness. "They'll collect it all one of these days" he said, sublimely about his art criticisms.

Wednesday 14 March

I cannot hold out any hope for the next fourteen days. There's the workmen everywhere; there's Nelly gay and garrulous as a lark. Can I do it? I must. I must. If only the fourteen days were over – and I in my bed again!

Monday 19 March

I cannot describe how the Nelly situation weighs on my spirits. I am determined not to discuss it with L. either. I couldn't imagine it would be so hard, and the worst to come. And to think none of this need have happened had I stuck to my guns three years ago! Now I must and will.

To dine with Nessa last night. Clive there. Nessa all ablowing and aglowing with the success of her show, and the money made. Then in came Lydia, all &c too, owing to her success; and I felt so old so cold so dumpish, nothing flowery or fiery glowing in me owing to Nelly, but not jealous: I don't think that. Maynard very flown too, and Duncan too, and Clive quiet.

Monday 26 March

'The worst is to come' – that is with Nelly. Well it is now coming very near – by this time – 3.30 – tomorrow it will be over. And then there'll only be the one dreadful day and we shall be off. I feel executioner and the executed in one. Meanwhile it is a brilliant spring day. Hugh, Stephen, William, Ott, and Vita all coming to tea and so on; I dine with Vita; then must ring up Elizabeth Bowen about our Irish tour, and so the immitigable day passes. I face up to it without any evasion: this has to be lived I say to myself.

Tuesday 27 March

The great scene with Nelly is now over, and of course much less violently than I supposed. She stood by the drawing room door in the full light, white and pink, with her funny rather foolish mulish face puckered up. And I made my speech correctly. She had one outburst, which I cut short and said we had agreed to part on good terms, gave her a cheque for £25 and a £1 note for my mending, and so she went upstairs and I came down here. I suppose some further lamentation and argument, with L. perhaps, is inevitable. But Lord what a relief now.

Wednesday 11 April

I am now back here with Nelly gone, and Mabel [Haskins], declared to be a treasure, coming to see me tomorrow. So this has been definitely accomplished, after all these years. The sense of freedom and calm – no more brooding; no more possessiveness; no more sense of being part of Nelly's world. How dazed and free and quiet I felt driving down to Lewes!

She has taken with her all the cookery books, except too elementary manuals, and the chair cover – a last spasm of possessive spite.

Wednesday 18 April
A curious little fact. Instead of smoking six or seven cigarettes as I write of a morning, I now, for three mornings, make myself smoke only one. And rather enjoy doing without.

Thursday 19 April
Oh but I'm much too sleepy to make even a brief note of the talk. It began at dinner. Tom and Maynard talking about his book [*After Strange Gods*]. You have brought up again one of the primal questions, and nobody has even tried to consider it. No, said Tom, much like a great toad with jewelled eyes. Morality. And Maynard said that he would be inclined not to demolish Christianity if it were proved that without it morality is impossible. "I begin to see that our generation – yours and mine, Virginia, owed a great deal to our fathers' religion. And the young, like Julian, who are brought up without it, will never get so much out of life. We had the best of both worlds. We destroyed Christianity and yet had its benefits." Well the argument was something like that. I pressed Tom to define belief in God; but he sheered off. Then Julian came. How will you live Julian, you who have no moral strictness? We, Julian said, miss your morality which has landed us in psychoanalysis, but I prefer my life in many ways. Maynard accused the young of being anxious to publish too soon. That's to make our names and make money. We want to chip in before the talk has changed, said Julian. Virginia: Its because you have no sense of tradition or continuity. I used to feel that the British Museum Reading Room was going on for ever. I felt I could take fifteen years over a book; I wanted to take longer and longer. Whereas you write and publish at eighteen. Tom agreed. Tom agreed to most of this, but reserved his idea of God. Elizabeth Bowen came in, rayed like a zebra, silent and stuttering. Had also been brought up to repress, by moral ancestors. Is thirty-four. L. said jews with great morality but no religion. Quoted his mother on immortality.

Maynard on becoming a Fellow of King's. The moving nature of the service; how they go to the Chapel and lock the doors and sit in their pews, and then the Provost asks Mr So and So to come up and put his hands in his hands and reads out a statement, about preserving the laws and traditions, and then they all shake hands and he is admitted to the brotherhood, a society for research, religion, and education. And thus he is accepted as a brother whom they will support and sustain. This is a great moment; and there is nothing very ceremonious; religious; only an admittance. I said did this society, this coming together move him, and Maynard said very much.

* * *

Monks House, Rodmell

Friday 18 May
I felt I suppose a little shiver. Can't be anything I said to myself after all
that holiday; but it was – the flue. So I had to resign all ideas – all flood of
Pargiters; all was blotted by the damp sponge; and now it is precisely a
week since I went to bed, and here we are for Whitsun at Monks. All is
calm and profoundly comfortable, owing to the absence for ever even in
the background of grumbling Nelly, and her replacement by the steady
silent unselfish Mabel.

Tuesday 22 May
At last today, after striking the match on the box despairingly, sterilely, a
little flame has come. Perhaps I'm off. I must be very leisurely and patient,
and nurse my rather creaking head and dandle it with French and so on as
cunningly as possible. We go back this afternoon, and the summer lap
therefore now begins in earnest. Out of sheer white mist we drove to
Charleston last night and my numbed torpor became slightly incandescent.
Clive Nessa Duncan Quentin all talking at once about [Stanley] Spencer's
pictures.

52 Tavistock Square, WC1

Monday 11 June
I went back, and again on Friday following shivered, and ached, was stiff
as a rod; bed; influenza, and so lay all that week; and then went to Rodmell;
and then there was the opera [Glyndebourne], the nightingale singing in
the ilex tree; and a very hot concert yesterday, so I cannot, no I cannot
write today.

Monday 18 June
Very very hot. A drought over the world. In flood with *Here and Now*, praise
be. I forgot we had Aldous [Huxley]: a most admirable cool, antiseptic
distempered, but humane and gentle man; has gone about the world,
completely sceptical, all the more humane, judging everything, yet nothing.
A little theoretical, about religion and sex; not for that reason a novelist;
infinitely elongated and bony; his blurred grey eye; his malice and wit. He
had spent a weekend at Welwyn with the Sex Reformers; taken off his
clothes among the cabbages and read *The Waste Land*. Necessary to say
penis and fuck; but that said, no change follows. He uses every instant to

the best advantage but has somehow solved the problem of remaining just, gentle – a very sympathetic mind.

Monday 2 July

Rung up by Osbert Sitwell just now. After hopping and jumping about he comes out with "And can't anything be done about this monstrous affair in Germany?" "One of the few public acts" I said "that makes one miserable." Then trying, how ineffectively, to express the sensation of sitting here and reading, like an act in a play, how Hitler flew to Munich and killed this that and the other man and woman in Germany yesterday. A fine hot summer's day here and we took Philip [Woolf], [his wife] Babs and three children to the Zoo. Meanwhile these brutal bullies go about in hoods and masks, like little boys dressed up, acting this idiotic, meaningless, brutal, bloody pandemonium. In they come while Herr So and So is at lunch: iron boots, they say, grating on the parquet; kill him; and his wife who rushes to the door to prevent them. It is like watching the baboon at the Zoo; only he sucks a paper in which ice has been wrapped, and they fire with revolvers. And here we sit, Osbert and I &c, remarking this is inconceivable. A queer state of society. If there were any idea, any vision behind it: but look at the masks these men wear – the brutal faces of baboons, licking sweet paper. And for the first time I read articles with rage, to find him called a real leader. Worse far than Napoleon. Established for a thousand year says somebody.

Wednesday 11 July

So dazed and dusty: I rather think of marking time till August and Rodmell; where we take Mabel, shall have Louie Everest I think as permanent. We saw her last week end – a merry little brown eyed mongrel who came running to meet us in the road.

Tuesday 17 July

I forgot to put in about the Colefax row, curiously enough. How she wrote me a violent letter – better to break altogether – can no longer have you in my life, because I put off dinner to meet Noel Coward.

This is one of the dryest and hottest of summers. And heat brings such lassitude; and people swarm. I have let them die out, be extinct: Osbert for instance; with his very sensual Royal Guelf face; his extreme uneasiness; his childish vanity always striking the two notes: rank and genius; so easily touched by praise, so eager. A sensitive man; voluble, august, uneasy; and gushing words. Still I like him – why I don't know.

Tuesday 24 July

Dinner last night at the Hutchinsons. Let me see. Praise of my dress – taken very philosophically. Desmond there and Tom. Dinner: not very good: one element of pleasure lessened. Talk frivolous at first. Mary describes a party: a champagne cocktail. Tom gravely attentive. Talk gets upon whether we frighten or are frightened. Tom said I made him feel I saw through all his foibles; which perhaps I do. Talk of [Coventry] Patmore. Desmond expatiated, praised, all in the *Sunday Times* agreeable manner. Jack robust, rather coarse. Tom remained on the verge; yellow, bony – so much melancholy in his face. Yes, and then, somehow to Hitler. And there was Leonard aquiline and lean; and so Desmond drew on to politics; and then, what with Jack's cross examination, and Tom's intentness, and Desmond burbling general goodwill and human love, and Leonard's specialised convictions, the argument blazed: how the Labour Party would come in: what it would do. But how can you make any such ridiculous claim Jack boomed. What is it going to do about unemployment, about agriculture? All these questions were put from the view of here and now, capable business men; L. ideal by comparison. How ten sensible men 'round a table', one of his phrases, could so manipulate the supply of locomotives and wheat that one country supplemented another. Oh if we were all men of good will, if we were all ready to be nice about it – Then Desmond as usual praised moderation, tact, the virtues of the defunct Liberal Party: how civilisation runs slowly in a great wide stream, and you must slowly facilitate its course, but by no means introduce whirlpools, cut precipices and so on. They heckled L. between them, and when the argument began to put its tail in its mouth, Mary asked if I would like to withdraw. We went upstairs, and she sat on the fender, and said how, being alone for the week end she had tried to write an ambitious biography. There was to be an outer story, and a second meaning; as far as I could gather. Then the others came; and Tom read [George] Barker's poems, chanting, intoning. He thinks there is some melody, some rhythm, some emotion lacking in the Audens and Spenders. Wants five shillings a week for this young man, who has a wife and child. So home at last.

MONKS HOUSE, RODMELL

Friday 27 July

Rodmell begins again: with this difference, we have Mabel just arrived; and Louie Everest, who is moving in [to the Woolfs' cottage] today. And the usual helter skelter, tidying, and nothing to settle to; must go at once to Worthing, then come back to a meeting.

Wednesday 1 August

Charleston yesterday. This morning, poor old Francis [Birrell] paralysed; another operation tomorrow, under which says Nessa, it is to be hoped he may die, since the cancer has come back. How I hate going through these thoughts again, and what a jumble of meanness and sordidity and the fine, one's feelings are.

Thursday 2 August

Louie's first morning here. A leap in the dark rather. Mabel making currant jam. Vast basins of black currants which she tops and tails. Mabel had a chicken that lived with her fourteen years and was called Old George.

Saturday 4 August

Waiting about to go to Annie's wedding. No signs yet. No bells ringing. So impossible to do anything, and here I am at 11 this hot August morning in full garden party dress. No news of Frankie.

Yesterday just as we had done tea, Adrian's gaunt form appeared; Karin's touseled shape, grown very thick and large. Her inferiority complex takes the form of praising Adrian. Clever old Adrian, she exclaims, if he bowls a good bowl. This is by way of saying – what? My marriage was not so bad after all? He remains perfectly unmoved, quiet, sensible; I suppose curiously immature, though able to go through all the actions correctly of a grown man, father, husband.

Tuesday 7 August

A rather wet Bank Holiday. Tea with Keyneses. Maynard had had teeth out, but was very fertile. "Yes, I've been three weeks in America. An impossible climate. In fact it has collected all the faults of all the climates. This carries out my theory about climate. Nobody could produce a great work in America. One sweats all day and the dirt sticks to one's face. The nights are as hot as the days. Nobody sleeps." So to German politics. "They're doing something very queer with their money. I can't make out what. It may be the Jews are taking away their capital. Let me see, if 2000 Jews were each to take away £2000 – Anyway they can't pay their Lancashire bill. Yet they're buying copper all the time. What's it for? Armaments no doubt. But of course there's something behind it. They're doing something foolish – no Treasury control of the soldiers." (But I am thinking all the time of what is to end *Here and Now*.)

Sunday 12 August

This is Saxon's week end. He is in the house, this windy cold gray day, playing chess with L. He has grown rather pink and chubby in face, and very mellow and in fact charming in mind. The old eccentricities have been melted in the sun – I cannot guess of what success. Anyhow he is not merely a bundle of dessicated separate remarks about toothbrushes and trains: he is continuous and even suggestive. I have spent an hour or so talking with him about Shakespeare, books in general, then people; and there is some virtue in these old friends: I mean conversationally; they enrich. Thus it was a good idea of mine to ask him. We had the Keyneses over. Old friends again.

News at first, through Julian, extremely optimistic about Francis. Now nothing, but perhaps more doubtful. Oh and the drought has broken; two carp are dead; there is the old ugly grey welter in the sky, which I'm afraid may now become 'weather'. Vita came over very late for dinner, having been kept by a row with her mother who, says Maynard, eats pâté de foie with a shoehorn.

Friday 17 August
Yes. I think owing to the sudden rush of two wakeful nights, making up early mornings rather, I think I see the end of *Here and Now* (or *Music*, or *Dawn* or whatever I shall call it). Its to end with Elvira going out of the house and saying What did I make this knot in my handkerchief for? And all the coppers rolling about –

Thursday 30 August
If I can't even write here, owing to making up the last scenes, how can I possibly read Dante? Impossible. Yesterday I found a new walk, and a new farm, in the fold between Asheham and Tarring Neville. Very lovely, all alone, with the down rising behind. Then I walked back by a rough broad overflowing grey river. The porpoise came up and gulped. It rained. All ugliness was dissolved. An incredibly 18th century landscape. A tremendous hailstorm after tea. Like white ice; broken up; lanced; lashing, like the earth being whipped. This happened several times. Black clouds while we played Brahms.

Sunday 2 September
I don't think I have ever been more excited over a book than I am writing the end of – shall it be *Dawn?* Or is that too emphatic, sentimental. I wrote like a – forget the word – yesterday; my cheeks burn; my hands tremble. I am doing the scene where Peggy listens to them talking and bursts out. It was this outburst that excited me so. Too much perhaps. Another lull; but very slight, caused partly by the great tea table talk yesterday – nine to tea. We arranged lots of little cakes on two tables. And some came early, others late. And they talked (as in my book that morning) about Civilisation.

Wednesday 12 September

Roger died on Sunday. I was walking with Clive on the terrace when Nessa came out. We sat on the seat there for a time. On Monday we went up with Nessa. Tomorrow we go up, following some instinct, to the funeral. I feel dazed: very wooden. Women cry, L. says: but I don't know why I cry – mostly with Nessa. And I'm too stupid to write anything. My head all stiff. I think the poverty of life now is what comes to me, a thin blackish veil over everything. Hot weather. A wind blowing. The substance gone out of everything. I don't think this is exaggerated. It'll come back I suppose. And I can't write to Helen [Anrep], but I must now shut this and try.

I remember turning aside at mother's bed, when she had died, and Stella took us in, to laugh, secretly, at the nurse crying. She's pretending, I said: aged thirteen. And was afraid I was not feeling enough. So now.

Saturday 15 September

I was glad we went to the service on Thursday. It was a very hot summer's day. And all very simple and dignified. Music. Not a word spoken. We sat there, before the open doors that lead into the garden. Flowers and strollers which Roger would have liked. He lay under an old red brocade with two bunches of very bright many-coloured flowers. It is a strong instinct to be with one's friends. I thought of him too, at intervals. Dignified and honest and large – 'large sweet soul' – something ripe and musical about him – and then the fun and the fact that he had lived with such variety and generosity and curiosity. I thought of this. They played Bach. Then the coffin moved slowly through the doors. They shut. They played again – Anon, I think; old music. Yes, I liked the wordlessness; Helen looking very young and blue eyed and quiet and happy. That is much to remember her for. I kissed her on the lips, in the courtyard. Then Desmond came up: said wouldn't it be nice to walk in the garden? "Oh we stand on a little island" he said. But it has been very lovely I said. For the first time I laid my hand on his shoulder, and said don't die yet. Nor you either he said. We have had wonderful friends, he said. We walked a little, but Molly was out of it, with her deafness. So we took them to Wellington Square and had tea. A merry natural talk, about Roger and books and people, all as usual. And it was roasting hot.

Very jaded; can't write. I must take a few days off. Ann and Judith [Stephen] upon us; then Dadie.

Tuesday 18 September

Ann and Judith came, strode in without their box. Great brown naked legged colts. Next day Angelica's party at Charleston. They acted. They acted very beautifully in Chinese clothes by the pond. Well I thought I can see this through Roger's eyes: its right to enjoy every tint. And yet how can one? This has gone out of the day – that laughter; that energy; and we were all thinned and stunted. So home. And then after Ann and Judith went – and I had begun to fidget because they don't wipe their mouths and eat so much – the Keyneses and Dadie came. We did not exactly repeat the funeral talk: but it loomed over us. Dear old Dadie very charming and affectionate. We talked about Cambridge; about teaching English; I held out a bare pole – I mean I extended my views rashly; he was donnish, serious, very measured; believes in education; in measuring the mind, and sending youth to Africa with 'an improved sense of leisure' and so on. But this rather broke down and he admitted that he means to leave as soon as he can afford it. Teaching without zest a crime.

Wednesday 19 September

I had a notion that I could describe the tremendous feeling at Roger's funeral: but of course I can't. I mean the universal feeling: how we all fought with our brains, loves and so on: and must be vanquished. A fear then came to me, of death. Of course I shall lie there too before that gate, and slide in; and it frightens me. But why? I mean, I felt the vainness of this perpetual fight, with our brains and loving each other, against the other thing; if Roger could die.

Thursday 20 September

But then, next day, the other thing begins to work – the exalted sense of being above time and death which comes from being again in a writing mood. And this is not an illusion, so far as I can tell. Certainly I have a strong sense that Roger would be all on one's side in this excitement.

Sunday 30 September

The last words of the nameless book were written ten minutes ago; quite calmly too. 900 pages: L. says 200,000 words. Lord God what an amount of re-writing that means! But also, how heavenly to have brought the pen to a stop at the last line, even if most of the lines have now to be rubbed out. Anyhow the design is there.

Tuesday 2 October

Yes, but my head will never let me glory sweepingly: always a tumble. Yesterday morning the old rays of light set in; and then the sharp, the very sharp pain over my eyes; so that I sat and lay about till tea; had no walk, had not a single idea of triumph or relief. L. bought me a little travelling ink pot, by way of congratulation. I wish I could think of a name.

So the summer is ended. Until the 9th of September when Nessa came across the terrace – how I hear that cry He's dead – a very vigorous, happy summer. Oh the joy of walking! I've never felt it so strong in me.

On Sunday we had Bunny [Garnett] and Julian; Bunny so thick and solid, like a beam out of an old tree; Julian rather smaller than usual. Bunny has grey wisps at his temples; talks like a heavy wardrobe; all heavy and angular sentences. I noted how my own rushing pace seemed too rushing, and after ten minutes had adapted itself to Bunny. Then Duncan and Helen came. It was rather fortunate that the first meeting should be among the flowers, vegetables, improvements. Then we went upstairs and talked and laughed about Roger, easily. I felt however the worn out, the used up feeling as if she were now feeling the shallows, after the exaltation; the shingle grating, the sordid – poor Helen.

Thursday 4 October

A violent rain storm on the pond. The pond is covered with little white thorns; bristling with leaping white thorns, like the thorns on a small porcupine; then black waves cross it: black shudders; a helter skelter rain, and the elms tossing it up and down; the pond overflowing on one side. Then completely smooth for a moment. Then prickled: thorns like glass; but leaping up and down incessantly. A rapid smirch of shadow. Now light from the sun: green and red: shining: the pond a sage green: the grass brilliant green: red berries on the hedges: the cows very white: purple over Asheham.

52 TAVISTOCK SQUARE, WC1

Thursday 11 October

A brief note. In today's *TLS* they advertise *Men Without Art* by Wyndham Lewis. Chapters on Eliot, Faulkner, Hemingway, Virginia Woolf . . . Now I know by reason and instinct that this is an attack; that I am publicly demolished: nothing is left of me in Oxford and Cambridge and places where the young read Wyndham Lewis. My instinct is, not to read it. Why do I shrink from reading Wyndham Lewis? Why am I sensitive? I think vanity. I dislike the thought of being laughed at, of the glow of satisfaction that A B and C will get from hearing Virginia Woolf demolished: also it will strengthen further attacks. Perhaps I feel uncertain of my own gifts: but then, I know more about them than Wyndham Lewis; and anyhow I intend to go on writing. Already I am feeling the calm that always comes to me with abuse: my back is against the wall. I am writing for the sake of writing: &c. And then there is the queer disreputable pleasure in being abused – in being a figure, in being a martyr. And so on.

Sunday 14 October
This morning I've taken the arrow of Wyndham Lewis to my heart. Well:
this gnat has settled and stung; and I think the pain is over. I'm glad that I
need not and cannot write, because the danger of being attacked is that it
makes one answer back – a perfectly fatal thing to do. I mean, fatal to
arrange *The Pargiters* so as to meet his criticisms. If there is truth in
Wyndham Lewis, well, face it: I've no doubt I am prudish and peeping,
well then live more boldly. But for God's sake don't try to bend my writing
one way or the other.

Monday 15 October
Walked with L. all round Serpentine and Kensington Gardens yesterday
(a fine blowy day: leaves falling) and asked him these questions: 1)
What is the sensible attitude to criticism? Not to read it. 2) What should
I do now of a morning – creation flagging? Read. 3) Does he feel I
have prevented him from going abroad? No. I have only prevented him
from lesser activities (I think this was the answer). We agreed to save
up for foreign travel on a large scale, to try to fly over America. Perhaps
to go to India and China. I now see us, far far away. A new civilisation
&c. Oh and L. was divinely good: so direct: what an immense relief to
talk to him! what a simplification. What an egress to open air and cold
daylight: how dignified: yes, and I have him every day, as I so often
think. So why – &c &c.

Tuesday 16 October
Quite cured today. So the Wyndham Lewis illness lasted two days. Helped
by old Ethel's bluff affection and stir yesterday, by buying a blouse; by
falling fast asleep after dinner. Writing away this morning.

Wednesday 17 October
I am so sleepy. Is this age? I can't shake it off. And so gloomy. That's the
end of the book. I looked up past diaries – a reason for keeping them – and
found the same misery after *Waves*. After *Lighthouse* I was I remember nearer
suicide, seriously, than since 1913. It is after all natural. I've been galloping
now for three months – well, cut that all off – after the first divine relief,
of course some terrible blankness must spread. This time Roger makes it
harder than usual. We had tea with Nessa yesterday. Yes, his death is worse
than Lytton's. Why I wonder? Such a blank wall. Such a silence. Such a
poverty. How he reverberated! And I feel it through Nessa. Now there's
the dullness, the cold to face and no protection. I'm so ugly. So old. No
one writes to me. I'm . . . Well: don't think about it, and walk all over
London: and see people; and imagine their lives. I can't read seriously. I

feel so drowsy, as if my brain were dilated: can't contract: then I suddenly lapse into sleep.

Margery [Fry] is going, Nessa thinks, to ask me to write about Roger. I don't feel ready to. I dread the plunge into the past.

Friday 26 October

Yesterday at Ottoline's. Old [W. B.] Yeats. I'm trying to get the Irish back to the great men of the 18th Century. Swift! But did Swift like Ireland? He started the whole Irish movement – made Irish different from English. Oh the bitterness against England. Must get them back to their own speech. You have always been rich and powerful. You create without hatred. The need of tragedy: some cause: that is what creates literature.

The Occult. That he believes in firmly. All his writing depends on it. Was walking with Robinson Ellis. The words came to him 'The world is the excrement of God': two minutes afterwards Robinson Ellis said them. This convinced Yeats of the existence of another mind. Neither religion nor science explains the world. The occult does explain it. Has seen things. His coat hanger advanced across the room one night. Then a coat on it, illuminated; then a hand in it. Is writing his memoirs. About [George] Moore and Lady Gregory. This went on for one and a half hours, I should say. I was too jaded to whip my brain: but felt Yeats's extreme directness, simplicity, and equality: liked his praise; liked him: but can't unriddle the universe at tea. He is older, less coloured and vigorous. Little burning eyes behind great glasses; ruffled hair; tweeds. Yeats said that in writing his memoirs he had to leave out himself, because no man could tell the truth about the women in his life. Also no man knew about himself.

Monday 29 October

Reading *Antigone*. How powerful that spell is still – Greek. Thank heaven I learnt it young – an emotion different from any other.

Wednesday 31 October

Too tired after dining with Helen last night and talking too much with Oliver [Strachey] about Roger and Bloomsbury – too tired to write. Helen by the way asked me tentatively to write Roger's Life. Julian to collect all the facts, make a skeleton; I to sum and compose. But Margery [Fry] wants to write it. Margery has the documents: is executor. I deferred. Isn't a 'Life' impossible? Yes, said Oliver. All sorts of people should put down recollections. And unprintable. So what's to come of it? I deferred. (What exactly does that word mean?)

Monday 12 November

What is uppermost now, is the question of writing Roger's life. Helen
came. Says both she and Margery wish it. So I wait. What do I feel about
it? If I could be free, then here's the chance of trying biography: a splendid,
difficult chance – better than trying to find a subject – that is, if I *am* free.
But Margery hesitates: I have heard nothing from her; and rather suspect
she wants to do it herself.

We were at Monks House in a great flood of rain and storm of wind this
week-end; which lifted yesterday. Home with the car all acrid and yellow
and red with crysanthemums. And so to hear [T. S. Eliot's] *Sweeney Agonistes*
at the Group Theatre: an upper attic or studio. I sat by Tom. The acting
made more sense than the reading but I doubt that Tom has enough of a
body and brain to bring off a whole play: certainly he conveys an emotion,
an atmosphere: something peculiar to himself; sordid, emotional, intense –
modernity and poetry locked together.

Thursday 15 November

And am now, 10.30 on Thursday morning, November 15th, about to tackle
re-reading and re-writing *The Pargiters*. An awful moment.

12.45. Well that horrid plunge has been made, and I've started re-writing
The Pargiters. Lord Lord! Ten pages a day for ninety days: three months.

Saturday 17 November

A note: despair at the badness of the book: can't think how I ever could
write such stuff – and with such excitement: that's yesterday; today I think
it good again. A note, by way of advising other Virginias with other books
that this is the way of the thing: up down, up down – and Lord knows the
truth.

Wednesday 21 November

Margery Fry to tea on Sunday. A long debate about the book on Roger:
not very conclusive. She says she wants a study by me, reinforced with
chapters on other aspects. I say, well but those books are unreadable. Oh
of course I want you to be quite free she says. I should have to say
something about his life, I say. The family – Now there of course I'm afraid
I should have to ask you to be careful, she says. Agnes is stone deaf; has
lived all her life in the family. I couldn't let her be hurt – and so on. The
upshot of all of which is that she's to write to the *New Statesman* asking for
letters; that I'm to go through them; that we're then to discuss – so it will
drag on these many months, I suppose.

Tom's head is very remarkable; such a conflict; so many forces have
smashed against him; the wild eye still; but all rocky, yellow, riven, and

constricted. Sits very solid – large shoulders – in his chair, and talks easily but with authority. Is a great man, in a way, now: self confident, didactic. But to me, still, a dear old ass: I mean I can't be frozen off with this divine authority any longer. Tom is larger minded than of old. "But that's only human" he said, when I asked him if he still liked seeing his own name in print.

Tuesday 27 November
Poor Francis lies in a hotel bedroom in Russell Square this rainy morning. I went in and sat with him. Quite himself with a lump on his forehead. May die under another operation, or slowly stiffen into complete paralysis. His brain may go. All this he knows; and there it was between us, as we joked. He came to the verge of it once or twice. But I can't feel any more at the moment – not after Roger. I kissed him. "This is the first time – this chaste kiss" he said. So I kissed him again. But I must not cry, I thought, and so went.

Tuesday 18 December
Talk with Francis yesterday. He is dying; but makes no bones about it. He was exactly as usual; no wandering, no incoherence. A credit to atheism. The soul deserves to be immortal, as L. said. We walked back, glad to be alive: numb somehow.

MONKS HOUSE, RODMELL

Sunday 30 December
End the year; with those cursed dogs barking. It has been the wettest Christmas, I should say, on record. I end every morning with a head full of ideas about *The Pargiters*. I am re-writing considerably. My idea is to contrast the scenes; very intense, less so; then drama; then narrative. I think it shall be called *Ordinary People*.

End of the year: and Francis transacting his death at that nursing home. The expression on his face is what I see: as if he were facing a peculiar lonely sorrow. One's own death – think of lying there alone, looking at it, at forty-five or so: with a great desire to live. And here we are, chafed by [Mabel's] lame leg and the dogs: yet as usual very happy I think: ever so full of ideas. L. finishing his *Quack Quack* of a morning. And Roger dead. And am I to write about him?

1935

Virginia's comedy Freshwater *was performed by a family cast before a receptive audience of friends in Vanessa's Fitzroy Street studio in January. Yet there was 'a vast sorrow at the back of life this winter', attributable to the loss of Roger Fry, which depressed her and, even more, Vanessa. The proposal that Virginia should write about him required Margery Fry's endorsement, but not until the summer did she make it clear that she expected a full-scale biography and begin to inundate Virginia with documents, followed by a demand that she speak at a memorial exhibition of Roger's pictures at Bristol.*

In the meantime London life was as demanding as ever; friends and relations, literary and political associates, converged on Tavistock Square. Among the most persistent was the editor of the New Statesman, *Kingsley Martin, constantly seeking Leonard's counsel. Also the indomitable Ethel Smyth, demanding affection, admiration, and attendance at performances of her music.*

Despite their growing awareness of the Nazi threat to European peace and the atrocities of anti-Semitism, on 1 May, avoiding King George V's Silver Jubilee celebrations, the Woolfs set out to drive via Holland, Germany and Austria to join Vanessa in Rome. They prepared for this rash journey by talking to a country neighbour, Ralph Wigram of the Foreign Office; but their best passport proved to be Leonard's pet marmoset Mitz, who bore a striking resemblance to Goebbels and disarmed officials and bystanders. They were away a month, returning through France. While in Rome, Virginia learned that the Prime Minister proposed to recommend she be made a Companion of Honour in the King's Birthday Honours; she declined.

During the summer, both in London and at Rodmell, Virginia's concentration on The Pargiters *– which she now decided to call* The Years *– was repeatedly broken by social distractions, headaches, and the increasing political tension abroad, leading up to Mussolini's invasion of Abyssinia and the imposition by the League of Nations of sanctions against Italy. In England the Conservative Stanley Baldwin succeeded Ramsay MacDonald as Prime Minister, and in November called a General Election which he won with a handsome majority. In October Virginia with Leonard spent a day at the Labour Conference at Brighton. These external concerns roused in her a wish to write a political pamphlet; but she was trying to finish* The Years, *and by the end of the year had embarked on the background reading for the biography of Roger Fry. The Woolfs spent Christmas at Rodmell.*

1935

Monks House, Rodmell

Sunday 6 January

Francis died on 2nd. It was a mercy, as we say, that it ended so soon. But a queer thing death. Last night I suddenly thought, how silly and indeed disgusting death, the decomposition of the body, &c. Why think of it as anything noble? We lunched with Maynard and Lydia, the first fine cold day since we came. We talked about Francis: Maynard said he was a case of arrested development; had been a most brilliant undergraduate, and remained one.

Friday 11 January

I have made a very clever arrangement on the new board that L. gave me for Christmas: ink, pen tray &c. I never cease to get pleasure from these clever arrangements. So death will be very dull. There are no letters in the grave, as Dr Johnson said. A very long, rather formal, I mean affected letter from Tom this morning, which I must put away, as it will be so valuable. Did he think that when he was writing it? This spring will be on us all of a clap. Already engagements are piling; and the lap ahead will be full of the usual jerks and strains. Tom suggests a fortnightly tea. And there's Helen . . . I never never invite anyone; but lie like an apron under an apple tree for fruit to drop.

52 Tavistock Square, wc1

Saturday 19 January

The play [*Freshwater*] came off last night, with the result that I am dry-brained this morning, and can only use this book as a pillow. It was said, inevitably, to be a great success; it is good to have an unbuttoned laughing evening once in a way. Angelica ravishing of course, but of course too grown up for my taste. That is, I rather dread Bloomsbury; and rather relish the clumsy directness, the hard fact of the Stephen girls: so clumsy and large.

But they will become workers – in the cause of – how the phrases one has written and listened to so many times run in the head! And Morgan said it was lovely, I mean the play.

Wednesday 23 January
I am taking a fortnight off fiction. My mind became knotted.

Friday 1 February
And again this morning, I'm too tired to go on with *Pargiters*. Why? Talking too much I daresay. I thought I wanted 'society': and saw Helen, Mary, [Louis] Gillet. Ann tonight. I think *The Pargiters* however a promising work. A day off today.

Saturday 2 February
Walked to Chancery Lane in a bitter rain about my spectacles. I wrote in praise of Rebecca's book to Rebecca [West], and have had no answer. This I did because of the talk at Charleston, when they said how much pleasure such letters gave. I expect I have (somehow) given pain. But its no great matter. My conscience, as they say, is clear.

Tuesday 5 February
Why should I mind so much Rebecca not answering my letter? Vanity largely, I suppose. I thought she would be glad &c. Never mind. She is a queer ill bred mind, with all the qualities I lack and fear.

Tom to tea yesterday. An admirable way of seeing him. And how he suffers! Yes: I felt my accursed gift of sympathy rising. He seemed to have got so little joy or satisfaction out of being Tom. A religious soul: an unhappy man: a lonely very sensitive man, all wrapped up in fibres of self torture, doubt, conceit, desire for warmth and intimacy. And I'm very fond of him – like him in some of my reserves and subterfuges. After abusing booksellers yesterday for some time, I said to Tom, do you ever buy a new book? Never, he said. And I said, I sometimes buy poetry, that's all. So this accounts for the problem, it strikes me, why authors don't sell: why booksellers don't stock &c &c.

Wednesday 6 February
I open this book to record the fact, with all its psychological implications – the fact that Rebecca's snub has now worn off. It lasted about four days: gave me a cold goose feather feeling every morning and every evening. It will now gradually fade out; and I shall dismiss her, and all that is implicit in that situation. But I should still be very glad if she did write to me. On

the other hand, the feeling of independence is even better than the feeling of pleasure would be.

Friday 8 February
Dine with Nessa; and oh dear, how the ghost of Roger haunted us. What a dumb misery life is for her. An extraordinary sense of him: of wishing for him; of vacancy. A letter from Margery, who is bringing documents, and wants to see me next week. No letter from Rebecca.

Tuesday 12 February
This should be the coldest day in the year, according to averages. Colefax came half an hour late: and we had it out. Lord what a drubbing you gave me in the summer, I managed to thrust in, after the usual patter about dining last night with somebody who had been dining with Lloyd George. Then her defences crumpled: she flushed and quickened; so did I. She sat on the floor by the way, and pulled down some white undergarment which had become creased. She only wears one undergarment and a small belt, by the way. And she twittered out how what had hurt her had been my thinking, or insinuating, that her dinner was merely a snob dinner to bring celebrities together. The truth was Noel [Coward] adores me; and I could save him from being as clever as a bag of ferrets and as trivial as a perch of canaries. And of course, I rather liked her. And she is so childishly ready to patter about her own simple love of sunsets, comparing herself to the worldly. That I stubbed by saying I admired and loved those who fill their sails with the spice breezes of the great world. So she had to trim and hedge; and admit that parties are a stimulus to the imagination; and that her chief pleasure is to tell herself stories, to make up a life, a picture, as she bustles and flits. This I think was intended to be in my manner – a tribute to the imaginative, artistic life: for indeed what she can't bear is to be rated a hard society woman: as she is, partly; but then we're all curates' eggs, as I was feeling: a mix.

Wednesday 20 February
A row with Clive which spoilt my dinner at the [Herbert] Read's; and sent me parched and throbbing up to that vast comfortless [Hampstead] studio, where none of the charm of Bohemia mitigated the hard chairs, the skimpy wine, and the very nice sensible conversation. Henry Moore, sculptor, and his Russian wife, something like Cordelia Fisher in the old days to look at; but more sympathetic. Respectable Bohemia is a little cheerless. Better have Sybil or the real thing. But all went decorously. Steel chairs, clear pale colours; talk of pots; brainy talk, specialists' talk. Read devitalised: possibly his look – a shop assistant. So this morning I can't write; only correct.

Thursday 21 February

A good party last night with old Hugh [Walpole]. Hugh on Hollywood. What was interesting though and rather horrifying was his account of his own pain: an agony of pain in his arm, like broken bones twittering incessantly. Agony agony agony – hadn't realised there could be such pain. Once he burst into tears and sat up shouting. Was conveyed across America in an aeroplane. And then, just as the pain was coming on at Hampstead, a parcel was delivered: a bottle of quack medicine called Cleano. And he took a dose, and slept; and next day he was better. And has had no pain since. But what was shocking was to see him an old man. All the buoyancy and taut pink skin gone. Something sunk and shuttered in him. I liked him. And I liked his capacity for miraculous rebirth.

A letter of explanation and conciliation from Clive.

Tuesday 26 February

A very fine skyblue day, my windows completely filled with blue for a wonder. And I have been writing and writing and re-writing the scene by the Round Pond. But Lord what a lot of work still to do! It won't be done before August. And here am I plagued by the sudden wish to write an anti-Fascist pamphlet. L. and I, after snarling over my cigarette smoking last night (I'm refraining altogether and without difficulty today) had a long discussion about all the things I might put in my pamphlet. He was extremely reasonable and adorable.

Friday 1 March

First of March: first of spring. Another blue day; and we're off to Walton on Thames.

Monday 4 March

It was a charming grey distinguished expedition too: to Walton; and we walked by the river, and said it was like a French picture. The grey trees, the weir churning, the bridge, the white cupola, and a lion in marble.

Yesterday I did not enjoy. What a guzzler old Ethel has become. She guzzled our very tough chops, till I could not sit still. She is a greedy old woman; I don't like greed when it comes to champing and chawing and sweeping up gravy. And she gets red, drinking. Then the concert. How long, how little music in it that I enjoyed! Beecham's face beaming, ecstatic, like a yellow copper idol: such grimaces, attenuations, dancings, swingings; his collar crumpled. In the artists' room afterwards there was Zélie with the red lips, and another ex prima donna and a dissolute musician, all waiting their turn to plague Beecham. And they hinted and shrugged that poor old Ethel was a well known imposition upon conductors. Out she came in her spotted cat's fur with her hat askew, carrying her brown cardboard despatch box, upon which they – the tight hard old prima donnas, fell on her and larded her with praise. (They had played *The Wreckers* overture). Who are they I said. Haven't an idea, she replied. So we had tea at the Langham, which I don't mind so much as meat and gravy. And then I could stand that stab of a voice emphasising, I don't know what, no longer; and said I must go. It was a Sunday evening drizzle in the street, an 1849 night, as we padded very slowly to the Tube; and thank God, she vanished. I was out of temper.

Monday 11 March
It was the bitterest Sunday for twenty-two years. We went to Sissinghurst: in the bitter wind with the country all lying in its June green and blue outside the window. Now that's an odd observation I have to make. My friendship with Vita is over. Not with a quarrel, not with a bang, but as ripe fruit falls. But her voice saying "Virginia?" outside the tower room was as enchanting as ever. Only then nothing happened. And she has grown very fat, very much the indolent county lady, run to seed, incurious now about books; has written no poetry; only kindles about dogs, flowers, and new buildings. Sissinghurst is to have a new wing; a new garden; a new wall. And there is no bitterness, and no disillusion, only a certain emptiness. In fact – if my hands weren't so cold – I could here analyse my state of mind these past four months, and account for the human emptiness by the defection of Vita; Roger's death; and no-one springing up to take their place; and a certain general slackening of letters and fame, owing to my writing nothing; so that I have more time on my hands, and actually ask people to come here now and again. (But the week fills unbidden mostly.) Coming back in the snowstorm from Vita's: the snow was like long ribbons of paper; whipping, mixing, getting entangled in front of the car.

Saturday 16 March
I have had three severe swingeings lately: Bloomsbury is ridiculed; and I am dismissed with it. And how little I mind, and how much; and how good my novel is; and how tired I am this morning; and how I like praise; and how full of ideas I am; and Tom and Stephen [Spender] came to tea, and Ray [Strachey] and William [Plomer] dine; and I forgot to describe my interesting talk with Nessa about my criticising her children; and I left out – I forget what.

And Rebecca West did answer yesterday, and signs yours ever, and had been ill, and no secretary, so that's done with. Tom's writing a play about Thomas à Becket to be acted in Canterbury Cathedral. In last week's *Time & Tide* St John Ervine called Lytton 'that servile minded man ... that Pandar' or words to that effect. I'm thinking whether, if I write about Roger,

I shall include a note, a sarcastic note, on the Bloomsbury baiters. No, I suppose not. Write them down – that's the only way.

Wednesday 20 March
Having just written a letter about Bloomsbury I cannot control my mind enough to go on with *The Pargiters*. I woke in the night and thought of it. But whether to send it or not, I don't know.

L. advised me *not* to send the letter. And after two seconds I see he is right. It is better he says to be able to say we don't answer. But we suggest a comic guide to Bloomsbury by Morgan and he nibbles.

Monday 25 March
Last night at Nessa's, talk all very chippy and choppy with Clive oddly inattentive, and a sense of unreality, and a great desire for Roger. Again the sense of him coming in with his great dark eyes, and his tie pin and his brown shoes and how, speaking in that very deep voice, he would have discussed Max Eastman and Epstein. We only flick the surface. And all would have been deepened, and made suggestive. But never mind. This is inevitable, and we must blow on the bellows.

Tuesday 26 March
A very nice dinner at MacCarthys last night. Desmond flung the door open and almost kissed me. But that's not our formula. So glad to see us – He looks firmer and pinker. And we talked of America. Very kind, quite untaught. Desmond never allowed to pay. He had enjoyed himself immensely. Only netted £150 though. Dear me, friendship is a very happy thing.

Wednesday 27 March
Yesterday we went to the Tower, which is an impressive murderous bloody grey raven haunted military barrack prison dungeon place; like the prison of English splendour; the reformatory at the back of history; where we shot and tortured and imprisoned. Prisoners scratched their names, very beautifully, on the walls. And the crown jewels blazed, very tawdry. And we watched the Scots Guards drill; and an officer doing a kind of tiger pace up and down – a wax faced barber's block officer trained to a certain impassive balancing. The sergeant major barked and swore: the men stamped and wheeled like machines: then the officer also barked; all precise, inhuman, showing off – a degrading, a stupefying sight, but in keeping with the grey wall, the cobbles, the executioner's block. People sitting on the river bank among old cannon. Ships &c. Very romantic; a dungeon like feeling.

Thursday 28 March

Spring triumphant. Crocuses going over. Daffodils and hyacinths out. Some chestnut leaves in the bird's claw stage in the park. The country trees and Square trees bare still. Little bushes all green. I want to make vegetable notes for my book. How soft and springy and fresh the air was yesterday – like the sea! And I think of being abroad. But we have not yet decided where to go.

Monday 1 April

We think of three weeks in Holland and France: a week in Rome, flying there. We went to Kew yesterday, and if vegetable notes are needed, this is to signify that yesterday was the prime day for cherry blossom, pear trees, and magnolia. So to walk through Richmond – a long walk by the ponds. I verified certain details. And it was 5.30 when we got back. And Mabel came in and said she had sat for two hours in the Piccadilly [Lyons'] Corner House, watching people and listening to the band. Many people do this, she said. They sit on and on, eating as slowly as possible. She was ashamed how long they had sat. But then they take a long time to bring things she said.

Friday 5 April

L. met James [Strachey] who says he means to set about a very long life of Lytton; and what he wants is that I should write a character of Lytton as introduction. Lytton and Roger – so my work as biographer is cut out – I wonder.

Tuesday 9 April

I met Morgan in the London Library yesterday and flew into a passion. "Virginia, my dear" he said. I was pleased by that little affectionate familiar tag. "Being a good boy and getting books on Bloomsbury?" I said. "Yes. And Virginia, you know I'm on the Committee here" said Morgan. "And we've been discussing whether to allow ladies –"

It came over me that they were going to put me on: and I was then to refuse: "Oh but they do –" I said, "there was Mrs Green . . ." "Yes yes – there was Mrs Green. And Sir Leslie Stephen said, never again. She was so troublesome. And I said, haven't ladies improved? But they were all quite determined. No no no, ladies are quite impossible. They wouldn't hear of it."

See how my hand trembles. I was so angry (also very tired) standing. And I saw the whole slate smeared. I thought how perhaps Morgan had mentioned my name, and they had said no no no: ladies are impossible. And so I quietened down and said nothing and this morning in my bath I made up a phrase in my book *On Being Despised* which is to run: a friend of mine, who was offered . . . one of those prizes – for her sake the great exception was to be made – who was in short to be given an honour – I forget what . . . she said, And they actually thought I would take it. They were, on my honour, surprised, even at my very modified and humble rejection. You didn't tell them what you thought of them for daring to suggest that you should rub your nose in that pail of offal? I remarked. Not for a hundred years, she observed. Yes, these flares up are very good for my book: for they simmer and become transparent: and I see how I can transmute them into beautiful clear reasonable ironical prose. God damn Morgan for thinking I'd have taken that . . .

The veil of the temple, whether academic or ecclesiastic I forget – was to be raised, and as an exception she was to be allowed to enter in. But for 2,000 years we have done things without being paid for doing them. You can't bribe me now. Pail of offal? No; I said; while very deeply appreciating the hon. . . . In short one must tell lies, and apply every emollient in our power to the swollen skin of our brothers' so terribly inflamed vanity. Truth is only to be spoken by those women whose fathers were pork butchers and left them a share in the pig factory.

Friday 12 April

This little piece of rant won't be very intelligible in a year's time. Yet there are some useful facts and phrases in it. I rather itch to be at that book. But I have been skirmishing round a headache, and can't pull my weight in the morning. It is now almost settled that we shall drive through Holland and Germany, concealing Leonard's nose, to Rome; and so back. A giant tour on our most heroic scale.

Last night I dined with Nessa, L. being at Kingsley's to hear the story of his divided mind. He can't make up his mind, and must display the separated parts, like a heaving oyster, to his friends.

Sunday 14 April

Let me make a note that it would be much wiser not to attempt to sketch a draft of *On Being Despised* until *The Pargiters* is done with. I was vagrant this morning and made a rash attempt, with the interesting discovery that one can't propagate at the same time as write fiction.

Wednesday 17 April

Tomorrow we go to Rodmell, and when [Donald] Brace, at 7, slowly put on his coat, and made some very polite remark about seeing us in New York – when all this happened, I sank back and thought the holiday has begun. I forget I had something in mind to write here, about 'the soul' perhaps. The soul – the soul – How far could I let myself go in an anti-Fascist pamphlet? I think of dashing off my *Professions for Women*, can I steal a moment between Roger, Lytton and proofs. All this about being so distinguished and cultivated might be knocked on the head.

Monks House, Rodmell

Saturday 20 April
The scene has now changed to Rodmell. Good Friday was a complete fraud – rain and more rain. I tried walking along the bank. At the same time through the rain I heard the cuckoo's song. Then I came home and read and read – Stephen Spender [*The Destructive Element*: 'A study of modern writers and beliefs']; too quick to stop and think; shall I stop to think; read it again? But I want to investigate certain questions: why do I always fight shy of my contemporaries? Do I instinctively keep my mind from analysing, which would impede its creativeness? I think there's something in that. No creative writer can swallow another contemporary. But I admire Stephen for trying to grapple with these problems.

In the public world, there are emphatic scares. L. brings home a bunch after every Committee meeting. Its odd how seldom I report them. One of these days they may come true. For instance, [Ernst] Toller says we are on the brink of war. Wants the Allies to declare war on Hitler. Belgium keeps its aeroplanes at active service level, all ready to rise into the air. But as Germany could be on them before they rose this seems useless. There is a dutiful perfunctory stir about the [Royal Silver] Jubilee. We have subscribed £3 towards buns and a bus shelter in Rodmell. The King is said to be almost comatose. Will he get through with his bowings? And – there are incessant conversations – Mussolini, Hitler, MacDonald. All these people incessantly arriving at Croydon, arriving at Berlin, Moscow, Rome; and flying off again – while Stephen and I think how to improve the world.

Monday 22 April
The [Ralph] Wigrams to tea; she something like an old daisy or other simple garden flower; if a flower could look very unhappy. He is very white toothed, blue eyed, lean, red cheeked – a nice rigid honest public school Englishman. Started almost at once telling us about Hitler. He had been at Berlin with [Sir John] Simon [Foreign Secretary]. Hitler very impressive; very frightening. Made speeches lasting twenty minutes without a failure. Very well coached. And all the time a tapping sound. Wigram thought an odd day to have the masons in. But it was the sentry marching up and

down the passage. Everything came out. We want ... I want room to move about Hitler said. Must be equal, and so on. A complete reversal to pre-war days. No ideals except equality, superiority, force, possessions. And the passive heavy slaves behind him, and he a great mould coming down on the brown jelly. Talks of himself as the regenerator, the completely equipped and powerful machine. Wigram and the rest frightened. Anything may happen at any moment. Here in England we haven't even bought our gas masks. Nobody takes it seriously. But having seen this mad dog, the thin rigid Englishmen are really afraid. And if we have only nice public schoolboys like Wigram to guide us, there is some reason I suppose to expect that Oxford Street will be flooded with poison gas one of these days. And what then? Germany will get her colonies.

And then we walked them round the garden, and they were, or said they were, envious and impressed. She thinks of cutting the London season and staying at Southease; where, I fear, we shall now be frequently asked, to help with the garden. And then Kingsley [Martin] rang up and is now imminent. So I intend to walk.

Tuesday 23 April

Kingsley coming at eleven of our first fine morning and staying till six has completely taken away any power I may have over the art of fiction. In order to ensure myself two hours of silence and air I went off to Muggery Poke and home by the river. And there was Kingsley eating cold veal and sweeping up his cauliflower on his fork. An effusive slippery mind: always on the fizz: but how without hardness or fineness of texture! And now of course all dissolved by personal anxieties into a chatter of egotism. "Is there anything more we can say about my affairs?" he remarked at three. No, I said to myself, there is nothing more. Should he stay or should he go? I could only amuse myself by probing the depths of his belief in the *New Statesman*. Directly I minimised its importance, he trotted out arguments to prove its immense value to the world. The only paper that tells the truth, the stay and bread of all the serious minded in Britain. Then, directly I'm alone with him, its his arthritis. True, he's not quite in his right mind; but how tiring this shambling through the hot sand is! And how undistinguished, with no ear or eye, no reflective faculty and catching at any straw to float on; garrulous, untidy, slovenly. It is like reading a living newspaper, talking to Kingsley. It is like listening to a perpetual leading article, so admirable, so well meaning, so shallow.

52 Tavistock Square, wc1

Thursday 25 April
Whether it was Kingsley or not, the usual headache wings its way about me, rather like a fowl soaring and settling and giving me a peck in my back: clouding the mind. I think I have earned a headache and a holiday.

Sunday 28 April
Very cold again. A black sky and the paper festoons looking purple and pink across the streets; large paper crowns and roses being delivered. Julian and Alix [Strachey] to dine, James having a cold. Conversation: whether one can give people a substitute for war. Must have the danger emotion: must climb mountains, fight bulls. Julian says all the young are communists in order to gratify their desire to do things together and in order to have some danger. Lust and danger. Can't cut them out at once. Must divert them on to some harmless object. But what? Some fantasy must be provided. I say many people have found life exciting without war and bull fighting. Has war ever won any cause? Alix says our Civil War. No talk of Lytton: all argument; but interesting.

Tuesday 29 April
I should be tidying the room, but I'm not. Everything scattered with winter's soot and cigarette ash. Everything is a little slack now I'm not writing. But I want to experiment with pure external living for a month – looking, sharing, taking in ideas and impressions. And then watch how the old trout at the bottom of the pond rise. I predict that the desire to write will become so frantic by the time we're on the way back that I shall be making up all along the French roads.

A fine spring morning, very quiet, birds chirping, all London busy wrapping up parcels for the Jubilee.

*   *   *

Monks House, Rodmell

Friday 31 May
Home again, and how queer, as we drove up there was Pinker's basket being carried up by Percy, and she had died yesterday: her body was in the basket. Just as we were saying that we should see her in a moment. A very silent breakfast. And I had been saying how she would put out my match and all the usual jokes. And the intensity of the sense of death – even for a dog – our feeling of her character – something pathetic, and the depression, and the, I suppose, fear of sentimentality and so on.

The usual tremor and restlessness after coming back, and nothing to settle to. The view as beautiful as any I've seen, by the way, even on a mud coloured day. We drove through Normandy yesterday and it was Bank Holiday owing to Ascension Day, so that all the people were dressed in respectable black coats and fur. A more ugly tribute to the spirit could not be. I am writing to steady the fidgets, to cover over the depression, and it is only eleven, and I can't take up my book. I think that an hour of reading some good author is prescribed. L. very depressed too, about poor dear Pink. Eight years of a dog certainly means something. I suppose – is it part of our life that's buried in the orchard? That eight years in London – our walks – something of our play private life, that's gone?

52 TAVISTOCK SQUARE, WCI

Wednesday 5 June
Back here again, and the grim wooden feeling that has made me think myself dead since we came back is softening slightly. It's beginning this cursed dry hard empty chapter again in part. Also, after the queer interlude, at once life – that is the telephone beginning – starts. So that one is forcibly chafed.

Saturday 15 June
We dined with Clive, and I felt very fond of him. He has great sympathy. Yes, I'm very fond of my old Clive. And L. was charming, genial, affable, urbane. Clive said, I always say you're half cracked (to me). We were saying how many Rogers and Lyttons there are. He said Segonzac thinks Nessa the best painter in England, much better than Duncan. I will not be jealous, but isn't it odd – thinking of gifts in her? I mean when she has everything else.

Thursday 20 June
I am so oppressed by the thought of all the books I have to write that my head is like a bursting boiler. Half an hour ago, Margery Fry rang up to ask me to open an Exhibition of Roger's paintings at Bristol; to speak for fifteen minutes. Oh we should all love it! she said. Then it appeared that they are counting on me to write a life. She is collecting papers. Helen [Anrep] tells me that the Stracheys are hurt that I never offered to write about Lytton. "But I wanted to and they never asked me!" I said. Oh but they didn't like to suggest it – James says they do want it. And here I am wedged – no, buoyant – in a floating storm of scenes at the end of my book. And we are incessantly asked to dine, lunch, and 'see' people.

Tom last night: supple and subtle, simple and charming. Stayed till 12.15. I never felt so much at my ease. He is a dear old fellow: one of 'us': odd: I felt I liked him as I liked Lytton and Roger – with intimacy in spite of God. We made a good dinner. Publishers' gossip. A story about a party to entertain the [Herbert] Reads. Tom bought fireworks; sugar that dissolved and let out small fish; and chocolates that he thought were full of sawdust. "They're very greedy," he said; "and by mistake the chocolates were full of soap. They set on me ... And it was not a success. So much so that I forgot the fireworks, until they were going. I then let them off on the doorstep." This was very amusing, and not as stiff as usual. Tom wants to give me all his works, but thought I didn't read them – would always have given me all his works.

MONKS HOUSE, RODMELL

Saturday 22 June
It has suddenly become full summer: droning, misting, with birds and bees. The cuckoo calling in the elm tree at three or four this morning so that I had to stop my ears. The heat came suddenly as we walked by the river on Friday. Instead of surveying all this in a torpid swoon of pleasure, Mrs Woolf and Harold [Woolf] came to tea. Then there were figures passing the window – Jack and [his son] Jeremy [Hutchinson]; whereupon she lost all interest in life, poor old lady, thinking that no one would listen to her family stories. She cannot stretch to take in any stranger. But they went on to the [Glyndebourne] opera. Harold and Mrs Woolf and I continued our rather burbling conversation: about highbrows, and then about maids, and the hotel. I heard all about L.'s father, and how he did not take silk till he was forty-five, and made his name over – I forget what case; so it comes over and again, the story of her life, with the usual comments. "And I ask myself, what for? And I am now so lonely. I have lived alone so many years now ..." So we droned, sitting on the terrace before this house – very successful as a sitting place on a hot day. Why does this talk smear my mind so that I can't settle in at 6.30 to do anything but march up and down the terrace? Poor old lady.

52 TAVISTOCK SQUARE, WC I

Tuesday 25 June
A curious and rather unpleasant scene with Mabel. She was in tears, because Mr Woolf never believes a word she says. And I think it is true. L. is very

hard on people; especially on the servant class. No sympathy with them; exacting; despotic. So I told him yesterday when he'd complained about the coffee. "If I mayn't even say when the coffee is bad &c." His extreme rigidity of mind surprises me; I mean in its relation to others: his severity; not to myself but then I get up and curse him. What does it come from? Not being a gentleman partly: uneasiness in the presence of the lower classes: always suspects them, is never genial with them. His desire, I suppose, to dominate. Love of power. And then he writes against it. It goes with great justice, in some ways; and simplicity too; and doing good things; but it is in private a very difficult characteristic. I must now get rid of Mabel, and find another; but I feel it's unfair on her.

Thursday 27 June
A good thing for old Bloomsbury to be shaken up no doubt: a good thing to dine with Rebecca West and Mr Andrews [her husband] last night in their flat in Portman Square with the view, with the £750 book case, and the fish carved out of a yew branch, and the modern pictures, period furniture, letter box in the wall and which don't work. But the electric light in the coat cupboard does work. And what's wrong? The plumber's nose – the miner's canary, again. I mean scenting out differences, and let us hope inferiorities. Of course its admirable in its way – impersonal, breezy, yes, go ahead, facing life, eating dinner at the Savoy, meeting millionaires, woman and man of the worldly. What's wrong then? Where does the gas escape? I think its the emptiness, the formality, the social strata they live on – the sense of Now we're having a dinner party and must talk till eleven. Nothing said of any naturalness or spontaneity. Yet that's not quite so: that one could go on having dinner every night and never know each other better. No intimacy at the end of that Oxford Street. Rebecca has great vitality; is a broad browed very vigorous, undistinguished woman; but a buffeter and battler: has taken the waves, I suppose; and can talk in any language; why then this sense of her being a lit up modern block, floodlit by electricity?

Friday 28 June
But dinner with the [David] Cecils last night was very good: free and spontaneous; they were all dressed for a party at the Herberts. Origo was there, whom I like. She is young, tremulous, nervous – very – stammers a little – but honest eyed; very blue eyed. Talk spurted. (I hope I did not try to be brilliant?) We talked about: fear of people; parties: they were all afraid. Up in the drawing room, Origo (her name is Iris) sat down on purpose by me. She has read my books, and was of course full of stumbling enthusiasm; so I made a rush, and talked about writing, spilling out ideas, of a kind.

She lives near Siena, in perfect country; they talk of the seasons; harvest; vintage; share with peasants. And we talked about biography and fiction; but with David pricking up his ears across the room. So he had to be drawn in; and I think we have said the same things before – about the relevant facts; biography as an art. And Origo was silent for half an hour, because of going to the party.

L.'s book [*Quack, Quack!*] selling now; and he is cheerful, and very contrite, in his way, about Mabel.

Sunday 30 June
We went to Swakeleys Farm [Ickenham] yesterday and bought a dog – Sally. She has a fine domed head; very globular eyes; a bloodhound's muzzle; very affectionate, thirteen months old, clasps L.'s breast, climbs on his chair, and is afraid of the basement stairs. She cost £18 – dear me. Still as we say, its nice to have a good dog. And we shall breed from her. She has already her own rather whimsical manner, is lighter, more nervous, perhaps less solid a character than Pinker. But so far she has no marked fault. Had her nose been the eighteenth of an inch longer, she would have been a champion like her sister, who fetched £2 or £300.

Monday 15 July
All this time the Bristol speech was weighing on me, and making me unable to get into my swing for the last lap: so I shut down, wrote it, learnt it, and went to Bristol, the hottest day of the year, on Friday and said it, dripping, to a large, but not I think very appropriate audience. It puzzles me why such displays, using up so much nerve power, should be needed. There was Roger's face on the canvas, smiling at me, and them. But oh the heavenly relief when we drove off in the hot evening to Bradford on Avon, and slept the night in an ancient workhouse in the valley; with a disordered garden, a stream with rotting sacks of old clothes, and the usual elderly ladies, retired business men, spaniels, bustling landladies and so on.

Tuesday 16 July
A curious sense of complete failure. Margery hasn't written to me about my speech. And it was for this that I ruined my last pages! I can't write this morning. Can't get into the swing. Innumerable worries, about getting people to dine and so on, afflict me. My head is all jangled. And I have to get that d—d speech printed, or refuse to. The director has written. Never again, oh never again. But oh this anxiety, and the perpetual knocking of the cup out of my hand.

Wednesday 17 July

Last night as I was sitting alone, L. dining with the Noel-Bakers, there were three rings, and I went down and let in Julian, who said "I have been given a professorship in China." He was very much excited, rather alarmed, naturally – it means that he must start in the middle of August and spend three years in China at Wu Jong, or some such place, alone on a flooded river. So we talked – intimately, I mean about the past and our lives, for the first time. I'm very sorry he's to go – the delightful, honest, bubbly yet after all so sympathetic and trusty young man. Still, obviously this is his first real experience. Then he will travel about China in his holidays, and come back a full grown mature man, with a place in the world. He wants to write on politics and philosophy and to enter politics seriously. He says politics have got more and more on his conscience. They're on the conscience of all his generation. So he can't be merely a poet, a writer. I see his dilemma. So he goes, and I'm sorry. Three years. He will be thirty and I fifty-six alas.

Friday 19 July

I go on getting preliminary headaches. It is no good trying to do the last spurt, these last days here. And we have Edith [Sitwell] and Eddie Playfair, and Ottoline and Julian and Quentin tonight.

Saturday 20 July

But it turned out very well last night: headache lifted. Old Edith singular – very, with her great bald face – so beautiful in some lights; and the thin fan shaped hands and their gestures, timid, appealing, attached to this large fat clumsy body in its black rather sack like dress. She has great wit and some sharp edge of character, a gay rambling butterfly mind; and a good deal of sting, and humanity. In came Ottoline, rather garish, and not so quick in the mind as the rest of us. Eddie a very good listener. Then Julian, with his poems, and Quentin. It was all demonstration on Edith's part, done for our amusement, very difficult to recapture. Looks like a Plantagenet tomb said Ott. So she does, with her high nose, in the air, and her thin lips and her little peering eyes – very medieval.

MONKS HOUSE, RODMELL

Saturday 3 August

So the summer ended; and now opens again here, with Nessa back; Charleston in being, though rather intermittent, with Duncan in Rome still, Clive going to Greece, Julian to China, and Nessa proposing to paint the

[SS] *Queen Mary* in London. And the harvest is positively orange on the hill, and the country divinely coloured, ripe ash coloured and gold.

Friday 16 August
I cannot make a single note here, because I am so terrifically pressed re-writing – yes, typing out again at the rate, if possible, of 100 pages a week, this impossible eternal book. I work without looking up till one: what it now is, and therefore I must go in, leaving a whole heap of things unsaid: so many people, so many scenes, and beauty, and a fox and sudden ideas.

Wednesday 21 August
Margery Fry comes on Friday with her hands full of papers, she says. Another book. Have I the indomitable courage to start on another? Think of the writing and re-writing. Also there will be joys and ecstasies though. Again very hot. I am going to re-paint this room.

Thursday 22 August
Worked in the morning. Went to Lewes, very hot day; and bought stores, also distemper. And went to the County Library; full of books. So hot after tea: walked along the river bank; a game of bowls; beaten; dined with Keyneses. Maynard not well – rather damp talk. Talk of Abyssinia.

Thursday 29 August
I had meant to write one matter of fact note daily, but have never had time. My brain all tossing after the morning's work. Julian is leaving Newhaven at this moment I suppose for three years. Piles of Roger's papers sent by Margery – a whole box. I have now three large boxes, but dare not look in.

Friday 30 August
For a wonder, my head is clear, and my hand does not shake. Now the book seems to me very good.
Last night they sang the Belgian anthem at the Prom: out of respect for the Queen [of the Belgians]; and after that, the news-reader announced, in his most penetrated with respectful sorrow voice, the death of the Queen in a motor accident. The car ran off the road into a tree, and she was flung out; struck her head. The King kissed her, as she died. "And as I could not do anything, I went on" says the most trustworthy observer, a passer by, this morning. That, in its way is a tragedy. I distempered – the colour is too blue, but better than the green; then we walked to the river, played bowls, and now expect, alas, a teaparty of the most ferocious description, and its a blowing rainy cold day too.

Saturday 31 August
Only the Wolves came however. Torrents and floods and rain and wind. Edgar [Woolf] like a corpse. Yawned behind his hand. Sylvia [his wife] nervous, cat faced, making conversation. Chiefly about gold fish, dogs and cars; I did my usual owl with Mrs Woolf and she said, as my reward, there was no talk she enjoyed more. Angelica did not come. Mercifully, as the party was damp and dismal, sitting till 6.30 in the dining room. How it rains, said Mrs W. Everybody talking about Abysinnia, which I cannot spell, nor can I form letters, though the morning has been fluent – too fluent.

Wednesday 4 September
The most critical day since August 4th 1914. So the papers say. In London yesterday. Writings chalked up all over the walls. 'Don't fight for foreigners. Briton should mind her own business.' Then a circle with a symbol in it. Fascist propaganda. L. said. Mosley again active. The Queen of Belgium's funeral. Flags at half mast. Bought an umbrella for 25 shillings. The first good umbrella I've had for years, with a tassel.

And I think I will call the book 'The Years'.

Thursday 5 September
I've had to give up writing *The Years* – that's what its to be called – this morning. Absolutely floored. Can't pump up a word. Yet I can see, just, that something's there; so I shall wait, a day or two, and let the well fill. I think, psychologically, this is the oddest of my adventures. Half my brain dries completely; but I've only to turn over, and there's the other half, I think, ready, quite happily to write a little article. Oh if only anyone knew anything about the brain. And, even today, when I'm desperate, almost in tears looking at the chapter, unable to add to it, I feel I've only got to fumble and find the end of the ball of string – some start off place – and my head would fill and the tiredness go.

A very sensational voice on the loudspeaker last night. Mussolini closes the door. Deep disappointment. What next? &c. I was also in a stew about war and patriotism last night. And when it comes to my thinking about my country!

Friday 6 September
Violent wind and rain: violent sun and light; and they go on talking, threatening, advancing and retreating at Geneva.

Sunday 15 September
A terrific downpour. Never was such rain, I think, as this year. Autumn showing through. Autumn birds chirping through the rain. I am thinking I

will broach the three boxes of Roger; very staidly, merely beginning to drop a few facts into my brain. But I swear I will not let it buzz me into excitement. Shall I ever have time enough to write out all that's in my head? Though suppose what's in my head becomes sillier and feebler? But why should it? Not if I vary it sufficiently: what with pamphlets, criticism, poetry, fiction, and as I think a play perhaps. But then I'm a very slow writer. And *The Years* will have taken me very nearly three years. And I never think, seriously, of dying.

Tuesday 17 September

So they came: I mean all the Bells, and Janie [Bussy], growing a little elderly, but very gayly dressed; Quentin like a large red and white sheep dog. London yesterday: a violent storm of wind all night. Garden a litter of apples and branches.

Friday 20 September

Yes it was a terrific storm; a storm to mark I suppose. We went to Seaford and saw the explosions of white water over the lighthouse. Sea coming over the road. Clive Angelica and Quentin yesterday; I'm ashamed to say I had longed for this week to be all alone; never had a quiet week all this summer, and the balm it would be – and even a tea party means apprehension, breakage. Poor old Clive a little battered I thought. He has a curious antiquity, premature age, sometimes: I suppose when the top doesn't spin. He had been spinning round Greece; enjoyed himself vastly. Clive is writing a letter to the *New Statesman* against war. War's so awful it can't be right anyhow – an argument for which I like him: his genuine humanity. Dislike of being uncomfortable himself: yes; but he dislikes other people's unhappiness too.

Two nights ago I started reading Roger. There's all the schoolboy letters to begin on: whether its wise, I don't know.

Monday 23 September

Reflections on Tom week end: that it is too long. Can't write. That he is more masterly; tells a story like one who has the right; is broader and bonier and more wild eyed – long almond shaped eyes; that he means to write modern verse plays; that he is self confident although going up Charleston Lane in the dark last night, he told me that he has no self confidence. We dined at Charleston. Nessa ordered eleven grouse, having doubled the number, thinking of them halved. Tom is magisterially accepting new experiences. Likes, more than we do, respectability. Went to service at 8 on Sunday: a wet morning. But he did his duty. A very nice man, Tom; I'm very fond of Tom, and at last not much knocked off my perch by him.

Sunday 29 September

Yesterday I saw the kingfisher again on the river. It flies across and across, very near the surface: it has a bright orange chocolate under side. And it is a tropical bird, sitting weighted on the bank. I have also seen a stoat – brown with a white tipped tail.

Wednesday 2 October

Yesterday we went to the Labour Party meeting at Brighton, and of course, though I have refused to go again this morning, I am so thrown out of my stride that I can't hitch on to *The Years* again. Why? The immersion in all that energy and all that striving for something that is quite oblivious of me; making me feel that I am oblivious of it. It was very dramatic: Bevin's attack on Lansbury. Tears came to my eyes as Lansbury spoke. And yet he was posing I felt – acting, unconsciously, the battered Christian man. Then Bevin too acted I suppose. He sank his head in his vast shoulders till he looked like a tortoise. Told Lansbury not to go hawking his conscience round. The women delegates were very thin voiced and insubstantial. On Monday one said, It is time we gave up washing up. A thin frail protest, but genuine. A little reed piping, but what chance against all this weight of roast beef and beer – which she must cook? All very vivid and interesting; but too much rhetoric, and what a partial view: altering the structure of society: yes, but when it is altered? Do I trust Bevin to produce a good world, when he has his equal rights? These are some of the minnows that go round my head, and distract me from what is, after all, my work. A good thing to have a day of disturbance – two days even – but not three. So I didn't go.

52 TAVISTOCK SQUARE, WC1

Tuesday 15 October

Since we came back I have been in such full flush, with *Years* all the morning, Roger between tea and dinner, a walk, and people, that here's a blank. Yes, it has been ten days of calm full complete bliss. London is quiet, dry, comfortable. I find my dinner cooked for me. No children screaming. Three days I got into wild excitement over *The Next War*. Did I say the result of the Labour Party at Brighton was the breaking of that dam between me and the new book, so that I couldn't resist dashing off a chapter: stopped myself; but have all ready to develop – the form found I think – as soon as I get time? And I plan to do this sometime this next spring, while I go on accumulating Roger. This division is by the way perfect, and I wonder I never hit on it before – some book or work for a book that's quite the other side of the brain between times. Its the only way of stopping the wheels and making them turn the other way, to my great refreshment, and I hope improvement.

Sunday 27 October

Yesterday we walked across Ken Wood to Highgate and looked at the two little old Fry houses. That's where Roger was born and saw the poppy. I think of beginning with that scene. Yes, that book shapes itself. Then there's my *Next War* – which at any moment becomes absolutely wild, like being harnessed to a shark; and I dash off scene after scene. I think I must do it directly *The Years* is done.

Tuesday 5 November

A specimen day, yesterday: a specimen of the year 1935 when we are on the eve of the Duke of Gloucester's wedding; of a general election; of the Fascist revolution in France; and in the thick of the Abyssinian war; it being mild warm November weather. At 2.30 we went to the BBC and listened to some incomparable twaddle – a soliloquy which the BBC requests me to imitate (a good idea, all the same, if one were free) with all the resources of the BBC behind one: real railway trains; real orchestras; noises; waves, lions and tigers, &c; at 3 we reach [the *Sunday Times* Book Exhibition]: a loudspeaker proclaiming the virtues of literature, the Princess Louise having just declared the show open and said that books are our best friends. There we meet old stringy Rose Macaulay, beating about, like a cat a-hawking odds and ends; home; at 5.15 telephone: the Baroness Nostitz has arrived early; up she comes: a monolithic broad faced Hindenburg, bulky; can't get in or out of my chair; says Germany is the better for Hitler – so they say; I want to get some young man to lecture on English poetry; has a rather hard, dominating impassive eye: must have been a beauty; statuesque; aristocratic. Then a card: in comes the Indian; stayed till 7.30. Was turned out of a carriage in Bengal. Liberty. Justice. Hatred of the British rule. Still, its better than the Italian. *You* are our allies. The British will be kicked out. And now Morgan rings up – May I lunch to discuss the French question. And so we go on. Another specimen day.

Sunday 10 November

Then, last night there was [Cecil] Day Lewis at the Book show, a man who makes queer faces; very nervous at first; with blurred eyes; a nice sensitive young man; but I think it would have been better read, his speech. All poets are misfits and therefore want communion with the common people. What exactly is poetry that is part the desire to communicate with the common people? Political poetry? Certainly it's not easy, one word Wordsworth poetry. Instead of 'The Leech Gatherer' the tank and poison gas. Too much theory: too little gift I think and too much public speaking. But then if he wants to be in touch with the common people he must talk at Book shows. Not very anxious I think to dine with us, for which I liked him. The usual hurry and scramble of literary gents; and Rose again hawking round the area railings for scraps.

Wednesday 27 November
Too many specimen days – so I can't write. Why can't I get quit of it all? Still happiness persists. And now for thirty minutes of Roger's letters to Helen – that vast sparkling dust heap, the best so far; but how to dig out? how to represent? I must read and read and wait on the moment of illumination. Cold frosty weather, dry for a miracle, and very sunny.

Wednesday 4 December
I must take ten – no five – minutes off before going up, and from reading Roger to Helen. I read and read and the packets hardly lessen, and I think of love, and L. and me; and the different lives. Yesterday Day Lewis wrote that his agent advises him to leave us for a larger firm, as he must make money. This revives the question of the Press – once again, once again. We both said walking at Ken Wood yesterday, we will now decide on a date and stop it. Yes: reading Roger I want to be free to travel as he was: free of MSS. Yet how keep our books? Or shall we try to hand it on to an intelligent youth? I rather doubt if such exist, or able to run it alone, and then we should still be tied.

Tuesday 10 December
I have promised to deliver *The Years* by 15th February. And had a bad morning's work in consequence. But if I want more time, I shall take it. I'm not time's fool – no. Nessa I thought very sad again, dining with Clive. What thin stuff we talk compared with what we used to talk. And then people say death doesn't matter.

Saturday 14 December
Dinner last night with the [Aldous] Huxleys; not altogether a sparkler. Julian [Huxley] and his wife, whom I did not recognise, but later understood from his eyebrows &c who he was. A very chirpy I don't know why I think dull, man. Full of scraps of information; and the same quickness that Aldous has – the same vivacity – but less sympathetic. Aldous in great flow: enjoys London; is getting on well with his novel; and thus juicy, sympathetic. He has a sense of the suffering, as well as of the infamy of the world.

Tuesday 17 December

How terrified I'm getting of Ethel [Sands]'s dressed dinner tomorrow! It makes a kind of ring round my mind. What I'm to wear: my velvet or chiffon: then my hair. When I'm there it'll be as easy as shelling peas – why this apprehension?

Friday 20 December

"It's because one changes one's values" Nessa said last night, when we discussed why we couldn't paint or write after a dinner party. And that's true. Only artists know how to live. She can't paint after a party. Can't get back into those proportions. Worse for women, because they have to be more active at parties: have to throw themselves into it. She won't go anywhere now where they make her dress.

Monks House, Rodmell

Saturday 28 December

Its all very well to write that date in a nice clear hand, but I cannot disguise the fact that I'm almost extinct; like a charwoman's duster; that is my brain: what with the last revision of the last pages of *The Years*. And is it the last revision? And why should I lead the dance of the days with this tipsy little spin? Its only half past eleven on a damp grey morning, and I want a quiet occupation for an hour. That reminds me – I must devise some let down for myself that won't be too sudden when the end is reached. Shall I ever write a long book again – a long novel that has to be held in the brain, at full stretch – for close on three years? Nor do I even attempt to ask if its worth while. There are mornings so congested I can't even copy out Roger. Goldie [Lowes Dickinson] depresses me unspeakably. Always alone on a mountain top asking himself how to live, theorising about life; never living. Roger always down in the succulent valleys, living. But what a thin whistle of hot air Goldie lets out through his front teeth. Always live in the whole, life in the one; always Shelley and Goethe, and then he loses his hot water bottle; and never notices a face, or a cat or a dog or a flower, except in the glow of the universal. This explains why his highminded books are unreadable. Yet he was so charming, intermittently.

Sunday 29 December

I have in fact just put the last words to *The Years* – rolling rolling, though its only Sunday, and I allowed myself till Wednesday. And I am not in such a twitter as usual. But then I meant it to end calmly – a prose work. And is it good? That I cannot possibly tell. Well there still remains a great deal to do. Anyhow the main feeling about this book is vitality, fruitfulness, energy. Never did I enjoy writing a book more, I think.

Monday 30 December

And today, no its no go. I can't write a word; too much headache. Can only look back at *The Years* as an inaccessible Rocky Island, which I can't explore, can't even think of. At Charleston yesterday. The great yellow table with very few places. Reading Roger I become haunted by him. What an odd posthumous friendship – in some ways more intimate than any I had in life. The things I guessed are now revealed; and the actual voice gone. Clive, Quentin, Nessa, Duncan. A little boasting. Some laughter. Politics – but carefully subdued.

A wild wet night – floods out: rain as I go to bed: dogs barking: wind battering. Now I shall slink indoors, I think, and read some remote book.

1936

Virginia had set herself to finish the revision of The Years *by the middle of February for publication in early summer; she restricted her social activities, and devoted the dismal winter days to a task which she found increasingly onerous and which brought on headaches and insomnia. The death of King George V and the manifestations of public mourning diverted her; but she was agitated by what seemed to her the incessant racket at home – the comings and goings, the telephone-ringings, the meetings – resulting from the worsening international situation and Leonard's political involvements. By early March (when Hitler's troops occupied the Rhineland), the decision was taken to have* The Years *set in galleys to accommodate the expectant American publishers, and Virginia began to despatch the typescript to the printers in sections as she finished them, the last batch being sent from Monks House at Easter. Racked by headaches, she was now close to total collapse, alarming Leonard who decided that proof-correction and publication must be postponed until the autumn, and she should have a complete rest. There are no diary entries between 9 April and 11 June. Virginia remained largely recumbent at Monks House, with brief intervals in London and a change of scene when Leonard drove her on a tour of the West Country as far as her beloved Cornwall. After two months she resumed work on the proofs of* The Years, *but again the effort and the pressures of London life threatened her nervous stability. The Woolfs retreated to Rodmell on 9 July and remained there until 11 October, Leonard going up weekly to attend to business at Tavistock Square. Virginia wrote no diary between 23 June and 30 October. At Monks House she rested, read, walked, played bowls in the garden, saw a few familiars, and laboured, an hour at a time, on her galley proofs; but it became apparent that autumn publication would be out of the question. Back in London, much improved in health, she struggled on, alternating between confidence and despair, and in the latter mood finally appealed for Leonard's verdict. He read the heavily worked-over galleys and, fearing the effect of adverse criticism on his overwrought wife, praised her book rather beyond his real opinion of its merit. The relief was immeasurable. She was able to finish the proofs by the end of the year and allow herself to turn eagerly to the writing of her long-simmering political work,* Three Guineas, *and to continue her preparatory reading for the biography of Roger Fry.*

Gradually Virginia picked up the threads of her social life. Events in the outer world also began again to engage her interest and concern (the Spanish Civil War had broken out while she was ill at Rodmell in July), none more so than the drama of King Edward VIII's abdication, which fascinated her. She was interested, and flattered too, when her girlhood friend Nelly's husband Lord Robert Cecil, now Viscount Cecil of Chelwood and President of the League of Nations Union, invited himself to tea at Tavistock Square and confided his opinion of world statesmen.

Curiously enough, throughout this ill-omened year, Virginia was sustained by Ethel Smyth's constant and open-hearted concern, expressed in numerous letters, to which she responded equally: over forty letters from Virginia to Ethel are preserved from this period.

1936

Monks House, Rodmell

Friday 3 January
I began the year with three entirely submerged days, headache, head bursting, head so full, racing with ideas; and the rain pouring; the floods out; when we stumbled out yesterday the mud came over my great rubber boots; the water squelched in my soles; so this Christmas has been, as far as country is concerned, a failure, and in spite of what London can do to chafe and annoy I'm glad to go back, and have, rather guiltily, begged not to stay here another week. I am content though because I think that I have recovered enough balance in the head to begin *The Years*, I mean the final revision, on Monday.

Saturday 4 January
The weather has improved, and we have decided to stay till Wednesday. So I have ordered a sirloin and we shall go for a drive. L. is happier: will now do his trees.

Tuesday 7 January
A pouring day. All the angles of the twigs have white drops on them. That's Hardy's gift by the way: minute obstinately individual observations. But how his reputation ever mounted, considering the flatness, tedium, and complete absence of gift of *The Trumpet Major*, I can't say; and would like to discover. I think he had genius and no talent. And the English love genius.

52 Tavistock Square, WC1

Friday 10 January
Back again. A great gale all yesterday and a dusk over everything and rain, so that the comfort I had expected was diminished. Origo to tea, and wants to dine next week. All the same I will keep my hands on the reins. For, to

391

tell the truth, this six weeks is going to be a most perilous enterprise. How on earth to finish, to get typed, to correct by the end of February?

Monday 13 January
The precious days are ticking over. About thirty now left me, and how much to do! But my new method is working I think: each hour mapped in bed, and kept to, so far.

Thursday 16 January
Seldom have I been more completely miserable than I was about 6.30 last night, reading over the last part of *The Years*. Such feeble twaddle – such twilight gossip it seemed; such a show up of my own decrepitude, and at such huge length. I could only plump it down on the table and rush up stairs with burning cheeks to L. He said This always happens. But I felt, no it has never been so bad as this. Now this morning, dipping in, it seems to me, on the contrary, a full, bustling live book.

Iris Origo to dine alone. At first I thought this too is going to be a wash out. But, chiefly owing to L.'s charm, and making myself a little drunk, we all chattered, and we both liked her. And she is to come again. A genuine woman, I think, honest, intelligent and, to my pleasure, well dressed; also being a snob, I liked her Bird of Paradise flight through the gay world. A long green feather in her hat suggests the image.

Sunday 19 January
I open this, forced by a sense of what is expected by the public, to remark that Kipling died yesterday; and that the King (George 5th) is probably dying today. The death of Kipling has set all the old war horses of the press padding round their stalls; and the papers have to eke out five or six columns with the very bare bulletin – condition causes anxiety – which they supplement with biographies of doctors, of nurses, pictures of Sandringham, remarks of old villagers, gossip about the little Princesses in their cherry coloured coats, a snow man, &c. But the fact remains that all the Princes have gathered together, and I suppose at any moment the butler may come in, just as they're finishing dinner, and say King Edward 8th, upon which – but I need hardly invent that scene having already so many on my hands.

I went up to an elderly stout woman reading the paper at *The Times* Book Club the other day. It was Margery Strachey. What are you doing? I said. 'Nothing!' she replied. 'I've got nowhere to go and nothing to do.' And I left her, sitting reading *The Times*.

Monday 20 January
And the King is not dead, but the same. It is a very fine bright day.

Tuesday 21 January

The King died last night. We were dining [in Pimlico] and drove back past Buckingham Palace. It was a clear dry night, rather windy and rather cold. As we turned the corner and came by the Palace we saw cars drawn up all along the Mall. On the white monument people were standing; there was a cluster like a swarm of bees round the railings. Some people were plastered against the railings, holding on to the bars. There was a discreet frame, like a text, holding a bulletin. We had to drive on past the Monument before the policeman, who spoke with weary politeness, would let us stop. Then we got out, and walked back and tried to shove our way through the crowd. But it was impossible. So I asked a policeman "What is the latest news?" (we had only seen Strength Diminishing on the placards as we drove out) to which he replied "His Majesty's life is drawing to a peaceful close." This he said without conviction, as if he were reciting words put into his mouth, but with a certain official tolerance. There was some agitation and excitement; many foreigners talking German; a large proportion of distinguished looking men, in semi evening dress. As we turned away, a firework – a silver gilt sputtering fizzing torch began bubbling up, like a signal, like a festival, but it was presumably a photographer's light. The crowd clustering on the rails became chalky white for a few seconds; and then we got into the car and drove home. The streets were very empty. But save for the occasional placard – it was now 'The King is Dying' – there was nothing out of the way. What I took for guns booming was only the banging of the loose door in the mews. But at 3 this morning, L. was woken by paper boys shouting in the street. The King had in fact died at 12.05. He was dead when we were outside the Palace.

Most of the men in Southampton Row wear black ties which are brand new, or dark blue ties, which are the nearest they can get. In the stationers' the woman spoke with a subdued kindness as if we were both mourning a great uncle we had never seen. A very fine cold day. Sun shining.

Wednesday 22 January

The people of America are mourning, as if for their own King; and the Japanese are in tears. So it goes on. But as a matter of fact the Prime Minister [Stanley Baldwin] – we are only allowed official announcements on the BBC, and if you turn it on you only hear the ticking of a vast clock – was rather fitting. He gave out the impression that he was a tired country gentleman; the King another; both enjoyed Christmas at home; and the Queen is very lonely; one left the other taken, as must happen to married couples; and the King had seemed to him tired lately, but very kind, and quiet as if ready for a long journey; and had woken once or twice on the last day and had said something Kind ('Kind' was the adjective always) and had said to his Secretary "How is the Empire?" – an odd expression. "The Empire, Sir, is well"; whereupon he fell asleep. And then of course, he ended with God Save the King.

The shops are all black. Mourning is to outlast the London Season. A black Ascot.

Monday 27 January
And I forgot to say we saw the coffin and the Princes come from King's Cross: the coffin with its elongated yellow leopards, the crown glittering and one pale blue stone luminous, a bunch of red and white lilies; after that three undertakers in black coats with astrakhan collars: 'our King' as the woman next me called him, who looks blotched and as if chipped by a stone mason; only his rather set wistful despair marked him from any shop-keeper – not an ingratiating face: bloated, roughened, as if by exposure to drink, life, grief, and as red as a fisherboy's. Then it was over. And I shall not try to see more. But the whole world will be afoot at dawn tomorow.

Tuesday 28 January
The King is at this moment being buried, and if I go up I shall hear the service. A fine mild morning. The sun is out, the streets almost empty. An occasional hoot.

Sunday 9 February
It is now the 9th of February and I have three weeks in which to finish my book. I work three hours in the morning; two often after tea. Then my head swells and I sleep.

Tuesday 25 February
And this will show how hard I work. This is the first moment – this five minutes before lunch – that I've had to write here. I work all the morning: I work from 5 to 7 most days. I have sworn that the script shall be ready, typed and corrected, on the 10th March. L. will then read it.

Saturday 29 February
Leap Year day. In these weeks of solitude, seeing no one, only going round to Nessa, refusing all parties, I become so absorbed in *The Years* that I take the other world as a kind of amplification, variation in another key. Nothing interferes for the moment; and I rush on. It is drizzling. It is a damp dismal day.

All Duncan's pictures have been refused – to give a scrap of upper air news – by the *Queen Mary*. A great Bloomsbury agitation set on foot.

Wednesday 4 March

Well yesterday I sent off 132 pages to Clark [Printers]. We have decided to take this unusual course – that is to print it in galleys before L. sees it and send it to America.

I can't help feeling in the subcutaneous way one does feel such things that we are slightly on the up grade again: old Bloomsbury. Its rather a nicer feeling than being on the down grade perhaps. The European situation developed on Saturday. We were at Monks House. Hitler has broken his word again.

Friday 13 March

We walked round Kensington Gardens yesterday discussing politics. Aldous refuses to sign the latest manifesto because it approves sanctions. He's a pacifist. So am I. Ought I to resign? L. says that considering Europe is now on the verge of the greatest smash for six hundred years, one must sink private differences and support the League [of Nations]. He's at a special Labour Party meeting this morning. This is the most feverish overworked political week we've yet had. Hitler has his army on the Rhine. Meetings take place in London. Another meeting tomorrow. As usual, I think Oh this will blow over. But its odd, how near the guns have got to our private life again. I can quite distinctly see them and hear a roar, even though I go on, like a doomed mouse, nibbling at my daily page. What else is there to do – except answer the incessant telephones, and listen to what L. says. Everything goes by the board. Happily we have put off all dinners and so on, on account of *The Years*.

Monday 16 March

For my own guidance: I have never suffered, since *The Voyage Out*, such acute despair on re-reading, as this time. On Saturday for instance: there I was, faced with complete failure; and yet the book is being printed. Yesterday I read it again; and I think it may be my best book. However ... A walk down the river and through Richmond Park did more than anything to pump blood in. Politics have slightly died down.

Tuesday 24 March

I'm so absorbed in *Two Guineas* – that's what I'm going to call it – I must very nearly verge on insanity I think. I get so deep in this book I don't know what I'm doing. Find myself walking along the Strand talking aloud.

Wednesday 1 April

I forgot though to make L. an April fool, and he forgot too. We went to tea with Gerald [Duckworth] yesterday, which was like visiting an alligator in a tank, an obese and obsolete alligator, lying like our tortoises, half in and half out of the water. I doubt that he much enjoyed seeing us, or has any capacity for enjoying anything left. We talked publishers' shop. And Gerald told me about his diseases, and threw cold water, sensible, business-man's very faded common sense – for he has failed as a business man – on all projects. There's nothing in it – nothing in it, he kept saying. Also, nothing doing, nothing doing whatever. I think felt us perhaps more in the swim than himself. I doubt he has any sentiment about the past. So we went, and walked in the park.

MONKS HOUSE, RODMELL

Thursday 9 April

Now will come the season of depression. The last batch was posted to Clark yesterday. L. is in process of reading. I daresay I'm pessimistic, but I fancy a certain tepidity in his verdict so far; but then its provisional. The horror is that tomorrow, after this one windy day of respite – oh the cold North wind that has blown ravaging daily since we came – after this one day's respite, I say, I must begin at the beginning and go through 600 pages of cold proof. Why oh why? Never again, never again. Dining at Charleston tonight, I'm glad to say.

And then there was Colefax – yes, instantly on us, the first day we arrived, for lunch: in a black beret, and grey tweed coat. Not improved by sorrow. Poor woman, what a hard nature, so that to lose [her husband] only liberates a little misty sentiment. And yet she's brave, I think; but still the hostess, the aspiring, restless, dissatisfied – running, running, like a dog behind a carriage that always goes too fast. We had polite conversation about notables over the fire, and then she left. Rolls Royce.

52 TAVISTOCK SQUARE, WC1

Thursday 11 June

I can only, after two months, make this brief note, to say at last after two months dismal and worse, almost catastrophic illness – never been so near the precipice to my own feeling since 1913 – I'm again on top. I have to re-write, I mean interpolate and rub out most of *The Years* in proof. But I can't go into that. Can only do an hour or so. Oh but the divine joy of being mistress of my mind again! Back from Monks House yesterday. Now I am going to live like a cat stepping on eggs till my 600 pages are done. I think I can – I think I can – but must have immense courage and buoyancy to compass it. This, as I say, my first voluntary writing since April 9th, after which I pitched into bed: then to Cornwall – no note of that; then back; then to Monks House; home yesterday for a fortnight's trial.

Sunday 21 June

After a week of intense suffering – indeed mornings of torture – and I'm not exaggerating – pain in my head – a feeling of complete despair and failure – a head inside like the nostrils after hay fever – here is a cool quiet morning again, a feeling of relief; respite; hope. I am living so constrainedly; so repressedly; I can't make notes of life. Everything is planned, battened down. I do half an hour down here; go up, often in despair. Lie down; walk round the Square; come back, do another ten lines. I see people lying on sofa between tea and dinner. A very strange, most remarkable summer. I am learning my craft in the most fierce conditions.

Tuesday 23 June

A good day – a bad day – so it goes on. Few people can be so tortured by writing as I am. Yet I think I can bring it off, if I only have courage and patience: take each scene quietly; I think it may be a good book. And then – oh when its finished! My brain is like a scale: one grain pulls it down. Yesterday it balanced: today it dips.

*　　　*　　　*

52 TAVISTOCK SQUARE, WC1

Friday 30 October

I do not wish for the moment to write out the story of the months since I made the last mark here. I do not wish, for reasons I cannot now develop, to analyse that extraordinary summer. Can I still 'write'? That is the question, you see.

Tuesday 3 November

Miracles will never cease – L. actually likes *The Years*! He thinks it so far as good as any of my books. I will put down the actual facts. On Sunday I started to read the proofs. When I had read to the end of the first section I was in despair: stony but convinced despair. I made myself yesterday read on to 'Present Time'. When I reached that landmark I said this is happily so bad that there can be no question about it. I must carry the proofs, like a dead cat, to L. and tell him to burn them unread. This I did. And a weight fell off my shoulders. It was cold and dry and very grey and I went out and walked through the graveyard with Cromwell's daughter's tomb down through Gray's Inn along Holborn and so back. Now I was no longer

Virginia, the genius, but only a perfectly insignificant yet content – shall I call it spirit? a body? And very tired. Very old. So we lunched, in a constraint: a grey acceptance. I was not unhappy. And L. said he thought I might be wrong about the book. Then ever so many strange men arrived. Then, after tea, we went to the *Sunday Times* Book Show. How stuffy it was! How dead I felt – Oh how infinitely tired! We went home, and L. read and read and said nothing; I began to feel actively depressed; and I fell into one of my horrid heats and deep slumbers, as if the blood in my head were cut off. Suddenly L. put down his proof and said he thought it extraordinarily good – as good as any of them. And now he is reading on, and tired out with the exertion of writing these pages I'm going up to read the Italian book.

Wednesday 4 November
L. who has now read to the end of '1914' still thinks it extraordinarily good: very strange; very interesting; very sad. But my difficulty is this: I cannot bring myself to believe that he is right. It may be simply that I exaggerated its badness, and therefore he now, finding it not so bad, exaggerates its goodness. If it is to be published, I must at once sit down and correct: but how can I? Every other sentence seemed to me bad. It is one of the most puzzling situations I have ever been in. Of course we might appeal to Morgan.

Thursday 5 November
The miracle is accomplished. L. put down the last sheet about 12 last night; and could not speak. He was in tears. He says it is 'a most remarkable book' – he *likes* it better than *The Waves*; and has not a spark of doubt that it must be published. I hardly know yet if I'm on my heels or head – so amazing is the reversal since Tuesday morning. I have never had such an experience before. Now it is pouring and we go down to Lewes for the fireworks.

Tuesday 10 November
I wonder if anyone has ever suffered so much from a book, as I have from *The Years*. Once out I will never look at it again. Its like a long childbirth. Think of that summer, every morning a headache, and forcing myself into that room in my nightgown; and lying down after a page: and always with the certainty of failure. But now I feel I don't care what anyone says so long as I'm rid of it. Madrid not fallen. Chaos. Slaughter. War surrounding our island.

Tuesday 17 November
Lord [Robert] Cecil to tea. He has grown large, but still has the angular twisting movements of a thin man. His face is moon shaped; brown and

pink – it used to be lank and cadaverous. He is more genial, and at his ease. A man of the world. A little frieze of still brown hair, very fine, at the back of his head. Bright merry eyes. In good spirits, in spite of the world. But he said, I think there is more vitality both in men and in institutions, than one expects. "We have failed (the League of Nations); no matter, we must try again. I'm convinced by Winston [Churchill]. An alliance of France, England and Russia. Bertrand Russell insane! Complete insanity! To tell us we are to submit to Hitler! Do what Hitler tells us! What do you think, Sally?" Caressed Sally [dog] with his long pointed fingers. Had been taken to see Mussolini. An absurd fellow. There he sat at the end of a very long room, making eyes at me (he made eyes). That doesn't impress me. Gave the impression of extreme well being: a saucepan gently simmering on the comfort and consideration of seventy years. Best type of English governing class I suppose: the flower of 19th century civilisation: urbane, broadminded, kind and hopeful. Much more cheerful than the intellectuals. Inclined to mock the earnest intellectual. Very nice of him to come of course. I was flattered. And it was raining and he went home in the Tube. Very poor he said. Couldn't afford a car. Anything else? Not much deluded I should say. Winston on side of Franco, because he has friends in that camp. But the people don't respect Winston. He changes his mind and policy. Baldwin a complete failure. That's about all.

Tuesday 24 November
Here I am cleft as usual in my little stick. So free and so cabined. Began *Three Guineas* yesterday. And liked it. Today the old symptoms – time of life: the swollen veins; the tingling; the odd falling; feeling of despair. Brain not fully blooded. Hot and cold. I'm glad, how odd, that I'm lunching with Clive. That I've a new black felt hat, bought yesterday after having Ethel Smyth to lunch. Glad too that Helen Anrep is dining with me: that I shan't be alone; alone I fall into those trances, comas, when I want to be clear and to read. But I've been on the whole vigorous and cheerful since the wonderful revelation of L.'s that night. How I woke from death – or non-being – to life! What an incredible night – what a weight rolled off!

Very cold and dank. We came up on Sunday through the fog. Figures suddenly emerged. Walked by the kerb all through Wimbledon and Wandsworth. The kerb ended. Here I was lost in a trackless mist. And so on and on. A little boy emerged – a street ruffian. People lined the pavement watching the lost cars. Another man led us. Just as we thought we must find a garage and come home by tube a bus driver told us that in two hundred yards it would be clear. So, miraculously, it was. Glass clear – lit up, and so home.

Friday 27 November

L. has a confidential story about the King and Mrs Simpson, told him in secret by Kingsley Martin.

Monday 30 November

There is no need whatever in my opinion to be unhappy about *The Years*. It seems to me to be a taut real strenuous book: with some beauty and poetry too. A full packed book. Just finished it; and feel a little exalted.

Monday 7 December

Now, we are – without a King? With a Queen? What? The Simpson affair is on the surface. It was on Wednesday 2 December that the Bishop [of Bradford] commented on the King's lack of religion. On Thursday all the papers, *The Times* and *Daily Telegraph* very discreetly mentioned some domestic difficulties; others Mrs Simpson. All London was gay and garrulous – not exactly gay, but excited. We can't have a woman Simpson for Queen, that was the sense of it. She's no more royal than you or me, was what the grocer's young woman said. But today we have developed a strong sense of human sympathy: we are saying Hang it all – the age of Victoria is over. Let him marry whom he likes. Harold [Nicolson] is glum as an undertaker, and so are the other nobs. They say Royalty is in Peril. The Empire is divided. In fact never has there been such a crisis. Spain, Germany, Russia – all are elbowed out. Parties are forming. The different interests are queueing up behind Baldwin or Churchill. Mosley is taking advantage of the crisis for his ends. In fact we are all talking nineteen to the dozen; and it looks as if this one little insignificant man had moved a pebble which dislodges an avalanche. Things – empires, hierarchies, moralities – will never be the same again.

Thursday 10 December

Has the King abdicated? I think so. At 3.30 Baldwin will speak. *The Times* reiterates No one has hurried the King. We sympathise but . . . it is for His Majesty to decide. Mrs Simpson at Cannes says she is ready to withdraw from an unhappy and untenable position. Cars, black cars, drive constantly to and from Fort Belvedere where the King is immured, some say drinking. Baldwin goes down constantly: the King is rude and drunk. Last night the Queen and Princess Mary went. A brake laden with luggage was seen to leave the fort. No royal engagements are kept. It is a time of mourning. The Queen visits old curiosity shops and is said to have bought a gold frog. Meanwhile 'the people' have swung round to a kind of sneering contempt. "Ought to be ashamed of himself" the tobacconist's young woman said. Last night Mary [Hutchinson] on the telephone said that to her certain knowledge the King was entirely possessed, against all friends' advice, of some bourgeois (her word) obsession about marriage: insisted, after two years of license, that the marriage service was essential – though Mrs Simpson did not wish it. She says all his friends think him insane. He could have gone on with Mrs Simpson as mistress till they both cooled: no one objected. Now he has probably lost her, and thrown away the Kingdom and made us all feel slightly yet perceptibly humiliated. Its odd, but so I even feel it. Walking through Whitehall the other day, I thought what a Kingdom! England! and to put it down the sink . . . Not a very rational feeling. *The Times* quotes, in its leader this morning, letters which beginning earlier in the week with hysterical sympathy, now say Our sons and brothers gave their wives and lovers and also their lives for the country. And can't even the King do this –? But everything now hardens into the certainty that the King can't do this, and will follow his luggage to Cannes. I am reluctant to end this page, because it is I think the last entry I shall make in this book on the subject of Edward the Eighth. If I write tomorrow, it will be in the reign, I suppose, of Albert the First – and he's not, so Mary says, a popular choice. Let it be. This afternoon I shall go down in the fog to the hub of the universe, and hang about the House of Commons.

[*Later*] This is the first hour, or since it is 5.30, and the abdication was announced at 4, the first hour and a half, of the new reign. Yes, I thought: I will go to Westminster. A bus took me to the top of Whitehall. There traffic was turned off and I dismounted. Whitehall was full of shuffling and trampling. Opposite the Horse Guards there was Ottoline, black, white, red lipped, coming towards me. She intercepted my impulse to escape. We turned and walked on, and on we wandered down the yellow brown avenue. That's the window out of which Charles the First stepped when he had his head cut off said Ottoline, pointing to the great lit up windows [of the Banqueting House] in their frame of white stone. I felt I was walking in the 17th Century with one of the courtiers; and she was lamenting not the abdication of Edward, but the execution of Charles. Its dreadful, dreadful, she kept saying. Poor silly little boy. No one could ever tell him a thing he disliked. But to throw it away . . . Still he hadn't yet, so far as we knew, thrown it away. However, she had a tea party: so we hailed a taxi. Have you any news? the man said. No . . . What do you think? I say he should. We don't want a woman thats already had two husbands and an American when there are so many good English girls . . . We were thus driving and talking when a newspaper car drove by with the word Abdication very large on a placard. It stopped near us; and the first papers in the bale were bought by Ottoline and me.

Sunday 13 December
Then we had the Broadcast. "Prince Edward speaking from Windsor Castle" as the emotional butler announced. Upon which, with slight stammer at first, in a steely strained voice, [he] began: "At long last . . . I can speak to you . . . The woman I love . . . I who have none of those blessings . . ." Well, one came in touch with human flesh I suppose. Also with a set pigheaded steely mind . . . a very ordinary young man; but the thing had never been done on that scale. One man set up in the Augusta Tower at Windsor addressing the world on behalf of himself and Mrs Simpson. Out in the Square there was complete emptiness. All the life had been withdrawn to listen, to judge. And then Edward went on in his steely way to say the perfectly correct things, about the Constitution, the Prime Minister, Her Majesty my Mother. Finally he wound up, God Save the King with a shout; after which I heard his sigh go up, a kind of whistle. Then silence. Complete silence. Then Mr Hibbert saying: And now we shut down. Good night everybody. Goodnight; and we were tucked up in our beds.

Thursday 30 December
There in front of me lie the proofs – the galleys – to go off today . . . a sort of stinging nettle that I cover over. Nor do I wish even to write about it here. A divine relief has possessed me these last days – at being quit of it – good or bad. Now for action and pleasure again and going about.

1937

The millstone of The Years *lifted from her shoulders, Virginia started the new year in a much happier frame of mind, free now to compose* Three Guineas*; and she had need of fortitude: two deaths, that of the sculptor Stephen Tomlin, and that of Miss West, the dependable manager of the Hogarth Press, affected her fairly closely; she endured acute anxiety – happily short-lived – when it seemed that Leonard might have a serious illness; she herself experienced disquieting symptoms which she ascribed to the menopause; her nephew Julian Bell was returning from China determined to fight against the Fascists in Spain; and over all loomed the approaching publication of* The Years *and the dread that it might be condemned. To her relief and some surprise it received very good notices, sold extremely well, and became a bestseller in America.*

Virginia always took pleasure in the company of the younger generation, and besides her nephews and nieces and their friends, liked to entertain young writers such as Christopher Isherwood and Stephen Spender. At this period conversation turned almost inevitably to politics and the Spanish Civil War. The Woolfs took their three-week holiday in May, avoiding the hubbub of the coronation of George VI, driving in Western France as far south as Albi. Not long after their return, Julian, having been dissuaded from joining the International Brigade, departed for Spain as an ambulance driver. Spain was never far from the surface this summer: Virginia saw refugees from Bilbao traversing the streets of Bloomsbury; she sat on the platform at an Albert Hall meeting called to raise funds for Basque children; and on 20 July the blow fell: news of Julian Bell's death reached London, and thenceforward Virginia devoted herself to the care of her stricken sister. The Woolfs drove her to Charleston and settled in at Monks House, Virginia going over almost daily to be with Vanessa. She was able to work at Three Guineas*, defining her ideas on her walks as though in argument with Julian, and reached the end of her first draft soon after returning to Tavistock Square on 10 October, when she at once began the rewriting. Towards the end of the year she had a little bout of temperature, but far worse, there was again a worry about Leonard's health. They went to Monks House for Christmas, but on 29 December his condition so alarmed them that they returned to London to consult his doctor.*

1937

Monks House, Rodmell

Sunday 10 January
Another windless perfectly brilliant day. And Tommy [Stephen Tomlin] is dead and buried yesterday, just as Clive was saying that no one had died lately. But Tommy's death is a queer piece of work. We said on the whole perhaps it was a good thing, because he seemed ravaged by his own misery, couldn't work, had been a failure; tore everyone and everything to bits in a kind of egotistic rage. My own intercourse with him broke over that bust, when I took a shudder at the impact of his neurotic clinging persistency, and perhaps behaved, though I didn't think so at the time, unreasonably, perversely. But the odd thing was that he had, years ago, great sensibility; a human charm, and sympathy. And he had a great gift for making people love him. But there was something twisted, deformed in him: some shudder and profound distaste, and uneasiness. A tragic, wasted life; something wrong in it; and wrong that we shouldn't feel it more.

52 Tavistock Square, WC1

Sunday 17 January
Home again. Poor L. grumbling, making Mabel a peg on which to hang his misery, oh dear. How quiet London is however. Not a sound. I must make up my mind to work. First I must tidy up: throw away all the old *Years* litter, get things clean and fresh. Lunch with Clive tomorrow to meet I don't know who. A great many MSS to read. I shall also go to the National Gallery and to the Zoo.

Thursday 28 January
Sunk once more in the happy tumultuous dream: that is to say began *Three Guineas* this morning, and can't stop thinking it. Dining with Hutchinsons to meet [H. G.] Wells.

Friday 29 January

Wells rather shrunk. Hair still brown, but has the dyed appearance of hair that is brown on an old face. Lines more marked; skin less plumped out. He was very affable. He sat by me, and was a little apprehensive of the highbrow at first I think. We made talk about Scotland; then switched off on to the poverty of authors. Then we got on to Russian politics, so, somehow to Tom Eliot. Tee Ess he called him with a hiss of despite; and then proceeded to say how he, which I think meant we, had been the death of English literature. Afraid of being vulgar, that's what was at the root of it. And Tom's religion. By that we came to the Archbishop. "I wonder – does Cosmo Gordon Lang ever alone at the dead of night face his Trinity? We all have to – But does he . . ." and so on. He likes to be listened to; and to chatter on, loosely generally, as he said to me when the gentlemen came upstairs. "We had a loose general kind of talk." Then he lay back in the armchair, put his tiny hands and still tinier feet together, and chirped away. It was old man's talk; mellower than I remembered; mischievous; eyes a little bleared; kindly in his way; merry. He gives the impression that on the whole he is a detached satisfied little man; conscious of his lack of distinction; prone to snap at any pretence; content I think with his position, and immensely interested still. Had one seen him behind a counter he would have seemed the very type of busy little grocer. And I suspect that when he faces his Trinity at dead of night there are a good many books that he thinks, justly, trash; but remembers that he has done a vast mass of work, and thinks it won't all die; and is amused at the place he has made – from Bromley, Kent to Regent's Park; and I suppose the greatest circulation in the whole world. A humane man in some corner; also brutal; also entirely without poetry.

Friday 12 February

Why should I write here? Only that I am devilishly anxious. L. is going to a Harley Street specialist at four today to get a report: whether the sugar means diabetes or prostate gland or nothing serious. And I must face facts: how to keep cool, how to control myself, if it is a bad report. Work is my only help. That is the conclusion I came to last night. Probably it is only a question of treatment. Anyhow we shall soon know, unless he keeps us hanging about. It is a very fine cold day and we are going straight on down to Rodmell where there is a Labour Party meeting and Quentin to dinner. I have been writing hard since January 28th at *Three Guineas*, and must simply keep at it – it is the one support. We had too the anxiety about Julian – he means to enlist for Spain. [Francis] Cornford's son was killed there last week. Nessa was in one of her entirely submerged moods on Monday when we went in. Always that extraordinary depth of despair. But I must fight, that's my instinct: but we are faced with a horrid afternoon. I feel like the man who had to keep dancing on hot bricks. Can't let myself stop. Hence I suppose I write here; which explains why Tolstoy and his wife kept diaries.

Monday 15 February

Oh it was heavenly driving down to Rodmell on Friday evening with that weight off us! I walked Harley Street up and down up and down for an hour. At last just before five L. came in his new light overcoat, and smiled. [Dr] Graham thinks it's only a case of diet: wouldn't even examine him for diabetes; said nothing about prostate gland; found all organs very healthy. So as I say we drove down, in that odd relieved state which seems as much physical as mental. Got to Monks House only at 7.30, had to dine hurriedly; Quentin rang up to say his car had broken down. The meeting. Quentin came at 9.30; in gum boots wet through; had dinner at 10.30; went back over the downs in the rain. And over us brooded the same delicious ease and content, as if another space of life had been granted us.

Thursday 18 February

A kind gentleman has troubled my peace with a copy of the *Saturday Review* (USA) in which I am called a maker of films and laces; a sitter in shaded drawing rooms, and so on. I am quite sure that the next lap of my life will be accompanied with whistlings and catcalls in this strain. The question I have now to settle is what 'attitude' to adopt. This kind of sneer has an inhibiting effect for the moment. But I must be quit of the need even of defending myself. I want to forge ahead, on my own lines. But in London where I am exposed all day and every day to criticism some plating of resolution is absolutely needed. And I think I've got it by the tip of the tail – a new kind of indifference. I experiment with snubs and sneers. How little they matter in the sum! how little they count with other people – how little the goodness or badness of my books affects the world.

Stephen Spender came to tea and dinner the other day. Rather a beautiful if too conventionally poetic young man: sunk cheeks, large blue eyes, skin always burning; great enthusiasm, but now tempered because, having married, his friend, the male, joined the Foreign Legion, is fighting in Spain; [his wife] sits at Brussels studying Spanish MSS in order, should he be killed in Spain, she may have a job to fall back on. A curious interpretation of marriage, dictated by the guns. I like him: told him not to fight. He argued that we cannot let the Fascists overrun Spain: then it'll be France; then us. We must fight. Stephen said the Communist Party which he had that day joined, wanted him to be killed, in order that there might be another Byron. He has a child's vanity about himself. Interesting to me at the moment, as I'm working out the psychology of vanity. Then he went to speak about Spain at the Friends' House, and we to *Uncle Vanya*. A very cold night.

Saturday 20 February

I turn my eyes away from the Press as I go upstairs, because there are all the review copies of *The Years* packed and packing. They go out next week. What do I anticipate with such clammy coldness? I think chiefly that my friends won't mention it, will turn the conversation rather awkwardly. I think I anticipate considerable lukewarmness among the friendly reviewers – respectful tepidity; and a whoop of red Indian delight from the Grig[son]s who will joyfully and loudly announce that this is the long drawn twaddle of a prim prudish bourgeois mind, and say that now no one can take Mrs W. seriously again.

Sunday 21 February

[Christopher] Isherwood and Sally [Chilver] last night. Isherwood rather a find: very small red cheeked nimble and vivacious. He said Morgan and I were the only living novelists the young – he, Auden, Spender I suppose – take seriously. For Morgan's books he has a passion. "I'll come out with it then Mrs Woolf – you see, I feel you're a poetess: he does the thing I want to do . . ." But I was satisfied with my share of the compliment which came very pat in these days of depression. Auden and he are writing away together. He does the prose, Auden the poetry. Auden wants innumerable blankets on his bed; innumerable cups of tea; then shuts the shutters and draws the blinds and writes. Isherwood is a most appreciative merry little bird. A real novelist, I suspect; not a poet; full of acute observations on character and scenes. One of the most vital and observant of the young; and a relief after the mute dismals of the others.

Tuesday 23 February

The doctor says L. is quite normal! So all that might have been spared us.

Wednesday 24 February

I'm off again, after five days lapse, on *Three Guineas*, and hope now to spin ahead. A quiet day for a wonder – no one seen yesterday: so I went to the Caledonian Market, couldn't find spoon shop; bought yellow gloves 3 shillings and stockings 1 shilling and so home.

Sunday 28 February

I'm so entirely imbued in *Three Guineas* that I can hardly jerk myself away to write here (here in fact I again dropped my pen to think about my next paragraph – universities –). Its a bad habit. Yesterday it was effectively broken by Desmond who came punctually at one, and stayed till 7.15; nor did we stop talking all that time. Nor was I once bored or wished it to stop. A greater tribute to Desmond couldn't be paid. He was well lit – dear old Desmond – as round as a marble: a paunch pendant; but nearly bald; with an odd 18th Century look, as if he had been dining at the Club with Johnson – a kind of Goldsmith or Boswell; a congenial spirit. And as full of human kindness as a ripe grape with juice. I think he had set himself now not to write a great book but to be nice to other people. What can I do for you, was his last remark on the stairs. Alas, he carried off *The Years*, which means – well, never mind.

Monday 1 March

I wish I could write out my sensations at this moment. They are so peculiar and so unpleasant. Partly Time of Life? I wonder. A physical feeling as if I were drumming slightly in the veins: very cold: impotent: and terrified. As if I were exposed on a high ledge in full light. Very lonely. Very useless. No atmosphere round me. No words. Very apprehensive. As if something cold and horrible – a roar of laughter at my expense were about to happen. And I want to burst into tears, but have nothing to cry for. And I cannot unfurl my mind and apply it calmly and unconsciously to a book. And my own little scraps look dried up and derelict. And I know that I must go on doing this dance on hot bricks till I die. Its the 15th March approaching I suppose – the dazzle of that head lamp on my poor little rabbit's body which keeps it dazed in the middle of the road. (I like that phrase. That gives me confidence.)

Tuesday 2 March

I'm going to be beaten, I'm going to be laughed at, I'm going to be held up to scorn and ridicule – I found myself saying those words just now. Anyhow these days of waiting must be a dull cold torture. I shall be happy enough this time next month I've no doubt.

Wednesday 10 March

The fatal day is approaching when my little reputation lies like an old cigarette end. But I'm too jaded with *Three Guineas* to care to find even the right metaphor. In my perhaps cowardly wish to have next week as an empty compartment, I've crammed this too full. On Friday we get off – the doomed discarded ridiculed novelist. What care I? I begin to whistle, but I'm too jaded.

Friday 12 March
Oh the relief! L. brought the *TLS* to me in bed and said Its quite good. And so it is; and *Time & Tide* says I'm a firstrate novelist and a great lyrical poet. And I can hardly read through the reviews: but feel a little dazed, to think then its *not* nonsense; it does make an effect. But now, my dear, after all that agony, I'm free, whole, round. And so stop this cry of content; sober joy. Off to Monks House. Julian back today.

Monks House, Rodmell

Sunday 14 March
I am in such a twitter owing to two columns in the *Observer* praising *The Years* that I can't, as I foretold, go on with *Three Guineas*. And when I think of the agony I went through in this room, just over a year ago ... when it dawned on me that the whole of three years' work was a complete failure: and then when I think of the mornings here when I used to stumble out and cut up those proofs and write three lines, and then go back and lie on my bed – its no wonder my hand trembles. Now at any rate money is assured: L. shall have his new car; we will be floated again; and my last lap – if I've only ten years of life more – should be fruitful. Work – work. But at the moment, the relief is so great, that I feel myself rocking up and down, like a bush a huge fowl sat on.

Dinner at Charleston last night. Julian a grown man – I mean vigorous, controlled, as I guess embittered, something to me tragic in the sadness now, his mouth and face much tenser; as if he had been thinking in solitude. Nessa said he hasn't altogether given up his idea of Spain: all depends on getting a job here. He comes to tea today.

Monday 15 March
Too much talk – Julian and Bunny – why do we live in such a way that the sight of our oldest friends and nephews back from China gives us a little shock of regret – I mean misery for the quiet evening gone? Julian set and rather self centred. Can only think what he ought to do. Still if what he ought to do is something for the world at large, one must excuse this grinding of an iron upon a granite slab.

52 Tavistock Square, wc1

Friday 19 March
Now this is one of the strangest of my experiences – 'they' say almost universally that *The Years* is a masterpiece. If somebody had told me I

should write this, even a week ago, let alone six months ago, I should have given a jump like a shot hare. How entirely and absolutely incredible it would have been!

Thursday 25 March

Yes, two days lying down, and can't write today. But a divine holiday. No reviews. And sales great. A rush before Easter. 280 sold yesterday. Boat Race at 11.30. Then we go tomorrow.

Monks House, Rodmell

Saturday 27 March

Merely scribbling here, over a log fire, on a cold but bright Easter morning; sudden shafts of sun, a scatter of snow on the hills early; sudden storms, ink black, octopus pouring, coming up: and the rooks fidgetting and pecking in the elm trees. As for the beauty, as I always say when I walk the terrace after breakfast, too much for one pair of eyes. We came down on Thursday, packed in the rush in London; cars spinning all along the roads; yesterday at last perfect freedom from telephones and reviews, and no one rang up.

Sunday 28 March

Yesterday a reporter for the *New York Times* rang up: was told he could look at the outside of 52 [Tavistock Square] if he chose. At 4.30 as I was boiling the kettle a huge black Daimler drew up. Then a dapper little man in a tweed coat appeared in the garden. I reached the sitting room – saw him standing there looking round. L. in the orchard with Percy [gardener]. Then I guessed. He had a green note book and stood looking about jotting things down. I ducked my head – he almost caught me. At last L. turned and fronted him. No Mrs Woolf didn't want that kind of publicity. I raged. A bug walking over one's skin – couldn't crush him. The bug taking notes. L. politely led him back to his Daimler and his wife. But they'd had a nice run from London – bugs, to come and steal in and take notes.

Monday 29 March

A man in an overcoat took notes in the field yesterday, and then someone banged on the door. I sat tight. L. was at Charleston. Julian, he says, very depressed.

Sunday 4 April

Another curious idiosyncracy. Maynard thinks *The Years* my best book. L. went to Tilton and had a long quiet cronies' talk. Maynard not well; cramp in the muscle of the heart. His toes curl up. Lydia anxious. Talk of what to do for Julian, who strikes everyone as depressed. Maynard said that he thought *The Years* very moving; more tender than any of my books; did not puzzle him like *The Waves*; very beautiful; and no more said than was needed.

52 TAVISTOCK SQUARE, WCI

Wednesday 14 April
I'm sunk in privacy, in quiet. How strange! It would be flat, if I were not so active in the head. Not a letter this morning: only ten or eleven perhaps about *The Years* since it came out. Nobody talks to me about it, nobody now writes about it. It seems to have sailed out of sight. Yet it sells – best of all my novels. Sold I think 9,300. Harcourt Brace in America have sold 12,000 before publication – easily my record. Honestly I do not know what to think of this book: is it good or bad? Tonight Kingsley Martin, Stephen Spender and Julian dine.

Thursday 15 April
And Stephen says *The Years* is the best of my books, and Kingsley also – but that don't please me. Stephen does. A long close political argument. Julian, Kingsley, Stephen – all calling each other by Christian names. What is our duty? What is the responsible man like Kingsley Martin to do? Can't be a pacifist; the irresponsible can. I sat there splitting off my own position from theirs, testing what they said, convincing myself of my own integrity and justice. Kingsley Martin very neurotic, dark eyed, melodramatic. Julian peppery and pithy – making his strange faces, suddenly hooting with laughter – uncouth rather, yet honest, yet undisciplined, yet keeping something up his sleeve. Obstinately set on going to Spain – won't argue; tight; hard fisted. Kingsley lives much in the military area: so we discussed hand grenades, bombs, tanks, as if we were military gents in the war again. And I felt flame up in me *Three Guineas*. Stephen runs on too fluent, too formless; but as I say gave me a shock of pleasure. Says *The Years* gives him the sense of time; and is so precise. So that's the young on my side.

Wednesday 21 April
On the whole Monks House was a good week end. Very cold wind. Went to tea at Charleston; and there found the whole family for once. Unfortunately Julian is dog obstinate about driving an ambulance; which casts a shadow over Nessa, and us too. There'll he be keeping us all on the tenterhooks – But it won't be for two months, and what's the use of looking

ahead? Summer time began on Sunday; and I look up and see my clock still an hour late.

Tuesday 27 April
Yes, that'll be nice – to sit out of doors and drink, in some French town, away from all this. Coronation impending. But on the 7th we're off.

Thursday 29 April
Well, we've decided to let the Hogarth Press lapse or change next June. Yes I think that is now definite. Many things have happened – a crowd of little engagements – the pleasantest, indeed a happy one, was the Memoir Club meeting. We dined in a kind of sitting room behind the Etoile [Restaurant] – and soon kindled, though it was a wet night: Duncan had a cold; Bunny the whooping cough. But Desmond was babbling as a nightingale – never have I known him in such jubilant good temper as this year. As if he worked only to enjoy, to radiate. And my thimble of vanity was filled instantly because Maynard praised *The Years* – a lovely book; and Desmond said he is going to write a long essay on me altogether (but he won't). And so round to the Studio. Duncan read a good account of his adventure at Florence, when he misrepresented Maynard. And then old Desmond 'obliged'. That is he had a few notes in his hand, took a comfortable chair, and gave us with perfect ease and fluency and form a character of Wilfred Blunt and his own shooting. And so on to the Trevelyans. Oh but it was beautifully done – and stopped when it might have gone on without boring us. Then Morgan read his condemned introduction to the [T. E.] Lawrence letters, which Bunny is now to do. And then we went off in the rain. Desmond said We're not a day older, and we enjoy our society as much as we ever did. And Morgan said I felt so fond of everyone, I almost wept.

Yesterday oh how Margery Fry snubbed me, by announcing, as she came into the room, that the reviews of *The Years* had been so sniffy she was afraid it must have influenced the sales.

Friday 30 April
So we have reached the last day of this agitating month – far better than I could have foreseen. If it weren't for Julian going to Spain I should be wholly content on our French journey. A very cold grey day; the Busmen threaten to strike tonight; streets laced across; camps and latrines in all the parks, like the Crimea; poles with silver hatchets along the pavements. The Queen told David [Cecil] that she went all ice at the thought of the Coronation; said the monarchy hadn't the same position as in the days of Victoria. All the fiddles are tuning up. The BBC is having a hundred and

fifty microphones and observers along the route. I shall try to listen in from some French café. Hugh Walpole is to be knighted. We are giving a youthful party on Monday; and leave on Friday – that is one week, in which I must settle the question of clothes. When I come back I shall instantly pounce on *Three Guineas* and see what I can do.

Tuesday 4 May
The day mother died in 1895 – forty-two years ago: and I remember it – at the moment, watching Dr Seton walk away up Hyde Park Gate in the early morning with his head bowed, his hands behind his back. Also the doves swooping. We had been sent up to the day nursery after she died; and were crying. And I went to the open window and looked out. It must have been very soon after she died, as Seton was then leaving the house. How that early morning picture has stayed with me! What happened immediately afterwards I can't remember.

I'm jaded after our youthful party – they stayed till 12.45. The Bus Strike on, so that they couldn't get buses – had to walk. The streets look odd, all aflutter with banners – white in Bond Street, red at Selfridges; and no omnibuses; a lower level in the streets; all taxis and innumerable private cars; and droves and herds trudging the pavement. The party though – jaded as I am I must refer to the party. Sally [Chilver]; Julian; bell rings: the Spenders; [Richard] Chilver; William [Plomer]. So we were crowded – no fire; a hot spring night. Julian was bitter at dinner against the Bloomsbury, habit of education. He had been taught no job; only a vague literary smattering. But I wanted you to go to the Bar, I said. Yes, but you didn't insist upon it to my mother, he remarked, rather forcibly. He now finds himself at twenty-nine without any special training. But then he objected, as I thought, to all professions. The Chilver sat all inhibited and nerve drawn, so I had to give him claret and sit by him and make party talk, about carpentering and bulbs. He would like to leave the Air Ministry and become a carpenter – make good chairs – but of course won't and can't, though Sally urges. Another aspect of the professional question. Air Ministry long hours, hard work; but regular and safe. Julian now all in favour of a settled job. He is learning the mechanics of lorries. Hadn't even been taught that at Cambridge – only the eternal [Alexander] Pope – which I scrambled through as a child. Poor old Julian – rather on a crazy edge of life I feel. And there was some well informed political talk.

Every moment till we go seems now numbered like stones in a building – and that's why I shall be so relieved on Friday – no numbers of any stones for almost three weeks.

*   *   *

MONKS HOUSE, RODMELL

Monday 1 June
I have at last got going with *Three Guineas*. But oh how my heart leaps up
to think that never again shall I be harnessed to a long book. No. Always
short ones in future. The long book still won't be altogether downed – its
reverberations grumble. Did I say that Harcourt Brace wrote and said they
were happy to find that *The Years* is the best selling novel in America? They
have sold 25,000 – my record, easily. The great desirable is not to have to
earn money by writing. 'Gibbon' was rejected by the *New Republic*, so I
shall send no more to America. Nor will I write articles at all except for the
TLS: for whom I am going now to do Congreve.

It has been August hot; Nessa came over and we had a long natural
gossip. Maynard has been very ill but is better. Must rest for six months.
Duncan in France. We stay here for one week's perfect solitude. Then a
London season, very hectic I guess. Mary Hutchinson asks me to dine to
meet the Duff Coopers. Courage bids me say Yes. But my hair? and my
dress?

52 TAVISTOCK SQUARE, WC1

Friday 11 June
Brain rather dried up after six days strenuous London. Very very hot. Very
noisy. And on top, Julian gone to Spain on Monday. So, a strain: which I
cannot now go into: and it must last – how long? A year? who knows?
Anything to keep talking, inventing, distracting.

Wednesday 16 June
I've seen: the Hutchinsons; Diana [Cooper] beautiful, veiled, easy going.
Desmond there. Then Ethel Smyth: with her rough old claws scratching.
Sniffing out *Three Guineas*. Then to the Coronation film, bits and bits; some
good; others not. Then to Herbert [Woolf]'s on Sunday; oh the ugliness of
that perfectly self-satisfied passive stockbroker's life: the orchard, the picture
– the coloured photograph – the mats, the maids; unreal, padded, easy . . .
and we walked at Staines. Then Adrian after dinner on a visit of friendship.
Then the Bowens, Bowras, Butts; then Helen . . . Now lunch.

Sunday 20 June
Last evening Ann Watkins forced her way in: offered me – I could see the
bait put on the hook – £1000 and all expenses if I would go to USA and
lecture three times weekly for three months. What about, I asked. That

they didn't mind. The more personal the better: for instance, about my experience of publishing, bringing in my marriage – a happy one. At this, your husband, who is sitting in the audience, will cry BOO! Well we declined. I was to repeat the same lecture – not to read it, but to speak it. That was very important. And Aldous and Gerald Heard, those apostles of the inner life and peace and goodness, are touring the States doing this in duet. Lord lord! what an example for the Soul ... and what a good quote for my book. I was amused by her perfectly frank commercialism. Money – money – money. What they want and Donald Brace wants is that I should come over and exhibit my person, and make money for Don and Ann. And what would they spend the proceeds of my personality on? Drink I should say, looking at Ann's cheeks.

Tuesday 22 June
Ann Watkins is now hot on the scent of magazine articles, and wants another talk. But here my gorge rises. No I will not write for the larger paying magazines: in fact, couldn't. In this way I put *Three Guineas* daily into practice.

Wednesday 23 June
I went shopping yesterday, and it grew roasting hot, and I was in black – such astonishing chops and changes this summer – often one's caught in a storm, frozen, or roasted. As I reached 52, a long trail of fugitives – like a caravan in a desert – came through the Square: Spaniards flying from Bilbao, which has fallen, I suppose. Somehow brought tears to my eyes, though no one seemed surprised. Children trudging along; women in cheap jackets with gay handkerchiefs on their heads, young men, and all carrying either cheap cases, and bright enamel kettles and saucepans, filled I suppose with gifts from some Charity – a shuffling trudging procession, flying – impelled by machine guns in Spanish fields to trudge through Tavistock Square, along Gordon Square, then where? – clasping their enamel kettles. A strange spectacle.

Thursday 24 June
A letter from Ott praising my Gibbon article. Now I have observed that any of my friends who disliked *The Years* always praise my articles, by way of urging me to give up fiction, and I suppose to make amends to me for not liking *The Years*. She has been *very* ill; almost thought she would have 'waved us adieu' but is recovering at Tunbridge Wells. Pipsy reads *Emma* to her, and she reads Henry James to herself.

Friday 25 June

To the Albert Hall meeting last night. The last I swear. Oh but I liked being introduced to Auden, a small rough-haired terrier man: slits for eyes; a crude face; interesting, I expect, but wire haired, yellowish white. Then speeches. Then semi jocular money collecting; then an auction of pictures. One by Picasso. All very stagey empty and unreal. The Basque children singing on the gramophone. [Paul] Robeson sang: a sympathetic, malleable nigger, expressive, uninhibited, all warmth and the hot vapours of African forests. I took several snubs and benedictions. Kingsley Martin uneasy – a man I don't like – so voluble, histrionic, and he drove us home, taking a hand off the wheel to gesticulate – a different style of driving from Leonard's. I'm hurrying. Can't analyse. Off to Monks House. Starting my Congreve: going to do it in three days at Monks House. Then back to *Three Guineas* refreshed.

Monday 28 June

Home is the hunter, home from the hill, and the Wolves are back from Monks House. And much refreshed into the bargain. Three solitary nights. Think of that! Not a voice, not a telephone. Only the owl calling; perhaps a clap of thunder, the horses going down to the Brooks, and Mr Botten calling with the milk in the morning. Up at 7.30 this morning, picked a rose, and drove up through Wimbledon, as Wandsworth Bridge is mending, but back by 10.30, and at work on the Second Guinea by 11. It is now started, and if I can drive my pen hard, might have it done by August. But there's a terrible lot of reasoning (for me) and fitting in of the right quotations. *Roger* waiting too.

Sunday 11 July

A gap: not in life, but in comment. I have been in full flood every morning with *Three Guineas*. Whether I shall finish by August becomes doubtful.

Monday 12 July

Alone with Nessa in the studio last night. We are very gingerly in our remarks about Julian, and Madrid, I notice. Always I feel the immeasurable despair just on t'other side of the grass plot on which we walk – on which I'm walking with such energy and delight at the moment. I went to Stoke Newington yesterday and found a study table in white stone on which James Stephen was carved, large and plain, as I suspect he was large and plain. A long inscription about Wilberforce and wife and family neatly filled with green moss on top of the study table. Next door to the old Church, which might be in a hollow under the downs, is Clissold Park, and one of those white pillared houses in which [great] Grandpapa studied *The Times* while She cut roses – now it smelt of Clissold Park mothers; and cakes and tea. I was much refreshed by all this.

Monday 19 July
Just back from Monks House. The kitchen a great success – now green and cool, and the new window shows a square of flowers. Why, all these years, I never thought to lay out £20 on a new cupboard, paint and window, I don't know. On Friday we went to Worthing. Mrs Woolf very plaintive. Then a [Labour Party] meeting at Monks House where the Major, who talks to mice, and holds toads in his hand, treated us to the most drivelling murmured muddle I ever heard – about force, and religion, which is heredity, and may I say with your permission, what I mean is, its all a question of thinking isn't it, and you can't talk to a Spaniard, but you can to a Mahommedan, and that's what I feel, religion's at the back of it, but Sir, if I may say so, its a question of heredity – but I can't reproduce the shell-shock Major; and could only keep from howling by fixing my eyes on a cigarette. L. summed up in a masterly flight; and so concluded. Quentin and I were dumb.

Monks House, Rodmell

Friday 6 August
Well but one must make a beginning. Its odd that I can hardly bring myself, with all my verbosity – the expression mania which is inborn in me – to say anything about Julian's death – I mean about that last ten days in London. That was a complete break; almost a blank; like a blow on the head: a shrivelling up. Going round [to Vanessa] that night; and then all the other times, and sitting there. An incredible suffering – to watch it – an accident, and someone bleeding. Then I thought the death of a child is a childbirth again; sitting there listening. No no, I will not go back to those days. The only thing was a kind of comfort in being there with Nessa, Duncan, Quentin and Angelica, and losing completely the isolation, the spectator's attitude, in being wanted. Then we came down here last Thursday; and the pressure being removed, one lived; but without much of a future. That's one of the specific qualities of this death – how it brings close the immense vacancy, and our short little run into inanity. Now this is what I intend to combat. How? Work of course. Directly I am not working, or see the end in sight, then nothingness begins. I have to go over though every other day to Charleston. We sit in the studio door. It is very hot happily. The thought of Julian changing so queerly: now distinct, now close; now of him there in the flesh; and so on. But how it curtails the

future: how it reduces one's vision to one's own life – save for Quentin and Angelica.

Well, there's *Three Guineas* to finish: the last chapter; now I suppose its stiff and cold. But I will try that tomorrow; then polish off Congreve; then earn £200, so they say, with a story; and so to *Roger* this autumn. Today we go to Charleston; Nessa is alone today. "I shall be cheerful, but I shall never be happy again."

Wednesday 11 August

Now we are in the worst of the time – I think I can recognise that. We don't talk so freely of Julian. We want to make things go on. Angelica and Quentin come over to play bowls. We beat up talk. We provide amusement, L. and I; this makes us rather quarrelsome when we're alone – the strain I suppose. The unbecoming stage of sorrow. On Monday I went by train to Charleston. Thus I left L. alone: have I the right to leave L. alone, and sit with Nessa? She was again in the submerged mood. An atmosphere of deep grey waters; and I flopping like a dilapidated fish on top. Very hard work. I shall have a long walk this afternoon, to Piddinghoe: walk myself serene; play bowls; read; and not think of little arrangements. Endless unwritten letters – sympathy about Julian who stalks beside me, in many different shapes.

Tuesday 17 August

Not much to say. Its true, the only life this summer is in the brain. I get excited writing. Three hours pass like ten minutes. At Charleston yesterday in the rain. I take the train to Lewes; shop; 4.35 bus; reach Charleston for tea. Its true I cannot write about Nessa; have to keep myself from thinking about her. Now and then she looks like an old woman. How can she ever right herself though? Julian had some queer power over her – the lover as well as the son. He was like her; yet had a vigour, a roughness, a kind of clumsiness, of Cambridge awkwardness, together with his natural gaiety. And that's all lost for the sake of ten minutes in an ambulance. I often argue with him on my walks; abuse his selfishness in going but mostly feel floored by the complete muddle and waste. I think I mean lack of judgement: obstinate and emotional. We should have respected him more if he had stayed in England and faced drudgery.

Sunday 29 August

Yes I am tackling Congreve, because I want to be quit of all articles and ready for *Three Guineas* on the 1st. How far would this energy of mind carry me – could I take this narcotic successfully if Leonard died, if Nessa died? I come out here at 10 and don't wake to anything but Congreve till one.

Go in with my head swaying like a captive balloon. The thing is there's no richness and security when I wake. No depth of happiness to refresh myself in. Considerable agility and gaiety and chatter. A very hot August again. Bowls have become a passion. I gave up a walk to play. But then I'm anxious to vary the day.

Thursday 2 September
Finished my Congreve, the end too crowded, but forced myself to take it to the post. And today's a holiday: letter writing, reading.

Sunday 26 September
Tom [Eliot] and Judith [Stephen] here: therefore I am not writing the end of *Three Guineas*, which has kept me completely submerged from ten to one every morning; and driven me like a motor in the head over the downs to Piddinghoe &c every afternoon from two to four. Then we play bowls from five to six. Then read. Then cook dinner. Then wireless. Then read. Then chocolates. Then bed. And so it begins again. But there have been so many interruptions. We went to Sissinghurst – unrecorded: Vita with that silent goodness, and Harold too, a sense of the human understanding unspoken. Many improvements: men digging: an Elizabethan drain being dug up.

Not a happy summer. That is all the materials for happiness; and nothing behind. If Julian had not died – still an incredible sentence to write – our happiness might have been profound. 'Our' – L.'s and mine, now that *The Years* has sold between 40 and 50,000 in America; now that we are floated financially, and privately as happy and rounded off as can be – but his death – that extraordinary extinction – drains it of substance. I do not let myself think. I cannot face much of the meaning. Shut my mind to anything but work and bowls. Now there's Tom and Judith. Tom is liverish looking, tired; but revives under the effect of Judith's fresh and downright and able but not sophisticated youth. She is a whopper: a strapper; yet with the usual complexities I think, submerged. I should however write a pack of letters.

52 TAVISTOCK SQUARE, WC1

Tuesday 12 October
Yes we are back at Tavistock Square; and I've never written a word since September 27th. That shows how every morning was crammed to the margin with *Three Guineas*. This is the first morning I write, because at 12, ten minutes ago, I wrote what I think is the last page of *Three Guineas*. Oh

how violently I have been galloping through these mornings! It has pressed and spurted out of me, if that's any proof of virtue, like a physical volcano. And my brain feels cool and quiet after the expulsion. So nothing was said here of the last weeks at Monks House. The weather was very fine. That objective statement sounds a little odd.

We have decided, gradually, completely, not to sell the Press; but to let it die off, saving for our own books. This is a good conclusion I think. It keeps the right to adventure; cuts off some money. We could not face writing for publishers.

Friday 22 October
No I didn't go to Paris. This is a note to make. Waking at three I decided I would spend the week end at Paris. Got so far as looking up trains, consulting Nessa about hotel. Then L. said he would rather not. Then I was overcome with happiness. Then we walked round the square love making – after twenty-five years can't bear to separate. Then I walked round the lake in Regent's Park. Then ... you see it is an enormous pleasure, being wanted: a wife. And our marriage so complete. To return to facts (though this 'fiction' is still radiant under my skin): walked to see Roger's Highgate birthplace: suddenly L. developed the idea of making the young Brainies take the Press as a Co-operative company (John [Lehmann]; Isherwood; Auden; Stephen). All are bubbling with discontent and ideas. All want a focus; a manager; a mouthpiece. Would like L. to manage it. Couldn't we sell, and creep out? That's the idea – and yet keep the soul, translated into this on the whole appropriate body? Anyhow, John was heard in the Press: consulted; interested; fights shy of money; £6,000; will lunch with Isherwood and discuss. And now telephones he will come on Monday. So that fat's a frizzling.

Monday 25 October
A terrific gale this week end. We went to Cuckmere, via Seaford. The sea over the front: great spray fountain bursting to my joy over the parade and the lighthouse. Right over the car. Then we walked down to the sea at Cuckmere; the birds came up like shots out of a catapult. We could not stand against the wind, the breath pressed out of us; nor see. We stood behind a shed, and watched the waves: a yellow rough light on them; pounding; a great curled volume roughened of water. Why does one like the frantic, the unmastered? So to Charleston, wet and soaking.

Monday 1 November
Dinner with Clive. I think poor old Clive even a little on the bare wheels; no blown up tyres. That to me is very ominous – if Clive's spirits should

give way – if he were to give up his enjoyment of life! We discussed education; dreams; Nessa and Angelica stitched at some private garment. Angelica alternately silent and decisive. Duncan came in. Not much boasting. An odds and ends evening, neither one thing nor another.

The Co-operative Press hangs: I think the young are eager to bite.

Wednesday 3 November
To Southwark and Lambeth, walking, yesterday. A great autumn for long City walks this.

Tuesday 30 November
Yes, its actually the last day of November, and they've passed like a streak of hounds after a fox because I've been re-writing *Three Guineas* with such intentness, indeed absorption. So I've never even looked at this stout volume. I have left out Cambridge; oh and people innumerable; the Book Show; and buying with some recklessness, fur boots, leather waistcoat, underclothes; for money once more brims the pot. And I'm paid £465 for a handful of old sketches. This a little shames me in comparison with Nessa's sales: but then I reflect, I put my life blood into writing, and she had children.

Wednesday 15 December
And then I had one of my little dips into the underworld – a temperature, sofa, three days recumbent, Monks House in a snowstorm; no walking; Foot and Mouth still dominant; back to our party. Young Newnham, all most free and easy, vigorous and inspiriting, all sitting on the floor; and then – writing, writing; the first chapter taken on Monday to the Chancery Lane typist; cold and rain; visits from Mrs Woolf and Herbert, from John yesterday; the Press question looms and lapses; and our views change: secretly we both wish to fade, not to sell; but John is eager to buy, yet stingy; must consult Isherwood and Stephen; and settle by mid January. Vita, who dined, more matronly and voluptuous than ever, won't go in with them: a parcel of hot headed and ignorant boys; – well, no use trying to pull this five minutes before lunch sentence together so I stop it.

Saturday 18 December
Oh this cursed year 1937 – it will never let us out of its claws. Now its L.'s kidneys: [Dr] Rau says it may be something wrong with the kidneys; possibly the prostate gland – that perennial horror. Its more likely, he says, to be a chill; but can't tell for a fortnight. So we go away with that hanging over us – The great cat is playing with us once more. How much do I mind death? I wondered last night, and concluded that there is a sense in which

the end could be accepted calmly. That's odd, considering that few people are more immensely interested by life: and happy. Its Julian's death that makes one sceptical of life I suppose. Not that I ever think of him as dead: which is queer. Rather as if he were jerked abruptly out of sight, without rhyme or reason: so violent and absurd that one can't fit his death into any scheme. But here we are, on a fine cold day, going to mate Sally at Ickenham: a saner proceeding than to analyse here.

1938

Leonard spent the first ten days of the new year in bed on a strict diet, awaiting the results of X-rays and tests for kidney disease; it was a false alarm and Virginia's relief was intense. She herself suffered her usual winter ailments, but by the beginning of February Three Guineas *was ready to be shown to Leonard and sent to press, although she still had a good deal of work to do on the notes. But these months were dominated by discussions about the future management of the Hogarth Press, which on the Woolfs had so often thought of giving up. Now finally it was agreed that John Lehmann should buy Virginia's half-share in the Press and become Leonard's partner, acting also as salaried managing director. Virginia continued to read and advise on manuscripts. This arrangement came into force in April.*

*In the Soviet Union, Stalin's opponents were being tried and executed; in Europe 11 March Hitler led his troops into Austria and proclaimed the Union (*Anschluss*) of Austria with Germany. The reverberations of these events were increasingly felt in Tavistock Square, where Leonard was deeply involved in attempts to persuade the Labour Party to agree to conscription and re-armament. Virginia was glad to turn to the past and to her biography of Roger Fry; but at Rodmell at Easter the exciting idea for a new book disturbed her concentration on the facts of his life. This was* Pointz Hall, *which was to develop during the next years into her last book,* Between the Acts.

Two more deaths particularly affected Virginia this spring. Although she had been in poor health for some time, the death of Lady Ottoline Morrell was unexpected; and even more so was that of Ka Arnold-Forster, who was five years younger than Virginia. Both of them had been her friends for nearly thirty years.

Three Guineas *was published early in June. Virginia was pleased by the plaudits of several eminent feminists and not unduly upset by the silence of close friends or the censure of detractors. The Woolfs set off on 16 June for a motoring holiday in the North of England and Scotland, crossing to Skye where they spent three days. Home again on 2 July, the remaining three weeks of their London season were exceptionally full and lively, though Virginia persevered in her work on Roger Fry, to which end she invited the painter Sir William Rothenstein – a fellow student of Roger's in Paris in the nineties – to dinner to talk about him.*

At Monks House, builders were constructing a new library for Leonard in the roof space, work which continued during the whole of their time there – time during which the international situation grew more and more desperate as Hitler increased his pressure on Czechoslovakia. Prime Minister Chamberlain's efforts to appease him and avert the imminent outbreak of war were dramatically (if temporarily) concluded by the Munich Settlement of 29 September, which was, for Virginia, deliverance from a nightmare. The Woolfs returned to London on 16 October.

Virginia Woolf was now a celebrity, which brought both pleasures and pains – the pleasure for instance of Max Beerbohm's flattering attention; the pain of finding that she was now regarded by younger critics as a has-been, rated lower than Forster or Eliot. But she enjoyed a nice old friends' evening with Tom Eliot, and probably ended the year with the feeling that in writing Three Guineas *she had said something that needed saying.*

1938

Sunday 9 January
Yes, I will force myself to begin this cursed year. For one thing I have 'finished' the last chapter of *Three Guineas*, and for the first time since I don't know when have stopped writing in the middle of the morning. How am I to describe 'anxiety'? I've battened it down under this incessant writing, thinking, about *Three Guineas* – as I did in the summer after Julian's death. [Dr] Rau has just been, and says there is still a trace of blood: if this continues, L. will have to go next week to a nursing home and be examined. Probably it is the prostate. This may mean an operation. He was suddenly worse at Rodmell; we came up on Wednesday [29 December]; since when its been a perpetual strain of waiting for the telephone to ring. He went to the hospital to be X rayed; has been, is still, in bed. There is a sense in which feelings become habitual, dulled; but only laid under a very thin cover. I walk; work, and so on. Nessa and Angelica and Duncan all at Cassis, which shuts off that relief, but why should she have this forced on her? Anyhow they come back in a fortnight, I suppose.

Saturday 15 January
In the five minutes left me before starting for Monks House I can't describe the relief of hearing at eight on Wednesday: Specimen completely normal. You can go away – That's where we are at this moment of a wet and windy January. Definitions, explanations can wait.

Tuesday 1 February
A week at Monks House hard at work. Nessa and Angelica back – dinner at Charleston. So home: then temperatures; bed; complete submersal, on the sofa, &c. Now down for final corrections. *Three Guineas* to be shown up to L. tonight.

Friday 4 February
L. gravely approves *Three Guineas*. Thinks it an extremely clear analysis. On the whole I'm content. One can't expect emotion, for as he says, its not

on a par with the novels. But I'm much more indifferent, that's true: feel it a good piece of donkeywork, and don't think it affects me either way as the novels do.

Monday 7 February
(Mother's birthday). A perfect week end [at Monks House], still, brisk spring: crocuses in the garden; birds rapturous; I was very happy: relieved of my book: and tossing ideas as I walked over the downs.

Thursday 10 March
Relieved of my book? What nonsense. Here am I working five hours a day to finish off those notes, those proofs, and severely warned by L. that unless I send off both in six days from this very Thursday, we must postpone till the autumn. But I've done my due today; and have said nothing here for so long: nothing about the Press; how ten days ago I signed my rights away to John [Lehmann]; how the last week has been June weather; and then all the people. I don't think I can add at this moment; and shall owl round the corner to buy a surreptitious packet of cigarettes.

Saturday 12 March
Hitler has invaded Austria: that is at ten last night his army crossed the frontier, unresisted. The Austrian national anthem was heard on the wireless for the last time. This fact, which combines with the Russian trials, like drops of dirty water mixing, puts its thorn into my morning: a pernickety one spent over notes. Privately I'm, as usual at the proof stage, bored with the book which was like a spine to me all last summer; upheld me in the horror of last August; and whirled me like a top miles upon miles over the downs. How can it all have petered out into diluted drivel? But it remains, morally, a spine: the thing I wished to say, though futile. Three USA papers have rejected it; but the *Atlantic* will pay £120 for 12,000 words. Their cable came when Morgan was here – blown in like thistledown – a very round and voluminous down he is now: but with a breeze behind him. And do I grudge it that *he* should be the best living novelist? He handed me a cutting in which he is thus saluted. And so, jealous as I am, rather mean always about contemporaries, I got my dejection, to run into the dirty drop. But this reminds me that our last Leonard and Virginia season is perhaps our most brilliant. Yes; if there is success in this world, the Hogarth Press has I suppose won what success it could. And money this year will fairly snow us under. In fact we have asked Mr Wicks [Lewes builder] to estimate for a library at Monks House in spite of Hitler.

Tuesday 22 March

The public world very notably invaded the private at Monks House last week end. Almost war: almost expected to hear it announced. And England, as they say, humiliated. And the man in uniform exalted. L. up to his eyes in the usual hectic negotiations. The Labour Party hemming and hawing. And I looked at Quentin and thought They'll take you. And then, just as in private crises, a sudden lull. The tension relaxes. And it was like June.

Now I must ward off the old depression: the book finished, what's the use of it, feeling. So yesterday I went to Wapping Old Stairs, and roamed through Shadwell and Whitechapel; a change, as complete as France or Italy. Then Tom to dinner, and to Stephen's *Trial of a Judge*. A moving play: genuine; simple; sincere.

Saturday 26 March

On Monday the galleys will go. So I can then seriously turn my mind off on to Frys, Highgate, the past. The crisis still shakes our telephone, the voice of Kingsley appealing to L. to have his mind made. But the lull is hushing us; not very profoundly though. When the tiger, i.e.: Hitler, has digested his dinner he will pounce again. I must take up life again on Monday: by which I mean ask Elizabeth Bowen to tea, buy a new dress, arrange one or two parties, and not let myself be submerged in *Roger* quite so completely as in *Three Guineas*.

Tuesday 12 April

Anyhow, on April 1st I think, I started *Roger*. Much of it donkey work; and I suppose to be re-written. Still there is twenty pages put down, after being so long put off. And it is an immense solace to have this sober drudgery to take to instantly and so tide over the horrid anti climax of *Three Guineas*. I didn't get so much praise from L. as I hoped. And I suspect I shall find the page proofs (due tomorrow) a chill bath of disillusionment. But I wanted – how violently – how persistently, pressingly, compulsorily I can't say – to write this book; and have a quiet composed feeling; as if I had said my say: take it or leave it.

Elizabeth Bowen to tea; cut out of coloured cardboard but sterling and sharpedged. Kingsley Martin still rings up, at inordinate length: I've time to change and write a letter while they talk; its about emigrating now from our doomed Europe. "If it weren't that I feel I must stay by the paper –"

Tuesday 26 April

We had our Easter at Monks House; but as for the sun, it never shone; was colder than Christmas; a grudging lead-coloured sky; razor wind; winter clothes; proofs; much acute despair; curbed however, by the aid of divine philosophy. Then Quentin rings up; to warn you: Have you had a letter from Pipsy [Philip Morrell]? Ottoline is dead. They told her Philip might die, and the shock killed her; and he's asking you to write about her. So I had to write. Yet in spite of that here am I sketching out a new book; only please don't impose that huge burden on me again, I implore – not yet awhile. But to amuse myself, let me note: why not Pointz Hall: a rambling capricious but somehow unified whole – a scenic old house – and a terrace where nursemaids walk? and people passing – and a perpetual variety and change from intensity to prose; and facts – and notes; and – but enough. I must read Roger; and go to Ott's memorial service, representing also T. S. Eliot at his absurd command. 2.30 at [St] Martin's in the Fields.

Wednesday 27 April

Ottoline's burial service. Oh dear, oh dear the lack of intensity; the wailing and mumbling, the fumbling with bags; the shuffling; the vast brown mass of respectable old South Kensington ladies. And then the hymns; and the clergyman with a bar of medals across his surplice; and the orange and blue windows; and a toy Union Jack sticking from a cranny. What had all this to do with Ottoline, or our feelings? Save that the address was to the point: a critical study, written presumably by Philip and delivered, very reasonably, by Mr [Robert] Speaight the actor: a sober, and secular speech, which made one at least think of a human being, though the reference to her beautiful voice caused one to think of that queer nasal moan: however that too was to the good in deflating immensities. So to Nessa's where we recounted the story; and yet I'm left fumbling for a house I shan't go to. Odd how the sense of loss takes this quite private form: someone who won't read what I write. No illumination in Gower Street. An intimacy abolished.

Thursday 28 April

Walked in Dulwich yesterday and lost my brooch by way of a freshener when confronted with the final proofs just today done; and to be sent this afternoon: a book I shall never look at again. But I now feel entirely free. No longer famous, no longer on a pedestal; no longer hawked in by societies: on my own, for ever. Well I've done my bit for that cause, and can't be bullied. And then, when they badger me, I can say Refer to *Three Guineas*.

Rain and dark. A lost dog in the Square; political lull. Income Tax up to five shillings and sixpence. Our earnings prodigious. Income last year about £6,000. John much impressed. Press worth £10,000. And all this sprung from that type on the drawing room table at Hogarth House twenty years ago. I can now give all my mind to *Roger*; also blow a few private bubbles of a morning; and don't wait publication day with any expectations. I shall

I feel forget this book completely. Yet I never wrote a book with greater fervour; under such a lash of compulsion. And it stood me in good stead.

Friday 29 April
The difficulty is that I get so absorbed in this fantastic *Pointz Hall* I can't attend to *Roger*. So what am I to do? This is however only my first day of freedom. I'm in a dazed state, hovering between two worlds like a spider's web with nothing to attach the string to.

Tuesday 3 May
My eyes ache with *Roger* and I'm a little appalled at the prospect of the grind this book will be. I must somehow shorten and loosen; I *can't* (remember) stretch out a long painstaking literal book: later I must generalise and let fly. But then, how can one cut loose from facts, when there they are, contradicting my theories? A problem. But I'm convinced I can't physically, strain after a Royal Academy portrait.

We take our treat on Friday now, and went to St Albans, in the grey blizzard; and saw Roman pavements, guarded by men in overcoats, attending upon imbecile sons. Had tea, and heard the local ladies discussing the Empire Day celebrations, which are to include a red white and blue cake decorated with flags. What will they say to *Three Guineas?*

Monday 9 May
This is written to fill up the usual distracted relics of Monday's broken morning: drove up [from Rodmell] in the clear May morning light. A rather patchy week end: bitter cold. Can't settle to my play (*Pointz Hall* is to become in the end a play) or to Roger's Cambridge letters. The truth is we want a holiday; and have to dribble along rather jaded, trying odds and ends to keep moving, till June 8th or so, when we escape. A social week ahead: lunch Clive; to Philip [Morrell] to choose a ring and emotionalise; two plays of Angelica's and God damn it, Saturday at Ray [Strachey]'s. L. rather on edge about that.

Thursday 12 May
Lunch Clive (balderdash, respectability rampant; hard superficiality); to Philip after tea. He pressed things on me. I felt rather uncomfortable: a vulture feeling; didn't want to take so much. But took the big green ring and pearl earrings, shawl and fan. Philip rather battered – simple, cheerful, with a vast black satin cravat. Had a bad heart, from an old rowing strain. The specialist thinking Ott an ordinary wife said "Do you want the truth?" Yes. "Well any shock will kill you. How old?" Sixty-seven. "You won't see sixty-eight – except you live like a potato." She burst into tears, which she seldom

did. Then he recovered, she got ill – paralysed – some nerve affection. They then told her of the Doctor's death: she was sick all night; recovered; and suddenly died in the early morning. A lovely thrush egg blue evening; domes and chimneys very pure and sharp walking home with my green shagreen box, the shawl and the fan. Ott's last gifts.

Friday 20 May

Time and again I have meant to write down my expectations, dreads, and so on, waiting the publication of *Three Guineas* – but haven't. What I'm afraid of is the taunt Charm and emptiness. The book I wrote with such violent feelings to relieve that immense pressure will not dimple the surface. That is my fear. But the fears are entirely outbalanced by the immense relief and peace I have gained, and enjoy this moment. Now I am quit of that poison and excitement. I am an outsider. I can take my way: experiment with my own imagination in my own way. The pack may howl, but it shall never catch me.

Tuesday 24 May

I'm pleased this morning because Lady Rhondda writes that she is 'profoundly excited and moved by *Three Guineas*'. A good omen; because this shows that certain people will be stirred; will think; will discuss; it won't altogether be frittered away. But as the whole of Europe may be in flames – its on the cards. One more shot at a policeman and the Germans, Czechs, French will begin the old horror. The 4th of August [1914] may come next week. At the moment there is a lull. L. says Kingsley Martin says we say (the Prime Minister) that we will fight this time. Hitler therefore is chewing his little bristling moustache. But the whole thing trembles: and my book may be like a moth dancing over a bonfire – consumed in less than one second. Now for the [Chelsea] Flower Show; dinner at the Hutch. What am I to wear? Aeroplanes growling overhead in the cloudy blue sky. They look like sharks, seen through our wavy window.

Wednesday 25 May

Ka [Arnold-Forster] is dead. I read it by chance in the *News Chronicle* yesterday before going to the flower show. No flowers, no mourning. Why did she die? And what do I feel? Oh that one could feel more for the deaths of one's friends! But it comes and goes, feeling. Always at first visual – Ka lying drawn and white, there with the flat sea underneath – the ships passing. Her own identical life ended when Rupert [Brooke] died. So I think. After that she was acting a part very carefully and deliberately chosen. Maternity, Will [her husband], public life. Hence some squint; she was never natural, never with me at least. And I was self-conscious; remembering how she had seen me mad. She used to come to Asheham: condescending, patronising, giving up her own pleasures to tend me and help L. I don't think I was ever at my ease with her. Yet we had an old affection; remembered things – Rupert &c – that we never spoke of. She had that irritating Quack Quack in her voice; as if she always must be impressing me with her busyness, her social standing; her responsibilities: how she was a JP on some Education Committee; doing actual things with important real people, while we frittered our time away writing books in London. In her house – a singularly ugly house in some ways – she was too much the hostess who keeps open house. But at the same time that was her role: to help; to lift lame dogs; to entertain, to arrange; manage; receive confidences. And what was wrong with all that? Only that after Rupert's death she was playing a part. Yet this is superficial. For there was a trustiness in her; a stable goodness; and a good deal of fortitude, patience, a determination to oar her way. I wonder, did she know she was dying? And what did she think of it all? And why? As usual, I regret: that she sent me cream at Christmas, and in the flurry of L.'s illness I never wrote and thanked; that she suggested coming, and absorbed in Nessa last autumn, I did not arrange it. But this is always so; and can't be helped. And I am thinking of her with affection – old Ka.

Thursday 26 May
Ka had a seizure and died without regaining consciousness. This is from a typed form sent by [her brother-in-law] this morning. She is buried today – rainy and dark: and I shall not go to the service. Will is in Canada.

Saturday 28 May
A pouring wet day as dark as November. May – this spring has been blotted from the calendar. The Buzz is beginning, though the little gadfly only emerges from its shell next Thursday. I can foretell that those who dislike will sneer at me for a well to do aesthete; and those who approve will echo Rhondda's 'most exciting, profoundly moving'. All reviews and letters will ring changes on those notes.

Monday 30 May
Nessa's birthday – the fifty-eighth I think it must be. She is at Charleston with Angelica and Quentin. Oh dear – Julian not there. And it rains hard – she says she is glad to be away. The Robson children and Tom at tea. A great spread; mostly eaten. The little boy crammed his mouth with sweets, and added one that Sally had already sucked. Tom came, most respectable; swallow tails and grey silk tie, having he explained to slip into his evening service in time to take round the plate – a churchwarden in South Kensington. Very friendly.

L. says I must expect some very angry reviews from men. I add, From women too. Then there'll be the clergy. But I think I can sit calm as a toad in an oak at the centre of the storm.

Tuesday 31 May
A letter from Pippa [Strachey]. She is enthusiastic. She says its the very thing for which they have panted. Now I can face the music, or donkey's bray or geese's cackle. Never have I faced reviews so composedly. Maynard may have a gibe; but what care I? And I shan't send copies to my family, and so they need say nothing.

MONKS HOUSE, RODMELL

Friday 3 June
This is the coming out day of *Three Guineas*. And the *TLS* has two columns and a leader; and the *Referee* a great black bar Woman Declares Sex War; or some such caption. Its true I have a sense of quiet and relief. But no wish to read reviews, or hear opinions. Oh it pleased me that the *TLS* says I'm the most brilliant pamphleteer in England. Also that this book may mark an epoch if taken seriously.

I talked to Nessa about Julian on Wednesday. She can hardly speak. What matters compared with that? Yet I was always thinking of Julian when I wrote.

Whit Sunday 5 June
Walked on the racecourse: bought cakes in Lewes. Charleston and Bunny to tea today, yesterday the first hot summer day. People in tails and white shirts tripping about Lewes. Glyndebourne in full flower. Windy today, but still fine, and the sun still active – after I suppose two months drought and darkness. The ugliest spring on record. So we were wise to save our holiday, though I'm so rested now. We shall attempt Skye, for if we don't now we never shall. L. says we are old. I say we are middle aged.

Saturday 11 June
On the whole *Three Guineas* is taken seriously: many high compliments; some snarls but generally kind, rather surprised, and its over – Off we can go to Scotland for a holiday that I don't really need, but still a freshener before *Roger* won't come amiss. No book ever slid from me so secretly and smoothly. Quit of all this, I've written an article on Walpole, very fast and free, for America. Walked several good walks. We go up this evening after

tea. Bowls. Bells. And the garden being planted by L. with some little help from me. And I must go in to cold mutton.

*   *   *

52 TAVISTOCK SQUARE, WC1

Tuesday 5 July

A thunderstorm, still further to distract my already distracted brain. How am I to calm and contract back again to *Roger*? We returned on Saturday.

Thursday 7 July

Oh the appalling grind of getting back to *Roger*, after these violent oscillations: *Three Guineas* and *Pointz Hall*. How can I concentrate upon minute facts in letters? But Gumbo [Marjorie Strachey] last night threw cold water on the whole idea of biography of those who have no lives. Roger had, she says, no life that can be written. I daresay this is true. And here am I sweating over minute facts. Is it to be done on this scale? I think I will go on doggedly till I meet him myself – 1909 – and then attempt something more fictitious. But must plod on through all these letters till then. Meanwhile I'm so raddled and raked with people, noise, telephones – have endless letters to write, long for peace.

Tuesday 19 July

What about yesterday as a specimen day? Work at *Roger* – fearful niggling drudgery to quarter to one. Robson to lunch. Isherwood wants to see me at three. I slip out; buy flowers, pâté de foie. Back at 3.15. Peep in at Stephen Spender, Chris [Isherwood] and John and L. all talking in John's room. Sit down upstairs. Visit Adrian. Tea on balcony. Dog playing, cars passing – Judith there. Ann to marry on Thursday. No invitations. Karin in and out. Look at house. Gossip and home. Will Rothenstein to dine. A respectable, suppressed, but I don't think quite such a snake as Duncan makes out. Only dimmed, tamed, I think on his guard. No enthusiasm for life – too much high nobility. Only . . . compared with Roger, how blunted, tolerant, and a little plausible. Gave me letters. Nothing vivid about Roger and Paris. All dim now. Fetched by a chauffeur and car.

Mercifully no one – I repeat *no one* – today. Today Julian was killed last year. And its hot again. I shan't say anything to Nessa. Oh dear – We go – this is an event for us – to the Ballet at Drury Lane in proper seats tonight. *Three Guineas* selling very slowly. Abusive or sneering letters the last two days.

Friday 22 July
Weather steamy but no longer blue. Sat in Gordon Square last night and Duncan and Vanessa were we thought unreasonable about Roger and Will Rothenstein and the Grafton [2nd Post-Impressionist Exhibition, 1911]. What a kettle of fish! And *Three Guineas* is once more selling; has now broached the six thousand. Ann was married yesterday. I gave her £15; L. £10.

Tuesday 26 July
Its very true that I have no time. I have simply dedicated the last fortnight to people – seeing people – not a day free from it. Always an engagement. If you let it fill your sails there's something to be said for it.

Monks House, Rodmell

Thursday 4 August
Came down on Thursday; almost mute with botheration: six from Charleston on Sunday; then Vita on Tuesday for the night and yesterday; Mrs Woolf, Edgar and Sylvia today. Yet we are very happy. I should add that we found a new gable thrown out in the roof, workmen hammering, Mr Wicks started work, without warning, and says he will be here three weeks which means five. It has been very hot with a strong hot wind. And I'm taking a gallop in fiction, after bringing Roger to his marriage. Rather a jerk and an effort, my work at the moment. Switching from assiduous truth to wild ideas. But I liked seeing Vita, so free and easy again. We sat out here and discussed her loves; death; Ben [her son]'s tears, on being scolded by Vita; Willy Maugham; Clive, who's writing a book, secretly, on war; Julian; Nessa; looking so ill; so many women have lost sons and lovers; I forget how it went. Also she brought a basket of peaches and half a bottle of Château Yquem from her mother's cellar. And off she went in her great black car that impresses Mrs Bartholomew so. She was much like old times.

Saturday 7 August
Yesterday I saw six tanks with gun carriages come clambering down the hill and assemble like black beetles at Rat Farm. Small boys playing idiotic games for which I pay. Harold [Nicolson] is very dismal, Vita says: predicts war, but not this week. A lull at the moment. And terrifically hot. A great purple black cloud massed itself behind Mrs Woolf, Sylvia and Edgar as they sat out here; then thunder; then rain, at last. And we had lights lit. Why they so rub the country bloom off – these family Woolves – I don't

know. Always a dusty feeling of Earl's Court and offices. Oh and the commonplaceness of the talk – mostly about [Woolf family] furniture: lovely silver mirrors, most artistic overmantels, suites of dining room chairs, coffee cups. She lies awake counting them, deciding who's to have what, and so falls asleep. Workmen tapping. Yesterday the men about the wireless. Too many gadgets and dodges perhaps in this house. And the children shrieking. But we go to Charleston for tea.

Wednesday 17 August
The old woman who lived up at Mount Misery drowned herself three days ago. The body was found near Piddinghoe – my usual walk. Her son died; she turned queer; had been a midwife in Brighton; lived in the broken windowed half of Mr Bradfield's house. She used to moon over the downs with a dog. Once she came to the shop late on Sunday to beg twopennyworth of paraffin – she was alone in the dark. They threatened to turn her out – farm wanted. She had killed her dog. So at last off she goes, on Monday perhaps when the tide was high in the afternoon, and jumps in. Louie says her brother found a drowned woman the other day at Barcombe Mills – a horrid sight. So I order dinner hastily and come out here to brew more *Roger*.

So, at supper, we discussed our generation: and the prospects of war. Hitler has his million men now under arms. Is it only summer manoeuvres or –? Harold [Nicolson] broadcasting in his man of the world manner hints it may be war. That is the complete ruin not only of civilisation, in Europe, but of our last lap. Quentin conscripted &c. One ceases to think about it – that's all. Goes on discussing the new room, new chair, new books. What else can a gnat on a blade of grass do? And I would like to write *Pointz Hall*; and other things; and have half a mind one of these days to explain what my intention is in writing these continual diaries. Not publication. Revision? a memoir of my own life? Perhaps. Only other things crop up.

Monday 22 August
I am in the wars, or shall be. Maynard sends for us on Wednesday; is said by Lydia to be very critical of *Three Guineas*. Now the thing to remember is that I'm an independent and perfectly established human being: no one can bully me: and at the same time nothing shall make me shrivel into a martyr or a bitter persecution maniac.

Tuesday 23 August
Its odd to be as nervous as I am at the idea of seeing Maynard tomorrow, and his heckling: dear old Hitler. But I won't be nervous.

Sunday 28 August
By the way Maynard never said a word. Some were unsaid. As for instance,
Lydia: we all put up with you Virginia, said significantly, kissing me at
parting. Maynard tired, extended, rather grim. Sunday is the devil's own
day at Monks House. Dogs, children, bells . . . there they go for evensong.
I can't settle anywhere. Beaten after three hard fights at bowls. Bowls is
our mania. Reading rather scamped. Ding dong bell . . . ding dong – why
did we settle in a village? And how deliberately we are digging ourselves
in! And at any moment the guns may go off and explode us. L. is very
black. Hitler has his hounds only very lightly held. A single step – in
Czechoslovakia – like the Austrian Archduke in 1914 and again its 1914.
Ding dong ding dong.

The autumn mists assemble. And I'm irritable with work and noise. We
dine at Charleston. Now its as quiet as the grave . . . all grey; the chestnut
leaves hanging heavy; birds on the telegraph posts. Letters fret me. Never
one that's disinterested. Requests always to speak, write, lecture, see people.
That's fame – dogs again. Yap Yap.

Wednesday 31 August
War seemed round the corner again. Question what Hitler will do, when
he'll do it. Cabinet Ministers summoned. And, of course, Kingsley Martin
ringing up, and annoyed that L. isn't in London to hold his hand, and make
it write an article. We were in London yesterday. Kingsley Martin to lunch.
Three possibilities. One of them European war. But not at once. A game
of bluff on Hitler's part, possibly. If there's war "my own solution is suicidal"
– while he munches mutton chops, and sweeps up fragments, scraping his
knife and fork round in a way I hate. So he burbled on: with his own article,
and his own figure, histrionically arrayed, in the centre. I walked off, bought
a pewter plate, a scissors, and a lustre globe, encouraged by a letter from
Brace [USA] reporting enthusiasm for *Three Guineas*, good advance orders,
and great praise.

Thursday 1 September
Politics marking time. A violent attack on *Three Guineas* in *Scrutiny* by Q.
Leavis. And I didn't read it through. But I read enough to see that it was
all personal – about Queenie's own grievances and retorts to my snubs.
Why I don't care more for praise or wigging I don't know. Yet its true.

Monday 5 September
Its odd to be sitting here, looking up little facts about Roger and the
Metropolitan Museum in New York, with a sparrow tapping on my roof
this fine September morning when it may be the 3rd August 1914 . . . What

would war mean? Darkness, strain: I suppose conceivably death. And all
the horror of friends: and Quentin ... All that lies over the water in the
brain of that ridiculous little man. Why ridiculous? Because none of it fits.
Death and war and darkness representing nothing that any human being
from the Pork Butcher to the Prime Minister cares one straw about. Not
liberty, not life ... merely a housemaid's dream. And we woke from that
dream and have the Cenotaph to remind us of the fruits. We may hear his
mad voice vociferating tonight. Nuremberg rally begun: but it goes on for
another week. And what will be happening this time ten days?

Saturday 10 September

I don't feel that the crisis is real – not so real as Roger in 1910 at Gordon
Square, about which I've just been writing. Of course we may be at war
this time next week. Seven ships are mobilised today. Meanwhile the
aeroplanes are on the prowl, crossing the downs. Every preparation is
made. Sirens will hoot in a particular way when there's the first hint of a
raid. L. and I no longer talk about it. Much better to play bowls and pick
dahlias. Today Morgan comes, and we have our crowded Memoir Club
week-end. It is at Tilton, in the afternoon, to suit Maynard, who is going
to read.

Sunday 11 September

Morgan here. He is writing in the garden. A very fine clear spruce blue
day. The news as black as possible. Hitler has at any rate cursed, and
Goering spat: nothing said till tomorrow. And now in to the house to tidy
rooms and hair.

Monday 12 September

Papers all say that we shall know the truth, one way or the other, tonight.
So there's nothing to do but wait. Memoir Club meeting had its little
sensation. Molly [MacCarthy] and Quentin lunched. After lunch, as she
came down stairs, Molly tripped and fell over the loose tile. Lay very white
in great pain. Obviously a bad twist. When we had to go, she couldn't
move. Ankle swollen. So we took her to [the doctor]; then the X ray; at
last to Tilton; carried her in. Maynard read a very packed profound and
impressive paper so far as I could follow, about Cambridge youth; their
philosophy; its consequences; what it lacked; what it gave; the beauty and
unworldliness of it. I was impressed. Then he had to rest; it turned grey
and cold. Molly had to be slowly conveyed – a bed made on the ground
floor at Charleston. Nevertheless a very human satisfactory meeting. Bunny,
Desmond, Quentin and Lydia, ourselves, Morgan, Clive, Nessa (in big hat:
much more herself than ever yet).

Tuesday 13 September
No war yet anyhow. Hitler boasted and boomed but shot no solid bolt.
Mere violent rant, and then broke off. We listened in to the end. A savage
howl like a person excrutiated; then howls from the audience; then a more
spaced and measured sentence. Then another bark. Cheering ruled by a
stick. Frightening to think of the faces. And the voice was frightening. But
as it went on we said anti-climax. This seems to be the general verdict. He
daren't cross the line. Comes up to it and stands bawling insults. How can
people stand this nonsense? Negotiations to go on, under threat that he
will use force if &c. Immense relief last night at Monks House, after a
gloomy dinner. Peaceful if depressed: anyhow a week or two without a
war.

Wednesday 14 September
Things worse today. Rioting in Prague. It looks as if Hitler meant to slide
sideways into war. Raises riots: will say Can't be stopped. But its a hopeless
war this – when we know winning means nothing. So we're committed,
for the rest of our lives, to public misery. This will be slashed with private
too. We – L. and I – can make out I suppose down here: vegetables and
fruit. And I've made some money. Needn't cringe. That's about all.

Friday 16 September
Chamberlain has flown to see Hitler. Universal relief and approval. No
news yet. They say this means Peace. War staved off for one year. Nessa
Duncan Angelica and Quentin start for Cassis tonight, driving across
France. We settle in for ten days alone. Dined at Charleston. All seemed
agreed that a country life is best. Clive is giving notice to Gordon Square.
We hear that Tavistock Square will be pulled down in three years. Shall
we not all provide ourselves with single rooms in London and live here?
Never make any fixed plans for life – that's my motto. Really, for the ten
years that remain, be free of the world.

Saturday 17 September
Chamberlain back. In a hard business man's voice told us, as he stepped
out of the plane at Croydon, that he was to meet Hitler again: that Hitler
was coming to meet an old man half way (is this symbolical?) and we
meanwhile not to believe rumour. No statement today. Cabinet meeting.
Just as in violent personal anxiety, the public lapses into complete indifference. One can feel no more at the moment.
    Dreamt of Julian one night: how he came back: I implored him not to
go to Spain. He promised. Then I saw his wounds. Dreamt of Roger last
night. How he had not died. I praised Cézanne. And told him how I admired

his writing. Exactly the old relationship. Perhaps easier to get this in dreams, because one has dreamt away the fact of his death, to which I woke as L. came in.

Thursday 22 September
The public fluctuates. Chamberlain flying today to Gotesberg (?). A strong opposition has risen. Eden, Churchill and the Labour Party all denounce serving Czechoslovakia on the altar and bidding it commit suicide. Czechoslovakia very dignified and tragic. The prospect of another glissade after a minor stop into abyss. All Europe in Hitler's keeping. What'll he gobble next? That's the summary of us in Sussex.

Wednesday 28 September
This may be the last day of peace; so why not record it, as I've twenty minutes and nothing to do? A tumultuous week end. Pouring wet Monday. L. came out to say Kingsley Martin begged him to come up, in order to act as liaison between the Labour Party and the Liberals. He was the only person &c. So we decided to go at once and spend the night. Drove up in the rain. Men digging trenches at Turnham Green. London crowded. L. went to see Kingsley, I to buy coffee &c. "Its a miserable day and our thoughts are miserable" the woman said. She said we should win; and that it would not be a long war. "But what is the point of winning?" I said, at which she exclaimed and shrugged her shoulders in agreement. Then Kingsley Martin to dinner; charcoal black round his eyes; as usual something histrionic. Hopelessly restless. Melodramatic in his gestures, perpetually looking at the time and ringing people up. No word of any possible plan or reason for summoning L. Stayed on, drinking, smoking. Then said he was going to walk the streets. Couldn't sleep. So to bed. Telephones all the morning. I went to the London Library. Sat in the basement and looked up *The Times* on [the Post-Impressionist Exhibition] in 1910. Old sweeper gently dusting. Came and said They're telling us to try on our masks. Have you got yours I asked. No not yet. And shall we have war? I fear so, but I still hope not. Oh they've laid in sand bags; the books will be moved; but if a bomb strikes the house ... May I dust under your chair? I looked in at the National Gallery being warned by a sober loud speaker to get my gas mask as I walked down Pall Mall. I looked at Renoir, Cézanne &c: tried to see through Roger's eyes: tried to get some solidity into my mind. So to lunch. Question what to do about the Press. Plans can only be sketched. We must settle into work at any rate. We must drive our pens and keep the Press going that way. We had a rather unpleasant farewell – they staying, we going. Its reasonable of course. But one doesn't like leaving them there: and yet they want to stay, for the money. A violent

rain storm; a great crowd in the streets. It was oddly peaceful and sane, getting out here after London. Mr Perkins brought gas masks about 10.30, and so at last we went to bed.

Thursday 29 September

We listened in yesterday at five expecting to hear that War was declared. Instead Mr Chamberlain made a sensational announcement. He has been invited by Herr Hitler to meet him tomorrow at Munich. Signor Mussolini and Daladier will be present. Mobilisation is postponed for twenty-four hours. It was like coming out of a dark room. Anyhow war for the moment is postponed. Perkins and Janson called last night to say fifty children arrive in Rodmell today and to note numbers of our rooms.

Friday 30 September

L. has just come in, it being 11.15, to say that he overheard a Broadcast when he was in the WC; dashed out: turned on our wireless; and heard that terms are being made at Munich. I can't go into them. But it means peace. They are agreeing to let some Germans into Czechoslovakia today; then English Italian and French are to enter and guarantee; then a three months' pause. Three months in which to settle the question, instead of bombs on London and Paris today! Such a reversal was never known. I will try and describe the reversal; which is soberly and truly life after death. For we, even if we escaped, should have had our noses rubbed in death; ruin; perhaps the end finally of all order. It would have meant our last fifteen years of life spent in battling for a thread of liberty; keeping the Press going among the deaths of the young. And now suddenly we can travel and move and use our normal faculties. No slaughter of the young beneath us. I wonder if we could have faced it even here – entertaining East End children in the hall; writing; getting all the dismal fag ends of things thrown at us; and reading Casualty Lists. Now of course one makes not new resolutions, but attacks the old with some fervour. Possibly – sanguinely – a new view will dominate. Hitler will sink instead of swell. But what a shave! A very fine day.

Saturday 1 October

A violent storm – purple ink clouds. L. is storing apples – finest harvest for perhaps some years. We were to live on apples honey and cabbage. Postman delivered an oration – "just my own thoughts" on War and Dictators. How all will worship Chamberlain now: but in five years' time we may be saying we ought to have put him, Hitler, down now. But now we can't help being glad of peace. Its human nature. Of course there's bound to be a turn against relief, as in violent illness. One turns peevish and has a sense of emptiness.

Sunday 2 October

Yesterday would have been the first day of the proclamation of war. It might be amusing to scribble down pall mall some higgledy piggledy of incidents: as they remain over; and will soon be forgotten. The BBC in a measured trained voice: how the public was to go with warm clothing: no glass: post cards: this interrupted by the Archbishop's prayers; then cold menace: a spaced dictated message from the Admiralty to ships. Obviously we'd sunk mines. Then the afternoon (Wednesday) when all foreign stations were jammed. Then the statement that all poisonous snakes at the Zoo would be killed, and dangerous animals shot – Vision of London ravaged by cobras and tigers. Sense of preparation to the last hair. All this mixture of minute detail; with invocations to God; with Hitler braying and the Germans howling; then the composed and cultured voice breaking in, say about not taking pets. Then over all a feeling of the senselessness, futility, so that there was a dilution of emotion. A child's game. Yet extreme physical relief when peace seemed twenty-four hours longer. Some instinctive self preservation. I felt this most when we drove away from 52 [Tavistock Square]. Some remorse at leaving the clerks exposed. Now rapidly other emotions chase each other; that peace seems dull, solid. Then that we must have a bone to gnaw. Some obliquity: after all we admired Chamberlain in the crisis. Is it fair to abuse him now?

Monday 3 October

The Keynes to tea yesterday. All a put up job between Chamberlain and Hitler, Maynard said. Never had been any chance of war. I wish I could get the ripples of all these complexities to land. Maynard and Lydia very congenial – dear old Maynard so sanguine, so powerful, somehow lovable too, and Lord how brilliant. I kissed him. A life time – what remains – of peace now. Reaction of shame beginning. *Daily Telegraph* decent, and starts a pro-Czech movement. *Times* disgraceful.

Thursday 6 October

Politics now a mere 'I told you so . . . You did – I didn't'. I shall cease to read the papers. Sink at last into contemplation. Peace for our life time: why not try to believe it?

Friday 14 October

Two things I mean to do when the long dark evenings come: to write, on the spur of the moment, as now, lots of little poems to go into *Pointz Hall*:

as they may come in handy; to collect, even bind together, my innumerable *TLS* notes: to consider them as material for some kind of critical book: ranging all through English literature as I've read and noted it the past twenty years. In fact I must clear my table, as L. calls it and does it – before we go on Sunday.

52 TAVISTOCK SQUARE, WC1

Sunday 30 October
Words, words, words, so many and so many – That I think is the vocalisation of my little sensation this morning. I am tired of writing. 'Words' refers partly to Vita's new poem, 'Solitude'. Does it jab on the nerve? Is it only sleek eloquence? The words I found on my lips were 'Suave and sumptuous'. I suspect there's a good deal more. But no doubt I'm at an angle. I don't want reflections on God: nor do I altogether forget her superficial view of *Three Guineas*: that she never troubled to think out what I meant. This is partly personal; partly not.

Nessa away slightly rasps me. I have no circumference; only my inviolable centre: L. to wit. A great deal on foot. Words words and now roast beef and apple tart. An evening alone.

Tuesday 1 November
Max [Beerbohm] like a Cheshire cat. Orbicular. Jowled. Blue eyed. Eyes grow vague. What he said was, I've never been in a group. No, not even as a young man. It was a serious fault. When you're a young man you ought to think There's only one right way. And I thought – this is very profound, but you mayn't realise it – 'It takes all sorts to make a world.' I was outside all the groups. Now dear Roger Fry who liked me, was a born leader. No one so 'illuminated'. He looked it. Never saw anyone look it so much. I heard him lecture, on the Aesthetics of Art. I was disappointed. He kept on turning the page – turning the page ... George Moore never used his eyes. He never knew what men and women think. He got it all out of books. Ah I was afraid you would remind me of *Ave atque Vale*. Yes. That's beautiful. Yes, its true he used his eyes then. Otherwise its like a lovely lake, with no fish in it.

About his own writing: dear Lytton Strachey said to me: first I write one sentence; then I write another. That's how I write. And so I go on. But I have a feeling writing ought to be like running through a field. That's your way. Now how do you go down to your room, after breakfast – what do you feel? I used to look at the clock, and say Oh dear me, its time I began my article ... No, I'll read the paper first. I never wanted to write. But I used to come home from a dinner party and take my brush and draw caricature after caricature. They seemed to bubble up from here ... he pressed his stomach. That was a kind of inspiration, I suppose. I have a public of about 1500 – Oh I'm famous, largely thanks to you, and people of importance at the top like you. I often read over my own work. And I have a habit of reading it through the eyes of people I respect. I often read it as Virginia Woolf would read it – picking out the kind of things you would like. You never do that? Oh you should try it.

Willie Maugham came in: like a dead man whose beard or moustache has grown a little grisly bristle after death. And his lips are drawn back like a dead man's. He has small ferret eyes. A look of suffering and malignity and meanness and suspicion. A mechanical voice as if he had to raise a lever at each word – stiffens talk into something hard cut, measured. Sat like an animal in a trap. And I could not say anything that loosed his dead man's jaw. Isherwood and I met on the doorstep. He is a slip of a wild boy: with quicksilver eyes. Nipped. Jockey like. "That young man," said W. Maugham "holds the future of the English novel in his hands." Very enthusiastic. In spite of Max's brilliance, and idiosyncracy, which he completely realises, and does not overstep, this was a surface evening. All kept to the same surface level by Sybil's hostesscraft.

Monday 14 November

So many pages, I see, about the Colefax party, and none about the incessant stream here. I use my old image. Trying to drink a cup of tea, and having it knocked out of one's hand.

A letter from Duncan. Complete bliss at Cassis, has a country life in view. Angelica perfect. So's the weather today. Jews persecuted, only just over the Channel. Here we feel a faint heat under us, like potatoes frying. But no more than that.

Tuesday 22 November

I meant to write Reflections on my position as a writer. Apparently I've been exalted to a very high position, say about ten years ago: then was decapitated by Wyndham Lewis and Miss Stein; am now I think – let me see – out of date, of course; not a patch, with the young, on Morgan; yet wrote *The Waves*; yet am unlikely to write anything good again; am a secondrate, and likely, I think, to be discarded altogether. I think that's my public reputation at the moment. It is based largely on Cyril Connolly's Cocktail criticism: a sheaf of feathers in the wind. How much do I mind? Less than I expected. I mean, I never thought I was so famous; so don't feel the decapitation. Yes I used to be praised by the young and attacked by the elderly. *Three Guineas* has queered the pitch. So my position is ambiguous. Undoubtedly Morgan's reputation is much higher than my own. So is Tom's. Well? In a way it is a relief. I'm fundamentally, I think, an outsider. I do my best work and feel most braced with my back to the wall. This is not the measured criticism of my position I meant to write. I'm not able to go deeply. For here's the usual stir and bother – Nessa back tomorrow.

Friday 25 November
L.'s birthday – 58? But I open this, to note, at the foot of the last pessimistic page, in two minutes, the fact that pessimism can be routed by getting into the flow: creative writing. So why not, when pessimistic, dandle the brain a little, until it gets into its circuit?

Sunday 11 December
We walked back from *Twelfth Night* (disappointing) on a clear cold night. Talked of death in Russell Square. L. said he had taught himself not to think about it. Two or three years ago fear of death became an obsession. I said I should not wish to live if he died. But until then found life what? exciting? Yes I think so. He agreed. So we don't think of death.

Very long hours of semi-drudgery on *Roger*. The war years. Mrs Woolf has had a heart attack. But her vitality may again pull her over. The Jews obsess her. This autumn reveals plainly our 'celebrity': that is, that we never get a day to ourselves; and attract a constant stream, from all quarters. Political, social, literary. I suppose this is secretly pleasing. I wonder. A month in winter fields will cool me down. The young all swarm, even if they criticise.

Monday 12 December
Rather a debauched Sunday evening at Clive's last night. Was he drunk? He was so quarrelsome and peevish, after dinner. A long tirade against motorists. Suddenly Nessa got quite red and said "This conversation is so foolish we'd better change it." But Clive wouldn't change it. Every change had its head snapped off. I thought of Roger and Lytton and how we used to talk of a Sunday evening. Now all personal gossip and these tedious bickerings.

Thursday 15 December
This is hell's Black Calcutta hole week.

Monday 19 December
I will spend the last morning – for tomorrow will be an odious scramble – in summing up the year. True, there are ten days or so to run; but the

liberty of this book allows these – I was going to say liberties, but my meticulous conscience bids me look for another word. That raises some questions about my concern with the art of writing. On the whole the art becomes absorbing – more? No, I think its been absorbing ever since I was a little creature, scribbling a story in the manner of Hawthorne on the green plush sofa in the drawing room at St Ives while the grown ups dined.

The last dinner of the year was to Tom Eliot last night. Physically he is a little muffin faced: sallow and shadowed; but intent (as I am) on the art of writing. His play – *Family Reunion* – was the staple of the very bitter cold evening. (The snow is now falling: flakes come through my skylight.) It has taken him off and on two years to write, is an advance upon *Murder [in the Cathedral]*: in poetry. When the crisis came, his only thought was annoyance that now his play would not be acted. And he hurried up the revision. Tom said the young don't take art or politics seriously enough. Disappointed in the Auden–Isherwood. A subtle, splitting mind: a man of simple integrity, and the artist's ingenuous egotism. Dines out and goes to musical teas; reads poems at Londonderry House; has a humorous sardonic gift which mitigates his egotism; and is on the side of authority. A nice old friends' evening.

This year I have worked at *Three Guineas*; and began, about April 1st, *Roger*: whom I have brought to the year 1919. I have also written 'Walpole'; 'Lappin and Lapinova', and 'The Art of Biography'. John says two cabinet ministers are in favour of giving me the OM. The reception of *Three Guineas* has been interesting, unexpected – only I'm not sure what I expected. 8,000 sold. Not one of my friends has mentioned it. I've written too 120 pages of *Pointz Hall*. I think of making it a 220 page book. A medley. I rush to it for relief after a long pressure of Fry facts. To be written for pleasure.

We shall find the new window in at Monks House. And its the coldest day for five years. Snow steadily falling. John temperamental. Another boil over on Saturday. A very bad season. Probable loss. Two years more of 52. The new flats going up in Southampton Row. Clive leaving 50 [Gordon Square]. Deaths this year: Ottoline, Ka. Mrs Woolf recovering.

1939

After spending nearly four weeks at Monks House over Christmas, in extremes of weather, the Woolfs returned to London on 15 January. At the end of the month they paid a courtesy visit to one of the Hogarth Press's most distinguished authors, Sigmund Freud, now a refugee living in Hampstead. The Spanish Civil War was coming to its end, and on 27 February General Franco's government was recognised by Great Britain and France, although Madrid did not fall until a month later. Virginia was working on Roger Fry, the first draft of which she finished in March, sometimes allowing herself the indulgence of writing her fiction Pointz Hall and thinking of a book encompassing the whole of literature. On 16 March Hitler marched into Prague, and in April Mussolini invaded Albania. European war now seemed inevitable. The Woolfs were at Monks House for almost the whole of April, and Virginia had days of extreme depression. A few days before her return to London, at Vanessa's prompting she began to write her memoirs, which she continued intermittently until January 1941.

Although the Woolfs' lease of 52 Tavistock Square ran until 1941, large-scale demolitions were proceeding all around them. The noise and dirt became insupportable. They found an alternative in 37 Mecklenburgh Square, some half a mile to the east, and negotiated a lease. But apart from four weeks from the end of May when they escaped to Rodmell and then across to Normandy and Brittany, they spent the high summer in their old London flat – and it was here that Virginia was subjected to the discomfort of being photographed by Gisèle Freund, a protégée of her wealthy and overbearing admirer, the Argentinian intellectual Victoria Ocampo. The London season ended with more deaths: Mark Gertler the painter committed suicide; and Leonard's mother, after another fall, died on 2 July, aged eighty-eight. The remaining days of July, before the Woolfs went to Monks House on the 25th, were intensely busy and sociable.

At Charleston, the prospect of war had prompted Vanessa to undertake various improvements. Clive Bell contributed the contents of his London flat, and the house was henceforward his, Duncan Grant's, Vanessa's and the children's main home, though the painters kept their studios in Fitzroy Street. In August the Woolfs went up from Rodmell on two successive weeks to supervise the removal first of the Hogarth Press and then of their own furniture and effects to their new home at 37 Mecklenburgh Square. The political crisis intensified with the signing of the German–Soviet Pact on 23 August; and on 1 September Hitler's forces seized Danzig and began their

446

attack on Poland. On 3 September the Prime Minister announced that Great Britain was at war with Germany.

The Woolfs settled in at Rodmell, going up to London from time to time to discuss the business of the Hogarth Press with John Lehmann, to try and make their new flat habitable, and to keep in touch with friends. Virginia's response to the anticipated privations of wartime was to take on more journalism to augment their diminishing income, and to offer weekend respites at Monks House to friends and to the staff of the Hogarth Press. It was the period of what came to be called the 'phoney' war, when, while Poland was overrun and partitioned between Germany and Russia, England waited uneasily and prepared for air bombardment; but action was confined to naval encounters. Petrol rationing had been introduced in September, and the Woolfs bicycled to Charleston for Christmas dinner.

1939

MONKS HOUSE, RODMELL

Thursday 5 January
So I take a new nib, and spend my last five minutes, this very fine January morning, in writing the first page of the New Year. We came down fourteen or fifteen days ago and found all pipes frozen. There was snow for five days – bitter cold; wind. We staggered for one hour through the blizzard. Chains were on our wheels. We ground over to Charleston and Tilton on Christmas Day. Then, two days later, woke to find green grass everywhere. The long spikes of ice that hung down the kitchen window had drops on their noses. They melted. The pipes thawed. Now its a June morning with an east wind.

Monday 9 January
Now that I have brought my brain to the state of an old washerwoman's flannel over *Roger*, I must expand, first on this irresponsible page, and then for four days I swear, before we go back on Sunday, in fiction. Though I've ground out most wish to write, even fiction. Rodmell is a grind on the brain: in winter especially. I write three solid hours; walk two; then we read, with intervals for cooking dinner, music, news, till 11.30. Weather now broken. Floods and gales; marsh under water. Charleston broken up. Maynard's father dying. And that reminds me of two obituaries I should have written, had I not been immersed: Jack Hills and Mitz [LW's pet marmoset]. Mitz was found dead on Boxing Day I think: her white old woman's face puckered; eyes shut; tail wrapped round her neck. L. buried her in the snow under the wall. Jack died the same day about – no Xmas Eve; and if I had a brain (but haven't) I could retell his life; as it affected ours, thirty years ago. Who he saw, where he lived even had long been lost to me. Yet of all our youthful directors he was the most open minded, least repressive, could best have fitted in with later developments, had we not gone our ways – he to politics and sport, we to Bloomsbury.

52 Tavistock Square, WC1

Tuesday 17 January
London on Sunday. Five minutes left of the morning. I wish I could distil some thoughts about 'the situation' into nuggets. The Spanish war is being won yesterday today tomorrow by Franco. I dreamt of Julian. A sniping article on him – 'The limitations of Bloomsbury' – by Janet Adam Smith. She advises life in a mining village as a remedy: what is her practice? At Clive's on Sunday. A good discussion of painting and music. Angelica sang a song. L. talked. So did Nessa. I'm taking four days holiday from *Roger*, writing *Pointz Hall*.

Wednesday 18 January
I am going walking and adventuring, going to see pictures of an afternoon; and often come face to face, after tea, at odd moments, with the idea of death and age. Why not change the idea of death into an exciting experience? – as one did marriage in youth? Age is baffled today by my creative gift – still abubble. And then the steady passion with which I now read ... A rainy day. Rain real wet drops: white splashing from the road. I must somehow ease my way back to *Roger* – shut *Pointz Hall* firmly.

Tuesday 24 January
On the placards this afternoon: Franco at the gate of Barcelona. Measures for Defence. This refers to our new voluntary service. The one is the cause of the other. And on the bus coming back from the Flower Show I described my new 'novel'; and we planned the books we should write, if we could live another thirty years.

Sunday 29 January
Yes, Barcelona has fallen: Hitler speaks tomorrow; the next dress rehearsal begins. I have seen Marie Stopes, Princesse de Polignac, Philip and Pippin [Woolf], and Dr Freud in the last three days. Also had Tom to dinner and to the Stephens' party. Dr Freud gave me a narcissus. Was sitting in a great library with little statues at a large scrupulously tidy shiny table. We like patients on chairs. A screwed up shrunk very old man: with a monkey's light eyes, paralysed spasmodic movements, inarticulate: but alert. On Hitler. Generation before the poison will be worked out. About his books. Fame? I was infamous rather than famous; didn't make £50 by his first book. Difficult talk. An interview. Daughter [Anna] and Martin [son] helped. Immense potential, I mean an old fire now flickering. When we left he took up the stand What are *you* going to do? The English – war.

Monday 30 January
Freud said It would have been worse if you had *not* won the war. I said we often felt guilty; if we had failed, perhaps Hitler would have not been. No, he said, with great emphasis; he would have been infinitely worse.

Last night Yeats's death announced. That great thick long jowled poet, whom I last met at Ottoline's. And we are all on tiptoe, waiting Hitler's speech tonight.

Tuesday 31 January
A very sensible day yesterday. Saw no one. Took the bus to Southwark Bridge. Walked along Thames Street; saw a flight of steps down to the river. I climbed down – a rope at the bottom. Found the strand of the Thames, under the warehouses – strewn with stones, bits of wire, slippery; ships lying off the bridge. Very slippery; warehouse walls crusted, weedy, worn. The river must cover them at high tide. It was now low. People on the Bridge stared. Difficult walking. A rat haunted, riverine place, great chains, wooden pillars, green slime, bricks corroded, a button hook thrown up by the tide. A bitter cold wind. Thought of the refugees from Barcelona walking forty miles, one with a baby in a parcel. So to Tower. Made a circuit: discovered St Olave's, Hart Street: Pepys's Church; too cold to explore; wandered about Fenchurch alleys, Billingsgate; walked through Leadenhall Market; so back by omnibus; the street and shops the product of this factory world; so home; left the kettle on; it blew out its connection; read Michelet; wrote to Desmond; L. out at Fabians; played gramophone; listened to Our Master's Voice, Hitler less truculent than expected; read; and so to bed.

Friday 17 February
Jangled with talk – nine hours solid, frothy, talk; varied by buying Michelet and [H. G. Wells's] *The Country of the Blind*. A hammer and a drill this morning exacerbate still further: they're pulling down Tavistock Square and building offices. So out in the brisk cold to buy note books. I'm starting my grand tour of literature. That is I'm going to write a book of discovery, reading as one pulls a string out; and must follow my trail through Sévigné, Michelet, Somerset Maugham &c. That's the idea; encouraged by that vast marsupial Margery Strachey, who implored me to do criticism; as indeed I've long wanted.

Tuesday 28 February
Yesterday, Franco was recognised. And Julian killed for this. Nessa though I suppose making herself live: succeeding: very busy.

Saturday 11 March
Yesterday I set the last word to the first sketch of *Roger*. And now I have
to begin – well not even to begin, but to revise and revise. A terrible grind
to come: and innumerable doubts, of myself as biographer: of the possibility
of doing it at all; all the same I've carried through to the end; and may
allow myself one moment's mild gratification. There are the facts more or
less extracted.

Thursday 16 March
Jack [Hills] I see in this morning's paper left £3,000 only. I see too that
Hitler has marched into Prague. This, says the Prime Minister 'is not in the
spirit of the Munich meeting'. My comment anyhow is superfluous. We sit
and watch.

Wednesday 22 March
Tom sent me his play, *Family Reunion*. No, it don't do. I read it over the
week end. It starts theories. But no . . . You see the experiment with stylised
chatter isn't successful. He's a lyric not a dramatic. But here there's no free
lyricism: is caught back by the character: as stiff as pokers. And the chief
poker is Tom. A cold upright poker. A clever beginning, and some ideas;
but they spin out; and nothing grips: all mist. A failure: a proof he's not a
dramatist. This is stated very politely by the papers this morning. We go
on Thursday. I'm of course for reasons I can't go into, selfishly relieved:
why? A mixture of motives. No, I can't write here. Politics lulled: but
Kingsley [Martin] vocal on the phone.

Wednesday 29 March
There can be no doubt that Tom knew that his play was a failure. He was
very yellow and heavy lidded. We talked about his cold, and I noted that
he said his lectures, on Church and State, were 'very bad', a proof, I think,
that all his work now seems so. But the evening was oddly successful.
Kingsley Martin invited himself, and privately told L. that German aeroplanes have been flying over London. Madrid surrendered. Kingsley says
war is inevitable.

Thursday 30 March
No, it was a good idea having Hugh [Walpole] alone. He gave me a
full account of his sexual life, of which I retain these facts. He only
loves men who don't love men. Tried to drown himself once over
[Lauritz] Melchior. Jumped into a river; stuck in mud; seized a carving
knife; saw himself in the glass; all became absurd. Reconciliation. Told
me too of the Baths at the Elephant & Castle. How the men go there.

Has had a married life with Harold for fifteen years without intercourse. All this piles up a rich life of which I have no knowledge; and he can't use it in his novels. They are therefore about lives he hasn't lived which explains their badness. Hasn't the courage to write about his real life. Would shock people he likes. Told me how he had had a father and son simultaneously. Copulation removes barriers. Class barriers fade. Lives at Hampstead with Harold's family and friends completely naturally. All this is a great deal better than his literary talk. Saw, at any rate, another Hugh. This lasted from 4.30 to 7.30; without a break. And I liked him and enjoyed it, though crushed in the head.

Friday 31 March
Yes I made a phrase last night about bearing the panoply of life, and being glad to lay it down. I wonder if its true. After a worried domestic day; then L. had a temperature and went to bed; the Memoir Club was imminent. I felt I was bearing up the panoply of life and would be glad to let it sink. I said to myself, Remember, this is the description of age coming. I'm on the qui vive to describe age: to note it. I often think of things in this way, but forget them. And as L. is normal and up and as its a fine morning, I'm not conscious of holding up my panoply, only distracted rather and can't settle in.

Monks House, Rodmell

Tuesday 11 April
Yesterday at Tilton; and Tilton's comfort, and quiet, all seem to make it harder for me to get on with revising *Roger*. Revising *Roger* at the rate of two weeks to a chapter will take me three months. Then there's the war. The finest Easter possible has this purple background. We wait like obedient children to hear what we shall be told when Parliament meets on Thursday. At Tilton we talked first medicine; Maynard's drastic cure; then politics; five minutes left for Tom's play. Maynard, even Maynard, can't find much that's hopeful now that Italy has nipped off Albania save that there's a unity of hatred. The men women children dogs &c are solid for war if war comes. But privately – how one rockets between private and public – his eyes are bluer, his skin pinker, and he can walk without pain. Lydia has devoted herself to the treatment.

Roasting hot: birds achirp: butterflies. I am reading Dickens; by way of a refresher. Also I'm reading Rochefoucauld. Chaucer I take at need. So if I had any time – but perhaps next week will be more solitudinous – I should, if it weren't for the war – glide my way up and up in to that exciting layer so rarely lived in: where my mind works so quick it seems asleep; like the aeroplane propellors.

Thursday 13 April
Two days of influenza. Now politics impend. Chamberlain's statement in the House today. War I suppose not tomorrow, but nearer.

Saturday 15 April
Its odd what extreme depression a little influenza and a cold in the head produces. Happily I'm interested in depression; and make myself play a game of assembling the fractured pieces – I mean I light a fire, and somehow dandle myself over it. Cooking is helpful. Oh but I was very down and dismal yesterday. And then noises and houses abuilding oppress: and there's always our dear old war – now postponed for a month.

52 TAVISTOCK SQUARE, WC1

Friday 28 April
Very much screwed in the head by trying to get Roger's marriage chapter into shape; and also warmed by L. saying last night that he was fonder of me than I of him. A discussion as to which would mind the other's death most. He said he depended more upon our common life than I did. He gave the garden as an instance. He said I live more in a world of my own. I go for long walks alone. So we argued. I was very happy to think I was so much needed. Its strange how seldom one feels this: yet 'life in common' is an immense reality.

   Oh such a dismal tea with Mrs Woolf yesterday. She is completely lifeless – like an old weed on a rock. And always recurring to the complaints. That was how, by the way, we came to discuss our deaths. L. said he hoped he would predecease me. Her lonely old age is so intolerable. But its lonely, he said, because she had adopted an unreal attitude. Lives in a sentimental make believe. Sees herself as the adored matriarch, and forces the children to adopt her attitude. This obsession of hers has also shut her off from all other interests: doesn't care for any impersonal thing – art, music, books. Won't have a companion or reader; must depend on her sons. Constant innuendoes therefore about the goodness of Herbert and Harold; inference that L. neglects her; hints that I have taken him away from his family; absorbed him in mine. So in that crowded pink hot room we sat for two hours trying to beat up subjects for conversation. And there were awful silences, and our heads filled with wool; and all was dusty, dreary, old, and hopeless.

Saturday 29 April
But what are the interesting things? I'm thinking of what I should like to read here in ten years time. And I'm all at sea. Perhaps literal facts. The annal, not the novel. Yesterday I went out in a fur coat, for it was bitter cold, to walk in London. I stopped by the Savoy Church; there were photographers. Soon the Bride arrived. The car glided on. Old sitters in the sun watching. Camera men. A little procession – rather skimpy and cold and not very rich I thought. Then I walked along the Embankment, up into the fur quarter behind Blackfriars. A smell of fur. Found some old City Company houses. So into Cannon Street. Bought a paper with Hitler's speech. Read it on top of Bus. Inconclusive. Everyone reading it – even newspaper sellers, a great proof of interest. So to Kingsway. Bought some folders. L. had four gents to discuss a memo. Read Chaucer. Enjoyed it. Was warm and happy. Nessa rang up. Bed.

Monday 1 May
A bad morning, because I'm dried up about *Roger*. I'm determined though to plod through and make a good job, not a work of art. That's the only way. To force myself on – But there's no blinking the fact that it is drudgery and must be; and I must go through with it.

Sunday 14 May
Its a fortnight I see since I had my few minutes margin between *Roger* and lunch. My head is a tight wound ball of string. To unwind it, I lie on my Heal chair bed and doze of an evening. But the noise worries me. The two houses next door are down; we are shored up. There are patches of wall paper where there used to be hotel bedrooms. Thus the Southampton Row traffic gets at me; and I long for 37 Mecklenburgh Square, but doubt if we shall get it. A talk about the future with John [Lehmann]. He is harrassed by the lean year. 37 is a large seeming and oh so quiet house, where I could sleep anywhere. But it don't do to dwell on it. And there would be the horror of the move in August. We are going to Brittany by the way after Whitsun. A whole two weeks rambling. Now that'll fill my dry cistern of a head.

Thursday 25 May
A queer little note to run off in a hurry: L. is bargaining for 37 Mecklenburgh Square upstairs; I'm packing. We're off: and very likely I shan't write much more in this now so tidy studio. I must pack upstairs. Brittany and Rodmell for three weeks.

Interrupted by parties come to see the house. The first day its in the agents' hands. Shall we end our lives looking in that great peaceful garden; in the sun? I hope so.

* * *

Friday 23 June
Back to London again after four weeks. Two spent driving about Brittany. The London uproar at once rushes in. We have 37 Mecklenburgh Square; and this is still unlet.

Saturday 24 June
Yes, London broke in fairly vigorously yesterday. [Victoria] Ocampo bringing Gisèle Freund and all her apparatus, which was set up in the drawing room. And the upshot is, a sitting – oh curse this petty vulgar photography-advertising stunt – at 3. No getting out of it, with Ocampo on the sofa, and Freund there in the flesh. So my afternoon is gone in the way to me most detestable and upsetting of all. A life sized coloured animated photograph – however L. is drawn in.

Monday 26 June
Talk at Nessa's last night. Much about [Mark] Gertler's suicide. He gassed himself two nights ago in his studio. He had got through to a new stage as a painter. This was true, Nessa and Duncan said; his last show, just over, was a great advance and very remarkable. So why did he turn on the gas, when his model left him? A most resolute serious man: intellectual; fanatical about painting, even if a fanatical egotist. And he seemed established. Poor of course, and forced to teach; and fundamentally perhaps too rigid, too self centred, too honest and narrow, to be content and happy. But with his intellect and interest, why did the personal life become too painful? His wife? We know no more.

Wednesday 28 June
Vita came to a late lunch; Mrs Woolf fell down and broke two ribs. L. to the nursing home after dinner. She will not die, so I assume. There is a terrible passive resistance to death in these old women. They have the immortality of the vampire. This is I suppose a cruel remark to make. But honestly, everyone would be relieved if she could make an end of it. Its so exhausting, and she has contrived to falsify all emotions, till the end is the only thing the family who are forced to be so devoted by her fantasy honestly wish for.

Thursday 29 June
A dismal day yesterday; shoe hunting in the Hall of Humbug, Fortnums. A Sale; but only of the unsaleable. And the atmosphere – British upper

classes: all tight and red nailed; myself a figure of fun, whips my skin. Noise here very great. Even if we lose our rent, no doubt its worth it – 37 will be heavenly quiet.

Monday 3 July

L.'s mother died last night. And its been jading and somehow very depressing – watching her die. She gradually ceased to breathe. It was like watching an animal die, L. said. It was a bright showery day. We walked in Regent's Park, after giving Kingsley Martin lunch. I always notice the weather in which people die, as if the soul would notice if its wet or windy. But I cannot do my article, and have a regret for that spirited old lady, whom it was such a bore to visit. Still she was somebody: sitting on her high backed chair with the pink cushion, all the flowers round her, a cigar always for Leonard, and plates of cakes which she pressed us to eat. But these feelings are mixed, scrappy, and I'm in the scraped state when writing don't work.

Thursday 6 July

[Mrs Woolf] was buried yesterday; and there was a service in the Synagogue. Women admitted, so I went. But its a compromise; and had nothing whatever to do with [her]. What was she like then? Let me see – She was small, narrow shouldered, and rather heavy. Her head nodded. She had stiff curled grey black hair. She would say as we came in "And Virginia?" My joke was, Conceal your disappointment at sight of me. Then she would laugh, kiss me, and give me a little pat. We were on friendly laughing terms, always at the same stock joke, which carried us through those two hour teas. "And tell me what you have been doing?" I would have some story ready. It was trumped up mostly. Yet there was something spontaneous about her. A great joy in family; in society. All was personal. She attaches to nothing in my own life. The truth was, age had taken everything that was real, I think: only age left the pathetic animal, the body that wanted to live. I know nothing of any interest about her now that I come to write, only little anecdotes; nothing that makes her a real person – save Is Virginia coming? which touches me.

Wednesday 12 July

For the first time for weeks, after being so damnably down in the mouth yesterday, I've worked with some pleasure at *Roger*. Yet how dumpish we were – starting off to the Movies, after dinner – L. asking me what I wanted to see, I not wanting to see anything – the crowds of deformed and stunted and vicious and sweating and ugly hooligans and harridans in the Tottenham Court Road – the sticky heat – all this brooded, till I was saying, step out, on, on, in my usual desperate way. Then instead we went to Nessa's. Angelica in bed. Clive there; Duncan bubbling; and we had a good laugh and gossip. Vanessa very silent, worried I suppose: yet 'cheerful' too. She will laugh and take part, even if she sinks again. Julian in the background. Oh dear. But a jovial sunny evening that rolled off my glooms effectively; perhaps L.'s. Its not a nice season in London.

Thursday 13 July

Two hours at Mecklenburgh Square planning, electric light, kitchen &c. The practical difficulty appals – all of our books carpets furniture and L. gloomy. A grim thought struck me: which of these rooms shall I die in? Which is going to be the scene of some – oh no, I won't write out the tragedy that has to be acted there.

Tuesday 25 July

On this page I should sum up reflections on leaving 52 Tavistock Square. But – Interruption.

MONKS HOUSE, RODMELL

Friday 28 July

I forget that we came down; and its been fine, rather; lovely on the marsh. Hay cutting. Figures spaced on the marsh. Reading Gide's diaries, recommended by poor death mask Eddie [Sackville-West]. An interesting knotted book. Its queer that diaries now pullulate. No one can settle to a work of art.

Sunday 30 July

Its fine; and our day's varied with what we enjoy. Such an expansion after the London pressure. I take my brain out, fill it with books, as a sponge with water – couldn't read a word in London. Taking a day or two with *Pointz Hall* to rest myself from *Roger*.

Monday 31 July

Human voices wake us and we drown – quotation on hearing the telephone yesterday asking us to Charleston. Bunny [Garnett] there; Angelica moody; conversation however well beaten up. Duncan's 480 canvases; new studio; Nessa's bedroom on the garden; Quentin's potting shed. Talk about rumours of war. Next Memoir meeting discussed. So home. Very cold and cloudy – yet the downs aglow with corn much to my liking. My poor old head very feeble – though why? Trying it on *Pointz Hall*. Age is it? or *Roger?*

Monday 7 August [Bank Holiday]
I have been thinking about Censors. How visionary figures admonish us. If I say this So and So will think me sentimental. If that . . . will think me Bourgeois. All books now seem to me surrounded by a circle of invisible censors. Hence their self-consciousness, their restlessness. A child crying in the field brings poverty: my comfort: to mind. Ought I to go to the village sports? Ought thus breaks into my contemplation.

Oh and I thought, as I was dressing, how interesting it would be to describe the approach of age, and the gradual coming of death. As people describe love. To note every symptom of failure: but why failure? To treat age as an experience that is different from the others; and to detect every one of the gradual stages towards death which is a tremendous experience, and not as unconscious, at least in its approaches, as birth is.

Friday 25 August
Perhaps it is more interesting to describe 'The Crisis' than Roger's love affairs. Yes we are in the very thick of it. Are we at war? At 1 I'm going to listen in. Its very different, emotionally, from last September. In London yesterday, there was indifference almost. No crowd in the train – we went by train. No stir in the streets. One of the removers called up. Its Fate, as the foreman said. What can you do against fate? Complete chaos at 37 [Mecklenburgh Square]. Museums shut. Search light on Rodmell Hill. Chamberlain says danger imminent. The Russian pact a disagreeable and unforeseen surprise. Rather like a herd of sheep we are. No enthusiasm. Patient bewilderment. I suspect some desire 'to get on with it'. Order double supplies and some coal. Unreal. Whiffs of despair. Difficult to work. Aeroplanes. One touch on the switch and we shall be at war. Underneath of course wells of pessimism. Young men torn to bits: Mothers like Nessa two years ago. The common feeling covers the private, then recedes. Discomfort and distraction. And all mixed with the mess at 37.

Monday 28 August
I stay out here, after bowls, to say – what? on this possibly last night of peace. Will the 9 o'clock bulletin end it all? – our lives, oh yes, and everything for the next fifty years? Everyone's writing I suppose about this last day. I walked on the downs; lay under a cornstack and looked at the empty land and the pinkish clouds in a perfect blue summer afternoon sky. Not a sound. Workmen discussing war on the road – one for it, one against. For us its like being on a small island. Neither of us has any physical fear. Why should we? But there's a vast calm cold gloom. And the strain. Like waiting a doctor's verdict. And the young – young men smashed up. But the point is one is too numbed to think. Old Clive sitting on the terrace,

says 'I don't want to live through it.' Explains that his life recedes. Has had the best. We privately are so content. Bliss day after day. So happy cooking dinner, reading, playing bowls. No feeling of patriotism. How to go on, through war? – that's the question. Yes, its a lovely still summer evening; not a sound. A swallow came into the sitting room.

Wednesday 30 August

Not at war yet. Negotiations. L. pessimistic more than I am this morning. He thinks that Hitler is making up his mind to spring. Raging voices began again last night in German. Last year's mad voice heard again, as if he were lashing himself up. Now I must listen to the 1 o'clock.

Red faced boys in khaki guarding Rodmell Hill. The soldiers in the village. Otherwise quiet and usual enough . . .

Friday 1 September

War is on us this morning. Hitler has taken Danzig: has attacked – or is attacking – Poland. This after a day in London, submerged doubts and hopes. Now at 1 I go in to listen I suppose to the declaration of war. A dull hot day. I don't know why I write this, or what I feel, or shall feel. All is hovering over us.

Sunday 3 September

This is I suppose certainly the last hour of peace. The time limit is out at 11. Prime Minister to broadcast at 11.15. L. and I 'stood by' ten minutes ago. We argued. If we win – then what? L. said its better to win. I suppose the bombs are falling on rooms like this in Warsaw. No children yet come. Maynard has given Quentin a job as tractor driver. This is a relief. No one knows how we're to fight. Rumours beginning. A flurry of people shopping in Lewes yesterday. Shops rather empty. People buying stuff for windows. Little girl says If we have a chink they'll spy us out. Two hours sewing [black-out] curtains. An anodyne: pleasure to do something: but so tepid and insipid. One's too tired, emotionally, to read a page.

Its now about 10.33. Of course I shall have to work to make money. That's a comfort. Write articles for America. Keep the Press going. So far plenty of petrol. Sugar rationed. So I shall now go in.

Wednesday 6 September

Our first air raid warning at 8.30 this morning. A warbling that gradually insinuates itself as I lay in bed. So dressed and walked on the terrace with L. Sky clear. All cottages shut. Breakfast. All clear.

All meaning has run out of everything. Scarcely worth reading papers. The BBC gives any news the day before. Emptiness. Inefficiency. I may as well record these things. My plan is to force my brain to work on *Roger*. But Lord this is the worst of all my life's experiences. Endless interruptions. We have done the curtains. We have carried coals &c into the cottage for the eight Battersea women and children. The expectant mothers are all quarrelling. Some went back yesterday. Yes, its an empty meaningless world now. Am I a coward? Physically I expect I am. Going to London tomorrow I expect frightens me. This war has begun in cold blood. One merely feels that the killing machine has to be set in action. So far, the *Athena* has been sunk. It seems entirely meaningless – a perfunctory slaughter, like taking a jar in one hand, a hammer in the other. No movies or theatres allowed. No friends write or ring up. Yes, a long sea voyage, with strangers making conversation, and lots of small bothers and arrangements seems the closest I can get. Of course all creative power is cut off. And for the hundredth time I repeat – any idea is more real than any amount of war misery. And what one's made for. And the only contribution one can make – This little pitter patter of ideas is my whiff of shot in the cause of freedom.

Monday 11 September

To London on Thursday. Pitiless fine weather. Over London a light spotted veil – the balloons. Very empty streets. A curious strained silence. At the Press, listening for sirens. Cases all empty but piled up. Mabel and I laid carpets. Sandwiches with John [Lehmann]. Stephen [Spender] came in. His great joints seemed to crack. Eyes stared. Is writing reams about himself. Can't settle to poetry. London after sunset a mediaeval city of darkness and brigandage. The darkness they say is the worst of it. No one can control their nerves. So I was glad to be on the road home. Poland being conquered, and then – we shall be attended to.

Saturday 23 September

Meanwhile Poland has been gobbled up. Russia and Germany divide it. An aircraft carrier has been sunk. But there have been no raids. And I – having said impulsively that I would write for the *New Statesman* by way of using my faculties patriotically – have written two and used up every morning to the margin. Also people have been staying here . . . oh such a fritter and agitation – solid weekends with Mrs Nicholls, Miss Perkins, Miss Woodward [Hogarth Press staff] – So distracted I've scudded over the surface of the days. And now Stephen is on us alone; and so we shall be lip sore and addle headed. Then there's John on Monday.

Civilisation has shrunk. The amenities are wilting. There's no petrol today: so we are back again with our bicycles at Asheham in 1915. And once more L. and I calculate our income. How much must we both earn?

Once more we are journalists. Then one begins stinting paper, sugar, butter, buying little hoards of matches. The elm tree that fell has been cut up. This will see us through two winters. They say the war will last three years. We had an S O S from Kingsley. He came for the night. What was it he couldn't say on the telephone? Nothing. Should he come out in favour of peace? Chamberlain has the terms in his pocket. All in the know say we are beaten. Nothing of the least importance is said though in his article.

I forget who else has been. Nessa painting L. Many games of bowls. No reading.

Sunday 24 September

Stephen scribbling diary – no, reading Proust in English in the drawing room. I've talked miles since last night, in spite of Stephen's colic. A loose jointed mind – misty, clouded, suffusive. Nothing has outline. Very sensitive, tremulous, receptive and striding; and walking the terrace, we plunged and skimmed and hopped – from sodomy and women and writing and anonymity and – I forget. At last I said I must write – and he must write; and so ordered boiled potatoes for his lunch; and sit in semi-retreat out here.

Freud is dead, the stop press says. Only these little facts interrupt the monotonous boom of the war.

Monday 25 September

The week end was sheer drudgery and has left me out of temper, out of mood. *Roger* seems hopeless. Yet if one can't write, as Duncan said yesterday, one may as well kill oneself. Such despair comes over me – waking early. And we're fretted and tormented with people.

Friday 6 October

Well I have succeeded in despite of distractions in copying out again the whole of *Roger*. Needless to say, its still to be revised, compacted, vitalised. And can I ever do it? The distractions are so incessant. Also there's the war: or rather the non-war. Nothing happens. All is held up. Nightly we're served out with a few facts, or a childstory of the adventures of a submarine. Hitler is said to make peace terms today. London is all agog; and also all aquiver. Here its distracted weather – hailstorms and gales and sun. Nessa is painting L. I have composed myself by tidying my room.

Saturday 7 October

Its odd how those first days of complete nullity when war broke out have given place to such a pressure of ideas and work that I feel the old throb and spin in my head more of a drain than ever. The result partly of taking up journalism. A good move, I daresay; for it compacts; and forces me to organise. I'm masterfully pulling together those diffuse chapters of *Roger* because I know I must stop and do an article. Ideas for articles obsess me. Why not try one for *The Times*? No sooner said than I'm ravaged by ideas. Have to hold the *Roger* fort – for I will have the whole book typed and in Nessa's hands by Xmas – by force.

We have a fortnight its said to consider Hitler's terms. If rejected, all the guns boom. So we may get a last safe week in London. And I don't much want to go.

Sunday 22 October

We have spent a week in London. The poster read, at Wimbledon: 'The War begins ... Hitler says, Now its on'. So as we drove to Mecklenburgh Square I said "Its foolish to come to London the first day of the war." It seemed as if we were driving open eyed into a trap. The flat was oh in such a mess – very small, very crowded. Whistles sounded. The dark was thick as Hell. One seemed cut off. No wireless. There we sat. And people came running in and out. We lunched with the [Sidney] Webbs. The old woman, wearing a white spotted headdress, was as alive as a leaf on an autumn bonfire: burning, skeletonised. I was so harassed and distracted that I could not expand my mind to receive impressions.

You never escape the war in London. People are all thinking the same thing. All set on getting the day's work done. Hitches and difficulties hold one up. Very few buses. Tubes closed. No children. No loitering. Everyone humped with a gas mask. Strain and grimness. At night its so verdurous and gloomy that one expects a badger or a fox to prowl along the pavement. A reversion to the middle ages with all the space and the silence of the country set in this forest of black houses. A torch blinks. An old gentleman revealed. He vanishes. That red light may be a taxi or a lampost. People grope their way to each other's lairs. We were talking in our lair about six hours daily. Great caterpillars dug up the Square. Gradually the sense of siege being normal replaced the fear – the individual fear. One's temper was rubbed by the sheer discomfort and perpetual need for clearing drawers, arranging furniture. The kitchen very small. Everything too large. Stairs bad. No carpets. The clerks scream like parrots. Rain poured – profuse unbridled mediaeval rain. Did nothing – was indeed in fretful useless distraction. So we came down and the world rises out of dark squalor into this divine natural peace. Alone today and for many days. It was an odd morbid week of many disagreeable sensations.

Wednesday 25 October

"The war begins today." So Ribbentrop said or rather howled last night. For so far its sporadic and halfhearted. How then can I say anything about it here? Here it peters out. I rode my cycle to Lewes yesterday. Now Nessa's come and is painting L. And its a blowy but sunny autumn day. And I'm screwed like a vice to the re-composing of the last chapter. Temptations to write other things fret me. As a journalist I'm in demand (not with the *TLS* though). To relax I read *Little Dorrit* and think of going on with my Autobiography. Never have I been so set on my own spinning.

Wednesday 1 November

It strikes me that Morgan probably keeps an admirable diary. I'd like to ask Morgan down. Our week ends are now taking the place of our dinners. Rather a laborious extension. But here we are settling in, very steadily, to a country life, and there's much to be said for it. The space, the concentration, the freedom. Every day on my walk I get a colour bath: the greens dying, the winter colours burnishing. Society too is fairly brisk. Tom comes for the week end. Eddie Sackville invites himself for next week. London and 37 recede. Dim voices reach us. No war news.

Thursday 9 November

Oh yes, Tom for the week end: more supple, less caked and rigid than of old. His teaching he told me, is that one improves with age. I suppose the working of the divine spirit which as usual he adored at 8 on Sunday morning. Last night we listened to the ravings, the strangled hysterical sobbing swearing ranting of Hitler at the Beer Hall. Today they say there was an explosion after he'd left. Is it true? There's no getting at truth now all the loud speakers are contradicting each other.

Monday 27 November

Since I wrote here, we have been in London, had a party, Adrian and Karin and Rose Macaulay; seen Colefax; and come back. It is all storm and rain now. Many ships sunk. Men out in boats. The magnetic mine active. Chamberlain speaking like a military shopwalker.

Wednesday 29 November

A nice dine and sleep visit from John [Lehmann], who pans out well under familiar scrutiny – dining in the kitchen &c – and things aren't doing badly: in fact stirring under the blanket of war. Ideas sprout. For a Bloomsbury Book Club ... for 'our' new magazine. Yes, the young do manage to pull along. And a long gossip ... bed wetting at Eton; its disastrous consequences. Repressions – homosexuality: this explains, I suppose, John's dash. John gets garrulous after wine.

Thursday 30 November
Very jaded and tired and depressed and cross, and so take the liberty of expressing my feelings here. *Roger* a failure – and what a grind . . . no more of that. I'm brain fagged and must resist the desire to tear up and cross out – must fill my mind with air and light, and walk and blanket it in fog. Rubber boots help – I can flounder over the marsh.

Saturday 2 December
Tiredness and dejection give way if one day off is taken instantly. I went in and did my cushion. In the evening my pain in my head calmed. Ideas came back. This is a hint to be remembered. Always turn the pillow. Began reading Freud last night; to enlarge the circumference, to give my brain a wider scope; thus defeat the shrinkage of age. Always take on new things.

I saw a Kingfisher and a cormorant the other day's walk in rubber boots. Planes very active. Russia attacking Finland. Nothing happens in England. There's no reason anywhere. Brutes merely rampant. Its like being in a temporary shelter with a violent storm raging outside. We wait.

Friday 8 December
Two days in London: a great distraction; leaving my mind in a torn state. Shopping – tempted to buy jerseys and so on. I dislike this excitement: yet enjoy it. Ambivalence as Freud calls it. Then Ethel [Smyth] and [William] Gillies. That upset me – Ethel's wig – five incongruous curls, that made her look babyish and foolish. Also she has gone downhill. She is now shut up quite alone in her old age – talks to herself, about herself. I felt this pathetic; also somehow ugly; humiliating; watching the old baby sucking its corals; compliments; the old story of her genius and its non-recognition. How hideous to be reduced to that kind of feeblemindedness – at eighty-four. I think it was pity more than anything that I felt; and all her clothes were undone; shaggy; untidy – like King Lear only without any tragedy or poetry. And the old charm in abeyance.

Saturday 9 December
It is a Saturday morning, and looks fine and still, after the broken whirlpool of weather yesterday. We took Louie to Lewes to have teeth out, and it was blackout driving for the first time. Like fog driving, one can't see people. All the cars have small red eyes. The margins of the road are lost. But I'm thinking of a dozen things as usual. Ideas pullulate, but escape when I try to catch them here. Freud is upsetting: reducing one to whirlpool; and I daresay truly. If we're all instinct, the unconscious, what's all this about civilisation, the whole man, freedom &c? His savagery against God good.

Saturday 16 December

The litter in this room is so appalling that it takes me five minutes to find my pen. *Roger* all unsewn in bits. And I must take fifty pages, should be a hundred, up on Monday. Can't get the marriage chapter right. But its true I don't fuss quite so much as over a novel. I learned a lesson in re-writing *The Years* which I shall never forget.

Horizon out; small; trivial; dull. So I think from not reading it. And now – oh now must I tidy up? London &c looms. And I've promised to lecture the WEA at Brighton.

Sunday 17 December

What the point of making these notes is I don't know; save that it becomes a necessity to uncramp, and some of it may interest me later. But what? For I never reach the depths; I'm too surface blown. Yes, ten minutes left – what can I say. Nothing that needs thought: which is provoking; for I often think. And think the very thought I could write here.

Oh the *Graf Spee* is going to steam out of Monte Video today into the jaws of death. And journalists and rich people are hiring aeroplanes from which to see the sight. This seems to me to bring war into a new angle; and our psychology. No time to work out. Anyhow the eyes of the whole world (BBC) are on the game; and several people will lie dead tonight, or in agony. And we shall have it served up for us as we sit over our logs this bitter winter night.

1940

On Twelfth Night Angelica's twenty-first birthday was celebrated with some flourish by a lively party at Charleston (at which Virginia obliged with a song), and for a time the eddies of social life reached Monks House. But gradually the privations and inconveniences of wartime – the black-out, food and petrol rationing, shortages and rising prices – became more evident. Virginia was polishing her Roger Fry, writing articles, mostly for the New Statesman, and preparing a lecture (later published as 'The Leaning Tower') for the Brighton Workers' Education Association, for which Leonard was already giving a series of twelve talks on 'Causes and Issues of War'. Every other week they drove to London and spent a few days in their Mecklenburgh Square flat dealing with Hogarth Press matters, Leonard's political concerns, and seeing friends. During most of March Virginia was laid low with influenza, but by 1 April was able to send Roger Fry to be printed; she finished correcting the proofs on 13 May and the book was published towards the end of July.

On 13 April the war suddenly erupted again, with the German invasion of Denmark and Norway; and from then onwards, with their assault on Holland and Belgium, their rapid advance across France to the Channel, the evacuation of British troops from Dunkirk, the occupation of Paris and the Franco-German Armistice of 22 June, Virginia observed and noted the unfolding military and political calamities with fatalistic clarity. She and Leonard had obtained the wherewithal to commit suicide should the Nazis invade England, as they had no doubt they would be marked down as Jewish anti-Fascists. Yet Virginia had no wish to die; she was again engrossed in writing Pointz Hall and, despite the day-to-day horrors of the war, was in good health and spirits. Inevitably, if in Virginia's case reluctantly, the Woolfs found themselves drawn further into Rodmell village life, Virginia helping to write and rehearse a play for the Women's Institute and even becoming its Treasurer, while Leonard, already a School Governor, undertook fire-watching duties.

As a prelude to the expected invasion, air attacks on Southern England (the Battle of Britain) began in earnest at the end of June, reaching a climax towards the end of August when they were redirected to the night-bombing of London. Rodmell was in the front line; the skies above were filled with warplanes. In September the Woolfs' London house was first made inaccessible and then uninhabitable by bombs; the Hogarth Press and its staff were moved to Letchworth in Hertfordshire; the Woolfs collected some of their more valued possessions, including Virginia's diaries, and at *the end of the year had the damp and dirty remainder brought to Rodmell and piled into Monks House and rented village store-rooms.*

In the autumn, still anticipating invasion, the Woolfs relinquished Mabel their live-in servant, and resigned themselves to their isolated country life with their daily help Louie. Virginia was working with confidence on Pointz Hall, *continuing her memoirs, reading, and, as always, delighting in the beauty of the countryside on her long daily walks, particularly when a bomb breached the riverbank and the entire Ouse Valley between Newhaven and Lewes became an inland sea. Vita came for a night; Kingsley Martin for another; some contact with Charleston and Tilton was maintained. Helen Anrep was lodging in the district; and so were David Garnett and Angelica, who were now living together to the dismay of some of her relations.*

When Virginia finished her first writing of Pointz Hall *at the end of November she was well pleased with her work but thereafter began to feel restless and dispirited, a condition she recognised from previous experience, and determined to counteract; but with diminishing success.*

1940

Monks House, Rodmell

Wednesday 3 January

This very large sheet begins a new year, on a new system. Evening over the fire writing, instead of end of the morning scrambling. Thus I hope to write a better hand, and more solidly. For unless I can put a little weight into this book, it'll have no interest, even for an old woman, turning the pages.

We have been out looking for skating. Its a long bitter winter frost – I forget how many degrees of a night – I think 22 below freezing. Figure an Italian sun yesterday; and hard white snow; and the street like glass; the butcher saying he'd had enough of it, which, as he has to be in the shop cutting joints at 6, I can follow.

I am oppressed and distracted with all my ideas. All the little cuckoos shoving the old bird – *Roger* – out of the nest. And here's L.

Saturday 6 January

Which of our friends will interest posterity most? Maynard? So that if I had any regard for the future I would use this hour to record what he said. Lying extended on the sofa the other night with the two fog lamps burning, and Lydia a sort of fairy tale elf in her fur cap. He is now supreme, mounted on his sick throne, a successful man – farmer, bursar, man of business, he called himself, applying for petrol. A heavy man with a thick moustache. A moralist. As interested in Patsy the black dog with the bald patch as in Europe. He was saying – odd how hard it is to remember – he was telling us about salt; water; heat and cold and their effect on the urine. About Roger. "Can I mention erection?" I asked Lydia. "What?" Maynard: "Stiff" (their private word). "No you can't. I should mind your saying it. Such revelations have to be in key with their time. The time not come yet." Is he right, or only public school? All is now so ordered, so royally arranged, that we had to go that Wednesday [27 December], because otherwise – "No Maynard says it is not convenient" Lydia on the telephone. But words are soon lost.

Mr Gwynne caught me at Piddinghoe on the down yesterday – a nobleman: lean, sporting, dried, with little wet pebble eyes; a severe man. I smiled; I was scrambling under the barbed wire in my wool helmet. "Where d'you come from?" "Only taking a walk." "This is private." "Hope I'm not spoiling your sport?" "Not at all. You can go on . . ." He'll ask his wife, what odd looking woman lives at Rodmell. She'll guess, Mrs Woolf. He'll say . . . Louie says he'll say he don't hold with the Labour Party. He had a row about the wood on his down. The villagers mustn't steal it.

Friday 19 January
I can't say that this after tea system has been good for this large page. But Sussex has been sociable. Angelica's twenty-first birthday party, and its legacy; then London, from which we came back this afternoon to frozen pipes. My London technique is improving. A concert at National Gallery; Hugh [Walpole] and William Plomer to dinner, Sybil [Colefax] to tea – all accomplished. And last night *The Importance of Being Earnest*, a thinnish play, but a work of art; I mean, its bubble don't break. Hugh is rather like the winter sun – his ruddy edges slightly blurred. He wore a red flower. William in a buff waistcoat, but sharpened, disappointed – life unsatisfactory; embittered. I diagnose some sense of defeat and strain, part private, part war. We talked – if I could face the labour of inverted commas – about *Horizon*: and about Humbert Wolfe; dead of overwork; and then Hugh told us the story of the [Joseph] Conrads, told it very well; so to diaries, and so to Dickens; and the Victorian hypocrisy, Thackeray hailing a prostitute in the street opposite the Garrick; Dickens and his mistress; (all spoken as if they were old friends – so they are – if you're in the Hugh tradition, but William and I aren't) – so to Trollope; and defamation of Wells; a mere scribbler; compare him with Conrad. A bitter cold night and they stayed till 12.30: then went into the moonlight, and left the door open.

Saturday 20 January
Smoking cigarettes over the fire and feeling – just because the rent of 37 is so high – that we were, for once, foolish. L. went and skated and I walked on the bank and home over the marsh. The beauty was etherial, unreal, empty. All silent, as if offered from another world. No birds, no carts, men shooting. This specimen against the war. This heartless and perfect beauty. The willows ruby red, no rust red; plumed; soft; and all the roofs orange and red; and the hills white. But some emptiness in me – in my life – because L. said the rent was so high. And then the silence, the pure disembodied silence, seemed to correspond to my own vacancy, walking muffled with the sun in my eyes. The men were waiting for widgeon – the quickest birds. Come down like an express. We sat in the sun on the bank.

All looked very distant, and picked out – the little stems of smoke – the wild duck – the horses huddled and still. No thoughts populated; I was somehow held in a pair of pincers, and came home to cook crumpets, to revise my article.

A fire at Charleston. Fire Engines called out on Wednesday night. No letters. A child crying in the school. What do I do to help?

Friday 26 January
These moments of despair – I mean glacial suspense – a painted fly in a glass case – have given way as they so often do to ecstasy. Is it that I have thrown off those two dead pigeons – my story, my 'Gas at Abbotsford' (printed today)? And so ideas rush in. I began one night, absolutely submerged, throttled, to read Julian. And off winged my mind along those wild uplands. A hint for the future. Always relieve pressure by a flight: hack an outlet. Often a trifle does.

What was I going to say? The thaw has set in, and rain and wind, and the marsh is soggy, and patched with white, and two very small lambs were staggering in the east wind. One old ewe was being carted off; and shirking the horror I crept back by the hanger.

Tuesday 30 January
Unable to go to London because of the worst of all frosts. A sudden return. Everything glass glazed. Each blade is coated, has a rim of pure glass. Walking is like treading on stubble. The stiles and gates have a shiny green varnish of ice. Ink frozen. On Sunday no cars could move. On Monday the electric light failed. Cooked breakfast on dining room fire. Came on at 12.30. Today all idea of travel impossible. Trains hours late or lost. No buses running. Walked to Lewes and back. Met snow plough; two or three cars; no walkers. Lewes very empty. Home by the short cut; which was painful. A great flight of wild geese. The grass is brittle, all the twigs are cased in clear brown cases, and look crystallised. Now and then the wireless reports a ship sunk in the North Sea. Almost out of meat, but at last the Co-op sent. Very still tonight. More snow? No papers till the afternoon.

Wednesday 31 January
It is thawing. There's a rush, like a mattress falling, as the snow slides off the roof. We walked on the marsh, and saw a half-devoured hare. Dabs of blood on the snow, and such a scrape of a wind, and such hobbling and tumbling over frozen tussocks into the snow that I cut the walk, and came home to type out my ten guinea Corelli. Vita is offered £1,850 for a 25,000 word story. My righteous backbone stiffens. I wouldn't for any money write 25,000 words. A little quick article I enjoy. Settled in for another

two weeks, and only village meetings and books; which are however very 'real'.

Friday 2 February

The snow remains, slightly pocked, but the road is clear. I forget to make extracts from the papers, which boom, echoing, emptily, the BBC. Hitler's speech – Churchill's – a ship sunk – no survivors – a raft capsized – men rowing for ten or twelve or thirty hours. How little one can explode now, as perhaps one would have done, had it been a single death. But the Black Out is far more murderous than the war. Prices rise by twopence then threepence. So the screw tightens gradually; and I can't even imagine London in peace – the lit nights, the buses roaring past Tavistock Square, the telephone ringing, and I scooping together with the utmost difficulty one night or afternoon alone. Only the fire sets me dreaming – of all the things I mean to write: the break in our lives from London to country is a far more complete one than any change of house. Odd how often I think with what is love I suppose of the City: of the walk to the Tower: that is my England; I mean, if a bomb destroyed one of those little alleys with the brass bound curtains and the river smell and the old woman reading I should feel – well, what the patriots feel.

Wednesday 7 February

(Mother's birthday; Nessa's wedding day.) Oh I had such a profound reflection on the tip of my tongue. It was to the effect that now, no longer in the movement, and remote in this water sogged country, now's the time to see if the art, or life, creed, the belief in something existing independently of myself, will hold good. Well, if it don't stand like a flagstaff, then its been a washout (word chosen in deference to the new movement). John for the night; and he plunges us in new this and that. Very nice – so eager and 'boyish' as the old women say. We had the Gardners to tea. The old wispy red veined blue eyed pussy purring Major. Very courteous, rather rambling. The children [Diana and Paul] bolt eyed and transfixed, partly in fear of what Papa might say. John obviously bored, but chivalrous. And then out with his documents, and his plans. Radiant hope for the *New Writing*; for the young. Clearly his metier to go on ringing his cowbell in advance. Oh and all the doings of the boys. The sink of buggery.

Thursday 8 February

Frau – Dr – yes she wasn't Frau though she looked it – [Rita] Hinden has just gone. She has gone back to London, to her house with its lounge and its modern Swedish furniture, in Hampstead Garden Suburb. Lunch lasted till 2.30. After that she and L. retired to the Library to discuss a Fabian treatise on South Africa, and I in rubbers and great coat plunged into the marsh, which was veiling, oh very effectively, for the wind blew, our unopened spring. Here I stop to insert a remark often occurring: how we're being led to the altar this spring: its flowers will I suppose nod and yellow and redden the garden with the bombs falling – oh its a queer sense of suspense, being led up to the spring of 1940. So I came back, and had to offer tea. Now at tea she shrivelled into the common, the lemon on steel acid vulgarity of the obvious, the cheap hard Jewess, which at lunch I hadn't seen. Confronted with Nessa's carpet, Duncan's table, she could only remember her Hampstead lounge; a transition which made me think of the future: and what'll it be, ruled and guided by these active and ambitious and after all competent, and I suppose, able Fabians – oh why don't they any of them embrace something – but what? Poetry, I suppose, the sensuous, the musical. Why must they always stress the ugliness of life; and yet be themselves so vital?

Friday 9 February

For some reason hope has revived. I've polished off, to the last gaiter button, the three d—d chapters for London on Monday; and though of course I shall get the black shivers when I reread let alone submit to Nessa and Margery [Fry], I can't help thinking I've caught a good deal of that irridescent man in my oh so laborious butterfly net. I daresay I've written every page – certainly the last – ten or fifteen times over. And I don't think I've killed: I think I've brisked. Hence an evening glow. Yet the wind cuts like a scythe: the dining room carpet is turning to mould. Now the wind rises; something rattles, and thank God I'm not on the North Sea, nor taking off to raid Heligoland. Now I'm going to read Freud.

Friday 16 February

This diary might be divided into London diary and Country. Just back from the London chapter. Bitter cold. This shortened my walk, which I meant to be through crowded streets. Then the dark – no lighted windows, depressed me. How silent it is there – London silent; a great dumb ox lying couchant. Dinner party: Tom and Saxon [Sydney-Turner]; Clive in afterwards. Tom's great yellow bronze mask all draped upon an iron framework. An inhibited, nerve drawn, dropped face – as if hung on a scaffold of heavy private brooding; and thought. A very serious face. And broken by the flicker of relief, when other people interrupt. But our talk? – it was about Civilisation. All the gents against me. Said very likely, more likely than not, this war means that the barbarian will gradually freeze out culture. Tom and Saxon said the Greeks were more thoroughly civilised. The slave was not so much a slave as ours are. Clive also pessimised – saw the light going out gradually. So I flung some rather crazy theories into the air. Saxon emitted some scholar's facts. It lasted till 12 I suppose. Then I suffered from my clothes complex acutely buying two new sets of clothes, and being persuaded into a blue striped coat by an astute and human woman at Lewises. "But I want you to have this – I don't want you just because you're in the country, to fling on anything. You've got to think of others" ... as if she guessed all my private life – queer: she seemed genuine. Of course I looked a shaggy dowdy old woman. Then to *Desire Under the Elms* [Eugene O'Neill]: disappointing; flat; elemental situation bare of words; like a scaffold. And Beatrix Lehmann not exciting: and the streets tunnels of gloom.

Monday 19 February

The snow came down on Saturday: thick white cake sugar all over the garden, blowing into my room in the night: door hinge frozen. Now the thaw has come: L. has his barometer: explains it to me. Walk over Mount Misery. Snow still thick, but the cart tracks run with rivulets. Oh and my new coat, the blue striped one, came, and its not too loud: I'm pleased.

Thursday 7 March

A fortnight – well on Saturday it will be a fortnight – with influenza. Up today for the first time. So it shows my inveterate – what's the word for love of writing? – that I open this. Head a white vapour: legs bent candles. All hope abandoned. Oh its the spring that's come while I was ill – birds chirping; Percy spraying apple trees; blue crocuses with snowdrops.

Wednesday 20 March

Yes, another attack – in fact two other attacks. What they call recurring with slight bronchitis. Yes. And the book [*Roger Fry*] read. One Sunday L. gave me a very severe lecture on the first half. We walked in the meadows. It was like being pecked by a very hard strong beak. The more he pecked the deeper, as always happens. At last he was almost angry that I'd chosen "what seems to me the wrong method". His theme was that you can't treat a life like that: must be seen from the writer's angle, unless the liver is himself a seer, which Roger wasn't. It was a curious example of L. at his most rational and impersonal: rather impressive; yet so definite, so emphatic, that I felt convinced: I mean of failure; save for one odd gleam, that he was himself on the wrong tack, and persisting for some deep reason – dissympathy with Roger? lack of interest in personality? Lord knows. Then Nessa came; disagreed; Margery's letter: 'very alive and interesting'. Then Nessa's note 'I'm crying can't thank you' – then Nessa and Duncan to tea up here; forbid me to alter anything; then Margery's final letter – 'Its *him*

... unbounded admiration.' There I pause. Well, I think I re-write certain passages, have even in bed sketched them, but how in time for this spring? That I shelve till tomorrow. Great relief all the same. And Lord to be quit of it and free – and Lord to have given Nessa back her Roger, lost since Julian died.

Easter Sunday 24 March

A curious sub-life has set in, rather spacious, rather leisured, and secluded and content. Still sleep in L.'s room; then I slowly bath and dress and sit in the sitting room, quietly, entering Margery's corrections. Not much bothered really, though I've so short a time. I can't help thinking, in spite of L., that its interesting. This is an egg shell life – so gingerly do I step to avoid rousing my temperature, which was 99 pt 4 and is again a little up. Wobbly like one of the spring lambs in my legs. And its refreshing and rejuvenating to see the gold thick clumps of crocuses, and the unopened green daffodils, and to hear my Asheham rooks dropping their husky caws through the gummy air. The twig carrying has begun, and this goes on while all the guns are pointed and charged and no one dares pull the trigger. Not a sound this evening to bring in the human tears. I remember the sudden profuse shower one night just before war which made me think of all men and women weeping.

Tuesday 26 March

A curious letter from Hugh [Walpole] this afternoon: 'As to my writing you and I are the opposite ends of the bloody stick. You are the supreme example of the aesthetic-conscience – there has never been such another in English fiction. But you *don't* write novels. What you write needs a new name. I am the *true* novelist – a minor one but a true one.'

Yesterday old Botten faded out under the eyes of Mrs West who's layer out and night watcher to the village. A frail old man; the last of the old villagers, talking the melodious Sussex, sprinkled with words like 'nard' for shoulder, wily and sly and grasping; yet poetic too. And a bore. Bringing the milk he'd stay talking, so we always cut at the sight of him.

Friday 29 March

What shall I think of that's liberating and freshening? I'm in the mood when I open my window at night and look at the stars. Unfortunately its 12.15 on a grey dull day, the aeroplanes are active, Botten is to be buried at 3. Well I recur what shall I think of? The river. Say the Thames at London Bridge; and buying a notebook; and then walking along the Strand and letting each face give me a buffet. For we're up in London on Monday. Then back here I'll saunter ... oh yes and we'll travel our books round

the Coast – and have tea in a shop – and look at antiques, and there'll be
a lovely farmhouse – or a new lane – and flowers – and bowls with L. and
May coming and asparagus, and butterflies. Perhaps I'll garden a little oh
and print, and change my bedroom furniture. I'm inducing a state of peace
and sensation feeling – not an idea feeling. The truth is we've not seen
spring in the country since I was ill at Asheham – 1914 – and that had its
holiness in spite of the depression. I think I'll also dream a poet-prose book,
perhaps make a cake now and then. Now, now – never any more future
skirmishing or past regretting – for in God's name I've done my share,
with pen and talk, for the human race.

Saturday 13 April
'The first crunch of the war' that's how Winston [Churchill] puts it. The
Germans have invaded Norway. Battles are going on. News leaks out.
Some say this is Hitler's downfall. A fine spring day in front; daffodils
luminous groups along the terrace. Aeroplanes overhead. Mine fields laid,
apparently to let us land our army. I write, because it is a crunch; after the
long lapse; also that I'm maggoty with lecture writing. Must ease my head.
Herbert Fisher was knocked senseless, had arm and ribs and skull fractured
two days ago by a lorry. On Tuesday, London: perhaps Sibyl Tom and
Desmond. No letters. Dinner in the oven. Meat bad and scarce. Eggs for
dinner. Fish for L.; maccaroni. And its time

Saturday 20 April
Desmond to dinner; London week. And we had Sibyl and Herbert [Woolf]
to tea. And came back yesterday. I remember Clive saying how he was
the only person who felt uncomfortable when a singer had a flybutton
undone. I had meant to note some such fragments. A stuffy evening. News
suspended. Herbert Fisher dead. Sibyl saw him the day before – of course.

Thursday 25 April
Herbert Fisher as a young man was almost ungainly: with his prominent
cheekbones and adam's apple. He had innocent blue eyes: a wisp of hair.
Much improved in dignity and distinction as he aged. Finally the very type
of culture and distinction. Composed, benevolent, wary. A crane like man.
Much like Adrian.
   Butterflies ball day three days ago. Cuckoo heard. Swallows come.

Monday 6 May
Nessa has just been and told us a "very tiresome piece of family news" –
A.'s affair with B. (I keep to the discretion of initials). A most astonishing
piece of news. Today they set off for two months alone in Yorkshire. Pray

God she may tire of that rusty surly old dog with his amorous ways and his primitive mind. It makes one feel oddly old: even to me comes the emptiness that Nessa feels, as I can guess. This blocks the way to my crowded London diary, and reduces it to fribble and patter. Clive's night; the police; and Mary's visit; Clive's unshaven cheeks; Desmond next day – all this I leave like torn scraps in a waste paper basket. Item my tea with Hugh; the sulphurous vista of the Green Park; the traffic; Hugh's sodomitic confession of affection; my lecture ['The Leaning Tower' at Brighton WEA]; two hundred about there; no fear on my part – and so home, last Friday, jaded and jangled, with my proofs – and this evening's work blown up, by this explosion of love; and the dream of the Yorkshire moors, and those two setting the supper in order, and retiring to the couch. Nothing will induce her to marry.

And we have withdrawn from Norway. The first defeat of the war. Compare Maynard's optimism three weeks ago. War practically over ... Kingsley of course croaks in triumph. Another lull.

The worst year we've ever had in the Press I gather. Its odd how much I thought of that lecture, and now its all forgotten – the agony and the sweat.

Monday 13 May

I admit to some content, some closing of a chapter, and peace that comes with it, from posting my proofs today: I admit – because we're in the third day of 'the greatest battle in history'. It began (here) with the 8 o'clock wireless announcing, as I lay half asleep, the invasion of Holland and Belgium. Apple blossom snowing in the garden. Churchill exhorting all men to stand together. "I have nothing to offer but blood and tears and sweat." Duncan saw an air battle over Charleston – a silver pencil and a puff of smoke. Percy has seen the wounded arriving in their boots. So my little moment of peace comes in a yawning hollow. But though L. says he has petrol in the garage for suicide should Hitler win, we go on. Its the vastness, and the smallness, that make this possible.

Tuesday 14 May

Yes, we are being led up garlanded to the altar. A soldier with his rifle. The Dutch Government and Court here. Warned of clergymen in parachutes. War war – a great battle – this hot day, with the blossom on the grass. A plane goes over –

Wednesday 15 May

An appeal last night for home defence – against parachutists. L. says he'll join. An acid conversation. Our nerves are harassed – mine at least: L. evidently relieved by the chance of doing something. Gun and uniform to me slightly ridiculous. Behind that the strain: this morning we discussed suicide if Hitler lands. Jews beaten up. What point in waiting? Better shut the garage doors. This a sensible, rather matter of fact talk. A thunderous hot day. Dutch laid down arms last night. The great battle now raging. Ten days, we say, will settle it. I guess we hold: then dig in: about November the USA comes in as arbitrator. On the other hand – No, I don't want the garage to see the end of me. I've a wish for ten years more, and to write my book which as usual darts into my brain. L. finished his [*The War for Peace*] yesterday. So we've cleared up our book accounts – though its doubtful if we shall publish this June. Hospital trains go by. A hot day to be wounded. Anyhow, it can't last, this intensity – so we think – more than ten days.

This idea struck me: the army is the body: I am the brain. Thinking is my fighting.

Monday 20 May

This idea was meant to be more impressive. It bobbed up in one of the sentient moments. The war is like a desperate illness. For a day it entirely obsesses; then the feeling faculty gives out. Then the battery is re-charged, and again – what? Well, the bomb terror. Going to London to be bombed. And the catastrophe – if they break through: Channel this morning said to be their objective.

Desmond and [G. E.] Moore are at this moment reading – i.e. talking under the apple trees. Moore has a thatch of soft unattached hair: red rimmed eyes, very steady; but less force and mass to him than I remembered. Less drive behind his integrity which is unalloyed, but a little weakened in thrust by the sense of age (sixty-five). So that our reverence is now what one might call retrospective. At tea yesterday with Nessa and Quentin we *remembered* his great influence: his silences. "I didn't want to be silent. I couldn't think of anything to say" he said, rebutting our charge that he had silenced his generation. Hence his dependence on Desmond; who started talking, to the towel horse, to the cat, when he was a baby, and was sent to school to silence him. Many old memories. These spin a kind of gauze over the war, which is broken by papers and at listening-in time. Moore munches like a chaff cutter; I guess has not a liberal table at home: takes a logical view of food; eats philosophically to the end: while Desmond sprinkles sugar and cream, also liberally but erratically. So the housekeeper in me rises into being, in this miserable life of detail and bombast.

Saturday 25 May

Then we went up to what has been so far the worst week in the war. And so remains. On Tuesday evening the BBC announced the taking of Amiens and Arras. On Monday they broke through. It seems they raid with tanks and parachutists: roads crammed with refugees can't be bombed. They crash on. Now are at Boulogne. What are the great armies doing to let this 25 mile hole stay open? The feeling is we're outwitted. They're agile and fearless and up to any new dodge. The French forgot to blow up bridges. The Germans seem youthful, fresh, inventive. We plod behind. This went on the three London days. Rodmell burns with rumours. Are we to be bombed, evacuated? Guns that shake the windows. Hospital ships sunk. So it comes our way. Today's rumour is the Nun in the bus who pays her fare with a man's hand.

Tuesday 28 May

And today at 8, the French Prime Minister broadcast the treachery of the Belgian King. The Belgians have capitulated. The Government is not capitulating. Churchill to broadcast at 4. A wet dull day.

Wednesday 29 May

But hope revives – I don't know why. A desperate battle. The Allies holding. L. has been in London. A great thunderstorm. I was walking on the marsh and thought it was the guns on the channel ports. We had our First Aid meeting. The [Women's Institute] plays rehearsed here yesterday. My contribution to the war is the sacrifice of pleasure: I'm bored: bored and appalled by the readymade commonplaceness of these plays: which they can't act unless we help. I mean, the minds so cheap, compared with ours, like a bad novel – that's my contribution – to have my mind smeared by the village mind; and to endure it, and the simper. So, if Margaret Llewelyn Davies says, how insolent we middleclass women are, I argue, why can't the workers then reject us? What's wrong is the conventionality – not the coarseness. So that its all lulled and dulled. The very opposite of 'common' or working class.

Began *Pointz Hall* again today, and threshed and threshed till perhaps a little grain can be collected.

Thursday 30 May

Walking today (Nessa's birthday) by Kingfisher Pool saw my first hospital train – laden, not funereal, but weighty, as if not to shake bones. Something grieving and tender and heavy laden and private – bringing our wounded back carefully through the green fields at which I suppose some looked. And the faculty for seeing in imagination always leaves me so suffused with something partly visual, partly emotional – the slowness, cadaverousness, grief of the long heavy train, taking its burden through the fields. Very quietly it slid into the cutting at Lewes. Instantly wild duck flights of aeroplanes came over head; manoeuvred; took up positions and passed over Caburn. No news today. Holding the line – heroism – all the usual perorations, in the usual highflown tense voice. Oh for a speaking voice, once in a way. And being beaten at bowls irritates me; and I'm strained writing *Pointz Hall* – so much more of a strain than *Roger*. And no meat today. And weeded this morning. And was very happy – the moment can be that: only there's no support in the fabric, there's no healthy tissue round the moment. Its blown out. But for a moment, on the terrace, no one coming, alone with L., one's certainly happy.

Friday 31 May
Raid, said to be warned, last night. All the searchlights in extreme antennal vibration. They have blots of light, like beads of dew on a stalk. Desperate fighting. The same perorations.

Monday 3 June
Leonard said, after Miss Griffiths [Hogarth Press clerk] went, "If it gives them so much happiness, we ought to put up with it from time to time." I said, But how, seeing she never spoke and was as unresponsive as a fish, could it have given her pleasure? "She leads such an awful life in Acton. She likes the food and sitting in the garden." This fairly sums up a very laboured week end: when we drew bucket up after bucket and nothing happened. But we made her sing, Monteverdi: and she sang quite simply. Will she marry? or fade? Again I'm struck with the helplessness of the lower orders. All of us on top. What can they get at –?

Four-fifths of the army over here now. A respite, a pause, perhaps. Perhaps Italy comes in . . . We have now been hard at it hero-making. The laughing, heroic Tommy – how can we be worthy of such men? – every paper, every BBC rises to that dreary false cheery hero-making strain. Will they be grinding organs in the street in six months? Its the emotional falsity; not all false, yet inspired with some eye to the main chance. Its the myth making stage of the war we're in.

Friday 7 June
Just back [from London] this roasting hot evening. The great battle which decides our life or death goes on. Up till 1.30 this morning, Kingsley diffusing his soft charcoal gloom. Question of suicide seriously debated among the four of us – Rose Macaulay the other – in the gradually darkening room. At last no light at all. This was symbolic. French are to be beaten; invasion here; fifth column active; a German pro-Consul; English Government in Canada; we in concentration camps, or taking sleeping draughts. The menace now is Ireland. Kingsley gives us about five weeks before the

great attack on England begins. I will continue tomorrow when less sleepy. Saw Stephen, Sibyl, John, Morgan, Judith, Raymond [Mortimer], Kingsley, Rose Macaulay, finally W. Robson – but can't discriminate.

Sunday 9 June

I will continue – but can I? The pressure of this battle wipes out London pretty quick. As sample of my present mood, I reflect: capitulation will mean all Jews to be given up. Concentration camps. So to our garage. That's behind correcting *Roger*, playing bowls. Another reflection: I don't want to go to bed at midday: this refers to the garage. What we dread (its no exaggeration) is the news that the French Government have left Paris. A kind of growl behind the cuckoo and t'other birds: a furnace behind the sky. It struck me that one curious feeling is, that the writing 'I' has vanished. No audience. No echo. That's part of one's death.

Monday 10 June

A day off. I mean one of those odd lapses of anxiety which may be false. Anyhow they said this morning that the line is unbroken – save at certain points. Anyhow its a day off – a coal gritty day. And cool mercifully after the furnace. Today, too, I sent off my page proofs, and thus have read my *Roger* for the last time. The Index remains. And I'm in the doldrums. The after book stage is on me.

Tuesday 11 June

Today or yesterday Italy came in: French said to be holding most lines; Government offices leaving Paris. Plays rehearsed, working till eyes blind at Index.

Wednesday 12 June

Black news. French apparently withdrawing but only guarded news. Percy says the little boats all summoned again, as if to fetch off more troops.

Thursday 13 June

If it weren't for – oh dear the retreat – Paris now almost besieged – 20,000 of our men cut off – still the French have gained five miles somewhere – if it weren't for this, today would have been a happy day. My Index sent off – so that's the very final full stop to all that drudgery. Up and down – up and down. No petrol at the pumps – providing for Invasion, only served a dribble, the man said.

Friday 14 June

Paris is in the hands of the Germans. Battle continues. We spent the day seeing Penshurst with Vita – picnicked in the park. Very fine and hot. The house of yellowish Oxford stone. Banqueting hall: disappointing furniture, like heavy and over ornamental Tottenham Court Road, only made 1314. Queen Elizabeth dancing. Elizabeth herself in another picture, delicate skinned, red haired, aquiline. Then the shell of Lady Pembroke's lute – like half a fig. Then some very ugly tables . . . a long panelled room with soft veined panels. Out into the garden, which has certain trim lawns, and long grass walks, then lapses into wilderness. Sidneys very poor – given up weeding. A great lily pond; the goldfish making an odd subacqueous tapping as they moved among reeds. Then through old pink courtyards to the car: but the butler came and said his Lordship wanted to see us. Vita went – we stayed. Then were summoned. Lord de L'Isle and Dudley is like a very old liver and white Sussex spaniel – heavy pouched, both eyes with cataract, eighty-seven but looks younger, waistcoat undone. Glad of company. Padded us into a small room; made us look at pictures said to be good. Can only keep a few rooms open. And those like seaside lodging rooms. Vita said he'd told her he was so poor he couldn't have people to stay: whole place run by two maids and a boy and butler; is alone – but d'you mind being alone? she asked. "Hate it" he said. Twice a week he goes to Tonbridge and plays Bridge. There this old snail sits in the corner of his tremendous shell. Odd to have seen this Elizabethan great house the first day that invasion becomes serious. But I like Monks House better.

Thursday 20 June
London diary: just back; and dinner so close and events so crowded that I must abstract. Monday lunch: John. The French stopped fighting; Kingsley Martin after dinner. Tuesday, dine with Adrian. They both off to air raid rehearsal at Middlesex Hospital. Adrian promises us a prescription. Churchill broadcasts. Reassuring about defence of England; not all claptrap. Now we're fighting alone with our back to the wall. Bombs first, then invasion. Ethel Smyth tea. Oh of *course* we shall fight and win. Monday ended in charcoal gloom. Kingsley Martin says we must and shall be beaten. He says perhaps four more numbers of the *New Statesman* will come out.

Here, as soon as we begin bowls, Louie comes agog. Harry [West, her brother] came back on Monday. It pours out – how he hadn't boots off for three days; the beach at Dunkirk – the bombers as low as trees – the bullets like moth holes in his coat – how no English aeroplanes fought; how the officer told them to take their shoes off and go past a pill box on all fours. Then went himself with a grenade and blasted it. At Dunkirk many men shot themselves as the planes swooped. Harry swam off, a boat neared. Say Chum, can you row? Yes, he said, hauled in, rowed for five hours, saw England, landed – didn't know if it were day or night or what town – didn't ask – couldn't write to his mother – so was despatched to his regiment.

Harry has had enough war, and is certain of our defeat – got no arms and no aeroplanes – how can we do anything?

Saturday 22 June
And the fighting goes on in France; and the terms aren't yet public; and its a heavy grey day, and I've been beaten at bowls, feel depressed and irritated, and vow I'll play no more, but read my book. I would like to find one book and stick to it. But I can't. I feel, if this is my last lap, oughtn't I to read Shakespeare? But can't. I feel oughtn't I to finish off *Pointz Hall*: oughtn't I to finish something by way of an end? The end gives its vividness, even its gaiety and recklessness to the random daily life. This, I thought yesterday, may be my last walk. The corn was flowing with poppies in it. And I read my Shelley at night.

Nightly raids on the east and south coast. Six, three, twelve people killed nightly.

Thursday 27 June
How difficult to make oneself a centre after all the rings a visitor stirs in one – in this case Elizabeth Bowen. These rough rapid twinkling ripples spread out and out – for some hours after Elizabeth is in the train. It is a disagreeable after-visit feeling. It has its connection too with too many cigarettes, with incessant knitting. Then a visit to Charleston threw another stone into the pond. And at the moment, with *Pointz Hall* only to fix upon, I'm loosely anchored. Further, the war – our waiting while the knives sharpen for the operation – has taken away the outer wall of security. No echo comes back. I have no surroundings. We pour to the edge of a precipice . . . and then? I can't conceive that there will be a 27th June 1941.

Elizabeth's stammer also had a disintegrating effect: like a moth buzzing round a flower – her whirr of voice as she can't alight on a word – a whirr of sound that makes the word quiver and seem blurred. We talked however – and very on the whole congenially. A very honourable horse faced, upper class, hard constricted mind.

Thursday 4 July
Again, back from London. But its here that the events take place. Louie, toothless, but all agog: yesterday at 5pm. pop, pop pop out over the marshes. She was picking fruit. Backfiring she thought. Told by someone it was a raid. So she went in. They bombed the train at Newhaven: the driver died this morning. Passengers lay under seats. Rails wrecked. Today a plane – ours – crashed at Southease. So, the Germans are nibbling at my afternoon walks. The French fleet has been seized and sunk. All Lewes listening to the wireless. In London, Kingsley Martin decreed that Tuesday,

or today, Thursday, was fixed for invasion. London very safe and solid in feeling. Pink brick fortresses – for ammunition? – in main streets. Wire mazes in Whitehall &c. We passed strings of ambulances coming down tagged with boughs. Canadians swarm – want to see Buckingham Palace.

Friday 5 July
Rumour, via Percy, has it that the streets of Newhaven were machine gunned. L. gets annoyed with Percy. I see the imagination – that should have turned a wheel, running to waste and foam instead. The French Fleet fought: Pétain cuts off diplomatic relations. So shall we be at war with our ally? Last month indissolubly determined to fight to the end.

Friday 12 July
How the grass shone pale emerald green when I walked off my temper on the marsh after dinner. The passages of colour, over Asheham, like the green backgrounds in Vermeer and then the little rusty grey church, and the cows, sun beaded, fringed with sun. We quarrelled about our communal feeling ... but we made it up. L. has given all our saucepans to Mrs Ebbs [the vicar's wife] to make aeroplanes with. I don't like any of the feelings war breeds: patriotism; communal &c; all sentimental and emotional parodies of our real feelings. But then, we're in for it. Every day we have our raids: at night the bloodhounds are out. I open my window when I hear the Germans, and the broad stalks of light rise all over the meadow feeling for them – a strange early morning spectacle. Then the drone buzz booms away, rather like a dentist's drill. No invasion so far.

Wednesday 24 July
I want at the moment, the eve of publication moment, to discover my emotions. They are fitful: thus not very strong – nothing like so strong as before *The Years* – oh dear nothing like. Still they twinge. Two strains, as usual, will develop: fascinating; dull; life-like; dead. So why do I twinge? knowing it almost by heart. But not quite. I shall of course be sneered at by those who sniff at Bloomsbury. I'd forgotten that. But as L. is combing Sally I can't concentrate. No room of my own.

Thursday 25 July
I'm not very nervous at the moment: indeed at worst its only a skin deep nervousness; for after all, the main people approve. What a curious relation is mine with Roger at this moment – I who have given him a kind of shape after his death – Was he like that? I feel very much in his presence at the moment: as if I were intimately connected with him; as if we together had

given birth to this vision of him: a child born of us. Yet he had no power to alter it. And yet for some years it will represent him.

Friday 26 July

I think I have taken, say a good second, judging from the *TLS* review. *Times* says it takes a very high place indeed among biographies. *Times* intelligent, but not room for more. By the way, I'm rather proud of having done a solid work. I am content, somehow. But its an incredibly lovely – yes lovely is the word – transient, changing, warm, capricious summer evening. Also I won two games.

When the twelve planes went over, out to sea, to fight, last evening, I had I think an individual, not communal BBC dictated feeling. I almost instinctively wished them luck. I should like to be able to take scientific notes of reactions. Invasion may be tonight or not at all. And – I had something else to say. But what? And dinner to get ready.

Sunday 28 July

Why do I mind being beaten at bowls? I think I connect it with Hitler. Yet I played very well. Such a curious peace; a satisfactory quiet. I shall see no one in London. Yes for a moment I believe that I can compass a season of calm weather. Yet 'they' say the invasion is fixed for August 16th. Yesterday at Charleston; Angelica there: I diagnose strain; a little defiance, restlessness. And feel in Quentin something heavy, mature, depressed. Almost a year he's been in the fields: all corn coloured and red poppied with his blue eyes for convolvulus.

Waiting for the Sunday papers in which *Roger Fry* will, or may, be disposed of by Desmond. I know that Desmond (who very likely won't do it) will if he does, gently hum and haw something about Mrs Woolf's charm and sympathy and then proceed to give his own version of Roger which will probably be more amusing than mine; and that'll fill his short column.

Friday 2 August

Complete silence surrounds that book. It might have sailed into the blue and been lost. 'One of our books did not return' as the BBC puts it. No review by Morgan, no review at all. No letter. Still I remain – yes honestly – quiet minded, and prepared to face a complete, a lasting silence. I'm so jaded after Philip Morrell, Pippa, and the London uproar – but with a sense of things forming, and freedom.

Sunday 4 August

Just time to record oh a great relief – Desmond's review really says all I wanted said. The book delights friends and the younger generation say

Yes, yes we know him; and its not only delightful but important. That's enough. And it gave me a very calm rewarded feeling – not the old triumph, as over a novel; but the feeling I've done what was asked of me, given my friends what they wanted. Now I can be content.

Tuesday 6 August
Yes I was very happy again when I saw Clive's blue envelope at breakfast this morning. Its Clive almost – what? – devout – no quiet, serious, completely without sneer approving. As good in its way as the best of my books – the best biography for years. So I'm really and truly immune, and feel, if only Louie's father hadn't died, and Mabel's lover hadn't gone to hospital so that I've all the cooking and washing up to do today, that I could go on to the next thing – to many next things. Is it an illusion that I'm freer and stronger, as a writer, than ever?

Men excavating gun emplacements in the bank. They look like swarms of busy ants, as I walk. Cementing floors; sandbagging walls. Great lorries of material go bursting down the Roman Road. No one pays any attention – so blasé are we. Guns along the river, boughs for camouflage, excite no one. *Roger* sells well. Talk of reprint.

Friday 16 August
They came very close. We lay down under the tree. The sound was like someone sawing in the air just above us. We lay flat on our faces, hands behind head. Don't close your teeth said L. They seemed to be sawing at something stationary. Bombs shook the windows of my lodge. I thought, I think, of nothingness – flatness, my mood being flat. Some fear I suppose. Then another came from Newhaven. Hum and saw and buzz all round us. A horse neighed on the marsh. Very sultry. Is it thunder? I said. No guns, said L., from Ringmer, from Charleston way. Then slowly the sound lessened. Mabel in kitchen said the windows shook. The All Clear, 5 to 7. 144 down last night.

Monday 19 August
Yesterday, Sunday, there was a roar. Right on top of us they came. I looked at the plane, like a minnow at a roaring shark. Over they flashed – three, I think. Olive green. Then pop pop pop – German? Again pop pop pop over Kingston. Said to be five bombers hedge hopping on their way to London. The closest shave so far. 144 brought down – no that was last time. And no raid (so far) today.

Friday 23 August
Book flopped. Sales down to fifteen a day since air raid on London. Is that the reason? Will it pick up? But I'm ravaged by Ann [Stephen] in house,

Judith Leslie Eleanor Camilla in and out of house. L. says he has a moral feeling of duty to young.

Wednesday 28 August
But well it taught me, that week of unintermittent interruptions, bowls, tea parties and droppings in, what public school is like – no privacy. A good rub with a coarse towel for my old mind no doubt. I should say, to placate VW when she wishes to know what was happening in August 1940 – that the air raids are now at their prelude. Invasion, if it comes, must come within three weeks. The harrying of the public is now in full swing. The air saws; the wasps drone; the siren – its now Weeping Willie in the papers – is as punctual as the vespers. We've not had our raid yet, we say. Two in London. One caught me in the London Library. Sales a little better.

Saturday 31 August
Now we are in the war. England is being attacked. I got this feeling for the first time completely yesterday. The feeling of pressure, danger, horror. Vita rang up at 6 to say she couldn't come. She was sitting at Sissinghurst, the bombs were falling round the house. I'm too jaded to give the feeling – of talking to someone who might be killed any moment. Can you hear that? she said. No, I couldn't. That's another. That's another. She repeated the same thing – about staying in order to drive the ambulance – time after time, like a person who can't think. It was very difficult talking. She broke off – Oh how I do mind this, and put the telephone down. I went and played bowls. A perfect quiet hot evening. Later the planes began zooming. Explosions. Planes very close. A great raid on London last night. Today quiet here. When I rang up Sissinghurst after dinner, someone cut in with "Restricted service. Things very bad there just now." Of course this may be the beginning of invasion. A sense of pressure. Endless local stories. No – its no good trying to capture the feeling of England being in a battle. L. sleeps sound all through it every night.

Monday 2 September
There might be no war, the past two days. A lull after the attacks on London. At Charleston yesterday a skeleton Memoir Club. We sat in the sun. It was hot. The apples hung red. Not a sound. Maynard what I call unredeemed Maynard, rather severe, snubbing, truculent. Talk about lives. Mine of Roger I gather is called by Maynard 'The official life'. I read my Dreadnought notes, not very well. Lydia wouldn't come. "She feels this is not the time for brains" said Maynard. Yet talk is interesting.

Thursday 5 September

Hot, hot, hot. Record heat wave, record summer if we kept records this summer. At 2.30 a plane zooms; ten minutes later air raid sounds; twenty later, all clear. Hot, I repeat; and doubt if I'm a poet. An idea. All writers are unhappy. The picture of the world in books is thus too dark. The wordless are the happy: women in cottage gardens. Now, in my nightgown, to walk on the marshes.

Saturday 7 September

An air raid in progress. Planes zooming. No, that one's gone over very quick and loud. Couldn't see if it were English. More planes over the house, going I suppose to London, which is raided every night.

Tuesday 10 September

Back from half a day in London – perhaps our strangest visit. Mecklenburgh Square roped off. Wardens there, not allowed in. The house about thirty yards from ours struck at one this morning by a bomb. Completely ruined. Another bomb in the Square still unexploded. We walked round the back. The house was still smouldering. That is a great pile of bricks. Underneath all the people who had gone down to their shelter. Scraps of cloth hanging to the bare walls at the side still standing. A looking glass I think swinging. Like a tooth knocked out – a clean cut. Our house undamaged. The garage man at the back – blear eyed and jerky – told us he had been blown out of his bed by the explosion; made to take shelter in a church. He said the Jerrys had been over for three nights trying to bomb King's Cross. So we went on to Gray's Inn. Left the car and saw Holborn. A vast gap at the top of Chancery Lane. Smoking still. Some great shop entirely destroyed: the hotel opposite like a shell. Heaps of blue green glass in the road at Chancery Lane. Men breaking off fragments left in the frames. Then to the *New Statesman* office: windows broken, but house untouched. We went over it. Deserted. Wet passages. Glass on stairs. Doors locked. So back to the car. A great block of traffic. The cinema behind Mme Tussaud's torn open: the stage visible; some decoration swinging. All the Regent's Park houses with broken windows, but undamaged. And then miles and miles of ordinary streets – all Bayswater – as usual. Streets empty. Faces set and eyes bleared. Then at Wimbledon a siren – people began running. We drove, through almost empty streets, as fast as possible. Horses taken out of the shafts. Cars pulled up. The people I think of now are the very grimy [Bloomsbury] lodging house keepers; with another night to face: old wretched women standing at their doors; dirty, miserable. Well – as Nessa said on the phone, its coming very near.

Wednesday 11 September

Churchill has just spoken. A clear, measured, robust speech. Says the invasion is being prepared. Its for the next two weeks apparently if at all. Ships and barges massing at French ports. The bombing of London of course preparation to invasion. Our majestic city – &c, which touches me, for I feel London majestic. Another raid last night on London. Time bomb struck the Palace. John rang up. Wants the Press moved at once. L. is to go up on Friday. Our windows are broken John says. Mecklenburgh Square evacuated.

We count now on an air raid about 8.30. Anyhow, whether or not, we hear the sinister sawing noise about then, which loudens and fades; then a pause; then another comes. "They're at it again" we say as we sit, I doing my work, L. making cigarettes. Now and then there's a thud. The windows shake. So we know London is raided again.

Thursday 12 September

A gale has risen. Weather broken. Terrific air traffic last night. But the raid beaten off by new London barrage. This is cheering. If we can hold out this week – next week – week after – if the weather's turned – if the force of the raids on London is broken – We go up tomorrow to see John about moving Press; to patch the windows, rescue valuables, and get letters – if that is we're allowed in the Square.

Friday 13 September

Just back from half day in London. Raid, unheard by us, started outside Wimbledon. Saw a pink brick shelter. Twice we left. More guns. Came back. At last started, keeping an eye on shelters and people's behaviour. Reached Russell Hotel. Loud gunfire. We sheltered. Started for Mecklenburgh Square: met John, who said the Square still closed; so lunched in the hotel. Decided the Press emergency – to employ Garden City Press [Letchworth] – in twenty minutes. Raid still on. Walked to Mecklenburgh Square. Refused admittance. John told us the story of Monday night. He rather white and shaky. Left him with distant guns firing. Started back. All clear in Marylebone High Street.

Saturday 14 September

A sense of invasion – that is lorries of soldiers and machines – like cranes – walloping along to Newhaven. An air raid is on. A little pop rattle which I take to be machine guns, just gone off. Planes soaring and roaring. Mabel comes out and looks. Asks if we want fish fried or boiled. As the result of a friendly cool talk it's settled, I think, that she leaves here. A great relief. I like being alone in our little boat. I like provisioning and seeing all's shipshape and not having dependants.

The great advantage of this page is that it gives me a fidget ground. Fidgets: caused by losing at bowls and invasion; caused by another howling banshee, by having no book I must read; and so on. I think I will begin my new book by reading Ifor Evans' sixpenny Penguin [*A Short History of English Literature*]. And whatever happens I will settle and sun on the moment. Fifty-eight – not so many more. I sometimes think about violent death. Who's whistling in the churchyard? Keep out the war from this page, now and then.

Sunday 15 September
No invasion yet. Rumours that it was attempted, but barges sunk with great loss. Raids over Brighton this afternoon. Mabel goes tomorrow; so pray God the Church Bells don't ring tonight. Now we go to our last Cook cooked dinner for I don't know how long. Could it be the end of resident servants for ever? This I pray this lovely fitful evening, as well as the usual Damn Hitler prayer.

Monday 16 September
Well, we're alone in our ship. Mabel stumped off, with her bunions, carrying her bags, at 10. Thank you for all your kindness, she said the same to us both. "I hope we shall meet again" I said. She said Oh no doubt – thinking I referred to death. So that five years' uneasy mute but very passive and calm relation is over.

To Charleston this afternoon, after provisioning for our siege in Lewes. Great air traffic all night – some loud explosions. I listened for Church Bells, thinking largely I admit, of finding ourselves prisoned here with Mabel. She thought the same. Said that if one is to be killed one will be killed. Prefers death in a Holloway shelter playing cards – naturally – to death here.

Tuesday 17 September
No invasion. High wind. Yesterday in the Public Library I took down a book of Peter Lucas's criticism. This turned me against writing my book. Turned me against all Lit. crit.; these so clever, so airless, so fleshless ingenuities and attempts to prove – that T. S. Eliot for example is a worse critic than F. L. Lucas. I dipped for five minutes and put the book back depressed. The man asked What do you want Mrs Woolf? I said a history of English Literature. But was sickened, I couldn't look. There were so many.

Wednesday 18 September
'We have need of all our courage' are the words that come to the surface this morning; on hearing that all our windows are broken, ceilings down,

and most of our china smashed at Mecklenburgh Square. The bomb exploded. Why did we ever leave Tavistock? – what's the good of thinking that? The Press – what remains – is to be moved to Letchworth. A grim morning. But I did forge ahead with *Pointz Hall* all the same.

Thursday 19 September

Another loud night. Another bad raid. Oxford Street now smashed. John Lewis, Selfridge, Bourne & Hollingsworth, all my old haunts. Also British Museum forecourt. A gale and rain here.

Saturday 21 September

We've just bottled our honey. Very still and warm today. So invasion becomes possible. The river high; all softly blue and milky; autumn quiet – twelve planes in perfect order, back from the fight, pass overhead.

Wednesday 25 September

All day – Monday – in London, in the flat; dark; carpets nailed to windows; ceilings down in patches; heaps of grey dust and china under kitchen table; back rooms untouched. A lovely September day – tender – three days of tender weather. John came. We are moved to Letchworth. *Roger* surprisingly sells. Invasion again withdraws.

Thursday 26 September

A talk on the phone with Nessa. [She] held the trump card. "Both our studios have been destroyed. The roofs fallen in. Still burning. Pictures burnt." So I had to pipe low. My fallen ceilings a trifle. Gathering apples all the afternoon. German raider comes over. Shots fired at Asheham. Bombs towards Seaford. Writing I remain unmoved. Only a German bomber? Oh that's all – No I didn't look out – Consider this remark last year – still more, ten years, still more fifty years ago. In flush with *Pointz Hall* thank God.

Saturday 29 September

A bomb dropped so close I cursed L. for slamming the window. I was writing to Hugh, and the pen jumped from my fingers. I was thinking (among other things): that this is a lazy life. Breakfast in bed. Read in bed. Bath. Order dinner. Out to Lodge. After rearranging my room (turning table to get the sun: Church on right; window left; a new very lovely view) tune up, with cigarette: write till 12; stop; visit L.; look at papers; return; type till 1. Listen in. Lunch. Read papers. Walk to Southease. Back 3. Gather and arrange apples. Tea. Write a letter. Bowls. Type again. Read Michelet and write here. Cook dinner. Music. Embroidery. 9.30 read (or sleep) till 11.30. Bed. Compare with the old London day. Three afternoons someone coming. One night, dinner party. Saturday a walk. Thursday shopping. Tuesday going to tea with Nessa. One City walk. Telephone ringing. L. to meetings. Kingsley Martin or Robson bothering – that was an average week; with Friday to Monday here.

I think, now we're marooned, I ought to cram in a little more reading. Yet why? A happy, a very free, and disengaged – a life that rings from one simple melody to another. Yes; why not enjoy this after all those years of the other?

Nessa rang up. A statue and frigidaire alone salved.

Wednesday 2 October

Ought I not to look at the sunset rather than write this? A flush of red in the blue; the haystack in the marsh catches the glow. Now a plume of smoke goes from the train under Caburn. And all the air a solemn stillness holds; till 8.30 when the cadaverous twanging in the sky begins; the planes going to London. Well its an hour still to that. Why try again to make the familiar catalogue, from which something escapes. Should I think of death? Last night a great heavy plunge of bomb under the window. So near we both started. A plane had passed dropping this fruit. We went on the terrace. Trinkets of stars sprinkled and glittering. All quiet. The bombs dropped on Itford Hill. There are two by the river, marked with white wooden crosses, still unburst. I said to L.: I don't want to die yet. Oh I try to imagine how one's killed by a bomb. I've got it fairly vivid – the sensation: but can't see anything but suffocating nonentity following after. I shall think – oh I wanted another ten years – not this – and shan't, for once, be able to describe it. It – I mean death; no, the scrunching and scrambling, the crushing of my bone shade in on my very active eye and brain: the process of putting out the light – painful? Yes. Terrifying. I suppose so – Then a swoon; a drum; two or three gulps attempting consciousness – and then, dot dot dot

Sunday 6 October

Never had a better writing season. *Pointz Hall* in fact pleases me; and so little to do now. Many letters to write.

Thursday 10 October

Rather flush of ideas, because I have had an idle day, a non-writing day – what a relief once in a way – a Vita talking day. About what? Oh the war; bombs; which house hit, which not; then our books – all very ample easy and satisfying. She has a hold on life, knows plants and their minds and bodies; [is] large and tolerant and modest, with her hands loosely upon so many reins: sons; Harold; garden; farm. Humorous too, and deeply, I mean awkwardly, dumbly affectionate. I'm glad that our love has weathered so well.

Saturday 12 October

If it were not treasonable to say so, a day like this is almost too – I won't say happy: but amenable. I can't stop looking: October blooms; brown plough; and the fading and freshening of the marsh. Now the mist comes up. And one thing's 'pleasant' after another: breakfast, writing, walking, tea, bowls, reading, sweets, bed. But I was thinking I must intensify. In London, now, or two years ago, I'd be owling through the streets. More pack and thrill than here. So I must supply that – how? I think book inventing. Scraps of memoirs come so coolingly to my mind. Wound up by those three little articles (one sent today) I unwound a page about Thoby.

But I want to look back on these war years as years of positive something or other. Queer the contraction of life to the village radius. All our friends are isolated over winter fires. No cars. No petrol. Trains uncertain. And we on our lovely free autumn island. But I will read Dante.

Thursday 17 October

Our private luck has turned. John says Tavistock Square is no more. If that's so, I need no longer wake in the night thinking the Wolves luck has taken a downward turn. A perfect day – a red admiral feasting on an apple day. The light is now fading. Soon the Siren; then the twang of plucked strings ... But its almost forgettable still; the nightly operation on the tortured London. We go up tomorrow. I must black out – the Siren, just as I had drawn the curtains. Now the unpleasant part begins. Who'll be killed tonight? Not us, I suppose. One doesn't think of that – save as a quickener. Indeed I often think our Indian summer was deserved: after all those London years. I mean, this quickens it. Every day seen against a very faint shade of bodily risk.

Sunday 20 October

The most – what? – impressive, no that's not it – sight in London on Friday was the queue, mostly children with suitcases, outside Warren Street tube. This was about 11.30. We thought they were evacuees, waiting for a bus. But there they were, in a much longer line, with women, men, more bags and blankets, sitting still at 3. Lining up for the shelter in the night's raid – which came of course. To Tavistock Square. With a sigh of relief saw a heap of ruins. Three houses, I should say, gone. Basement all rubble. Only relics an old basket chair (bought in Fitzroy Square days) and Penman's board TO LET. Otherwise bricks and wood splinters. I could just see a piece of my studio wall standing: otherwise rubble where I wrote so many books. Open air where we sat so many nights, gave so many parties. So to Meck. All again litter, glass, black soft dust, plaster and powder. Books all over dining room floor. Only the drawing room with windows almost whole. A wind blowing through. I began to hunt out diaries. What could we salvage in this little car? Darwin, and the silver, and some glass and china. Then lunch off tongue, in the drawing room. John came. I forgot *The Voyage of the Beagle*. No raid the whole day. So about 2.30 drove home. Cheered on the whole by London. Damage in Bloomsbury considerable; but miles and miles of Hyde Park and Queen's Gate untouched. Now we seem quit of London. Exhilaration at losing possessions – save at times I want my books and chairs and carpets and beds – how I worked to buy them – one by one – And the pictures. But to be free of Meck. would now be a relief. But its odd – the relief at losing possessions. I should like to start life, in peace, almost bare – free to go anywhere.

I must add that today is as hot as August: walked on downs; heard gunfire at Dover? – shelling Calais; summer clothes. Too hot for fire. Mist rising, must black out.

Tuesday 22 October
The vast ideas that float are never caught. I thought: how L. sees people in the mass: I singly. I thought, I will write supports and additions for my old *TLS* articles; a good deal about manners, and our class; about my rug; about a prayer for the Victorian scene in *Pointz Hall*; if I wait the thought may return. A lovely almost a red admiral and apple day; twenty-four volumes of diary salved; a great mass for my memoirs.

Wednesday 23 October
Heard the whistle of bombs for the first time today. About 5 – windy, cloudy: playing bowls. Suddenly heard a plane: suddenly heard a whistle. Like a toy pig escaping – rather; then I saw smoke, over the field path. Then four separate thuds – said to be at Iford. Went into village. Then Annie and two children appeared. In the bus from Lewes they had seen the bombs fall near. No one hurt – as far as known.

Tuesday 29 October
Today I cycled to Newhaven – city of the Dead. Sepulchred shops empty; silent, dour men. Baker boasted of the raid – at 5.30 yesterday twenty-five Germans descended: dropped twenty-five bombs – houses ruined – little girl killed. "And not a Spitfire anywhere near . . ." The gloomy self-consequence of the newly bombed. Home by Tarring Neville. The loveliest of low views.

Friday 1 November
A gloomy evening, spiritually: alone over the fire – L. in bed with influenza cold: caught off Percy. So I am alone; and by way of conversation, apply

to this too stout volume. The relics of my distracted morning were spent tightening the wretched £150 story, 'The Legacy'. Well, I combed and tidied it – so far as 'it' has any hair on its head. Then dipped into my memoirs: too circuitous and unrelated. All the same, I can weave a very thick pattern, one of these days, out of that pattern of detail. Early in the morning Annie came, asked me to stand for the Women's Institute Committee. "No" I cried too violently. The poor don't understand humour. I repented; went round later and found her in the sunny parlour and said I would. Then I carried L.'s lunch. Then I pumped my bicycle. Then I rode to Lewes.

Sunday 3 November

Yesterday the river burst its banks. The marsh is now a sea with gulls on it. L. (recovered) and I walked down to the hanger. Water broken, white, roaring, pouring down through the gap by the pill box. Today the rain is tremendous. Flood deeper and fuller. Bridge cut off. Water made road impassable by the farm. So all my marsh walks are gone – until?

Tuesday 5 November

The haystack in the floods is of such incredible beauty . . . When I look up I see all the marsh water. In the sun deep blue, gulls caraway seeds; yellow islands; leafless trees; red cottage roofs. Oh may the flood last for ever – a virgin lip; no bungalows; as it was in the beginning. Now its lead grey with the red leaves in front, our island sea. Caburn is become a cliff.

I was thinking: the University fills shells like H. A. L. Fisher and [G. M.] Trevelyan. They are their product. Also: never have I been so fertile. Also: the old hunger for books is on me; the childish passion. So that I am very 'happy' as the saying is; and excited by *Pointz Hall*.

Thursday 7 November

Morgan asks if he may propose me for the London Library Committee. Rather to my pleasure I answered No. I don't want to be a sop – a face saver. This was a nice little finish to a meeting with Morgan years ago in the London Library. He sniffed about women on the Committee. One of these days I'll refuse I said silently. And now I have. Bad bombing last night – four thuds at 7 – said to be Glyndebourne. London tomorrow.

Tuesday 12 November

Chamberlain is dead: and if we hold on till March we have broken the back (or whatever the phrase is). These two facts sum up the papers. I could add about Greece . . . Hitler's speech . . . no: time goes so heavy and slow, that nothing marks the days. A bomb fell at lunch yesterday. There is nothing new. Eastbourne bombed. London.

Friday 15 November

As I cannot write if anyone is in the room, as L. sits here when we light the fire, this book remains shut. A natural slimming process. A screw over the end of *Pointz Hall* made me rather sink into the disillusions yesterday. We have been a bit pressed. Michael MacCarthy to lunch; L.'s lecture; Nessa to lunch – two hard shopping days, in one of which I bought blue serge slacks – all this has rattled my head; so I plunged into the past this morning, wrote about father; and then we walked in top boots and trousers through the flood. Increased again. Lewes this evening with two lights showing looks like a harbour – like a French town spreading its skirts round a bay. Coventry almost destroyed. The usual traffic last night. All the hounds on their road to London. A bad raid there. When I am not writing fiction this fact seeps in.

Sunday 17 November

Butter stolen yesterday; Louie says "You are too well liked for any villager to take it." This flatters us. The butter disappeared when we were playing bowls. A man's voice heard, and the card of St Dunstan's found in the door. Assumption then that the voluntary Collector took it.

Saturday 23 November

Having this moment finished *The Pageant* – or *Pointz Hall?* – (begun perhaps April 1938) my thoughts turn, well up, to write the first chapter of the next book (nameless). *Anon,* it will be called. The exact narrative of this last morning should refer to Louie's interruption, holding a glass jar, in whose thin milk was a pat of butter. This was a moment of great household triumph. I am a little triumphant about the book. I think its an interesting attempt in a new method. I think its more quintessential than the others. More milk skimmed off. A richer pat, certainly a fresher than that misery *The Years*, I've enjoyed writing almost every page.

The flood is less today. Yesterday a raider came popping over the hill; L. saw smoke rise. In fact it was shot down at Tarring Neville.

Friday 29 November

Many many deep thoughts have visited me. And fled. The pen puts salt on their tails; they see the shadow and fly. I was thinking about vampires. Leeches. Anyone with £500 a year and education, is at once sucked by the leeches. Put L. and me into Rodmell pool and we are sucked – sucked – sucked. I see the reason for those who suck guineas. But life – ideas – that's a bit thick. We've exchanged the clever for the simple. The simple envy us our life.

John has written – wobbly: wants limelight and bouquets. Third impression of *Roger*: and I not told.

Friday 6 December

And then what they call real life broke in. Vans arrived in a deluge. Oh, we unpacked standing in the rain. Monks House gorged with old jugs and lidless pots. And the [rented store] room laden with four tons of old damp books. Real life is a helter skelter, healthy for the mind doubtless. I see what a working woman's life is. No time to think. No silence. I cannot concentrate on Ellen Terry. Rather depressing – old papers, letters, note-books: I'm going to bind the survivors tonight; and in coloured paper they may refresh my eye. All this writing – what a deluge of words I've let loose – on paper only: I mean not printed.

Sunday 8 December

I have only five minutes after a struggle with Ellen Terry to say that the war – yes I have only five minutes to fill in that omission – the war goes on. In ten years I shall ask, what was happening to the war? It is better. The Greeks are driving the Italians out of Albania. Perhaps this is the turning point in the war. But it dribbles out in such little drops. One can't always catch them. The war slowly enacts itself on a great scene: round our little scene. We spend fifty-nine minutes here; one minute there.

Monday 16 December

Exhausted with the long struggle of writing 2,000 words about Ellen Terry – interrupted by four days of furniture moving – distracted by the chaotic state of our possessions – oh the huddle and hideousness of untidiness – oh that Hitler had obliterated all our books tables carpets and pictures – oh that we were empty and bare and unpossessed – I take my pen to drawl and drowse a little. The year draws to an end; and I am harassed, damp: but I will take the matter in hand: scrub and polish and discard; and make our life here as taut and bright and vigorous as it can be. Its rather a hard lap: the winter lap. So cold often. And so much work to do. And so little fat to cook with. And so much shopping to do. And one has to weigh and measure. Then Kingsley comes and devours sugar and butter. I will write memoirs, I think: then *Reading at Random*. Measure, order, precision are now my gods. Even my hand shakes. One day last week we lunched at King's Cross with John. He was polite, impersonal – the Prince Consort. A ceremonious lunch. Why are we hooked to that large, rather pretentious livid-bellied shark? And must I spend my last years feeding his double row of teeth? I forget. I forget what I wished to say.

Kingsley Martin effusive but less distasteful. He ruined two days, now I come to think of it. Yes, its like going to the films – the film of December 1940 talking to Kingsley. I sit with my eyes dazed. Then at meals he scrapes and sops. I cook in the damp kitchen. And the village keeps tugging and jogging. The Women's Institute party tomorrow. My old dislike of the village bites at me. I envy houses alone in the fields.

Thursday 19 December
1940 is undoubtedly coming to an end. The shortest day comes this week: then the days draw out. It would be interesting if I could take today, Thursday, and say exactly how the war changes it. It changes it when I order dinner. Our ration of margarine is so small that I can't think of any pudding save milk pudding. We have no sugar to make sugar puddings: no pastry, unless I buy it ready made. The shops don't fill till midday. Things are bought fast. In the afternoon they are often gone. Meat ration diminishes this week. Milk is so cut that we have to consider even the cat's saucer. I spent an hour making butter from our skim of cream – a week's takings provides about half a pound. Petrol changes the day too. Nessa can only come here when she goes to Lewes shopping. All prices rise steadily. The screw is much increased since the summer. We buy no clothes but make do with the old. These are inconveniences rather than hardships. We don't go hungry or cold. But luxury is nipped off, and hospitality. It takes thought and trouble to feed one extra. The post is the most obvious inconvenience perhaps. It takes two days to get a London letter; four to get a parcel. I bicycle to Lewes instead of driving. Then the black out – that's half an hour daily drudgery. We can't use the dining room after dark. We are of course marooned here by the bombs in London. This last week the raids are so few that we forget to listen for a siren. That used to come at 6.30 punctually. What's Hitler got up his sleeve next – we ask? A certain old age feeling sometimes makes me think I can't spend force as I used. And my hand shakes. Otherwise we draw breath as usual. And its a day when every bough is bright green and the sun dazzles me.

Friday 20 December
We have been shopping in Brighton. It is a raw cold day, with the wind rising now. We bought a duck for our Christmas luncheon. We bought some buns and a wedge of cheese. Yesterday we went to the village school. They make things. I sat beside the flushed and cushioned Mrs Janson; and invited Mrs Ebbs to tea.

Sunday 22 December
How beautiful they were, those old people – I mean father and mother – how simple, how clear, how untroubled. I have been dipping into old letters and father's memoirs. He loved her – oh and was so candid and reasonable and transparent – and had such a fastidious delicate mind, educated, and transparent. How serene and gay even their life reads to me: no mud: no

whirlpools. And so human – with the children and the little hum and song of the nursery. Nothing turbulent; nothing involved; no introspection.

Tuesday 24 December

I note with some dismay that my hand is becoming palsied. Why I can't say. Can I make clear straight lines any more? It seems not.

We lunched with Helen [Anrep, at Alciston]; and again 'I could have fancied living there.' An incredible loveliness. The downs breaking their wave, yet one pale quarry; and all the barns and stacks either a broken pink, or a verdurous green; and then the walk by the wall; and the church; and the great tithe barn. How England consoles and warms one, in these deep hollows, where the past stands almost stagnant. And the little spire across the fields ... L. is now cutting logs, and after my rush of love and envy for Alciston farm house, we concluded this is the perfect place. L. says it is exactly right, for we needn't be cumbered with possessions here. Which reminds me. We are very poor; so I must write. Yes, our old age is not going to be sunny orchard drowse. By shutting down the fire curtain, though, I find I can live in the moment; which is good; why yield a moment to regret or envy or worry? Why indeed?

Sunday 29 December

There are moments when the sail flaps. Then I ride across the downs to the cliffs. A roll of barbed wire is hooped on the edge. I rubbed my mind brisk along the Newhaven road. Shabby old maids buying groceries, in that desert road with the villas, in the wet. And Newhaven gashed. But tire the body and the mind sleeps. All desire to write diary here has flagged. What is the right antidote? I must sniff round. I detest the hardness of old age – I feel it. I rasp. I'm tart.

> The foot less prompt to meet the morning dew,
>   The heart less bounding at emotion new,
>   And hope, once crush'd, less quick to spring again.

I actually opened Matthew Arnold and copied these lines. While doing so, the idea came to me that why I dislike, and like, so many things idiosyncratically now, is because of my growing detachment from the hierarchy, the patriarchy. When Desmond praises *East Coker* [T. S. Eliot], and I am jealous, I walk over the marsh saying, I am I; and must follow that furrow, not copy another. That is the only justification for my writing and living.

How one enjoys food now: I make up imaginary meals.

1941

The year began with snow and bitter cold. Virginia felt harassed by the straits and exigencies of wartime and generally dejected. She was copying the manuscript of Pointz Hall *and reading for her projected work – a survey of the whole of literature. She enjoined herself to take pleasure in her writing; but her diary-writing became more laconic, less fluent, and less frequent.*

Octavia Wilberforce, *a Brighton doctor and a distant relative, drew on the connection to make fairly regular visits to Monks House with offerings of milk and cream from her Sussex farm, with which Virginia made butter. Every ten days or so Leonard would go by train to London for the day, sometimes accompanied by Virginia, who would wander, forlornly, among her bomb-devastated haunts. In February they made an expedition to Cambridge, dining one night with Pernel Strachey, the retiring Principal of Newnham, the next with Dadie Rylands in King's, spending the intervening day at Letchworth where their Hogarth Press was now accommodated. Elizabeth Bowen came to stay a night at Monks House on their return, followed by Vita Sackville-West, whom Virginia had persuaded to lecture to the Women's Institute.*

On 26 February *Virginia notes that she has finished* Pointz Hall – *now to be called* Between the Acts – *which she gave Leonard to read. She was désoeuvré; she attempted to spring-clean and tidy up the house; one day she and Leonard bicycled to Brighton; another they went there by car when he had to lecture. There was still a great deal of enemy air-activity over Sussex, and solemn warnings were being given to prepare for the German invasion before Easter. Virginia was irritable and depressed. On 14 March she and Leonard met John Lehmann in London. He was told of Virginia's new book, about which she was clearly worried. But she sent him the typescript with a deprecatory note, asking him to judge whether it was fit to be published. He had no hesitations about it; but she subsequently wrote to tell him she could not publish it as it stood, and that she would revise it and try and pull it together before the autumn. Leonard was now seriously alarmed by her state of mind and health, and took her to see Octavia Wilberforce as a doctor. But Virginia was convinced that she was now so far down the remembered road to madness there would be no getting over it, and next day, leaving notes for Vanessa and Leonard, she walked across the water-meadows to the river Ouse and threw herself in. Her body was not retrieved until three weeks later. Leonard buried her ashes beneath the great elms which stood at the edge of Monks House garden and which they had called Leonard and Virginia.*

499

1941

MONKS HOUSE, RODMELL

Wednesday 1 January
On Sunday night, as I was reading about the Great Fire in a very accurate detailed book, London was burning. Eight of my city churches destroyed, and the Guildhall. This belongs to last year. This first day of the new year has a slice of a wind – like a circular saw. Leslie H[umphrey]. came to lunch; said um-um so often I nearly goggled; he was discussing the foundations of communism, having come chiefly to pick L.'s brain. Then old Octavia [Wilberforce] came, with her market woman's basket. Great white bottles of milk and cream. L. looking at the comet. Rather a strong moon, and so can't identify the constellation. And now its close on cooking time. A psychologist would see that the above was written with someone, and a dog, in the room. To add in private: I think I will be less verbose here perhaps – but what does it matter, writing too many pages. No printer to consider, no public.

Thursday 9 January
A blank. All frost. Still frost. Burning white. Burning blue. The elms red. I did not mean to describe, once more, the downs in snow; but it came. And I can't help even now turning to look at Asheham down, red, purple, dove blue grey, with the cross so melodramatically against it. What is the phrase I always remember – or forget. Look your last on all things lovely.

Yesterday Mrs Dedman was buried upside down. A mishap. Such a heavy woman, as Louie put it, feasting spontaneously upon the grave. And today she buries the aunt whose husband saw the vision at Seaford. Their house was bombed by the bomb we heard early one morning last week. And L. is lecturing and arranging the room. Are these the things that are interesting? that recall; that say Stop you are so fair? Well, all life is so fair, at my age. I mean, without much more of it I suppose to follow. And t'other side of the hill there'll be no rosy blue red snow. I am copying *Pointz Hall*. I am economising. I am to spend nothing. Is it difficult now to string tight? The great change isn't that but the change to the country.

Miss Gardner instead of Elizabeth Bowen. Small beer. But space, silence; and time.

Wednesday 15 January
Parsimony may be the end of this book. Also shame at my own verbosity, which comes over me when I see the twenty is it – books shuffled together in my room. Who am I ashamed of? Myself reading them.

Then Joyce is dead – Joyce about a fortnight younger than I am. I remember Miss Weaver, in wool gloves, bringing *Ulysses* in typescript to our tea table at Hogarth House. Roger I think sent her. Would we devote our lives to printing it? The indecent pages looked so incongruous: she was spinsterly, buttoned up. And the pages reeled with indecency. I put it in the drawer of the inlaid cabinet. One day Katherine Mansfield came, and I had it out. She began to read, ridiculing: then suddenly said, But there's something in this: a scene that should figure I suppose in the history of literature. He was about the place, but I never saw him. I bought the blue paper book, and read it here one summer I think with spasms of wonder, of discovery, and then again with long lapses of intense boredom. This goes back to a pre-historic world. And now all the gents are furbishing up opinions, and the books, I suppose, take their place in the long procession.

We were in London on Monday. I went to London Bridge. I looked at the river; very misty; some tufts of smoke, perhaps from burning houses. There was another fire on Saturday. Then I saw a cliff of wall, eaten out, at one corner; a great corner all smashed; a Bank; the Monument erect; tried to get a Bus; but such a block I dismounted. A complete jam of traffic; for streets were being blown up. So by tube to the Temple; and there wandered in the desolate ruins of my old squares: gashed; dismantled; the old red bricks all white powder. Grey dirt and broken windows; sightseers; all that completeness ravished and demolished.

Monday 20 January
I will be curt, compressed. A mood like another. Back from a damp, perhaps rather strained, visit to Charleston. Nessa and Quentin; Adrian has almost died of pneumonia. Visit from Oliver Strachey. All stocky gloom. Civilisation over for 500 years. I say to Nessa, Do you find painting gets slower? Yes. And money? Never think of it. And Helen? She does nothing. How can one do nothing? All the same Monks House is somehow cheerful. I am reading – oh all lit. for my book.

Sunday 26 January
A battle against depression, routed today (I hope) by clearing out kitchen; and by breaking into *Pointz Hall* two days, I think, of memoir writing. This

trough of despair shall not, I swear, engulf me. The solitude is great. Rodmell life is very small beer. The house is damp. The house is untidy. But there is no alternative. What I need is the old spurt. "Your true life, like mine, is in ideas." Desmond said to me once. But one must remember one can't pump ideas. I begin to dislike introspection.

We are going to Cambridge for two days. There's a lull in the war. Six nights without raids. But Garvin says [in *The Observer*] the greatest struggle is about to come – say in three weeks – and every man, woman dog cat even weevil must girt their arms, their faith – and so on. Yes, I was thinking; we live without a future. That's what's queer, with our noses pressed to a closed door.

Friday 7 February

Why was I depressed? I cannot remember. A week of broken water impends. Cambridge; then Elizabeth Bowen; then Vita and Enid [Bagnold]. The snow came back. Marshes in the thaw a swamp. We were in London, and had to come home, owing to a bomb, by Dorking. London streets are very empty – Oxford Street a wide grey ribbon. At Charleston Clive was stockish, like a Bell. I said "What a risk Nessa ran in marrying him!" The third week in March is fixed for invasion. Now black out.

Sunday 16 February

In the wild grey water after last week's turmoil. I liked the dinner with Dadie best. All very lit up and confidential. Then Letchworth – the slaves chained to their typewriters, and their drawn set faces and the machines – the incessant more and more competent machines, folding, pressing, glueing and issuing perfect books. They can stamp cloth to imitate leather. Our Press is up in a glass case. Very long train journeys. Food skimpy. No butter. No jam. Elizabeth Bowen arrived two hours after we got back, and went yesterday; and tomorrow Vita.

Wednesday 26 February

Finished *Pointz Hall, The Pageant: The Play* – finally *Between the Acts* this morning.

Yesterday in the ladies lavatory at the Sussex Grill at Brighton I heard: She's a little simpering thing. I don't like her. But then he never did care for big women. He has wonderful white teeth. He always had. Its fun having the boys ... If he don't look out he'll be court martialled. They were powdering and painting, these common little tarts, while I sat, behind a thin door, p—ing as quietly as I could. Then at Fuller's. A fat, smart woman, in red hunting cap, pearls, check skirt, consuming rich cakes. Her shabby dependant also stuffing. They ate and ate. Something scented, shoddy, parasitic about them. Where does the money come to feed these fat white slugs? Brighton a love corner for slugs. The powdered, the pampered, the mildly improper. We cycled. Irritated as usual by the blasphemy of Peacehaven. No walks for ever so long. People daily. And rather a churn in my mind. And some blank spaces. Food becomes an obsession. I grudge giving away a spice bun. Curious – age, or the war? Never mind. Adventure. Make solid. But shall I ever write again one of those sentences that gives me intense pleasure? There is no echo in Rodmell – only waste air. No life; and so they cling to us. This is my conclusion. We pay the penalty for our rung in society by infernal boredom.

Saturday 8 March
No: I intend no introspection. I mark Henry James's sentence: Observe perpetually. Observe the oncome of age. Observe greed. Observe my own despondency. By that means it becomes serviceable. Or so I hope. I insist upon spending this time to the best advantage. I will go down with my colours flying. This I see verges on introspection; but doesn't quite fall in. Occupation is essential. And now with some pleasure I find that its seven; and must cook dinner. Haddock and sausage meat. I think it is true that one gains a certain hold on sausage and haddock by writing them down.

Oh dear yes, I shall conquer this mood. Its a question of letting things come one after another. Now to cook the haddock.

Monday 24 March
When we came in she was sitting perched on a three cornered chair with knitting in her hands. An arrow fastened her collar. And before five minutes had passed she had told us that two of her sons had been killed in the war. This, one felt, was to her credit. Sitting there I tried to coin a few compliments. But they perished in the icy sea between us. And then there was nothing.

A curious seaside feeling in the air today. It reminds me of lodgings on a parade at Easter. Everyone leaning against the wind, nipped and silenced. All pulp removed.

This windy corner. And Nessa is at Brighton, and I am imagining how it would be if we could infuse souls.

Octavia's story. Could I englobe it somehow? English youth in 1900.

L. is doing the rhododendrons . . .

INDEX

Index